DE PACE REGIS ET REGNI.

viz.

A Treatiſe declaring which be the great and generall Offences of the Realme, and the chiefe impediments of the peace of the King and the Kingdome, as *Menaces*, *Aſſaults*, *Batteries*, *Treaſons*, *Homicides*, *and Felonies*, *Ryots*, *Routs*, *Vnlawfull aſſemblies*, *Forcible entries*, *Forgeries*, *Periuries*, *Mainteinance*, *Deceit*, *Extortion*, *Oppreſſion*: And how many and what ſorts of them there be, and by whome, and what means the ſayd Offences, and the Offendors therein are to bee reſtrained, repreſſed, or puniſhed.

Which being reformed or duly checked,

Florebit pax Regis & Regni.

Collected out of the Reports of the Common Lawes of this Realme, and of the Statutes in force, and out of the painfull workes of the Reuerend Iudges Sir Anthonie Fitzharbert, Sir Robert Brooke, Sir William Stanford, Sir Iames Dyer, Sir Edward Coke, Knights, and other learned Writers of our Lawes, By

FERDINANDO PVLTON of Lincolnes Inne, Eſquier.

THE LAWBOOK EXCHANGE, LTD.
Clark, New Jersey
2007

ISBN-13: 978-1-58477-697-0
ISBN-10: 1-58477-697-8

The quality of this reprint is equivalent to the
quality of the original work.

THE LAWBOOK EXCHANGE, LTD.
33 Terminal Avenue
Clark, New Jersey 07066-1321

Please see our website for a selection of our other publications and fine facsimile reprints of classic works of legal history:
www.lawbookexchange.com

Library of Congress Cataloging-in-Publication Data

Pulton, Ferdinando, 1536-1618.
De pace regis et regni : a treatise declaring which be the great and generall offences of the realme, and the chiefe impediments of the peace of the king and the kingdome ... / by Ferdinando Pulton.
p. cm.
Originally published: London : printed for the Companie of Stationers, 1609.
ISBN-13: 978-1-58477-697-0 (alk. paper)
ISBN-10: 1-58477-697-8 (alk. paper)
1. Criminal law--Great Britain. I. Title.
KD7869.P84 2005
345.42--dc22 2006019390

Printed in the United States of America on acid-free paper

DE PACE REGIS ET REGNI.

viz.

A Treatiſe declaring which be the great and generall Offences of the Realme, and the chiefe impediments of the peace of the King and the Kingdome, as *Menaces*, *Aſſaults*, *Batteries*, *Treaſons*, *Homicides*, *and Felonies*, *Ryots*, *Routs*, *Vnlawfull aſſemblies*, *Forcible entries*, *Forgeries*, *Periuries*, *Mainteinance*, *Deceit*, *Extortion*, *Oppreſſion*: And how many and what ſorts of them there be, and by whome, and what means the ſayd Offences, and the Offendors therein are to bee reſtrained, repreſſed, or puniſhed.

Which being reformed or duly checked,

Florebit pax Regis & Regni.

Collected out of the Reports of the Common Lawes of this Realme, and of the Statutes in force, and out of the painfull workes of the Reuerend Iudges Sir Anthonie Fitzharbert, Sir Robert Brooke, Sir William Stanford, Sir Iames Dyer, Sir Edward Coke, Knights, and other learned Writers of our Lawes, By

Ferdinando Pulton of Lincolnes Inne, Eſquier.

LONDON,
Printed for the Companie of Stationers.
An. Dom. 1609.

Cum Priuilegio.

The Preface to the Reader.

SEeing wee all haue receiued, and allowe it for truth, That the ignorance of the Law doth excuse none of offence; and also, That the Law doth helpe the watchfull, and not the slothfull man: therefore it behoueth each person, first to seeke the knowledge of those Lawes vnder which he doth liue, and whereby he is to receiue benefit, or to sustaine perill, and next with al, industry to frame his obedience vnto them, or humbly to submit himselfe to the censure of them. And though wee find by experience, that some men by the sluggishnesse of their natures, others by the carelesnesse of their owne welfares, and a third sort wholly giuen ouer to pleasures and vanities, do little respect to know, and lesse to obey our criminal and capitall Laws, being things of great moment and importance, and therfore doe ofttimes tast the smart of them, and repent their follies when it is too late: Notwithstanding, for that there be many others which do endeuour to read them, and imploy their industrie to conceiue them; some for the increase of their knowledge, others, in their actions to be directed by them, and many for the eschewing of the penalties of them, & yet do not wholly addict themselues to the studie of the Law: therefore, as neere as I can, to satisfie the desires, and to giue contentment to al the persons aforesaid, I haue done my endeuor in this Treatise, to lay open to all them that are willing to read, and thereby to know, which be the offences that the Law doth in generall tearmes condemne, and do most tend to the breach or blemish of the peace of the Realme, and to the dislike of all the good members thereof, and what punishments she hath imposed vpon the transgressors therein, and by whom, & in what maner to be inflicted. If one man do pretend title vnto, & sue to recouer any land, lease, or goods of anothers, all strangers stand indifferent, and meddle no further, but onely wish well to him that hath the best title, & desire that iustice may be done, and right may preuaile: but if a Treason, Murder, Burglarie, Robberie, Theft, notorious Riot, Forgerie, Periurie, Extortion, or Oppression be committed, then each man in conceit maketh it his owne case, & doth in a sort take it to bee done to himselfe; and all persons generally do find fault with the transgressors therein, they exclaime of them, condemne thẽ, & in their hearts cry Crucifige *vpon them. And therefore the crimes aforesaid, & such like, may bee tearmed generall offences, partly, for that they do redownd to the generall dislike of all the good members of the realm; and partly for that they tend to the breach or blemish of the peace, being a thing generally imbraced or wished for, & which the king & all his good subiects are bound, and in a sort haue vndertaken to maintaine: and therefore as the king hath an interest in them, or iurisdiction ouer them all, to punish the offendors in them, as transgressors of his lawes, and disquieters of his peace, and people, so hath euery other well gouerned member of the Commonweale, a care and regard of them, foreseeing that he may receiue the like wrong, and tast the same abuse, by the said, or other such malefactors meanes; and for that cause doth proclaime open warre against them, and is as desirous to root them out, as the husbandman his thistles out of his good corne, or the gardner his nettles from his sweet flowers. Wherefore, seeing a guiltie person in any of the crimes aforesaid, is persecuted, in deed, or consent, by all wishing well to the Weale publique, or their owne priuat estates: it is requisit that good men which eschew to offend for the loue of vertue; and euill men, which feare to offend for the dread of punishment, should both know those lawes which they are to make vse of, and the penalties which be threatned to the infringers thereof, to the intent that the good man hauing a will to stand, may trust to his feet, remaine firme, and continue his integritie; and the euill minded man beginning to stagger, may bend his endeuour to stay, and slide no further. All which by this worke (good Reader) I labour to performe, to the intent, that the well meaning man being made the better,*

ter, and he that before was lewdly disposed, the lesse hurtfull, may both at the last meet and ioyne in seeking and furtherance of that peace which will be comfortable to the King and Realme, and pleasing both to God and man. The question may be asked me, Wherefore I intitle my Booke, De pace Regis & Regni, *and yet do chiefly make mention therein, of those crimes which doe most disturbe the peace of the King and the kingdome, and so make the Booke and the title as it were* oppositum in subiecto? *Whereunto I answer, That the peace whereof I do write, is not obtained by the said offences committed, but by the lawes that do punish or restraine them, which lawes also I haue set downe at large in this Treatise, being the principall marke that I desire the Reader to behold: As, many Physitians haue written large volumes of seuerall infirmities in mans bodie, and then expressed which bee the Medicines to cure them; not to the intent to allure the Reader to seeke the disease, but how to preuent it before he hath it; or how to be rid of it when he hath taken it. And seuerall Diuines haue composed whole Tomes, of Pride, Malice, Couetousnesse, and such like offences, not to the intent to intice the fraile man to fall into them, but to shew the enormities of them, how grieuous they bee in Gods sight, and how hee hath threatned deepely to plague the offendors therein, to the end they might dehort and discourage transgressors from them, and might allure and winne them to humilitie, forgiuenesse, patience, charitie, repentance, and other vertues. And so I name my Booke of the quiet euent, and not of the persecuting cause; of the patient cured, and not diseased; of the sinner reclaimed, and not persisting in vice; of that peace which I would haue, and wish might flourish, and not of those Lawes that by awe do worke it. For these Lawes whereof I doe write, and some others, doe preserue the peace of the King, in that they doe assure vs who is our King; doe settle and continue the Crowne on his head, do put the Sword and Scepter in his hand, doe attributo to him seuervll Regall Titles, Honours, and Prerogatiues, doe bind his Subiects to performe all loyaltie, duetie, and obedience vnto him, and lay heauie punishments vpon the withstanders or deniers thereof. These Lawes bee as his Priuie Counsellours, incessantly respecting the preseruation of his person, peace, Crowne,*

How the Lawes doe preserue the peace of the King.

and

and dignitie: These be as his Gentlemen Pentioners, attending daily in his presence, to do him all princely honor and seruice: These bee as the Yeomen of his guard, waiting day and night to protect his person in peace, from all forcible assaults, and other perils: These bee as his great and goodly Shippes, which lye houering on the Seas, and his strong castles and forts of defence, which stand firmly vpon the land, wherewith he doth preuent forrein hostilitie, represse inward tumults, and so keep himself and his people in peace: these be as the Iudges, Iustices, Sherifes, Constables, and other Officers, watching euerie houre and moment in all the Shires, places, corners, and creekes of the Realme, to represse outrages, and to maintain his peace: And lastly, these be to him as his mynt, by which he doth coyn gold and siluer to defend himselfe and his people in the time of warre, and to support his honour and royall estate in the time of peace. And also by the protection of these Lawes euerie good member of the whole kingdome doth receiue the like benefit of peace: for in feare of them each person doth enioy his life and limmes in peace, and is defended from the bloudie minded murderer, and manqueller, and the rage of the furious quareller and fighter: And in feare of them the housekeeper resteth in peace, with his wife and family vnder his owne roof, without being assaulted by burglers: And in feare of them the traueller iournieth in peace from one country to another, without being spoiled by robbers: And in feare of them the Grasiers cattell do feed quietly in his pasture, without being stolne by theeues. The terrour of the Lawes do ofttimes restraine cholericke or contentious spirits from Batteries, Riots, Routs, Forcible entries, and other outrages; and couetous and greedy persons, from practising or procuring of forgeries; and godlesse and irreligious people, from persuading or committing of periuries; and false and guilefull persons, from putting in vre of frauds and deceits; and impudent and shamelesse men, to wrest from others by briberie, extortion, or oppression. And diuers there be, who neither by the lawes of God, of nature, or reason, will be bridled and reduced to vertue, yet by the penalties & feare of some of our capital and criminal laws, do yeeld to be curbed, & refrain from the practise of their vicious liues, of whom the saying of the Poet may be verified, Oderunt peccare mali formidine pœnæ. *And so I may truly verifie, that the Lawes whereof I do write, be the meanes of the peace*

How the Lawes doe preserue euerie person in peace.

the

of the K. and the kingdom: And so long as the offences in this Treatise specified shall be reformed, or duely checked by these Lawes, Florebit pax Regis & Regni. *But though peace be mine end, and peace the marke that I roue at, yet there be some that thinke, that the diuulging of our criminall and capitall Laws, in our mother tongue, will not be a meane of that peace which I do so much ayme at, for that, as they surmise, the same Lawes may then be misconstrued by euerie ignorant and vnlearned person, that can read English, and the sence and meaning thereof may be mistaken, the reader himselfe may be led into errour, and others may be misinformed by his imbecilitie of iudgement, seeing the same reader is able only to looke into the letter of the law, and not to discerne of the intent of the makers, or of the true sence thereof: And do alledge for their reason, the same that was obiected at the making of the Statute of* Anñ 34. H. 8. *ordained for the* St. 34 H. 8. *restraint of seuerall persons to read the Scriptures in the English tongue, for feare of raising of heresies and schismes in* Gods *church, surmising then, that ignorance was the mother of deuotion, as these men now would make her of obedience: But if the same parties will looke backe, they shall find the said Statute repealed, and by the lear-* St. 1. E. 6. 12 *ning and practise of the former, & our present age, the reason aforesaid refelled. Men may not surcease to read the Scriptures, because the diuell misconstruing the Psalme, would haue persuaded thereby* Psal. 90. *Iesus Christ the sonne of God, to cast himselfe downe headlong from* Math. 4. *the pynacle of the Temple: Nor for that the Saduces being deceiued in a place of Deutronomie, would haue inferred by the woman which* Deut. 25. *maried seuen brethren, that there is no resurrection of the dead: Nor* Math. 22. *for that S.* Paul *in his Epistles did write certaine obscure things to be* 2. Pet. 3. *vnderstood, which vnlearned and vnconstant men depraued as they did other Scriptures, to their owne destruction: For this deprauing, misconstruing, or wresting of the lawes of* God, *or man, out of their true meaning, & proper sence, doth conuince the reader of ignorance, pride, selfe loue, or folly, and doth nothing impeach the credit of the same laws, nor the necessitie or conueniencie of them, nor the considerat iudgement of the law-makers. We perceiue by the questions, demurrers, & argumẽts, which oft do arise amongst the reuerent Iudges, and learned men in the lawes of our Realme, touching the construction and true meaning of diuers of our Statutes and common*

lawes,

lawes, that the old Prouerbe is true, Nemo nascitur artifex, viz. *No man is borne vnto, or at the first can obtaine the perfect vnderstanding of any learning, science, or art whatsoeuer, but euerie person beginneth in ignorance, & then increaseth in knowledge by little & little, according to his capacitie and diligence: For, as the Pomander doth giue a pleasant sauour only whe it is rubbed, and the flint doth yeeld fire onely when it is beaten; so knowledge in all lawes and other learnings, is obtained onely by much studie, due consideration, & deep digestion thereof, as an hole is made in the hard stone, by the often dropping of the soft and liquid water. And therfore, if the buse searcher of other mens knowledge, and carper at their ignorance, will with the eyes of his mind looke into the old and new Testament, and euery booke, place, and particle thereof, and into the workes of euerie Rabbie, Counsell, Father, Doctor, and other Expositor of the same, thereby to learne which parts of the said Testament be written Hystorically, which prophetically, which metaphorically, which hyperbolically, and which literally, and how euery of them are to be construed & takē: and into al the books of controuersies in religion, which haue bin written in all former ages, and this our present time, and all the reasons produced for the maintenance of each seuerall persons opinion, and then will bend his care vpon the church of God, and learne by the report of the Ecclesiasticall Hystoriographers, related from the first creation of man vntill this day, when, where, by whom, & whose meanes she hath flourished and increased, and again, when, where, & by what meanes she hath bin obscured and blemished: And also will haue respect to the Cosmographers and Chroniclers of the seuerall kingdomes and prouinces of the world, who did describe the scituation of them, the nature and disposition of the people of each countrey, their forme of gouernment, their seuerall laws and customes, the fertilitie and barrennesse of their soyls, and how in times they haue flourished and decayed: And further, will reuolue in his mind the hundreds of volumes which haue bin written of the Common and Ciuile Lawes, and of the rites of other kingdomes, nations, and cities: And also will take notice of the infinit number of singular men, which in seuerall ages haue written learnedly and profoundly, of Grammer, Logicke, Rhetorick, Philosophy, Physick, Arithmetick, Geometry, Musicke, and Astronomie, and published to all posteritie the seuerall*

grounds,

grounds, principles, and maximes of euerie of them: And moreouer, will diligently hearken vnto the number of volumes collected in seuerall ages, of the procreation, nature, and course of life, of all the beasts of the field, the wormes of the earth, the fowles of the ayre, and the fishes of the sea: and of the beginning, increase, & vertue of all trees, hearbs, roots, plants, & things vegetatiue: and of the operation of all stones, mynes, quarreyes, metals, and other things which grow vpon the face of the earth, or lye hidden in the ground: And further, will take a view in his memorie of the millions of bookes which haue been written in the Syriake, Chaldie, Hebrew, Greeke, and Latin tongues, for the increase of all sorts of learning and knowledge: And lastly, will giue his heart leaue to thinke of the huge multitude of Treatises, which haue beene composed in verse, mytre and rime, in a sweet and harmonicall tune: and then if the same curious carper at other mens ignorance, after his said due consideration had of all the writings and writers aforesaid, and of their seuerall deepe wisedoms, knowledges, and vnderstandings in the arts, sciences, and things aforesaid, and how necessary, beneficiall, or comfortable they be to man, will returne home againe, and looke into his owne breast and bosome, and examine himselfe seriously what he doth lacke of all the artes and sciences aforesaid, and also how farre from perfection he is in his owne profession, I doubt not but whatsoeuer before he thought of himselfe, he wil now find that he hath but a small drop, sparke or particle of learning or knowledge, in respect of that he wanteth, and which hee may perceiue to haue beene in some others, and that hee hath no cause to maligne the ignorance of others, but rather to pitie his owne, and to say with the old Philosopher, Hoc solum scio quod nihil scio. *Many* *Cratippus.* *wholly deuoted to their owne opinions, do desire to maintaine Paradoxes, & to strain all their wits to defend them, though their assertions seeme neuer so improbable, and their arguments neuer so weak to others: as appeareth by* Rodolphus Agricola, *who did write a book* De vanitate scientiarū, *which the whole wisdome of the world in all ages hath so much admired and honoured: and by* Erasmus Roterodamus, *who compiled a Treatise* Of the prayse of folly, *attempting therein, to proue by a farre fetched argument, that the folly of man and woman together, is the onely cause of the propagation and continuance of mankind vpon the face of the earth, and that*

the

the fault and folly of Adam *in eating of the forbidden apple, contrarie to Gods commaundement, being the breach of the peace betweene God and man, was the cause that moued Iesus Christ the son of God, to descend from the bosome of his father, to take flesh of the blessed virgin* Marie, *to suffer his passion for the sinnes of man, and so to renew peace betweene God and man. And therefore we must not insist vpon the priuat conceits, or particular phantasies of a few opinatiue persons, but shall do well rather to obserue what care our fathers from one age to another, did take, and what ordinances they established in Parliament, that seuerall penall, criminall, and capitall lawes and statutes should be read or proclaimed in Churches, in Faires, in Markets, at the generall Assises, and Quarter Sessions of euerie countie, at Leets, and Lawdayes, and in the Halls of euerie Inne of Court, and Chauncerie, and how the same is continued, and duely put in practise at this day, to the intent that the same lawes, and the penalties thereof, should be heard, learned, knowne, and vnderstood by all sorts of persons willing to perceiue and apprehend the same. But if there be any, who persuading themselues that they doe search further into the bowels of reason or experience, than all our foresaid law-makers and others haue done, and will by disputes encounter the publishing or reading of our foresaid lawes in the English tongue, I must and will patiently content my selfe, suffer them to affirme what they please, and say with mine old Schoolemaster* Cato, Arbitrij nostri non est quid quisq; loquatur.

St. 25. E. 1. 3
St. 7. R. 2. 6
St. 33. H 8. 9.
St. 5. El. 1.

¶ Of Menaces, Assaults, Batteries, Imprisonments, and Maihems.

Vndertaking to write of the peace of the King, and the
Kingdome, and the chiefe impediments thereof, and to
declare which be the great and generall offences of the
Realme, I haue thought it good to begin with the verie
root and principall cause of the same, which are mena-
ces, threatnings, and other bitter wordes, beeing as
streames gushing out of contentious spirits, and veni-
mous tongues, their naturall fountaines and spring *The euill fruits of menaces.*
heads, from whence doe ensue sometimes assaults, batteries, riots, routs, vn-
lawfull assemblies, forces, and forcible entries; some other times forgeries,
periuries, and oppressions; and ofttimes maihems, manslaughters, and mur-
ders. And therefore king Dauid, hauing felt the sting of the bitter curses, op-
probrious slaunders, and sharpe menaces of king Saul, Shemei, Nabol, and o-
thers, did verie aptly and effectually decipher euill tongued persons by these
wordes: Sepulchrum patens est guttur eorum; linguis suis dolose agebant, ve-
Psal. 13. nenum aspidum sub labijs eorum: Quorum os maledictione & amaritudine
plenum est: Veloces pedes eorum ad effundendum sanguinem: Contricio &
infoelicitas in vijs eorum, & viam pacis non cognouerunt. And againe, speaking
Psal. 11. in their persons, he saith, Qui dixerunt, linguam nostram magnificabimus, labia
nostra a nobis sunt, quis noster dominus est? And for that cause the same king,
well obseruing the sea of mischiefes, miseries, and calamities, which daily doe
flow from euill tongues, made his humble prayer vnto God, to graunt him
power to be watchfull of his owne tongue, saying, Pone custodiam ori meo, et
Psal. 140. ostium circumstantiæ labijs meis. And when he perceiued that God had heard
Psal. 38. his prayer, he said ioyfully, Dixi, custodiam vias meas vt non delinquam in lin-
gua mea, viz. I haue made a full resolution, and promise to my selfe, that I wil
so vse and gouerne my speech, that I will neuer offend in my tongue. And the
said king telleth vs plainely, that there is no other meanes to haue the com-
Psal. 33. fort of this life, and to enioy good daies in this world, but to restraine the tong
from speaking of euill, the lips from powring out mischiefe, and to seeke peace
Prou. 18. and follow it. And his sonne, king Salomon, confirmed the same, saying, Vita
est mors in manibus linguæ. And though slaunderous speeches, and menaces,
be but wordes, and may be taken but only as a smoke, a breath, or blast of wind
and so to vanish and be dispersed in the aire like dust; yet experience doth teach
vs, that by the imbecilitie of mans iudgement, and the corruption of his na-

 ture,

ture, they be vsed as firebrands of priuat and open grudges, quarrels, conspiracies, & most other tragicall & turbulent stratagems: and therby a verbis ad verbera peruentum est. And we seldome heare of any yͤ said enormities effected, but they tooke their beginnings of menaces, threats, slanders, or other euill words: which offences growing by menaces, & other spéeches tending to contention, and the breach of the peace, the whole bodie of this realm hauing déeply tasted the smart therof, & desirous to preuēt the like, by a stat. made an̄ 18. E. Stat. 18. E. 3.
3. did ordain, that the K. Justices, amongst other articles, shalbe sworn, in case any of what estate or condition they be coms before thē in their Sessions with force & armes, or otherwise, against the peace, or against the form of the statute Sta. 2. E. 3. 3.
therof made, or disturbe execution of yͤ common law, or to menace the people yͭ they may not pursue the law, they shall cause their bodies to be arrested & put in prison. And in case they be such, yͭ they cānot arrest them, the same Justices shall certifie the K. of their names, & of their offence speedily, so yͭ he may therof prouide conuenient remedie.

Menacers shalbe imprisoned.

There is another foule puddle that ouzeth frō the same corrupt gogmire, & distilleth out of a heart likewise infected with malice & enuie, but is deuised and practised by another mean thā the former, which is by libelling, secret slandering, or defaming of another: for this priuie backebiter doth not by words impeach his aduersarie in so manifest and turbulent maner, as the cholerick menacer in his furie doth, but seeming to sit quietly in his studie, he doth more déeply pinch him, & infixeth a more durable wound into his fame, & credit, than the other boistrous fellow doth into his bodie, who in a moment threatneth to do more, than peraduenture he after is willing, or dareth to performe in an age. The menacer layeth open his name, & his grief, and standeth in the face of his enemy, & discouereth the corasiue of his mind, & doth thereby giue a forewarning to his aduersarie to prouide for, & defend himselfe: But this secret canker the libeller, concealeth his name, hideth himselfe in a corner, & priuily stingeth him in fame, reputation, & credit, who then neither knoweth from whom, or vpon what cause he receiueth his blows, nor yet hath means therin to defend himselfe. Co. li. 5. 125
And whether this libelling, secret slandering or defaming, be against a publike magistrat, or a priuat person, yet it may tend to the breach of the peace, to the raising of quarels, & effusion of blood, & so may be a speciall impedimēt of that peace which all good policie endeuoreth to maintaine.

The enormities of priuie defaming and libelling.

For if it be against a publike magistrat, it is a great scandall & offence to the king, his chief magistrats, & the whole gouernment of the realm, to assigne such an officer to rule and gouerne others, who himselfe is void of gouernmēt, and shall deserue to be impeached with such crimes as he shalbe taxed with, or shalbe imputed vnto him by such an infamous libell. And if it be but against a priuat person, yet seeing that a libel, or other note of infamie, is inuented to defame him, to tread his honor & estimation in the dust, to extirpate and root out his reputation & credit from the face of the earth, to make him a scorne to his enemies, & to be derided & despised by his neighbors, it doth greatly kindle the wrath of him, & of such as be of his kindred, alliance, & true friendship, & vrge them to reuenge: whereupon do ofttimes ensue grudges, quarels, fraies, combats, & manslaughters. Sometimes the malicious defamor powreth out his venim in writing, by a scandalous booke, ballad, epigram, or rime, either in mitre or prose: some other times by songs, scofs, iests, or taunts: & diuers times by hanging of pictures of reproach, signs of shame, or tokens of disgrace, néer yͤ place where the party therby traduced doth most conuerse: as the picture of the gallowes, pillorie, cucking stoole, hornes, or other such like. In which cases the law hath prouided, that the partie delinquent, when he is found out & discouered, shalbe sharply punished: for he may either be indicted for the same of-

fence

fence by the ordinarie course of the common Law: Or else a Bill may be exhibited against him in the Starre chamber, where he shal be punished according to the qualitie of his demerits, by fine & imprisonment; and if it be an exorbitant offence, then by Pillorie, losse of his eares, whipping, or &c. or the party greeued may haue an Action vpon the case against the offendor, & recouer his damages. And in this case it is not material whether the Libel be true or false, or the party scandalized thereby be lyuing or dead, or be of good name, or euill: for though the libell be true, & the party defamed be euill, yet our good Lawes be deuised to punish him, & such like euill men by a due course of iustice, after his offence is presented, inquired of, tried, & proued to his face before lawfull magistrates thereunto assigned, and he is not to be carped at, accused, & condemned in a corner behind his backe by any other priuat person, who intrudeth himselfe without warrant to be a censor of manners, & rather seeketh the discredite of the partie, then the reformation of his faults: for this secreat searching into, & sifting of other mens conditions, dyuing into their offences, & diuulging them to their discredites, doth conuince the offendor to be a man of lewde disposition, to haue made shipwracke of his conscience, & doth brand him during his life with the name of an infamous Libeller, or slaunderous backbiter. And therefore by Gods owne commandement it is specially giuen in charge to euery of his people: *Non maledices principi populi tui. Non fasias calumniam proximo tuo.* And king Dauid saith, *Detrahentem secreto proximo suo, hunc persequebar.* And God doth threaten, that he himselfe will take reuenge of the slaunderer, saying: *Sedens aduersus fratrem tuum loquebaris, & aduersus filium matris tuæ ponebas scandalum, hæc fecisti, & tacui, existimasti inique quod ero tui similis, sed arguam te, et statuam contra faciem tuam.* And as infamous libelling, & secret defaming, be oft times the causes of grudges, seeking of reuenge, and thereby of quarrels, in like sort words of slaunder, or speeches of disgrace, openly published to the face of an other, or behind his backe, be also firebrands of variance, dissention, fighting, and the shedding of bloud, and so be speciall meanes of the breach of the peace. As it may partly appeare by the words of the kings writ allwayes inserted in an action vpon the case, brought by one person against an other for speaking of slaunderous words, in which writ it is supposed that the words were spoken, Ad graue damnum ipsius querentis, & contra pacem nostram. And the same is further proued by the words of the statute of Añ 2. R. 2. whereby it is ordeined, That because publishing of false newes, tales, and lyes of Prelates, Dukes, Earles, Barons, & other noble and great men of the Realme, or of the Chauncellor, Treasorer, Clerke of the priuie Seale, Steward of the kings house, Iustice of the one Bench, or of the other, or of other great Officers of the Realme, debate, discord, or matter of discord or slaunder may rise betweene the Lords & commons, whereof great perill may come to the Realme, and speedy subuersion & destruction of the same: therefore it was enacted by the said statute, That if any do commit the before specified offence, he shall be taken & imprisoned (according to the statute of Westm 1.) vntill he hath brought forth him which did speake the same. And further by an other statute made Añ 2. R. 2. it was moreouer enacted, That when the said offendor is taken & imprisoned, and can not find him that spake the words, then he shall be punished by the aduise of the Councell. And to the intent that such euill disposed persons, which by their lewde speeches & slaunderous words or reports, do indeuor to breake or disquiet the peace of the Realme, might the sooner be inquired of, found out, & punished, By a stat. made Añ 1. & 2. P. & M. it was further established, That the Iustices of

Margin notes: The punishment of a secret Defamor. — Lib. Intr. fol. 13. — Psal. 100. — Psal. 49. — Action vpon the case for slaunder is contra pacem. — St. 2. R. 2. 5. — Slaundering of Noble men or great Officers. — St. 3. E. 1. 34. — St. 12. R. 2. 41. — Sta. 1. & 2. P. & M. 3.

of peace in euery shire, citie, & towne corporat, within the limits of their seuerall commissions shall haue full power to examin heare & determine the causes abouesaid in the said 2. acts of 3. E. 1. & 2. R. 2. specified, & to put the said 2. stat. & euery branch in them conteyned in due execution that condigne punishment be not deferred from such offendors. And besides the before mentioned penalties assigned to be inflicted vpon transgressors by the foresaid stat. euery noble man, or great officer of the realme, against whom any scandalous words, false newes or lies be spoken, may prosecute against the offendor an action De scandalis magnatū, & recouer damages against him. And in like sort may euery inferior person for any such like words of infamie spoken against him pursue an action vpon his case against ỹ offēdor & recouer his damages. And further if one person shall exhibit a bill in the Starre chamber against an other, & amongst other things charge him with murder, piracy, robbery, or other felony, or to be a procurer thereof, or accessory thereunto, or with any other offence which is not examinable in the said court, the defendāt in the said bil may prosecute against the complainant therein an action vpon the case & recouer his damages; for this bil was exhibited of malice by the complainant to remaine of record in the said court, to the infamie & slander of the defendant, & not to punish him for the said offences suggested in the sāe bil by a course of iustice, seeing the court of Starre chamber hath no authoritie to inquire of, or punish the same offences. But if the complainant doth suggest in his said bill of complaint any matter against the defendant which is examinable in the said court, then no action vpon the case is maintenable against him by the defendant therefore, though the matter surmised be meerely false, for it is done in a course of iustice: Et sub iudice lis est, whether the matters suggested be true or false, vntil they be proued. And in former ages speeches tēding to the reproch of others were so odious that K. Edgar ordeined that his tongue should be cut out which did speake any infamous or slaunderous words of an other. But though it be true (as is aforesaid) that infamous libels, secret defamations, or publick slanders, or reproches, be oft times more offensiue to the party taxed therby, then open menaces and threates of violence are: Yet seeing for the most part menaces springing out of distemperat & cholericke humors do more hastilie break forth into further fury & extremities tending to the breach of the peace, then libelling & secret defamation doe, which must haue a breathing time to be inquired of, bolted forth, and then to be punished, Therefore I will omit to write any further of libelling or defamation & goe forward with menaces &c. & tota sequela sua.

11. El. Dy. 285.
Co. li. 4. 12.

Edg. Lex. 4.

2 Menaces, assaults & batteries be things of seuerall natures, & yet for the most part they tend to one effect, viz. to hurt him against whom they are bent, menacing is a threatening of some hurt to be done or procured by the speaker or some other by his meanes to the person of the hearer, or his wife, seruant, tenant or other, whereby he receiueth losse, or hurt. Assault is an attempt to execute the thing menaced by force & violence. Battery is the performing of the thing before threatened, viz. the beating of him that was first menaced, & then assaulted. Menacing beginneth the quarrell, assaulting doth increase it, & battery accōplisheth it: menacing laieth togither fire & coales in the house of peace, assault bloweth it & maketh it burn. And battery doth endeuor to consume the whole building to ỹ ground. And therfore because some sorts of menacing, assaulting, & battery be professed enemies to the peace wherof I do write, I will endeuor plainly to expres which be those menaces, &c. that ỹ law doth inhibit, & in what sort, & by what means she doth restrain, & punish ỹ offēdors therein.

The differēce of menace, assault and battery.

3 The law hath allwayes had that speciall regard to the preseruation of the peace of the Realme, and of euerie member thereof, that she could not endure

dure, neither would suffer one person so much as to menace or threaten another of life, or member, or of any thing tending to the breach of the peace: And therefore she hath not only assigned in all countries & places of this realm, Sherifes, Justices of peace, Constables, Thirdboroughs, and diuers other officers, to be as watchmen, continually attending, & bending their cares & industries, to preserue the peace, and to defend each person from the violent sting of menace, assault, or batterie: but also she hath giuen and prouided for him who is

40.E.3.40. only menaced, an action of Trespas (as she hath done for him who is assaulted or beaten) wherby he shall recouer his damages: so that the same menacing do tend to the hurt of him who was menaced, his seruant, tenãt, or any other person, by whom he liueth, or receiueth benefit. And therefore the plaintife in an action of Trespas of menace, may declare, That he is an Atturney, and that in respect of the defendants menace, he durst not attend his clients suites, from such a day in M. vntill such a day in O. or that he is a husbandman, and could not attend or ouersee his husbandrie: or that he is a bailife, or collector of rents, and could not in respect of such menace, by the space of many monethes, attend

The declaration in Trespasse of Menace.

37.H.6.3. his bailiwick, collection of rents, or other businesses: or that in regard of such

30.Ass. p.14. menacing, he was not able, nor durst trauell abroad, to apply his trade, or get his liuing, without such force and defence, as his estate was not able to maintaine. As the collector of a fifteene brought an action of trespas for the king and

27.Ass. p.14. himselfe, against one, and declared, That the defendant did so rebuke him, that he durst not tarie in the towne to gather vp the fifteene, for feare least the defendant would haue beaten him. And though the defendant did not beat him, yet this rebuke was adiudged an assault, and the plaintife recouered an C.s. in damages. And in like sort one brought a bill of trespas in the Cõmon pleas,

Rebuke in Assault.

30.Ass. p.14. for the king and himselfe, and declared, That whereas hee was comming towards the Commõ pleas, to answer in a plea of land, the defendant came, and did so beat, assault, and menace him, that hee durst not bring his writings, or come thither, without great charges, in contempt of the king, contrarie to his peace, & to the damages of the plaintife &c. Whereunto the defendant pleaded not guiltie. And the defendant was compelled to find pledges of his good behauior, & for the peace, & ỹ he should not meddle with the plaintife, by himself, nor

Fitz. Trespas 159. by any others, openly nor secretly. In an action of Trespas the plaintif declared, That the defendant so menaced him in one county, ỹ he could not do his businesse in another county: and this was adiudged a good declaration, and it

37.H.6.2. was ordered, ỹ the issue shold be tried in the county where the menace was, for there was al the trespas cõmitted, & ỹ other county was put in only to increase the damages.

Li. Intr. 592. 22.Ass. p.76. 20.H.7.5. 4 And in like sort, if one man do menace or threaten the seruant of another, of life or member, in such sort as the same seruant doth depart frõ his master, wherby ỹ master doth for a time lose the seruice of his said seruant: in this case the master shal haue an action of trespas, & declare against him ỹ did so menace his seruant, That he made assault vpon his seruant, did beat him, wound him, and euil intreat him, & so often menaced to kill & dismẽber him, & did him so many iniuries & wrongs, ỹ his said seruant durst not for such menaces, & for feare of being killed or maimed, attend his businesse (viz. the bailiwike of his husbãdry, his seruice in husbãdry, or keeping of his horses, beasts, sheep, &c.) And so his said busines & seruice lay vndone, & ỹ said pl. lost the seruice of his said seruãt, frõ ỹ 20. day of M. vntil ỹ 20. day of N. thẽ next following, to his great damage, & against ỹ K. peace, whereof he cõplaineth, that he is endamaged 20.l.

Menacing a seruant, whereby he departeth.

And so note, that a man shall not haue an Action of Trespasse for menace one- 7.E.4.24.
ly, vnlesse he hath also thereby some other losse or hurt: for the menace and 27.Ass.
the hurt which the partie doth sustaine thereby, doe make the Trespasse, and p.11.
doe giue cause of the action of Trespasse. But it is otherwise, if a man beat 20.H.7.5.
the wife or villaine of another, for in those cases, the partie wronged, viz.
the husband, or Lord, shall haue an action of Trespasse, though hee hath recei-
ued no losse, nor hindrance in commoditie: For hee must ioyne in suit with
his wife, to recouer recompence for the batterie and wrong done vnto her
by the trespassor: and also hee may punish him by action of Trespasse,
who beateth his villaine, as hee may doe him who beateth his horse, cow,
ore &c.

Menacing a tenant, whereby he departeth.

5 And the same law is, if one man doe so menace of life and member, the Li.Intr.592.
tenants of another, which doe hold of him certaine lands and tenements at 20.H.7.5.
will, paying to him therefore certaine yearely rent and seruices; in respect of 9.H.7.7.
which menace, the same tenants doe depart from their said tenements, and
leaue the said rents vnpaid, and the same seruices vndone: In this case the
Lord, or owner of the same tenements, may haue an action of Trespas against
such menacer, in the Kings Bench, or Common Pleas, and declare of the sayd
menacing of his tenants at will, of their departure from his tenancies there-
by, and the losse and preiudice that he hath sustained by his rents vnpaid, and
seruices vndone, and he shal recouer damages accordingly. And in this case it
is a good plea for the defendant, to plead, That those tenants of the plaintifes,
which departed from their tenancies, were the freeholders, and the freehold te-
nants of the plaintifes, and not his tenants at will: For if it be so, the plain-
tife shall recouer nothing against the defendant, because hee hath other suffici-
ent remedie to recouer the seruices of his freeholders, or the land in stead of the.
And so it is, to plead, that the tenants which departed, were tenants for terme 21.H.6.31.
of yeares.

Menacing a Lords freeholder.

6 In the cases aforesaid, he that is wronged in his owne person, his ser-
uants, or tenants, by the menace of another, whereby hee sustaineth losse, shall
haue his action of Trespasse against the offendor, for the said menace, and the
hurt which he receiueth thereby; and the king also shall haue a fine of the of-
fendor, for that the menace was of life and member, and suggested to bee done
vi & armis, and so tended to the breach of the peace. But if it bee such a me-
nace as doth not tend to the breach of the peace, then the law is otherwise: for
then the partie menaced, shall neither haue an action of Trespasse, or other re-
medie against the menacer, neither shall the king haue a fine of him. As, if a
man dye seised of certaine lands, and a stranger will abate, and then the heire 22.H.6.48
of him who dyed seised, will enter vpon the stranger, and menace and threaten 21.H.6.26.
him, That if he will not depart from the possession of the same land, that then 9.H.7.7.
hee shall repent it, as the law will allow: this is menace iustifiable, for that he
hath said no more, than the law will allow him to performe. And in like sort, if
A. be disseised of his freehold, eiected out of his terme of yeares, dispossessed of Li.Intr.555
his goods, beaten, assaulted, or euill intreated by B. if in this case A. will say
vnto B. That he will not endure those wrongs, nor put them vp at his hands,
but will prosecute suit according to the law of the Realme, in the sharpest ma-
ner that he can, for the redresse of those iniuries, and for the due punishment of
B. this is menace iustifiable, and nothing tending to the breach of the peace:
for A. hath said nothing, but that the law will permit him to doe. And in these
cases

Menace which is iustifyable.

cases the menacer doth yeeld to make the law iudge of his wrongs, and that also in peaceable manner: but in the former cases, the menacer doth threaten to be the reuenger of his owne iniuries, and so to be his owne iudge, and that also in a forcible and vnlawfull sort. And so it is, if one man owe money to another, and at the time assigned doth not pay, if the creditor do say to the debtor, that he will sue him according to the course of law, and imprison him for his
16.E.4.7. debt, this is menace iustifiable, for the law doth allow him to doe it.

7 As menace in words is accounted in many cases to be a meane of the breach of the peace, and so punishable by the lawes of the realme: so menace by deeds, by behauiour, gesture, wearing of armour, or vnusuall and extraordinarie number of seruants or attendants, is accounted to be in affraie and feare of the people, a meane of the breach of the peace, and so punishable: for the law doth intend, that he which in a peaceable time doth ride or goe armed, without sufficient warrant or authoritie so to doe, doth meane to breake the peace, and to doe some outrage: seeing shee is able, and wil be alwaies ready to defend euery member of the common weale, from taking or receiuing of force or violence from others, if himselfe doe not giue cause to the contrarie: Whereupon by a
St.2.E.3.3. Statute made at Northhampton, anno 2.Ed.3. it was enacted: That no man great nor smal of what condition soeuer he be (except the kings seruants in his presence, & his ministers in executing of the kings precepts, or of their office, and such as be in their companie assisting them, and also vpon a Crie made for armes to keepe the peace, and the same in such places, where such acts happen) be so hardie to come before the kings Iustices, or other the kings ministers in doing their offices, with force and armes: nor bring no force in affraie of the peace, nor to goe nor ride armed by day nor by night in faires, markets, nor in the presence of the Iustices, or other ministers, nor in no part elsewhere, vpon paine to forfeit their armour to the king, & their bodies to prison, at the kings pleasure. And that the kings Iustices in their presence, Sherifes, and other ministers in their bailiwicks, Lords of franchises, & their bailifs in the same, & mayors & bailifs of cities & boroughs within the same cities & boroughs, & borough-holders, & wardens of the peace within their wards, shal haue power to execute this act. And that the Iust. assigned, at their cōming down into the coūtrey shall haue power to inquire, how such officers & Lords haue executed their offices in this case, & to punish them whom they find haue not done that which
St.7.R.2.13 pertained to their office. And after by a statute made anno 7.R.2. it was ordai-
20.R.2.1. ned, That no Lord, knight, nor other, little, or great, shall go nor ride by night or by day armed, nor beare sallet or skull of yron, nor other armour, vpon the paine of forfeiture thereof to the king (except the kings officers and ministers in doing their offices:) And by the same statute it was also assented, that none should ride or goe with Launcegaies (beeing an armour defensiue then vsed) in affraie of the people, but that the same Launcegaies should be for euer put out.

Menace by going or riding armed.

Launcegaies.

8 And shortly after, the same Statute of 2.Ed.3. was put in execution: for a knight was attached and arraigned in the kings Bench, for that hee did weare armor vnder his vpper garment in the kings palace, and in Westmin-
24.E.3.33. ster hall: who pleaded that there was debate betwéen him and another knight, who did that weeke strike him, and yet did menace him, and that for feare of further perill, and to saue his life hee did weare the same armour: But this was adiudged no plea, for the court did award, that hee should forfeit his armour, and be committed to the marshalsey. And though he desired to be let to

Wearing of a priuie coate.

mainprise,

mainprise, he was not admitted thereunto untill the kings pleasure was knowne. And the other knight his aduersarie, was sent for into the kings Bench, and there commanded upon paine of all that he could forfeit, that hee should not meddle, nor doe any thing but that which was good to his said aduersarie.

Labourers shall weare no weapons.

9 And because seruants in husbandrie, labourers, artificers, and other persons of meane degree, should take no incouragement nor occasion to breake the peace, nor weare any weapons therewith to menace, threaten, or terrifie others: Therefore by a Statute made anno 12. R. 2. it was ordained, That no seruant in husbandrie, or labourer, nor seruant of artificer, or victualler, shall beare any Buckler, Dagger, or Sword, upon paine of forfeiting of the same (except it be for the defence of the realme in the time of warre, and then by the suruey of Arraiers for the time beeing, or in trauelling with their masters, or on their masters businesse.) And Sherifes, Mayors, Baylifes, and Constables shall haue power to arrest all offendors against this Statute, and seize the said Bucklers, Swords, and Daggers, and keepe them untill the Sessions of the Justices of peace, and the same shall present before the same Justices in their Sessions, together with the names of them that did beare the same. But this shall not be preiudiciall to the franchises of Lords touching forfeitures due to them. By the foresaid two Statutes of 2. Ed. 3. and 12. R. 2. it doth appeare, that the meaning of the makers of those lawes was, not onely to preserue peace, & to eschew quarrels, but also to take away the instruments of fighting and batterie, and to cut off all meanes that may tend in affraie or feare of the people.

St. 12. R. 2. 12.

Assurances made by menace.

10 As menace of life and member giueth cause of an action of trespasse, to him that receiueth losse or hurt thereby, & intituleth the king to a fine: in like sort an obligation, a release, or deed of annuitie made, and granted by menace, are voidable by the law, so that the same menace be of life, member, or libertie: viz. of some hurt to be done to his body by death, maiheming, or imprisonment, and not to his lands or goods: for if A. will menace B. that if he will not make him an obligation of xx. l. that then he wil disseise him of such land, or dispossesse or take from him such goods: in this case if B. doe make and deliuer ye said obligation of xx. l to A. in an action of debt brought by A. against B, upon the said obligation, B. shall not auoyd this obligation, in respect of this menace, because this menace did not tend to the hurt of the person of B. but to preiudice him in his lands, or goods: for the redresse and recouerie whereof, the law would haue giuen B. a sufficient remedie, if A. should haue done him ye wrong which he menaced. And he that will take an aduantage to auoid his deed by menace, must in this plea expresse, how and in what sort the other partie did menace him: viz. that he drewe his sword against him, and threatened to kill him, if he would not seale and deliuer such an obligation, release, annuitie, &c. If A. doe menace B. in one countie, that he will kill or maihem him, if hee doe not seale him an obligation of xx. l, or stand to the arbitrement of C. in a cause depending in question betweene them: And after B. beeing at libertie in another countie doth seale the same obligation, or doth stand to the arbitrement of C. this obligation or arbitrement is void, for it shall be intended to bee done by force of the first menace. And if A. doe menace B. that he wil kil him, imprison, maihem, or beate him, if he doe not make an obligation of xx. l to C. if in this case B. do become bound by obligation to pay unto C. xx. l. in an action of debt

20. Ass. p. 14
28. H. 6. 8.
7. Ed. 4. 21.
4. H. 4. 2.
39. H. 6. 51.
Fitz. Dures 13.
33. H. 6. 24.
2. H. 5. 10.
39. H. 6. 36.
Co. li. 2. 9.

debt brought upon this obligation by C. against B. the same B. may avoid this Obligation which he made by this menace of A. though the menace was made by one man, & the Obligation was made to an other; for that the menace was the cause of the making of this Obligation, which the law doth respect and punish, and not only the partie to whom the Obligation was made.

What is assault and batterie.

11 Assault & batterie be for the most part an accomplishment of that which menace did threaten, & a performance by deedes of that, which the other forewarned by words: that is to say, a violent & forcible abusing, or attempting to abuse by blowes and stripes the person of an other, contrary to the peace of the Realme, and the law of the same; which hath ordeined, that no person shall be Judge or revenger of his own wrong, but leave that to the censure of the law, that is alwaies readie to heare & redresse every mans iust complaints: for he that doth attempt to assault or beat an other, to satisfie his own turbulent spirit, or to revenge his owne privat iniurie, doth as much as in him lieth to wrest the sword of governmēt out of the K. hands, to take from the law her equal censure in iustice, & to make himself both Judge, & executioner in his own cause; & because this disordered person contemning the iustice of the Law, hath assaulted or beaten an other without warrant of law, & broken thereby the peace of the realm; the law hath devised a quiet & peaceable course, to reduce him again to order, in punishing him by an action of Trespas of assault & batterie, wherin being convicted, he shal satisfie the party grieved his damages, & pay to the K. a fine, & his body shal be committed to prison, untill he hath satisfied it. Though the party menaced shall not have his remedy by action of Trespas, unlesse the same menace was of life & member, and also that the party menaced received some losse or preiudice therby in his livelyhood, or estate; for that the menace, & the hurt which the party doth receive thereby, being ioyned together do make the trespas, & give cause of the action of Trespas: Yet in an action of Trespas of Assault & battery, where it is proved & found, that the offendor did make an assault only (as one did strike at an other with a hatchet) but did make no batterie, or hurt the person of any other, it is otherwise: for seeing assaulting doth
22. Ass. p. 60 tend to the breach of the peace, & he that maketh an assault, doth his indevor to
42. Ed. 3. 7. hurt, the law doth give to him that is assaulted an action of Trespas to recover
40. Ed. 3. 40. his damages, & to the K. a fine: for by the assault, the party assaulted is put in
6. H. 7. 1. feare, evill handled, & hindred of his busines. And if he be divers times assaulted, he may have one action of Trespas for all those assaults, & shall recover da-
45. E. 3. 24. mages, according to the number and grievousnes of them. And for an assault
22. Ass. p. 60 made to the wife, the husband & the wife shal have an action of Trespas against
46. Ed. 3. 6. him that made the assault, & the declaration shal be ad damnũ ipsorum, though the husband only shall recover the damages.

Justifying of beating in his owne defence.

12 But as he that is assaulted or beaten, shal have his remedie by action of Trespas against him that did assault or beat him, & also the K. shall have a fine therefore, if he that made the assault or battery did it without cause, & offered therein iniurie to the party assaulted; because the kings peace is broken, & one
16 Ed. 4. 11. member of the cōmon weale hath abused & done wrong to an other: So on the
19. H. 6. 47. other side, if he that was so assaulted or beaten, did first make an assault upon
6. H. 7. 1. him that after did beat him, & would have beaten, wounded, or &c. and in his
34. H. 6. 15. said assault did receive from the other some stripes or blowes, the def. may iu-
43. Ed. 3. 23. stifie his said assault & batterie, as a thing done in defence of his owne person from imminent & present perill, & wherin the Law will protect & defend him: And therfore in yͤ case the def. doth answer the pl. declaration, & pledeth in bar, that yͤ pl. did assault him, & would have beaten him, & he defended himself, & the hurt which the pl. received was by his own assault. And yͤ pl. in his replication

doth

doth plead, that the defendant did with force & armes, & of his owne wrong,
make assault vpon him, beate him, & euill intreate him, contrary to the Kings
peace, without any such cause, as the defendant hath alledged; And so the
issue is ioined, whether the assault was begun and made by the plaintife vpon
the defendant, or by the defendant vpon the plaintife: for if the assault & bat-
terie, or assault only was first made and begun by the defendant vpon the 38.Ed.3.6.
plaintife; Then the defendant did it with force & armes, and against the kings
peace, & is to answere damages to the plaintife, according to the hurt which he
receiued, & to pay a fine to the K. for vsing force & violence, & breaking his peace:
for at all times in an action of Trespas vi & armis brought against any person, 19.H.6.8.
if the defendant be conuict, he shall pay a fine to the King. But if the plaintife 8.Ed.4.15.
made the first assault, and the defendant in his own defence (& rather then he
would be beaten or wounded) did beate, strike, or wound the plaintife, Then
the plaintife shall recouer no dammages against the defendant, but shalbe a-
merced to the King for his false suit: Neither shall the defendant be charged to
pay to the king any fine. And if one man wil assault, & offer to beate two, three, 12.Ed.4.6.
or more persons, & they in their own defence doe beate or wound him, he shall
haue no action of Trespas or other remedie against them, & one of them may
defend & helpe the other. But it is to be obserued in this case, that if one man
doe assault an other, if he which is assaulted may escape with his life, or with- 2H.4.8.
out being wounded or maihemed, it is not lawfull for him to beate or wound 33.H.6.18.
the other who made the assault.

13 As the law doth accompt it no breach of the peace for one man to beate
Iustifying of beating in defence of others — an other in the defence of his own person from killing, wounding, or beating,
but a thing iustifiable: So doth she impute it no fault punishable for the hus-
band to beate him, that doth assault, & would beate, wound, or euil intreate his 19.H.6.31.
wife, being both one flesh: or for the wife to beate him, that doth assault, and 66.
would beate, wound, or euil intreate her husband: Or for the sonne or daugh- Lib. inf 553.
ter to beate him that doth assault, & would beate, wound or euil intreate his or
her father or mother: Or for the father or mother to beat him that doth assault, Lib. inf 554
& would beate, wound, or euil intreat his or her sonne or daughter, being then
within age, & not able to defend him or her selfe: Or for the Lord to beate him
that doth assault, & would beate, wound or euil intreat his villaine: Or for the
seruant to beate, him that doth assault, & would beate, wound, or euill intreate 35.H.6.51.
his master or mistris; or to take any weapons wherewith the assailant would 11.H.6.19.
beate, wound, or euil intreat his master, & to keepe them vntil his rage be swa- 12.Ed.4.6.
ged; for the seruant is bound to performe vnto his master & mistris protection
& dutie, & he may kill a man in defence of his master, if his said master cannot
otherwise escape. But the seruant cannot iustifie the beating of him, that doth 21.H.8.39.
assault, & attempteth to beate, wound, or euil intreate the father, mother, bro-
ther, sister, son, or daughter of his master or mistris for he oweth no obedience 9.Ed.4.48.
or duty to any of them. Neither can the master iustify the beating of him, that
doth assault, & would beat, wound, or euill intreat his seruant. But though the Fitz. Iustification 3.
master cannot assault & beat an other that doth assault, & would beate, wound, 19.H.6.30.
or otherwise euill intreat his seruant; Yet he may with a sword, staffe, or other 66.
weapon aide & defend his seruant assaulted, from being beaten, & that in respect
of the losse of his seruice. And also after his seruãt is beaten, he may haue an ac- 22.H.6.43.
tiõ of Trespas against him that did beat, wound or euil intreat his said seruãt 21.H.6.9.
The masters remedy for the beating of his seruant. — (vnles it were vpon ye same seruants own assault) & recouer so much in dama- Fitz. Trespas 46.
ges against the offẽdor, as he receiued preiudice, or hinderance by ye losse of his 20.H.7.5.
said seruants seruice: for if the seruant be but so beaten, that he is able to do his Cook, lib.5. 108.
ser-

seruice, as well as he was before, the master shall recouer no damages for that beating. And as the master may haue an action of trespas against the offendor, & recouer so much in damages as he doth lose by the want of his said seruants seruice: so likewise the same seruāt may haue another action of trespas against the offendor, & recouer so much in damages, as he shall receiue hurt on his bodie, by ẏ said assault & beating. In an action of trespas brought by ẏ master for beating of his seruant, wherby he did lose his seruice, it is a good plea for the defendant to say, that he was not the plaintifs seruant, or that he was the defendants seruant, and not the plaintifs: or that he was farmor, tenant, neighbor, or soiourner with the plaintife, and not his seruant: or that the partie beaten was the plaintifs wife. And in the said action of trespas of assault and batterie for the beating of his seruant, he need not declare of the retainet of the same seruant, for if he did but serue his master at his pleasure, yet the master shall haue an action of trespas for the losse of his seruice.

Fitz Tre. spas. 210. 21.H.6.8. 34.H.6.54. 34.H.6.28. 43. 22.H.6.43.

14 As the law doth allow a man to beat another in defence of his person, from extreame peril: so doth she tollerate one man to beat another for the preseruation of his goods from rapine and spoile: for as it standeth not with the peace of the realme, that one man without some lawful cause should beat another: so it standeth not with the iustice of the realme, that one man should take anothers goods iniuriously from him. And he that will attempt by force and violence to take away another mans goods wrongfully from him, may iustly by force & strong hand be resisted: And if in that case he that shall make an assault to take those goods, be in the encounter beaten by the owner of the same goods, the law will excuse the owner therin, & protect him to defend those goods, wherof he hath a lawfull propertie. And the same law is, if a man hath no propertie in goods, but onely a possession by the bailement of another, to bee redeliuered when they shall be required: if in this case a stranger will assay by force to take the same away, he that hath the possession of the same goods (though it be but a bloodhound) may defend the same by force: And if the said stranger shalbe hurt or beaten in that assault, he shall haue no remedy by action of trespas, or otherwise, against him that had the said possession, for he may iustifie the defence of the goods so bailed vnto him, in respect that he hath the lawful possession of thē, and standeth chargeable to redeliuer them, or the very value of them to him, ẏ bailed them vnto him, whensoeuer he shall be required. And so it is if one hath a mill whereunto a riuer or spring of water doth run, and hath run time out of the remembrance of man, and another would stop the course of that water, & turne it another way, & the owner of the mill doth disturbe him therein, whervpon that other doth assault and attempt to beat him: In this case, if the owner of the mill for his owne safegard, and for the defence of his auncient water course, doth beat him againe, it is iustifiable: for this beating was not an intended breach of the peace, but to defend him from violence offered to his person, and iniurie to his freehold or terme. And the same law is in euery case of batterie of another, who doth menace or assault the right owner, and attempt to beat him for the lawfull defence of his owne freehold, or terme, or from his lawfull high way.

Battery in defence of his goods.

9.E.4.28. 19.H.6.31. 65. Kel.p.92.

Lib.Intr. 553.

Battery in defence of his land, lease, or way.

3.H.4.9.

Lib.Intr. 554. 11.H.6.33. 10.E.4.6.

15 If one man do make assault vpon another attempting to beat him, & so to breake ẏ peace, if a Iu. of peace do command him ẏ maketh ẏ assault to keep ẏ peace, & to surcease his assault, & he wil not do it, or wil answer ẏ he will not: ẏ Iust. of peace may lay his hands vpon the offendor, & arrest him to find sureties of his good behauiour: and if the offendor doe make rescue, and resist the arrest

9.E.4.3.

Battery in resisting a Iustice of peace.

arrest by force, and then be beaten, hee shall haue no remedie against the same Iustice of peace, who hath done nothing but that which belonges to his office, and dutie: and the offendor first in breaking the peace, and after in resisting the Iustice of the Law, being beaten by the Iustice of Peace, or any other in his company, hath worthily tasted the due reward of his owne disobedience. And also the Iustice of peace may in this case commit the offendor to prison, vntill he hath found sureties to keep the peace: A Iustice of peace may arrest one to find suretie of peace, and though he doth let the same partie after to goe at libertie, without finding suretie of peace, yet he shall haue no action or other remedy to punish the same Iustice, because he is Iustice of Record. 21.H.7.22. 9.E.4.3.

A schoolemaster beateth his scholler.

16 In an action of trespasse of assault and batterie, it is a good plea for the defendant to plead, that he is a schoolemaster, and a teacher & instructer of children, and that the plaintife put himselfe to be scholler with him, & to be taught & instructed in his booke; and because the plaintife was carelesse and negligent in learning of that whereof he was instructed, or did beat & abuse other schollers his schoole-fellows, the defendant did beat him with a rod, as it was lawfull for him to doe. 21.E.4.6. Li.Intr.556

A master beateth his prentice.

17 And likewise in an action of trespasse of assault and batterie, it is a good plea for the defendant to plead, that he is a free man of the citie of London, occupying the trade of a draper: & that the plaintife beeing aboue the age of xiiij. yeares, put himselfe apprentise vnto him, to serue him in that trade, by ẏ space of vij. yeares: And because the plaintife was negligent in learning his trade, he did strip him, and beat him with a rod, as it was lawful for him to do: and if he did not sufficiently beat him for his offence at one time, hee may beat him againe: And in like sort, if a villaine wil not be iustified by his Lord, nor obedient vnto him, it is lawfull for the Lord to chastise and beat him, or to imprison him, or to inflict any reasonable punishmẽt vpon him, so that he do not maihem or kill him: for in the foresaid cases, the schoolemaster, master, and Lord haue a ciuill power and authoritie ouer the scholler, seruant, and villaine. Some doe hold that if an apprentice or seruant be aboue the age of xxj. years, and then do his seruice negligently, that his master ought not to beat him therefore, but to haue an action of couenant against him. But note the forme of the Indenture of an apprentice touching chastising him: And it appeareth by the Statute of 33. H.8.12. that the master may strike his seruant with his hand, fist, small staffe, or sticke for correction, and though he do draw blood. S.Br.28. 21.E 4.6. & 53. Stat. 33. H. 8.12.

Beating of a man that is franticke.

18 If a man be franticke, furious, or mad, and attempteth being at liberty to burne an house, or to doe some other mischiefe, or to hurt himselfe, or others: it is lawfull for his parents, kinsmen, and other friends, to take him, put him into an house, to bind him, and to beat him with rods, & to doe any other forcible act to reclaime him, or to keep him in a house or place alone, where he shal do no hurt: And he shall haue no action of trespasse of assault and batterie, action of false imprisonment, nor other remedie against them: for in this case, and the others before rehearsed, the peace of the realme was not broken, but a lawfull punishment was inflicted vpon those who had deserued it, to the end they should be reformed, and hereafter doe their duties the better. 22. Assise p. 56. 22.E.4.45.

Beating of one that will not yeeld to arrest.

19 If one man do enter a plaint against another in a court hauing iurisdiction to hold plea of that suit, and the Sergeant of the court doth arrest the defendant 2.E.4.6. 21.H.7.39.

fendant, and the defendant will draw his sword to defend himselfe, and after doth run away, with intent to escape from the Sergeant, if in this case, the Sergeant and he that did enter the plaint, do pursue him, beate, & hurt him, if he will not be apprehended and yeeld to the arrest, they may iustifie the same in an action of Trespas of assault and batterie; for they haue not broken the peace, nor offended the Law, in seeking to iustifie him, who doth attempt to flie from the iustice and indifferent triall of the law. But if the partie had not been arrested, the Sergeant, nor any other with him could haue iustified the beating of him.

38.H.6.25. 20 In an action of Trespas of assault and batterie, the defendant pleaded, that the plaintife was his seruant retained, & departed out of his seruice, and that he laid hold vpon him, and led him home to his house to doe his seruice: But this was adiudged no plea; for it is not lawfull for the Master in this case to beate, or forciblie to compell his seruant against his will to returne and do his seruice; but to require him to do it, and if he will not, then the Master may haue an action of Couenant against his seruant, and recouer so much in dammages, as he hath receiued hinderance by the losse of his seruice. But by Sta.5.El.4. the statute made An 5. Eliz. it is ordeined, That if any seruant retained to serue in husbandry, shall depart from his master, mistresse, or dames seruice, before the end of his terme, vnlesse it be for some reasonable and sufficient cause to be allowed by a Iustice of peace of the Countie, or the Maior, or other head officer of the Citie, borough, or towne corporat, wherein the said Master, mistresse, or dame inhabiteth: Or if any seruant at the end of his terme depart from his master, mistresse, or dames seruice, without one quarters warning giuen before the end of his terme, and before two lawfull witnesses; Then vpon complaint made by the said Master, &c. to two Iustices of peace of the Countie, or to the Maior, or head officer of the citie, borough, &c. they or any of them shall haue power to heare and examine the matter, and finding the said seruant, or the partie so refusing, faultie in the premisses, vpon such proofes and good matter, as to their discretions shall be thought sufficient, to commit him to ward, there to remaine without baile or mainprise, vntill he shall be bound to the partie to whom the offence shall be made, to continue with him for the wages limitted by this statute, and then to be discharged vpon his deliuerie, without paying any fee to the Gaoler where he shall be so imprisoned. And as the Master cannot by beating, nor by force compell his 38.H.6.25. 22.Ass.p.85 seruant, to serue him against his will: No more can a Lord compell his ward, by beating, or by force to come vnto him, or to tarie with him against his will: But if he doe depart from him, then his Lord is to haue his action against him.

Beating of a seruant departing out of his seruice.

A Gardian may not beat his ward.

22.Ass.pla. 59. 27.Ass.p.4. Fitz.Trespas 238. 21 H.6.39. 21 If A. commaund, procure, or hyre B. to smite, or beate C. and he doth assault and beate C. in the presence of A. In this case, C. may haue an action of Trespas of assault and batterie against A. and recouer dammages against him, or against A. and B. together; for here the peace was broken, and wrong done to C. by the meanes and perswasion of A. And B. had not striken with his weapon, if A. had not first striken with his tongue. And the same law is, if A. go to fight with C. and desireth B. to go with him, and after doth meete with C. and doth assault and beate him; In this case C. may haue an action of Trespas against A. and B. together, or against B. alone, though B. did not assault C. nor giue him any

Commaundement of batterie.

blowe, and recouer dammages against him, because he came in company with one, that intended to breake the peace, and to doe an vnlawfull act.

Hurting at some exercise.

22 If two or more doe agrée together to runne at tilt, iuste, barriers, or to play at backsword, bucklers, footebal, or such like, & one of them doth beat, bruise, or wound an other; the party grieued shal not haue an action of Trespas of assault & batterie against the other: for that it was a combate by consent, & put in practise to try their strength, valour, or agilitie, & not to break the peace. But if the same day or some other after that the pastime is at an end, & they departed a sunder, one will assault or beate an other, in respect of some wrong conceiued to be receiued in the time of the said play; then an action of Trespas of assault & battery may be pursued by him that is so beaten against the trespassor. Fitz. barre 244.

Whipping of a Vagabond.

23 In an action of Trespas of assault & battery, it is a good plea for the defendant, to plead, that the plaintif was by the stat. made An. 39. El. (intituled an Act for punishment of Rogues, Vagabonds, & sturdy beggers) declared to be a Rogue, Vagabond, or sturdy begger, & that he was taken begging, vagrant, & misordering himselfe at L. in the County of N. & that vpon his apprehension, by the appointment of A. B. one of the Iustices of peace of the said County of N. or of the Constable, Headborough, or Tithingman of the same parish of L. he was by this defendant stripped naked from the middle vpward, and openly whipped vntill his body was bloudy. And the same law is if any Iustice of peace, Maior, Bailife, or other head officer shall commit any offendor which shall cut or vnlawfully take away any corne or graine growing, or robbe any orchards or gardens, or breake or cut any hedge, pales, railes, or fence, or digge, pul vp, or take vp any fruit trées, or trées in any orchard, garden, or elsewhere, to the intent to take & cary the same away; Or shall cut or spoile any woods, or vnderwoods, poles, or trées standing, not being felony by the lawes of this Realme: Or shall be a procuror or receiuor knowing the same (contrary to the statute therefore made An. 43. El. intituled, an act to auoid and preuent diuers misdemeanors in lewd and idle persons) shalbe committed by a I. of Peace, or by a head officer of a city, borough &c. to some Constable or other inferiour officer of the city, borough, Towne, or Hamlet, where the offence shall be committed, or the partie apprehended, to be whipped. If in this case the said Constable, or other inferior officer shall whip the same offendor vntill his body shalbe bloudie; the same offendor shall neither haue an action of Trespas of assault & battery, nor other remedy against the said Constable or officer: for in the foresaid cases, & in all other cases, where an offendor is punished for petit Larceny by whipping, & for other offences by the pillorie, the stocks, the tumbrell, or otherwise, for any offéce committed by him contrary to any of the lawes or statutes of the Realme, there is no peace broken, nor blame to be imputed to him or them which do execute that punishment; for it is the iustice of the law, which doth inflict those punishments vpon offendors for transgressing the law, & the executioners of those punishments be but the instruments of the law; as the axe is in the Carpenters hand.

St. 39. El. 4.

Sta. 43. El. 7.

Punishments by the order of law.

Battery for disobeying of a Writ or Warrant.

24 In an action of Trespas of assault & battery, it is a good plea for the def. to plead, that he had a warrant to arrest the plaintife, and that by force of that warrant he did arrest him, & then the plaintife made assault vpon him, & therefore ẏ hurt which he receiued, was by his own assault: for euery subiect is boũd to obey the K. writs, & all mandates, precepts, & warrants awarded by his Iusti- 21. H. 7. 39. Fitz. Trespas 108.

stices, shiriffes and officers sufficiently authorized: And he that doth resist them, or denyeth to obey them, encountreth the iustice of the law; and therefore the beating of him who refuseth to submit himselfe to the obedience of the Law, is no breach of the peace, but a meane to performe the law.

25 Though the Law hath a regard to preserue peace betwéen all persons, and in all places, and caryeth a vigilant eye, that one person shall not menace, assault, beate, maihem, or imprison another (but in certaine cases, and for some speciall causes) and imposeth an heauie burden vpon such as shall breake that peace by any of the meanes aforesaid; Yet she hath a more speciall respect to some ceraine places, to some tymes, and to some persons; and caryeth that reuerend and due care and consideration of them; that she inflicteth a more sharpe and bitter punishment vpon such as shall violate the peace in them, or to the offence of them. And therefore for the auoiding of the disturbance of the peace in the Church (where God is to be honoured and all peace to be preserued) and to continue peace to preists, clerks, and others, whilest they are doing diuine seruice; There was a statute made Anno 50. E. 3. and after rehersed and continued Anno 1. R. 2. whereby it was enacted; That if any of the Kings officers, or other person, doe arrest any priest, clerke, or other, which is doing any diuine seruice in the Church, Churchyard, or other place dedicated to God, he shall be imprisoned, and punished at the Kings pleasure, and further shall recompence the partie arrested. But no people of the Church, shall kéepe them within the Church, or Sanctuarie by fraud or collusion.

Sta. 50. E. 3. 1. R. 2. 15.

Arresting one in a Church doing diuine seruice.

26 And because it is most necessarie in euery Christian common weale to prouide that peace and tranquility may be preserued and continued among the people, and specially in holy Church in the time of diuine seruice, and preaching, and that all things being contrary thereunto, or that are or may be in disturbance thereof may by forsight be eschewed and auoyded, and remedy therefore prouided. By a like statute made Anno 1. Reg. M. it was ordeined, That if any person of his owne authoritie, shall willingly and of purpose by open words or déeds, maliciously or contemtuously disturbe, or by any other vnlawfull wayes disquiet or misuse any Preacher allowed to preach by the Quéene, or by any Archbishop or Bishop of this realme, or by any other lawfull Ordinary, or by any of the Uniuersities of Oxford and Cambridge, or otherwise lawfully authorized, or charged by reason of his cure, benefice, or spirituall promotion, or charge, in his open sermon, preaching, or collation, that he shall preach or pronounce in any Church, Chappell, or Churchyard, or in any other place vsed or appointed: then euery such offendor, his aydors, procurors, or abbettors, immediatly after any of the said misdemeanors committed, or at any time after, shal be arrested by any Constable or Churchwarden of the said parish, towne, or place where the said offence shal be so committed, or by any other officer, or by any other person then being present at the time of the said offence, and carried to any Justice of peace within the said shire, or within any City, borough, Libertie or towne corporat, wherein Just. of P. be, where the said offence shalbe so committed: And the said Justices vpon due accusations thereupon made by the apprehendor, or other person, of the offendor, forthwith shal commit him to safe kéeping: & within 6. days immediatly after the said accusation so made, the said Just. with one other Just. of P. within the shire, city, borough, liberty, or town corporat shal diligently examin the

Sta. 1. M. 3.

Disturbance of a preacher in his sermon.

the offence aforesaid. And if the said two Justices shall upon their examination find the person so accused guiltie of any of the said offences, whereof he shall be accused, and that by two sufficient witnesses, or by his confession; then they shall commit him to the Gaole of the said Shire, City, Borough &c. where the offence was committed; there to remaine without baile or mainprise by the space of thrée moneths then next ensuing, and further to the next quarter sessions &c. at which sessions the said person upon his reconciliation & repentance before the said Justices at the said sessions, shall be delivered out of prison upon sufficient surety of his good abearing, and behauiour, to be then and there taken by the said Justices for one whole yeare then next ensuing, as by the discretion of the said Justices then and there being, or of the more part of them shall be thought conuenient. And if the said person will not be reconciled, and repent at the said quarter sessions, then he shall be further committed to the said Gaole by the said Justices; there to remaine without baile or mainprise, untill he shall be reconciled and be penitent &c. And if any person or persons of their owne authoritie willingly and unlawfullie doe rescue any offendor so apprehended, or will disturbe the said offendor to be apprehended; then euery of the said Rescuers or disturbers shall suffer like imprisonment as is aforesaid, and further shall pay for euery of his offences v. l. to the Quéene. If any of the offendors aforesaid be not apprehended in time conuenient but doe escape, then the said escape shall be lawfully presented before the Justices of peace at the next quarter sessions &c. and the Inhabitants of the parish where the said escape was suffred, shall forfeite to the Quéene &c. for euery such offence v. l. to be leuied and taken as other like amerciaments and fines be leuied upon any village, hundred, or towne, for the escape of any murderer, or other felon, for not making pursuit upon huy and cry, according to the Statute of Winchester, and the statute of 3. H. 7. 1. This Act shall not extend to take away the authority and punishment of the Ecclesiasticall lawes standing in force, for the punishment of any of the offences aforesaid: But they shall be used in euerie thing, as though this act had neuer ben made. Whatsoeuer person offending in the premisses, shal for any the offences afore recited, receiue punishment of the Ordinary, hauing Testimoniall thereof under the said Ordinaries seale, shall not for the said offence eftsones be conuicted before the Justices: Et é conuerso.

Rescuing the offendor, or disturbing the arrest.

The punishment of the Town where the offendor dothe scape.

Punishment by Ecclesiasticall laws.

27 To the intent utterly to take away all quarreling, brawling, fraying, and fighting openly in Churches and Churchyards, by a statute made An. 5. & 6. E. 6. it was ordained; That if any person whatsoeuer doe by words only quarrell, chide, or brawle in any Church or Churchyard; Then it shall be lawfull to the Ordinary of the place, where the offence is done, and proued by two lawfull witnesses, to suspend him being a Layman ab ingressu Ecclesiæ, and being a clerke from the Ministration of his office, so long as he thinketh méete, according to the fault. And if any person or persons shall smite or lay any violent hands upon any other, either in any Church, or Churchyard; then ipso facto euery person so offending shall be déemed excommunicat, and be excluded from the fellowship and company of Christs congregation. And if any person shall maliciously strike any person with any weapon in any Church or Churchyard, or shall draw any weapon in any Church or Churchyard, to the intent to strike an other with the same weapon; then euery person so offending, and thereof being conuicted by verdict of xij. men, or by his owne confession, or by two lawfull witnesses before the Justices of assise, Justices of

Sta. 5. & 6. E. 6. 4

Chiding in a Church or Churchyard.

Smiting in a Church or Churchyard.

Drawing or smiting with a weapon in a Church.

oyer

oyer and determiner, or Justices of peace in their sessions, shall be adiudged by the same Justices before whom such person shall be conuicted, to haue one of his eares cut off. And if the person or persons so offending haue none eares, whereby they should receiue such punishment, as is aforesaid; Then he or they to be marked and burned in the cheeke with an hot yron hauing the letter F. whereby he or they may be knowne and taken for fray makers, and fighters; and besides that, euery such person to be and stand ipso facto excommunicated as is aforesaid.

28 As the law hath alwaies had a principall and most speciall regard, that there should be no breach, or disturbance of the peace, to those persons, places, and tymes, which be dedicated and deuoted to the seruice of God, to the Ministration of his Sacraments, and preaching of his worde: So hath she a secondarie respect, that the King the head of the Realme and chiefe fountaine of peace, may haue tranquillitie and peace, at the time, and in the place, where he doth rest, and in person make his aboade: whereupon by a Statute made Anno 33. H. 8. it was enacted, That if any person shall maliciously strike any other person, whereby bloud shall be shed in any of the Kings houses or pallaces, or in any other house, where the Kings Maiestie his heires &c. shall be at that tyme abiding in his royall person, (viz. within any edifices, courts, places, gardens, orchards, or houses within the Porters warde of any the houses aboue rehearsed, or within any gardens, priuy walkes, orchards, tiltyards, woodyards, tennis playes, cockfights, bowling allies, neare adioyning to any of the houses aforesaid, and being part of the same, or within 200. foote of the standard of any outward gate, or gates of any of the said houses, commonly vsed for passage from any of the houses &c. and shall be thereof indicted, arraigned, and attainted according to the Statute in that case prouided, he shall haue his right hand stricken off, be imprisoned during his life, and make fine to the King at his pleasure. But this act, nor the paines and forfaitures before rehearsed, shall not extend to any Noble man, or other person that shall strike his seruant within the said pallaces or houses, or the limits of the same, with his hand, or fist, or any small staffe, or sticke for correction for any offence committed; Nor to any of the Kings officers, that in executing his office shall strike any person with his hand or fist, or small staffe, sticke, or tipstaffe; Nor to any other person, that in doing seruice at any triumphe, or any other time of seruice, by the King, or any of his Councell, or other his head officers commaundement, shall for the executing of his said seruice, strike any person, with his hand, fist, small staffe, or sticke, or any tipstaffe within the same pallace, house &c. although by reason of the same stroake or stroakes there happen to be any bloud shead of such person as shall be so striken, except the person so stricken dye of the same stroake within one yeare next after. Long time before the making of this statute King Alured ordeined a law, That if any man did strike or drawe a weapon of iron to strike in the Kings pallace, the King might, if he pleased, put him to death.

Stat. 33. H. 8. 12.

Drawing of bloud within the Kings pallace.

Leges Aluredi cap. 7.

29 Because they which vpon the Kings commaundement do come to his councell, or vpon his summons doe resort to his Parliament, doe make their repaire thither to further the wealth and peace of the Realme; it hath been therfore thought reason that during the time of the said councel & Parliament they should not be depriued of that peace which they endeauor to procure to

Assault vpon one which cōmeth to the Parliament. — *Stat.11.H.6.11.*

others and themselues. Wherefore by a Statute made Anno 11.H.6. it was ordeined: That if any assault or fray be made vpon any Lord Spirituall, or Temporall, Knight of the Shire, Citizen, or Burgesse, which commeth to the Parliament, or to the Kings Councell by his commaundement, and there being and attending; then Proclamation shall be made in the most open place of the Towne where the fray was made by three seuerall dayes, that the partie which made such affraye or assault shall yeeld himselfe in the Kings Bench within a quarter of a yeare next after the Proclamation made, if it be in the Terme tyme, or otherwise at the first day of the Terme following the said quarter. And if he doe not, he shall be attainted of the deede, and pay to the party grieued his double dammages, to be taxed by the discretion of the Justices of the same bench, or by the inquest if it be needfull, and shall make fine and ransom at the Kings pleasure. And if he come, and be found guiltie by inquest, by examination, or otherwise, of such affray or assault, then he shall pay to the partie grieued his double dammages found by the inquest, or to be taxed by the discretion of the said Justices, and make fine and ransom at the Kings pleasure.

Assaulting the seruant of a Parliament man. — *St.5.H.4.6.*

And by the Statute made Anno 5.H.4. it was enacted, That he shall haue the like punishment which maketh assault or fray, in the Parliament tyme, vpon any meniall seruant of any Knight of the Parliament, Citizen, Burgesse etc. which doth come to the Parliament with his master.

The libertie of the Clergie as a conuocation. — *St.8.H.6.1.*

And by the Statute of Anno 8.H.6. it was prouided, That al the Clergie, which be called to the conuocation by the Kings writ, and all their seruants, and familiars, shall fully vse, and enioy such libertie, or defence, in comming, tarying, and returning, as the great men and Commons of the Realme haue, or are wont, or ought to enioy, which are called to the Parliament.

30 Seeing the wealth and peace of the Realme doth chiefely consist in the due execution of Justice, which cannot be ministred without meete persons, and places ordeined therefore; for that cause the Law hath specially prouided, that those persons and places which be designed to the same Administration of Justice, shall be so guarded and protected from force and violence offered vnto them, or in them, that shee hath inflicted deeper and more greiuous punishments to those who shall breake or disturbe the peace, in the presence of those Magistrates, or in those places, than to them who shall breake the peace in the Kings own pallace, where he is in person abiding, or in the Parliament time ordeined for the making of Laws.

Assaulting a Judge or Juror. — *22.Ed.3.13.*

And therefore it hath bene adiudged; That if one draw his sword to strike a Justice assigned sitting in place of iudgement, and be thereof found guiltie, he shall forfeite his lands and chattels, and haue his right hand cut off. And likewise if one in the presence of the Justices doe strike a Juror, he shall forfeite his lands and goods, haue his right hand striken off, and be committed to perpetuall prison. And the same Law is, if one of the Kings Justices assigned doth arrest any person, which hath made a fray before him, and a straunger will rescue that prisoner, whereby he doth escape, in this case, as well the prisoner, as he that made the rescous shall be disherited, and be perpetually imprisoned, for that the attachment of such a Justice is the Kings owne attachment in the construction of the Law.

Striking in time or place of Justice. — *Fitz: Cor. 280. 2.& 3.P.&.M. Dy.188.*

And if one doe strike an other in Westminster Hall, during the time that the Kings Courts do sit, hee shall forfeite to the King his lands and goods, haue his right hand cut off, and bee committed to perpetuall prison.

4.H.7.2. 31 In an action of Trespas of assault and batterie, the defendant pleaded, that there were divers felonies committed in those parts where he dwelt, and he being watching in his house, came into the high Streete, where the plaintife was at eleuen of the clocke in the night, and the defendant came vnto him, and laid his hands in peaceable maner vpon him to see his face, and when he perceiued that he was a true man, he left him & departed, which was the same assault and batterie: And this was allowed to be a good iustification; for by the statute of Winchester, watchmen may arrest Nightwalkers, and also may appose them from whence they come, and what they be; but they must be such watchmen, as be appointed by the Towne: And so euery man may arrest Nightwalkers, for it is for the good of the Common wealth. The same
4.H.7.18. law is in an action of Trespas brought of the assault and batterie of his ser-
5.H.7.5. uant, whereby he did lose his seruice 3. daies, and the defendant pleaded, that
2.Ed.4.8. A. was robbed at midnight, of goods to the value of xl. s. whereupon the said A. came to the Constable, and prayed him to search for suspicious persons, and to apprehend and arrest them, and accordingly he did search, and found the same seruant walking suspiciously in the streete in the night, and therefore he would haue arrested him, but the said seruant fled, and would not yeeld to the arrest, and the defendant by the Constables commaundement pursued and tooke him: This was adiudged a good plea in barre; for when a felonie is committed, the Constable, or any others may arrest suspitious persons: and if any that is arrested will not yeeld, but assault him or them that do arrest him, they may iustifie the beating of him, for that he doth resist the peace, and iustice of the Realme, when he doth forcible striue to flie, and not to be iustified by it. Arresting by watchmen.

32 If a man be assaulted and beaten, and then be outlawed in an action Trespas for batterie before outlawrie.
30.Ed.3.4. 29.Ass.p.63. of Trespas, and after doth purchase his Charter of pardon, which is allowed;
28.Ed.3.92. he may haue an action of Trespas against the offendor, for the assault & bat-
6.H.4.7. terie made before the Outlawrie, for the said outlawrie shall not extinguish his action, nor cause that offence, which before was punishable to be vnpunished: And if the partie beaten should not haue his Action, the iniurie done vnto him should be vnpunished: for the king shall haue no remedy to recouer
29.Ass.p.47 damages for this batterie done to the person of him that was outlawed, as he
63. might haue had, if any debt had been owing, or any goods had been taken from the outlaw before his outlawrie: And the Law doth expect, that for the peace broken, and the wrong done to the partie grieued, the same partie shall vpon his action of Trespas brought, be recompenced by the recouerie of his damages, and the king satisfied for his peace broken by a fine.

33 In an action of Trespas of assault and batterie, the defendant pleaded A man first indicted of batterie, and after sued for the same trespas.
11.H.4.65. not guiltie, the plaintife replied, that the defendant was before that time in-
9.H.6.60. dicted before the Iustices of Peace of the same Countie, of the said assault and
27.Ass.p.57 batterie, and thereupon proces was awarded against him for the kings fine, who then appeared, and pleaded, that the hurt which the plaintife receiued was by his owne assault, and thereupon they were at issue, and before the verdict, the defendant appeared, and confessed the Trespas, and submitted himselfe to the kings fauour, and made his fine; and demaunded iudgement, if he should be allowed to plead not guiltie, contrarie to his owne confession: and this was adiudged a good Replication, and an Estoppell of the said plea in barre. And then the defendant pleaded, that the hurt which the plaintife receiued

receiued was by his owne assault, vpon which plea the plaintife demurred, seing the defendant before had pleaded that plea against the King. And then he also waiued that plea, and confessed the trespas: whereupon a writ was awarded to inquire of dammages. And so for this assault and batterie the king was first intituled to a fine by the Indictment, and after the partie grieued recouered dammages, by an action of Trespas.

What imprysonment is.

34 Imprisonment is where a man is arrested by force, & against his will, and is restrained of his libertie, and put in a common Gaole, or other gaole, in a cage, or in the stockes, or otherwise kept in the high streete, or open field, if he be in restraint, and cannot go at libertie when he will, but is bound to become obedient to the will of the Law, and is in the custodie of the Law. And in all the cases aforesaid, the partie so restrained, is said to be a prisoner, so long as he hath not his liberty, freely to go at all times, when he will, without baile, mainprise, or other restraint: And therefore if one person do arrest, imprison, or otherwise restraine an other person of that libertie, without sufficient and lawfull cause, the partie grieued may haue an action of False imprisonment, or an action of Trespas against him that doth so arrest, or imprison him, and recouer damages against him. And the King shall also haue a fine of him, for that his law is contemned, and his peace is broken, in that one of his subiects presumeth to imprison an other without sufficient warrant of him, or his law; seeing imprisonment of an other by only act, will, or commaundement (without offence of the Law) is one of the kings most royall prerogatiues, and only annexed to the maiestie, dignitie, and imperiall Crowne of this Realme: For by the Statute of Magna charta it was specially ordeined, That no man shall be taken or imprisoned, or disseised of his freehold, or liberties, or free customes, or be outlawed, or exiled, or any other wayes destroyed, neither shall any passe or sit in iudgement vpon him, but by lawfull iudgement of his Peeres, or by the Law of the land. And by the statute of An 28. Ed. 3. it was enacted, That no man shall be put out of his land or tenement, nor imprysoned, nor disherited, nor put to death, without being brought in aunswere by due proces of the Law. And therefore whereas the Maior and Burgesses of a towne corporate (being before authorized by the Kings letters patents to make ordinances for the good gouernment of the same Towne) did condiscend amongst themselues, to leuie a summe of money for the charges of a lawfull and necessarie act to be done in the same Towne, and did further agree, that if any of them did refuse to pay his part of that contribution money so assessed, to be paied, that then he should be committed to pryson vntill he had paid it: and after one of the Burgesses of the Towne which before had agreed to the same assessement & ordinance, refused to pay the money which he was by the residue assigned and assessed to pay: whereupon the Maior of the same Towne committed him to pryson, against whom the same Burgesse brought his action of False imprisonment, and recouered dammages against the same Maior: for though the same Burgesse, & all others of the same Corporation might haue submitted himselfe to haue paid a summe of money, to haue been leuied by distresse, or action of debt, if he or they had not performed the same order, & paid his part of that contribution: yet the libertie or imprisonment of his bodie resteth in the censure & iudgement of the Law, and not in his owne disposition. As if B. do promise C. or be bound by Obligation vnto him, that if he do not paie vnto the same C. xx. li. within sixe monethes, that then C. shall take and impryson him, vntill he hath paid it: notwithstanding B. do not pay to C.

Lib. Intrac. fol. 319.

An action of False imprysonment.

Stat. 9. H. 3. 29.

Stat. 28. Ed. 3. 3.

Co. Lib. 5. 64.

Voluntarie consent, no cause of imprysonment.

to C. the same xx.l. at the time assessed, C. may not imprison B. for it, though it was his owne promise, agreement, or bond: for that B. is not iudged by his peeres or condemned by the law of the land according to the foresaid statute of Magna Charta. Neither is he brought to answere by due Proces of the law according to the purport of the before specified statute of An 28.E.3.

35 But in many cases one person may arrest, imprison and restrayne an other of his libertie and no action of false imprisonment, action of Trespas, or other remedie will be had against him. As first it is a lawfull imprisonment which is done by the absolute commaundement of the King, the chiefe Soveraigne head of the common weale by his owne mouth, or by the privie Councell, (which speake and direct by his Authoritie) or by the absolute commaundement of the Kings Iustices: Or for the forrest: Or for the detestable offence of wilfull murder. And the common law doth prohibit the prisoner to be mainpernable in all the foresaid cases, as it appeareth by the statute of Westm 1. Imprisonmēt by the commaundment of the King, his Iustices, &c.

Stat. 3. E. 1. 15.

36 He is lawfully imprisoned as a speciall disturber of the peace, who is committed to prison, for any great and notorious offence, viz. such as we doe call Mala per se, which be hated, abhorred, and persecuted in all Kingdomes, Provinces, Cities, and well governed common weales: As Treasons, murders, rapes, burglaries, robberies &c. And it appeareth by the statute of West. 1. that he is lawfully imprisoned which before was outlawed: And he which is an approver: And that felon which is taken with the manner: And he which hath broken the Kings prison: And he which is a theefe openly defamed, and knowen: And he which is appelled by an approvor: And he which is taken for burning of a house feloniously done: Or for false money: Or for counterfeiting the Kings seale: And he which is excommunicat taken at the Bishops request: And he which is taken for a manifest offence, or for Treason touching the King: in which said cases the offendor shall be committed to prison and not be let to baile or mainprise. And if any person shall be once convicted that he did take upon him by witchcraft, inchantment, charme, or sorcerie to declare in what place any treasure of gold or silver might be had, or where things lost, or stollen, should be found, or to the intent to provoke any person to unlawfull love, or whereby any cattell or goods of any person shall be distroyed, wasted, or impaired, or to hurt or distroy any person in his or her body, although the same be not effected: Then he shall suffer imprisonment one whole yeare without baile, or mainprise, and shall stand upon the Pillorie &c. for he that declareth the things aforesaid, by any of the meanes aforesaid, receiveth his knowledge therein, and practiseth to effect the same, by the inspiracion of the Devill, the professed enemie of mans peace, and so committeth a great and notorious offence, and worthily deserveth imprisonment.

Imprisonmēt for notorious & great offences.

Stat. 3. E. 1. 15.

Sta. 1 Iac. 12.

Witchcraft, charme, sorcery.

S. Felony by Statute.

37 He is lawfully imprisoned who is found by verdict, or by his owne confession convicted for any offence done vi et armis and against the Kings peace: for the law hath ordained that all things shall be done, and all sutes prosecuted betwene one member of the common weale and an other with all tranquilitie and quietnes, and he that doth any thing in perturbation of that tranquilitie, breaketh the Kings peace, and so shal be committed to prison, as a disturber of the peace, untill he hath paied unto the King a fine. And therefore in an action

Imprisonmēt for offences done vi & armis.

action of Trespas or false imprisonment, if the plaintife do declare against the defendant, that he did such an offence, or made such a trespas, vi & armis & contra pacem, the defendant doth first and principally seeke to auoyd that, to cleare him selfe of force, and the breach of the peace, and doth plead thereunto Quoad venire vi & armis & quicquid est contra pacem non est culpabilis &c. Accordingly in an Assise brought against foure men, it was found by verdict that one of them came with force and armes, and all foure were committed to prison because in Trespas all be principals, and none be accessories; and yet if any of them had bin within age, then he should not haue been imprisoned. But if a woman couert be found a disseisoresses with force, she shall be committed to prison, And if an action of Trespas of battery be brought against the husband and wife, and it be found by verdict that the wife was guiltie of the battery, but not the husband, the wife shall be imprisoned, and not the husband. If he that is proued to be a disseisor in an assise be found to haue carried away any goods, this is an attainder of force, and he shal be imprisoned without further inquiry of the force, for so it is ordayned by the statute of Anno 4.H.4. If a man do giue councell to others to do a disseisin with force, whereby they do it, this shall be adiudged a disseisin in him, and he shall be imprisoned. In an Assise, if the defendant do pleade a plea wherein an Ouster is not denied, which is found against him, he shall be imprisoned, though he doth not confesse the Ouster: And he that confesseth an Ouster, if the Issue be found against him shalbe imprisoned. In an action of Trespas brought for fishing by force and armes in his seuerall fishing, the defendant was found guiltie, and was committed to prison. In an assise of rent charge against three terre tenants, it was found that the rent was behinde, and the plaintife distrayned, and one of them made rescous, and therefore they were all adiudged disseisors, but none were imprisoned but he that made the Rescous. And in euery case of force where any Trespas is found vi & armis, false imprisonment, or assise, the iudgement shall be, quod defend' capiatur, for he shall be imprisoned for the Kings fine, and when he doth pay the Kings fine he shall be deliuered.

[Margin: 2.Ass.p.8. 12.Ass.pla. 33. 14.E.3.18. 16.Ass.p.7. 22.ass.p.87. 11.H.4.17. St.4.H.4.8. 17.Ass pla. 14. 28.Ass.p.15 40.Ass.pla. 16. 19.H.6.8. 39.Ass.p.4. 9.Ass.p.7. 22.Ass.pla. 87.]

38 As one person may be imprisoned who menaceth, assaulteth, or beateth the person of an other, or with force and armes entereth vpon his lands or tenements or violently taketh away his goods or chattels; so by the statute of Anno 2.H.5. where three persons or more be attainted of great and heinous Riots, they shall haue one whole yeares imprisonment at the least, without being deliuered by baile or mainprise, or in any other manner during the said yeare: And if the Rioters be attainted of petit Riots, they shall haue imprisonment as the King and his Councell shall thinke good. And by the statute made Anno 1.M. it was enacted, that if any persons aboue the number of two, and vnder the number of twelue being assembled together, shall intende, practise, or put in vre, with force of armes vnlawfully, to murder any of the kings subiects, or to breake downe the pales, hedges, ditches, wales, or other inclosure of any parke or other ground inclosed, or the bancke of any fish pond or poole, to the intent the same should remaine open, or to doe any other vnlawfull act, prohibited by that statute, and being required by a Iustice of peace, or shirife of the said County, or by the Maior or chiefe officer of the city or towne corporat to returne to their inhabitations, do not, but attempt to put in vre any of the said things. Then euery of the same persons shall be imprisoned one yeare without baile or mainprise: for the offendors in both the

[Margin: Imprisonmēt for Riots. St.2.H.5.8. S.Riots 11. St.1.M.12. S.Riots 36.]

the caſes aforeſaid, putting in practiſe their outrages with a multitude of perſons bee great diſturbers of the peace, and Tranſgreſſours of the law.

21.H.6.5. 39 In an action of Falſe impriſonment, the defendant pleaded that the plaintif held the manor of D. by force and B. C. a Iuſtice of peace of the ſame County did take him, recorded the force, and ſent him to the defendant being Gaoler of the ſame County to be impriſoned, and this was allowed a good iuſtification, though he was committed to priſon but by one Iuſtice of peace. And in like ſort if the action of falſe impriſonment had bin brought againſt the Iuſtice of peace who committed the offendor to warde, the ſame had been St.8. H.6.9. a good plea in barre for him, for that the ſtatute of Añ 8. H. 6. doth warrant him ſo to do, & giueth that authority to one Iuſtice alone, or to more then one. Impriſoning him that holdeth land with force.

29.Ed.3.9. 40 If a Huy and Cry be leuied and purſued that a horſe of ſuch a colour or 5.H.7.4. marke, ſo many beaſts of ſuch a ſort, or age, or ſo many ſheepe of ſuch a brand be ſtolen, & one is taken leading or driuing of the ſaid horſes, beaſts, or ſheepe: it is lawfull for any man to apprehend and ſtay him, and to commit him to the Conſtables of the Towne where he is apprehended, and by them to be put into the ſtockes, or ſafe kept, vntill he be deliuered by due courſe of law, though he be not of euill fame, or name, but a man of good credite: for ſeeing the law by the Huy and Cry hath accuſed him, by a courſe of law, he muſt be againe acquited and diſcharged: And in this caſe he that is ſo taken though he be after acquit of the felony, ſhall not haue an action of Treſpas, falſe impriſonment, or other remedy againſt him, that did apprehend him. Impriſoning of one purſued by Huy & crie.

Fitz. barre 202. 3.H.4.9. 41 In an action of Treſpas of aſſault, battery and impriſonment, the defendant pleaded that the plaintife menaced to kill him, and therefore he requeſted the Conſtables to arreſt the plaintife to find ſuerties of his good abearing, and the Conſtables, and the defendant with them, did come and arreſt him, and put him into the ſtockes vntill he did finde ſuerties: and this was al- 5.H.7.6. lowed to be a good iuſtification. And in like ſort if one do make an aſſault vpon a Conſtable, the ſame Conſtable may arreſt and impriſon him, vntill he hath found ſuerties to keepe the peace, though the Conſtable be the ſame perſon vpon whom the ſaid aſſault was made: for in this caſe he doth nothing but preſerue the peace, and obſerue the Law, which is to be done aſwell in his own 13.H.7.10. caſe, as any others: And moreouer if a Conſtable be informed, that a lewd man is in a ſuſpected houſe, with a woman of euill name, for incontinencie, he may take ſo many of his neyghbors with him as he will, and arreſt the ſaid man and woman to find ſuerties of their good behauior. And they, nor eyther of them ſhall haue any action of Falſe impriſonment or other action therefore againſt the ſaid Conſtable, or any other of his aſſiſtants; for the Conſtable 10.Ed.4.17. was ordeyned to keepe the peace, and to repreſſe felons. And he may take ſuertie by Obligation, if he find any commiting of a fray, but vpon no penaltie. And if the partie will not find ſuerties, the Conſtable may impryſon him, vntill he hath found ſuerties. Impriſoning him that doth breake the peace. Arreſting ſuſpected perſons.

9.Ed.4.26. 42 In an action of Treſpas of aſſault, battery, and impriſonment, the defendant pleaded, that the plaintife lay in waite in a high way leading from the towne of A. to the towne of B. to rob ſuch perſons as trauailed in that way, and aſſaulted to rob one L. and drew his ſword, and commaunded the ſame L. Impriſoning him that doth attempt to rob.

to

to deliuer his purse, whereupon L. fled and leuied Huy and Cry, and this defendant being trauailing that way, pursued the plaintife, and toke him, and committed him to the Constable to be put in the stockes, who did it accordingly: and this was adiudged a good iustification: for euery man may arrest and imprison him that doth commit a felony, or him who maketh it apparant, that he doth intend, and goe about to commit a felony: for that he doth manifest him selfe to be a principall breaker of the law and peace of the realme.

Assisting to arrest by warrant.

43 In an action of false imprisonment against two, one of them pleaded 19.H.6.43.
that he had a precept to arrest the plaintife which he did accordingly, And the 56.
other defendant pleaded that he came in company with the other to ayde and assist him to arrest the plaintife. And this was allowed a good Iustification in them both: for any straunger may assist a Sherife, his Baylifes or any other that hath authority to execute the Kings writs or proces, and he that wil not assist him being required shall paie a fine to the King: And the Sherife
may take as many persons as he will to aide him to execute the Kings writs, 3.H.7.1.
for it is in furtheraunce of Iustice and no breach of the peace. 17.E.4.5.

Breaking a house to arrest

44 If a man be indicted of Trespas, and a Capias pro fine awarded to the 27.Ass. pla.
Sherife to take the body of the same person, The Sherife may breake open 35.
his house, or close to arrest and imprison him, & it is a lawfull imprisonment. 18.E.4.4.
But the Sherife may not breake any house or chest to make execution by vertue of a fieri facias to him directed. S. Force 32.

The Sherife arresteth and doth not retorne his writ

45 If the Sherife haue a Capias to arrest a man, and he doth arrest him, and after doth not retorne his writ, the partie arrested may haue an action of false imprisonment against the Sherife, and recouer damages for his wrongfull arrest or Imprisonment: for the Capias is, ita quod habeas corpus eius &c. and so if he haue not the parties body in the Kings Court at the day of the retorne of the writ, it shall be intended that he did not arrest him by force of that writ, nor according to the purport of it, but of his owne wrong. But if
the Sherifes Baylie doe arrest the man, and the Sherife doth not retorne the 11.H.4.58.
writ, the partie arrested shall not haue an action of false imprisonment against 21.H.7.22.
the Bailie: for the Sherifes offence shall not preiudice the Baylie, and the Baylie can not compell the Sherife to returne the writ: for a Shirife or a Bailie errant which is knowen and sworne may arrest a man without shewing

A knowne officer may arrest without shewing his warrant.

his warrant, for euery man is bound to take knowledge of them; But where the Sherife doth make a precept to an other to arrest, he must shew his war-
rant. And if a Capias be awarded to the Sherife without an originall to take 21.H.7.22.
a man, and he doth take him, yet the partie grieued shall not haue his action 11.H.4.36.
of false imprisonment against the Sherife, for that he did it by warrant of the

Arresting a man by a Capias without an originall.

Kings writ, for it is a good plea in an action of False imprisonment to say that
he is Shirife of the Countie of M. and that he did arrest the plaintife by force 22.E.4.47.
of a Capias directed to him, which is the same imprysonment.

Arresting vpon suspicion of felony.

46 In an action of False imprisonment, it is no plea for the defendant to 7.H.4.35.
plead, that it was told him, that the plaintife had brought cattell to the towne, 27.H.8.23.
and put them in a blind corner, and that there was great cause of suspicion that the plaintife had stollen them, whereupon he did arrest him; for suspicion only without a felony committed, is no cause to arrest an other. But if a felonie be done in those parts, and one doth suspect an other to haue committed

the

the same felony, then he may arrest him: for a Justice of peace can not
14.H.8.16. arrest an other of suspition of felonie, vnlesse he himselfe doth suspect him to haue committed felonie, And somuch an other may doe that doth suspect one to haue committed felony viz. if he himselfe doth suspect him to haue committed the felony. The common voyce and fame of the Country
2.H.7.15. is a great cause of suspition of felony where a felonie is committed. And
5.H.7.4. therefore in an action of false Imprisonment, the defendant pleaded that
11.E.4.4. there was a felonie committed, and the common voyce and fame of the Countrie was, that the plaintife was a man of euill behauiour, and had done the same felony: whereupon he that was robbed, came to the Constable and requested him to arrest the plaintife, and the Constable came to the defendant and desired him to assist him, to arrest the plaintife, the which he did, and they arrested him. And this was allowed a good iustification, and sufficient cause to arrest the plaintife, seing there was a Robbery committed, and the common voyce and fame of the Countrie
5.H.7.4. accused the plaintife thereof. And in like sorte in an action of false imprisonment the defendant pleaded that J. S. was poysoned, and that the common voyce and fame of the Countrie was that the plaintife had poysoned him, whereupon the defendant apprehended the plaintife, and committed him to prison, as it was lawfull for him to doe: And this was also adiudged a good Plea in barre of the said action, for seing a felony was committed and the common voyce and fame of the Countrie had accused the plaintife thereof, euery person who him selfe hath suspition that the plaintife hath committed the same felony may arrest him thereof. And so it is if in an action of false imprisonment, the defendant doe pleade, that before the im-
7.Ed.4.10. prisonment A. B. was slaine at C. and the plaintife was in the company of
7.Eliz. Dy. 236. those who killed him at the time of the felony committed, and the common voice and fame of the Countrie at C. was that the plaintife was partie to the felonie, whereupon the defendant found the plaintife at C. and arrested him for suspition of felonie, and committed him to the Sherife, which is the same imprisonment. And this was allowed a good and sufficient Plea and not double, though the defendant did alledge the common voice and fame of the country: and the being in company with those that killed A. B. for where a man doth iustifie for suspition of felonie, he may shew as many causes of suspition as he can. And it is a good cause of suspition to say, that huy and crie was leuied after a felony committed, and that the plaintife was a man suspected, Or to say that the plaintife was a vagarant, exercising no trade to get his liuing by, and no laborer, Or to pleade that parcell of the goods stollen were taken in the possession of the plaintife.

The common voice & fame of the countrey, cause of suspition.

Suspected of poysoning.

Suspected of Manslaughter.

Causes of suspition.

38.Ed.3.6.
10.H.7.20. 47 In an action of false imprisonment, the defendant pleaded that the plaintife had so beaten and wounded an other man, that he was in great perill and daunger of death, and that vpon the same huy and cry was leuied, whereupon the defendant being Constable did arrest and imprison the plaintife foure dayes, vntill it might be knowen whether the partie wounded were like to liue, or dye, and when he perceiued that the partie beaten was like to
24.Ed.3.9. liue, he did let the plaintife go at libertie: and this was adiudged a good plea in barre. And in the like case in an action of False imprisonment brought against one, the defendant pleaded, that the King had directed a Commission to certaine persons to apprehend those that were notoriously slaundered for felonies, or great trespasses, notwithstanding they were not indited thereof,

Arresting vpon doubts of Manslaughter.

and that the plaintife had most dangerously wounded J. S. whereupon the Commissioners directed their warrant to the defendant, to apprehend the plaintife, which he did accordingly: And this was allowed a good iustification, and the plaintife was barred of his action; for in both these cases the peace was broken, and at the time of the arrest it was vncertaine whether the offence would proue felonie or not.

A Iustice of peace warrant to arrest a felon.

48 In an action of False imprisonment, the defendant iustified, for that a Iustice of peace directed a warrant vnto him to arrest the plaintife for felony, which he did. And it was holden that a Iustice of peace cannot make a warrant to arrest a Felon, vnlesse he be indicted, for he is a Judge of record, and he must haue a record whereupon hee doth award his proces. But if a Bailife serue his warrant, it is a good iustification for him, though the Iustice of peace did erre in the awarding of the proces. And the same law is, if the Shirife doth erre in any warrant that he doth direct to the Bailife of a Libertie. 14.H.8.16.

Arresting an offendor, & deliuering him to the Constable.

49 If a man do arrest an other, who he knoweth hath committed a robberie, manslaughter, or other felony, & do deliuer him to the Constable to carrie to the gaole, and the Constable will set him at libertie, or doth not carrie him to the gaole, or that the same person arrested be rescued out of the possession or custodie of him that did arrest him; yet in neither of the foresaid cases, he that was arrested shall haue an action of False imprisonment against him that did arrest him, for that there was no default in him, that the offendor was not imprisoned according to his desert. 10.Ed.4.17.

Imprisonmēt vntill he hath made an Obligation.

50 An action of False imprisonment was brought for imprysoning the plaintife, vntill he had made an Obligation of xl. pounds to the defendant and others vnknowen by duresse, and this was adiudged maintenable, for if the plaintife did not know their names, he could not expresse their names, for the Obligation is not the effect of this suit, but the imprisonment, and he shall not recouer dammages for the Obligation, but for the imprisonment, for that he is not yet damnified by the Obligation; because when that is sued, he may plead, that it was made by duresse of imprysonment, and so auoid it. But if the action of False imprisonment be brought of an imprisonment, vntil he had made a fine, he shall recouer dammages for both, for he is presently grieued by the fine, and so is he not by the Obligation. 2.Ed.4.19.

The seruant not chargeable for the masters offence.

51 If a master do imprison a man in a house, and deliuer the key of the dore of that house to his seruant, the partie imprysoned cannot haue an action of False imprysonment against the said seruant for the keeping of the key. But if the seruant that hath the key do know that the same partie were wrongfully imprysoned, then he ought to let him go at libertie: for the seruant is bound to obey his masters commaundement, but in those things that be lawfull onely. And if the seruant which kept the key did not know that the same partie was imprysoned in that house, then vpon his plea of not guiltie, he shall be excused in an action of False imprisonment brought against him by the partie imprisoned. 22.Ed.4.45.

Imprisonmēt by force of a Iusticies.

52 If a writ of Natiuo habendo, or a Iusticies be directed to the Shirif, he can not iustify the impris. of any man by force therof, for they be but commissions to 2.H.4.24.

hold

hold plea. And the bodie of a man shall not be arrested or taken, but by proces awarded out of a court of record, and by those Commissions the Shirifes court is not made a court of record.

9.Ed.4.30. 53 In an action of False imprisonment, it is a good iustification for the defendant to plead, that a Supplicauit came to the Shirife to apprehend the plaintife, who made his warrant to the defendant to take him, which he did accordingly. And yet the Shirife can not giue his authoritie to an other to take suertie of him. A warrant vpon a Supplicauit.

5.H.7.6. 54 A Iustice of peace can not direct a warrant to apprehend him who hath broken the peace, for he is to be punished by inditement, at the Kings suit, or by action of Trespas of batterie at the partie grieued his suit. But he may direct his warrant to apprehend him who he doth doubt meaneth to breake the peace in time to come, and to bring him before himselfe, or some other Iustice, or else to commit him to prison; for one Iustice of peace alone may doe his endeuor to preserue the peace before it be broken: but being once broken it must be punished by inditement in the presence of diuers Iustices of peace, or by action at the common Law. Arresting him who would breake the peace.

Sta.5.El.4. 55 If any seruant, workeman, or laborer, shall wilfully or maliciously make any assault or affray vpon his master, mistresse, or dame, or vpon any other that shall at that time haue the charge or ouersight of him, or of the worke wherein he is appoynted, or hired to worke and beeing thereof conuicted before any two of the Iustices of peace, Maior, or head officer of a towne corporat where the offence is committed, or before either of the Lords Presidents of the North, or Wales, by the confession of the said seruant, workman, or laborer, or by the witnesse and oath of two honest men: Then euery such offendor shall suffer imprisonment by the space of one whole yeare, or lesse, by the discretion of two Iustices of peace (if it be without a towne corporat) & if it be within a towne corporat, then by the discretion of the Maior or head officer of the same towne corporat, with two others of the discreetest persons of the same corporation at the least. And if the offence shall require further punishment, then to receiue such other open punishment (so as it extende neyther to life or limme) as the Iustices of peace in open Sessions, or as the more part of them, or the said maior or head officers, or vj. or iiij. at the least of the discreete persons of the same corporation, before whom the offence shall be examined shall thinke conuenient, for the qualitie of the said offence so committed. Imp. of a seruant for assaulting of his master.

56 By which foresaid cases, and many more, it appeareth that imprisonment is lawfull, and sufficiently authorized by the Common Lawes and Statutes of this Realme in diuers respectes, and for many crimes, and there is by it no breach of the peace, nor offence to the Law, when it is inflicted by the warrant of the law: for it aduaunceth as much the iustice and peace of the Realme to haue offendors punished, as to haue the innocent protected. But the imprisonment which tendeth to the breach of the peace, and the offence of the law is, when one person or more vpon his or their owne authoritie, eyther in reuenge of some supposed wrong receiued, or in hope of a priuat gaine expected, or for some other cause, will Where imprisonment is lawfull, and where not.

of his or their owne authoritie imprison or arrest an other; for the redresse whereof the party grieued shall haue an action of false imprisonment, or an action of trespas, & recouer his damages. And the same offendor which before did wrongfully imprison an other, shall then vpon his conuiction by verdict, or his owne confession, be himselfe lawfully imprisoned, vntill he hath paid to the king a fine.

Imprisonmēt for offences done to the iustice of the Realme.

57 As in the cases aforesaid, imprisonment of offendors is both tollerable & requisit, when it is inflicted for misdemeanors done to the peace of the Realme: so in many other cases it is as necessary when it is imposed for offences done to the law & iustice of the Realme, being the foundation & principall piller of the same peace, and without the due execution whereof there can not be a general and perfect peace. And amongst many other transgressors who doe offend contrarie to the iustice of the Realme, and yet in a sort doe preserue the peace, the law doth principally note foure kinde of persons worthy for their offences to be imprisoned. Whereof the first be they who doe commit some acts that 1.
be wrongfull, iniurious, and prohibited by the common lawes, or Statutes of the Realme: The second be they who doe attempt and prosecute vniust and 2.
wrongfull actions or suits, to molest, trouble, or charge others: The third be 3.
they who being impleaded vpon iust and good causes, doe plead false, or dilatorie pleas, in retardation of iustice and hinderaunce of the due and ordinarie course of the law: The fourth be they who vpon stubbornesse, contumacie, 4.
or wilfulnesse, refuse to doe that which they know the law doth require at their hands, and may enforce them vnto: of euery of which amongst many, I will insert some fewe cases. As to the first by the Statute of Anno 5. Eliz. 1.
he shall be imprisoned, and set vpon the pillorie, who doth falslie forge, or wil- Sta. 5. El. 14.
lingly assent, or cause to be forged, or made, any false deede, charter or writing sealed, Court Roll, or the will of any person in writing, to the intent S. Forgery 3
that the estate of freehold or inheritance of any person in any lands should be recouered or charged &c. for forging of deeds is an iniurious and wrongfull act, and alwaies hath bin hated, detested, and persecuted in this Realme. By the Statute of Westm. 2. If the master do assigne auditors to any Bailifes, Sta. 13. E. 1. 11.
Seruants, Chamberlaines, or other receiuors which are bound to yeeld accompt, and it chaunce them to be found in arrerages (all things being to them allowed) they shall be arrested, and by the testimonie of those auditors committed to the next Gaole which the King hath in those parts, and shall be receiued by the Sherife, or his Gaoler, and prisoned, fettered in irons, liuing of their owne goods, vntill they haue fully satisfied their master of all the arrerages; for detayning of the arrerages of an accompt is a plaine and manifest wrong to the master: And this imprisonment must be 27. H. 6. 8.
presently after the accompt taken, and not any distance of tyme after. And he that doth a disseisin, or maketh an entrie contrarie to his owne deede, Or 14. Ass. pla. 12.
is conuicted for the imbeziling of an Exigent, or for some other notorious deceits, committeth open and manifest iniurie, and therefore shall be imprisoned. If one man do make a lease of a Tenement by writing to an other 8. Ass. p. 20.
for terme of life of the lessee, whereupon the lessee doth enter and enioyeth it, 28. Ass. pla.
and after the lessor doth enter and disseise the lessee for life, and then the lessee 28.
do bring an Assise against the lessor, and recouer against him the Tenement leased: in this case the same lessor shall be imprisoned, for that he made an entrie contrarie to his owne deede, and so willingly committed

Imprisonmēt for cōmitting vnlawful acts. Forging of deeds.

Accomptants found in arrerages.

Disseison contrarie to his owne lease.

an

18. Ass. p. 3. an open and manifest wrong. The same law is, if a man do make a disseisin of land, of his whole title wherein he hath before made a release, or confirmation to the tenant of the same land, in this case he shall be imprysoned. And if a Gardian do take a feoffement of his wardes land, being within Fitz. Assise 395. age, he shall be imprisoned therefore, for this, and all the former be iniurious acts, and knowen to the offendors to be prohibited by the law. As touching the second point; they be also worthy to be imprisoned, who do 2. attempt or prosecute unlawfull suits, to the trouble & vexation of others: As 50. Ed. 3. 1. if one do bring an Appeal against an other, and that appeal do abate by the plaintifes nonsuit, or by any other default of his, he shall be imprisoned. A 9. H. 4. 2. woman brought an Appeal of the death of her husband against one, who was attainted and hanged at her suit; and after shee brought an appeal against an other man of her said husbands death, who pleaded the attainder of the first man in barre, whereupon the appeal was abated, and the woman committed to pryson for her wrongfull vexation and suit. A woman brought an appeal 8. H. 4. 18. against a man of the death of her husband, and her said husband was brought into the court, and shee was examined if that were her husband, who said yea, but shee supposed that he had been dead, and therefore shee was imprisoned for her false appeal. If one do bring an appeal against an other, for a Murder, Burglarie, Robberie, or other felony committed in W. in the County of N. and there is no such W. in that County, the appeal shall abate, and the plaintife shall be imprisoned: for it is manifest, that this suit was commenced upon malice, and to put the defendant to vexation and trouble, and not upon any iust cause. Thirdly, they are worthy to be imprysoned, who do plead false, or dilatorie pleas, in hinderance of suits, and retardation of iustice. As if a man 33. H. 6. 54. in his plea do denie his owne deed; or do plead a false deed made to himselfe, 45. Ed. 3. 11 which is found against him by verdict; or do plead a deed that is rased, enter-6. Ass. p. 4. lined, or otherwise suspicious that is adiudged against him, he shall be im-24. E. 3. 74. prisoned. By the statute intituled De coniunctim feoffatis, if the tenant in Sta. 34. Ed. 1 Assise do plead iointenancie of the land in demaund with his wife, or a stranger, and sheweth a deed to testifie the same, to the intent to abate the plaintifes writ: and if it be found by the Assise that the exception was maliciously alleaged to delay the plaintifes right, the said tenant shall be one yeare imprysoned, though the assise passe for him against the plaintife. And if that tenant in the assise be an Enfant, who doth plead iointenancie, yet if that 37. Ass. pl. 1. plea be found against him, he shall be imprysoned: for that the said statute 3. H. 6. 51. is generall, and doth not except an Enfant. By the statute of Westm̄ 2. if St. 13. Ed. 1. he that is named a disseisour in an Assise, do personally alleage any false ex-25. ception, whereby the taking of the assise is deferred, viz. that at an other time an assise of the said tenements passed betweene the said parties, or that a writ of higher nature is depending betweene them of the said tenements, and doth vouch any rols or records to warrant the same, and at the day giuen he faileth of his warrant, he shall be adiudged a disseisour, without recognizance of the assise, and shall restore double dammages of that which shall be found, and for his falshood shall be one yeare imprysoned. And fourthly, a 4. man in divers cases shall bee imprysoned for his stubbornesse, wilfulnesse, disobedience, and contempt to subiugate, and submit himselfe to the censure and iudgement of the Law, and to performe & accomplish that which the law doth expect at the hands of him and all others being in his case. As if a Quid iuris clamat, or Per quæ seruitia, be brought against a man, who doth appeare in Court, and will not atturne to the plaintife, nor plead in barre, he shall be

Imp. for prosecuting unlawfull suits.

Imp. for false or dilatory pleas.

Imprisonmēt for false pleading of iointenancie.

Imp. for failing of a record pleaded.

Imp. for not atturning.

Imprisonmẽt for not doing his true seruice.

imprisoned for his stubbornes. And if the tenant that ought to do homage or fealtie to his Lord, do appeare in Court, and will not do such of the said seruices as be claimed of him, neither plead in barre thereof, he shall be imprisoned vntill he will do his foresaid seruices, for his wilfull contempt of the law, and disobedience to iustice. And if a writ of Estrepement be directed to the Shirife to prohibit him to commit wast in lands against whom a reall action, or action of Wast is depending, for, or touching the same lands: the Shirife by force of the same writ may resist him who would do wast, And if he cannot otherwise redresse the offence, he may imprison him, & if néed be, he may take the power of the Countie to assist him; for this disobeying of the Kings writ, and resistance of the Shirife, is a wilfull frowardnesse and contempt of the law in the offendor, and therefore he deserueth to tast the smart of the Law by imprisonment for his contumacy. And in like sort by the statute of Añ 27. H.8. & Añ 32. H.8. it was ordeined, That if any person after sentence difinitiue giuen against him, by the Ordinarie, his Commissarie, or other competent minister, or lawfull Judge, do obstinatly refuse to pay his Tythes, or duties, or such summes of money adiudged, wherein he is condemned for the same: Then two Justices of the peace of the same Shire (whereof one to be of the Quorum) shall haue authoritie vpon information, certificat, or complaint made in writing by the ecclesiasticall Judge that gaue the same sentence, to cause the same person so refusing to be attached, and committed to the next Gaole, and there to remaine without bayle or mainprise, vntill he hath found sufficient suerties to be bound by Recognizance, or otherwise, before the same Justices, to the vse of the King to performe the said sentence. In the same maner may any one of the Kings Councell, or two Justices of peace, vpon an Information or request made to them by the Ordinary, commit any offendor to ward, for any contempt, contumacie, disobedience, or any other misdemeanour of his in any suit, for subtraction of Tythes, offerings, and other duties of the Church, vntill he hath found suerties &c. vt gladius gladium iuuet.

Fitz. Per q seruitia 23.

Co. Lib. 5. 105.

Stat. 27. H. 8. 20.

Stat. 32. H. 8. 7.

Imp. for obstinate refusing to performe the Ordinaries sentence.

St. 27. H. 8. 20.

what is Maihemingٍ.

58 Maiheming is an other gréeuance in the Realme, and a speciall cause to disturbe the peace: And that is when one member of the Common weale shall take from an other member of the same, a naturall member of his bodie, or the vse and benefit thereof, and thereby disable him to serue the common weale by his weapons in the time of warre, or by his labour in the time of peace, and also diminisheth the strength of his body, and weaken him thereby to get his owne lyuing, and by that meanes the common weale is in a sort depriued of the vse of one of her members.

How many sorts there be of maiheming.

59 This maiheming is a dismembring of a man, or taking away some member, or part of his body, or the vse thereof; As when a wound, blow, or hurt is giuen or done by one person or more to an other person, whereby he is the lesse able to defend himselfe in the time of warre, or to get his lyuing in time of peace: And therefore, if a man do put out the eye, or cut off the hand, or foote, or any ioynt of the hand, or foote of an other, it is a Maihem, though it be done by chaunce medley. (But if one man of malice pretended, do cut out the tongue, or put out the eyes of any of the Kings subiects, it is Felonie) And if one man do crush the mouth, or head of an other, or break out his fore téeth, it is a maihem, for with them he may defend him selfe in battaile: but to breake his hinder téeth, or to cut off his Nose, or Eares, whereby he loseth his hearing, is no maihem, but a deformitie, or blemish

Sta. 5. H. 4. 5.

Fitz. Corone 458.

blemish of his bodie, and no weakning of his strength. It is a Maihem to pull any boane out of a mans head, or to cut off any finger of a mans hand, or to breake any of them so, that they become shronke vp, or dried vp, or dead, or croked. Gelding of a man is also a maihem; though it be in a secret place, yet it maketh him more feeble, and vnable to defend himselfe in in bataile, or to worke for his liuing. If by any wound receiued the sinewes, or vaines of a man be shronke vp, it is a maihem. To cut off the cheeke or iawbone of any person, or so to crush, or breake any of them that the same person is the lesse able to take his meate or drinke is a maihem. If one person or more doe take an other person by force, and put him in the stocks or otherwise bind him fast, and after poure so much skalding what oyle, and vinegar, or hoat melted lead, or other skalding licor vpon any part of his body, and so continue it vntill it doth wast, and consume the flesh of the same part, and drie vp and mortifie the veynes and sinewes of the same parte, it is a maihem. If A. do strike at B. and the weapon wherwith he striketh, breaking, or falling out of his hand by the force of the blow doth put out the eyes of D. this shalbe adiudged a maihem, for that A. had an intention at the first to do some hurt in striking at B.

28.Ed.3 94. Lib.int.fol. 45.

Lib. int fol. 45.

13.H.7.14.

60 The greatnesse or smalnes of the wound in some of the cases aforesaid doth make the difference, whether it be a maihem or not, which is to be examined by the Iustices of the court before whom the appeal of maihem is depending, and by them to be decided, if they be requested by the defendant in the appeall and will condiscend to do it. And they may award the kings writ to the shirif of the countie where the fact was done, to warn two expert surgeons of that Countie, citie or towne, to appeare in the same court at a day prefixed, to informe the court what they thinke of the wound, and whether they conceiue it to be a maihem or not: And if the wound be fresh, and new, and thereby hardly to be discerned, whether it will proue a maihem or not, the Iustices need not presently to examine it though the defendant in an appeal of maihem doth desire it, or notwithstanding he doth plead that it is no maihem. And if in an appeall of maihem the defendant doth plead not guilty, without requesting that the maihem may be examined by the court, by this the defendant hath allowed that it is a maihem. But if in an appeall of maihem the defendant doth pray that the maihem may be examined, if the Iustices and the surgeons, (that they will call vnto them) be in doubt whether it be a maihem or not, the Iustices may refuse the examination, and compell the defendant to put him selfe vpon the triall of the countrie: And yet in that case, if the defendant do praie that the maihem may be examined, by the court, if the Iustices do adiudge it a maihem, it is peremptorie to the defendant, for he shall not after plead not guilty, or any other plea in Barre, seeing by his plea he hath allowed it to be a maihem. But the court can not view the wound, and examin whether it be a maihem or not, vnlesse the defendant in the appeal will request it and referre it to their iudgement. If in an appeall of maihem the defendant doe plead not guiltie, without requesting that the maihem may be adiudged by the court, though the Iurie who are to try the issue doe desire to see the plaintife if he be maihemed or not, the plaintife need not to shew his wound, for by pleading not guilty the defendant hath allowed that it is a maihem though he hath estraunged himselfe from the committing thereof.

Examination of a maihem.

28.Ass.p.5. 28. E.3.94.

41.Ass.pla. 27.

22.Ass. pla. 82.

21.H.7.40.

6.H.7.1. 22.Ass.p.99

28.Ass.p.8.

22.Ass.p.82

9.H.4.2. 61 If seuerall men do at one time assault one man, and one of them doth mai-

Diuers appels of maihẽ for one offence

maihem him in one part of his body, and an other in an other part, he may haue seuerall appeals of Maihem against them: for that they be seuerall maihems which he hath receiued: And yet if seuerall men do murder or otherwise kill a man, there may be but one appeall of murder maintained against them all, for that a man can haue but one death. But if a man sue an appeall of maihem against seuerall persons, whereof against some as principals, and some others as accessories, and after apparance he is nonsuit, he can not pursue an other appeall of maihem against the same persons, and charge those as accessories, which before he had named principals, nor those principals who before were suggested to be accessories. 40. Ass. p. 14

Principal and accessorie in maihem.

62 In an appeall of maihem the plaintife may choose to make all principals, or els to make him principall that did first strike him, and the residue accessorie. The Law was holden in auncient time that the plaintife in an appeall of maihem, must haue declared against all the defendants as principals: But now he may choose and make some principals, and some accessories: for an appeall of maihem is in effect but an action of Trespas wherein the plaintife shall recouer damages, according to the quality & quantitie of the offence, and the defendant shall be imprisoned. And if the plaintife do bring an appeal of maihem whereas it doth appeare to the court that by the blow which was giuen him he is not maihemed, he shall paie a fine. 40. Ass. p. 9. 41. Ass. pla. 16. 8. H. 4. 21.

Maihem is a Trespas. The iudgemẽt in appeall of maihem.

Mainprise in an appeall of maihem.

63 In an appeall of maihem if it do appeare to the court that the maihem is very apparant, grœuous, bloudy, and extreame, as if a mans legs or armes be broken, or that the partie maihemed is in great perill of death, the defendant shall not be let to mainprise, no more then he should be in an appeall of murder, or burglarie. But if the maihem be not apparant, or that it is doubtfull, and questionable whether it be a maihem or not, then the defendant in an appeall of maihem may be let to mainprise. And that also appeareth by the statute intituled officium Coronatoris: whereby it is ordained, that vpon an appeall of maihem, if the wounds be mortall, they which be appealled shal forthwith be apprehended, and kept vntill it be knowen whether he that is hurt shall recouer or not: if he die they shall be retained, if he liue, they shall be attached by foure or sixe pledges according to the bignesse of the wound, if it be for a maihem then there shall be no lesse then foure pledges, if a small wound two will serue. 6. H. 7. 1. Stat. 3. E. 1.

Why maihem is supposed to be done feloniously.

64 In an appeall of maihem the plaintife doth declare that the defendant did maihem him felonice vt felo domini Regis: and so it may be called felony as petit Larcenie is called felony, or it may be termed felony, for that the blow which caused the maihem may be a meane of his death within the yeare and day after the stroke stricken, and then it will be felony, or for that he which did giue the blow had then a murdring mynd and so a felonious intent. 40. Ass. pla. 40. 6. H. 7. 1.

Barres in appeall of maihem.

Iustifiing in his owne defence.

65 It is a good plea in barre in an appeall of maihem for the defendant to plead, that the plaintife at the place aforesaid, and at the day and yeare aforesaid, did make assault vpon the defendant, and would haue beaten and killed him, vnlesse the defendant had then and there quickly defended himselfe against the plaintife, and so the hurt and dammage (if any were) that then and there did come to the plaintife was of the plaintifes owne assault and in defence of the defendant. And likewise it is a good plea in barre in an appeall Li. int. f. 45.

of

of maihem for the defendant to plead the plaintifs release made unto him after the supposed offence done of all actions personals, or of all actions, or of all appeales, or of all demaunds: for in this case the plaintife is but to recouer dammages. The plaintifes release.

7.H.4.30. 66 If an appeal of maihem be brought against diuers, & one of them doth appeare in court and confesse the maihem, and is committed to the Marshalsea, and the plaintife hath iudgement against him, he can not sue against the residue, vnlesse he will suffer him that hath confessed the maihem to goe at liberty: for if he hath iudgement, and the body of him who confessed the maihem to remaine in prison, that shall be an execution for this whole maihem. Execution in appeal of maihem.

67 The Sages and Iudges of the land in former ages did hold it for law, that if one doe assault, beate, and maihem an other, and the partie maihemed doth bring an appeall of maihem against the offendor, and recouer dammages against him, yet after he may haue an action of Trespas of assault and battery against the same offendor, and recouer dammages for his beating: and the recouerie of dammages in the appeal of maihem shalbe no plea in barre against the plaintife, for the appeal doth only medle with the maihemimg, & not with the beating. But if the plaintife do bring an appeal of maihem in the Kings bench, and after apparance be nonsuit in the same, and then doe bring an action of Trespas of assault and batterie for the same fact, Then the defendant may plead the same appeal and nonsuit in barre against the plaintife, and it is a good plea. But of late yeares, viz. Añ 31. Eliz. it was adiudged, that in this and all cases, when the plaintife for one wrong and iniurie is but to recouer dammages, he shall not be for that cause satisfied twice for one offence: And in these two actions of appeal of maihem and trespas, the plaintife shall onely recouer dammages. And therefore it was adiudged a good plea in barre in an appeal of maihem to plead, that the plaintife had before brought an action of Trespas against the defendant of assault, battery, & wounding, and had recouered dammages therein, and to auerre that the same assault, batterie, and wounding, and this maiheming were all one offence.

Fitz.Coroñ 110. 22.Ass.p.82 43.Ass.p.38 41.Ass.p.16 Co.Lib.4. 43.

An action of Trespas after an appeal of maihem.

68 As the law hath prouided remedies to punish those who by menace, assault, battery, imprisonment, or maiheming, do breake the peace, So hath it alwaies had a vigilant eie by anticipation to preuent many others that would breake the peace by any of the meanes aforesaid, and therefore hath from age to age, appointed meet magistrates and watchmen, to whose charge specially (as selected Sentinels) she did commit the preseruation of the peace, who in times past before the raigne of King Edward the third were called Conseruators of the peace, and sithence they haue been termed Iustices of peace, because they be Iudges of record, or otherwise they be named Commissioners of the peace, because they haue and deriue their authority by the Kings Commission: who him selfe being the chiefe and generall Conseruator and Preseruer of the peace throughout all his Dominions, doth by his seuerall Commissions commit some particles of his authoritie, touching the continuance of the peace, and maintenance of certaine of his Lawes, to some chiefe and select men in all the parts of the Realme, whom he taketh to be the most meete men for the same, in respect of their integritie, wisdome, learning, courage, and liuelyhood. The forme of so much of which Commission as toucheth the Peace and good Abearing

Restraint of affraies by Iustices of peace.

Stat. 1.E.3. 16.

Abearing is this. Iacobus &c. prędilecto & fideli Conciliario nostro Thomę domino Elsmere domino Cancellario, nec non prædilectis, A.B.C.D.E.F.G. H.I.L.M.N.O.P.&c. Sciatis quod assignauimus vos coniunctim & diuisim, & quemlibet vestrum Iusticiarios nostros ad pacem nostram in Comitatu nostro Buck. conseruand', ac ad omnia ordinationes & Statuta pro bono pacis nostrę, ac pro conseruatione eiusdem, & pro quieto regimine, & gubernatione populi nostri ædita in omnibus & singulis suis articulis in dicto comitatu nostro (tam infra libertates quam extra) iuxta vim, formam, & effectum eorundem custodiend', & custodire faciendum. Et ad omnes contra formam ordinationũ vel Statutorum illorum aut eorum alicuius in comitatu prædicto delinquentes, castigandũ & puniendum, prout secundum formam ordinationũ & Statutorũ illorum fuerit faciendum. Et ad omnes illos qui alicui vel aliquibus de populo nostro, de corporibus suis, vel de incendio domorũ suarum minas fecerint, ad sufficientẽ securitatem, de pace vel bono gestu suo, erga nos & populum nostrũ, inueniendam, coram vobis seu aliquo vestrum venire faciendum: Et (si huiusmodi securitatem inuenire recusauerint) tunc eos in prisonis nostris (quousque huiusmodi securitatem inuenirent) saluo custodire faciendum. Et ideo vobis & cuilibet vestrum mandamus, quod circa custodiam pacis, ordinationum, Statutorum, & omnium & singulorum cęterorum prẹmissorum diligenter intendatis; Et ad certos dies, & loca, quę vos vel aliqui duo, vel plures vestrũ (vt prædict' est) ad hoc prouideritis, super prẹmissis faciatis inquisitiones, & premissa omnia & singula audiatis & terminetis, ac ea faciatis & expleatis in forma prædicta, factur inde quod ad Iusticiam pertinet, secundũ legem & consuetudinem Regni nr̃i Angliæ, saluis nobis amerciamentis, & alijs ad nos inde spectantibus.

The Commission of the Peace.

69 And though there be many other offences mentioned in the said commission which the Justices of peace are by force of the said Commission to enquire of, heare, and determine, and to punish the offendors therin, according to the lawes and Statutes of the Realme: Yet as it appeareth by the words of the said commission, the same hath his chiefe care and respect of the peace, & to the preseruation thereof. And to the intent that the said Justices, or commissioners should the better remember and respect their charge and dutie, they are called Justices or commissioners of the peace, and not commissioners of justice, of conscience, or equitie &c. And so their names, together with their offices, and duties be in a sort written in their foreheads. And the restraining or punishment of all the other offences mentioned in the said commission, do only tend to the maintenance of justice, the roote, foundation, and supporter of peace. And whereas the King by the words of the said Commission doth appoint the persons therin named his Justices to preserue his peace, and to keepe and cause to be kept all ordinaunces, and Statutes made for the conseruation of the peace, and the quiet gouernment of his people: These Statuts amongst many others chiefly be intended, the Statutes of Anno 2. Ed. 3. 18. Ed. 3. & 34. Ed. 3. by which it is ordained, that Justices of peace shall haue power to heare and determine at the Kings suit all manner of felonies, and Trespasses, committed against the peace in the same County: and to restraine offendors, riotors, & all other barretors, and to pursue, take, and chasten them, to imprison and punish them according to their Trespas and offence, and to informe them according to the said Justices discretion: And to inquire of all those that haue been pillers and robbers beyond the Sea and be come againe, and goe wandring, and will not labour as they had

The Commission doth chiefely respect the peace.

Why they be called Justices of Peace.

Sta. 2. E. 3. 6. 18. E. 3. 2. 34. Ed. 3. 1.

had wont to doe: And to take and arrest all those, which they can find by inditement, or suspition, and to commit them to prison: And to take of all those which be not of good fame in the place where they remaine sufficient suertie and mainprise of their good abearing or behauiour towards the King and his people, and the other duelie to punish, To the intent that the people be not by such Rioters troubled, or endammaged, nor the peace broken, nor any passengers by the way disturbed, or put in perill. But the fines which Iustices shall assesse vpon any person shall be reasonable, hauing regard the quantitie of the Trespas, and the cause.

Binding persons suspected to their good behauiour.

7 So that it appeareth both by the words of the said Commission of peace, and also by the foresaid Statutes, That a Iustice of peace by vertue of his office hath authoritie to preuent the breach of the peace, both by taking suertie for the keeping of it, and for the good behauiour of the offendors, And that he may do either of his owne motion, or discretion, or els at the request or praier of an other. And by his owne discretion he may cause a common Barretor, Rioter, or one that maketh an affray in his presence, or other person to him suspected to be inclyned to the breach of the peace, or men menacing one to hurt or kill an other, or contending in whote words, to finde suertie of the peace. And he may perswade one man to require the suertie of peace against an other man, and he himselfe after may graunt it: for it is no more then he might haue done of his owne authoritie: which suertie of the peace, is a recognizance taken by the said Iustice of peace of the partie and his suerties to the King, for the keeping of the peace. And as a Iustice of peace may take this suertie of peace, or suertie of good abearing, as a Iudge by vertue of his office; So may he doe it as a minister by force of a Supplicauit directed vnto him out of the Chauncerie; in which case he is then only to direct his precept to compell the partie vpon the writ to finde suertie of the peace. Which Supplicauit out of the Chauncerie is sometime directed to one Iustice of peace alone, sometime to mee, and sometime to the Shirife, and sometime to him with others: And then the same Iustice or Iustices of peace, or Shirife must make retorne of the said writ of Supplicauit, and a Certificat of his doing into the Court from whence the same was awarded. And if the said Iustice of peace shall take the said Recognizance for the keeping of the peace by vertue of his office, then by force of the Statute of Anno 3.H.7. he shall certifie, sende, or bring the same Recognizance at the next Sessions of the peace where he is, or hath bin Iustice that the party so bound may be called. And if the partie make default, the same then there to be recorded: And the same Recognizance with the record of that default shall be sent and certified into the Chauncerie, the Kings Bench, or into the Exchequer. And the suertie of good abearing is graunted by authority of the foresaid commission of peace, & by the warrant of the before rehearsed Statut of 34.E.3. aswell as the suerty of peace is, & it is ordained for the preseruation of the peace, & it doth differ in nothing frō that of the peace, but that there is more difficultie in the performance of it, and the party bound may sooner slide into the peril & danger of it. The suerty of good abearing is most commonly granted in open sessions, or by two, or thrée Iust. of P. Or vpon a Supplicauit, & great cause shewed, & proued: it is granted in the Chancery or K. Bench. And though one Iustice of peace alone may grant it if he will, yet it is seldom done so, vnles it be to preuent some great, sodain, & imminent enormity or danger. The suerty of peace is most times taken at the request of one for the preseruation of the peace chiefely against one, But the suerty of good abearing is

A Iustice taking suertie of the peace.

9.E.4.3.

What the suertie of the peace is.

Taking suertie of the peace by a Supplicauit.

Sta.3.H.7.1

Certificat of a Recognizance

Suertie of good abearing.

9.E.4.3.
Kel.fo.41.

is oftentimes graunted at the suit of diuers, and those must be men of credit, and to prouide for the safetie of many: for the effect and purport thereof is that the partie bound shall demeane himselfe well in his port, behauiour, and company, and doe nothing that may be the cause of the breach of the peace, or in putting the people in feare or trouble: And it is chieflie graunted against common Barretors, common rioters, common quarrellers, common peace breakers, and persons greatly defamed for resorting to houses suspected to maintaine incontinentie or adulterie, and against those that be generally feared to be robbers or spoilers of the Kings people, or which doe endamage, disturbe, trouble, or put in peril passengers by the way: And therefore if one doe exhibit Articles to Justices of peace against a certaine person, comprehending diuers great abuses, and misdemeanors, not onely touching the Petitioner himselfe, but many others, to the intent that the same person may be bound to his good behauiour: in this case the partie so accused shall not for any matter conteined in the said Articles maintaine a action vpon the case; for the party or parties who exhibited the said Articles haue pursued an ordinarie course of Just. & nothing was attempted but the reformation of the mans conditions, and to haue the peace and good behauiour continued. And though this suerty of good abearing is chiefely prouided for the continuance of the peace, yet by force of seuerall Statutes it is also grauntable in some other cases. As if the King do graunt to any person a charter of pardon of any felony, then he shall come within three Monthes before the Shirife and Coronors of the same Countie where the felony was done, & finde sixe sufficient Mainpernours (for whom the said Shirife and Coronors will answere) that he from thence forth shall beare him selfe well and lawfully. And if any man disturbe a Preacher in his Sermon he shall be bound to his good abearing for one yeare. And he shall be bound to his good abearing for seauen yeares who doth vnlawfully hunt and steale deare, or conies or take away wrongfully any haukes, or haukes egges, or shall vnlawfullie distroy or breake the head or damme of any pond, poole, moate, stagne or stew whereas fish are put, or shall wrongfully fish in any of them, to the intent to steale or take away any of them, against the will of the owner or possessor of the same, not hauing lawfull authoritie so to doe. And he shall be bound with two sufficient sueties in CC. l. to the good behauiour which doth absent himselfe from the Church by the space of twelue moneths &c.

[Margin: Articles exhibited to haue good abearing granted.] [Margin: Co.li.4.14.] [Margin: The suertie of good abearing in other cases then for the peace.] [Margin: St.10.E.3.3] [Margin: Sta.1.M.3] [Margin: St.3.Iac 19. 5.El.21.] [Margin: Sta.23.El.1.]

71 Because it appeareth by the words of the foresaid commission of peace, that the said Justices of peace shal cause al those to finde suerty of peace which doe threaten any of the Kings people to hurt them in body, or to burne their houses: Therefore all lay persons vnder the degree of Lords or Peers of the Realme; and also Ecclesiasticall persons, if they be not attendant vpon diuine seruice may be arrested to finde suerty for the peace. And if the husband do threaten to kill his wife, or outragiously to beate her, or that she hath any notorious cause to feare that he will doe so, she may demaund the suertie of the peace against him, and she shall haue it graunted. And in like sort and for the like causes many the husband demaund suertie of the peace against his wife, in which case shee her selfe shall not be bound, but others shal be bound for her. And a Justice of peace vpon his owne discretion may in either of the foresaid cases grant suertie of peace. And one Justice of peace may vpon his owne discretion, or at the request of an other graunt the suertie of peace, against an other of his felow Justices of peace of the same county. And one Justice of peace

[Margin: For whom & against whom the suertie of peace is to be graunted.] [Margin: Fitz. Nat. Bre.80.239.]

peace may demaund suertie of peace of an other of his fellow Iustices against an other man. A man attainted of Treason, or Felony, or in a Premunire, or abiured, or conuict of Heresie, a dumbe man, or an Enfant within the age of xiiij. yeares, may demaund & ought upon cause to haue suertie of peace. And so may a Willeine haue suertie of peace against his Lord, least that his Lord should maihem him, & the Lord may haue suertie of peace against his villein. A dumbe man, or an Enfant aboue the age of xiiij. yeare may also be inforced to find suerties for the kéeping of the peace: but then themselues are not to be bound, but some others for them: Or else they must be committed to prison untill they can find suerties. A Iustice of peace cannot graunt suertie of peace against a Baron of the Realme, nor any other aboue the degrée of a Baron: But the party who would haue the peace against him, must bring him by Subpoena into the Chauncerie, & there he must be bound to the peace. A man that is frantike shall not haue the suertie of peace of his owne demaund, because he hath not discretion to request it. But a Iustice of peace upon his own discretion may bind an other to kéepe the peace against him, if he sée cause thereof. Neither shall he who is a Alien borne, & no Denizen, nor in friendship with the King & the Realme haue suertie of peace graunted him.

A man attainted. An Heretike. A Dumb man An Enfant. A Willeine. A Baron. Fitzh. Subpoena 20. A mad man. An Alien.

17. Ed. 4. 4. 72 If a man do threaten an other to imprison him, the partie threatned shall not haue the suertie of peace against him that did so menace him, for that after he is imprisoned, he may haue against the other a Homine replegiando, or an action of false imprisonment, and recouer damages, & so be recompenced for his imprisonment. But if one man do threaten an other to beate him, the partie threatned may haue the suertie of peace against him: for that beating may tend to the maiheming or killing of him, which the suertie of peace might haue preuented. If a man do feare that an other will kill him, maihem him, hurt him in bodie, or burne his house, or procure, or cause the same to be done, and will come before a Iustice of peace, & take his corporall oath to that effect, the Iustice of peace is to graunt him the suertie of peace against the man complained of: for that may satisfie the conscience of the said Iustice, that the partie doth complaine upon mére feare, and not upon malice or vexation. And though the partie against whom the peace is demaunded may séeme to the Iustice of peace to be a simple person, weake, féeble, impotent, or far unable to incounter by force and strength with him that demaundeth the suertie of peace, yet he may procure, or cause the other to be slaine, maihemed, beaten, or his house to be burned: And further if the party that doth complaine and desireth the suertie of peace, will sweare that he doth feare, where indéed he neither doth feare, nor hath cause of feare, yet his oath doth therein discharge the conscience and oath of the Iustice of peace. And the whole fault (if any be) shall be iustly imputed to the complainor.

Upon what cause the suertie of peace is to be graunted. Fitz. Na. B. 79.

73 And whereas the words of the kings Commission be, That the said Iustices of peace shal cause all those to find suertie of peace, which do threaten any of the kings people to hurt them in bodie, or to burne their houses. It is to be obserued, that in some cases a Iustice of peace may by his owne word only cause suertie of peace to be found, & sometime he must do it by writing: As if one man do in the presence & hearing of a Iust. of peace, threaten to kill, maihem, wound, or beate an other, or to burne his house, or in his presence do

Suertie of peace inioyned by word or writing.

 offer

offer to strike, or beate an other, the Justice of peace may commaund him by word to find suertie of peace: Or if one man will demaund of a Justice of peace, the suertie of the peace against an other man, who is then in the presence of the said Justice of peace, and will then and there be sworne that he is affraid of him, the Justice of peace may by word commaund the same partie to find suertie of peace: or otherwise he may commaund the Shirife, Bailife, or some knowen officer, or his owne seruant being then present, to arrest the same partie, and to bring him before him to find suertie of peace. But if the partie against whom the peace is demaunded, or the Shirife, or Baylife be absent, and not at that time in the presence of the Justice of peace: Then the same Justice must make a warrant or precept in writing to the Constables, Boursholders, Tythingmen, &c. or to any other man (though he be no Officer) to arrest the same partie, and to bring him before him, or some of his fellow Justices to find suertie of peace. In which Precept must be conteined the cause why the peace was graunted, and at whose suit, to the intent that the partie to be bound may prouide his suerties ready, and take them with him to the Justice of peace. And the warrant ought to beare date of the place where it was made, to the intent that if an action of False imprisonment be brought against him that made the same arrest by force of that warrant, the defendant in his plea must shew the place where it was made. If suertie of peace be required of a Justice of peace of one County (which at that time remayneth out of the Countie where he is Justice) against a man of the Countie where he is Justice, the same Justice may graunt a precept to be serued in the Countie where he is Justice: But when the partie shall be warned to find suerties, the officer must not carrie him out of that Countie to the Justice that made the precept, but to some other Justice of that Countie: for a Justice hath no authoritie but in the Countie where he is Justice.

Suertie of peace commaunded by writing. 14.H.8.18.

A Justice remayning out of the countie. Plow.Com. fol.37. 13.Ed.4.8.

The seruing of proces for the peace.

74 If a Precept be made by a Justice of peace (either as he is a Judge, or as he is a minister) to two men to arrest a man to find suertie of the peace, yet one of them alone may do it: If it be directed to the Shirife, he may commaund his Undershirife, Bailife, or other sworne or knowen officer to serue it, without any precept by writing: But if he will commaund an other man that is no knowen officer to serue it, he must deliuer him a precept in writing, for otherwise he doth it not by sufficient warrant, & so a writ of False imprysonment will lie against him for the arrest. And if a Just. of peace do direct his warrant to the Shirifes Bailife, his owne seruant, or to a stranger, to arrest one for to find suertie of the peace, the partie to whom that warrant is made must serue it himselfe, for he can commaund none other to do it, either by precept or word. A sworne & knowen officer, be he Shirife, Undershirife, or Bailife, &c. need not to shew his warrant to a man when he commeth to serue it vpon him, for his knowen office doth authorize him. But if a Justice of peace will direct his warrant to his seruant, or to an other stranger to serue, he must shew his warrant to the partie (if he will demaund it) or otherwise the partie may make resistance, and need not to obey it. And if the party against whom the suertie of the peace is graunted, will vpon the seruing of the Justices precept, refuse to come to be bound to the peace, the partie to whom the warrant is directed, may commit him to the gaole of the same Countie, there to remaine vntill he will find suerties. The forme of which warrant for the peace is this, viz. Anthonius Greenway Miles, vnus Iusticiariorum domini Regis nunc, ad pacem in Comitatu prædicto conseruandam assignatus, Vicceco-

Who may serue a warrant without writing, who not.

Who may serue a warrant without shewing of it, and who not. 8.E.4.14. 20.H.7.13.

Refusing to obey the Justices warrant.

A warrant for the peace. *Buck.*

vicecomiti comitatus prædicti. Nec non omnibus & singulis Balliuis, Constabularijs ceterisq; Dñi Regis ministris, tam infra libertates quam extra in eodem com̃ salutem. Quia A. B. de Bechampton in comitatu prædicto Taylor venit coram me, & sacramentũ pręstitit corporale, quod ipse sibi metuit damnum vel malum de vita & mutilatione membrorum per R. C. de Stonistratford in comitatu prædict' Butcher, vel per alium per eius procurationem fieri. Ideo vobis & cuilibet vestrũ ex parte dicti Domini Regis mando quod capiatis, seu vnus vestrum capiat p̃fatũ R. C. ita quod habeatis, seu vnus vestrũ habeat corpus eius coram me, vel aliquo sociorum meorum Iusticiaoɽ dicti dñi Regis ad pacem in p̃dict. Comit̃ conseruandã assignat̃ quã cito capi possit ad inueniendã sufficientẽ securitatẽ, quod ipse aliquod malum vel damnum de vita seu mutilitatione membrorũ dicto A. B. non faciet nec fieri procurabit quouismodo. Et si hoc facere recusauerit tunc ipsũ R. C. Gaole dicti dñi Regis in comitatu p̃dict' duci faciat, seu vnus vestrum duci faciat, ibidem moraturum, quousque hoc gratis facere voluerit. Et qualiter hoc pręceptũ fuerit executum scire facias dictis Iusticiarijs ad proxima generalem Sessionem pacis in com' pædict' tenendam, & habeas ibi tunc hoc preceptum. Dat. apud Lecomstead &c.

21. H. 7. 21. Co. li. 5. 59. 75 If a Justice of peace doe direct his warrant to a Constable or other officer, to arrest one, and to bring him before the same Justice, or some other of his companions to find suertie of the peace, and he doth arrest him accordingly, but will not bring him before such a Justice of peace as the partie arrested will nominate, but before some other, yet notwithstanding the party arrested shall not haue an action of false Imprisonment, or an action of the case, nor other remedy against the same Constable, or officer: for it is in the discretion of the same Constable, or officer, to bring the party arrested before which Justice of peace of that County that he will, so that he dwell within a conuenient distance, and not too farre from the parties owne habitation. But if a Supplicauit of the peace be directed to the Justices of the peace, the Justice to whom the writ is first deliuered shall only make the precept to apprehend the partie to find suerty of the peace, and that precept shall be retornable before him only, and he only shall take the suerties, and only make the retorne without the others. And a Justice of peace may if he will make a warrant to the Co. lib. 5. 59 Constable to bring the partie before himselfe. *To which Justice of peace the partie arrested is to be brought.*

5. Ed. 4. 12. 76 If a Justice of peace doe direct his warrant to the Constable, or some other to cause A. B. to finde suerties to keepe the peace, The same Constable or &c. must first require the same A. B. to find suerties to keepe the peace, and if he doe refuse it, then he may arrest the same A. B. for if A. B. will finde suerties, then the said Constable may not arrest him, because the purport of the precept is performed (which is if he refuse so to doe, that then he shall conuey him to the Gaole.) And if the Constable shall arrest A. B. after that he hath found suerties according to the precept, the same A. B. may haue an action of false imprisonment against him, for that he hath arrested and imprisoned him without warrant, or cause. And likewise if the Constable 5. E. 4. 6. do arrest A. B. and doe not carrie him before some Justice of peace, to find suerties to keepe the peace or if he resist, or refuse so to doe, then if he doe not carrie him to the Gaole, A. B. may haue an Action of false Imprisonment against the Constable: And when the partie commeth to the Justice of peace by force of a warrant, he must offer suerties to the Just. of P. or else he may 14. H. 7. 5. commit him to prison: for the Just. needeth not to demaund suertie of him. *A warrant to find suertie to keepe the peace* *The partie must offer his suerties.*

Suerty of the peace dieth with the king

77 The suertie of peace is discharged by the kings death, for the band is to obserue the peace of the King, and when he is dead it is not his peace: So doth the death of the recognisor, & so doth also the death of him at whose suit it was taken, discharge the suertie of the peace if in those cases it were not forfeited before. And in like sort when the King by his commission doth appoint Justices of peace and after dieth, or giueth ouer his crowne, the Authoritie of the same Justices doth cease: for he maketh them Iusticiarios suos, and therefore when he dieth their authority endeth. 1.H.7.13.

The Justices authoritie dieth with the King.

The suertie for the peace must be named.

78 When a Justice of peace doth take suerties for the peace, it is not sufficient to say, that I. N. hath found sufficient suertie for the peace without naming the names of the suerties: but he must name their names and surnames. 2.H.7.4.

He that is bound to the peace must appeare &c.

79 If a man doe finde suerties to kéepe the peace, and hath day vntill a time prefixed, he must appeare the same day (although he who demaunded the peace doe not appeare) or otherwise, he shall forfeit his band. But it is otherwise where a suit is betwéene party and party, and the defendant being taken by a Capias is bound to appeare vpon a day appoynted. 39.H.6.26.

A Supersedeas for the peace.

80 When the suertie of peace is graunted against a man by a Justice of peace, he will sometime rather desire to be bound to the peace by an other Justice, then by him that graunted the same, and made the warrant: And therefore he may offer himselfe to become bound to the peace to some other Justice of peace of that County if he will, & then procure a Supersedeas from that other Justice before whom he is bound to all other Justices of that Countie to be discharged of any other arrest to be made of him, for the law doth not require that he should be seuerall times bound for one cause. And this Supersedeas is sufficient although it neither name the suertie, nor contein the summes wherein they are bound, but yet it is a better forme to expresse them both, as the Chauncerie and Kings Bench doe. And when a man doth heare of such a precept awarded or granted against him by a Just. of peace of the County where he dwelleth, he may go & eyther giue suertie of the peace in the K. Bench or els in the Chancery, & thereupon may procure a Supersedeas from the court where he is bound, to restrain the Just. of peace of the County to take any suertie of peace of him. And then the Justices of peace of that County must forbeare to make any warrant for the peace against the partie; and if any of them haue awarded it, he must make a Supersedias to discharge it. But a Just. of peace of the county by a Supersedeas cannot discharge a precept that is awarded by his felow Just. by force of a Supplicauit directed to him out of the Chancery or the K. Bench to take the suertie of peace of one resident in that County. If any officer hauing a warrant from a Just. of P. to arrest a man to find suerty of the peace shall receiue a Supersedeas, out of the Chancery, or the Kings Bench, or from any Justice of the Kings Bench or from any Justice of peace of that County where he is commorant, to discharge the same suerty of peace, wil neuertheles vrge that partie against whom the same warrant is granted to find new suertie for the peace, he may refuse to giue it: And if the said officer will therupon vnder ye color of his warrant commit him to prison, the party imprisoned may haue an action of false impris. against him: for yt the said warrant is discharged by as great authoritie, or greater, as it was made, and the thing

A precept awarded by force of a Supplicauit.

for

for the which it was made is effected. The forme of which Supersedeas graunted by a Justice of the peace is this, viz:

Thomas Denton Miles; vnus Iusticiariorum dñi Regis nunc ad pacem in Comitatu p̄dicto conseruandam assignat̃, Vicecomiti comitatus prędicti: Nec non oibus & singulis Balliuis, Constabularijs, ceterisq; dicti dñi Regis ministris, tam infra libertates quam extra in eodem Com̃ Salutẽ. Quia A. B. de Pountdon in com̃ prædict' Laborer venit corã me, & invenit sufficientẽ securitat̃ qd; ipse comparebit ad proximã generalẽ Sessionẽ pacis in com̃ prædicto tenend'. Et quod ipse interim pacẽ dicti Dñi Reg. erga ipsũ dominũ Reg. & cunctũ populũ suũ, & precipue erga C. D. de Twyford in com̃ prædicto Husbandman conseruabit ideo ex partæ dicti dñi regis vobis & cuilibet vestrũ mando, quod de arrestando, imprisonando, seu aliqualiter molestando prædictũ A. B. ex causa p̄dicta Supersedeatis, & quilibet vestrũ Supersedeat omnio. Et si eũ ex dict' causa, & non alia ceperitis, seu imprisionaueritis, seu aliquis vestrũ ceperit, seu imprisonauerit, tunc à prisona illa siue delatione deliberari faciatis, datũ apud Hilsdon &c. But if a man be arrested in the common place for the suertie of peace, and he is lett to baile, to a certaine day, at which day he doth bring a Supersedias out of the Chauncerie, that he hath found suerties in the Chauncery: that is not allowable, because he was by baile, which is an imprisonment in law, and therefore the suertie in the Chauncery will not serue. And it may be that the suerties in the Chancery be not sufficient, and that the King and the Court was deceiued therein. And yet the common place hath no authority to take suerty of peace, but of the peace broken before them.

Buck. A Supersedeas for the peace.

22.H.6.59. Supersedeas in the Chancery for one bound in the common place.

2.H.7.2.

81 When the partie against whom the precept is awarded to find suerties for the keeping of the peace, doth come before the Justice of peace to be bound to the peace, then it resteth in the discretion of the same Justice of peace (if he deale in this cause as a Justice of peace by force of the generall commission of peace, and so as a Judge) to assigne what number of suerties he will accept to be bound with the party, in what summe of money the party & his suerties shall be bound, to allow, or disallow of the sufficiencie of those suerties, to limit the time how long the party shall be bound, and to determine vpon some such other circumstances touching that matter. But if the same Just. of peace be commanded as a minister in the execution of the writ of Supplicauit, to take the peace of any person, then he must do as the writ doth direct him, which sometime is to take sufficient suertie to be bound in a summe prescribed, and some other time not, & then it resteth in his owne discretion. The most vsuall maner is for a Justice of peace to take two suerties, besides the partie himselfe, to be bound by Recognizance to the King, viz. Domino Regi, and that must alwaies be for the keeping of the peace. The forme of which Recognizance for the keeping of the peace is as followeth, viz.

A Recognizance for the keeping of the peace.

Memorandum qd' nono die Augusti, Anno regni dñi nostr̃ Regis Iacobi dei gratia &c. 5. A. B. de Padburie in Comitatu p̄dict' Husbandman, in ꝑpria persona sua venit coram me Richardo Ingalsby Milite, vno Iusticiariorũ dicti dñi Regis ad pacem in dicto Comitat̃ conseruandam assignatorũ, & assumpsit pro seipso sub pœna xx. li. et D. E. & H. I. de C. in Comitat̃ prædict' Husbandmen, adtunc & ibm̃ in ꝑprijs personis suis similiter venerunt, & manuceperunt pro prædicto A. B. viz. quilibet eorum seperatim sub pœna x. li. quod idem A. B. personaliter comparebit coram Iusticiarijs dicti domini Regis ad pacem ad ꝑximam generalẽ Sessionem pacis in Com̃ p̄dicto adud Buck. tenendam,

Buck.

 ad faad faciendum & recipiendū quod ei per Curiam tunc & ibidem iniungetur. Et quod ipse interim pacem dicti dñi Regis custodiet erga ipsum dominū Regem & cunctum populū suum, & pręcipue versus L.M. de O. de comitatu prædict. Et quod damnum vel malum aliquod corporale, aut grauamen pręfat L.M. nec alicui de populo dicti domini Regis quod in lęsionem aut perturbationem pacis ipsius Domini Regis seu præfati L.M. cedere valeat, quouismodo non faciet, nec fieri procurabit. Quam quidem summam xx. l'. prædict' A.B. & quilibet manucaptorum prædictorum prædictas seperales summas x. l'. recognouerunt se debere dicto domino Regi, de terris & tenementis bonis, & catallis suis, & cuiuslibet eorum ad opus dicti domini Regis fieri & leuari ad quorumcunque manus deuenerunt, si contigerit ipsum A.B. præmissa vel eorum aliquid in aliquo infringere, & inde legitimo modo conuinci. In cuius rei testimonium ego pdictus Richardus Ingolsby sigillum meum apposui. Dat apud Lethenborow die & Anno supradict'.

And the forme of the Recognizance for the good abearing is this, viz.

A Recognizance for the good abearing.

Memorandū &c. & quod ipse A. B. interim se bene geret erga Dñm Reg. & cunctū populū suū, & pręcipue erga L. M. Et quod ipse non inferet nec inferri pcurabit per se nec per alios, damnū aliquod seu grauamen pfato L.M. seu alicui de populo ipsius dñi Regis de corporibus suis, per insidias, insultus, seu aliquo alio modo quod in lęsionem seu perturbationem pacis dicti dñi Regis cedere valeat quouismodo, viz. vterq; prædict' D. E. et H. I. sub poena 50. libr, et prædict' A. B. sub poena 100. libr &c. And this may be done by a single Recognizance in Latin, with a Condition thereunto added in English for the keeping of the peace, or the good Abearing, and for the day and place of the parties apparance at the Quarter Sessions.

A Releas of the suertie of peace.

82 A Justice of peace who upon his owne discretion compelleth one to find suertie of the peace untill a certaine day, may upon the like discretion release the same before that day: But if a Justice of peace do graunt the peace at the request of an other, viz. at the suit of A. and that the Recognizance be taken to keepe the peace against A. then may the same A. only releas it, and none other, before the same Justice of peace, or any other Justice, that will certifie the same releas before the Justices of peace at the next quarter Sessions; for that certificat being of record will discharge it, which a releas by deed can not do, the suertie of peace being a Recognizance, and so of it selfe a record. And though the Recognizance be versus cunctum populū, & precipue versus A. yet may the same A. releas it: for though it may seeme populer, and that others should haue equall interest therein with A. yet as it appeareth by the word precipue, it was specially taken for his safetie. But though in some case a Justice of peace may releas the suertie of the peace, & in some other case the partie, yet the King can in neither of the said cases releas it untill it be forfeited, for the mischiefe that may come to A. thereby, though the Recognizance be taken domino Regi, for that it is not a debt unto him untill it be forfeited: But being forfeited, then the King, and none other may releas & pardon the forfeiture. And in the cases aforesaid, though the Just. of peace, or the party may releas the suertie of the peace, yet the Recognizance before taken for the suertie of the peace must not be cancelled, least the peace was broken before the releas made, & so the Recognizance was forfeited. And the forme of the Justice of peace releas of the peace is this: Ego pfatus Paulus Risley armiger,

Buck. The Justices release of the peace.

miger, vnus Iuſticiariorū dñi Regis nunc ad pacem in Com̄ p̄dict̄ conſeruãdam aſſignat̄, qui S. T. de Preſton ad ſecuritatē pacis inueniendam mea diſcretione compuli eandem ſecuritatem pacis, quantū in me eſt, in mea diſcretione 10. die Maij An̄ 5. Reg. Iac. &c. remiſi & relaxaui. Dat' apud Chetwood &c. And the forme of the releaſe of the party before the ſame Iuſtice that tooke the Recognizance of the peace is this: Memorandum quod 10. die Iulij Anno 5. Regis Iacobi &c. A. B. venit coram me Franciſco Cheney Milite, vno Iuſticiariorum dom̄ Regis nunc ad pacem &c. & gratis remiſit & relaxauit (quantum in ſe eſt) prædictam ſecuritatem pacis per ipſum verſus ſupranominatum S. T. petitam. In cuius rei teſtimonium, ego p̄fatus F. C. &c. Dat̄ apud Cheſſam Bois &c. And in like ſort the Iuſtice or Iuſtices of peace may doe, which tooke ſuretie for the good abearing, if they ſee cauſe. The parties releaſe of the peace.

83 The peace or good abearing is broken, & the Recogniſance taken for the keeping of the ſame, is forfeited by violent, extreame, malicious, and vnlawfull menacings, aſſaults, affrayes, batteries, ſtrikings, or impriſonments: as if a man bound to the Peace, doe wrongfully and malitiouſly menace, aſſault, beat, or impriſon another: or doe forcibly thruſt him into a riuer, well, or pond, whereby he is in danger of drowning: or doe rauiſh a woman againſt her will: or doe commit manſlaughter, burglarie, or robberie, Br.peace 20 or treaſon againſt the perſon of the King. And if a man be bound to the peace, & after he doth procure another to breake the peace, this is a cauſe of forfeiture of his recognizance, taken for the ſurety of the peace, for that the peace is broken 18.Ed.4.28. by his meanes. And if one be bound to the peace, & after doe menace I. S. to his face, & in his preſence to kill or beate him, this is a breach of the peace. But if I. S. be abſent when he is menaced, then is it no breach of the peace, vnles the ſame partie doe, according to his menace, lie in waight to kill or beate I. 22.Ed.4.35. S. for then alſo it is a breach of the peace. And though the ſuertie of the peace 2.H.7.2. be not broken without fighting, beating, impriſoning, or extremity of menacing, yet the ſuertie of good abearing may be forfeited by the extraordinary 10.H.7.12. number of people, that the partie bound hath attending vpon him, or by his wearing of harneis, or other weapons more then before he hath vſually done, or be meete for his degree or eſtate, or by vſing of rigorous or terrible words, or threatenings tending or inciting to the breach of the peace, or indemeaning himſelfe in his behauiour, company or geſture, or doing of any thing which ſhall tend to the breach of the peace, or to put the people in dread or feare. Cauſes of the breach of the peace, or good abearing.

84 As the wiſdome of the Realme hath ordained Iuſtices of peace to be preſeruors of the peace, and men wholy or ſpecially deuoted & aſſigned to that office. So hath ſhe made choice of other magiſtrates, who with their other offices haue the conſeruation of the peace annexed to their charges, & as a thing incident or inſeperable from their other functions, and goe continually lincked arme in arme with them: As euery Shirife in his County, euery Coroner, high conſtable of any lath, rape, wapentake, hundred or fraunchiſe, and euery petit Conſtable, Borſhoulder, Tithingman, Headborough, Boroughhead, Thirdborough, and chiefe pledge in euery Towne, Village, & hamlet, is within his limits and the precincts of his authoritie a conſeruator of the peace. And ſo is the Steward in euery Leete, and view of franck pledge, & the Steward of euery Court of Pipowders a conſeruator of the peace, and if an affray be made in their preſence ſitting in their Court, each of them may commit the offen- The Shirife, Conſtable, &c. conſeruators of the peace.

offendors to prison. And they all are in dutie first to bend their care & foresight to preuent the breach of the peace, next to imploy both their owne valor and strength, & to commaund the helpe & force of others to pacifie those who by word or deed are in breaking of the peace: And thirdly to punish those who haue broken the peace, according to the law. And therefore any of the St.5.E.3.14.
officers aforesaid may take, and arrest suspected persons which walke in the night, and sleepe in the day, and carrie them before a Justice of peace to finde suerties of their good behauiour. And if any be taken by watchmen in the night Sta.13. E.1.
watch that is suspected of euill behauiour, they may take him and imprison him, vntill he be deliuered by the ordinarie course of law. And if any doe goe or ride armed by day or night in fayers, or markets, or other places, (sauing the Kings seruants in his presence, or in executing of his precepts, or such as doe pursue huy and cry where offences be done) any of the same officers may take their armor from them to the Kings vse, and commit them to the gaole. And if any assemblies, Rout, or rumor shall be begun, the Shirifes and other St.17.R.8.
the Kings officers, shall take the power of the County and disperse them, and shall commit the offendors to prison vntill they be duely punished according to the law. And if any do threaten to kill maihem, or beate an other, or doe attempt or goe about to doe it; then any of the said officers may arrest the offendor to come before a Justice of peace, to finde suertie for the keeping of the peace, or els the same officer may commit him to prison. And if either of 1.H.7.7.
the said officers shal perceiue any other in his presence to be in breaking of the peace, eyther by drawing of their weapons, or by assaulting or striking one of an other, or by assaulting himselfe, he may commaund them vpon paine of imprisonment to surcease, or else he may with his weapon part & keepe them 5.H.7.6.
asunder, and call and procure others likewise so to doe. And then he may carrie them before a Justice of peace to find suertie of the peace, which if they refuse to doe, he may commit them to prison, or els the Constable may 3.H.4.9.
take suerties of them by Obligation to keepe the peace. And if any of the offendors doe flee into a house, the said officer may breake open the dores 13.Ed.4.9.
and arrest him, and so he may doe if the offendor doe flee into another Countie, for that the arrest is for the benefite of the commonweale. And likewise if any of the said officers shall learne that certaine persons be fighting or quarreling in a house, in such sort that they are like to breake the peace, or that a man and a woman be in a house together committing addultery or fornication, he may breake open the dores and arrest them to come before a 7.E.3.10.
Justice of peace to find suertie of the peace, or otherwise if he will, he may 1.H.7.6.
commit any of the said offendors to prison. And if any of the parties to an affray haue receiued any daungerous wound, then the officer must arrest the offendor, and carrie him to a Justice of peace, who is eyther to commit him 22.Ass.p.56
to prison, or to let him to mainprise vntill the next Gaole deliuery, that it be knowen whethir the partie wounded will liue or die thereof: or els the officer himselfe may commit him to prison vntill the same be knowen: for if the par- 38.Ed.3.6.
tie wounded doe die, the offence wil be felony. If the common voice and fame of the County be that C. D. hath committed a felony, any of those officers that doe suspect him thereof may arrest him for it. And so he may search within the limits of his authority for any persõs suspected of felony, for it is a chiefe parte of the Constables dutie to preserue the peace and represse felons. And if any of the officers before mentioned do arrest an offendor, or any person suspected for any of the causes aforesaid, who ought to be carried to the Gaole, or before a Justice of peace, the same officer neede not carrie him presently to the

Gaole,

22.Ed.4.35. Gaole, or before the Iustice, but he may put him in the stocks, or some other safe custody for a time, untill he can provide sufficient company to assist him to conduct the same offendor to the Gaole or to the Iustice: Or if the partie 2.Ed.4.9. arrested be so sicke, diseased, or wounded that he cannot be presently carried without daunger of death, the officer may stay him untill he be recouered.

85 But the peace of the Realme hath béen so precious to all ages; and Treasons, Felonies, assaults, batteries, and other forcible violences and offences so odious, that the Lawes and Statutes of the Realme, and the wisedome of our forefathers haue made and appointed (besides the Magistrates and officers before mencioned) all sortes of able persons, in some sort, and to some purposes, preseruers of the peace; intending that as all the members of the common weale, doe taste swéet comfort, and pleasant repose by the benefit of peace, so they should be all partakers, when néede requireth of the paines to maintaine and continue the same peace, and to punish Sta.3.E.1.9. the transgressors thereof. And therefore by the Statute of Westm 1. it is ordained, That all men generally shall be ready at the commaundement and summons of the Shirifes, and at the crie of the country, to pursue and arrest felons, when néede shall be, aswell within fraunchises as without; and they that will not, and be thereof attainted, shall make a grieuous fine to the Sta. 3.Ed.1. King. By the statute intituled Officium Coronatoris it is enacted, That upon all Homicides, Burglaries, men slaine, or put in great daunger, huy and crie shall be leuied, and euery man shall follow the huy and crie, and the offendors steppes if it may be: and whosoeuer doth not, and is thereupon conuicted, shall be attached to appeare before the Iustices of Gaole deliSt.5.E.3.14. uerie. By the Statute of Anno 5.Ed.3. it is established, That if any man suspect lewd persons (then termed robertsmen, wasters, or drawlatches) of any manslaughters, felonies, or robberies, be it by day, or night, they shall incontinently be arrested by the Constable of the towne, and if it be within franchise deliuered to the Bailifes of the franchise, and if in guildable to the shirife, and kept untill the comming downe of the Iustices of Gaole deliuerie, who St.17.R.2.8. shall procéede to the deliueraunce of them. By the Statute of 17.R.2. it is defended to all the Kings people aswell Lords as others, that none shall make assemblies, Riots, or Rumors against the peace. And if any such assemblie be begun, as soone as the Shirife and other Ministers may haue knowledge thereof, they with the strength of the country shal disturbe such offendors, and put them in prison untill the law be executed upon them. And all Lords and other liege people of the Realme shall be attending with all their strength and St.2.H.5.8. power to the Shirifes and Ministers aforesaid. By the Statut of An 2.H.5. it is prouided, That the Kings people being able to trauaile in the Countie where Riots, assemblies, or routs against the law be shalbe assistant to the Iustices, Commissioners, Shirife, or undershirif of the same Countie, when they shall be reasonably warned, to ride with the said Iustices, Shirife &c. in aide to resist such Riots, Routs, and Assemblies, upon paine of imprisonment, and St.15.R.2.2 to make fine and ransom to the King. By the Statute of 15.R.2. it is ordeined, That if the Shirife, or any other of the Countie doe not attend upon a Iust. of peace, to arrest such offendors as doe make forcible entries into lands or tenements, he or they so offending shall be imprisoned, and pay a fine to the Sta.1.M.12. King. By the Statute of An 1.M. it is established, That if any person being aboue the age of xvii. yeares, and under the age of lx. being able to serue, and not sick, lame, or impotent, shall be required by any Iustice of peace, or any Shirife

Euery able person is a Conseruator of the peace.

Shirife of any County, where any unlawfull assembly of xij. persons or aboue shall be to do any unlawfull act prohibited by that statute; or by any Maior, Bailife, or other head Officer of any Citie, Borough, or towne corporat; or by any other by the commaundement of any such Justice, Shirife, Maior, &c. to go with him or them to suppresse the persons unlawfully assembled: Then euery person, which so being able and required, doth willingly and obstinatly refuse so to doe, shal suffer imprisonment for one yeare without baile or mainprise. And as in al the cases aforesaid euery able person is bound upon request to assist the Justices, shirifes, & other the Kings officers, to pursue, apprehend, arrest, and imprison Manquellors, robbers, felons, or other disturbers of the peace, and so to do his whole endeuor to be a conseruator of the peace of the Realme: In like sort is euery able person bound by the common law, and by the Stat. of Westm̃ 1. & Westm̃ 2. to be attendant upon the Shirife, or undershirife, in the execution of the kings writs, and by that meanes to be a supporter of the justice of the Realme.

Euerie person must assist to execute the K. writ.

St. 3. E. 1. 17. S. 13. E. 1. 39.

These offẽces punishable in the Starre Chamber.

86 Menaces, assaults, batteries, imprisonments, and maihems committed by some persons, to some persons, at some times, in some places & in some manner, forme, sort, and with some circumstances (besides the penalties aforesaid inflicted upon the offendors therein) are also punishable in the Kings high Court of the Starre chamber as other offences hereafter mentioned be, as it doth more at large appeare in Oppressions 35.

Of

Of Riots, Routs, vnlawful and rebellious Assemblies.

Riots, Routs, vnlawfull & Rebellious assemblies haue bin so many times pernitious, & fatal enemies to this kingdom, the peace, & tranquillity thereof, & haue so often shaken the foundation, and put in hazard the very forme and state of gouernment of the same, that our lawmakers haue been enforced to deuise from age to age one law vpon an other, & one stat. after another for the repressing & punishing of them, & haue endeuoured by all their wits to snib the sprouts, & quench the very first sparkes of them: as euery man may easily perceiue there was cause thereof, who will looke back, and call to his remembrance, what that small Riot begun at Dartmouth in Kent in the raigne of King Richard the second between the collector of a subsidy, and a Tyler and his wife, about the payment of one poore groat did come vnto, which being not repressed in time, did grow to so great a rebelliō, that after it put in hazard the life of the K. the burning of the Citie of London, the ouerthrow of the whole Nobility, gentlemen, and all the learned of the land, and the subuersion of this goodly Monarchy and forme of gouernment: Or if they will call to mind the small Riot, or quarrell begun in the raigne of King Henry the sixt between a Yeoman of the gard and a seruingman of Richard Neuils, Earle of warwick, which so farre increased for want of restraint, that it was the roote of many wofull tragedies, and a meane to bring to vntimely death, first Richard Plantagenet Duke of Yorke proclaymed successor to the Crowne, and the chiefe pillar of the house of Yorke, and after him King Henry the sixt, and Prince Edward his sonne, the heires of the house of Lancaster; and to ruinate with the one, or the other of them, most of the Peeres, great men, and gentlemen of the realme, besides many thowsands of the common people. And therefore King Edward the first did well ordaine, That no Shirifes shall suffer Barretors or maintainers of quarrels in their Counties: And that to all parliaments, Treatises, and other assemblies, each man shall come peaceably, without any armor: and that euery man shall haue armor in his house according to his ability to keepe the peace. And King Edward the third prouided, that no man shall come before the Justices, nor goe or ride armed. And that suspected, lewd, and riotous persons, shall be arrested and safely kept vntill they be deliuered

The enormitie of Riots.

West. 1. 3 E. 1. 32. Sta. 7. Ed. 1. St. 13. E. 1. 6.

St. 2. E. 3. 3. St. 5. E. 3. 14.

Statutes ordained to preuent forces or Riots.

uered by the Iustices of Gaole deliuery. And that Iustices of peace shall re- St.34.E.1.3.
straine offendors, riotors, and all other Barretors, and pursue, take, and cha- Sta.2.R.2.6.
sten them, according to their Trespas and offence. King Richard the second Sta.5.R.2.6.
did prohibit Riots, Routs, and forcible entries into lands, that were made in St.15.R.2.2
diuers counties and partes of the Realme. And that none from thenceforth St.7.R.2.13
should make any Riot, or Rumor. And that no man shall ride armed, nor vse 20.Rich.2.1
Launcegaies. And that no laborer, seruant in husbandry, or Artificer, or vict- St.12.R.2.6
ualer, shall weare any buckler, sword, or dagger. And that all the Kings of-
ficers shall suppresse and imprison such as make any Riots, Routs, or vnlaw- St.17.R.2.8.
ful assemblies against the peace. King Henry the fourth enacted, That the Iu-
stices of peace, & the Shirife shall arrest those which commit any Riot, Rout,
or vnlawfull assembly; shall enquire of them, and record their offences. King St.13.H.4.7
Henry the fift assigned commissioners to enquire of the same Iustices & Shi- St.2.H.5.8.
rifes defaults in that behalfe, and also limited what punishment offendors at-
tainted of Riot should sustaine. King Henry the seauenth ordained, that such Sta.19.H.7.
persons as were returned to enquire of Riots should haue sufficient freehold
or copihold land within the same Shire. And that no maintenance should
hinder their Inquisition. And in the Raigne of Queene Mary, there was Sta.1.M.12.
a necessary Statute established to restrain and punish vnlawfull and rebelli-
ous assemblies raised by a multitude of vnruly persons, to commit certaine
violent, forcible, and Riotous acts.

2 As the said Lawes & Statutes were deuised in seueral ages by the wise-
dom of the Realme, to enquire of, and restraine Riots, Routs, vnlawfull, and
rebellious assemblies, and to checke violences, and forces, before they should
grow to a head: So haue our prouident forefathers erected the most honorable
Court of Starre chamber, to examine and punish those, and other offences, (The Court of Starre chambers authoritie to punish Riots, &c.)
when they breake out to extremities, viz. to great and haynous Riots, or
such like enormities, thereby to keepe euery person in awe, and so the whole
Realme in peace. As appeareth by the Statute of Anno 3. H. 7. whereby
it is inacted, That the Chauncellour, and Treasorer of England for the
time being (and the President of the Kings Councell, and the keeper of the St.3.H.7.1.
Kings priuy seale, or two of them) calling to them a Bishop, and a Tempo- Stat. 21. H. 8.22.
rall Lord of the Kings most honorable priuy Councell, & the two chiefe Iusti-
ces of the K. Bench, and common place for the time being (or other two Iust.
in their absence) vpon bill, or information put to the said Chauncellor for the
King, or any other against any person (for any misbehauing by vnlawfull
maintenances, giuing of liueries, signes and tokens, retainers by Inden-
tures, oathes, writings or otherwise, embracery of the Kings subiects, vntrue
demeanings of Shirifes, in making of pannels, and other vntrue returnes,
by taking of money, by iniuries, by great Riots and vnlawfull assemblies)
haue authority to cal before them by writ, or by priuy seale, the said misdoers
and they, and other, by their discretion by whom the truth may be knowne, to
examine, and such as they finde therein defectiue, to punish them according to
their demerits, after the forme and effect of the Statutes thereof made, in like
manner and forme, as they should or ought to be punished, if they were there-
of conuict after the due order of the law. And though the Iustices of peace
doe assesse a fine in the Country vpon some that haue committed a Riot there,
yet the Lords in the Starre chamber, may assesse vpon the said offendors for
the same Riot, a greater penalty, if they see cause; for in this case the offendors
be not twice punished for one offence, but part of the due punishment is infli-
cted

ded at one time, and part at another: And the Lords doe sufficiently punish an offence, which was but remisly done by the Iustices.

3 A Riot is where thrée persons or aboue do assemble themselues together, to the intent to beate or maihem a man, to pul downe a house, wall, pale, hedge, or ditch wrongfully, to claime or take common or way in a ground, to destroy any parke, warren, douehouse, pond, poole, barne, mill, or stacke of corne, or to doe any other vnlawfull act with force and violence, and against the peace, and they doe it. If a man goe abroade with his houshold seruants which he hath commonly of his owne familie (though they be more then his abilitie or degrée is to maintaine) and doth make a fray by the way, this is no Riot, vnlesse the Master did before make his seruants priuy, that hée meant to make an affray: for it is no riot, except there be an intent before to doe some violence and hurt. If thrée, foure, or more doe enter into landes with force, vppon the possession of an other, though their entrie be lawfull, yet is it a Riot, for the Statute of Anno 5. Richard. 2. doth prohibite entrie into Landes and Tenements with force, or a multitude of people. — *What is a Riot.* — *St. 5. R. 2. 7.*

4 An vnlawfull assembly is, where thrée persons, or aboue, doe assemble themselues together, to the intent to doe any of the Actes aforesaide, or any other such vnlawfull act, with force and violence against the Peace, although they doe it not indéede, but after their assemblie they departe by their owne consent, vpon some feare conceiued, or other cause, without doing of any outrage, for their intent of assembling was vnlawfull, though the act subsequent did not ensue according to the same. — *What is an vnlawfull assembly.*

5 A Route is, where thrée persons or aboue doe assemble themselues, for the reuenge of their owne common quarrell. As, if the Inhabitants of a Towne doe assemble together to pull downe a house, wall, pale, ditch, or other inclosure, of a parke, pasture, or close, or the head of a poole, where they wrongfully pretend to haue title of common, or a way, or to beate, or maihem one man, or more, that haue done to them all some publike offence. If they once méete, procéede, and goe forward, towardes the execution of any of the Actes aforesaide, and doe shew by Armour, Gesture, or Spéech, that they meane to doe any violence, or to terrifie or feare any of the Kings people, it is a Rout, whether they put their intended purpose in execution, or not: But if a Maior and Aldermen, or Bayliffe and Burgesses, or the fellowes of any societie doe assemble in their common quarrell, and make a Riot, Rout, or Unlawfull assembly, this shall be punished in there owne priuate naturall persons, and not in the body politike, for it was their priuate persons that assembled to offend the Lawe, and not the bodie politike. If a man goe to the Sessions, Market, Faire, or other assemblie of company, with his seruants in Harnesse, though he hath no intent to fight, or to commit any Riot, yet this is a Rout by the manner of his comming, and is contrary to the Statute of 2. Edw. 3. which hath ordained, That no man shall bring any force in affray of the peace, nor shall go armed in faires, markets, or elsewhere, vpon paine of imprisonment, and forfeiture of his Armour. — *What is a Rout.* — *17. Ed. 4. 4* — *Rout by wearing of Armour.* — *St. 2. Ed. 3. 3*

F 6 An

Lawfull assemblies of thrée persons, or more.

6 An Assembly of thrée persons or more, which is not to the terrour of the
people, nor to doe some Act with force and violence against the peace, is not
vnlawfull nor prohibited by any of the Statutes before mentioned. The
watch in London vpon Midsummer night is lawfull, and so be such like in
other Cities and Townes. Assemblies be lawfull that be vsed vppon Maie
day, to fetch in Maie boughs, or floures; and so be assemblies at Church-
Ales, Whitson, or Midsummer-Ales. Assemblies at the fetching home, set-
ting vp, or dauncing about a Maie-pole, and assemblies at the bayting of a
Bull, or Beare, or at the mowing or making of Dole or Reuell meade, and
assemblies of Minstrells and their fellowes at certaine places, and times of
the yére, allowed by old and ancient customes are also lawfull: And Assem-
blies to play at Cardes, Tables, Bowles, Clash, Bucklers, Wasters, halfe
Sword, Tennis, Quoits, Cailes, or such other games be likewise by the
common lawe tollerable (though some of the same games be prohibited vp-
on some penalties by Statute to be vsed by some persons) and assemblies to St.33.H.8.9
runne at Quintall, Sand bagge, Base, Foteball, Stoleball, Handball,
or such like disports be also lawfull: For these assemblies be not made with
the intent to breake or disturbe the Peace, or to offer violence, force, or hurt
to the person of any; but either to trie Actiuity, or to increase societie, ami-
tie, and neighbourly friendship. And if in any of the said assemblies, any of
the parties the same, shall make a fray with a stranger, that is no Riot, nei-
ther doth it make the residue of the same company Riotors, who came thither
for their disports, and not to any euill or vnlawfull intent. But if any of the
same company shall fall out with a stranger, or some others of their owne
associates, and then some of them doe take one parte, and some of them an-

An Assembly lawfully begunne doth end riotously.

other, whereby a Riot is committed: then so many of both sides as shall
take sides, and be parties to that quarrell, shall be adiudged Riotors, but
not the residue; for the Riot did not take his beginning at the first méet-
ing, when they did all assemble for any of the sportes before mentioned,
but when the taking of parte with those that did quarrell beganne. And
therefore they onely, who made themselues parties to that quarrell, shall
be punished as Riotors, and none other. And so it is, if a Iurie be char-
ged to trie an Issue, if some of them fall out, and fight; this is no Riot
in the residue assembling to a lawfull end. And it is lawfull for the She- 22.H.6.37
riffe, Vndershériffe, or Bayliffe to take the power of the Countie, what 3.H.7.1.&
number they shall thinke good, to execute the Kings processe: And so may 10.
any Iustice or Iustices of Peace, and the Sheriffe, and the Vndershe- St.17.R.2.8.
riffe, take any power of the Countie to repressé Riots, Routes, vnlaw- St.1.M.12.8
full or Rebellious Assemblies: Or to remoue such persons, as by In- St.3.H.4.17
quisition are found to haue made forcible Entries into other mens posses- St.2.8.H.6.9.
sions, or to detaine them with force. And so may a Iustice of Peace, St.3.Ed.1.9.
Sheriffe or Constable take of the Countie any number that they will to
pursue and apprehend Traytours, Murderers, Robbers, or other felons,
or such as doe breake, or goe about to breake, or disturbe the peace: For
though in the cases last specified there be thrée or aboue assembled together,
yet it is to execute the iustice of the Lawe, and by that meanes to pre-
serue peace. And it is a lawfull assembly which is gathered together to runne
at Tilt, Iusts, or Barriers by the Kings commaundement: for the cause, be-
ginning, and end thereof, doe tend to obedience, the laudable exercise of true
valour,

valour, and manhood, and to the encouragement and enabling of the actors therein to defend the Realme, and the peace thereof.

7 And though by the before specified Statute of Anno 34. Edw. 3. it is ordained, that Iustices of Peace shall restraine offendors, Riotors, and all other Barrators, and pursue, take, chasten, imprison, and punish them according to their trespasses and offences, to the intent that the people bee not by such Riotors troubled, or indammaged, nor the peace broken, nor any passengers by the way disturbed, or put in perill: Yet by force of that Statute the Iustices of Peace could not require the helpe of the Sherife, nor commaund St. 17. R. 2. 8. the power of the countie to helpe to assist them, to repress the said Riotors. Whereupon by the before mentioned Statute of Anno 17. R. 2. it is defended, That none shall make assemblies, riot, or rout against the peace in any wise. And if any such assembly be begun, as soone as the Sherifes and other the Kings ministers may haue knowledge thereof, they with the power of the countie, where such case shall happen, shall disturbe such malice with all their power, and shall apprehend all such offendors, and put them in prison, vntill due execution of the law be made of them: and all Lords and other liege people of the Realme shall attend with their whole strength and power, the Sherifes and ministers aforesaid. Disturbing of riotors.

8 But because the said Statute of 17. R. 2. or any other Statute or Law before that time made, doth not enable the Iustices of Peace, and Sherife to record that, which they shall find done in their presence against the law, nor to make enquirie thereof, nor to heare and determine the same, nor to make certificat thereof to the King and his counsell, if the truth cannot be found: Nor doth assigne what Proces shall bee awarded against the offendors, nor doth inflict any penaltie vpon the Iustices which shall not execute the law: St. 13. H. 4. 7 Therefore by the before rehearsed Statute made Anno 13. H. 4. it was established, that if any riot, assemblie, or rout of people against the law be made in any part of the Realme, the Iustices of peace, three, or two of them at the least, and the Sherife or Vndersherife of the shire, where such riot, assembly, or rout shall be made, shall come with the power of the countie, if need bee to arrest them. And the Iustices, Sherife, or Vndersherife, shall haue power to record that which they shall find done in their presence against the law: And the same trespassors and offendors shall bee conuict by the Record of the same Iustices, Sherife, or Vndersherife, in manner and forme as is contained in the Statute of forcible entries. The forme of Recording of which riot is this; viz. Memorandum quod primo die Martij anno regni regis Domini nostri Iacobi dei grat̄ &c. tertio, Nos Franciscus Goodwin miles, & Alexander Hamden miles Iusticiarij domini Regis nunc ad pacem in comitatu prædicto conseruandam, necnon &c. assignati, & Richardus Ingolsby miles adtunc vicecomes eiusdem comitatus, ad querimoniam A. B. de Wadsdon in com̄ prædicto yeoman in proprijs personis nostris accessimus ad domum mansionalem ipsius A. B. apud Wadsdon prædict̄; & ibidem inuenimus quosdam C. D. E. F. G. & alios malefactores, & pacis dicti domini Regis perturbatores ignotos, ad numerum octo personarum modo guerrino arraiatos, viz. cum gladijs, baculis, arcubus, & sagittis riotosè, & illegitime aggregatos, & eandem domum sic custodient̄, in magnam perturbationem pacis dicti domini Regis & populi sui terrorem, & contra formam statuti in Parliamento domini

The Iustices and Sherifs shall arrest Riotors.

Buck. Recording of a riot.

Henrici nuper Regis Angliæ quarti, Anno Regni sui decimo tertio tento, editi. Et ideo nos præfati F. G. & A. H. corpora pdictorũ C. D. E. F. G. adtunc arrestauimus, ac proxime Gaole dicti domini Regis in Com' pdicto duci fecimus p recordum nostrum de transgressione prædicta conuictos in præsentia nostra, ibidem moraturos, quousq; finem dicto domino Regi p transgressione sua prędicta fecerunt. In cuius rei testimonium huic recordo nostro sigilla nostra apposuimus. Dat apud Wadsdon prędict' die & Anno prædictis.

Inquirie of a Riot by the Iustices, &c.

9 By the same Statute of 13. H. 4. it is further ordained, That if it happen such Trespassors and offendors be departed before the comming of such Iustices, and Shirife, or vndershirife, the same Iustices, three, or two of them shall diligently inquire within a moneth after such Riot, assembly, or Rout of people so made, and the same shall heare and determine according to the lawes of this Realme: And because the said Iustices of peace, Shirifs &c. are by this braunch of the Statute, to make inquiry of the Riot, which must be done by a Iury returned by the Shirife, the forme of the said Iustices precept to the Shirife to returne the said Iury is this, viz. Henricus Longuile miles, & Willihelmus Anderous miles Iusticiarij Domini Regis nunc ad pacem in Comitatu prędicto conseruandam, nec non ad diuersas felonias, transgressiones, et alia malefacta in eodem Comitatu audiendum & terminandum assignati, vicecomiti Comit prædicti salutem. Ex parte dicti Domini Regis tibi præcipimus firmiter iniungentes, quod non omittas ppter aliquam libertatem in Balliua tua, quin eam ingrediaris, & venire facias coram nobis apud Cauluerton in Comitatu prędicto 10. die huius mensis Ianuarij 24. pbos & legales homines Comitat prędicti, quorum quilibet habeat terras & tenementa infra dictũ Comitatum liberi tenementi per chartam ad valorẽ viginti solidorum, aut per Copiam Rotulorum curie ad valorem 26. s. 8. d. aut de vtroque vltra omnes reprisas; ad inquirendum pro dicto dño Rege de quodam Riotto apud C. in comitatu pdicto nuper commisso, vt dicitur, & qd' sup quemlibet Iuratorũ pdictorũ tunc returnes in exitibus xx. s. Et hoc nullatenus omittas sub pena xx. li. quam noueris te incursurum, si in executione pmissorum tepidus seu remissus fueris. Et habeas ibi hoc præceptum, Testibus nobis pfatis H. L. & W. A. quarto die Martij, An regni dñi nostr Regis Iacobi dei gratia &c. tertio. And when the Shirife hath returned his precept at a day and place, then two Iustices of peace at the least (without the Shirife, who is not to sit vpon the Inquisition) are to make enquiry by the same Iury returned, the forme of which Inquisition is this. Inquisitio pro Domino Rege capta apud Wynslowe in Comitatu prædicto, primo die Octobris Anno Regni dicti domini nostri Regis Iacobi &c. quinto, coram Roberto Dormer milite, & Anthonio Tiringham milite, adtunc Iusticiarijs dicti Domini Regis ad pacem in Comitatu prædicto conseruandam, necnon ad diuersas felonias &c. assignatis super sacramentum A. B. C. D. E. F. G. &c. Qui dicunt super sacramentũ suum quod H. I. K. L. M. N. de Addington in Comitatu prædicto husbandmen &c. simul cum alijs malefactoribus, & pacis dicti Domini Regis perturbatoribus ignotis, ad numerum decem personarũ vi & armis, modo guerrino arraiati, viz. cum gladijs, Bacculis, Arcubus & Sagittis, vicesimo die Septembris, Anno quinto supradicto, inter horas septimam & vndecimam ante meridiem eiusdem diei, domum mansionalem cuiusdam S. T. de Wynslowe prædict fregerunt & intrauerunt & in ipsum S. T. adtunc & ibidem insultum fecerunt, & ipsum verberauerunt, vulnerauerunt, & maletracta-

St. 13. H. 4. 7

Buck.

A precept to the Shirife to returne a Iurie to inquire of a Riot.

Buck.

The forme of an inquisition of a Riot.

tractauerunt, ita qd' de vita eius desperabatur, in magnam perturbationem pacis dicti domini Regis, & populi sui terrorem, ac contra formam statuti de Riotis, Routis, & illicitis congregationibus, in parliamento domini Henrici nuper Regis Angliæ quarti, Anno regni sui decimo tertio, ęditi.

St.13.H.4.7 10 By the foresaid Statute of 13. H. 4. it is moreouer established, that if the truth cannot be found in maner aforesaid, then within a Moneth next after, the same Iustices, three, or two of them, and the said Shirife, or Vndershirife, shall certifie before the King and his Councell, of the whole fact, and the circumstances thereof: which certificat shall be of the same force, that a presentment by twelue men is: Upon which certificat, the said trespassors and offendors shall be put to aunswere, and they which shall be found guilty, shall be punished by the discretion of the King and his Councell. And if the same trespassors and offendors do trauerse the matter so certified, the same certificat and trauerse shall be sent into the Kings Bench, there to be tried and determined according to the order of the Law. Certifying a Riot. Trauerse of a Certificat.

St.13.H.4.7 11 The same Statute of 13.H.4. hath also prouided, that if the said trespassors and offendors do not come before the King, and his Councell, or into the Kings Bench, at the first precept; then an other precept shall be deliuered to the Shirife of the Shire to take the said trespassors and offendors, if they may be found, and to bring them at a certaine day before the King and his Councell, or into the Kings Bench: And if they cannot be found, the Shirife or Vndershirife shall make proclamation in his full Countie next insuing the said second precept, that they shall appeare before the King and his Councell, or in the Kings Bench; (or in the Chauncerie in the time of vacation) within three weekes then next following. And if the offendors do not appeare, as is aforesaid, and the proclamation be made, and returned, they shall be attainted and conuicted of the Riot, Assemblie, and Rout aforesaid. Proces against offendors.

St.13.H.4.7 12 By the said Statute of 13. H. 4. it was lastly enacted, that the Iustices of peace, which dwell neerest in euery County, where such Riot of people shall be, together with the Shirife, or Vndershirife of the same Countie; And also the Iustices of assise, for the time that they shall be in their Sessions (in case any such Riot, assemblie, or Rout be made in their presence) shall doe execution of this Statute, euery one vpon paine of C. li. to be paied to the King, as often as they shall be found in default of execution of the same Statute. The forfeiture of the Iustices, which do not inquire of Riots.

13 Because it was not prouided by the foresaid Statute of 13.H.4. that the partie grieued should haue any other remedie, if default should be in the said Iustices, Shirife, or Vndershirife, where such Riot, assemblie, or rout should be made, nor at whose costes the same riot should be repressed, neither was it limitted what punishment the parties attainted of such Riots should suffer: Therefore by an other Statute made Anno 2. H. 5. it was established, That if default be found in the said two Iustices of peace, or Iustices of Assise, and the Shirife, or Vndershirife of the Countie where such Riot, assemblie, or rout shall be made, touching the execution that they ought to make by vertue of the said statute of 13.H.4. and whereof the said Statute maketh mention: Then at the instance of the partie grieued, the kings commission shall be awarded vnder the great Seale, to inquire aswell of the truth St.2.H.5.8. A commission to inquire of the Iustices, &c. default.

truth of the case, and of the originall matter, for the partie complaynant, as of the default or defaults of the said Justices, Shirife, or Undershirife in this behalfe supposed, to be directed to sufficient and indifferent persons, at the nomination, and by the aduise of the Chauncellor of England. And the said Commissioners incontinently shall send into the Chauncery the Enquests and matters before them in this behalfe taken and found.

Upon the Commission the coronors shal returne the Jury. *What issues shalbe returned upon the Jurors.*

14 The Coroners of the same Countie for the time being, in which Countie such Riot, Assemblie, or Rout shall be made, shall make the panell upon the said commission retornable for the time, that the Shirife so supposed in default shall returne no persons, but only such which haue lands, tenements or rents to the value of x.l. by the yeare at the least. And also the same coroners shall return upon every of the said persons impannelled at the first day when issues be to be lost xx.s. at the least; at the second day xl.s. at the least; and at the third day C.s. at the least; and at every day after the double at the least; which issues so returned because of non-appearance of such persons impanneled, shall be forfait to the King and leviable to his use. And if default be found in the said coronors touching the returne of such persons, to be impanneled, or touching the returne of such issues as afore is said, every of them shall pay to the Kings use forty pounds. St.2.H.5.8.

Where the shirife shal return the Jury and not the coronors.

15 And if the Shirife so reputed in default be discharged of his office, at the time that such commission shall goe out of the Chauncerie, then the new Shirife of the same County, his successor mediate or immediate, and not the coronors, shall make the pannell upon this commission returnable in manner and forme as the said coronors should doe in time when the Shirife so reputed in default stood in his office. And the same Shirife shall incurre like paine of xl. li. to the King, if any default in him be found, touching the returne of other persons by him impannelled, which haue not lands, tenements or rents to the value of x.li. by the yeare, or of returning such issues as the said coronors be above charged to returne, as the said coronors be to lose to the King in this behalfe. St.2.H.5.4.

A writ directed to enquirie of a Riots.

16 The Chauncellor of England, as soone as he may haue knowledge, of such Riot, assemblie, or Rout, shall cause to be sent the Kings writ to the Justices of peace, and to the Shirife or undershirife of the County, where they be so made, that they shall put the foresaid Statute of 13.H.4. in execution upon the paine contained in the same. And though such writ come not to the said Justices, Shirife, or undershirife, they shall not be excused of the paine (of 100.pounds) aforesaid, if they make not execution of the said Statute. St.2.H.5.8.

Riots shalbe inquired of at the Kings costs.

17 The Justices and other officers aforesaid shall doe their offices at the Kings costs, in going, tarrying, and returning in doing their said offices, by payment thereof to be made by the Shirife of the same County for the time being, by Indentures betweene him and the said Justices, and other officers aforesaid, to be made of the payment aforesaid, whereof the said Shirife upon his accompt in the Exchequer shall haue due allowaunce. St.2.H.4.8.

18 Such

St.2.H.5.8. 18 Such Riotors, attainted of great and haynous Riots, shall haue one whole yeares imprisonment at the least without being let out of prison, by baile, mainprise, or in any other manner during the yeare aforesaid: and the Riotors attainted of petit Riots shall haue imprisonment as the King and his Councell shall thinke good. *The punishment of Riotors.*

St.2.H.5.8. 19 The Kings liege people being able to trauaile in the Countie where such Riots, assemblies, or routs shall be made, shalbe assistant to the Justices, commissioners, Shirife or vndershirife of the same County, when they shalbe reasonably required, to ride with the said Justices, Shirife, or vndershirife, in aide to resist such Riots, Routs, and assemblies, vpon paine of imprisonment, and to make fine and ransom to the King. *Each man shall helpe to represse Riots.*

St.2.H.5.8. 20 The Bailifes of franchises shall impannell sufficient people as before, vpon paine to lose xl.li. to the King, in case that such sufficient persons may be found within the said franchises. And like ordinances and paines shall hold place and take effect in Cities, Boroughs, & other places, and townes enfranchised, which haue Justices of peace within them. *Bailifes of Franchises. Corporat townes hauing Justices.*

21 Forasmuch as in the before rehearsed Statute of 13.H.4. it is not expressed of what sufficiency the Jurors impannelled by the Shirife to inquire of Riots should be, Nor what issues they should lose, if they appeare not, Nor any mention is made of any punishment the mainteinors, and embraceors of the Jurors that so shall be impannelled, should haue for their misdemeanor, *A Jury to enquire of Riots*
St.19.H.7.13. if any should be: Therefore by a Statute made Ann 19.H.7. it was enacted, that if any Riot, Rout, or vnlawfull assemblie be committed within this realme, the Shirife hauing a precept directed to him shall returne xxiiij. persons dwelling within the Shire where such Riot, &c. shall be so committed whereof euery of them shal haue lands and Tenements within the same shire to the yearely value of xx.s. of Charter land or freehold, or xxvj.s.viij.d. of copihold, or of both, aboue all charges, for to inquire of the said Riot, Rout, or vnlawfull assemblie. And he shall returne vpon euery person so by him impanelled in issues at the first day xx.s. at the second xl.s. (if that they appeare not and be sworne to enquire of the premisses at the first day.) And if default be found in the Shirife, or vndershirife, for returning of other persons, being not of the same sufficiency, or for not returning issues in forme aforesaid, then the said Shirife shall forfeit to the King for either twenty pounds.

St.19.H.7.13. 22 If the said Riot, Rout, or vnlawful assemblie be not found by the said Jury, by reason of any maintenance or embracery of the Jurors, then the same Justices, and the Shirife, or vndershirife (beside such certificat that they be bound to make according to the foresaid Statute of 13.H.4.) shall in the same certificat certifie the names of the mainteinors and embraceors in that behalfe, if any be, with their misdemeanors that they know, vpon paine of euery one of the said Justices and Shirife or vndershirife to forfait xx.li. if they haue no reasonable excuse for not certifying of the same: which certificat so made shall be of like force and effect in the law, as if the matter contained in the same were duly found by the verdit of xij.men. And euery person duly proued to be a mainteinor or embraceor of the same, shall forfeite to the King xx.l. and shall be committed to ward, there to remaine by the discretion of the Justices. *Maintenance whereby a Riot is not found.*

23 One

What one Justice of peace may doe alone in a Riot.

23 One Justice of peace alone can neither make inquiry of a Riot, Rout, or vnlawfull assemblie, when it is done, nor assesse any fine, nor award any proces for it, nor otherwise meddle with it in the nature of a Riot, or Rout, but only as a trespas against the peace, or vpon the statute of Northampton, or the Statut of 34. Ed. 3. or vpon the Stat. of forcible entries; for the wordes of the foresaid Statute of 13. H. 4. be: That if such trespassors or offendors be departed before the comming of the said Justices, Shirife, or &c. the same Justices, three or two of them shall diligently enquire &c. So that there must be two of them at the least to make such inquirie. But if one Justice of peace doe heare of any Riot, Rout, or vnlawfull assembly, he alone with his seruants may goe to the place, where the assemblie is reported to be made, and if he finde any riotously gathered together, he may arrest them to finde suerties of their good behauiour according to the Statute of 34. Ed. 3. & he may take their weapons from them, and retaine them vntill their hot bloud be cooled. And if they refuse to finde suerties of their good behauiour, he may commit them to prison. But this must be done presently vpon the act doing, for if there be any meane time, he hath then no authority to commit them to prison. And if he come to the place, whither he doth vnderstand, that some persons will repaire to commit some Riot, Rout, or violent act against the peace, and the same persons be not yet come thither, he may leaue his seruants there, to restraine them from committing their intended Riots, or other offences, or else to arrest them to finde suerties of their good behauiour, if they doe offer to commit any Riot, or to breake the peacce. And so may he also doe, if he shall be sicke and heare of any Riot &c. intended to be done; he may send his seruants to represse it, or to bring the offendors before him, or some other Justice of peace, to finde suerties to keepe the peace, or else to commit them to the Gaole. So that one Justice of peace alone may by the warrant of the said Statute of 34. Ed. 3. doe much in preuention of a Riot &c. before it be done, & for the staying of it, whilest it is in doing, but nothing to punish it as a Riot, when it is done: for that statute of 34. Ed. 3. was made for the common profit of the Realm, speedily to interrupt, and preuent present mischiefes, & to disperse malefactors, Barretors, and other Riotors in their very first meeting and encounter, and so farre as may be to parte and cut off the quarrell, before it grow to any head or extremity, which peraduenture would not be easily pacified, if one Justice should doe nothing, vntill some other of his fellowes came to assist him therein. And a Justice of peace may by word only, without warrant in writing, commaund his owne seruants, or any of them, to apprehend those, that are about to commit a Riot in his presence: And they may iustifie the taking of them, though those Riotors be gone or fled away out of the presence of the same Justice, before his said seruants can lay hold on them.

7. Ed. 4. 18.

14. H. 7. 9.

Kel. fo. 41.

24 Although this Statute of 13. H. 4. doth not make that mention which the Statute of 8. H. 6. of Forcible entries doth, touching complaint to be made to the Justices of peace, of a Riot, Rout, or vnlawfull assemblie, but doth binde the next Justices of peace to doe execution of this Statute, euery one vpon pain of C. li. yet the Sages of the Realme, and the wisedom of the interpreters of the law, haue thought it reason, that notice should be giuen vnto the said next Justices thereof, before they should incurre the said penaltie of C. li. vnles it be some great, notorious, and very perilous Riot, which by common intendment, euery person in those parts may take knowledge of; for as the said Statute of 13. H. 4. doth relate to the Statute of 8. H. 6. touching the

The Justices must haue notice of the Riot.

4. El. Dy. 210.

con-

conuiction of offendors by the record of the Iustices: So it is like, that the meaning of the makers thereof was, it should doe, in giuing notice, or making of complaint of the wrong receiued.

25 If the Iustices doe assemble themselues, the Shirife, and the Iurie to make inquirie of a Riot within a moneth, according to the Statute, and after at the parties request, they do not inquire of it, but doe dismisse the Iurie, for that the parties haue agréed betwéene themselues; Yet the Iustices shall pay a fine to the King, although none doe giue euidence for the King vpon that Riot: for they ought to take and charge an enquest, and to make enquiry of that Riot, whereof they were enformed, or of all Riots, séeing, it may be, that the Iurors themselues haue knowledge of the Riot. And moreouer they must make proclamation, if any will enforme the Kings Iustices of any Riots, Routs &c. And the said Statute of 13. H. 4. which giueth authoritie to the Iustices and Shirife &c. to inquire of the Riot, and to heare and determine it, according to the law, was ordained to punish Riotors for breaking of the Kings peace, and thereby to make them an example to others, and also to intitle the King to a fine. And therefore the law will not permit, that the satisfaction of the parties grieued should depriue the King of his fine, or ease the offendors of their due and deserued punishment, and also yéeld incouragement to others, vpon hope of agréement, to put in practise the like Riots or other outrages. The parties agréement, no discharge of the inquisition.

St. 13. H. 4. 7 26 And whereas the said Statute of 13. H. 4. hath ordained, that if any Riot or &c. against the law shall be made, the Iustices of peace, the Shirife or vndershirife shall come with the power of the Countie, if néede be, to arrest them: That power of the County is expressed before by the Statute of 17. R. 2. viz. Al Lords and other liege people of the Realme, as Knights, Esquires, gentlemen, yeomen, laborers, seruants, apprentises, villaines, and all others of the age of 15. yeares or aboue (which be not of the Clergie, decrepite, or women) whereof the said Iustices and Shirife may take so many to assist them as they shall thinke good to arrest the offendors, and to cary them to the Gaole. And if the Iustices of peace be informed of a Riot committed at such a place, and they go with the power of the Countie to suppresse it, and finde no Riot there, yet they are not to be blamed or fined for the leuying of the power of the Countie. What power of the County the Iustices shall vse to represse Riots.

St. 13. H. 4. 7 27 By the said Statute of 13. H. 4. the Iustices of peace, Shirife or vndershirife, haue power to record that which they shall finde done in their presence against the law, and the trespassors and offendors shall be conuict by the Record of the same Iustices; which recording must either be grounded vpon a thing done in their owne presence, or else by inquirie vpon the oath of other men: And therefore if two Iustices of peace assisted with the Shirife or vnder Shirife, doe sée a Riot, they may commaund the Riotors to be arrested, & then record the Riot, without other inquirie. But it is otherwise, if they do not sée it, for then they must first inquire of it by a Iury, and after the same being found by inquisition, they must make a record thereof, which record that the said Iustices doe make, must be in writing, and is to remaine with one of them. And they and none other of the Iustices ought to commit the Riotors to prison, and to assesse their fines, and to cause the same to be estreated into the Exchequer. And if the Iustices do record a Riot of their owne sight, the parties The Iustices record of a Riot.

No trauerse to the record of a riot made of the Iustices own sight.

parties charged therewith shall neuer be allowed to trauerse it, though indeed there was neuer any such Riot: for their sight of the Riot being Iudges of record, maketh that record in the iudgement of the law, as strong and effectuall, as if the supposed offendors had confessed the Riot before them; and (touching the restrayning of trauerse) more effectuall, then if the Riot had béen found by a Iury vpon the euidence of others. And if the Iustices of peace doe sée the Riot committed, they may record the riot, though the Riotors doe escape for that the fact is done in their presence, which is the ground of their record. And if the same Riotors doe escape from the Iustices at that time, they cannot apprehend them at an other time; for the apprehension and punishment of them must be whilest the Riot is committing, or presently after, and as it were, whilest the blood is hot. Neither in that case, if the Riotors doe escape, the Iustices can make any proces vpon their record; neither ought it to be kept amongst the records of the peace, but must be sent into the Kings Bench, that proces may there be made vpon it: And in that case, the offendors are not to be admitted to their trauerse, but are of necessity to make fine for it. 36.H.6.25. If two Iustices of peace or more, and the Shirife or vndershirife, doe méet at a place appointed about the Kings seruice, the affaires of the country, or their owne priuate busines, and any others to the number of thrée or aboue will make an assault in Riotous manner vpon them, or any of them, or vpon any other in their presence, they may arrest the offendors, commit them to prison, and record the Riot, aswell as if they had come of purpose to sée and arrest Riotors; but if they which doe begin a Riot doe flie into an other Countie before they doe commit the Riot then the Iustices must not meddle with them. And this recording of a Riot by the Iustices of peace, the Shirife, or vndershirife is of that credit in the iudgement of the Law; That if a man be bound by Recognizance to kéepe the peace, and after such a record of being partie to the committing of a Riot is entred against him, in a Scire facias awarded against him, vpon his Recognizance, he shall not be allowed either to iustifie the fact, nor plead not guiltie thereunto.

The credit of the Iustices record of a Riot.

28 Whereas the said Statute of 13.H.4. hath ordeined, that if the truth cannot be found, then within a Moneth next after, the same Iustices, thrée, or two of them shall certifie, before the King and his Councell, the whole fact, and the circumstances thereof, which words (viz. the same) haue relation to the Iustices of the Shire; So that if two Iustices of the Shire, and the Shirife, or &c. go to sée the Riot, any other two Iustices may make inquirie of it, and then they together, or the first two, or the last two may make certificat thereof, within a moneth after that inquisition taken. But if the inquiry be made within a moneth after the Riot, or &c. committed, and the certificat not made within a moneth after that, then is not the certificat good, nor according to the said Statute; And yet if the Iustices do make an inquirie within a moneth after the Riot committed, and then do giue day to the Iury to deliuer their verdict after the moneth expyred, that is a good inquisition and according to the Statut; for by that day giuen the Iury may enquire further, and receiue more euidence to informe them of the truth of the matter. If an enquest doe finde that a Riot was committed by x. persons and the Iustices doe certifie, that it was committed by xx. persons, then the certificat, and not the inquisition shall be taken, for by that certificat of the Iustices it appeareth, that the truth was not found by the inquisition. And so it is, if the inquisition be of x. persons, and the certificat be of x. persons in harneis. And like-

St.3.H.4.7

Certificat of a Riot.

likewise if ẏ inditement be of a riotous assault only, and the certificat bee of a riotous assault, battery, & maiheming: for though in the cases aforesaid the enquest haue found a truth, yet they haue not foūd the whole truth, neither that which is most for the Kings aduantage, nor fully performed the meaning of the said statute: but if the inditment and the Iustices certificat do vary in the day of the committing of the riot, then the inditment shall be preferred before the certificat; for the day doth alter nothing to qualifie or aggrauat the offence. And yet seeing the said certificat is but only in the nature of a declaration, to cause the parties accused to make answer thereunto, the same certificat ought to comprehend the certaine yeare, and day, though not the addition of the parties, being not within the words of the statute of Additions made An̄ 1. H. 5. 5.

St.13.H.4.7. 29 And though the said Statute of 13. H. 4. doth only make mention of a Capias, yet it seemeth by the words of the same, that first there ought to be awarded a Venire facias against the offendors, and if they do not appeare, then a Capias: for the words of the Statute be, if they do not come before the King and his councel, or into the Kings Bench at the first precept, then another precept shal be deliuered to the Sherife to take the said offendors &c. And this proces must be returned before the Kings councell, or in the Kings Bench: but if there be awarded against the offendors, a Subpena, or a priuie seale, it shall be void. *The proces against riotors.*

St.13.H.4.7 30 Notwithstanding the said Statute of 13. H. 4. hath inflicted a penalty of C. l. vpon the next Iustices of the county where such riot shalbe committed, if the execution of that Statute be not done: yet if other Iustices of the same county do performe that office, then the next Iustices shall be excused, and the same penaltie shall be saued: for the Statute doth wholy or chiefly respect, that the offendors shalbe arrested or disturbed, their offences inquired of, recorded, and punished, and by that meanes the peace preserued: for all the Iustices of peace within the commission, how farre off soeuer they dwel (so that they dwel within the said countie) if they haue notice of such a riot, rout, or vnlawfull assemblie, ought to enquire of it, to record it, and to suppresse it, or otherwise they may be fined by the Lords in the Star chamber, though the penaltie of one C. l. shalbe inflicted onely vpon the two next Iustices, for that they are intended most likely and soonest to haue knowledge of it. But if the Sherife or Vndersherife should not come to the Iustices, being sent for to assist the same Iustices, and to further the repressing of that riot, and the performance of that seruice, then all the said Iustices dwelling neere or remote shalbe excused of the same penaltie of C. l. or any other, for ẏ said statute doth giue him equal authoritie, and as it were ioyne him in commission in the copulatiue with them. *The penaltie of C. l. for not executing this Statute.*

St.13.H4.7. 31 It appeareth by ẏ said stat. of 13. H. 4. that if the offendors & trespassors do trauerse the matter certified by the Iustices of peace, to the King & his councell, the same certificat and trauerse shal be sent into the K. Bench, and there be tried & determined according to the law. And in like sort, if the trespassors & offendors do trauerse the matter found by Inquisition before the Iu. of peace in the countie, the same Inquisition shalbe sent to the Iustices of peace at the next Quarter Sessions of the same countie, city, borough, or towne corporat, hauing Iustices of Peace within themselues, & there the trauerse shalbe tried and determined according to the Law: the forme of which trauerse taken in a towne corporat is this; Aliàs, scilicet ad Sessionem pacis tentam apud Buckingham in comitatu predicto die Lune proximo post festum Sancte Trinitat, *Trauerse to an Inditement of Riot.*

Anno

A trauerse to an Inditemēt of riot.

Anno regni dñi nr̄i Regis Iacobi dei grat̄ Angliæ &c. secundo, coram Iohanne Nichols generoso Balliuo Burgi & parochiæ de Buckingham prædicta, & Francisco Fortescue milite, Thoma Denton milite, Richardo Ingolsbie milite, Willihelmo Androwes milite, Roberto Iohnson milite, Paulo Risley armigero, & Simone Lambard generoso, & alijs socijs suis Iusticiarijs dicti domini Regis ad pacem in dicto Burgo & parochia conseruandam, necnon ad diuersas felonias, transgressiones, & alia malefacta in eisdem Burgo & parochia perpetrata, audienda, & terminanda, assignatis, per sacram duodecem Iuratorum extitit presentatum, Quód A.B.C.D.E.F. de Galcot, cum diuersis alijs malefactoribus & pacis dicti Domini Regis perturbatoribus modo guerrino arraiati, vniti, & assemblati, vicesimo die Maij, hora quarta post meridiem eiusdem diei, Anno eiusdem domini Regis nunc secundo, vi & armis, viz. baculis, gladijs, pugionibus, falcastris, & alijs armis tam inuasiuis, quam defensiuis apud Prebend-end in Buckingham prædicta clausum cuiusdam L. M. vocatum Bonehill close, illicitè, riotosè, & routosè fregerunt, & intrauerunt, & decem carractatas feni ad valenc' quatuor librarum de bonis & catallis dicti L. M. adtunc & ibidem iniuste & illicite ceperunt, & asportauerunt, contra pacem dicti domini Regis, & contra formam statuti inde editi & prouisi. Per quod præceptum fuit Iohanni Crooke subballiuo, quod non omitteret propter aliquam libertatem &c. quin venire faceret eosdem A.B.C.D.E.F. ad respondēdum &c. Posteaque scilicet die Lune proximo post festum sancti Michaelis Archang' anno regni domini Regis nr̄i Iacobi secūdo corā præfatis Iusticiarijs venerūt p̄dicti A.B.C.D.E.F. in proprijs personis suis, & habito auditu Indictamenti p̄dicti, seperatim dicunt, quod ipsi non sunt inde culpabiles. Et de hoc ponunt se super patriam: Et H. I. qui pro domino Rege in hac parte sequitur similiter. Ideo veniunt inde Iurat̄ coram Iusticiarijs dicti dñi Regis ad pacem in Burgo & parochia p̄d conseruandam assignatis &c. ad Sessionem pacis apud Buck. p̄d die Lune proximo post Epiphaniam dñi tunc proximo futuro tenēdam. Et qui &c. Ad recog. &c. Quia tam &c. Idem dies datus est tam prefato H. I. qui sequitur p Dño Rege, quam p̄fat̄ A.B.C.D.E.F. Ad quas quidem Sessiones pacis tentas apud Buck. p̄d in com̄ p̄d dicto die Lune proximo post festum Epiphaniæ domini, Anno regni dicti Regis dñi nostri Iacobi tertio, coram dicto Balliuo & dictis F.F.T.D.R.I. & socijs suis Iusticiarijs dicti Dñi Regis ad pacem in dict' Burgo & parochia conseruandam, necnon ad diuersas felonias, transgressiones, & alia malefacta in eodem Burgo & parochia perpetrata, audienda, & terminanda assignatis, venerunt tam p̄fatus H. I. qui pro dño Rege in hac parte sequitur, quam p̄fat̄ A.B.C.D.E.F. in proprijs personis suis: Et Iuratores p subballiuum Burgi & parochie p̄d ad hoc impannellat̄ & exacti; viz. E. F. Mercer. O. P. Draper, &c. similiter venerunt, qui ad veritat̄ de p̄missis dicendam triati & iurati dicunt super sacrum suum: quod p̄d A.B.C.D.E.F. culpabiles sunt, & eorū quilibet culpabilis est de transgressione, contemptu, & riotto p̄d in Indictamento p̄d superius specificatis, modo & forma prout superius versus eos supponitur. Ideo cōcessū est p cur̄, q̄ p̄d A.B.C.D.E.F. capiantur ad satisfaciendum dicto domino Regi de finibus suis occasione transgressionis, contemptus, & riotti prædicti. Qui quidem A. B. C. D. E. F. adtūc & ibid̄ p̄sentes in cur̄ petierūt se ad finē cū dict' dño Rege occasione p̄d admitti. Et inde poñ se seperat̄ in misericordia dñi Regis. Et assessat̄ finis eiusd̄ A.B. per Iusticiar̄ p̄d ad 5. li. Et assessatur finis eiusdem C.D. ad 3. li. &c. bone & legalis monet̄ Angliæ ad opus & vsum dicti dñi Regis.

32 Though the lawes & statutes before rehearsed, or mētioned did take sufficiēt order for ẏ inquiring of, repressing, & punishing of such as did cōmit riots, routs,

routs, or vnlawfull assemblies, by xij.iiij.v. or some small number of persons, and then were apprehended, or dispersed by the Iustices of Peace, the sherife, or vndersherife, with the help of the countrie, when need required: Yet there was no sufficient law deuised to suppresse, and punish such, as did assemble in great numbers, routs, and tumults, and would in contempt of the law, and in rebellious manner, put in practise, vnlawfull, forcible, and violent acts, and being by authoritie of the same law, in calme manner required to the contrary, would yet stand at the staues end with the peace of the realme, and the iustice of the law, and as it were in despite of all gouernment and gouernors proceed in their furie: Therfore to continue peace and tranquilitie in the common weale, and by a more sharpe corrasiue to bridle or punish so great maladies, by a statute made Anno 1. M. it was enacted, That if any persons to the number of xij. or aboue, being assembled together, shall intend, goe about, practise, or put in vre by force of armes, vnlawfully, and of their owne authoritie, to alter, or change any lawes made or established for religion by authoritie of Parliament, which stand in force, or any other laws or statutes of this realm, or any of them, the same number being commanded or required by the sherife of the shire, or by any Iu. of peace of the same shire, or by the mayor, sherife, I. of peace, or by the baylifs of any citie, borough, or towne corporat, where such assemblies shalbe vnlawfully had and made, by proclamation in the Queens name, to retire, and repaire to their owne houses and habitations, or places frō whence they came; and they or any of them, notwithstanding such Proclamation, shall remaine, and make their abode and continue together by ye space of one whole houre after such commandement or request made by Proclamation, or after that shall willingly in forcible and riotous manner attempt to do or put in vre any thing aboue specified: Then as well euery such abode or continuing together, as euery such act or offence, that after such commandement or request by Proclamation had or made, shalbe attempted to be done, practised, or put in vre by any of the persons being of the number aforesaid, shalbe iudged felonie in all and singular those persons, that so shall make their abode or continue together, or shall attempt or commit any act. And the offendors therein shalbe adiudged felons, and shall suffer only execution of death, as in case of felony.

St. 1. M. 12. — Twelue or aboue assembled to change lawes.

St. 1. M. 12. 33 If any persons to the said number of twelue, or aboue, shall intend, goe about, practise, and put in vre, in manner and forme aforesaid, to ouerthrowe, cut, breake, cast downe, or digge vp the pales, hedges, ditches, or other inclosure of any Parkes or Parke, or other grounds or ground inclosed, or the bankes of any fish-pond or poole, or any conduits for water, conduit heads, or conduit pipes, hauing course of water, to the intent, that the same or any of them from thenceforth should remaine open, not inclosed, or voyd, or vnlawfully to haue common or way in the same Parkes or Parke, or other groundes or ground inclosed, or in any of them, or to destroy in manner and forme aforesaid the Deere in any Parks or Parke, or any warrens or warren of Conies, or any Doue-houses, or any fish in any fish-pond or poole, or to pull or cut downe any houses, barnes, milles, or bayes, or to burne any stackes of corne or graine, or to abate or diminish the rents or yearely value of any mannors, lands, or tenements, or the price of any victuall, corne, or graine, or any other thing vsuall for the sustenance of men, & being required or commanded by any I. of peace, or by the Sherife of the countie, or by the mayor, bailife, or bailifs, or other head officers of any citie or towne corporat, where such assemblie shall

Practising to destroy parks, ponds, conduits.

Common or way.

Destruction of deere, conies, doue-houses, fish. Pulling downe houses, burning stacks of corne, abating of rents.

shall be had by proclamation to bee made in the Quéenes name, to retire, & returne in peaceable maner to their places and houses from whence they came, and they or any of them (notwithstanding such proclamation) shall remaine or make their abode, or continue together by the space of one whole houre after such cõmandement or request made by proclamation; or after that shall in forcible maner do, or put in vre any of those things last before mentioned: Then aswell euery such abode, or continuing together, as euery such act, that after such commandement or request by proclamation, or request had or made, shall be done, practised, or put in vre, by any of the persons being aboue the number of twelue, shalbe adiudged felonie, and the offendors therein shall be adiudged felons, and shall suffer only the execution of death, as in case of felonie.

Raising of vnlawfull assemblies by some acts or words.

34 If any person or persons vnlawfully, and without authority, by ringing of any bell, or bels, sounding of any trumpet, drumme, horne, or other instrument whatsoeuer, or by fiering of any beacon, or by malitious speaking or vttering of any words, or making of any outcrie, or by setting vp, or casting of any bils or bil, or writing whatsoeuer, or by any other déed or act, shall raise or cause to be raised or assembled any persons to the number of twelue or aboue, to the intent, that the same persons should doe, or put in vre, any of the things aboue mentioned; & that the persons to the number of twelue or aboue so raised and assembled after request or commandemẽt had or giuen in forme aforesaid, shall make their abode, or continue together, as is aforesaid, or vnlawfully and in forcible manner perpetrate, doe, commit, or put in vre any the acts or things abouesaid: Then all and singular persons, by whose speaking, deed, act, or any other the meanes aboue specified, any persons to the number of twelue or aboue shall be raised or assembled, for the doing, committing, or putting in vre of any the acts or things aboue mentioned, shalbe adiudged for his so speaking or doing a felon, & shall suffer executiõ of death, as in case of felony. 1.M.12.

Releiuing them which be assembled.

35 If any wife, or seruant of any of the same persons, or any other person whatsoeuer, shall willingly and without compulsion, bring, send, deliuer, or conuey, any money, harnesse, artillerie, weapon, meat, bread, drinke, or other victuall to any person or persons so beeing assembled as is aforesaid, during such time as he or they shall so be assembled, or be together, as is aforesaid: then euery wife, seruant, or other person, so bringing or conueying &c. any of the foresaid things to the same persons so beeing assembled together in forcible manner, or to any of them, and not departing to their houses or dwelling places, vpon request or commandement made vnto them as is aforesaid, shall bee adiudged a felon, & shal suffer execution of death, as in case of felonie. 1.M.12.

Vnlawful assemblies aboue two and vnder twelue.

36 If any persons aboue the number of 2. and vnder the number of 12. beeing assembled together, shal intend, goe about, practise, or put in vre with force of armes vnlawfully, & of their owne authoritie, to murder, kill, or slay any of the kings subiects, or to ouerthrowe, cut, breake, or cast downe, or dig vp the pales, hedges, ditches, wall, or other closure of any parkes or parke, or other ground inclosed, or the bankes of any fish-pond or poole, to the intent that the same or any of them from thenceforth should remaine open, not inclosed, or void, or to haue common or way in the same parks or parke, or other grounds or ground inclosed, or in any of them, or to destroy any parkes or parke, or fish-pond, or poole, or any warrens or warren of conies, or any doue-houses, or to pul, or cut down any house, barne, or mil, or to burne any stacke of corne 1.M.12.

or

or graine, or to alter, defaulke, or abate the rents, or yearely value of any mannors, lands, or tenements of any of the Kings subiects, or the price of any victual, corne, or graine, or any other thing vsuall for the sustenance or apparell of men, and being required or commanded by any Iustice of peace, or the sherife of the countie, or by any mayor, bailife, or bailifes, or other head officer of any citie or towne corporat, where such assembly shall be had, by Proclamation to be made in the Kings name, to retire or returne to their habitations, places, or houses: and they so required by such proclamation shall not so do, but after that shall in forcible manner in forme aforesaid, attempt to do or put in vre any of the things last aboue mentioned: then euery of the same persons beeing aboue the number of two and vnder the number of twelue, shall suffer imprisonment of his or their bodies by the space of one whole yeare, without baile or mainprise. And also if any person or persons shall be damnified or hurt by the doing, committing, or putting in vre of any vnlawfull act or thing aboue mentioned, then all and singular persons so damnified and hurt shall recouer and haue dammages with the costs of their suit susteined in that behalfe trebled against the offendors therein.

The remedie of the parties grieued.

1.M.12. 37 If any persons aboue the number of two shal vnlawfully & of their own authoritie assemble together, to the intent with force and armes to do, practise, or put in vre any of the things aboue mentioned: Then it shall be lawfull to euery Iustice of peace, & to euery Sherife in any countie, beeing within the K. dominions, and to euery mayor, bailife, and other head officer of any citie, or towne corporat, for the time he shall be in office, or any other person or persons hauing the K. commission, or Letters from his highnes, as wel to raise and assemble the kings louing subiects in maner of warre to be arraied in such great number, as he or they then shall thinke meet or able, to the intent by violense of strength to suppresse, apprehend, and take the said persons that shall bee so vnlawfully assembled. And if the said persons so vnlawfully assembled, after such cammandement or request by proclamation made, shal continue together and not endeauour themselues to returne towards their habitations, houses, or places from whence they came, in as short time as they may conueniently: Then it shall be lawful to euery I. of peace, sherife, and also euery mayor, bailife, and other head officer of any citie or town corporat, & to euery other person hauing authoritie as is aforesaid, after such commandement or request by proclamation made, and to such persons as shalbe assembled with any Iustice of peace, or sherife, or with any mayor, bailife, or other head officer of any citie or town corporat, and with euery other person hauing authoritie as is aforesaid, to suppresse, apprehend, & take those persons so vnlawfully assembled, which after such proclamation made, shall continue together, and not endeauour thēselues to returne towards their habitations &c. And if the said persons so vnlawfully assembled together, or any of them shall fortune to be killed, slaine, maihemed, or hurt, in, or about the suppressing or taking of them, then euery such Iustice, Sherife, Maior, &c. and euery other person hauing authoritie as is aforesaid, and all and singular persons by him or them assembled shalbe free, discharged, and vnpunishable: as well against the king, as against all and euery other person and persons, of, for, or concerning the killing, maiheming, or hurting of any person or persons so vnlawfully assembled, that shall be killed, slaine, maihemed, or hurt about or by occasiō of taking or suppressing of thē &c.

Raising of power to suppresse vnlawful assemblies.

1.M.12. 38 All and euery Copieholder and Customary holder, being a yeoman, artificer,

A copieholder being required refuseth to serue.

tificer, husbandman, or labourer, & being of ẏ age of xviij. yeares, or more, & vnder ẏ age of lx. years, not sicke, impotent, lame, maihemed, neither hauing any other iust or reasonable excuse or cause to the contrary, and beeing required by the sherife, Iustice, or Iustices of peace, or other hauing authoritie by this act, or by commission, or letters &c. they declaring their said authoritie, or being required by the immediat Lord or Lords of whom such copie or customary holds then shall be holden, to serue the King, for any the causes aboue rehearsed, and refuse so to doe, shall (only during the life of such person or persons so refusing) forfeit to his Lord or Lords, of whom such copie or customarie holds then shal be immediatly holden, & should be holden during the life of such person or persons so refusing, in case he had not refused, all their copie & customarie holds: And it shalbe lawful to euery such Lord, &c. his heirs or assignes of whom such copy or customary holds shalbe immediatly holden, & should haue bin holden, in case that such person or persons had not so refused, to enter & take into his or their hands or possessions all such copie & customarie holds so holden of thē, or any of thē immediatly, & to retain the same during only the life of such offēdor or offendors, in such maner as he or they should haue had ẏ rents or seruices of such copy or customary hold, in case such person or persons so refusing, had not refused.

A farmer required refuseth to serue.

39 All & euery farmer being a yeoman, husbandman, artificer, or labourer, & beeing of the age of xviij. yeares, or more, & vnder the age of lx. years, not sick, impotent, lame, maihemed, nor hauing any other reasonable excuse or cause to the contrary, & being required by the sherife, Iustice, or Iustices of peace, or other hauing authoritie by this act, or by commissiō, or letters &c. they declaring their said authoritie; or being required by their said Landlord or Landlords for the time being, to whom the rents of such farmes shalbe then rising, growing, or comming, to serue ẏ king, for any the causes aboue rehearsed, and refuse so to doe, shall (during only the life of such farmer or farmers so refusing) forfeit and lose to such Landlord and Landlords as should haue had the rents of such farmer during the life & liues of such person & persons so refusing, all their said farmes. And it shalbe lawfull to euery such Landlord &c. their heires and assignes to whom the rents of such farmes should haue bin due, during the life of such person or persons so refusing (in case he or they had not refused) to enter & take into his or their hands or possessiō al such farms, & to retain the same only during the life of euery such offēdor or offendors. But after the death, expiration, or determinatiō of the interest or terme of yeares of euery such copyholder, customary holder, or farmer, as so shal offēd, & forfeit any of the said copi-holds, customary holds, or farmes, as is aforesaid: thē euery such person as should, or ought to haue had the copy holds, customary holds, or farmes, after, or by the death, expiration, or determination of the interest, or terme of years of such copie-holder, customarie holder, or farmer (in case such copie-holder, customarie holder, or farmer, had not so offended ne forfeited) shall and may haue the same copie-hold, customarie holds, and farmes by entrie, action, admission, or otherwise, in like manner, forme, and condition, and by such meanes, as they and euery of them should, might, or ought to haue had, if no such forfeiture or offence had bin had, done, or committed. 1.M.12.

Disclosing a commotion when one is moued.

40 If any person shalbe spoken vnto, moued, or stirred to make any cōmotion, insurrection, or vnlawfull assembly for any of ẏ intents aboue mētioned, and doe not within 24. houres next after he shalbe spoken vnto, moued, or stirred (vnlesse he haue good and reasonable cause of excuse) declare the same 1.M.12.

vnto

vnto one Iustice of the peace, or Sherife of the said countie, or to the Mayor, Sherifes, Bailifes, or other head officers of any citie or town corporat, where such commotion &c. shall be had; he shall suffer imprisonment by the space of thrée moneths, without baile or mainprise, vnlesse he shall be discharged by 3. Iustices of peace (whereof one to bee of the Quorum) of the same shire where the offence shall be committed.

1.M.12. 41 If any person béeing aboue the age of eightéene yeares, and vnder the age of thrée score, beeing able to serue, and not sicke, lame, or impotent, shall be required by any Iustice of peace, or any Sherife of any Countie, where any such assembly shall be, or by any Mayor, Bailife, or other head Officer, of any citie, borough, or towne corporat, or by any other by the commandement of any such Iustice, Sherife, Maior, &c. to goe with him, or them, to suppresse the persons vnlawfully assembled in manner and forme aforesaid: then euery person which so béeing able, and required, doth willingly and obstinately refuse so to doe, shall suffer imprisonment for one whole yeare, without baile or mainprise.

An able person required refuseth to serue.

1.M.12. 42 If the King shall by his Letters patents make any Lieutenant in any Countie or Counties of this Realme, for the suppressing of any commotion, rebellion, or vnlawfull assemblie; then as well all Iustices of peace, and the Sherife and Sherifes of the same, as all Maiors, Baylifes, and other head officers, and all inhabitants and subiects of any Countie, Citie, Borough, or towne corporat, within euery such Countie, shall vpon declaration of the said Letters patents and request made, bee bound to giue attendance vpon the same Lieutenant, to suppresse any commotion, rebellion, or vnlawfull assemblie, vnlesse hee so required haue any reasonable excuse for his not attendance, vpon paine of imprisonment for one whole yeare.

Attendance vpon a lieutenant.

1.M.12. 43 The order and forme of the Proclamation that shall be made by the authoritie of this Act, shalbe as hereafter followeth, or with the like order and words in effect, viz. The Iustices or other persons authorized by this Act, to make the said Proclamation, shall make or cause to be made an Oyes, and after that shall openly pronounce or cause to be pronounced these wordes, or to the like effect: The King our Soueraigne Lord chargeth and commandeth al persons being assembled, immediately to disperse themselues, and peaceably to depart to their habitations, or their lawfull businesse, vpon the paine contained in the act, lately made against vnlawfull and rebellious assemblies: And God saue the King.

The forme of the Proclamation.

1.M.12. 44 If any person or persons doe, or shal molest, let, hinder, or hurt any person or persons, that shall proclaime, or go to proclaime, according to the proclamation and order aforesaid, whereby such proclamation shal not be made; then euery such person so molesting or hurting, &c. and hauing knowledge of his message, shall incurre such daunger, and suffer such paines and forfeitures, the persons assembled, to whom the proclamation should haue beene made, should by this Act incurre, for not obeying the Proclamation (if it had béene made,) or for doing after the Proclamation of any the things before expressed. And also all such persons beeing assembled to the number aforesaid, to attempt or doe any the things aforesaid, to whom Pro-

Hinderance of the Proclamation.

clamation should or ought to haue beene made, if the same had not beene let, shall likewise in case they doe after put in vre, and doe any the things aforesaid, hauing any ways knowledge of the let so made, or by any meanes procuring the same let, incurre like danger, and suffer like paines and forfeitures aforesaid, in euery their degrees, as though the proclamation had beene made: any clause, article, &c. in this Act &c. notwithstanding.

Other mens right saued.

45 All and euery the heire and heires of all and euery the offendor and offendors in any the cases aforesaid, and all and euery person and persons, bodies politicke and corporat, their heires, successors, and executors, and euery of them (other than such person and persons onely, as shall be attainted, conuicted, and outlawed of any the foresaid offences of felonie) shall haue, hold, & enioy all such right, title, entrie, interest, leases, possessions, rents, conditions, profits, and aduātages, as they, or any of them shall, or of right ought to haue, in, or to any mannors, lands, rents, reuersions, seruices, or hereditaments whatsoeuer; or in, or to any part thereof, in as large manner to all intents, as if such attainder had neuer beene had: any thing in this act &c. notwithstanding &c. Sauing to euery person and persons, bodies politicke and corporate, and their successors, their liberties and franchises in such maner, as if this act had neuer beene made. 1.M.12.

Procuring others to offend.

46 If any person or persons doe moue, stirre, or procure any person or persons, to commit any of the offences in this Act specified: then euery such person and persons which shall procure, stirre, or mooue any person or persons so to offend, shall suffer such punishment by imprisonmēt, without baile or mainprise, as is before expressed in this Act against counsellors of such offendors. 1.M.12.

Unlawful assemblies by xl. or aboue.

47 If any persons to the number of fourtie or more, shall assemble together in forcible manner vnlawfully, and of their owne authoritie, to the intent to execute, doe, or put in vre any of the things aboue specified, or to doe any other felonious or rebellious act or acts, and so shall continue together by the space of three houres after proclamation shall bee made, at or nigh the place where they shall be so assembled, or in some market towne thereunto next adioyning, and after notice to them giuen thereof: Then euery person so willingly assembled in forcible manner, and so continuing together by the space of three houres after such proclamation made, and notice thereof giuen, shall bee adiudged a felon. 1.M.12.

A lieutenant shall not appoint a deputie.

48 No lieutenant that shall bee made by authoritie or colour of this Act, or for to execute this Act, shall constitute vnder him, or in his place, any deputy, nor shall call or appoint to appeare before him, by the onely authoritie of lieutenancie, or of commission of lieutenancy any person for any cause or matter whatsoeuer, saue onely for the causes and matters expressed in this Acte, and for none other. 1.M.12.

Ayding of the offendors after the offence

49 No person or persons shall bee put to any losse, forfeiture, paine, or punishment, of life, land, or goods, as accessorie to any person or persons, that shall commit any of the offences contained in this act, for receining, 1.M.12.

uing,comforting, or aiding of any ſuch offendor, after ſuch act committed or done.

1.M.12. 50 No attainder or conuiction of any perſon or perſons, for any offence or offences herein contained, ſhall be any corruption of blood betwixt the offendor and any of his anceſtors, or ſuch perſon or perſons as ſhould haue beene heire to ſuch offendor, if no ſuch attainder or conuiction had bæne had: ſauing to euery perſon and perſons, bodies politicke and corporat &c. their liberties and franchiſes, in ſuch manner as if this Act had neuer beene made.

The attainder of thoſe offences no corruption of blood.

Of Force, forcible Entries, and forcible retayning of possessions.

Unlawfull force an enemy to peace.

1 FOrce and violence executed without warrant of Law, be so meere contrarie to the peace and justice of the Realme, as disobedience is to loyaltie, and contempt to government: for whosoever doth make a Forcible entrie into lands in the possession of an other, doth secretly revolve in his mind, and distrust to himselfe, that there is no Law in the Realme to redresse his wrong, or no ministers to execute the same; and therefore he will sit in iudgement of that cause himselfe, and take into his owne hands the distribution of justice, and assume into his possession by the strength of his arme, what the phantasie of his head shall resolve to be his due; whereas the Law in convenient time would truely satisfie him, whether the land in question, by the rules of justice be his, or not, and also assigne him a milde and calme course to recover all his whole dutie, with valuable damages for the time he is iniured. And because this force and forcible entrie into lands, is so opposite and meere repugnant to the peace and justice of the Realme, and tendeth so much to the dishonour of the King, and his Crowne, and the discredit of the Law, that any person by byrth and oath devoted to the obedience of the King, and his Lawes, should presume of his owne authoritie, by force, and strong hand to resist them both, and as it were in contempt of them, violently to intrude himselfe into an other mans possession, before the law hath decided his title therein: Therefore the wisedom of the Realme, hath by the space of many generations first provided to restraine those forces, and forcible Entries, and next to inflict condigne punishment upon them, which were offendors therein: Whereupon by a Statute made An 5. R. 2. the King defended, that none from thenceforth should make any Entrie into any lands and tenements, but in case where entrie is given by the Law, and then not with strong hand, nor with multitude of people, but only in a peaceble course & maner. And if any from henceforth do the contrary, and thereof be duely convict, he shall be punished by imprysonment of his bodie, and thereof ransomed at the Kings pleasure.

There shal be no forcible entry into lands.

St.5.R.2.7.

2 But for that the said Statute of 5.R.2. did give no speedie remedie to those which were expelled out of their lands or tenements, nor assigned any speciall persons to suppresse the said disorder: Therefore by an other Statute made

St.15.R.2. made Añ 15.R.2. it was further ordained, That when any such forcible entrie shall be made into lands or tenements, or into any Benefices or offices of the Church, and the complaint thereof come to the Justices of the peace, or any of them, that the same Justices or Justice take sufficient power of the County, and go to the place where such forcible entrie is made, & if he or they find any that holdeth such place forcible after such entrie made, they shall be taken, and put into the Gaols, there to abide conuict by the record of the same Justices, or Justice, untill they haue made fine and ransom to the King. And all they of the Countie, aswell the Shirife, as other, shall be attending upon the Justices to go and assist the same Justices, to arrest such offendors, upon paine of imprisonment, and to make fine to the King. The penaltie of forcible entrie into lands or benefices.

3 And forasmuch as the said Statute of 15.R.2. doth not extend to Entries into tenements in peaceable manner, and after holden with force, nor if the persons which enter with force into any lands or tenements be wholy remoued and departed before the comming of the said Justices, or Justice; Neither is there any paine ordained, if the Shirife do not obey the precepts of the Justices in this behalfe: Therefore by an other Statute made Añ 8. H. 6. it was ordained, that the said former Statutes should be continued and executed. And further, that where any do make such forcible entrie into lands, tenements, or other possessions, or hold them forciblie, after complaint thereof made within the said Countie where such entrie is made, to the Justices of peace, or to one of them by the partie grieued, that the Justices or Justice so warned, within a conuenient time cause the said Statute to be executed, and that at the costes of the partie so grieued. And whether such persons making such Entries be present, or gone before the comming of the said Justices or Justice, presently the same Justices or Justice in some good Towne next unto the tenements so entred, or in some other conuenient place, according to their discretion, shall haue authoritie to inquire by the people of the same Countie, aswell of them that made such forcible entries into lands or tenements, as of them which hold the same with force. And if it be found before any of them, that any doth contrarie to this Statute, then the said Justices or Justice shall cause the lands or tenements so entred or holden as aforesaid to be reseised, and shal put the partie so put out, in full possession of the same lands or tenements so entred or holden, as before they were entred or holden. And if any person after such entrie into lands or tenements holden with force, make a feoffement or other discontinuance to any Lord, or other person to haue maintenaunce, or to take away and defraud the possessor of his recouerie in any wise, if after in an Assise, or other action thereof to be taken or pursued before Justices of Assise, or other the Kings Justices whatsoeuer they be, by due inquirie thereof to be taken, the same feoffements and discontinuances may be duely proued to be made, for maintenance, as is aforesaid, then such feoffements or other discontinuances so as before made shall be void. And if any person be put out or disseised of any lands or tenements in forcible manner, or put out peaceablie, & after holden out with strong hand, and armes, against the Justice of peace; or after such entry, any feoffement or discontinuance in any wise thereof be made, to defraude & take away the right of the possessor, the party greiued in this behalfe, shall haue an Assise of Nouel disseisin, or a writ of Trespas against such disseisor. And if the party grieued recouer by Assise, or by action of Trespas and it be found

St.8.H.6.9.

Holding possession by force.

Feoffement of lands for maintenance.

An Assise or action of trespas against a disseisour by force.

found by verdict, or in any other manner by due forme of the Law, that the partie defendant entred with force into the lands & tenements, or them after his entrie did hold with force, then the plaintife shall recouer treble dammages against the defendant, and moreouer the defendant shall make fine and ransome to the King. And the Maiors, Justices and Justice of peace, Shirifes, and Bailifes of Cities and Boroughes hauing fraunchise, shall haue in the said Cities, Townes, & Boroughes, like authoritie to auoid such Entries, and in other articles aforesaid, rising within the same, as Justices of peace and Shirifes in Counties and Shires haue.

The authority of officers of Cities and Townes enfranchised.

4 As by the foresaid Statute of 8. H. 6. if any person after entrie into lands or tenements holden with force, shal make any feoffement or other discontinuance thereof to any Lord or other person, to haue maintenance, or to defraud the possessor of his recouery, then the same feoffements & discontinuances shall be void: So by an other Statute made before that Anno 4. H. 4. it was inacted, That if any man in his owne right to his vse, or in an other mans right to his vse, doth make any forcible entrie into an other mans lands by way of maintenaunce, or doth take or carry away any goods of the possessors of the freehold after any such forcible entrie; then if the partie grieued or other lawfull man will affirme, that the entry was made in such forcible manner, the Chancellor of England may graunt to the partie greiued a speciall Assise: And if the disseisor be attainted of such forcible disseisin, he shall be one yeare imprisoned, and pay to the partie grieued his double daunmages, and also dammages for his goods. And one of the Justices of the one Bench, or of the other, or the chiefe Baron of the Exchequer (if he be learned in the law) shall be named in euery such speciall Assise. And no Supersedeas shalbe granted to the contrarie of such Assise. St. 4. H. 4. 8.

A speciall Assise against a disseisor with force.

5 Wherefore, if a man be disseised by force of any lands or tenements by way of maintenance, or that his goods be taken or carried away after such entrie made: Or that he be put out, or disseised of his lands in forcible manner: Or that he be put out peaceablie, and after holden out with force against a Justice of peace: Or after such entrie, any feoffement or discontinuance be made to defraud and take away the right of the possessor; then the partie grieued (as his case requireth) may haue a speciall Assise against the disseisor, and recouer his double dammages, and dammages for his goods, and the disseisor shall be one yeare imprisoued, according to the foresaid Statute of 4. H. 4. Or else he may haue an Assise of Nouel disseisin, or an action of Trespas against the disseisor, and recouer treble dammages; and moreouer, the disseisor shall make fine and ransom to the King, according to the before rehearsed Statute of 8. H. 6. Or if the plaintife will omit the benefit of recouerie of his dammages, he may only craue and vse the assistance of a Justice of peace, to see and remoue the force, to record it, to inquire of it, and to make him restitution, according as the truth of his case shall appeare to the said Justice vpon his owne sight, or be found by inquisition, according to the former prouision of the said Statute of 8. H. 6. Or lastly, he that is put out, or holden out of his lands with force, may haue a writ directed out of the Chauncerie to the Shirife only, or to the Shirife and the Justices of peace vpon the Statute of Northhampton made An 2. Ed. 3. commaunding that proclamation may be made vpon that Statute. St. 4. H. 4. 8. St. 8. H. 6. 9. St. 2. E. 3. 3.

Seuerall remedies for seuerall offences by force.

6 And

6 And for that it is conuenient, that he who is with force expelled out of his lands, or by force detained from the same, should not be long kept out of possession thereof, but that there should be a spéedie redresse to restore him to his owne: and also because it is meant, that the inquisition of that force should be made by men of good estate, and so the more like to be indifferent, of better vnderstanding, and to declare the truth in those cases: Therefore by the foresaid statute of Anno 8. H. 6. it was moreouer ordained, That when the said Iustices or Iustice shall make such inquiries, as are beforesaid, they shall cause their warrants and precepts to be directed to the Shirife of the same Countie, commaunding him on the Kings behalfe to cause to come before them, and euery of them, sufficient and indifferent persons, dwelling next about the lands so entred vpon as before; to enquire of such entries, whereof euery man that shall be impannelled, and may inquire in this behalfe, shall haue lands or tenements to the value of xl. s. by the yeare at the least aboue reprises, and that the Shirife returne issues vpon euery of them at the day of the first precept returnable xx. s. and at the second day xl. s and at the third day fiue pounds, and at euery day after, the double. And if any Shirife or Bayliffe within a fraunchise, hauing the returne of the Kings writs be slacke, and make not execution duly of the said precepts to him directed to make such inquiries, he shall forfeit to the King xx. li. for euery such default, and moreouer shall make fine and ransom to the King. And aswell the Iustices or Iustice aforesaid, as the Iustices of Assise, and euery of them, at their comming into the Countrey to take Assises, haue power to heare and determine such defaults, and negligences of the said Shirifes, and Bailifes, and euery of them, aswell by bill at the sute of the party greiued for himselfe, as for the King, to sue by Inditement only to be taken for the King. And if the Shirife or Bailife be duly attainted in this behalfe by Indictment, or by bill, he which sueth for himselfe, and for the King, shall haue the one moitie of the forfaiture of xx. li. together with his costs and expences. And the same proces shall be made against such persons indited, or sued by bill in this behalfe, as should be against persons indited or sued by writ of Trespas with force and armes against the Kings peace.

Sta. 8. H. 6. 9.

A precept to the Shirife to impannell a Iurie.

Shirifes forfaiture.

The proces.

7 The forme of which precept by a Iustice of peace, to the Shirife to returne a Iurie, to enquire of Forcible entries is this. Edwardus Tirrell miles vnus Iusticiariorum dñi Regis, ad pacem in Comitatu Buck. conseruandam assignatorum vicecomiti eiusdem Comitatus salutem: Ex parte dicti Domini Regis tibi mando, quod venire facias coram me apud Thornborough in Comitatu prædicto 10. die Octobris proximo futuro 24. probos, sufficientes, & legales homines de viceneto de Thornborough prædicto, quorum quilibet habeat 40. solidos terrarum & tenementorum, vel redditnum per annum ad minus vltra reprisas, ad inquirendum super sacramentum suum, si A. B. de Adstock in dicto Comitatu Buck. blacksmith, & alij malefactores, & pacis dicti domini Regis perturbatores, in vnum mesuagium & 20. acras terræ & alia tenementa de C. D. husband. de T. prædict' manu forti super possessionem dicti C. D. ingressi sunt, aut eadem cum fortitudine adhuc tenent & occupant. Et videas quod super quilibet Iuratorum in hoc parte impannellandorum xx. s. ad primum diem returnes; & hoc nullatenus omittas sub pena xx. li. quam noueris te incursurum, si in executione præmissorum tepidus aut remissus fueris. Et habeas ibi hoc præceptum. Dat' apud Thornton xx. die Septemb. Anno Regni domini nostri Regis Iacobi &c. tertio.

Buck.

The forme of a Precept to the Shirife to returne a Iurie.

8 The

8 **The forme of an inquisition or verdit of the Jury which are returned and sworne to enquire of forcible Entrie into lands or tenements, or of the forcible detayning of them taken by a Justice of peace is this.** viz. Inquisitio pro domino Rege capta apud Buckingham in Com̃ prædicto xx. die N. Anno Regni domini nostri Regis Iacobi &c. quarto, super sacramentum A.B.C.D.E.F.G. &c. coram Thoma Temple milite vno Iusticiar̃ dicti domini Regis ad pacem in dicto Comitatu conseruandam assignatorum: Qui dicunt, quod vbi H. I. de Tyngswicke in Comit̃ prædict husbandman, qui legitime & pacifice seisitus fuit in dominico suo vt de feodo, de vno mesuagio cum pertinentijs in Tyngswick prædicto, & possessionem suam sic continuauit, quousq; L. M. de Maydsmoorton in Comitatu prædicto laborer, & alij malefactores, & pacis dicti domini Regis perturbatores xxx. die O. iam vltimo elapso, vi & armis, viz. cum baculis, gladijs, arcubus, sagittis, fustibus, gunnis, & balistis in mesuagium prædictum &c. intrauerunt, & ipsum H. I. inde expulerunt, & idem mesuagium &c a prædicto xxx. die O. vsq; ad diem captionis huius inquisitionis &c. cum huiusmodi fortitudine & potentia tenuer̃, & occupauerunt, in magnam pacis dicti domini Regis perturbationem, & contra formam statuti in tali casu ęditi & ꝓuisi, vbi nullus eorum, nec aliquis alius cuius statum ipsi aut aliquis eorum habuerunt, aut habuit, aliquid in eodem mesuagio &c. aut aliqua inde parcella habuerunt, aut habuit infra tres annos proximos ante ingressũ suum prædictũ, neque aliquo tempore pręcedente ad notitiam Iuratorum ꝑdictorum.

Buck. **The forme of an Inquisition of forcible entrie.**

9 **And for that the said Statute of** 8. H. 6. **hath ordained, That if it be found before any of the said Justices of peace, that any doth contrarie to that Statute, then the said Justices or Justice shall cause the lands or tenements so entred, or holden with force to be reseised, and shall put the partie so put out in full possession of the same lands, so entred or holden as before they were entred or holden: Therefore, when the Justice of peace shall by the said Inquisition be informed, or by the view of his owne eye perceiue, that any such forcible entrie into any lands hath been made, or after the same lands be holden with force, he is either himselfe to reseise the same lands, and put the partie in possession againe, who was so forciblie expelled or kept out of possession, or else he is to make his Precept to the Shirife of the same Countie to make restitution to the same partie. The forme of which warrant or precept is this,** viz. Georgius Throckmorton Miles, vnus Iusticiariorum dñi Regis ad pacem in dicto Comitatu conseruandam assignatorum, Vicecom̃ eiusdem Comitat̃, salutem. Cum per quandam Inquisitionem patriæ coram me captum apud East-Claydon in Comitatu ꝑdicto 2. die Dec. Anno regni dñi nostri Iacobi quarto, sup sacr̃m A.B.C.D.E.F. &c. ac per formam statuti in hmodi casu ꝓuisi compertũ fuerit, qd' L. M. de Horwood magna in Com̃ ꝑdict' husb. & alij malefactores, & pacis dicti dñi Regis perturbatores, 26. die No. añ dicti dñi Regis nunc quarto, in quoddam messuagiũ &c. N. T. in East-Claydon ꝑdicta, vi & armis ingressi fuerunt, ac ipsum N. T. inde expulerunt, & ꝑdictũ mesuagiũ &c. a ꝑdicto 26. die &c. vsq; ad dictũ secundũ diem Decemb. manu forti & cum potentia tenuerunt, ꝓut per Inquisitionẽ ꝑdictam plenius liquet de recordo: Ideo ex parte dicti dñi Regis tibi mando, & pręcipio quod ad hoc debit̃ requisitus, vnà cum posse Comitat̃ tui, si necesse fuerit, accedas ad mesuagiũ & cætera premissa, ac eadẽ cum ptinentijs reseisiri facias, & ꝑfatũ N. T. ad & in plenam possessionẽ suam inde, ꝓut ipse ante ingressũ ꝑdictũ fuerat, restituas, & mitti facias, iuxta formã dicti statuti, de Ingressibus manu forti factis æditi & ꝓuisi. Et hoc nullatenus omittas sub ꝑiculo incumbent̃. Teste me ꝑfato G. Throckmorton. Datum apud Fulbrooke &c. tertio die Decembris &c.

Buck. **A warrant to the Shirife to make restitution.**

7.Ed.4.18. 4.H.7.18. 15.H.7.5. 10 If a man be indited before the Iustices of peace in the County, for that he did with force expell, and put another out of his possession of certaine lands within the same County, and after this inditement is remoued into the kings bench by a Certiorari, the Iustices of the same court may award a writ of Restitution to the shirife of the same County, to restore possession to the party so expelled, though the words of the statute of 8.H.6. doe giue that authority only to the Iustices of peace of the County, where the forcible entry is made: and if he be indited before Iustices to heare & determine, and after the record is remoued into the K. Bench, the Iustices of the same court may award restitution: for that they who haue supreme authority, and do represent the K. person, now haue before them the record whereby the party was indited. Restitution awarded out of the K. bench

11 By the words of the foresaid statute of 8.H.6. it doth appeare, that one Iustice of peace alone may remoue the force, and also enquire thereof, & so may diuers Iustices. But by the aforesaid statute no restitution can be made to the party put out of possession, if the said expelling or putting out of possession be not found by inquisition: nor but in case, where the words of the Inditement vpon the statute of 8.H.6. be, adhuc extratenet. No restitutiō, but where the force is found by inquisition.

21.H.6.5. 14.H.6.16.

12 In the foresaid statute of 8.H.6. there is a prouiso, That they which keepe their possessions by force in any lands and tenements, whereof they or their auncestors, or they, whose estate they haue in such lands or tenements, haue continued their possession by the space of three yeares or more, be not endammaged by the force of the said statute. And by one other statute made Anno 31. Eliz. for the explanation and declaration of the meaning and intent of the said prouiso, and of the law therein, it was ordained, declared, and enacted, That no restitution vpon any inditement of Forcible entry, or holding with force, shalbe made to any person or persons, if the person or persons so indited hath had the occupation, or hath beene in quiet possession by the space of three whole yeares together, next before the day of such inditement so found, & his, her, or their estate or estates therein not ended nor determined: which the party indited shall and may alledge, for stay of restitution, and restitution to stay vntill that be tried, if the other will deny or trauerse the same. And if the same allegation be tried against the same person or persons so indited, then the same person or persons so indited to pay such costs & damages to the other party, as shalbe assessed by the Iudges or Iustices before whom the same shal be tried, the same costs and dammages to be recouered and leuied, as is vsuall for costs and dammages contained in iudgements vpon other actions. If a man hath beene in quiet and peaceable possession of lands three yeeres or more by a good title, and then is expelled and disseised of them, and the party offending is therefore indited vpon the statute of 8.H.6. and the disseisee who was expelled, is restored to his possession by a writ of Restitution, and is in possession accordingly; in this case he cannot iustifie the detainer of the possession of those lands, by force of the foresaid prouiso contained in the statute of 8. H.6. because his possession was interrupted & discontinued, for that possession must be three whole yeeres together without interruption, before the said party may by the said prouiso keepe his possession by force. And likewise if he that is a iust and lawfull possessor of lands by the space of twenty yeeres together, be once clearely & wholly remoued from the possession of the same land, he cannot come againe with force, and a multitude of people to put himselfe in possession thereof, and detaine the same with force, by vertue of the prouiso in the said statute

St.31.El.11. Where no restitutiō against three yeares possession.

4.& 5.P.& M Dy.141.

3.& 4.P.& M. Dy.141.

of 8.H.6. because his possession was interrupted. Neither in this case, if he be indited of a Forcible entry, according to the statute of 8.H.6. shall he be relieued touching his restitution by the foresaid statute of 31.El. for that he had not the occupation, nor had béene in quiet possession by the space of thrée whole yeares together of the same lands next before the day of such inditemēt found. But if a man be seised of a lawfull possession by the space of thrée yéeres of any land without interruption, he may kéepe his possession by force against all others. And he is neither to be remoued from his possession by a Just. of peace, though it be found by inquisition, that he held that land by force, nor yet by an action of Forcible entry brought against him vpon the said statute of 8. H.6. Otherwise it is of a disseisor, or of a man that commeth to land by a wrongful and vnlawfull title: for if he hath detained the land by force, thrée yeares, or twenty yeares, he may be indited by vertue of the statute of 8.H.6. before a Justice of peace, of forcible detaining of the same land, and that being found, the said Justice of peace is to reseise the land, and to award restitution to the party disseised or expelled thereof. And also the same disseisor shall make fine and ransome to the King (cui nullum tempus occurrit) whose peace is brokē by this long and vnlawfull detaining of the possession of another mans land by force. But the party disseised, expelled, or kept out of possession, cannot in this case maintaine an action of Forcible entry vpon the said statute of 8.H.6. against the said disseisor, séeing he hath omitted his time, & suffered the disseisor to gaine of him thrée yeares possession, & therby the benefit of the same prouiso contained in the said statute of 8.H.6.

22.H.6.18. Fitz. Na. B. 249.

Where restitution not withstanding thrée yeares possession.

14.H.7.28.

13 If a man who hath made an Entry vpon the possession of another of any lands or tenements by force, or doth hold lands by force, after a peaceably entry made, doe doubt, that he shalbe thereof indited before a Justice of peace vpon the statute of 8.H.6. and that restitution will be thereupon awarded, he may haue a Certiorari out of the Kings Bench ready, and when the Bill of Inditement is found, he may presently deliuer it to the court, and that shalbe a Supersedeas to stay Restitution, for that by this Certiorari the inditement shalbe remoued. And though the inditement be found after the Teste of the writ of Certiorari, it is not materiall, for they be both the Kings Courts. And when an inditement vpon the said statute of 8.H.6. is remoued into the kings Bench, and that the party indited doth tender to trauerse the same, the Justices of the same Bench may graunt or stay restitution, at their discretion, according as the truth of the Title shall appeare to them. But if a speciall sessions be procured to inquire of a Forcible entry, or detaining of possession, according to the said statute of 8.H.6. and the Justices to whom complaint is made, do repaire to the place supposed to be entred vpon, or holden with force, and doe sée the same according to the said statute, & after they do inquire thereof, and that is found, and thereupon they graunt restitution; no other Justice of peace can graunt a Supersedeas to stay the same restitution: for by the said statute no other Justice hath authority to graunt restitution, but he or they to whom the complaint is made, and before whom the force is found, & the writ shalbe graunted vnder the Teste of one of them onely, sauing the Justices of the K. Bench, who haue supreme authority, and where the law doth intend, that the King himselfe doth sit.

1.R.3.4.

A Supersedeas to stay restitution.

2.& 3.P.& M.Dy.122.

2.& 3.P.& M.Dy.187.

14 Whereas the words of the foresaid statute of 8.H.6. be: If it be found before any of the Justices or Justice of peace, that any doth contrary to this statute

Sta.8.H.6.9

statute (viz. enter vpon, or hold lands with force) then the said Iustices or Iustice shall cause the lands or tenements so entred or holden to be reseised, and shall put the party so put out in full possession of the same landes or tenements so entred or holden, as before they were entred or holden. And therefore if the father be put out of possession of lands by force, and dieth before or after inquisition thereof, his heire shall not haue restitution thereof vpon the said statute of 8. H. 6. for that he was not the same person which was put out. And the same Law is, if after the death of the father, dying seised of certaine lands, a stranger doth abate, and holdeth the same lands by force against his heire, before he had gotten any possession indeed, and that force is found before a Iustice of peace by an inquisition, the same heire shall not haue restitution by the words of the said statute, for that the same heire had but a possession in law, and was not in actuall possession of that land, neither is hee that party who was put out. And so it is, if tenant for terme of yeeres of certaine lands be put out of his terme by force, and die, though after his death the force be found by inquisition taken by a Iustice of peace, his executors shall not be restored to the possession of that land by the same Iustice of peace, causa qua supra. But yet in the cases aforesaid the offendor shall be punished by imprisonment & fine to the K. for by his forcible entry he hath broken the peace. Where force found, and no restitution.

St. 15. R. 2. 2. 15 Whereas by the before rehearsed statute of 15. Rich. 2. it is ordayned, That when any forcible entry shalbe made into lands, and complaint thereof come to a Iustice of peace, he shall go to the place where the entry was made, and if he find any that hold any such place forcibly after such entry made, they shalbe taken and put into the Gaole &c. The forme of which Iustice of peace Mittimus, whereby he shall send the same offendors to the Gaole, is this, viz.

Buck. A Mittimus to send to the gaole such as do hold land by force.

Francis Fortescue knight, one of the Iustices of peace of our Soueraigne Lord the King, within the county of Buckingham, to the keeper of his Ma. Gaole in Aylesbury in the said county, and to his deputie and deputies there, and to euery of them greeting: Vpon complaint made to me by A. B. of Whaddon in the said county husbandman, that C. D. E. F. of S. in the said county labourers, and other malefactors and disturbers of the Kings peace had forcibly and with strong hand entred into his house &c. in Whaddon aforesaid, and him expulsed, & the same yet held with force, I went this present day to the said house, and there found the said C. D. E. F. holding the said house &c. with swords and bucklers, bils and staues, to the great disturbance of his Ma. peace, and against the forme of the said statute in that behalfe ordained. And therefore I send you by the bringers hereof the bodies of the said C. D. E. F. conuicted of the said forcible holding by my record: commanding you and euery of you in his Ma. name, that you receiue them, & safely keepe them in your said Goale, vntill they shall haue made their fine and ransome to the King, and be deliuered thence by the order of the law. Hereof faile you not, vpon the perill that will fall thereof. Dated at Salden the 30. day of I. in the third yere of the raigne of our soueraign Lord K. Iames &c.

16 And though ỷ words of the before rehearsed stat. of 8. H. 6. be, Vpõ cõplaint made to ỷ I. of P. or one of thẽ &c. yet those words do not alwais bind a I. of P. to expect ỷ cõplaint of ỷ party grieued, or to omit to do his duty in inquiring of, repressing, & punishing of force, because ỷ party grieued by the forcible entry, or detaining of possessiõ, is ignorãt in seeking lawful redres for his receiued iniury, or doth intẽd to take his remedy by other means: but a I. of P. hauing notice

A Justice may inquire of forcible entries without complaint.

of such forcible entry, or detaining of possession by force (though it be by others 7.E.4.18.
and not by the party grieued) may and of duty ought to goe to the place where
the same force is committed, & to make inquisition thereof; and if the force be
found, to make restitution to the party expelled or put out by force. And so by
his meanes the offendor shall be punished according to his desert, the partie
wronged shal be restored, & the king shall be intituled to a fine, all which with-
out the said Justices diligence would be omitted.

An action of forcible entry.

17 If a man that is seised of lands or tenements of an estate in fee simple, Fitz.Na.B.
fee taile, for terme of his owne life, or for the terme of anothers life, be disseised 248.
or expelled thereof by force, he may haue an action of Trespas of forcible entry
vpon the foresaid statute of 8.H.6. against him or them that did so disseise or
expell him thereof: and so he may, if he be put out, or disseised of his lands or 6.H.7.12.
tenements peaceably, and after the disseisor, or he that doth expell him, doth 14.H.6.1.
hold them with force. And in like sort he may haue the same action, if any doth 3.E.4.19.
enter into his said lands or tenements with force, & after doth defend and hold 10.E.4.11.
them by force, then he which is so put out and holden out with force, may haue
this action, though the words of the statute be in the disiunctiue, viz. disseised
with force, or disseised quietly & after holden out with force: for that the intent
of the statute was to punish all such forces, whether it were vpon the entry &
disseisin made, or vpon the holding and detaining of the land with force: in all
which cases, he who is so disseised or put out, may haue an action of forcible en-
try vpon the said statute of 8.H.6. and shall recouer his damages and costs to
the treble of that which shalbe found by the Enquest, that he is endammaged, 19.H.6.6.

The writ of forcible entry must be Vi & armis.

& hath spent in his suit, & as wel for the occupation as for the first entry. And it 22.H.6.57.
is to be noted, that the writ & declaration in an action of forcible entry, must be, 9.H.6.19.
that the def. entred vi & armis, and not illicitè, or by any other such words: for
if the writ be otherwise, it shall abate; seeing a writ of forcible entry is al-
waies vi & armis, and proces of Outlawry lieth in it: and the declaration must 37.H.6.23.
expresse the certainty of the lands, whereupon the defendant did make his for- 38.H.6.1.
cible entry, and which they be, and not suggest, that he did enter vpon certaine
lands in D. And in this action of Forcible entry, and in all actions Quare vi et 35.H.6.6.
armis, a Capias doth lie, and where a Capias doth lie in the proces, there after 49.Ed.3.2.
iudgement a Capias ad satisfaciendum doth lie, and there the king shall haue a Co.lib.3.12
Capias pro fine.

Who may bring an actiō of forcible entry.

18 None can pursue or maintaine this action of Forcible entry, but he who Fit.Na.B.
hath freehold at the least in the lands or tenemēts so entred vpon: for tenant for 248.
terme of yeeres, or a copyholder, cannot maintaine this action, for ẏ the words
of the said stat. of 8.H.6. be, If any person be put out, or disseised of any lāds &c. Sta.8.H.6.9
and the words of the writ grounded vpon the said statute be, Expulit et disseisi-
uit: and tenant for terme of yeeres, or a copyholder, cānot be disseised, seeing dis-
seisin is alwaies of a freehold, which neither of them haue in that land. But if
tenant for terme of yeeres, or a copiholder, be put out by force, or put out peace-
ably, & after holden out with force of land which either of them doth hold by the
said estate: then vpon cōplaint made by the party grieued to a J. of peace, after
inquisition thereof by a Jury, & the same force found, the said Just. may reseise
the said lands, & cause restitution thereof to be made to the party so put out: for
in this case the same cōplaint may be made to the said J. of P. aswell by him in
ẏ reuersiō, as by ẏ tenāt for terme of yeres, or copiholder: seeing he in ẏ reuersiō
who is disseised of his freehold by this forcible entry, is & may as well be termed

the

the party grieued, as the tenant for terme of yeeres, or the copyholder for their
said particular estates. And when the Justice of peace hath made restitution,
the particular tenant for terme of yeares, or copyholder, and also he or they in
4.& 5.P.& reuersion shall hold and enioy their said seuerall estates in the same lands, in
M.Di.f.142 such sort as they did before the said Forcible entry made. But if tenant for
terme of yeares be expelled out of that land which he so holdeth for the terme
of yeeres, he in the reuersion cannot bring an action of Forcible entry vpon the
statute of 8.H.6. for the same, although it be a disseisin to him, for that the ex-
pulsion is not done immediatly to him.

Fit.Na.Br. 19 If a man do enter by force into lands or tenements, whereunto he hath — He that hath title entreth by force.
248. right or title to enter, & doth put out him who hath ye freehold of the same lãds,
9.H.6.19. in this case he who is so put out by force, cannot maintaine an action of trespas
of forcible entry against him, who hath title to enter, for that his entry was no
disseisin to ye other, who was not lawfully seised thereof: but he may indite him
for this forcible entry, & this inditement being found, he shalbe restored to his
possession againe by a Just. of peace by vertue of the said statute of 8.H.6. And
22.H.6.18. after that, he that did first enter forcibly by lawful title, may again enter peace-
ably, or bring an assise of Nouel disseisin at his pleasure.

Fit.Na.B. 20 If a man do enter into lands or tenements, & disseise one with force, and — He that hath possessiõ sueth a writ of forcible entry.
249. after the disseisee doth reenter againe, yet the same disseisee may pursue an actiõ
22.H.6.37. of Trespas of forcible entry against the disseisor, & recouer his treble damages,
though he be seised of the land at the time of the writ brought. And therefore it
is not a sufficient plea in a writ of forcible entry, for the def. to plead, that the
plaintife was seised of the same land the day of the said writ brought.

20.H.6.12. 21 A man may haue a writ of Forcible entry of a rent, as well as of land: — Forcible entry of a rent or common.
22.H.6.23. for one may distraine with force for rent, and that doth counteruaile an entry
with force. And one may haue a writ of Entry of a rent, which doth suppose,
that the def. did enter into the rent. And in an Assise of rent, the disseisin may
39.Ass.p.4. be found to be done by force. If there be three iointenants of land, out of the
which there is a rent going, & vpon a distresse taken, one of thẽ maketh rescous
by force, he only shalbe imprisoned, & yet the others be disseisors. And the like
law is of a commõ of pasture, for a commoner may by force be expelled or kept
out of his common. And a man may keepe his beasts in another mans ground
27.Ass.p.30 by force, claiming common where he hath no common, and that is disseisin by
force. And in either of the cases aforesaid, a Just. of peace vpõ complaint to him
made, may remoue the force, but not award restitution, because they are to be
taken & vsed in another mans land.

2.H.7.16. 22 If diuers do enter with force to the vse of another, who himself doth not — Forcible entry to the vse of another.
17.Ass.p.14 enter, but after doth agree to this entry to his vse, this agreement doth make
him a disseisor, or a trespassor: but he shall not thereby be punished for ye force,
for there can be no forcible entry without an actuall entry. And yet there may — Forcible detaining by words only.
be a forcible detaining of possession by words only, without act: as if he ye hath
wrongfully but peaceably entred into another mans house, & expelled and put
out the owner thereof, shall say to the same owner, if he do come thither againe
to enter, he will kill him, this is a forcible detaining of possession.

23 If there be two iointenants or tenants in common of certaine lands, &

one of them doth expell & put forth the other out of possession of the said lands by force, he that is so expelled, may haue an action of Trespas of forcible entry against his companion that did so expell him, upon the said statute of 8.H.6. for the words of the writ may be verified, Expulit & Disseisiuit, and therupon he shall haue a writ of Restitution to restore him to his former estate. But if one iointenant or tenant in common of lands doe expell the other by force out of the same lands, he that is so expelled, cannot maintaine a writ of Entry upon the statute of 5.R.2. against his companion that so put him foorth, and suppose that he did enter into the same lands vbi ingressus non datur per legẽ: for that his entry and possession in that land is lawful through the whole land in respect of his owne moitie or estate: and further, seeing by that action the plaintife is to recouer but only dammages as in an action of Trespas, and not to be restored to his possession: which action of Trespasse one iointenant or tenant in common cannot maintaine against another, for any Trespas done in the land so holden by them.

Iointenants or tenants in common expelling each other by force.

8.Ed.4.9. & 19. 10.H.7.27. Fit.Na.Br. 249. 21.E.4.10. 18.H.6.5.

24 None can maintaine a writ of Entry upon the said statute of 5.R.2. vbi ingressus non datur per legem, but onely tenant in fee simple, tenant in fee taile, or tenant for terme of life at the least: for tenant for terme of yeares, a copyholder, or a tenant at will cannot pursue and maintaine it, seeing they haue but the manurance and occupation of the land. Neither can the King bring the said Action, nor an Assise, Eiectione firmæ, nor action upon the statute of 8.H.6. Nor any other action which doth proue him out of possession of the land.

Who may bring a writ of Entry upon the statute of 5.R.2.

8.E.4.9. & 19. 4.H.7.1.

25 If a man do enter into another mans ground, and turne away by force an ancient watercourse, which he hath running to his myll, the party grieued may haue a speciall Assise of Nusance upon the statute of 4.H.4. against the offendor, & recouer his double damages, & yet he was not put out, nor disseised of his freehold, but a Nusance was done to the dammage thereof.

Turning a watercourse by force.

Plow. Com. 467.

26 In a writ of Forcible entry, the defendant may plead not guilty, & that shalbe a good plea. But if the defendant doe plead some matter in barre, yet he must in the end of the barre trauerse and deny the entry with force, which is alledged against him, as to say, without that he did enter with force &c. And the plaintife must answer to that speciall matter alledged in the barre, without answering to the Trauerse of the force, and upon that speciall matter, the issue must be ioyned, and not upon the force. And if that speciall matter alledged in the barre be found by verdict with the defendant, he shalbe excused, and the force shall not be inquired of. But if it be found with the plaintife, and against the defendant, then the defendant shalbe attainted of force, and render treble dammages, and treble costes, without inquirie of the force. As, one brought an action of Forcible entry upon the statute of 8.H.6. and supposed that the defendant with force and armes entred into a messuage &c. Whereunto the defendant pleaded, That a stranger was seised of the same messuage &c. and enfeoffed him thereof, by means whereof he entred peaceably, without that, that he entred by force. And the plaintife made a title, and trauersed the barre, and the issue was found for the plaintife: and thereupon it was adiudged, that the force should not be inquired of: For seeing the title is found against the defendant, he shall be conuict of the force, as on the other side, if the barre had beene found for the defendant, the force should not haue beene inquired

The plea of not guilty in forcible entry.

The finding of the speciall matter, doth charge or discharge the def. of force.

Lib. int fol. 330. Fit.N.B. 249. 14.H.6.16. 22.H.6.57. 22.H.6.17. 9.H.6.19. 21.H.6.39. 15.H.7.17. 1.H.7.19.

red of: for that if the title of the plaintife be not good, although the defendant doth enter with force, the plaintife hath no cause of action; and yet in that case, he that entreth with force, shalbe indited thereof, and shall pay a fine to the K. therefore. And if the defendant doth enter peaceably, where his entry is not lawfull, he may plead, that he did not enter contra formam statuti, and by that meanes the force and the disseisin shalbe inquired of. But if he make a title to the land by pleading in barre, as is aforesaid, then it shalbe adiudged his owne folly. As, in a writ of Forcible entry, when the defendant doth plead in barre, yet he must trauerse the force: So in a presentment of Forcible entry before the Iustices of peace, it was found and presented, that A. was seised of the manor of B. in his demesne as of fee, vntill C. did enter vpon the said manor, and put him out with force and armes against the kings peace. And this presentment being remoued into the kings bench, and proces being awarded for the king against C. he appeared and pleaded to the force and armes, & all that is against the peace, not guiltie. But the court enforced him to plead to his entry, and then he iustified his entry by reason of a remainder intailed to his father of the same land, and that his father entred and died seised thereof, & that he as heire to his father did enter. And so it is, if a man be indited for the taking away of certaine goods by force and armes, he shal answer to the taking, and if he be found guilty of the Trespas, there shalbe no inquirie made of the force and armes.

7.H.6.13. — Presentment of forcible entry.

27 A man brought an action of Forcible entry against diuers others vpon the statute of 8.H.6. and counted, that they did with force & armes enter vpon his land, and put him out, and so declared according to the statute, whereupon they were at issue. And it was found by verdict, that some of the defendants entred vpon the land with force and armes, and did not hold it with force, and some others of them did enter peaceably into the same land, and held it with force and armes: and so the Iurie taxed the dammages seuerally vpon both those points: vpon which verdict it was adiudged, That the plaintife should recouer treble dammages against those that entred forcibly, and also should recouer treble dammages against those that entred peaceably, and held with force, and the costs of his suite: and further, that the said plaintife should bee amerced, for that he supposed that all did enter with force, which was found against him. And in like sort, if two be indited of Forcible entry and detayning with force, and vpon their Trauerse it is found, that one of them entred with force, and the other detained with force, yet restitution shall be awarded to the party put out of possession.

19.H.6.32. — One action for entring & detaining with force.

28 And further if a man do enter by force, or detaine by force any lands or tenements, the partie grieued may haue a writ out of the Chauncery, directed to the Sherife of the Countie onely, or to the Sherife and Iustices of peace, or some of them, vpon the statute made at Northampton anno 2. Ed. 3. The form of which writ is this, viz. Iacobus Dei gratia &c. vicecomiti Buck. Salutem; Quia datum est nobis intelligi, quod quamplures malefactores, & pacis nostræ perturbatores, in conuenticulis congregati, armati, & modo guerrino arraiati apud Westburie accederunt, et clausuras, et domos quorundam legiorum nostrorum ibidem per vim & potentiam armati intrauerunt, & res, redditus, & prouentus, ac alia bona sua quæcunque de quibuscunque possessoribus suis ibidem prouenientia capere consenserunt, & asportare intendunt, & ad hoc parant in nostri contemptum, ac quorundam de populo nostro ibidem terrorē & commotionē mani-

Fit. Na. B. 249. — Sta. 2. E. 3. 3. — A writ vpon the statute of Northamptō.

manifestam, ac contra formam statuti apud Northampton de armis contra pacẽ domini Edwardi nuper Regis Angliæ tertij, progenitoris nostri, non portandis editi, & contra pacem nostram. Nos statutum prædictum inuiolabiliter obseruari, & idem infringentes iuxta vim & effectum eiusdem statuti castigari facere volentes, & puniri: Tibi præcipimus quod apud villam de Westbury, et alibi in comitatu tuo vbi necesse fuerit publice proclamari, & ex parte nostra firmiter inhiberi facias, ne quis cuiuscunq; status seu conditionis fuerit ibidẽ armatus cõtra pacem nostram, ac contra formam statuti prædicti accedat, nec armatam potentiam, nec quicquid aliud ibidem, seu alibi facere, per quod pax nostra, seu statutum prædict' lædi, vel populus noster turbari, terreri, aut indebitè grauari poterit quouismodo sub pœna amissionis armorum suorum, & incarcerationis corporũ suorum ad voluntatẽ nostram, prout in statuto prædicto plenius continetur. Et omnes illos quos post & contra proclamationẽ et inhibitionem pdictam inueneris contraria facientes, vel per inquisitionem per te modo & forma debita capiendam inueneris fecisse, vnà cum armis, & armaturis suis secum inuentis, arrestari, & capi; & corpora ipsorum arrestatorum in prisona nostra, quousque aliud à nobis pro deliberatione sua habueritis in mandatis, saluò custodiri, et arma & armatur prædicta appreciari, & nobis inde responderi facias. Nos verò in Cancellaria nostra sub sigillo tuo, de nominibus arrestatorum prædictorum, & de armis, & armaturis suis, & quæ & cuiusmodi fuerint, & de pretio, & de vero valore eorundẽ, ac de toto facto tuo in hac parte reddatis distinctè & apertè sine dilatione certiores, hoc breue nobis remittentes. Teste &c. When the Shirife or Iustice or Iustices of peace to whom the foresaid writ is directed, hath caused thrée proclamations to be made according to the purport of the said writ, then he or they may enter and make search in the house, houses, or place suspected, and search whether there bee any force of armour or weapons worne, borne, or vsed against the said proclamation, or otherwise he is warranted by the said writ to inquire thereof by a Iurie. And if any such armour or weapons be found, he must imprison the offendors, and seise and praise their armour and weapons so found with them to the Kings vse. And if vpon the proclamation they doe depart in peaceable manner, then he hath no warrant by the writ to commit them to prison. But by this writ the Shirife or Iustices haue onely authority to remoue the force, but not to put the party expelled in possession againe. S. Manasse &c. 7.

What shalbe said to be force

29 Because I haue written of force, forcible entry, and forcible detaining of possession, it is conuenient that I should somewhat declare, what the law doth accompt to be force, and what acts, and in what manner done to be forcible. This forcible entry or forcible detaining of possession, which the statutes before rehearsed do prohibite, must be done with somé weapons either offẽsiue or defensiue, as with swords, bucklers, pykes, iauelines, bills, clubs, pitchforkes, staues, halberts, bowes & arrowes, crossebowes, gunnes, harneys, casting of stones or blocks, pouring of hot coales, scalding water, or lead, or with any other thing wherewith one man may hurt the person of another. And further, if a man doth enter vpon the possession of another, or doth kéepe a possession taken with more seruants or attendants, then he doth cõmonly maintaine, it is force, and it shalbe adiudged in him a forcible entry, or a forcible detaining of possession. And so it is, if diuers do come with bowes, bills, gunnes, or other weapons to a ground, or to a house, and enter without the disturbance of any, this is an entry by force: for the words of the statute of 5. R. 2. be, That none shall enter with multitude of people, but only in a peaceable manner. And in like

Force by number of seruants. 10. H. 7. 11.

Sta. 5. R. 2. 7

like sort, if a man doe enter peaceably into a house, and after doth bring into the same more weapons then he and his ordinary family do commonly & usually weare (besides those weapons that he doth find in the house, whereof he must make no use to defend his possession) it is a forcible detaining of possession. And moreouer, if complaint be made to a Justice of peace, that one hath entred forcibly into a house, and doth detaine the same with force, and the said Justice of peace doth goe thither, and findeth the dores shut, and him or those within denying him to enter, this is a detayning of possession with force, though there be no weapon shewed or used, and though there be but one person within ẏ house, for in this case the offendor doth use the dore as his buckler to keepe the possession. If the Justice of peace doe find in the house any great number of people, or any persons in harneis, or hauing harneis lying by them, this is a detainer with force. Wherefore in all the cases aforesaid the Justice of peace may take the power of the County, breake open the dores, & commit the offendors to prison. And if a man do mowe, reape, sheare, or sickle corne or grasse (or by such other labor which cannot be done without the hands of man) wherunto he hath no title, this shalbe adiudged an entry & disseisin with force. If a man do keepe his beasts by force in another mãs seueral ground, claiming common therein, whereas he hath no common there, this is a disseisin of the land by force. And if a man do enter into the possession of another mans land, and after doth fell or lop wood there, this is a disseisin by force. If a man do enter into another mans house or land, & disseise or expel him thereof, & after doth carry away certaine goods of the disseisee, this is a disseisin with force & arms, and the disseisor shalbe imprisoned for it.

Force by nūber of weapōs. 11. Ass. p. 25. 27. Ass. p. 30. 30. Ass. p. 50. 11. H. 4. 16.

16. Assis. p. 7. 14. Ass. p. 18. 12. H. 4. 22. 22. Ass p. 33.

30 A woman couert may commit a disseisin with force, and be imprisoned therfore: and so may an infant of the age of 18. yeeres or aboue commit a disseisin by force, & be imprisoned. But if he be of tender age, he shal not be adiudged a disseisor with force, nor be imprisoned. Who may cōmit a forcible entry.

31 Though force being opposed against the law, is a professed enemy to the peace of the Realme, yet being used in the maintenance of the law, it is a principall protector of the same peace: for the law doth put the sword of iustice into the kings hand to protect himselfe and euery of his subiects from the violēce and oppression of others, and to relieue each one that hath iust cause of complaint, and thereby to yeeld him peace. Wherefore force is to be resembled to fire, which being abused, may consume the whole house, and being wel guided is a meane to yeeld sustenance and comfort to euery person therein. And so force may be lawfully used by all the kings Officers, Ministers, and Subiects thereunto deputed (with the helpe of all others to assist them when need shall require) to execute or aduance iustice, or the iudgements of the Law. It is lawfull force, wherby all offendors in Treason, Felony, & other great crimes, be apprehended, caried to prison, brought to their answers, & receiue condigne punishments, inflicted upon them for their offences. It is lawful force, wherby the Shirife, his Undershirife, Baylifes, or Deputies doe with strength apprehend any person by uertue of the kings writs, to answere or satisfie the purport of the same writs. It is lawfull force whereby Justices of peace doe remoue those unlawfull Entries, or unlawfull detainings of possession which one man doth make into another mans land, contrary to the Laws and Statutes abouesaid, and whereby they doe put him againe in possession, who was wrongfully disseised or expelled thereof. And it is lawfull force which Justices of What force is lawfull to the persons of mē. 7. E. 8. 16. St. 8. H. 6. 9.

of peace, Shirifes, Coroners, Constables, Tithingmen, Headboroughes, Boroughholders, & al other charged and authorized to preserue the peace (together with their assistants, deputies, or assignées) shall vse in apprehending or committing to prison such as doe attempt to disturbe or breake the peace within their iurisdictions, or being commanded, wil refuse to put in sufficient sureties for the kéeping of the same peace.

Where the house of a man may be broken by force, and where not.

32 As in the causes aforesaid force may be lawfully vsed to the persons of men, so in some other cases forces may be vsed, & forcible entries may be lawfully made into the lands and tenements of others. As for Treason, or Felony, or suspition of Felony, one may by force breake open a house, if the dores be shut, to apprehend the Felon: For as a Felon is an enemy to the Commonwealth, so is it for the benefit of the Commonwealth to apprehend him: And the King as head of the Cōmonwealth hath interest in felony to punish it, and so a house doth not defend an entry to pursue and arrest one that hath committed felony, or is suspected therof. 13.E.4.9. As if one hath wounded a man, whereby he is in perill of death, and the offendor doth flie into a house, the Constable or those that do pursue him, may breake open the house to apprehend him, if the dores be shut. 7.E.3.16. And in like sort, if a fray be made, or a quarrell be moued in a house, whereof the dores be shut, whereby the peace is broken, or like to be broken, the Shirife, a Iustice of peace, or a Constable may by force breake open the dore of the house to appease that quarrell, or to take surety of the offendors to kéepe the peace. And if a man be outlawed of Treason or Felony, or in a personall action, whereby a Capias vtlagatum is directed to the Shirife to apprehend and take him, the Shirife may breake open the dores of the house, if they be shut, apprehend the same Outlaw, and commit him to prison. And if it be found by an inquisition before a Iustice of peace, that one hath entred into another mans house by force, or doth detaine it by force after peaceable entry made, he may breake open the house by force to reseise the same land, and to put the party so put out in possession againe; and so may the Shirife doe, hauing the Iustices warrant. If a man be indited of Trespas, and a Capias pro fine is awarded to the Shirife to take him, the Shirife may breake open the house to take him, if the dores be shut. 27.Ass.p.35 And in all cases where the king is party, the Shirife may breake the house of the party offēding, or the house where he is, to apprehend him, or otherwise to execute the Kings proces, if the dores be not open, or that he cannot otherwise enter: Co.li.5.91. 13.Ed.4.9. for where the King hath interest, the writ or action is in the nature of a writ of Non omittas propter aliquam libertatem. But this is to be obserued, that alwaies before the Shirife or other Officer doth breake open the house or dores of any man, he must signifie the cause of his comming, and desire that the dore may be opened vnto him: Fitz.Execution 252. for if there be no default in the owner, the law doth condemne the breaking of a house, which was prouided for the dwelling and safetie of men. And therefore in any of the cases aforesaid, if the Shirife doe breake open the house, where some of the dores of the same be open, whereby he may enter, or that he may open the dore by the key, or without breaking, he is a Trespassor, and is chargeable therefore to the owner of the house in an action of Trespas. If one man doe distraine another mans cattell, and after doe put them into a Castle, Fortresse, or other strong hold, house, or place, and then the owner of the cattell doth sue a Repleuin directed to the Shirife, to make deliuery to him of yͤ same cattell: Sta.3.E.1.17 13.Ed.1.38. then if the same Castle, Fortresse, House, or Hold, be not opened to the Shirife vpon his solemne request, when he commeth to make deliuerance of

of the cattell, according to the purport of his writ, he may take the force and power of his County, and breake downe the same castle, fortresse, or house &c. and make deliuerance of the same cattell: for it would tend to the dishonor of the King & his Crowne, that the Shirife hauing the kings writ, should be resisted with force by any of his owne subiects to execute the same, and to make deliuerance of the cattell. When any house is recouered by one man against another in any reall action, or by an Eiectione firme, the Shirife hauing the K. writ of Habere facias seisinam or possessionē, may breake open the same house, if the dores be shut, to deliuer seisin or possession to the demaundant or plaintife: for after iudgement the house in right & by the censure of the law is none of the tenants or defendants. But it is not lawfull for the Shirife at the suit of any common person to breake the house of the defendant in the same suit, to execute proces (though he doe make request and be denied it) for thereupon might ensue great inconuenience, that vpon colour of any fained suit, a man should haue his house (being his castle of defence) broken by day or by night, by any Vndershirife or Baylife, being many times of small abilitie. And therfore if in that case the Shirife breake any mans house to make execution of any proces at the suit of a common person, he is a trespassor to the owner of the same house, who may haue an action of Trespas against him therefore, as against any other person, and shall recouer his dammages. But notwithstanding, the execution, which the said Shirife shall then and there make, is good. And yet the house of a man is a castle, and place of priuiledge, but for himselfe, his wife, seruants, and ordinarie resiants, and for his owne goods: for it will not protect any other man which will flie into his house, or the goods of any other person which shalbe brought into his house, to preuent lawfull execution, and to escape the ordinary proces of the law. And therefore in any of those cases, if the Shirife hauing proces to doe execution vpon the body or goods of a man, do make request to haue the dore opened, or to haue the body of the party flying thither, or the goods of another brought thither, to be deliuered vnto him, and it be denied him, or that it be not done, the Shirife may breake the house, and execute the proces.

Co.lib.5.91

18.E.4.4.

Co.li.5.93

33 As force is to be vsed lawfully, where it is for the benefit of the king, or to auaile the Commonwealth: so euery man being of himselfe a little world, & his family a small Commonwealth, & he the head thereof, may in diuers cases defend the same Commonwealth by force. As, if theeues or robbers do come to a mans house, to rob or murther him, he may defend his house by force, and if he or his seruants do kill any of them, they shall receiue no hurt thereby. And if a man being in his house, doe heare that another will come to his house to beat him, he may lawfully assemble his neighbors and friends, to assist and aid him in the defence of his person: for his house is his castle, and place of protection & defence, where he must dwell. But if a man be threatened, that if he come to such a Market or Fayre, or to such a place, that then he shall be beaten, in this case he may not assemble his neighbours and friends to go thither, in safegard of his person, for there is no necessitie that he should go thither, seeing it would rather be a meane to seeke a quarrell, then to eschew it: but in that case he may take his remedy by surety of peace. And if there be an attẽpt made to maihem, wound, or beat a man, his wife, father, mother, or any of his children within age, or to disseise him of his land, or to dispossesse him of his goods, or to disturbe him of his high way, or to turne an ancient watercourse from his mill, he may lawfully vse force to resist it.

Cok.lib.5. 91. 26.Ass.p.23 & 32. Fitz.Cor. 303.305. 22.Assise p. 55. St.24.H.8.5 21.H.7.39.

16.Ed.4.17. 9.E.4.28. 19.H.6.31. 6.H.7.1.

In what cases any person may defend himselfe and his by force.

34 As the law hath prouided by the before rehearsed statute of 15. R. 2. that whẽ any forcible entry shalbe made into any benefices or offices of the church, a Iustice of peace shall take the power of the county, and commit the offendors to the gaole: So hath it further deuised, that if there be debate betwæne two persons for one church, and one of them doth enter into the church with a great power of lay men, and holdeth out the other by force and armes, then he which is holden out, shall haue a writ of Vi laica remouenda directed to the Shirife, commaunding him that he shal remoue the power which is within the church: and the shirife shalbe further commaunded, that if he doe find any that doe resist, he shall take with him the power of the county, and attach the bodies of all the resisters, and commit them to prison, so that he may haue their bodies before the King at a certaine day to answer for their contempt. But by this writ the Shirife ought not to remoue the Incumbent, who is in possession of the church, be he in possession by right or wrong, but only to remoue the force, and to suffer the Incumbent to inioy his possession, for if he do remoue the Incumbent, the same Incumbent shall haue a writ to the Shirife, to restore him to it againe.

St. 15. R. 2. 2.

The writ of Vi laica remouenda to remoue force.

Fitz. Na. B. 55.

35 If the King do bring a Quare impedit against the disturber and the Incumbent, and the Kings title is found for him, whereupon his clarke is instituted by writ, and after the first Incumbent doth enter by force, & great number of people, and doth take the profits, the Kings Incumbent shall not haue the Kings writ to the Shirife to remoue the force, for that when the iudgemẽt giuen by the court is executed, the court hath no more power to deale in that cause. But if the defendant had disturbed the Bishop to admit the Kings Incumbent, then he should haue had such a writ.

Where force shal be remoued for the K. incumbent, where not.

Br. force 20

For-

Forgerie.

1 Hauing vndertaken to write of the great and generall maladies of the Realme, and the chiefe impediments of the iustice and peace of the kingdome, I shall not farre digresse from my theame, by treating of Forgerie, Periury, Maintenance, Deceit, Extortion, and Oppression, wherein though a man be not assaulted by the rapier and dagger, pike-staffe, or bilbow-blade, as he is in a fray, forcible entrie, or riot, yet a forged deed that conueyeth his land from him, a false othe which depriueth him of his lease, or vnlawfull mantenance that wresteth his credit or goods from him, do longer disturbe the peace of his mind, stick in his stomacke, and infixeth a deeper and more durable impression of sorrow into his heart, than a boxe on the eare, a dust in the necke, or a blow with a cudgell giuen on the sodaine, will doe: For the griefe of these later stripes is short, and doe weare out of mans mind by little and little, as his choller ceaseth, and his hot bloud cooleth: but the discontent, and the wants which he receiueth of the former blowes, doe continue with him, and yeeld him most dislike, when he is most patient, and best aduised. And therefore the wisedome of this Realme hath from age to age taken great care by lawes and statutes, to represse them, and to inflict vpon the offendors in euerie of them, penalties correspondent to their deserts. Our lawes doe chastise those that breake the peace by frayes, assaults, batteries, riots, or routs, with imprisonment of their bodies, vntill their hot blouds be cooled, and their distemperat humors be qualified: but they doe impose sharper and more durable punishments vpon such as doe forge deeds, commit or procure periurie, or bee maintainers of other mens suits, or quarels; accounting these last offences to tend more and for a longer time to the breach or blemish of the peace, or hinderance of the iustice of the Realme, than the former doe: As hee that committeth forgerie in some cases, shall bee set vpon the pillorie, lose his eares, haue his nostrels slit, and pay to the partie grieued his double costs and dammages: And in some other cases, shall be hanged as a felon: He that committeth periurie, shall in some cases be one yeare imprisoned, be set vpon the pillorie, and neuer after be allowed as a witnesse: And hee that maintaineth other mens suites, shall in some cases be three yeres imprisoned, and further punished at the kings pleasure: And in some other cases sustaine other disgraces. And therefore the preamble of the statute of anno 1.H.5. doth truely informe vs, that forged deeds do trouble and change the lands of good people, intending to be in peace. And the statute of anno 32.H.8. doth teach vs, that the suborning of witnesse for to maintain any matter or cause, is to yͤ disturbāce or hinderance of iustice.

Forgerie, periurie, & maintenance, doe tend to the breach of the peace.

St.1.H.5.3.

St.32.H.8.9

The enormity of Forgerie.

2 The forging of false sealed Deeds, Euidences, or Writings, or of Court Rols, or of the will of any person, or of any Obligation, Bill obligatorie, Release, or other discharge, or the pronouncing, publishing, or giuing in euidence of the same, wherby any person shalbe molested, troubled, charged, or defeated of his land, lease, annuitie, debt, accompt, action, suit, or demaund, is no lesse perillous and preiudiciall to the party thereby wronged (if it be not discouered, preuented, or auoided) then the wresting and euicting from him of the same land, lease, annuitie, debt, or demaund. And the offendors therein do as iniuriously, and with as small colour of iustice, wrest from the party grieued his said land, lease, annuitie, debt, &c. as the robber doth take a purse from the traueller by the way, or the burglarer his intended prey from the houskeeper in the night. And if those reall dueties or things in action, were conuerted into things personall, the vndue conueying of them in this vnlawfull manner, would deserue to be accounted and punished amongst other felonies; as in some sort it is ordained so to be by the statute of anno 5. Eliz. And because diuers persons did forge false deeds and miniments, and did cause them to bee openly pronounced, published, and read, to trouble, change, or vndoe the lands of other persons, and to vndoe and troble the possessions and titles of the kings people: therefore by a statute made anno 1. H. 5. it was ordained, that the partie grieued thereby, shall haue his suit in that case, and recouer his dammages, and the partie conuict shall make fine and ransome at the kings pleasure. But forasmuch as the wicked and daungerous practise of making, forging, and publishing of false and vntrue deeds and writings, was much more practised and put in vre, in all the parts of this Realme, than in times past it had beene, to the disherison of diuers persons, and the great subuersion of iustice, which hath growne chiefely by that the paines and punishments limited for such great offences, by the lawes and statutes of this Realme, before time were so small and easie, that such euill people were not afraid to enterprise the practising and doing of such offences: Therefore by a statute made anno 5. El. it was enacted, That all other statutes before that time made and prouided for forger of false deeds, charters, miniments, or writings, and all and euerie penaltie appointed for the same, should from the first day of Iune then next following, be void.

St. 5. El. 14.

St. 1. H. 5. 3.

The repeale of former statutes of Forgerie.

St. 5. El. 14.

Forging of a deed, whereby anothers freehold shalbe troubled.

3 To the intent that condigne, or some sharper punishment might bee ordained for such as should bee offenders in that crime of forgerie, than in time past had beene, by the sayd statute of anno 5. Elizab. it was established, That if any person or persons after the first day of Iune then next following, vpon his or their owne head and imagination, or by false conspiracie and fraud with others, shall wittingly, subtilly, and falsly, forge, or make, or subtilly cause, or wittingly assent to bee forged or made, any false deed, charter, or writing sealed, court roll, or the will of any person or persons in writing, to the intent that the estate of Freehold or inheritance of any person or persons, of, in, or to any lands, tenements, or hereditaments, freehold or copihold, or the the right, title, or interest of any person or persons, of, in, or to the same, or any of them, shall or may bee molested, troubled, defeated, recouered, or charged: Or shall pronounce, publish, or shew forth in euidence, any such false and forged deed, charter, writing, court roll, or will, as true, knowing the same to bee false and forged, as is aforesaid, to the intent aboue remembred, and shall bee thereof conuicted, either vpon any action or actions of Forger of false deeds, to bee foun-

St. 5. El. 14.

Publishing of a forged deed.

ded

ded vpon this statute, at the suit of the partie grieued, or otherwise according to the order and course of the lawes of this Realme, or vpon Bill or Information to be exhibited into the Court of Starrechamber, according to the order and vse of the Court, he shall pay vnto the partie grieued his double costs and dammages, to bée found or assessed in the Court where such conuiction shall bée, and also shall be set vpon the Pillorie in some open market towne, or other open place, and there to haue both his eares cut off, and also his nostrels to be slit, and cut, and seared, so as they may remaine for a perpetuall note or marke of his falshood, and shall forfeit to the Queene her heires and successors, the whole issues and profits of his lands and tenements during his life, and shall suffer and haue perpetuall imprisonment during his life. The same dammages and costs to bée recouered at the suit of the partie grieued, as is aforesaid, to be first paid, and bee leuied of the goods and cattels of the offendors, and of the issues and profits of the said landes, tenements, and hereditaments of such partie conuicted, or of one, or both of them, the sayd title of the Queene, her heires and successors to the same notwithstanding.

Stat.5,El.14 4 If any person or persons after the said first day of June next, vpon his or their owne imagination, or by false conspiracie, or fraud, had with any other, shall wittingly, subtilly, and falsly, forge or make, or wittingly, subtilly, or falsly, cause or assent to bee made and forged, any false Charter, Deed, or Writing, to the intent that any person or persons shall or may haue or clayme any estate or interest, for terme of yeares, of, in, or to any Mannours, Lands, Tenements, or Hereditaments (not beeing Copihold) or any Annuitie in Fee simple, Fee tayle, for terme of life, liues, or yeares: Or shall, as is aforesayd, forge, make, or cause or assent to bee made or forged any Obligation, or Bill obligatorie, or any Acquitance, Release, or other discharge of any Debt, Account, Action, Suit, Demaund, or other thing personall: Or shall pronounce, publish, or giue in euidence, such false or forged Charter, Déed, Writing, Obligation, or Bill obligatorie, or any Acquitance, Release, or discharge, as true, knowing the same to bee false and forged, and shall bee thereof conuict by any of the wayes or meanes aforesayde: Then hee shall pay to the partie grieued his double costs and dammages, to bee found and assessed in such Court where the sayde conuiction shall bée had, and also shall bee set vpon the Pillorie in some open Market Towne, or other open place, and there haue one of his eares cut off, and also shall suffer imprisonment by the space of one whole yere, without baile or mainprise.

Forging a déed, whereby a lease or annuitie may bee claimed.

Stat.5,El.14 5 The partie and parties grieued by reason of any the offences aforesaid, shall and may at his and their pleasure haue and sue his action of forger of false déedes, vpon this Statute against any of the offendors in the same, by originall writ out of the Chauncerie, and shall haue like Proces vpon the same, as in cases of trespas at the common law; Or may at his pleasure take his suite against any such offendors in any the premisses by Bill in the Kinges Bench, or in the Exchequer: In which sutes no Essoine,

Seuerall remedies for the partie grieued.

Forgerie.

Iniunction, or Protection shall be allowed for the party Defendant.

Not twice impeached for one offence.

6 If the Defendant shall be conuict for any of the offences aforesaid, ac- St.5.Eli.14.
cording to the order and forme aboue limited, and shall haue receiued thereupon punishment corporall according to this Act, then he shall not eftsoones be impeached for the same offence.

The plaintifs release shal onely discharge his owne remedy.

7 Although the partie or parties plaintife in any such Action, or Bill to be St.5.Eli.14.
sued as is aforesaid, shall after verdict past against the Defendant, or Defendants, happen to release or discharge the iudgement or execution vpon the same, or otherwise suffer the same to be discontinued: yet neuerthelesse the same release, discharge, or discontinuance, shall extend onely to discharge such costs and dammages as the same plaintife should haue had against the defendant; And the Iudges before whom the said action or suite shall be taken, shall and may proceede to iudgement of and vpon the residue of the said penalties, and forfeitures, and commaund execution vpon the same, the saide release, discontinuance, or other discharge had, made, done, or suffered by the partie plaintife in any wise notwithstanding.

The punishment for the second offence.

The right of others saued.

No forfeiture of Dower or corruption of blood.

8 If any person or persons being hereafter conuicted, or condemned of a- St.5.Eli.14.
ny of the offences aforesaid, by any of the wayes or meanes aboue limited, shall after any such his or their conuiction or condemnation eftsoones commit or perpetrate any of the said offences in forme aforesaide: Then euery such second offence or offences shall be adiudged felony, and the parties being conuicted or attainted according to the lawes of this Realme, shall suffer paines of death, losse and forfeiture of their goods, cattels, lands, and Tenements, as in cases of felony by the common lawes of this Realme ought to be lost or forfeited, without hauing any aduantage or benefit of Clergie or Sanctuarie: Sauing to euery person and persons, body politique and corporate, their heires and successors (other than the said offendors, and such as claime to their vses) all such rights, titles, interests, possessions, liberties of distresses, leases, rents, reuersions, offices, and other profits and aduantages, which they or any of them shall haue at the time of such conuiction, or attainder, of, in, or to any the lands, tenements, or hereditaments of any such person, so as is aforesaid conuicted or attainted, or at any time before, in as large & ample maner, to all intents and purposes, as if this Act had neuer bin made. Prouided alwayes, that any such conuiction or attainder of felony as is aforesaid, or any forfeiture by reason of the same, shall not in any wise extend to take away the dower of the wife of any such person attainted, nor to the corruption of blood, or disherison of any the heire or heires of any such person or persons so attainted: This Act or any thing therein contained, or any other statute, law, or custome notwithstanding.

Iustices of Oire and Determiner and Iustices of Assise.

9 All and euery Iustices of Oire and Determiner, and Iustices of Assise St.5.Eli.14.
in their circuits, and euery of them shall haue full power and authoritie in euery of their open and generall Sessions, to inquire, heare, and determine of all and euery of the offences aforesaid, committed or done within the limits of their Commission, and to make Processe for the execution of the same,

as

as they may do against any person beeing indicted before them of Trespasse, or lawfully conuicted thereof.

Stat. 5. El. 14 10 If any person or persons whatsoeuer hath of his or their owne head, or by false conspiracie or fraud with any other, wittingly, subtilly, and falsly, forged or made, or shall before the first day of June next comming, forge and make any false déed, charter, or writing sealed, or the will of any person in writing, or any court roll, to the intent that the estate of Freehold or inheritance, or the right, title, or interest of inheritance or freehold of any persons, of, in, or to any Mannors, lands, tenements, or hereditaments, being freehold or copihold: Or that by any such forged déed, charter, court roll, or writing, before the said first day of June, shall or may be molested, troubled, or defeated of any of the said estates of any lands, tenements, or hereditaments being fréehold or Copihold: Or if any person or persons haue heretofore published or shewed forth in euidence, or before the said first day of June shall publish or shew in euidence, for the prowfe of any title, any false and forged déed, charter, writing, will, or Court Roll, as true, knowing the same to be false and forged as aforesaid, to the intent aboue remembred, and shall be thereof attainted or conuicted according to the order of the law, either in an Action of forger of false faits, or in an Action vpon the case, at the sute of the party grieued, his heirs, executors or assignes: Then the party so conuicted shall yielde and pay dammages, and costs of sute to the plaintife, as shall be assessed according to the law of the Realme, in any such like Action or sute, and shall suffer imprisonment, and pay fine and ransome at the pleasure of the Quéene, her heires, or Successors. And if any person or persons shall after the said first day of June next comming, pleade, publish, or shew forth in euidence, or otherwise for the prowfe of any title, any false and forged déed, charter, writing, will, or Court Roll heretofore falsly made and forged, or to be falsly made and forged before the said first day of June as true, knowing the same to be false and forged, to the intent to haue or claime thereby any estate of inheritance, fréehold, or lease of yeares, in, or to any mannors, lands, tenements, or hereditaments, or any annuitie, rent, or profit forth of any mannors, lands, tenements, or hereditaments: Or to the intent to alter, defeate, molest, trouble, charge, or recouer the estate of inheritance, fréehold, or lease for years of any person, in any mannors, lands, tenements, rents, or hereditaments: Then euery person and persons that so shall offend, and shall be thereof conuicted in forme first aboue remembred, shall pay vnto the partie grieued double costs and dammages, and shall haue imprisonment, losse of Eares, slitting and searing of Nose, and forfeiture of lands in the same maner and forme as aboue is limited for any person that shall offend by forging or publishing of any false déede, or writing, as aforesaid, after the said first day of June.

Forging of deeds before the statute.

Pleading a forged deed made before the statute.

Stat. 5. El. 14 11 This Act or any thing therein contained, shall not extend to charge any Ordinarie, or any their Commissaries, Officials, Registers, or any other their Officers, or Ministers, with any the offences aforesaid, for putting their seale of office to any will to be exhibited vnto them, not knowing the same to be false or forged: or for writing of the said will, or probate of the same. Neither shall this Act or any thing therein contained, extend or be hurtfull to any Proctor, Aduocate, or Register of any Ecclesiasticall Court within this realm, for

Persons not chargeable by this statute.

for the writing, setting forth, or pleading of any Proxie made according to the Ecclesiasticall lawes or customes heretofore allowed and vsed by the Ecclesiasticall Courts of this Realme, for the apparance of any person or persons, beeing cited to appeare in any of the said Courts Ecclesiasticall: Nor to any Archdeacon, or Officall, for putting their authentique seale to the said proxies, or proxie: Nor yet to any Iudge Ecclesiasticall, for admitting of the same: but they and euerie of them may hereafter doe in all poynts concerning the same, as they and euerie of them might lawfully haue done before the making of this Act. Neither shall this Act extend to any Attourney, Lawyer, or Counsellor, that shall for his client plead, shew forth, or giue in euidence, any false and forged deed, charter, will, court roll, or other writing, for true, being not partie nor priuie to the forging of the same, for the pleading, shewing forth, or giuing in euidence of the same. Neither shall this Act extend to any person or persons, that shall plead or shew forth any deed or writing exemplified vnder the great Seale of England, or vnder the great seale of any other authentique Court of this Realme. Nor shall extend to any Iudge or Iustice, or other person that shall cause any seale of any Court to bee set to any such deed, charter, or writing inrolled, not knowing the same to bee false and forged: Any thing in this Act to the contrarie notwithstanding.

Officiall. Attourney. Counsellor. Exemplification. A Iudge. A Iustice.

Forging of a customarie booke. — *15.Eliz.Dy. 322.*

12 If one or more tenants of a Mannor, wherein there bee seuerall Copiholders, doe make a customarie booke or roll of the same Mannor, in parchment, or paper, and doe insert therein diuers customes, whereof some be false, and doe set his or their owne seales thereunto, and the seales of some other Copiholders of the same Mannour, and the same customarie booke or roll is intituled and pretended to be collected, renewed, set forth and allowed by the Lord, and all the Freeholders and Copiholders of the said Mannour, where in truth it is set forth and made without the priuitie or consent of the Lord of the same Mannour, or of the residue of the Copiholders thereof: This is a forgerie, and false making of a writing sealed, to the intent to benefit themselues, and to disinherit the Lord of the Mannor, and therefore punishable by the open and shamefull punishment contained in the foresayd Statute of 5. Elizab.

The proces to leuie costs and damages of a forger. — *15.Eliz. Dyer 323.*

13 Whereas the sayd Statute of 5.Elizabeth. hath ordayned, That if any person shall bee conuicted or forging of a false deed vpon a bill, or information to bee exhibited into the Court of the Starre chamber, according to the order and vse of the Court, hee shall pay vnto the partie grieued his double costs and dammages, to bee assessed in the same Court: Therefore when any man is attainted of Forgerie in the Starre chamber, for the recouerie of the double costs and dammages taxed by the Court a writ in English shall bee made, and directed to the Sherife of the Countie where the offendor doth dwell, reciting the Statute, and the conuiction, commaunding the Sherife to leuie the said costs and dammages of the goods, cattels, and profits of the lands and tenements of the offendor, and to bring the money into the Starre chamber: Which writ shall bee sealed with the great Seale, and vnder the Teste of the King. And there by the order of the Court the money shall be deliuered to the partie grieued.

The kings pardon of forgerie. — *15.Eliz. Dyer 323. Co.li.5.50.*

14 If a man be attainted of Forgerie in the Starre Chamber, or in an action of Forger of false deeds, founded vpon the said statute of 5.Eliz. the king may

may pardon his corporall punishment of setting vpon the pillorie, slitting his nostrels, and perpetuall imprisonment, viz. so much of the penaltie of the sayd statute, as is to be inflicted for a terrour or example to his people, for that hée onely hath interest therein, as hée hath in the issues and profits of the said offendors lands. And as he may pardon the second offence of him, who béeing once conuicted of forgerie, doth eftsones commit the same againe, and thereby doth become a felon: And as the plaintifes release, discharge, or discontinuance, by the words of the said statute, shall discharge the defendants iudgement or execution touching such costs and dammages, as the plaintife should haue had against the defendant: So may the kings pardon discharge the same defendant of any penaltie or forfeiture, that the same statute doth giue vnto him, which be the corporall punishments, and the issues and profits of the defendants lands.

13.El. Dy. 302. 15 Whereas the said Statute of 5. Elizab. hath ordained, That if any shall forge the will of any person in writing, to the intent &c. That then hée shall be punished as is aforesaid: Yet if one do forge the Testament of another person, whereby any lease for yeares shall bée conueyed, hée is within the danger and penaltie of the said statute, though no mention bee made in the statute of a Testament, and he shall be charged onely in respect that hée hath forged a writing sealed. But of a will concerning fréehold, or inheritance, there is speciall mention made in the same statute. Forging of a Testament.

12. Eliz. Dyer 288. 16 If a Clerke doe write the will of another man which is deadly sicke (and after the Testator is become speechlesse, and past memorie) doth insert some article or clause in the same will, which the Testator did not direct him to doe, yet this is no forgerie punishable by the sayd statute of 5. El. nor within the meaning of the makers of the same: For the principall déed or writing, which was the wil of the Testator, was not forged, neither was any false déed, charter, writing, or will, though the article or clause inserted therein, hauing no sufficient warrant, was false, and therefore not the Testators wil, nor part thereof, nor to be proued therewith. Inserting more in a will than is directed.

17 And though the said statute of 5. Eliz. doth repeale as well the before mentioned statute of 1. H. 5. and all other statutes before that time made and prouided for forging of false deeds, and hath ordained a new action of forger of false deeds, to be founded vpon that Statute, and other new remedies, yet seeing both those statutes were made and prouided to one end, viz. to auoid and punish the enormities of forgerie of false deeds, to the disherison or hurt of others, though vpon seuerall penalties: Notwithstanding in some cases the like reason, and so the same law is to be retained in the said statute of 5. Elizab. which was before in the first mentioned statute of 1. H. 5. As in action of Forger of false deeds, brought vpon the said statute of 1. H. 5. it is a góod plea in barre, for the defendant to plead not guiltie, or that he did not forge that deed, or to plead, that he gaue to the plaintife a gallon of wine in satisfaction of the said offence, which he did accept. And so it is a good plea in barre, in an action of forger of false deeds, brought vpon the statute of 5. Elizab. and the same plea being confessed by the plaintife, or found by verdict, shall not onely barre the plaintife of the recouerie of his double costs and dammages, but shall also discharge the defendant of all corporall punishments to be inflicted, and of the forfeiture of the issues and profits of his land to the king. For this is not a release

Lib. int. fol. 359.

9. H. 6. 26. 20. H. 6. 11. 19. H. 6. 29. 21. H. 7. 15. 37. H. 6. 37.

Pleas in barre of forgerie.

lease or discharge after verdict, but a discharge before verdict, whereby the whole Action and sute is discharged, and so not within the compasse of the said statute of 5.Eliz.14. touching the plaintifes release or discharge after verdict.

Where one shall haue an Action of forgery, though he hath but a right to the land.

18 There be some cases where a man shall haue an Action of forger of false déeds, though he hath neither possession, reuersion, or remainder, but onely a title to the land. As if a man die seised of certaine land, and a stranger doth abate, and enter vpon the same land before the entrie of the heire, and holdeth out the heire, and after the same abator doth forge some charter, deed, or other writing sealed of the same land, to the intent to disturbe, trouble, or defeate the estate of the heire in the same, in this case the heire may haue an Action of forger of false deeds against the same stranger, though he hath then no possession, reuersion, or remainder in the same land. And so it is, if one man doe disseise another man of land, and after doth forge false deedes &c. of the same land, to the intent aforesaid, the disseisee may maintaine an action of forger of false deeds against the disseisor vpon the Statute of 5.Elizab. as he might haue done before vpon the Statute of 1.H.5. for that his right and title to the same land is molested, troubled, defeated, recouered, or charged by the same forged deed. And the same law is, if a man doe bring a reall Action against an other of certaine land, and before iudgement one claiming a lease for the terme of yeares of the same land, praieth to be receiued to saue his terme according to the Statute of Glocester, and doth shew his said lease, which lease is forged: In this case the Demandant in the saide Action may haue a writ of forger of false deedes, against him that claimeth the said terme, though he hath as yet nothing in possession, reuersion, or remainder in the same land, but onelie a right, for this lease is forged to the intent to defeate him of his right, viz. of his present possession.

4.H.6.25. 22.H.6.15. 15.Ed.4.24. 9.Ed.4.37. Stat.6.Ed.1 11.

Where no Title no Action of forgerie.

19 If a man hath neither possession, reuersion, remainder, or title, of, in, or to land, and yet will bring against another an Action of forger of false deedes of the same land, it is a good plea in barre for the defendant to pleade, that hée himselfe is seised of the same land, without that the plaintife hath any thing therein: for if the plaintife hath nothing in the freehold, or inheritance of the land, nor any estate for yeares, copihold or annuity in the same, then he cannot be the party grieued in that Action, neither his right, title, or interest, of, in, or to the same can be molested, troubled, or defeated, recouered or charged. And the same law is, if a man hath in land no mediate or immediate estate expectant vpon any lease or leases for life, liues, or yeares, nor profit, right of entry, but onely a possibilitie: As if A. doe giue land to B. and the heires of his body lawfully begotten, the remainder thereof to C. and his heires for euer: If E. doe forge a deed containing that A. gaue the same land to the said B. & the heires of his body lawfully begotten, the remainder thereof to him the said E. and his heires for euer: In this case C. cannot pursue an Action of forger of false deedes against E. during the liues of B. or of any of the heires of his body lawfully begotten, for the said forgery, séeing that during the said time, his right, title, or interest into that land is not molested, troubled, defeated, recouered, or charged, for that he hath therein during that time but onely a possibilitie, which possibilitie it may be shall neuer come into Esse. And further, C. cannot for the said forgery recouer double costs and dammages according to

21.H.6.51. 8.H.6.34. 33.H.6.22.

No Action in respect of a possibilitie.

to the said Statute of 5. Eli. for that he is not as yet a partie grieued, nor dammified, nor hath sustained any dammages, neither peraduenture euer shall, if B. and his heires doe continue from one generation to another, and not die without issue of their bodies, &c. And of a bare possibilitie no value can be made, neither single or double dammages assessed.

18.H.6.5. 9.H.6.26. Kel.fol.114 20 If there be two Ioyntenants, or tenants in common of land, and a stranger doth forge a deede concerning the same land: if one of those Ioyntenants, or tenants in common doe bring an Action of forger of false deedes against the offender, and the Defendant doe pleade that another hath an estate in Ioyntenancie, or in common with the plaintife who is in full life, this writ shall abate: for seeing this Action is but in the nature of an Action of Trespas, wherein the plaintifes are onely to recouer dammages, Ioyntenants and tenants in common must ioyne in the same Action, for though their right in the land be seuerall, yet their possession touching the profit thereof is ioynt. And this Action is founded vpon the possession. And whereas both the Statute of 1.H.5. and 5. Eliz. doe ordaine that the partie and parties grieued, shall and may at his and their pleasure, haue and sue this Action of forger of false deedes, in this case both the Ioyntenants and tenants in common be the parties grieued, for that their land is molested, troubled, recouered or charged by this forged deed. But if there be two Ioyntenants or tenants in common of certaine land, and one of them doth forge a false Release, or other Deede, whereby the whole land is intended to be conueied to himselfe, in this case the other Ioyntenant or, &c. may haue an Action of forger of false deeds against his said ioyntenant or, &c. for that forged and false deede was made, to the intent that the right or title of the forgers companion in estate should be molested, troubled, defeated, or recouered. And in this case he is the partie grieued, to whose onely disherison the said forgery doth trench. Forging of a deed touching ioyntenants land. Fitzh. Forger.5.

21.H.6.4. 21 In an Action of forger of false deedes, the Defendant pleaded that the Plaintife being seised of certaine land, did couenant with a stranger to enfeoffe him of the same land, whereupon the same stranger came to the defendant being a Clerk, and requested him to make a deed of feoffment of the same land, which he did: and after by the plaintifes commaundement he sealed the same deede, and after did reade the deede at the time of the liuerie and seisin, which is the same forgerie, and proclamation: and that was adiudged a good Plea: for when the defendant sealed the feoffement by the plaintifes commaundement, and in his presence, it was the plaintifes owne act and deede, and his owne sealing, and not the defendants: for the plaintife did vse the defendants hand but as his instrument therein: as men vnlearned doe vse an others mans hand to helpe or direct them, to subscribe their names to a Deede. One sealeth a deed by an others commaundement.

9.H.6.26. 7.H.6.34. 22 If the father do forge a deede, and after dieth, and then his sonne doth find the same deede, and doth pronounce, publish, or shew forth in euidence the same deede, knowing the same to be false and forged, to the intent the estate of freehold or inheritance of any person of, in, or to any lands, &c. should be molested, troubled, defeated, or recouered: this is forgerie in the sonne, and he shall be punished according to the foresaid Stat. of 5. El. And the same law is if one man One forgeth and another doth publish.

man do forge a deed, or &c. and an other man knowing thereof shall publish it, to any of the intents aforesaid: this is forgerie prohibited by the same statute: for the same stat. of 5. Eliz. is in the disiunctiue, viz. if any person shall forge or publish.

Forgerie by antedating of a deed

23 If a man doe make a feoffement to one person of certaine land, and doth deliuer possession therof accordingly, and after he doth make a feoffement to another person of the same land, bearing date before the first feoffement, but doth not deliuer it, this last feoffement is not the feoffors deed: But yet if hee do publish it to be his deed, the first feoffee may haue an action of forger of false deeds against him: for when he had made the first feoffement of the land, hee then had nothing left in him of the same land. And therefore when hee made the second antedated deed of that land, it was a false and forged deed, and then after publishing, pronouncing, or shewing it forth to be his deed, it was with intent to molest, trouble, defeat, recouer, or charge the land of the first and lawfull feoffee, and so he is punishable according to the foresaid stat. of 5. El. as hee was before by the stat. of 1. H. 5. 27. H. 6. 3.

24 Though the foresaid two statutes of 1. H. 5. and 5. Eliz. were ordained to punish those who should forge any false deed, or &c. to the intent, to molest, trouble, charge, or recouer the right or title of any person in his lands, tenements, or hereditaments, or to the intent that any person should claime any lease for yeares, or annuitie, or should forge any Obligation, Bill obligatorie, Release, Acquitance, or other discharge of any debt, account, action suit, demaund, or other thing personall: yet was there no prouision in either of them to punish those who should get into their hands any money, goods, cattels, iewels, or things of any other persons, by colour of a false token, or forged or counterfeit letter: for the redresse whereof by a statute made anno 33. H. 8. it was St. 33. H. 8. 1.
enacted, That if any person or persons, of what estate or degree soeuer hee or they be, shall falsely and deceitfully obtaine or get into his or their hands or possession, any money, goods, cattels, iewels, or other things, of any other person or persons, by colour or meanes of any false toke, or counterfeit letter, made in another mans name, that then euerie such person & persons so offending, & being thereof lawfully conuict by witnesses taken before the L. Chauncelor of England for ye time being, or by examination of witnesses, or confession taken in the Star chamber before the K. honorable Counsel, or before the Iust. of Assise in their circuits for the time being, or before the Iust. of peace within any part of the K. dominions, in their generall Sessions, or by action in any of the K. courts of record, shal haue & suffer such correction, & punishment by imprisonment of his body, setting vpō the pillorie or otherwise, by any corporal pain (except pain of death) as shalbe vnto him or them limited, adiudged, or appointed by the person and persons before whom he shalbe so conuicted of the said offences, or any of them.

Getting of other mens goods by counterfeit tokens or letters.

Suspected persons called before the Iustices.

25 As wel the Iust. of Assise for the time being, as also ij. Iust. of peace in euerie countie, wherof one to be of ye Quorū, shal haue power & authoritie, to call and conuent by proces, & otherwise, to the said Assises or generall sessions any person or persons, being suspected of any of ye aforesaid offences, & to cōmit him or thē to ward, or to let him or thē to baile vntil ye next Assises or general sessiōs, there to be examined, and further to be ordered by their discretions, as is abouesayd: Prouided alwayes, that the Iustices of peace within euerie Citie, St. 33. H. 8. 1.

Borough,

Borough, Towne, and Franchise within this Realme, or other the kings dominions, shall haue like iurisdiction, power and authoritie, at their generall Sessions, and otherwise, to do and execute all and euerie thing and things in all points, as other Iustices of Assise in their circuits, or Iustices of peace in the Counties, by vertue of this Act be limited and appointed to do and execute for the punishment and correction of like offendors, as beforesaid is limited. Sauing to the partie grieued by such deceit, such remedie, by way of action, or otherwise, of & for the same money, goods, cattels, iewels, or other things so obtained, as he might haue had, if this Act had neuer bin made. Any thing in this Act &c. notwithstanding. *The remedie of the partie grieued.*

26 Forgerie of writings hath béene alwayes so hatefull in this realme, that our law-makers haue pursued the practisers therof with sharpe and bitter punishment, though in some cases the same was not put in vse to molest or euict any man of his land, lease, annuitie, debt, account, action, suit, or other demaund, nor to get into his hands any others goods, cattels, or iewels, but only to escape the ordinance and censure of the law: As, by a statute made anno 5. Eliz. it is established, That no person retained in husbandry, or in certain inferior arts or faculties (in the said statute mentioned) shal depart out of one citie, towne, or parish, into another, nor out of the Lathe, Rape, Wapentake, or Hundred, nor out of the County or Shire where he last serued, to serue in another Citie, Towne, &c. vnlesse he haue a Testimoniall of the said Citie or towne corporat from whence he departed, or of the Constable or other officer, &c. And if any such person shall be taken with any counterfeit or forged testimoniall, then he shalbe whipped as a vagabond. *St. 5. El. 7.* *Forging of a testimoniall.*

Per-

Periurie, Subornation of witnesses.

Truth tried by the othes of men.

1 The Law of the Realme desirous to trie out truth in all causes called in question before her, to the end she might procéed in iudgement, and execute iustice accordingly, hath in all ages prooued it to bee the best meanes to search out this truth by the othes of honest, lawful, and indifferent persons: intending that the man who doth professe God to bee his Creator, Redéemer, and Sanctifier, and hopeth to be saued by his blood, when hee doth come in the presence of that God, and his people, and doth aduisely sweare, that he will declare the trueth, according to his knowledge, in that matter in question, as God shall help him: (which is to say, as he will expect the blessing of God in this life, and eternall saluation in the life to come) is void of all partialitie and priuat affection, in all respects to be credited, and will tell the whole truth, and nothing but the truth. And therefore an othe is aptly termed Sacramentum, a holy band, or sacred tie, or godly vow: some do call it firmamẽtum veritatis, the foundation & ground of truth; and some other, vinculum pacis, a meane of the knot or lincke of peace. And if it be taken and found by a whole Iurie, consisting vpon twelue persons or aboue, it is called veredictum, viz. a presentment of truth. And others doe hold it a ceremonie instituted by God, wherein himselfe is a partie, and therefore he will see it verified, or sharply punished. Wée know, that the proofe of most of our acts, déeds, and writings, doe depend vpon the othes of others, and whatsoeuer men do for their owne particular account most certaine, is altogether in most cases vncertaine, vnlesse it may be iustified by the othes of others. As if one doe commit murder, rape, burglarie, robberie, or other offence whatsoeuer, and it be denied and cannot be prooued by the othe of some other, the offendor shall escape vnpunished for it. And likewise if a man do buy land of another, if the feoffor doe make him a déed of feoffement thereof, do seale and deliuer it, and giue him possession, and after will denie it, vnlesse it can be prooued by the othe of some other, the feoffée shall loose his land and money. And so it is of leases, annuities, releases, acquitances, obligations, bargaines, contracts, couenants, promises, offences, entries, disseisins, and other matters in fait, if they be denied, trauersed, and called in question, the proof and validitie of them doth depend wholly vpon the othes and testimonie of others. And there is no case so plaine, which commeth in question betweene partie and partie, but one of

The credit of an othe.

of the parties to the sute may pleade such a plea as shall come to be tried by the othes of others.

2 Therefore as the Lawe doth reuerently respect the othes of men, taketh her intelligence of matters in fait from them, doth cleaue & leane vnto them, and giueth such credite and approbation vnto them, that shée doth found and build her iudgements in most cases of greatest importance vpon them: So shée retaineth a vigilant and carefull eye, that those othes be taken by men of sinceritie of life, and maturitie of iudgement, persons not stained with Periurie, or other gréeuous or foule offences, men indifferently affected, and such as will in swearing respect the trueth of their knowledge, and not the face of the person: for if shée espie any of those defects in him, she doth either wholly reiect his othe, or else shée giueth little or no credite vnto it, and further inflicteth condigne punishment vpon him, according to his desert. What sorts of persons are to be deposed.

Mag. Char. 9. H. 3. 29. 3 And because the King himselfe at his Coronation is sworne, that iustice shall be solde, deferred, or denied to no man: nor that any man shall be condemned but by lawfull triall: and euery of his Iudges be sworne, that

Sta. 18. Ed. 3 hée shall doe equall Lawe and execution of iustice to all the Kings Subiects, rich and poore, without hauing regard to any person: Therefore the law hath deuised that those Iudges before whome any cause is called in question, and is brought to an issue, shall be informed of the trueth of that issue, by the othes and verdict of twelue Iurors, who are impannelled, returned, and sworne to trie that issue, to the end the same Iudges may ground their iudgement thereupon, and so doe equall iustice to the parties, according to their oathes: and also that the saide Iurors shall be ascertained of the veritie of the fact, by the Othes of witnesses, or other euidences, that they may giue their verdict thereupon, according to their Othes. And séeing those Iurors being the greatest number of persons that be vsually sworne, for the furtherance and execution of iustice, be returned by the Shiriffe of the Countie where the cause dependeth in question, his vndershirife, or the Bailife of some Libertie, or for some default in them, by the Coroners: Therefore the Lawe hath further ordained, that the saide Shiriffe, Vndershiriffe, or &c. shall be indifferent persons of themselues, and also deale vprightly in returning of those Iurors, lest by their partialitie, Truth may be concealed, Periurie committed, and so iustice subuerted. And for that cause the prouidence of the Lawe doth not allow that Shiriffe, Vndershiriffe, Bailiffe of Franchise, Coroner, or other person as indifferent, or méete to impannell a Iurie, who is a partie to the sute or matter in question: or who doth maintaine either of the parties plaintife, or defendant in the same sute: or is of councell with either of them in that sute then in issue: Nor who is within the distresse, receiueth the yéerely fée, or weareth the liuerie or robe of any of the parties to that sute: Nor who is of kinred by nature, or of affinitie by marriage, to any of the parties to that sute: Nor who doth returne that Enquest, or any of the Iurors therein, at the denomination, or by the procurement of any of the parties to the same sute, or of any other person whatsoeuer: Nor who doth impannell that Enquest, or any of the Iurors therein, for the fauour which he doth beare more to the one partie than to the other: Nor who was an Arbitrator in that cause in question, and to be in triall, and did treate and conferre of the same: Nor who is then in sute of lawe with either of the parties to this question or triall, for any matter of trespasse, malice, or euill will: Nor who did bap-

All the parties to the execution of iustice sworne.

Causes of suspition in Shiriffes in impannelling of Iuries.

Fitz. Challenge. 113. 7. Ed. 4. 56. 33. Ass. p. 12 12. Ass pl. 1. 26. Ass. p. 56 12. Ass. p. 36. 44. Ass. p. 18 Plo. Com. fol. 425. 29. Ass. p. 2. 28. Ass. p. 22 7 H. 4. 10. Fitz. Challeng. 94. 99. 8. H. 5. 5. 20. H. 6. 39. 11. H. 4. 26. 38. H. 6. 6. 24. Edw. 37.

tize the childe of any of the parties to this sute and triall, or any of the parties to the same sute did baptize his childe. All which the Lawe doth suspect as causes of favor and affection in the Shiriffe, his Undershiriffe, &c. and to be mooners, fauourers or consentors to Periurie, and therefore upon challenge of the Array so being inpannelled, and the same proued, the whole Array shal be quashed. 4.Ed.4.11.

4 As the Lawe hath great care that Shiriffes, Undershiriffes, Bayliffes of Liberties, Coroners, and all others hauing authoritie to returne enquests should therein be voide of all partialitie, or presumption or cause thereof, to the intent that a gappe should not be left open by their meanes, to those that be willing to enter into corruption of conscience, and so to commit Periurie: In like sort hath shee vigilantly foreseene, that those Jurors which be returned by the said Shirifes, &c. may be so sifted, tried, and examined, that they may be found in all respects Probi & legales homines, viz. honest, upright, and lawfull men in the eie and iudgement of the Lawe, and that none of them be an Alien, a villaine, or outlawe, an excommunicate person, and thereby not legalis homo, nor conuicted in a Writ of Conspiracie, or an Attaint, and by that meanes not probus homo, and so to be challenged in euery cause, and by euery person: and further, that they may be proued to bee men of indifferencie, and voide of all partialitie, and such as will wholy respect the trueth of the cause in question, and in their verdict nothing regarde any that is partie thereunto. And therefore if there be any lawfull cause to feare particular fauour and affection in any of the Jurors, and that hee will rather incline to Periurie, than giue eare to the trueth of the cause, the Lawe doth allow to the partie grieued, or suspecting the same, seuerall Challenges to the same Juror, and thereby to haue him drawne and remooued out of that Enquest.

Euery Juror must be an honest and lawfull man. 33.H.6.55. 26.Ass.p.28 14 H.4.19. 9.Ed.4 16. 11.H.4.4.

Challenges of Jurors suspected.

5 As if a man be a witnes in a cause in question, he can not be a Juror in the same cause, for the witnes doth testifie upon his certaine knowledge, and the Jurors of an Enquest must giue their verdict according to their euidence. And besides, he that produceth a witnesse, expecteth at his hand a fauourable deliuery of his euidence, or otherwise he would not produce him, which favor euery Juror must be wholy voide of, if he will auoide Periurie.

A witnesse. 23.Ass.p.11 12.Ass.p.12 11.Ass.p.19

6 If a Juror after he is returned, and before he is sworne, will say that he will passe for the plaintife, or defendant, and doth speake it for the fauour which he beareth to the one partie, or the hatred which he hath to the other, (and not in respect of his owne knowledge of the trueth of the cause) the Law doth feare periurie in him, and therefore shee will remooue him out of that enquest, if he be challenged therefore.

Periurie suspected by deliuering his verdict before hand. 20.H.6.39. 8.Ed.3.69.

7 If one that is impannelled of a Jurie doth goe to the Assises with one of the parties to the issue, and doth eate and drinke with him at his charges, the Law doth suspect the same Juror of partialitie, and so of inclination to Periurie, in recompence of that kindnes receiued, and therefore shee will remooue him out of that Enquest if he be challenged therefore.

Periury suspected by lying at the charge of one of the parties. 8.Ed.3.69 13.H.4.13. Fitz.Challenge.177.

8 If

20.H.6.39. 9.Ed.4.46. 7.H.7.18. 8 If two men be in question for any cause, and then do refer the matter in debate to be heard & ended by two Arbitrators, whereof the one doth make choice of one Arbitrator, and the other of an other, which Arbitrators doe méete together, and confer of the cause, but do not agrée, whereupon the party grieued doth prosecute the said suit to an issue, and one of the same Arbitrators is returned of that Enquest, the law doth suspect the same Iuror of partialitie, and so of inclination to Periurie, and therfore she will remoue him out of that Enquest, if he be challenged therefore; for when he was chosen by one of the parties alone, this election maketh him in a sort of councel with him that did chose him, and so fauorable vnto him, but if he had bin chosen by the consent of both the parties together, the law would haue made other construction of him, and adiudged him indifferent. 3H.6.25. Periurie suspected by an Arbitrator in the cause in question.

34.Ass.p.6. 9 If two men do combine themselues by Oath, bond, couenant, or faithfull & aduised promise, that one of them will take an others part, be his friend, and assist him in all causes whatsoeuer: And after there is a sute commenced betwéene one of those parties & a straunger, and they come to issue, & the other partie who made the same combination is returned vpon the Enquest to trie the matter in issue betwéene his companion and that stranger, the law doth suspect him of fauor and periurie, & so will reiect him, if he be challenged therefore, for she doth feare that his old friendship & former league with the party to that issue hath suncke déeply into his brest, and will further preuaile with him, then the truth of a straungers case to be presently examined and tried will doe, be it neuer so apparant. Periurie suspected by combination.

Fitz.Chal. 106. 8.H.5.11. 10 If two men be at controuersie, and in sute of law, and depending that sute, there is an other controuersie, and sute in law commenced betwéene one of those parties & a stranger, and they discend to an issue, and the other party to the first sute is returned one of that Enquest: In this case the law doth suspect him of malice, and will remoue him out of that enquest, if he be challenged therefore by his former aduersarie: for she doth feare that the grudge which he hath conceiued in his hart against his aduersarie vpon the first sute, will moue him to reuenge, which is one of the grounds and causes of periurie. Periury suspected if one of the parties & a Iuror be at sute in law.

8.H.4.3. 27.Ass.p.13 11 If two persons or more doe conspire and agrée betwéen themselues to indite an other of felonie, and accordingly they doe procure him to be indited of the same felony, of which felony vpon his arraignement he is acquit; if the partie indited doe bring a writ of conspiracie against the said conspirators, and they doe come to an issue to be tried by a Iury, if any of those who were the Inditors of the same person be returned vpon the enquest to trie the conspiracie, the law will suspect him of partialitie, and not admit him to be sworn to try the conspiracie, for feare of periurie: for she conceiueth that he will doe his indeuor to iustifie and maintaine that which before he had found vpon the inditement, though it be false, for the sauing of his owne credit. And the like law is, if a man be one of those who doe indite an other of felonie; and after when the partie indited hath pleaded not guilty, and doth submit himselfe to be tried by the Country, the same Inditor is returned vpon the enquest, to trie innocencie or guilt of the man, vpon the challenge of him by the partie indited, he shall be remoued: for the law will suspect him of periury, and that he will rather respect his owne credit, and iustifie his former oth and the inditement to be true, then regard his euidence the life of the man arraigned, 7.E.4.4. 12.Ass.p.36 Periury suspected for that the Iuror passed against him before.

and the truth of the case in triall. And it is specially prouided by the Statute of Añ 25. Ed. 3. That no Inditor shall be put in Enquests vpon the deliuerance of the Inditees, if hee be challenged for the same cause by him which is indited. St. 25. E. 3. 3

Periurie suspected in respect of Subiection or gouernment.

12 And the Lawe doth suspect one that is returned of a Jurie of partialitie and fauour, who is within the distresse of either of the parties to that sute, or that is within the Jurisdiction of the Court Hundred, or Court Leete of the plaintife or defendant, or of any other, in whose right, to whose vse, or, by whose commaundement either of them do claime: for if he hath any land in his owne right, or his wiues, or that any other is seised to the vse of him or his wife of any land whereof he taketh the profit, which is holden mediately or immediately of either of the parties to that sute, the Lawe doth suspect him of Periurie, and being challenged therefore, hee shall be drawen, and not sworne of that Enquest. And so it is if any of the persons returned to be of a Jurie be seruant to either of the parties to that Issue, the Lawe doth suspect him of Periurie, for that hee is at the commaundement, and vnder the correction of his Master, and therefore being challenged, hee shall be drawen out of that Jurie. And the like Lawe is if either of the parties to the sute, be seruant to any of the Jury, and that Juror be challenged therefore, hee shall not be sworne for feare of Periurie, which hee may commit for his seruants benefit.

Fitz. Challenge. 19. 27. 46. 61. 4. H. 6. 25. 44. Ed. 3. 5. 38. Ed. 3. 25. 22. Ed. 4. 1. 2. H. 4. 13.

Periurie suspected in respect of kinred, aliance, or profite.

13 The Lawe doth also perceiue, that Nature and priuate profite be oft times speciall motions to Partialitie, Fauour, and Periurie. As if any person be returned of a Jury, who is neere of kinred or affinitie to either of the parties to that sute, or to his wife, viz. within the degrees of Marriage, and specially, if the same Juror may by any presumption, or likeliehoode, after take benefit of the thing in question: Or if either of the parties to that Issue, may be heire to the Juror, or the Juror or his heire be heire to the said partie: then the Lawe vpon Challenge doth reiect that Juror for feare of Periurie. But if the kinred or aliance betweene the partie to that sute, and the Juror be farre off, and many degrees asunder: Or that one be a kinsman on the fathers side, and the other of the mothers side, or one be a kinsman to the other of the halfe blood, or a Bastard, or otherwise, in such sort that the land of the one can not by the course of inheritance, and the rules of the Lawe discend to the other: Or if the alliance be such, that the sonne of the one hath married the daughter of the other, and not betweene themselues: then the Lawe doth not feare Periurie in the same Juror, but hee may be sworne to trie that Issue. And if there be a sute commenced betweene a Corporation and a priuate person, and that doth come to be tried by a Jurie, if any of the same Jurie be neare of kinred, or alliance to any person of that Corporation, or to any principall Officer of that Corporation, the Lawe doth suspect him of Periurie therefore, and if hee be challenged for that cause, hee shall be drawen out of that Enquest. The Lawe doth account it a kinde of affinitie, if one of the parties to the sute haue baptized, and beene godfather to a childe of one of the Jurors, and that the Juror in respect thereof doth beare an extraordinarie affection, and is to make a recompence to the same partie, and that therefore in this triall hee will fauour him, and be a

8. H. 6. 15. 7. H. 6. 40. 40. Ass. p. 20. Fitz. Challenge. 102. 3. Ed. 4. 12. 34. Ass. p. 6. 7. Ed. 4. 4. 2. H. 4. 15. 10. H. 6. 24.

One godfather to the others child.

meane of Periurie: and therefore if the Iuror be challenged for that cause, he shall be drawen: And some doe affirme the same cause of challenge and feare of Periurie to be, if a Iuror hath beene godfather to either of the parties
7.H.6.40. 19.H.6.66. to that triall, or to any childe of his.

14 The Lawe expecting to be satisfied per Veredictum Iuratorum of the trueth of such causes as doe come to an issue, doth carefully foresee, that those Iurors who are to deliuer the trueth by their verdict, should either before the time of the triall vpon their owne priuate knowledge, or by their Euidence at the time of the triall, be certainely informed of that trueth of the thing in question, lest by ignorance, mistaking falshoode for trueth, they should slide into Periurie. And because those that be dwelling, or haue some land, where the land, lease, or thing in question doth lie, are more likely to haue intelligence of the trueth of the cause in question, both to satisfie themselues, and informe their Companions, than other strangers of the same Countie are, who dwell farre off, the Lawe hath ordained by the Statute of Anno 27 Elizab. That there shall be sixe sufficient Hundredors impannelled vppon euery Issue ioyned, which is to be tried in any of the
St.27.El.6. Courts of the Kings Bench, Common Pleas, and the Exchequer, or before the Iustices of Assise, in all cases where euerie Iuror by the auncient lawes of this Realme ought to haue fortie shillings of freeholde at the least. And that at, or vppon the triall of any personall action, there shall two sufficient Hundredors at the least appeare. And for that cause, if in those cases there be not so many Hundredors at the least, the Lawe doth conceiue, they be ignorant of the truth of the Issue in triall. And to that end for the auoiding of Periurie, she will reiect the whole Iurie, if they be challenged. And so it is in an Assise, where the plaintife is to be put in possession per Visum
8.Ed.3.69. Iuratorum (if he recouer) or in any action where the Iurie is to haue the
Fitz. Chall. view of the land in question; if the same Iurors, or some of them had not the
102.169. view of the land in question, nor did know it before, the Lawe will suspect that they will commit Periurie, if they should be sworne, seeing they be ignorant of the land, and know it not in specie. And therefore vpon challenge they shall be remooued.

Periurie suspected in respect of ignorance of the cause.

want of Hundredors.

want of the view.

1.R.3.4. 15 Because our Law-makers haue in seuerall ages found by experience, that nothing is a greater motiue, enticement, or rather inforcement to Periurie than neede and pouertie: Therefore they haue endeuoured by many Statutes to prouide, that such as be returned of Enquests, should not onely be men of good behauiour and credite, but also of conuenient liueliehoode, estate, and abilitie to liue of themselues, for that Necessitie (which hath no lawe nor bridle) should not compell them to sell truth for rewardes, nor to plunge themselues into Periurie for bribes. And for the preuention of this Periurie in poore persons, and such as bee of
St.21.Ed.1 meane and weake estate, by a Statute made Anno 21.Ed.1. it was ordained, That no Shiriffe, Vndershiriffe, or Bayliffe of Libertie, shall put in any Recognisaunces of Assises, Iuries, Enquests, or Attaints, that shall passe out of their proper County, any person of their Bayliwickes (except he hath lands and tenements to the yearely value of a hundred shillings at the least) or that shall passe within the Countie (except hee hath

Periurie in respect of pouertie.

Iurors impanelled that shal passe out of their owne Counties.

lands to the yearely value of xl.s. And for the same cause, & upon the same reason of preuention of periurie in poore and needy persons, by a Statute made Anno 3. H. 5. it was established, That no persons shall be admitted to passe in any enquest upon triall of ye death of a man, or in any enquest betweene partie and partie, in plea reall, or in plea personall, whereof the debt or dammages declared do amount to xl. Markes, if the same person hath not lands and tenements of the yerely value of xl. s. aboue all charges, so that he be challenged for that cause by the party. But by the Statute of An 23. H. 8. euery person being the Kings naturall subiect borne, which by the name of a Citizen, a freeman, or any other name, doth inioy the liberties of any Citie, borough, or town corporat where he dwelleth, being worth in goods to the cleere value of xl. li. shall be admitted in triall of Murders, and felonies, in euery Sessions, and gaoles of deliuery, kept in, and for the libertie of such Cities, Boroughes, or Townes corporat, albeit he hath no freehold. But this Act extendeth not to any Knight, or Esquire, dwelling, abyding, or resorting in, or to any such citie, borough, &c. And by the Statute of An 27. Eliz. it was enacted, That in all cases where any Iuror to bee returned for the triall of any issue or issues, ioyned in any of the Courts of the Kings Bench, common Pleas, & the Exchequer, or before Iustices of Assise, by the Lawes of the Realme now in force, ought to haue estate of freehold in lands, tenements, or hereditaments, of the cleere yerely value of xl. s. in euery such case the Iurors that shal be returned, shall euery of them haue estate of freehold in lands, &c. to the cleere yearely value of foure pounds at the least, out of auncient demesne within the Countie where the issue is to be tried. By the Statute of 11. H. 7. it is prouided, That no person shal be impannelled, summoned, or sworne in any Iury or Enquest in Courts within the citie of London, except he be of lands, tenements, goods, or cattels to the value of xl. Markes. And no person shall be impannelled, summoned, or sworne, in Iuries or Enquests in any Court within the said Citie, for lands or tenements, or action personall wherein the debt or dammages amounteth to the summe of xl. markes, except he be in lands, tenemets, goods, or cattels, to the value of one hundred marks. By the Statute of Anno 19. H. 7. it was ordained, That euery of the xxiiij. persons dwelling within the shire where any riot, rout, or unlawfull assembly shall be committed, which shall be returned by the Sherife to enquire thereof, shall haue lands and tenements within the same shire, to the yearely value of xx. s. of Charter land, or freehold, or twentie sixe shillings eight pence of copiehold, or of both, aboue all charges. But in that case, by the Statute of Anno 2. H 5. if they be returned by the Coroners, then euery of them shall haue lands and tenements, or rents to the yearely value of tenne pounds at the least. By the Statute of Anno 1. R. 3. it was enacted, That no officer shall returne in any panell to be taken or put in, or upon any inquisition or inquirie before the Sherife in his Turne, other than such which bee of good name and fame, and which haue lands or tenements of freehold within the same countie to the yearly value of xx. s. at the least, or else copyhold lands to the yearely value of xxvj. s. viij. d. at the least, aboue all charges. By the Statute of An 8. H. 6. it was prouided, That euery person which shall be returned to inquire of any forcible entrie into lands, or detayning of lands by force, shall be a sufficient & indifferent person, and shall haue lands and tenements to the cleere yearely value of xl. s. By the Statute of An 1. H. 8. it was established, That euery Iuror which is returned before any escheator, or commissioner, to inquire of lands or tenements, or some other to his use, shall haue lands or tenements of the

yearely

Margin notes (left): Iurors to try felonies in corporat townes. — Where Iurors must haue 4. li. land. — Iurors in London. — Iurors to enquire of riots. — Iurors in the Sherifs Turne. — Iurors to inquire of forcible entrie. — Iurors returned before Escheators.

Margin notes (right): St. 3. H. 5. 3 — St. 23. H. 8. 13. — Sta. 27. El. 6. — St. 11. H. 7. 21. — St. 19. H. 7. 13. — St. 2. H. 5. 8. — St. 1. R. 3. 4. — Sta. 8. H. 6. 9 — Sta. 1. H. 8. 8.

yearely value of xl. s. aboue all charges in the same shire where the inquirie shall be made. And by the stat. made An 11.H.7. An 23.H.8. An & 37.H.8. The Iurors returned vpon an attaint in London, or els where, shalbe of more or greater ability in lands, tenements, goods or cattels then is before specified.

St. 11. H. 7. 21. 23.H.8.3. 37.H.8.5.

16 The law hauing first vsed al good deuises to cause shirifes, vndershirifes, Bailifes of liberties, coroners, & al others authorized to return & impannel Iuries to be indifferent, & to returne the said Iuries & Iurors without al partiality, & that they shalbe no furtherers, maintainors, nor assistors to periury, subornation, or embracery, & also hauing prouided that all those Iurors which be so returned vpon Enquests, & to try issues betwéen party & party, may again one by one be sifted, tried, & examined, whether they standing vnsworne be indifferent, or not: She doth then expect to receiue from those Iurors Veredictū a true tale, that is to say, a true verdit or presentment of such things as be giuen them in charge, according to their euidence. But if the same Iurors will decline from truth, and make a false presentment, contrarie to their euidence, then is it not to be termed Veredictum, but Periurium, and it will be returned to them as Maledictum: for by the common Law, they being attainted by the verdict of xxiiij. other Iurors, shall receiue a cursed and villanous iudgement therefore, viz. the said Iurors shall lose the fréedom of the Law, their wiues & children shall be thrust out of their houses, their houses shall be pulled downe to the ground, their orchards & gardens shall be supplanted, their trées shall be digged vp by the roots, their meadowes shall be eyred vp: All the goods & cattels which they had at the time of the Attaint brought, or at any time after, shal be forfeited to the King: The King shall haue all the profits of their lands during their liues: And they shall be committed to perpetuall prison. Which iudgement was deuised, & many yeres put in execution, to the intent it might be knowen how much the common Law did detest and punish willfull Periurie and falshood, in those who shée trusted in place of iustice, and from whom shée accompted to receiue truth.

Fit.Ass.396. 46.Ed.3.23. 42.Ed.3.26 6.Assi.p.7. 30.Ass.p.24 40.Ass.p.20. 41.Ass.p.18. Li.Int.fo 92

The iudgement in an at the common law of a Iury proued periured.

17 But sithence by the Statute of An 11.H.7. and An 23.H.8. the said iudgement against a petit Iurie attainted, is in some cases altered and qualified, for by the Statute of 11.H.7. it is ordained, That the party grieued by any false verdict giuen in any of the Courts of the Citie of London, shall and may sue Attaint by Bill in the Hustings of London, holden for common Pleas before the Maior & Aldermen of the same Citie. And if the graund Iurie sworne in the same Attaint, find that the petit Iurie haue giuen an vntrue verdict, then the iudgement shal be against the defendant, as is vsed in attaint sued by writ at the common Law: And the iudgement shall be against the petit Iurie, that euery of them shall lose xx.li. or more, by the discretion of the Maior and Aldermen of the said Citie kéeping the Hustings, to such vses as other issues and penalties béen forfeited in any action or plaint commenced before the Mayor and Aldermen of the said citie; and his bodie to bee imprisoned, there to remaine without baile or mainprise vj. moneths, or lesse, by the discretion of the Mayor and Aldermen; and to be disabled for euer to be sworn in any Iurie before any temporall Iudge: But the iudgement in such Attaint shall not extend to any lands or tenements, ne to other punishment of the petit Iurie. And by the before mentioned Statute of Anno 23.H.8. it was enacted, That vpon euery vntrue verdit giuen betwéene partie and partie in any suit, plaint, or demaund, before any Iustices or Iudges of Record, where the

Sta. 11.H.7. 21.

The iudgement in Attaint in London.

St. 23.H.8.3 An. 13. El. 25.

An attaint where the thing extendeth to xl. l. the thing in demaund, and verdict thereupon giuen extendeth to the value of fourtie pounds, and concerneth not the ieopardie of mans life, the partie grieued by the same verdict shall haue a writ of Attaint against euery person so giuing an vntrue verdict, and euery of them, and against the partie which shall haue iudgement vpon the same verdict. And euery one that shall passe in the same Attaint, shall haue lands and tenements to the value of twentie markes by yeare of freehold, out of auncient demesne. And if the graund Iurie find that the petit Iurie gaue an vntrue verdict, then euery of the said petit Iurie shall forfeit twentie pounds, whereof one halfe shall be to the King, and the other halfe to him that sueth, to be leuied by Capias ad satisfaciendum fieri facias, or Elegit, or by Action of Debt against euery person of the petit Iurie so forfeiting, and against his Executors and Administrators, hauing then sufficient goods of their said Testator not administred. And euery of the said petit Iurie shall seuerally make fine by the discretion of the Iustices before whom the said false Serement shall be found, after their seuerall offences, defaults, and sufficiencie of them. And those of the petit Iurie so attainted shall neuer be after of any credit, nor their oath accepted in any court. And if a false verdict be giuen in any action, suit, or demaund before any Iustice, or Iudge of Record, of any thing personal, as debt, trespas, and other like, which shall be vnder the value of xl. pounds, then the partie grieued shall haue an Attaint. And if the petit Iurie be attainted, then euery of them shall forfeit fiue pounds to the King and the partie after the forme aforesaid, and also shall make fine by the discretion of the Iustices. And euery person that may dispend fiue markes by the yeare of freehold, out of auncient demesne, or is worth an hundred markes in goods, is able to passe in the same Attaint.

Attaint wher the thing doth not extend to xl. l.

18 The Law doth so hate Periurie, and so much endeauour to extirpate the very roote thereof, that shee doth sometime punish it in the onely will, and intention of a man, though that will neuer come to effect, so that the same will and meaning may bee laid open vnto her, by due proofe; as it appeareth by a braunch of the before specified Statute of Anno 11. Hen. 7. whereby it is ordained That if it be found by the graund Iurie that the petit Iurie haue giuen a true verdict, in any of the courts of the citie of London, in a suit whereupon an Attaint is brought, then the graund Iurie shall haue authoritie to inquire if any of the petit Iurie hath receiued any summe of money or other reward, or promise of money or other reward, of the named defendants, or tenants in the same Attaint, or of any other person by the commandement, couin, or assent of any of them, for the intent of their verdict giuing, whereupon the same Attaint is grounded: And after any such corruption by the said graund Iurie found, then the Iuror that is so found defectiue in taking money, or rewards &c. shall pay to the plaintife named in the said Attaint, tenne times the value of the summe, or other reward so taken, or promised, and shall suffer imprisonment without Baile or Maineprise sixe moneths, or lesse, by the discretion of Mayor and Aldermen of the said citie, and shall bee disabled for euer to bee sworne in any Iurie before any temporall Iudge. And such defendant and tenant in the same Attaint, shall pay, to such vse as other penalties bee forfeited within the same citie, tenne times the value of the summe of money, or other reward by him so giuen to any of the said petit

The meaning to commit periurie punished.

St. 11. H. 7. 21.

Decies tantū.

petit Jurie, and shalbe imprisoned without Baile or Maineprise during sixe moneths, or lesse, by the discretion of the said Mayor and Aldermen. And in like sort, and for the same cause the Statutes of Anno 34. Edw. 3. & 38. Edw. 3. were prouided, whereby it was enacted, That if any Iuror sworn in Assises, or other Enquests to be taken betweene the King and the partie, or betweene partie and partie, doe by himselfe or any other take any thing of the plaintife, or defendant, to giue his verdict, and thereof is attainted at the suit of the partie, which will sue for himselfe, or for the King, or of any other person (entring his plaint by Bill immediately before the Iustices before whom the Iurie was sworne) the said Iuror shall pay tenne times so much as he hath receiued. And all those which bee Imbraceors to lead and procure such Enquests in the Countrie, to make a gaine and profit thereof, shall be punished as the Iurors. And if the Iuror or Imbraceors so attainted haue not wherewith to make recompence in forme aforesaid, he shalbe one yeare imprisoned; which imprisonment shall not be pardoned for any fine: and the partie grieued may haue his action before other Iustices if hee will. But no Iustice or other officer shall inquire of office upon any of the points of this Statute, but onely at the suit of the partie, and of others as aforesaid. By which foresaid Statutes it doth appeare, that the Law doth punish Periurie, not onely in such Iurors as doe commit it, but also in those persons who bee the Imbraceors, Perswaders, or Procurers of it: and not onely in those who doe commit or procure it, but likewise in those who giue or take rewards to haue it done, though it bee neuer effected: for shee accounteth, that when a man hath giuen his heart leaue for a reward to bee sworne, it is the reward he respecteth in his oath, and not the truth of the cause; which reward will lead him blindfold into the dungeon of Periurie, and therefore hee deserueth to be punished as a periured person. S. Maintenance &c. 6.

St. 34. E. 3. 8. 38. E. 3. 12.

Decies tantū.

Imbraceors.

19 Because diuers did resort to Iurors in Wales, and the Marches thereof, and suborned them to acquit Murderers, Felons, and Accessories openly knowne: therefore by a Statute made Anno 26. H. 8. it was enacted, That forthwith upon the charge giuen to any Enquest, to bee taken and sworne before any Iustices, Steward, Lieutenant, or other officer within Wales, or the Marches of the same, of, for, or upon any Trauerse against the King, or the triall of any Recognizance broken, or any other forfeiture forfeited to the King, or of, for, and upon the triall of any Murderer, felon, or accessorie of felonie or murder, an officer shall be sworne for the keeping of the same Iurors. And if the same Iurors doe acquit any such felon, murderer, or accessorie, upon whose triall they shall be charged, or giue any untrue verdict against the King, upon the triall of any Trauerse, Recognizance, or other forfeiture, contrarie to the good and pregnant euidence ministred to them by the persons sworne before the said Iustice, Steward, Lieutenant, or other officer: Or that the said Iurors or any of them doe eate, drinke, or speake to, or with any person, or persons, than to such as be sworn with them, or otherwise misdemeane themselues after they be sworne, and before they haue giuen their verdict: Then the Lord President or other of the Councell of the Marches for the time being, upon notice or complaint thereof to be made, shall not onely haue authoritie to call such Iurors before them, but also the same Iusticiar, Steward, or other officers, afore whome any

St. 26. H. 8. 4.

The punishment of periurie committed by an enquest in Wales.

any such acquitall, vntrue verdit, or misdemeanors shall happen to be made, shall haue full power to compell such Iurors, and euery of them, vpon paine of imprisonment, to be bound by Recognisance in a certaine summe of money, by their discretion to be limited, that the same Iurors, and euery of them shall personally appeare at a certaine day by the same Iusticiar, Steward, or other officer to be limited, before the Lord President, and other of the Councell aforesaid for the time being, then, and there to abide, and stand to such direction and order, as the same councell shall make, ordaine, and decree, of, in, and vpon the same. And the same councell shall thereupon haue authoritie by examination, or otherwise, to heare and determine all and euery such cause, and shall haue like authoritie to commit euery of the same Iurors to prison, or other punishment, as shalbe thought meet by the discretion of the said counsel, or otherwise assesse, or taxe euery such Iuror to his fine and ransome by the same discretion, to be paied and leuied of their lands, goods, and cattels, to the vse of the King.

Periurie committed by witnesses.

20 Hauing written of the restraint and punishment of periurie in Iurors consisting of twelue persons at the least, impannelled or sworn to deliuer their verdict according to their euidēce, I am now to expresse what punishments ye law doth inflict vpon such, which doe come one by one, as deponents, or witnesses, to testifie the truth, and to informe the Iudge, or the Iurie of the veritie of the matter in issue or question, according to their knowledge, whereof euery man by himselfe may be called singularis testis, though there be more witnesses sworne in that canse. And seeing that iustice cannot be executed without the knowledge of the truth of the cause in question, & that truth is in most cases only to be deliuered by the othes and testimonies of such parties as were witnesses, priuie, or best acquainted with the matter in variance: Therefore first it is to be obserued, that the wisdom of the law hath thought it necessarie, to prouide that such witnesses may be compelled vnder a great paine to appear in court, and testifie their knowledge concerning such matter in question: as

A witnes vpon proces serued shall appeare.

by the Statute made Anno 5. El. it was ordained, That if any person vpon St. 5. El. 9.
whom any proces out of any of the courts of Record within this Realme, or St. 29. El. 5.
Wales, shalbe serued, to testifie or depose concerning any matter depending in any of the same courts, and hauing tendered to him according to his countenance, or calling, such reasonable sums of money for his costs and charges, as (hauing regard to the distance of the places) is necessarie to be allowed in ye behalfe, doe not appeare according to the tenor of the said Proces, hauing not a lawfull and reasonable let to the contrarie; then the partie making default shall forfeit for euery such offence x. l. and shall yeeld such further recompence to the partie grieued, as by the discretion of the Iudge of the court out of the which the said proces shall be awarded, according to the losse and hindrance ye the partie which procured the said proces shall sustaine, by reason of the non appearance of the said witnesse: the said seuerall summes to be recouered by ye partie so grieued against the offendor by A. I. B. P. &c. in any of the K. courts of Record, wherein no W. E. or P. &c.

21 There were seuerall statutes made during the raignes of king H. 6. K. H. 7. and K. H. 8. against Periurie, and the procurers and committers of periurie: and lastly one was ordained Anno 32. H. 8. against such as should sub- St. 32. H. 8. 9
orne witnesses, to the hindrance of Iustice, and the procurement of periurie: Sithence the making whereof, for that the penaltie therein is small towards the

the offendors in that behalfe, the said offence of subornation, and sinister procurement of false witnesses did neuerthelesse greatly increase, and by reason of the wilfull Periurie committed by the same suborned witnesses, diuers persons did sustaine disherison, and great impouerishment, as well of their lands and tenements, as of their goods and cattels: for the redresse and more sharpe punishment whereof, by a Statute made Anno 5. El. it was enacted, That all and euery person and persons which shall vnlawfully, and corruptly procure any witnes, or witnesses, by Letters, Rewards, Promises, or by any other sinister and vnlawfull labour, or meanes whatsoeuer, to commit any wilfull and corrupt Periurie, in any matter or cause whatsoeuer, depending in suit and variance by any Writ, Action, Bill, Complaint, or Information, in any wise concerning any lands, tenements, or hereditaments, or any goods, cattels, debts, or dammages, in any of the courts of the Chauncerie, Starre chamber, White hall, or in any other of the Kings Courts of Record, or in any Leet, view of Franke pledge, or Law day, Auncient demesne Court, Court Hundred, Court Baron, or in the Court or Courts of the Stannerie in the countie of Deuon, and Cornewall: Or shall likewise vnlawfully and corruptly procure, or suborne any witnesse, or witnesses, which shall bee sworne to testifie in perpetuam rei memoriam: Then euery such offendor or offendors, shall for his, hers, or their said offence, being thereof lawfully conuicted or attainted, forfeit fourtie pounds to the King and the partie grieued, hindered or molested by reason of any of the offences aforesaid, that will sue for the same by A. B. P. or I. in any of the Kings Courts of Record, wherein no W. E. P. or I. shall bee allowed. And if it happen any such offendor or offendors being so conuicted or attainted as is aforesaid, not to haue any goods or cattels, Lands or Tenements to the value of fourtie pounds, then euery such person or persons so conuicted or attainted of any of the offences aforesaid, shall suffer imprisonment one halfe yeare, without Baile or Maineprise, and stand vpon the Pillorie one whole houre in some Market Towne, neere, or next adioyning to the place where the offence was committed, in open market there. And no person being so conuicted or attainted shall bee from thenceforth receiued as a witnesse to bee deposed in any court of Record within any of the Kings dominions of England, Wales, or the Marches of the same, vntill the Iudgement, giuen against him, or them, shall bee reuersed by Attaint, or otherwise. And vpon euery such reuersall, the parties grieued shall recouer his or their dammages against all and euery such person and persons, as did procure the said iudgement so reuersed to bee first giuen against them, or any of them, by action to be sued vpon his or their case, according to the course of the common Law.

St. 5. El. 9. 29. El. 5.

The penaltie for procuring of wilfull periury in witnesses.

22 If any person or persons, either by the subornation, vnlawfull procurement, sinister perswasion or meanes of any others, or by their owne Act, Consent, or Agreement, shall wilfully and corruptly commit any manner of wilfull periurie, by his, or their deposition, in any of the Courts before mentioned, or being examined ad perpetuam rei memoriam: Then euerie person or persons offending, shall for his or their said offence lose and forfeit twentie pounds to the King and the partie grieued, hindered, or molested by reason of any of the offences before

St. 5. El. 9.

The penaltie for committing of wilfull periurie.

before mentioned, that will sue for the same by A. B. P. or I. in any of the Kings courts of Record, wherein no W. E. P. or I. shall be allowed, and shall haue sixe months imprisonment without Baile or Maineprise. And the oath of such person or persons so offending from thenceforth, shall not bee receiued in any court of Record within England, or Wales, or the Marches of the same, vntill such time as the iudgement giuen against the said person or persons shall be reuersed by Attaint, or otherwise. And vpon euery such reuersall, the parties grieued, to recouer his or their dammages against such person and persons as did procure the said iudgement so reuersed to be giuen against thē, by action to be sued vpon his case. And if the said offendor haue not any goods or cattels to the value of xx. l. then he shall be set on the Pillorie in some market place within the shire, citie, or borough, where the said offence shall be committed, by the Sherife, or his ministers, if it be without any citie or towne corporat: and if it be within any citie or towne corporat, then by the head officer or officers of the same citie or &c. or by his or their ministers, & there shall haue both his eares nailed, and from thenceforth be discredited & disabled for euer to be sworne in any of the courts of Record aforesaid, vntill the iudgement shall be reuersed; and thereupon shall recouer his dammages in manner and forme before mentioned.

In what courts Periurie shall be punished.

23 As well the Iudge and Iudges of euery such of the said courts where any such suit is, or shall be, and whereupon any such periurie is or shal happen to be committed, as also the Iustices of Assise, and gaole deliuery in their seuerall circuits, and the Iustices of the peace in euery countie within this realm, or in Wales, at their Quarter Sessions, both within liberties and without, shall haue authoritie by vertue hereof, to enquire of all and euery the defaults and offences committed contrarie to this act, by inquisition, presentment, bill, or information, before them exhibited, or otherwise lawfully to heare and determine the same, and thereupon to giue iudgement, award processe, and execution of the same, according to the course of the lawes of this Realme. Sta. 5. El. 9.

Proclamatiō of this Statute.

24 The Iustices of Assise of euery circuit within this Realme shal in euery countie within their circuits two times in the yeare, viz. in the time of their sittings, make open Proclamation of this Statute, or of the effect thereof, to the intent that no person shalbe ignorant of the penalties herein contained. St. 5. El. 9.

Periurie punished in the spirituall court.

25 Prouided that this Act, or any thing therein contained, shall not extend to any spirituall or Ecclesiasticall court within this Realme of England, or Wales, or the Marches of the same; but all and euery such offendor and offendors as shall offend in forme aforesaid, shall and may be punished by such vsuall and ordinarie lawes, as heretofore hath bin, and yet be vsed in the said Ecclesiasticall court: any thing in this Act &c. notwithstanding. St. 5. El. 9.

Periury punishable in the Starchāber.

26 Prouided that this Act shall not extend to restraine the power or authoritie giuen by Act of Parliament made An̄ 11. H. 7. to the Lord Chauncelor, and others of the Kings Councel, to examine, and punish riots, routs, hainous Periuries, and other offences (which haue vsed to heare and determine such matters in the Starre-chamber at Westminster) nor to restraine the power of the Lord President and Councell in the Marches of Wales, or in the North, nor of any other Iudge hauing absolute authoritie to punish Periurie before the making of this Statute: But they

Sta. 5. El. 9.
St. 11. H. 7. 25.

But they and euery of them shall procéede in the punishment of all offences heretofore punishable, in such wise as they might haue done and vsed to do before the making of this Act, to all purposes, so that they set not vpon the offendors lesse punishment then is contained in this Act.

27 Because by the said statute of 5. Eliz. 9. there is no Ordinance made for the punishment of those Bankrupts, who being sworne and examined vpon Interrogatories by Commissioners thereunto authorized, shall commit Periurie: Nor for the punishment of those witnesses, who either by the procurement of others, or by their owne consent shall commit Periurie, being examined by the said Commissioners touching Bankrupts goods or debts: Therefore by a statute made Anno 1. Iac. it was ordained, That it shall be lawfull for the Commissioners authorized vnder the great Seale of England, or the greatest part of them, to take order with Bankrupts bodies, lands, tenemēts, and hereditaments, money, goods, cattels, wares, and debts, to examine the said offendor or offendors vpon such interrogatories, touching the lands, tenements, goods, cattels, and debts, bils, bonds, bookes of accompt, and such other things as may tend to disclose his, her, or their estate, or the secret graunts, cōueyances, and eloigning of his, her, or their landes, tenements, goods, money, and debts, as they shall thinke meet. And if therein the offendor or offendors shall refuse to be examined, or to answer fully to euery interrogatorie, to him to be ministred by the said Commissioners, or the greater part of them, it shall be lawfull for the said Commissioners, or the greater part of them, to commit the said offendor or offendors to some strait or close imprisonment, there to remaine, vntill he, she, or they shall better conforme him or her selfe. And if vpon his, her, or their examination it shal appeare, that he, she, or they haue committed any wilfull or corrupt Periurie, tending to the hurt or dammage of the creditors of the said Bankrupt, to the value of tenne pounds of lawfull money of England, or aboue, the party so offending shall or may thereof be indited in any of the Kings Courts of Record, and being lawfully conuicted thereof, shall stand vpon the Pillory in some publike place by the space of ij. houres, and haue one of his eares nailed to the Pillory and cut off. And by the same statute of Anno 1. Iac. it is further established, That if any person or persons (other then the Bankrupt) either by subornation, vnlawfull procuremēt, sinister persuasion or meanes of any others, or by his owne act, consent, or agréement, shall wilfully and corruptly commit any manner of wilfull Periury, by his deposition to be taken before the said Commissioners, or the greater part of them, as is aforesaid: Then the party or parties so offending, and all and euery person and persons that shall vnlawfully and corruptly procure any such vnlawfull, wilfull, and corrupt Periurie, shall or may therefore be indited in any of the Kings Courts of Record, and after his or their conuiction thereof, shall incurre such forfeiture, and receiue and haue such paines and punishment as are limitted by the statute made concerning Periury, Anno 5. Eliz. 9.

St. 1. Iac. 15.

Periury punished in Bankrupts.

Periury committed by witnesses for Bankrupts.

St. an̄ 5. El. 9.

28 A man cannot be indited for Periurie vpon the foresaid statute of 5. El. for giuing false euidence on his oath to the Enquest at a Sessions, vpon an Inditment of Riot: For the statute was ordained against procurers of Periurie, in a matter depending in suit and variance, by any Writ, Action, Bill,

Co. li. 5. f. 99

Periury committed vpon an inditment of Riot.

Complaint, or Information, and so procurement of Periurie upon an inditement is out of this braunch of the said statute. And the second braunch of the same statute touching committing of Periury, shal haue the same construction which the first hath, though it be not there in words, and shall haue reference to the first: And it shalbe expounded as if the words of the statute had béene, If any person shall wilfully and corruptly commit any wilfull Periurie in any cause depending in suit by any Writ, Bill, Action &c. And the same law is, if a man commit wilfull Periury, upon euidence giuen to the great Enquest upon an inditment of Felony, he is not to be punished by force of the foresaid statute of Anno 5. Eliz.

Periury upon an inditement of Felony.

29 If wilfull Periurie be committed in the Kings bench, by any witnesse produced to proue a Suggestion, for a Prohibition there graunted against an Ecclesiasticall Judge, according to the statute of 2. & 3. E. 6. whereby the party is staied of this consultation, this shall not be examined and punished in the Starre chamber: for the statute of 3. H. 7. which maketh mention of such things as the Court of Starre chamber is to hold plea of, prouideth no more punishment by speciall words for Periurie, then it doth for Murder or Rape. There is a prouiso in the foresaid statute of Anno 5. El. That the Lord Chancelor and others of the Qu. Counsell shall and may procéed in the punishment of all offences, in such wise as they might haue done, and used to do, before the making of the said Act to all purposes, so that they set upon the offendors no lesse punishment then is contained in the said Act.

Periury in prouing a suggestion for a prohibition.

7. & 8. Eliz. Dyer 243. St. 2. E. 6. 13 St. 3. H. 7. 1

30 A Bill of Periurie may be sued in the Chancery for a periurie committed in the same Court, contrary to the foresaid statute of Anno 5. El. and if the defendant do plead unto it not guilty, he shall be sworne to his plea, and also shall answer to Interrogatories, as it is usually done in the Starre chamber, for the L. Chauncellor had absolute power before the said statute of Añ 5. El. to punish Periury. And therefore by a prouiso in the said statute, his power therein is not restrained by the same statute. And if the Court of Chauncery will examine Periury committed there, it must be done by a bill in Latin, and pleaded in Latin, and the issue shalbe ioyned there, and tried in the K. Bench, as it is used in the like cases.

A suit upon periury in the Chancery.

12. El. Dy. 288.

31 There is no remedy or punishment for Periurie in a spirituall Court against inditors, that do endite a man of felony, which be periured, or against a Jury which doth giue a false verdict betwéene party and party: And if a suit be commenced in the spirituall court against an offendor in Periurie, in either of those cases, he may haue a prohibition; for this periury doth rise upon a cause that is temporall, viz. the Treason, or Felony, Debt, Trespas, or plea of land: and for this periury the offendors shall be punished by attaint by the common law, or otherwise. And so it is, if a man be defamed by a false inditment, there is no remedy in the spirituall Court for his defamation, for that it groweth upon a matter which is temporall. But where the Periury doth rise upon a matter which is spirituall (as upon a Testament, Matrimony, or Legacie, or such like) then the spirituall Judge hath authority to punish it, and in that case a Prohibition will not lie. And as there is no punishment in the Ecclesiastical Court for Periury that doth rise upon a cause that is temporall: So the Law hath prouided, that defamation (which is another euill fruit of a malicious

Where periury shalbe punished in the temporall court, & where in the spirituall.

22. H. 8. Kel. 39.

Defamation. Co. lib. 4. 20

and

and corrupt heart, and of a leud and venomous tongue) shall not be punished in the Ecclesiasticall Court, vnlesse it concerne matter that is meerely spirituall, and determinable in the Ecclesiasticall Court, as to call a man Hereticke, Schismaticke, Adulterer, Fornicator &c. and vnlesse it doth concerne matter that is meerely spirituall onely: For if such a defamation doe concerne any thing that is determinable at the common Law, the Ecclesiasticall Judge shal not hold plea thereof. And yet if such a defamation be meerely spirituall, and onely spirituall, notwithstanding he that doth sue in the Ecclesiasticall Court for being defamed, cannot sue there for recompence or dammages, but only for the punishment of the offence.

Maintenance, Champertie, Embracerie, and Buying of Titles.

What maintenance is, & the enormities thereof.

Maintenance is, where a man giueth to another (that is demaundant, or tenant, plaintife or defendant in any suit, or to any other in his behalfe, or to his vse) any summe of money, or other reward for to maintaine his plea or suit: Or otherwise vseth persuasion, or maketh labour for him, or vseth other meanes to countenance, aid, or assist him, when he himselfe hath nothing therewith to doe. Which is an offence that the wisdome of the Realme from age to age hath condemned, and hath indeuored to inflict diuers punishments vpon the transgressors therein, as it may appeare by the statutes of West.1. West.2. 28.Ed.1. 33.Ed.1. 8.H.6. 19.H.7. 32.H.8. & 18.El. The law doth so greatly desire the continuance of peace betwéene one member of the Commonweale and another, & so much condemneth variance & suits without cause, that many times and in many causes the plaintife is amerced for commencing a wrongfull suit: for the law doth intend those suites to be pursued for vexation & trouble: and likewise in some other cases the def. is amerced for the wrongfull detaining of that which is not his owne, and for inforcing the plaintife by suit in law to séeke & recouer his owne. But as in all cases the vnlawfull maintainor of suits is in fault, so is he in euery such case punishable. For though the case of the plaintife or def. which he vndertaketh to maintaine, be iust and lawfull in him, who prosecuteth or defendeth the suit, & whose the cause is, yet in the maintainor it is vnlawfull, for it is not his owne suit, neither is it pursued or defended for the recouery or protection of ẏ which he pretendeth to be due to himself; and so in a sort he maketh complaint where he hath no wrong, or maketh defence where none séeke to hurt him, whereby, opposing himselfe against others who do not contend with him, he laboureth to disturbe the ordinary course of iustice, and therewith to blemish the peace of the Realme: for as it appeareth partly by the statute of Anno 1.Ed.3. and Sta.1.E.3.14
specially by the preamble of the statute of Anno 32.H.8. Nothing conserueth St.32.H.8.9
the people in more peace & good concord, then the due administration of iustice, and the indifferent triall of titles and issues, according to the Lawes of this Realme, which being hindered & letted by Maintenance, Embracery, Champertie, Subornation of witnesses, sinister labour, and buying of titles, there will of necessitie insue thereof great periurie, vnquietnesse, oppressions, troubles, wrongs, and disheritances.

2 And because this Maintenance is as an euill Tree hauing growne out of it many corrupt branches: therefore the wisdome of the Realme hath frō time to time prouided seuerall statutes (as it were sharpe hatchets) to loppe or shred those boughes when they did spring and shoot out. As King Ed. 3. perceiuing that his Counsellors, Magistrates, and Officers in his house, & certaine great men of the Realme, by sending of Letters, Messengers, giuing of Liueries, & by other means, did sollicite matters, and maintaine quarrels, and tooke parts in the Countrey, by a statute made Anno 1. of his raigne, and another Anno 20. of his raigne, did ordaine, That common right should be done to all persons, as well poore as rich: and that none of his said Officers, nor any Noblemen, nor any other great or small, should take vpon him to maintaine quarrels, or to take parts, to the let or disturbance of the common law: Nor that any should take in hand, or meddle with quarrels or questions, but their owne. And because there was no speciall punishment ordained by the said statute of Anno 1. Ed. 3. for those who should transgresse that Law, therfore King R. 2. by a statute made in the first yeare of his raigne established, That if the kings Counsellors or great Officers should take vpon them to sustaine any quarrell by Maintenance in the Countrey, or elsewhere, he so offending should indure that paine which should be inflicted by the King himselfe, by the aduise of the Lords of his Realme: and other inferior officers and seruants of the kings, in the Exchequer, and other Courts: and his meniall seruants shall lose their offices and seruices, and be imprisoned, & be ransomed at the kings pleasure, euery of them according to his degree, estate, and desert: and all other persons of the Realme, of what estate soeuer they be, shalbe imprisoned and ransomed as the other aforesaid.

Maintenance by men of authority.

St. 1. E. 3. 14
20. Ed. 3. 3.
St. 1. R. 2. 4.

3 The statute intituled Definitio de conspiratoribus, made Anno 33. E. 1. doth decypher another sort of Maintainors, which there be called conspirators in this sort, viz. Conspirators be they that bind themselues by oath, couenant, or other alliance, that euery of them shall helpe and sustaine the other, falsely & maliciously to indite, or falsely to moue or maintaine pleas: and also such as cause children within age to appeale men of felony, whereby they are imprisoned & sore grieued: and such as retaine mē in the country with liueries, or fees, to maintaine their malicious enterprises; and this extendeth aswell to the takers as to the giuers: and stewards and bailifes of great lords, which by their seigniorie, office, or power, vndertake to vphold or maintaine quarrels, pleas, or debates, that concerne other parties then such as touch the estate of their lords, or themselues.

St. 33. Ed. 1.
St. 1. R. 2. 7.

Maintenance by cōbination

Maintenance by noblemens officers.

4 There is also another kind of Maintenance, which is called Champerty, and the offendors therin be called Champertors, whom the foresaid statute of Anno 33. E. 1. doth define in this maner, viz. Champertors be they that moue pleas and suits, or cause to be moued, either by their owne procurement, or by others, & sue them at their proper costs, for to haue part of the land in variance, or part of the gaines: which Champertors were accounted great maintainors of suits, and professed enemies to peace: whereupon it was ordained by the statute of West. 1. That no Officer of the kings by themselues, nor by other, shall maintaine pleas, suits, or matters hanging in the Kings Court, for Lands, Tenements, or other things, for to haue part or profit thereof, by couenant made betweene them, and he that doth, shall be punished at the kings

Maintenance by champerty.

Who be champertors.

St. 33. Ed. 1.
St. 3. E. 1. 25.

pleasure: and after by the statute of Westm. 2. the same was expressed more at large, by the which it was enacted, That the Chauncellor, Treasurer, Justices, nor none of the Kings Councell, no Clarke of the Chauncerie, nor of the Exchequer, nor of any Justice, or other Officer, nor none of the Kings house, Clarke, nor Lay, shall receiue any Church land nor tenement by gift in fee, nor to farme, nor for purchase, nor otherwise, so long as the thing is in plea in the Kings Court, or before any of his Officers, nor shall take reward therefore: and hee that doth contrary to this Act, eyther himselfe, or by any other, or make any bargaine, shall bee punished at the Kings pleasure, as well he that doth purchase, as he that doth giue. And because other Officers were not bound by the foresaid Statutes as well as the Kings, and to the intent some certaine and more sharpe penaltie might bee imposed vpon the transgressor of the said statutes, then before time had beene prouided, Therefore by a statute made Anno 28. E. 1. intituled Articuli super Chartas, it was ordained, That no Officer, nor any other (for to obtaine part of the thing in plea) shall maintaine any matter that is in suit: Nor none vpon such couenant shall giue vp his right to another, and if any doe and bee attainted thereof, the taker shall forfeit to the King so much of his lands and goods, as doth amount to the value of the part that he hath purchased for such Maintenance: and to obtaine that, any person that will, shall be receiued to sue for the king, before those Justices before whom the suit doth depend, and the iudgement shalbe giuen by them. But it may not be vnderstood in this case, that a man may not haue counsell of pleaders and learned men for his fee, nor of his next friends. And after, to the intent to impose a sharper punishment vpō such as should be offendors in Maintenance, Champerty, or ẏ like, by a statute made Anñ 33. E. 1. it was enacted, That if any person do take vpō him for Maintenance, Champerty, or the like bargaine, any manner of suit or plea against another, & is attainted of such assumption, suit, or bargaine, or of consent thereunto, he shalbe three yeares imprisoned, and further punished at the kings pleasure.

[Margin: St. 13. E. 1. 48 — St. 28. Ed. 1. 11. — Pleaders may giue counsell for their fees. — St. 33. Ed. 1. — The punishment of champertors.]

8 And so it appeareth by the foresaid statutes, that it is Champerty, where a man by couenant or agreement made by writing or word, doth bargaine to haue parcell of the land, debt, or other thing which is in suit, if it be recouered to aid and maintain the party to that suit: and in this case, he that is the other party to that suit, & oppressed or grieued by this Maintenance, may prosecute a writ of Champerty against the same offendor, or a writ of Maintenance at his choice, for euery Champerty is Maintenance, but euery Maintenance is not Champerty. And in this case of Champerty, he that selleth his land, or demiseth his land for life or yeares, or any part thereof, during the time that the same land is in suit, shall be punished according to the foresaid statute of 28. Ed. 1. as well as he that purchaseth the same land. And the writ of Champerty may be brought against the buyer alone, or against the seller alone. And it is all one penalty where he selleth his land for mony or other consideration, and where hee freely doth giue his land: for if it be giuen during the time that the land is in suit, it is Champertie: for the Law doth prohibite euery man to obtaine land when it is in suit. But if a man purchase land after iudgement, it is no Champertie, for then there is no suit depending touching that land: and if a man that is learned in the Law, and doth giue counsell therein, doe take part of the land that was in variance of his client

[Margin: What is chāperty, & what not. — Fit. Nat. Br. 171. — 7. Ed. 3. 9. — Fit. champ. 6. — 9. H. 6. 64. — Fit. champ. 5. — 30. Ass. p. 5. — 8. Ed. 4. 13. — 13. H. 4. 19.]

client for his fees, after the same is recorded, this is no Champerty: So that the bargaine be made after the recouery of the land, and not depending the suit. And if a man doe bring an action against another, and do recouer the
47.E.3.9. 7.E.4.15. thing in question against the defendant, yet the plaintife may haue an action of Maintenance against euery person that shall maintaine the defendant in that suit, though he hath lost nothing by that Maintenance, for that the same Statute of 28.Edw.1. is a prohibition of Champertie. And if a man doe bargaine for land before any suit is commenced for the same,
Fit.champ. 15. and after a suit is prosecuted against the tenant of the land for the same, if the same tenant doe make a feoffement or other assurance to the purchasor, according to his bargaine of the same land, during the time of the same suit, yet this is no Champertie: For in this case the seller did not assure this land to the purchasor, vpon couenant to haue Maintenance, but to performe his former bargaine, and the sale was before the suit, though the performance thereof was after. And if a man doe make a feoffement of land to others to his owne vse, during the time that a suit is depending
8.E.4.13 for the same land, this is no Champertie: for the feoffement was not made to haue Maintenance in that suit, but to haue the possession of the land to bee transferred to others, and yet to the same vse it was before. And a man may giue land to his sonne in Franke-marriage, or for the terme of
6 E.3.33. his life, during the time that a suit is depending against him of the same land, and it is no Champertie: for that the words of the statute of Anno 28.Edw.1. be, But it is not intended, that a man shall not haue counsell of pleaders, and of learned men for his fee, nor of his next friends: and the father is bound to relieue and helpe his sonne as much as he may, and it is no Maintenance nor Champertie in him to assure the land to his sonne,
21.Ed.3.52. nor in the sonne to take it. And in a writ of Champertie it is a good plea for the defendant to plead, That he purchased the land of him who recouered it for his money, and not for Champertie to maintaine the suit. And if a man
Fit.champ. 14. doe make a lease for the terme of life of land, and after the tenant for life is impleaded for the same land, and depending that plea, the tenant for life doth surrender his estate for life to him in Reuersion, this is no Champertie.

6 Maintenance may also bee committed in other sorts then be aforesaid, viz. by Embraceors, and by Juries. By the Statute of Anno 33.Edw.1. *Maintenance by Embracery*
St.33.Ed.1. an Embraceor is described to be one that commeth to the barre with the party, and speaketh in the matter, and is there to suruey the Jurie: And
Fit.Nat.Br. 171. he is accounted an Embraceor, who will threaten the Jurie, or any of them, if they doe not giue their verdict by his direction: and he also, who
13.H.4.19. is a procuror of a Jurie to appeare, that is commonly called a leader of Enquests. And the punishment of Maintenance both in Embraceors and Jurors, is assigned by the Statutes of Anno 34.Edw.3.& Anno 38.Edw.3.
St.34.E.3.8 38.Ed.3.12. whereby it is ordained, That if any Juror sworne in Assises, or other Enquests, to be taken betweene the King and the party, or betweene party and party, doe by himselfe, or any other, take any thing of the plaintife, or defendant, to giue his verdict, and thereof is attainted at the suit of the party, which will sue for himselfe, or for the King (or of any other person entring his plaint by Bill immediatly before the Justices before whom the Jurie was sworne) the said Juror shall pay tenne times so much as he hath receiued. *Maintenance by Jurors.*

And

The penalty of Maintenance in Jurors and Embraceors.

And all those which be Embraceors to lead and procure such Enquests in the Countrey, to make a gaine and profit thereof, shalbe punished as the Jurors. And if the Juror or Embraceor so attainted haue not wherewith to make recompence in forme aforesaid, he shall be one yeare imprisoned, which imprisonment shall not bee pardoned for any fine: and the party grieued may haue his action before other Justices, if he will. But no Justice or other officer shall inquire of office vpon any of the points of this Statute, but onely at the Suite of the partie, or of others, as is aforesaid. See Periurie 18.

Maintenance punished by a Decies tantū.

7 Upon the foresaid Statutes of 34. Edw. 3. & 38. Edw. 3. is the writ of Decies tantum grounded. By the which writ the party grieued by any such Maintenance and taking of money by a Juror or Embraceor, shall recouer against the offendor tenne times so much as he hath taken, whereof the King shall haue the onely halfe, and the same party who doth recouer, the other halfe. And a man may haue one writ of Decies tantum against all the Jurors of an Enquest, if they all did take money to giue their verdict, or against so many of them as did take money. And so he may haue one writ against the Embraceors and the Jurors, and recouer against euery of them tenne times so much as he receiued to giue his verdict, or to embrace: as if one of them tooke tenne shillings, another twenty shillings, a third 5. pounds &c. and the dammages shall be taxed against euery of them seuerally. And therefore when one action is brought against seuerall Jurors, for taking of money to giue their verdict, euery of them must plead his plea seuerally, and by himselfe. If a Juror doe take money to giue his verdict on the one part, if after he doth giue no verdict, or if hee with his companions doe giue a true verdict, or such a verdict as the party who bringeth the writ receiueth no hurt thereby, or if the plaintife be nonsute, yet a Decies tantum may bee brought against him: For it is not the giuing of the verdict which the Law doth respect, and punish, but the taking of the money to giue his verdict, and so to doe an vnlawfull act. But otherwise it is of an Embraceor, for if he take money to embrace, and yet doth not embrace, no action will lye against him: for he is no Embraceor, if he doe not embrace. In a writ of Decies tantum, if the Jury find, that one of the Jurie in the former Issue did take land for fortie pounds lesse then it was worth, to giue his verdict, the same Juror shall forfeit to the King and the party tenne times so much, viz. foure hundred pounds. And so shall the Embraceor forfeit tenne times so much, if he hath the land for lesse then it is worth, after the Jurie hath giuen their verdict by his meanes or persuasion. And the one moytie which is due to the King in this case, according to the foresaid Statute of Anno 38. Edward. 3. is a fine to the King for his offence, and not a debt to the King, and therefore the partie grieued shall be first satisfied of his moytie, and after him the King shall bee payed in the receit of the Exchquer. Men that be learned in the Law, may for their fees speake to the Jury, and enforce their clients euidence vnto them so much as they can openly, vpon the triall of the cause: But they may not otherwise labour to the Jury to giue their verdict, and receiue money to that end, for then they be Embraceors. If he that is the party grieued, who may haue against any Juror a Decies tantum for taking of money, doe release to the same Juror all actions, this will not auaile the same Juror,

40.E.3.33. 41.Ed.3.9. Fitz. Decies tantum 1.

21.H.6.20.

37.H.6.31.

41.E.3.9.

41.Ed.3.15. Fitz. Decies tantum 12.

44.Ed.3.36.

6.E.4.5.

Juroꝛ, foꝛ by the said statute any person that will, being a stranger, may haue a Decies tantum against the same Juroꝛ. But if the King doe release befoꝛe any suit commenced, it is a good barre against all persons, as it is in other popular actions: and yet if the party hath begun his suit, the Kings release wil not discharge it, but foꝛ his owne part: foꝛ that which was befoꝛe popular, is now become his priuat action: and a condemnation oꝛ acquitall at his suit is a discharge against the King and all others.

1.H.7.3. 5.E.4.2.

8 There is another kind of Maintenance by Juroꝛs, that the Law doth pꝛohibite, which is, when a Juroꝛ doth take money oꝛ other thing of the one part and the other, who is commonly called Ambidexter: foꝛ the punishment of whom, by a statute made An.5.E.3. it was oꝛdained, That if any Juroꝛ in Assises, Juries, oꝛ Enquests, take of the one part, and of the other, and be thereof duly attainted, he shall not after be put in any Assises, Juries, oꝛ Enquests, but shall be sent to pꝛison, and further punished at the Kings pleasure. And the Justices befoꝛe whom such Assises, Juries, & Enquests shall passe, haue power to inquire and determine, accoꝛding to this statute. As this greedie Ambidexter doth offend two Lawes, so it is pꝛouided to impose two seuerall punishments vpon him: vpon a wꝛit of Decies tantum bꝛought against him, he shall be compelled to pay to the King and the party grieued ten times so much as he hath receiued to giue his verdict, accoꝛding to the statute of 38.E.3. And shall be no moꝛe put in Enquests, but sent to pꝛison, and punished at the Kings pleasure, accoꝛding to the foꝛesaid statute of Anno 5.Ed.3. But no person shall be punished accoꝛding to the said statute of Anno 5.Ed.3. vpon any wꝛit of Decies tantum bꝛought against him, but only vpon an Jndictment at the Kings suit. If any Juroꝛ doe take money of eyther of the parties to a suit after his verdict giuen, foꝛ giuing his verdict, without making couenant therefoꝛe befoꝛe hand, he shall not be punished accoꝛding to any of the foꝛesaid statutes of Anno 5.E.3. 34.Ed.3. oꝛ 38.E.3. foꝛ he is out of the danger of the wꝛit of Decies tantum, and he shall not be impꝛisoned by foꝛce of the statute of Anno 5.Ed.3. foꝛ he did not take mony contrary to the meaning of that statute: But in that case he shall pay a fine to the king.

Maintenance by Ambidexter.

St.5.E.3.10

44.E.3.39. Fit.Dec. tantum 12.

39.Ass.p.19

9 As it is Champertie, and therewith Maintenance, to haue part of the land oꝛ thing in variance: so it is Maintenance to take part in any quarrell depending in suit in the Kings court, oꝛ to woꝛke any fraud whereby iustice may be hindered; as it appeareth by the statute of West.1. whereby it is oꝛdained, That if any Clerke of the kings, oꝛ of any Justice, do receiue the pꝛesentment of any Church, foꝛ the which any plea oꝛ debate is in the K. Court, without the kings speciall licence, he shal loose the Church and his seruice. And if any Justices oꝛ Shirifes Clerke, take part in any quarrell depending in the Kings Court, oꝛ doe woꝛke any fraud, whereby common right may be delayed oꝛ disturbed, he shall loose his seruice, and be further punished, if the Trespas doe require. And after by a statute made Anno 32.H.8. there was a greater penalty imposed vpon those who shall be maintainoꝛs of suits: By which statute it was oꝛdained, That no person oꝛ persons whatsoeuer, shall vnlawfully maintaine, oꝛ cause oꝛ pꝛocure any vnlawfull maintenance in any action, suit, demaund, oꝛ complaint in any of the Kings Courts of the Chauncerie, Starre-chamber, White hall, oꝛ elsewhere, within any of

Westm.1. 3.E.1.28.

The penalty foꝛ maintaining of suits.

St.32.H.8.9

of the K. dominions of England, or Wales, or the marches of the same, where any person or persons haue authoritie, by vertue of the K. Commission, Patent, or Writ, to hold plea of lands, or to heare, examine, or determine any title of lands, or any matter of witnesse, concerning the title, right, or interest of any lands, tenements, or hereditaments: Or shall vnlawfully retaine for maintenance of any suit or plea, any person or persons, or embrace any freeholders or Iurors, or suborne any witnesse by letters, rewards, promise, or by any other sinister labour or meanes, for to maintaine any matter or cause, or to the disturbance or hinderance of iustice, or to the procurement or occasion of any manner of Periurie, by false verdict, or otherwise, in any of the Courts aforesaid, vpon paine of forfeiture for euery such offence x. pounds to the king and Inf. to be recouered by him that will sue for the same in any of the kings Courts of Record, by Action of Debt, Bill, Plaint, or Information, wherein no W. E. P. &c. if the suit be commenced in any of the kings Courts within one yeare next after any such offence committed, or els not.

Retaining for maintenance, or imbracing, or suborning of Iurors.

10 As it is Maintenance to haue by agreement part of the land in variance, or part of the gaines of the suit in question, so is it Maintenance to buy a pretenced right or title of another, of, or to lands or tenements, whereof the seller hath no possession, for it is oft times the cause of Subornation of witnesses, procurement of Periurie, and of the subuersion of iustice; For the redresse whereof, by the last specified Statute of Anno 32. H. 8. it was first enacted, That all Statutes heretofore made concerning Maintenance, Champertie, and Embracerie, or any of them, then standing in force, should be put in due execution, according to the effects of the same. And also by the same statute it was ouer that ordayned, That no person or persons, of what estate, degree, or condition soeuer he or they be, shall bargaine, buy, or sell, or by any meanes obtaine, get, or haue any pretenced rights or titles, or take promise, graunt, or couenant to haue any right or title of any person or persons, in, or to any Manors, Lands, Tenements, or other Hereditaments: but if such person or persons which shall so bargaine, giue, graunt, couenant, or promise the same, their auncestors, or they by whom he or they claime the same, haue beene in possession of the same, or of the reuersion or remainder thereof, or taken the rents or profites thereof, by the space of one whole yeare next before the said bargaine, couenant, graunt, or promise made, vpon paine that he that shall make any such bargaine, sale, promise, couenant, or graunt, shall forfeit the whole value of the Lands, Tenements, or Hereditaments, so bargained, sold, promised, couenanted, or graunted, contrary to the forme of this Act. And the buyer or taker thereof knowing the same, shall also forfeit the said value of the said Landes, Tenements, or Hereditaments, so by him bought or taken, as is aforesaid: the one halfe of the said forfeitures to be to the king, and the other halfe to the party that will sue for the same, in any of the kings Courts of Record, by Action of Debt, Bill, P. or I. &c. wherein no W. E. P. or I. &c. if the suit be commenced by A. B. P. or I. in any of the kings Courts, within one yeare next after any such offence committed, or els not. Prouided alwayes, That it shall be lawfull to any person or persons, being in lawfull possession, by taking of the yearely ferme, rents, or profites of any Manors, Lands, Tenements, or Hereditaments, to buy, obtaine, get, or haue by any reasonable meanes the pretended right or title of any other per-

St. 32. H. 8. 9

Maintenance by buying of pretenced titles

The possessor purchaseth a pretenced title.

person or persons to be made to, of, or in any such lands, tenements, or hereditaments, whereof he shalbe so in lawfull possession: Any thing in this Act &c. notwithstanding.

22 & 23. El. Dyer 374. 6. Ed. 6. Dy. 74. Plow. Com. 87.

11 If a man make a lease or promise a lease for the terme of certain yeeres to another of land, contrary to the foresaid statute of Anñ 32. H. 8. viz. of those lands, whereof neither he himselfe, nor any of his auncestors, nor any by whõ he doth clayme the same land, haue beene in possession of the same, nor of the reuersion, nor remainder thereof, nor taken the rents or profits thereof by the space of one whole yeare before the said bargaine, graunt, and demise made, he is within the danger of the foresaid statute of Anno 32. H. 8. as well as if hee had made an estate for the terme of life, in taile, or in fee simple of the same lãd: for that the scope and effect of the statute is vtterly to root out Maintenance, and bargaines and promises of Titles, for the which the words of the statute be, That no person shall sell or buy any pretenced rights or titles. And a lease is no more lawfull for one yeare, then for an hundred yeares: and some man will be as ready to maintaine to haue a lease for yeares, as to haue a greater estate. Wherefore he that doth make a lease for yeares, or make promise of a lease for yeares of lands, whereof he hath but a pretenced right or title, shall forfeit to the King and him that will sue, the whole value of the inheritance of the land, as well as if he had bargained and sold the fee simple thereof. But it is specially to bee respected in that case, that he hath but a pretenced right or title at the time of his Lease made: for if he hath a good title in the same land at the time of the said Lease, then is he not within the danger of the said Statute, though neither hee himselfe, nor any of his auncestors, nor any by whom he doth clayme the same land, haue beene in possession thereof, nor of the reuersion or remainder thereof, nor haue taken the rents or profites thereof by the space of one whole yeare before the said Lease made: For if a man doe enter into lands that be holden of him, for an alienation in Mortmaine: Or if hee doe recouer lands by a reall action, hee may sell the same land, or make a Lease of the same land within a yeare after the Entry or Recouerie, though neyther hee, nor his auncestors, nor they by whom hee claymeth the same land, haue beene in possession thereof, nor taken the Rents or Profites thereof, by the space of one whole yeare before. And so it is, if a man doe morgage his Land for diuers yeares, vpon condition of repayment of money at a certaine day, or vpon any other condition. If after hee doe redeeme his Land, hee may sell it, or Lease it within one yeare after, though he hath not beene in possession thereof, nor taken the Rents or Profites thereof by the space of many yeares before: For the meaning of the Statute is not to restraine the bargaining, buying, or selling of good and cleare Rights, but of pretenced Rights and Titles. And this pretenced Right or Title is, when one man is in possession of Lands or Tenements, and another man who is out of possession of them, doth clayme them, or doth sue for them: for hee is not aptly sayd to haue title to land, who is in possession of the same. And therefore if he that is out of possession of land, doth bargaine, sell, or make any Agreement, Couenant, or Promise to depart from the same land, or to make any assurance thereof, after hee shall recouer the said Land, hee is within the danger of the said Statute, whether he hath a good title to the same land, or not. And so it is, if one who hath a pretenced Right or Title to copyhold Lands, doth

What is selling of a pretenced title.

Br. Maint. 38 6. E. 6.

What is a pretenced title.

doth bargaine and sell it to another, he is within the compasse and danger of the foresaid statute of Anno 32.H.8. For the words of the statute be, If any doe bargaine, buy, or sell &c. any right or title in or to any lands or tenements: So that those words (any right or title) doe extend to all manner of rights or titles, and consequently to copyhold lands. And seeing a great part of the land of the Realme is graunted by copie; Therefore the meaning of the makers of the said Statute of Anno 32.H.8. was to include them, for the auoiding of Suits, Maintenance, and Champertie, and not to leaue all copyhold estates to the mischiefes mentioned in the preamble of the sayd Act. Co.lib.4.2.

Maintenance by giuing of Liueries and retaining.

12 Giuing of Liueries, Badges, Signes, and Tokens, and retayning of vnnecessarie seruants, is an euill budde springing out of the foresayd Branch of Maintenance, being put in practise by men of great countenance, authoritie, and estate, and it hath beene from age to age accounted a meane to stirre vp quarrels, to boulster Suites, to procure Periurie, and to subuert iustice. And therefore the chiefe Gouernours of this Realme haue endeuoured by many Acts of Parliament to represse or snibbe it: as by the Statute of Anno 1.R.2. & 7.Hen.4. it was ordained, That if any person shall giue any Chaperons, Hats, or such like Liueries to any man for maintenance of quarrels, or other confederacies, he shall forfeit an hundred shillings for euery such Liuerie: and he which receiueth such Liuerie, shall forfeit fortie shillings. And by the statute of 8.H.6. it was enacted, That if any person of his owne authoritie and proper costs doe buy, or weare for his clothing any Clothes or Hats, called Liueries, of the sort or suit of any Lord, Ladie, Knight, Esquire, or other person, to haue supportation, succour, or maintenance in any quarrell, or in any other matter, and being thereof lawfully conuict, he shall forfeit fortie shillings, and be one yeare imprisoned. And by the statute of Anno 1.H.4. it was prouided, That if any which is a Knight or Esquire, meniall of the Kings, or who is of his retinue, to whom his Maiestie shall giue his honourable Liuerie, doe weare his said Liuery in the countrey or Countie where he is resiant or dwelling, or in any other place of the Realme out of the Kings presence (sauing in going or comming from the Kings house) and is thereof duly attainted, he shall lose his Liuerie, and forfeit his fees for euer. And by the statute of Anno 8.Ed.4. it was established, That no person by himselfe, or any other for him, shall giue any Liuerie, or Badge, or retaine any person, other then his meniall Seruant, Officer, or learned man in the one Law or in the other, by any writing, oath, or promise: And if any doe the contrary, hee shall forfeit for euery such Liuerie or Badge giuen an hundred shillings. And he which doth retaine or take of any other such oath, writing, or promise, or is retained by Indenture, shall forfeit an hundred shillings for euery moneth that any person is so retayned with him, by Oath, Writing, Indenture, or Promise. And euery person which is retained by Writing, Indenture, Oath, or Promise, for euery moneth that he is so retained, shall forfeit an hundred shillings. But this act shal not extend or be preiudiciall to any Gift, Graunt, or Confirmation made of any Fee, Annuity, Pention, Rent, Lands, or Tenements by the King, or any others, to any person or persons, for their counsell giuen, or to be giuen, or for their lawfull seruice done or to be done (and for no other vnlawfull cause, or vnlawfull intent) although the person to whom such gift, graunt, or con-

St.1.R.2.7. 7.H.4.14. Sta.8.H.6.4 St.1.H.4.7. Sta.8.E.4.2. Sta.1.H.4.7.

confirmation is made, be not learned in the one law or the other: Neither doth it extend to any libertie giuen at the Kings or Quéenes coronation, or at the installment of any Archbishop, or Bishop, or erection, creation, or mariage of any Lord or Lady of estate, or at the creation of any Knights of the Bathe, or at the commencement of any clerke in an Uniuersitie, or at the creation of Serieants of the law, or giuen by any Fraternitie, Guild, or Mysterie corporat, or by the Maior, Sherife, or other chiefe Officer of any Citie, Borough, Towne, or Port of this Realm of England for the time being, during that time, for the executing of their office or occupation: Nor to any Liueries or Badges, giuen in the defence of the King and his Realme: Nor to the Constable or Marshal for giuing any Badge, Liuerie, or token, for any feats of armes to bee done within this Realme: Nor of any Wardens of the Marches toward Scotland, for any Badge, Liuerie, or token by thē giuen, frō Trent Northward, at such time onely as shall be necessarie to leuie people for the defence of the Marches. And by the stat. of anno 7. H. 4. it was ordained, That no congregation or companie shall make any Liuerie of cloth, or of hats, at their owne costs, vpon paine that euerie of the same congregation or companie, shall forfeit fortie shillings (except Guilds and Fraternities, and also people of Artes and Sciences within Cities and Boroughes, which be ordained to a good intent.

St. 7. H. 4. 14

13 As the wisedome of the Realme hath established from one age to another the foresaid lawes and statutes, for the repressing or snibbing of Champertie, Embracerie, buying of titles, and all other sorts of Maintenance: so hath she prouided trumpets to sound out and publish those laws into the ears, and sinke them into the hearts of all people: and secondly shee hath assigned watchmen and sentinels, to sée who infringed those lawes: and lastly she hath ordained Censors and Judges to punish the offendors therein; as it appeareth by the before specified statute of anno 32. H. 8. wherby it is enacted, That the Justices of Assise shall in euerie Countie within their circuits, two times in the yeare, viz. in the time of their sittings for taking of Assises, or deliuerie of the Gaoles, cause open proclamation to be made as well of the said statute, and euerie thing therin contained, as also of all other statutes heretofore made against vnlawfull maintenance, champertie, embracerie, or vnlawfull retayners, to the intent that no person hearing the same, should be ignorant, or misconisant of the dammages and penalties therein contained. And by the former rehearsed statute of anno 8. E. 4. it is ordained, That euerie person which will sue against any other, for any offence committed contrarie to that statute, or any other of the premisses (viz. any other ordinance or statute before that time made against any persons for giuing or receiuing of Liueries or Badges) before the Kings Justices in his Bench, before the Justices of the Common Pleas, Justices of peace in their Sessions, Justices of Oier and Terminer, and Gaole deliuerie, Justices of the countie Palantine of Lancaster and Chester, and in the Court of Heramshire, and in the Court of the Bishop of Durham in the countie Palantine of Durham, shal be admitted thereunto by the discretion of the said Judges, to giue information for the king of any of the premisses committed within the iurisdiction of the same Courts. And euerie Informer shall be admitted to sue for the King and himselfe, action or actions vpon the same, by information in any of the said Courts, against as many such offendors in one Bill of Information as liketh him, which Information shall be in stead of a Bill, or originall writ, wherein such Proces shall bee awarded,

Publishing, inquiring of, and punishing of maintenāce

St. 32. H. 8. 9

St. 8. Ed. 4. 2

M j. as in

as in an originall writ of Trespasse (but that in the Counties Palantine of Lancaster and Chester, nor in Duresme, no Exigent shall be awarded upon any information, suit, or proces, to be made by force of this ordinance.) And if any be, or any Outlawrie thereupon pronounced, the same shalbe void without any writ of Error. And if any of the offendors be present in any of the said courts, any of the Iustices may cōmaund him to be brought to answer to such bill upon such information (by an othe first to be taken upon a booke by such informer, before some one of the Iudges, that his complaint is true) without any other or further proces therein. And everie of the same Iudges within his iurisdiction may by his discretion examine everie of the defendants upon such information, and iudge him convict as well by examination, as by triall, and the King shal have the one halfe of the forfeiture (if it be not in a citie or towne corporat, that hath the same by the grant of the king, or &c.) and the informer the other halfe, which also shall recover his costs by the Iudges discretion, and execution thereof, as in recoveries upon debt or trespas, wherin no Essoine or Protection shall lye. And the Maior, Sherife, Bailife, or other chiefe officer of everie citie, borough, towne, or port within this realm, having power to heare and determine personall pleas in the court holden before them, or any of them, within any such towne, have authoritie to receive information of any person which offends in the premisses, and to heare & determine as wel by examination as by triall, all things done concerning the same, by, or to the inhabitants within the iurisdictiō of the same court, & to put this stat. for those offences provided, in execution. And the King shal have the one moitie of all penalties forfeited by the said stat. and the Informer & chiefe officers of such citie, borough, &c. shall have the other moitie, equally to be divided betwixt them. And the said chiefe officers part shalbe imployed to the use of the said citie, borough, towne, or port, &c. And sithence the foresaid lawes & statutes, by one other stat. ordayned an. 33. H. 8, and confirmed an. 37. H. 8. it was enacted, That Iust. of peace at their Quarter Sessions, shal have authoritie to inquire as wel by the othes of xij. men, as by information given to them, by any person or persons, of defaults, contempts, & offences cōmitted against the lawes & statutes made and provided concerning, or in any wise touching retainers, giving of liveries, signs, tokens, or badges, maintenance, embracerie, &c. and every of them, & to heare & determine the said defaults, offences, &c. And upon any information touching the penalties, or any of them, to make proces by Venire fac', one Capias & an Exigēt under their seals, against every such person & persons against whom such information or presentment shalbe had, for their appearance before them in their Sessions, to answer to such information or presentment as shall be there made. And if the person or persons so accused by information or presentment shalbe convicted upon such information or &c. by confession, or verdit of xx. men, then the said Iust. have power to give iudgemēt, against every such offendor so convicted, of imprisonment, forfeiture of money, or both of them, as are limited by the said severall statutes for such offences whereof they are convict, and to cause execution therof to be made accordingly.

Iust. of peace may inquire of and punish maintenance.

St. 33. H. 8. 10. 37. H. 8. 7.

14 Maintenance, Champertie, buying of titles, & Embracery, have bin accounted so offensive & professed enemies to the iustice & peace of the realm, that though by the stat. of an. 18. El. it is ordained, That every informer upon any other penall stat. shal exhibit his suit in proper person, & pursue the same onely by himselfe, or by his Atturney in court: and that none shalbe admitted to pursue against any person upon any penall stat. but by way of information or originall

Why the pursuing of maintenance is left out of the stat. of 18. El.

Stat. 18. El.

ginall writ, and not otherwise, nor shall haue any deputy at all. And that vpon euerie such information which shalbe exhibited, a speciall note shall be made of the very day, moneth, & yere of the exhibiting therof into any office, or to any officer which lawfully may receiue the same, without any maner of antedate to be made thereof: And that vpon euery such proces shalbe indorced aswel the parties name that pursueth the same proces, as also the stat. vpon which the information in that behalfe made, is grounded, and that no Informer or plaintife shall compound or agree with any person that shall offend, or shalbe surmised to offend against any penal statute, for such offence, but after answer made in court vnto the information or suit in that behalfe exhibited or prosecuted: nor after answer, but by the order or consent of the court, in which the same information or suit shalbe depending: Yet in the said stat. of 18. El. there is a prouiso, That it shalbe lawfull for any person or persons grieued by means of any maintenãce, chãpertie, buying of titles, or other embracery, to pursue vpõ any stat. prouided against maintenance, champerty, buying of titles, or embracery, as he or they might haue done before the making of the said act. Which prouiso was made to the end that all persons grieued by reason of any maintenance, champertie, buying of titles, or embracery, should be left at libertie to pursue & chasten the offendors therin, by all such means as former laws haue authorised thẽ, & not be restrained by any of the ordinances or articles before rehearsed, for that the said offẽces were by the makers of the said stat. adiudged to be greater impedimẽts & obstacles to the execution of iustice, than other penal stat. were.

15 As the policie of the realme hath deuised the foresaid popular actions and suits to enable euery person ẏ will, in diuers cases to pursue & prosecute maintainors, champertors, buyers of pretenced rights, &c. to the intent the sooner to root out & extirpat those offendors who indeuor to wrest the execution of lawes out of their due course, to subuert iustice, & thereby to hinder the peace of the realme: so hath it in some cases gone further, & ordained, that some assurances made for maintenance, shalbe presently void: as it appeareth by the stat. of an. 8. H. 6. wherby it was enacted, That if any person after his entry into lands or tenements, holden with force, do make a feoffement or other discontinuance to any Lord, or other person, to haue maintenance, or to toll & defraud the possessor of his recouerie in any wise: If after in an Assise, or other action thereof to be takẽ or pursued before the Iust. of Assise, or other the kings Iustices whatsoeuer they be, by due inquiry therof to be taken, the same feoffements and discontinuances may be duly proued to be made for maintenance, as is aforesaid, that then such feoffements or other discontinuances, so as before made shall be void, & holdẽ for none. And by the stat. made an. 4. H. 4. it was established, That if any man, great or small, of what estate or condition they be, make any forcible entry in his own right, or to his own vse, or in anothers right, to his vse, by the way of maintenãce, & therof is attainted at the suit of the party grieued, he shalbe one yere imprisoned, & pay to the partie grieued his double dammages: And also he shall answer to the partie grieued damages for his goods & cattels, if vpon the said forcible disseisin he tooke away any.

Assurances to haue maintenance void.

St. 8. H. 6. 9

Lands gotten by force assured to haue maintenance.

St. 4. H. 4. 8.

Lands forcibly gotten by maintenance.

16 As by the before mentioned stat. maintenance, champerty, embracerie, & buying of titles, be in generall termes deciphered, together with their seuerall penalties, so haue the learned Iudges & Sages of the law expounded the particular branches of euery of those stat. as they grew in question, & were prosecuted in suit before them, & also resolued what maintenance is punishable, and what iustifiable, who may pursue an action, writ, bill, or information &c. of

What maintenance is punishable, and what iustifiable.

maintenance, champerty, &c. against whom the same is to be brought, for what offence or cause the same is maintenable, what pleas are to be pleaded to ye writ, or in bar of the said actions, writs, informations, &c. & what iudgemēt shall ensue thereupon. As euerie champertie is an vnlawful maintenāce, prohibited by the foresaid stat. of West. 1. & West. 2. and punishable according to the before rehearsed stat. of An. 28. E. 1. and euerie chāpertie is a maintenance, & the partie grieued may haue aswel a writ of Maintenance as of Champertie, for by that meanes the champertor hauing bargained to haue part of the land or thing in question, doth ofttimes moue & further the suit, suborneth witnesses, corrupteth the Jurie, and so subuerteth iustice: but there must be a suit depending before it can be adiudged maintenance in any sort: for if one man wil giue money to another to beginne and prosecute a suit against a third person, this is no maintenance, for that this mony was giuen when there was no suit depending: and if there be a writ brought and neuer returned, it is no maintenance. 9.H.6.64. St.28.E.1. 11. 3.H.6.55. 8.H.5.8. 10.Ed.4.19. 30.Ed.3.3.

No maintenance in a Juror for giuing his verdict.

17 If there be a suit depending betwéene two, and they do ioyne an issue, which is tried by xij. men, & found for the plaintife: in this case the defendant cannot haue an action of maintenance against the said Jurors, or any of them, for this verdit giuē, for that they gaue their verdit according to their euidence, and their knowledge of the truth of the matter: and besides they did not thrust thēselues into that cause, but were compelled to appeare by an ordinarie course of law, being impanelled & returned by the Sherife, or some other lawfull officer: but if after the verdit giuen any of the Jurie wil solicit or labor to ye Judge or Judges of the court where the said suit is depending, to giue iudgement for the plaintife, then the def. may haue an action of Maintenance against him, for that the same iudgemēt is a thing wholly belonging to ye office of a Judge, and not of a Juror, & therfore he doth therin intermeddle with another mans office and another mans cause, more than he hath to do or may iustifie, and so hath committed vnlawfull maintenance. 18.E.4.2. 28.H.6.6.

Maintenance by a Juror suing for iudgement.

Maintenance in a Juror.

18 If a Jurie be charged to inquire of a matter in issue, one Juror may perswade his cōpanions, or any of them, to passe for ye plaintife or def. as he conceiueth the truth of the cause to be, or as their euidence doth induce them, & this is no maintenance: but if one of the Jurors will giue or promise money to another of his fellowes, to giue his verdit for the pl. or def. this is vnlawfull maintenance, though he doth wage him to giue his verdit according to truth, and right of the cause in issue. 17.E.4.5. 18.Ed.4.4.

Maintenance by speaking of words.

19 If a man of great authoritie in a country will in the presence of a Jurie, and the standers by at the tryall of an issue say openly, that he will spend mony in the cause in question, in the behalfe of the pl. or the def. or that hee will giue money to labour the Jury, or wil speake other great or high words, in fauor of one of the parties, this is vnlawful maintenāce in him, though he do spend no mony in that cause, nor doth labor the Jury therin: for it may be, that whē the Jury do by his words know his meaning, they dare not in respect of his authoritie or greatnesse in that coūtie, giue their verdit otherwise thā he would haue them. And for the preuention of that kind of maintenance, by a stat. made An. 20. R. 2. it was ordained, That no Lord, or other of the country, great or small, shall sit vpon the bench with the Just. of Assise in their Sessions, in any of the Shires of England, vpon paine of a great forfeiture to the King: neither the Justices shall suffer the contrarie to bée done. And in like sort if a man of great authoritie in the Countie where an Issue is to be tried, hauing nothing to doe in that cause, doth come to the barre with the plaintife, or defendant, that is one of the parties to an Issue that is then to bée tryed, and standeth 22.H.6.5. 13.H.4.19. St.20.R.2. 13. 22.H.6.6.

None shall sit with the Just. of Assise on the bench.

Maintenance in comming to the barre with one of the parties.

by

by him, this is an vnlawfull maintenance in him, though hee neither doth, nor yet speaketh any thing in the matter: for his presence and companie with the one partie, doth shew to the Jurie his particular affection to the same partie, and doth ofttimes induce them to fauour, as much as labour and persuasion by words could doe. And though the Jurie doe not respect him, but giue their verdict for the other partie to that suit, according to their euidence and the truth of the cause in question, yet he hath done what in him lyeth to the contrarie.

21.H.6.15. 22.H.6.5. 28.H.6.7. Dyer fo.95. 20 And so it is if two be in suit, and do ioyne in issue, and the Master of one of the parties to that issue, or any other will deliuer money of his owne to a stranger, to labour the Jurie impanelled to try that issue, to giue their verdit for his said seruant or friend: this is maintenance vnlawfull in the Master or other, though the partie to whom the money was giuen, did neuer deliuer it to the Jurie, nor did not labour vnto them in such sort as hee was directed, or though the Jurie did giue their verdict against his said seruant: for when the Master had deliuered the money to the stranger, and told him to what purpose he should vse it, he had done as much as he could do in that suit, to hinder the course of iustice, though his direction tooke no successe according to his desire. And also it is vnlawfull maintenance, if one giue money to a man that is impanelled of a Jurie to giue his verdict on the one side, though that partie impanelled doth not appeare, or do appeare, and is drawne out by challenge or otherwise. And it is maintenance vnlawfull, if one do threaten to kill or beat a Juror, if he do not giue his verdict for the one part to that issue, which hee doth name, though the same Juror do otherwise. 22.H.6.6. Maintenance by giuing of money to labour a Jurie.

28.H.6.6. 21 If a Jurie do come to a mans house, and desire him to informe them of the truth of a matter whereof they do doubt, and he doth informe them thereof, this is iustifiable: But if one do come to a Jurie, or of himselfe do labour to informe them of the truth of a cause in question, this is maintenance vnlawfull, and therefore punishable. And so it is, if the Court be informed by the plaintife or defendant when an issue is to be tryed, that there is a man at the bar, or in that place, who doth know the truth of the matter in issue, and doth desire that the same man may be examined by the Court to testifie the truth of that cause in question to the Jurie, and the Court doth cause him to be called to testifie his knowledge therein, and he at the commaundement of the Court deliuereth that which he doth know in that matter, this is maintenance iustifiable: But if the same partie will come to the barre of his owne head, and testifie for the plaintife, or the defendant, this is vnlawfull maintenance, and hee may be punished therefore. What is maintenance in a witnesse, and what not.

22.H.6.6. 22 If one man do labour to indict another, by force whereof he is indicted: in this case hee that is indicted may haue a writ of Maintenance against the procurer of that indictment, and yet this is no quarrell, but it is a taking of a part, and so prohibited by the stat. of anno 1.E.3. and it is in the nature of an action betweene the King and the partie indicted: and the foresaid statute is generall, that it shall not be lawfull to any person great or smal, to maintain quarels, or to take parts, to the let or disturbance of the Common law. St.1.E.3.14. Maintenance by procuring of an indictment.

What is maintenance in a mainpernor.

23 If a man be arrested, indicted, or sued, so that he is compelled to become bound with mainpernors for his apparance, the mainpernor may come into the Court and see the apparance of the same partie recorded, and iustifie the same in a writ of Maintenance brought against him: but he cannot retaine or intreat a man learned in the law to be of counsell with the principall partie, nor meddle further in that cause, than to see the mainprise performed, and himselfe discharged. 34.H.6.25. 14.H.6.6. 18.E.4.12.

Maintenance in respect of his interest in the land.

24 Euerie person that hath any interest in land, may meddle and maintain him who is impleaded for the same land, and not bee punished therefore in a writ of Maintenance: As if tenant for terme of life, or in taile of land, bee impleaded for the same land, or any part thereof, he in the reuersion or remainder thereof, may at his owne charges maintaine him in that suit, for the safegard of his owne estate; for it is in a sort his owne case, and the defence of it is to his owne benefit, and the euiction to his owne disheritance. But this maintenance must be after tenant for terme of life hath atturned vnto him in the reuersion: for if he maintaine the suit before, it is punishable in him. And so it is, if a man being seised of land, hath issue a daughter, who is maried to another, if the father in law be impleaded of that land in a reall action, the sonne in law may maintaine him at his owne charges; for that by possibilitie that land may after the decease of his father in law descend to his wife, and so come to him in her right. But if the daughter dye without issue of her bodie begotten by the said husband, before the said suit commenced, then the sonne in law cannot maintaine the father in law in that suit: Neither can hee maintaine him during the life of his wife, if an action of Debt, couenant, account, or any other personall action be brought against him: for he is neither to take benefit or losse by any of those suits. And if a man seised of land make a lease for certaine yeares of the same, and after a suit is commenced betweene the said lessee for yeares, and a stranger, touching the same land, or any part thereof, the lessor may giue euidence for the lessee, vpon the triall of the cause in question, or otherwise may maintaine him in that suit, at his owne charges, for it tendeth to his owne priuat benefit or losse. And in some case a man may maintaine a suit lawfully, though he be neither heire to the land, nor in possession, reuersion, or remainder thereof: As if a man being seised of land, doe make a lease thereof to another, for the terme of the life of the lessee, and after doth grant to a straunger, that if the said tenant for terme of life doe dye during the same lessors life, that then the same stranger shall haue and enioy the same land for the terme of xx. yeares after the death of the same tenant for life; if in this case the tenant for life be impleaded for this land, the same stranger may maintaine him for the sauing of his owne estate for yeares, and yet he hath no certaintie, but a possibilitie of a terme for yeares, which peraduenture will neuer chance. And likewise in some other case a man may maintaine a suit lawfully, though he be neither in possession, reuersion, remainder, or possibilitie of the thing in question: As if a man be seised of a rent going out of another persons land, to him and to his heires, and by his deed doth graunt the same to another and to his heirs, with clause of warrantie, and the tenant of the land out of the which this rent is issuing, doth atturne to the grauntee of this rent, if after the grauntee be impleaded of this rent, vpon tryall of the issue the grantor may come into the Court, and shew to the Jurors such euidence as he hath to proue the title of this rent; and it is lawfull maintenance, and not punishable in him,

Bro. Maint. 53. — 9.H.6.64. — 14.H.7.2. 6.E.4.5. 19.E.4.3. — 6.E.4.2. 39.H.6.20.

Maintenance in respect of his possibilitie. — 9.H.6.64.

Maintenance in respect of his warranty — 11.H.6.49.

though

though he was neither called into the Court by voucher to warrantie, or by Warrantia Chartæ. And so might he haue done, if he had beene called to warrantie by any of the meanes aforesaid, vpon a warrantie made of land or rent: for it is to preserue himselfe out of daunger, and from recompencing in value of that whereof before he had made warrantie.

25 As it is in lands and leases, so is it in rents, goods, and debts, for euerie person that hath interest in them may meddle, and maintaine and defend him who is impleaded or prosecuted by suit, or doth implead or prosecute by suit any other, for any matter or cause concerning him, or whereupon hee doth depend, so that the same suit doth tend to impeach, preiudice, or trouble his estate therein, or may redound to his benefit or profit, or may be a meane thereof: As if a man haue a rent charge in fee out of certaine lands, and another 9.H.6.64. man hath in custodie a boxe of writings concerning the same rent, and after hee that hath the rent doth graunt it to a stranger and his heires, to the which graunt the tenant of the land charged doth atturne; and moreouer, the grantor of that rent charge, doth graunt to the assignee of the same, that if he can recouer the same boxe of writings, that then the same assignee shall haue them: If after this graunt the grauntor doth pursue a writ of Detinue against him that hath the custodie of this boxe of writings, he to whom the same rēt charge was graunted, may lawfully maintaine him in that suit, for that by promise he is to haue the same boxe of writings, if it be recouered, for the preseruation 11.H.6.47. of his estate in the said rent charge. And a Lord may maintaine his tenant if he be impleaded for his freehold, in respect of his rent and seruices that he is to receiue and haue of him. And so it was before the Statute of Uses, made anno 27.H.8. if a man had made a feoffement of land to others, to his owne vse, the feoffor might maintaine the freehold tenant which held of his feoffees, in respect of the vse which he hath in the rent and seruice of that tenant.

Maintenance in respect of his rent.

A Lord may maintaine his tenant.

15.H.7.2. 26 And the same law is touching debt: As if A. do owe vnto B. xx.l. and C. doe owe to A. xx.l. due by Obligation, and A. will deliuer vnto B. the same Obligation, in satisfaction of the xx.l. which he doth owe him: In this case B. may sue an Action of Debt vpon this Obligation against C. in the name of A. and retaine an Attourney and learned counsell, and pursue and maintaine the suit, and so may A. for either of them hath interest in this debt: and one of them may aid, assist, and maintaine the other, to recouer his debt against C. in respect of their seuerall interests in the same debt. But if in this case A. had promised to B. but part of this debt, to haue prosecuted and maintained this suit, then it had beene Champertie, and vnlawfull maintenance in B. And the 34.H.6.30. same law is, if one man be bound by Obligation to pay another man xx.l. to the vse of a third man: the Obligee, and hee to whose vse the Obligation was made, may both meddle in the suit of this Obligation.

Maintenance in respect of debt.

27 And so it is in goods: for he that hath any propertie, title, or lawfull 39.H.6.20. possession in goods, may maintaine a suit that is prosecuted against another touching the same goods: As B. brought an action of Debt against A. in London, and the Sherife returned that A. had nothing &c. Wherupon at the plaintifes surmise, certain goods of A. were attached in the hands of I. according to the

Maintenance in respect of his title to goods.

the custome of the said Citie, and a Scire facias was awarded against the same I. to answer for those goods, in which A. did maintaine the same I. in nominating vnto him a learned man in the law, to whom by his aduice he went for his counsell, and this was awarded maintenance iustifiable, for that the propertie of the goods so attached in the hands of I. were, and did continue in the said A. So it is if one man doe deliuer a deed or other writing to another to be kept, if a straunger will bring an action of Detinue against him to whom the same was deliuered, the partie who deliuered that writing, may lawfully maintaine him in that suit, for the interest hee hath in the same writing. And yet the recouerie of that writing would not haue bound him that did deliuer it, but hee might haue had his action for the same against him that did recouer it.

Maintenance in detaining of a writing deliuered in trust.

Maintenance in respect of his ioynt interest with others.

28 As euerie person may lawfully maintaine any suit that shall be prosecuted, which concerneth his priuat and particular land, lease, rent, debt, or goods, so may he maintaine a suit touching any land, or other thing, which hee hath ioyntly or in common with others: As the Parson of a Church brought an action of Trespasse against one of his Parishioners, for digging of his ground, and spoyling of his grasse: Whereunto the defendant pleaded, That the place where the Trespasse was supposed to be done, is a Churchyard, consecrate by the Bishop, and that he, and all those who are inhabitants in the same Parish, haue vsed to haue their Sacraments and buriall for their dead there: And that one of the inhabitants of the same Parish dyed, and hee with others brought his bodie to the Church, and after made a graue for him in the same Churchyard, and there buried him, which is the same digging whereof the plaintife hath conceiued his action: Whereupon they were at issue: In this case it was agreed by all the Iustices, that euerie inhabitant of the same Parish may lawfully giue euidence, and otherwise maintaine this issue, though they be not parties thereunto: for euerie of them hath the like interest in the Churchyard, as the partie to that suit. And the same reason and law seemeth to be, if there be a suit commenced betweene one or more inhabitants of a village, Hamlet, or Parish, and some other person or persons, for a common or way, or for the digging of a pit of stone, marle, grauell, morter, sand &c. vsed, or claimed to belong, or of right to bee due to the inhabitants of the same Village, Hamlet, or Parish; after issue ioyned touching the right or title of the same common, way, or pit, the residue of the inhabitants of the said Village, Hamlet, or Parish, may aide, and assist their neighbour or neighbours partie to that issue, and it is lawfull maintenance, for it tendeth to the benefit or preiudice of all the said inhabitants, and is in a sort their owne case. 18.E.4.2.

Maintenance by all the inhabitants of a parish.

Maintenance of a poore man in his suit.

29 In a Writ of Maintenance the plaintife supposed that the defendant did maintaine one A. in an action which the plaintife brought against the sayd A. Whereunto the defendant pleaded, That the same A. was a poore man, and had nothing to defend himselfe in the suit which the plaintif had commenced against him, and that the defendant of his almes gaue him xx.s. which is the same maintenance. This was allowed a lawfull maintenance, and iustifiable for any man to doe: for whereas vnlawfull maintenance is in case when a man doth maintaine a suit, to haue the whole or parcell of the land, or thing in question, or to haue some other consideration to further or vphold that suit, 32.H.6.35. 21.H.6.15. 9.H.6.64.

or

or where a man hauing nothing to do, nor colour to meddle, yet wil undertake for euill will to maintaine that cause in question; this giuing mony to a poore man to defend his right, is not to either of the intents aforesaid, but bestowed upon a charitable disposition, to search out truth, and further the execution of iustice: which appeareth by the stat. of 11. H. 7. wherin the king and the whole parliament willing indifferent iustice to be ministred, according to the common laws, as wel to the poore as to the rich, and perceiuing that the poore were not of abilitie to sue according to the law of the realme, for the redresse of their iniuries and wrongs, ordained, that the king himselfe, the L. Chancellor, and some of each profession towards the law, should in a sort aid and assist them: the words of which stat. be these, viz Euerie poore person which shall haue cause of action against any other, shal haue by the discretion of the Chancellor, writs originall, & writs of Subpena, according to the nature of his cause, nothing paying to the K. for the seales of the same, nor to any person for ÿ writing of ÿ same writs. And the said Chancellor shall assigne such of the clerkes, which shal use the making and writing of the writs, to write the same readie to be sealed, and also learned Counsell & Atturneyes for the same, without taking any reward therefore. And after the said writs be returned, if it bee before the King in his Bench, the Iustices there shal assigne to the same poore person counsel learned by their discretions, which shall giue their counsell, nothing taking for the same. And likewise the Iustices shall appoint Atturneyes for the same poore person, & all other officers requisit to be had for the speed of the said suits, which shall do their dueties, without any rewards for their counsels, helpe, and businesse in the same. And the same law and order shalbe obserued in all such suits to be made before the K. Iustices of his Common pleas, & Barons of his Exchequet, and all other Iust. in Courts of Record, where any such suits shal be.

St. 11. H. 7. 12

Proces, counsellors, and Atturneyes assigned to aid the poore.

30 As Maintenance in the cases aforesaid is lawfull and iustifiable, in respect of the parties priuat profit or interest in the thing in question, or when it is done without malice or hope of profit, upon a charitable disposition, so is it in diuers cases allowable, in regard of the linke or bond of nature, whereby one person is by loue or dutie tied to another: as the father may maintaine his son and heire, and giue money of his owne in defence of him, or his title, or suit, for he is bound to find him: but so he may not doe for another kinsman. And the sonne may maintaine the father and mother, and one brother another, and one neere kinsman another, and one ally another, in some cases, and in some sort: as if a man be impleaded, another that is his brother, or kinsmã, or of his alliance, may go to the bar with him, & stand by him, & comfort him: or he may ride to his counsell with him, or he may request a man that is learned in the law, to bee of counsell with him in that cause: but he must not retaine that learned man, nor giue him any mony of his own to be of counsel, neither must he giue or promise money to the Iurors, or any of them, to giue their verdict for him, for then it is unlawfull maintenance in him: & so it is in a stranger, who hath nothing to do in that cause; if he doe goe to the barre with him that is impleaded, or do stand by him of purpose, for to countenance the cause in question, or doe request a learned man in the law to bee of counsell with him, or doe giue money to any of the Iurors for their verdict, this is unlawfull Maintenance in him. And in the cases aforesayd, and all other cases of Maintenance, this unlawfull Maintenance is a continuall Maintenance during that suit, unlesse the partie grieued doe in the meane time release the same. But if the same Maintenance bee in respect of alliance, and that hee who is supposed to bee the

Maintenance in respect of kindred or alliance.

34. H. 6. 26. 6. Ed. 3. 33.

21. H. 6. 16. 14. H. 7. 2. 20. H. 6. 1. 19. Ed. 4. 3. 21. H. 6. 16.

9. Ed. 4. 32.

Unlawfull maintenance is continuall.

the maintainor, hath maried the daughter, sister, neece, or other kinswoman of one of the parties to the first suit wherein the maintenãce was supposed to be, he must pleade, that his wife was living at the time of the maintenance supposed to be: for if she were then dead, the alliance betweene them is dissolved, and then he had no cause to maintaine that suit, but shalbe punished as a stranger. And yet in that case, if the same woman hath any issue of her bodie begotten, who may inherit the land of him whose suit that husband of the deceased woman, and the father of that issue did maintaine, then is the maintenance lawfull in any action brought against the same partie, in respect of the kindred, and also of the benefit that may come to his owne issue. And in a writ of maintenance it is a good plea for the defendant to plead, that hee was gossip to him whose cause he was supposed to maintaine, for that gossiprie is in law adiudged a kind of affinitie.

6.Ed.4.

14.H.7.2.

Maintenance in respect of gossiprie. 6.Ed.4.5.

Maintenance in respect the partie could not speake English.

31 A. brought a writ of Maintenance against B. and supposed, that the same B. did maintaine L. in an action which he brought against the said L. on the part of the said L. Whereunto the sayd B. pleaded, that the same L. was a Dutchman, borne out of the Kings obedience, and could not speake the English or Latine tongue, and therefore being acquainted with B. the defendant, who could speake the Dutch tongue, he desired him to bring him to some man learned in the law, to be of his counsell in that suit, and to informe that learned man of the truth of his cause in question: whereupon hee brought him to one M. a man learned in the law, and opened the truth of his case unto the said M. as he received it from the said L. in Dutch, which is the same maintenance. And this was adiudged a good plea in barre, and a lawfull maintenance: for it is a deed of charitie to aid and helpe him who could not helpe himselfe. And the Dutchman had no meanes to helpe himselfe, being a straunger borne, and not understanding the English nor Latine tongue, but by the assistance and information of some English man.

34.H.6.26. 15.H.7.2.

Maintenance in a professor of the Law.

32 If a Serieant at law, an Apprentice, or other Councellor, being retained for his fee, doe give unto his Client the best counsell that he can for the recoverie or defence of the suit which he undertaketh, according to the ordinarie course of the law; or doth enforce the evidence at the barre so much as he can, at the tryall of his clients cause, this is lawfull maintenance, and iustifiable: But if he doe pay or promise money to any of the Iurie, to give his verdit for his client, or do threaten any of them to be killed, beaten, or otherwise evill intreated, if they do give their verdit against his client: or if he do spend, or do offer to spend his own mony in defence of his clients cause, this is unlawful maintenance, & punishable according to the before rehearsed stat. of ann. 1. R. 2. for those things he doth not as a lawyer, or according to the course of the law, nor by the warrant of law, but by iniustice, and upon his owne corruption and wrong. But in the first specified case, if a man that is not learned in the law, having himselfe no interest in the cause in question, will declare to the Iurie, or to the partie, or to his counsell, the cause in question, and the circumstances thereof, as a man learned in the law, this is unlawfull Maintenance in him, though hee doe it as well as a man learned in the law: for hee doeth it upon Maintenance, where the learned man doeth it for his fee. And so it is, if a man that hath land in suit or question, will bring and

6.Ed.4.5.

22.H.6.6. 11.H.6.13.

22.H.6.5.

and shew his evidences and writings to a Nobleman, Gentleman, or other Fitz.Maint. 21.
man of countenance, that is not learned in the law, and request his opinion of them, whether they will serue to defend his title in the cause in suit, and the partie doth affirme them to be good and sufficient in law, to iustifie and maintaine his cause, this is vnlawfull maintenance in that person who giueth this counsell, for by this meanes the partie may be encouraged to prosecute or defend a suit which the law will not warrant him to effect. And if L. being a man Co.li.1.177
that is not learned in the law, will publish that B. hath good right and title to the Mannor of D. wheras in truth B. hath no good right & title thereunto, but C. hath the onely right & title to the same: in this case because L. hath taken vpon him the knowledge of the law, and intermedled in a matter wherin he hath nothing to do, C. may haue an action vpon the case against the said L. for slandering of his title, and shall recouer his damages against him, and his ignorance of the law will not excuse him.

33 In an Action of Maintenance the plaintife declared, That the defen- Maintenance by an Atturney.
36.H.6.37. dant maintained one B. in the court of L. in an action of Couenant, which the plaintife brought against the said B. in the same court. Whereunto the defendant pleaded, That he was retained to be the Atturney of the same B. in the said suit which the plaintife did prosecute against him, by force wherof he came to a man learned in the law, by the commandement of the said B. his client, and desired him to be of counsel with the said B. and gaue him his fee of the money of the said B. the which is the same maintenance. And this was adiudged maintenance iustifiable: for when an expert and learned man is Atturney for another, he is to do all lawfull things which he can touching that suit, for the benefit of his client, with the priuitie or direction of his client, as in retaining of learned counsell, suing forth of originall or iudiciall proces, procuring a Iu-
Kel.fol.50. rie to be impanelled, and returned by the Sherife, by obtaining a Supersedeas
13.H.4.19. for his client, when cause doth require it, and he may giue euidence to the Iury vpon the tryall of his clients cause: and also he may request any of the Iurors impanelled for the triall of the said cause, to appeare, for the speedy end of the said suit. But neither the same Attourney who is retained for that only cause,
34.H.6.26. nor a generall Attourney that is constituted by any person in al his causes, ac-
St.13.E.1. 10. cording to the stat. of West. 2. may do any vnlawfull thing in his clients behalfe, as to giue or promise money, or other reward, of his owne, or his clients, to a Iuror, to giue his verdict for his client, or to threaten him if hee doe other-
21.H.6.10. wise, or to defend or offer to defend his clients cause at his owne charges: or to procure the Sherife to returne a Iurie at his denomination for the tryal of his clients cause: for in all these cases last specified, the maintenance is vnlawfull and punishable; for he cannot do them as an Attourney, but as a straunger, a maintainor, and of his owne wrong. And if a man do maintaine a suit by an
22.H.6.14. Atturney, an action of Maintenance doth lye against the Master. And if the Maintenance in a Sherife or his bailiffes.
Sherife of any Countie, his Vndersherife, or any Bailife, do any of the things
13.H.4.19. aforesaid, in any suit prosecuted betweene partie and partie, other than impanell a Iury, and summon them to appeare at a day & time prefixed by the kings writ, it is vnlawfull maintenance in him.

22.H.6.35. 34 In an action of Maintenance the defendant pleaded, That he whō it is Maintenance in respect of neighborhood.
supposed that he maintained, is his neighbour, and that hee came vnto him, and told him that the plaintife had procured a Capias to arrest him, & therefore

prayed

praied the defendant to giue him counsell, what he were best to doe, and hee this defendant aduised his said neighbour, to goe to London, and to yeeld his bodie to the Iustices, and to procure a Supersedeas, which is the same maintenance whereupon the action is brought. And this was adiudged no vnlawfull maintenance, but a neighbourly and friendly counsell, which euerie person may giue to another. For if a husbandman, or any other doe come to his neighbour, and tell him that a stranger doth owe him money, or doth detaine his goods from him, and request his counsell, that neighbour may aduise him to bring an action of Debt or Detinue against the same straunger: Or if one 12.Ed.4.14.
neighbour shall tell another, that hee hath a cause to put in suit, and desire that 19.Ed.4.3.
hee will instruct him what learned man in the law he doth know to whom he may repaire for counsell, his neighbour may informe him of such one as hee taketh to bee learned, and also may goe with him to that learned man, and bee present when he doth retaine him of his counsell, and open his case vnto him, and also, hee being a meane man and of small countenance or authoritie in the countrey, may goe to the barre, and stand by him at the tryall of his cause in question: but if that neighbour shall giue any money to the counsellor, to be retained with his neighbour, or shall giue any money or other reward to the Sherife, or Vndersherife, or to any Bailife, to arrest the other partie in his neighbours behalfe, or to answer his suit, then is it vnlawfull maintenance in him, and hee is by action of Maintenance to bee punished therefore.

Where the master may maintaine his seruant.

35 In an action of Maintenance brought by A. against B. the plaintife 31.H.6.8.
declared, that where he brought another action before against C. the said defendant did maintaine the same C. in the same first action: whereunto B. the defendant pleaded, That the same C. is his seruant, retained in his seruice for one whole yeare, and therefore he retained one M. an Apprentice of the law, to be of counsell with the said C. his seruant, and paid the said M. his fee, with part of the wages due to the said C. which was the same maintenance: and this was adiudged a good plea in barre, and lawfull maintenance; for it is law- 22.H.6.35.
full for the Master to request a man that is learned in the law to be of counsel 9.H.6.64.
with his seruant in his suit, and to pay the same counsellor his fee, with part of 28.H.6.12.
the wages of his said seruant, and to goe with his seruant to the barre at the 19.Ed.4.3.
tryall of his cause in question, which the law doth allow him to doe, in respect 19.H.6.30.
the sooner to deliuer his seruant from suit and trouble, that hee may not loose the benefit of his seruice, for the longer he doth lacke his mans seruice, the greater is the Masters losse. And if the seruant be arrested in any priuiledged place, the Master may maintaine him, and spend his owne money to deliuer him, in respect that otherwise he should loose his seruice: for by that meanes he doth maintaine him in his owne behalfe, and to auoid his owne hinderance. But if the seruant be impleaded in a reall action, wherein he may appeare, and answer by Attourney, and that his owne presence is not requisit, then the ma- 21.H.7.40.
ster may not maintaine him therein, for that the Master shall receiue no preiudice if the land in question shall be recouered from his seruant. And in like sort the seruant may maintaine the Master, in any suit commenced by or against his said Master in all lawfull manner: As, he may trauaile in furtherance of his Masters suit, he may retaine his counsell with his Masters mo- 19.H.6.31.
ney, and shew his counsell, or the Iurie, vpon the tryall of his Masters cause 19.Ed.4.3.
in question, his Masters euidence: for he is bound to doe his Master his diligent

How the seruant may maintaine his Master.

gent seruice, and that which his Master commaundeth him to do touching his suit, is his Masters seruice. But that seruant which may iustifie to maintaine his Master in such sort as is aforesaid, must be a seruant who is retained
39.H.6.5. with his Master for a yeare, or some long time, and to do all such seruices as he shalbe imployed in by his said Master: for if he be a seruant onely hired for a day, two, or three, or to ride but some one iourney, or to do but some one speciall seruice, then if he do maintaine his Master, or his Master maintaine him in any sort, as aforesaid, it is vnlawfull maintenance in him. But if in either of the cases aforesaid, the Master for his seruant, or the seruant for his Master, shall giue or promise money, or other reward, to any of the Jurie, to giue his verdict, or do threaten any of them to be killed, beaten, maimed, dispossessed of
12.E.4.14. their farmes, or do giue his owne money to the Sherife to arrest the other par-
19.H.6.31. tie to that suit, then it is punishable by action of Maintenance, in him that shal so offend.

Deceit, Couin, Collusion, Fraud.

1 DEceit, Couin, Collusion, and Fraud, bee great offences to the Commonweale, and speciall impediments of the iustice and peace of the Realm, whereof there be so many, and of so generall sorts and kinds, as there be wicked deuises in the hearts of men, and lewd persons to put them in practise. And it were a worke almost as infinite, to diuulge the particulars, and to reduce into writing all the Deceits, Couins, Collusions, and Frauds, which in time haue beene inuented and effected, as it were to poise the weight of the sands of the sea, or to decipher the number of the starres of the element: for by how many meanes a man may trust, by so many and more hee may bee deceiued. And therefore I will vndertake to treat of no more than our common and statute lawes haue detected, and accused to bee deceits, frauds, &c. and amongst others, but of those which the makers, expositors, and Sages of our lawes haue noted to be chiefely offensiue, and most opposite to the due execution of iustice, vpon which this peace, whereof I doe write, doth chiefely depend. For the wisedome of this Realme, first in the making of our lawes, and after in expounding them, haue bent their chiefe care to crush and beat downe Deceit and Fraud, plainely seeing, that the greatest part of the crimes which bee committed in this kingdome, from the highest treason to the smallest trespasse, haue some intermixture with them: And that if they with their dependants could bee fully extirpat, both iustice and peace would more brightly flourish. And notwithstanding they doe not begin their quarrels with rapier and dagger, sword and buckler, as some other of the offences before mentioned do, yet is there grafted in the root of them as much gawle and venim, and more durable and bitter extremities do spring from them, than doe ensue by the Canon shot, the light horsemans staffe, or the footmans bill: For though some part of euerie kings raign hath had a calme and repose from war and hostilitie, yet neuer any age or yeare was cleerely freed of falshoods, corruptions, deceits, and frauds.

The multitude and enormitie of Deceits and Frauds.

2 The wisedome of the Realme perceiuing how necessarie a thing iustice is, and how opposite and repugnant vnto it deceits and frauds bee, doth there-

therefore specially prouide to make choyce of such men of all sorts, to execute the same iustice, as she is persuaded by their learning and experience can, & by their vertue & integritie will performe to euerie person his due, and tread & beat downe fraud, whose pains she doth requite with reuerend respect, liberal rewards, titles of credit, & large priuiledges. But if she do find any of the said officers whom she putteth in trust, to deceiue her expectation, and to practise falshood or guile, then she doth as sharply punish them, as she did before munificently wage them: As appeareth by the stat. of An. 8. R. 2. wherby it was ordained, That if any Iudge or Clerke do make any false entring of a plea, rase any rol, or change any verdict, whereby any person receiueth disheritance, & he be thereof conuict before the K. and his Counsell, he shal be punished by fine & ransome at the K. pleasure, and satisfie the partie: And for the recouerie of the inheritance, the partie shall sue by writ according to the law. And for the auoyding of corruption which may happen in officers in those courts & places, wherein there is requisit to be had the true administration of iustice; & to the intent that worthy persons should bee preferred to the places of iustice, & none other should attaine the same for fee or reward, by a stat. made An. 5. & 6. E. 6. it was enacted, That if any person bargaine or sell any office, or deputation of office, or take any mony, fee, reward, or other profit, directly or indirectly, or take any promise, agreement, couenant, bond, or assurance, to receiue or haue any mony, reward, &c. for any office, or the deputatiõ of any office, or any part of any of thẽ, or to the intent that any person shold enioy any office, or the deputation of any of thẽ, or any part or parcel of any of them, which office, or any part of it doth concerne ye administration or execution of iustice, or which shall cõcern any clerkeship, to be occupied in any court of record, wherin iustice is to be ministred: then he so offending, shall not lose onely all his right & estate, which hee shall then haue of, in, or to the sayd office, or deputation; but also he that shal giue or promise any money, fee, or reward, for any such office, or deputation, shall immediatly vpõ the said gift, or promise, be adiudged a disabled person in the law to all intents, to haue or enioy the said office or deputatiõ. And euerie such bargain, sale, bond, couenant, promise, and assurance, shall bee void, to and against him by whom the same is made. But this Act shall not be preiudiciall to the chiefe Iust. of the K. Bench & Common pleas, or to the Iust. of Assise, but they may do in euerie behalfe concerning any office to be granted by any of thẽ, as they might haue done before the making of the same Act. And because the prouidence of the realm did conceiue some iealousie & suspition in those learned men in the lawes of this realm, who by their owne means & industrie, & for their own cõmoditie and ease, obtained to be Iust. of Assise in the counties where they were borne, or did dwell, and did feare that affection & fauor towards their kinsmen, allies, neighbors, and friends, might sometime allure thẽ to decline from the beaten path of iustice, therfore by one stat. made An. 8. R. 2. & another An. 33. H. 8. it was enacted, That no Iustice, nor other man learned in the laws of this realm, shal exercise the office of Iust. of Assise within the countie where he was borne or doth inhabit, vpon pain to forfeit for euery offence done contrary to this act C. l. to the K. & him that will sue by B. P. I. or actiõ of debt, wherin no W. E. P. But this stat. doth not exted to any Clerk of Assise, associat to any Iust. of Assise: nor to the Iustices, Iustices Clerks, or Clerk of Assise withi[n] the Duchie, and County Palantine of Lancaster: nor to the I. of the one Bench or the other, for taking, hearing, & determining of Assises in the said courts: nor to any Iust. that shal take any Assise vpon adiournment, for difficultie of ye same: nor to any Maiors, Sherifes, Recorders, Stewards, Bailifs, Sutors, or other officers in any citie, borough, or towne, but they may be I. of Assise, of Fresh force, and of other Assises, in the same towne &c. where he or they do dwell, or were borne, as they might haue bin before. And in like

Margin notes:

The reward for paines and punishments for deceit of officers towards the law.

St. 8. R. 2. 4. — A Iudge, A Clerke.

Stat. 5. & 6. E. 6. 16. — No office of iustice shalbe sold or bought.

St. 8 R. 2. 2. St. 33. H. 8. — No man shal be iustice of Assise in his owne countie.

A Sericant, A Pleader. like sort by the stat. of W.1. it was established, That if any Sericant, Pleader, or other, do any deceit in the K. court, or do consent therunto, to beguile the court, or the partie, & is therof attainted, he shalbe imprisoned a yeare & a day, and being a counsellor, he shal not any more be receiued to plead in the K. court for any man, and if he be any other than a pleader, he shalbe imprisoned as aforesaid. And if the trespas require a greater punishmēt, it shalbe at the K. pleasure. And by the stat. of An.10.H.6.& An.18.H.6. it was enacted, That if any Philozer, Exigenter, or any other officer of the K. Bench, or Common pleas, do make any entry in any suit, that the plaintife in the same suit hath offered himselfe in his owne proper person, except the pl. in yͤ same suit (before such entrie be made) do appeare in his own proper person before some of the Just. of yͤ place where yͤ plea is depēding, & there be sworn vpō a book, yͭ he is yͤ same person in whose name yͤ said suit is pursued, or yͭ some other credible person of the K. counsell wil take such oth for him, yͭ said philozer, exigenter, &c. shal forf. xl.s. to yͤ K. euery time yͭ he shalbe attainted by yͤ examinatiō of any of yͤ J. of yͤ same place where any such entry or record is. St.3.Ed.1.2 A Philozer, An Exigēter. St.10.H.6.4 18.H.6.9.

3 And because Atturneies be also necessary mēbers in the cōmonweale, & special means to solicit & further yͤ executiō of iustice, therfore the law hath had a careful regard that they should be men of integrity, vertuous, and of good name; and hath prouided seueral stat. to punish such of thē as shall cōmit any notorious falshood, guile, fraud, slacknes, ignorance, omissiō, or contempt of dutie: As by yͤ stat. of An.4.H.4. it was ordained, That all Atturnies shalbe examined by yͤ Just. & by their discretiōs their names shalbe put in yͤ rol, & they yͭ be good, vertuous, learned, & of good name, shalbe receiued & sworne wel & truly to serue in their offices, & specially, yͭ they make no suit in a forein coūty. And if any such Atturney be notoriously found in any default of record, or otherwise, he shal forsweare yͤ court, & neuer after be receiued to make any suit in yͤ K. courts. And this ordinãce shalbe performed in yͤ Exchequer after yͤ discretiō of the treasurer & the barōs there. And accordingly by one other stat. made an.3.Ia. it was enacted, That none shall from henceforth be admitted Atturneies in any of yͤ K. courts of record at West. but such as haue bin brought vp in yͤ same courts, or otherwise wel practised in soliciting of causes, & haue bin foūd by their dealing to be skilful, & of honest dispositiō: and none to be suffered to solicit any cause or causes in any of yͤ courts aforesayd, but only such as are known to be men of honest dispositiō. And no Atturney shal admit any other to follow any suit in his name, vpō paine yͤ both yͤ Atturney & he that followeth yͤ suit in his name, shal each of thē forf. for such offence xx.l. to yͤ K. and yͤ party grieued, to be recouered in any of yͤ said courts of record, by A.B.P. J. wherin no W.E.P. &c. And yͤ Atturney in such case shalbe excluded frō being an Atturney for euer hereafter. By yͤ stat. of an.18.H.6. it was enacted, That in all cases wherin proces of Capias & Exigēt lyeth, if yͤ Atturney haue not his warrant of record, yͤ same terme yͭ the Exigent is awarded, he shal lose xl.s. to the K. if he be attainted therof by examinatiō of yͤ Just. And by yͤ stat. made an.32.H.8. & an.18.El. it was established, That euery such person which shalbe Atturney for any other person or persons, being demandant or plaintife, tenāt or defendāt, in any actiō or suit cōmenced in any of yͤ K. courts of record at West. & plead to an issue in yͤ same, shal deliuer or cause to be deliuered, his lawfull warrant of Atturney, to be entred of record for euery of yͤ said actions or suits wherin he is named an Atturney, to yͤ officer or his deputy ordained for yͤ receit or entring therof, in yͤ same terme whē yͤ issue is entred of record in yͤ said court, or before, vpon paine of forf. of x.l. for euery default, for not deliuery of yͤ said warrāt: the one moity to the K. his heirs & successors, yͤ other to such officer, to whō, or in whose office yͤ same warrāt shold be deliuered, entred, or filed, to be rec. by A. of det. B.P. or J. wherin no W.E.P. &c. & also he shal suffer such imprisonmēt as by yͤ discretiō of yͤ J. of yͤ St.4.H.4.18 St.3.Iac.7. Who shalbe Atturneyes. Soliciters. Following a suit in anothers name. St.18.H.6.9 St.32.H.8.30. St.18.El.13.

Court

Fit.N.B.96 Court (where any such default shall be made) shall be thought good. If a man make an Atturney in a real action brought against him, & after by couin agreed vpon betweene the demandant and the said Atturney, the same Atturney maketh default, whereby the tenant doth lose his land: then the same tenant who lost his land, may haue a writ of Deceit against the Atturney. *Deceit by an Atturney.* And so it is, if a man bring an action of Trespasse against two others, and the plaintife and an Atturney by couin agreed vpon betweene them, doe cause two straungers, not parties to the writ, to come into the court, and to say, that they be the same two defendants named in the writ, and that they do constitute the same man to be their Atturney in that suit: whervpon the same Atturney, as Atturney to the defendants named in the writ, do plead to an issue, and after suffer the enquest to passe by his default, by which meanes the plaintife doth recouer against the defendant: in this case they who be indeed defendants, and against whom the same action of Trespasse was brought, may haue a writ of Deceit against the same Atturney, that appeared as Atturney for them, and shall recouer their dammages. (Register fo. 113. Fit.N.B.96.) If an Atturney be informed by his client, to plead a false plea, which he cannot in conscience plead, he may procure this Entrie to bee made, Quod non fuit veraciter informatus, ideo nihil &c. to defend him in a writ of Deceit brought against him by his said client. (10.Ed.4.9. 20.Eliz. Dyer 367.) If an Atturney do sue forth a Capias where there was no originall writ before, he shalbe committed to prison, and thrust out of his place in that and all other Courts. (20.H.6, 39.)

4 As the law doth punish her Officers who do practise or commit any deceit or fraud, in stead of truth, in place of iustice, so doth she renounce and condemne all acts of greatest importance, if they be intermixt with guile and falshood: *The law reiecteth fraudulent acts.* For though Iudiciall acts, as Fines, Recoueries, Warranties, deedes inrolled, &c. being of their owne natures iust and lawfull, and meanes to settle titles, to appease controuersies, and to yeeld each person his due, bee therefore greatly respected and fauoured in her sight; yet if any of them be deuised, or executed by couin, or to deceiue, then she doth vtterly reiect them, and adiudge them void. As a man was Lord of the Mannor of D. wherein there was a tenant which had some parcels of freehold land in fee simple: (Co.li.3.77.) the Lord demised certaine lands, parcell of the demesnes of his said Mannor to the said freeholder, for xxi. yeares, reseruing certaine rent, and demised some other lands, parcell of the said demesnes, to the same freeholder at will, reseruing another rent, and graunted by copie of Court roll certaine other lands, parcell of the same Mannor, to the sayd freeholder, for the terme of life, according to the custome of the sayd Mannour, reseruing a third rent: And after the same freeholder demised all the sayd lands, which hee held by lease, for yeares, at will, and by copie in D. to a straunger for the terme of life: and then the same freeholder leuied a fine with proclamations, of so many messuages, so many acres of land, medow, pasture, &c. as he had by lease for yeres, at will, by copie of Court roll, & of his owne inheritance in D. by couin & fraud, to barre ẏ lord of his inheritance. All the proclamations were made, and the fiue yeres were past, the same freeholder continued in possession of the land which was graunted to him by lease for yeres, at will, and by copie, and paid to the Lord yerely his seuerall rents for the same. And after the stranger to whom the freeholder made the lease for life, died, and the lease which the Lord made to the freeholder for xxi. yeares expired. And then the same freeholder claimed the inheritance of all the land which the Lord demised vnto him for yeares, at will, & by copie, inten-

intending to barre the Lord thereof, by force of the fine with proclamations, & the fiue yeares past. But this fine was adiudged void against the Lord, and that it did not barre him to clayme and enter vpon his land, for that it was leuied by him, who had but estate in those lands for yeeres, at will, or by copy of court Roll, and that neither had nor could pretend any title to the inheritance of the land, but only by fraud practised the disheritance of the leassor. And whereas the meaning of the makers of the statute of Anno 4. H. 7. was (as it may appeare by the preamble of the same) that fines ought to be of the greatest strength to auoid strifes and debates, when the lessee for yeares, at will, or copyholder shall make an assurance by fraud and couin, to the intent a fine may be leuied, to disherit the right owner of his land, this is not a meanes to auoid or appease strife, but to begin it, where none was before: and therefore the same statute did not intend to ratifie such an estate begun by deceit. And further, the meaning of the makers of the said statute was not, That he who could not leuie a fine of this land, in respect of the debilitie of his estate therin, should be enabled by his owne practise and deceit to leuie a fine therof, to barre him who had a lawfull title therein, and a right to leuie a fine thereof. And the same lessee for yeares, tenant at will, and copyholder contriued his fraud in so secret manner, that by his couert practise he depriued his lessor of the remedy which the said statute of Anno 4. H. 7. did giue him, viz. to make his entry, or to pursue his action within fiue yeares, which he could not do, being ignorant of the lease for life which his tenant had made of this land to a stranger: and also conceiuing that the lessee hauing land of his owne fee simple in the same towne, he leuied a fine of that land, which hee might lawfully doe. And the deceit and fraud in this case is the more odious, because it was practised by the lessee against his lessor, and by the copyholder against his Lord, who is by the law bound to do fealty to the lessor and Lord, which is a bond of confidence, and a linke of trust. And if a man seised of land in fee, do make a lease to another thereof for terme of life, and the lessee for life doth leuie a fine thereof to a stranger, he in the reuersion may enter into the same land for a forfeiture, and put forth the conusee in the fine, and auoid the fine, for it was leuied by deceit, to defraud him of his reuersion. If a fine be leuied of lands to secret vses to deceiue the purchasor of the same land, it may be auerred to be leuied by fraud, and so by the statute of 27. El. 4. auoided. And so if a fine be leuied vpon an vsurious contract, and that be auerred, the same fine shalbe void by the stat. of 13. Eliz. 8.

Margin notes: St. 4. H. 7. 24 — A fine leuied of land to defraud the right owner therof. — Fit. Fines 120. — St. 27. Eli. 4. — St. 13. Eli. 8.

5 The law is as prouident to protect mens seigniories, rents, and seruices from euiction by deceit, as she is their lands and tenements: & knowing that a fine in some cases leuied by couin of the one, may be as preiudiciall to his inheritance, as of the other, hath therefore ordained seuerall remedies to redresse seuerall wrongs: as if a man seised of lands in ancient demesne, do leuy a fine thereof at the common law to another, this is a deceit to the lord of that manor of whom the said lands be holden, & therefore he may haue a writ of Deceit against the cognisor and the tenant of the lord, & thereby auoid the said fine, and then he that leuied the said fine shall be restored to the possession, and the title which he had before in the same land, and also the same land shall returne and become auncient demesne as it was before, for that the said fine shalbe vtterly void. And he that is lord of a manor of auncient demesne but for the terme of his life only, may maintaine this writ of Deceit. And so may he in reuersion, if tenant for the terme of life doe not bring it during his life, and either of them

Margin notes: A fine leuied of ancient demesne lands to defraud the Lord. — 21. Ed. 3. 20 Fit. Nat. Br. 98. — 21. Ed. 3. 56.

by

by his said writ may auoid the same fine: for by the leuying of a fine at the com-
8.E.4.6. mon law of lands in ancient demesne, or by recouerie of them at the common
law, the same lands do become Franke fee, and pleadable at the common law,
and so the lord should be deceiued of his right, and lose his seigniorie in them.
And the writ of Deceit will auoid the said fine or recouerie, because the fine
was leuied, and the recouerie was suffered coram non iudice, in deceit of the
Lord, viz. not before that Iudge, nor in that Court where they ought to haue
17.Ed.3.31. béene. But if a man seised of lands, whereof parcell be auncient demesne, and
7.H.4.44. parcell Franke fee, doe leuie a fine at the common law of both parcels: in this
8.H.4.23. case though the Lord of the auncient demesne doe by his writ of Deceit auoid
Fitz.Na.Br. the fine for so much as is ancient demesne, yet the residue of those lands which
98. be Franke fee, shall continue in force: for a fine leuied of them was no wrong
or deceit to any.

6 And the same law is where land is recouered by deceit: as if one man do A writ of Deceit to auoid a recouery.
bring a Præcipe quod reddat against another, and demaund certaine land, by
force whereof the tenant ought to be summoned to be before the Iustices at a
certaine day, and the shirife doth returne the tenant of the land, against whom
Fit.Nat.Br. the said Precipe is brought, summoned, whereas in truth he was not summo-
97. ned: by which false returne and deceit of the shirife, the demaundant doth vp-
on the Graund Cape recouer seisin of the land by default of the tenant: in this
3.E.3.28. case the tenant to whom this deceit is done, may after iudgemēt giuen for the
Fitz.Deceit demaundant, haue a writ of Deceit against him that did recouer, and against
49. the shirife for his false return. And by this writ of Deceit the tenant shalbe re-
18.E.4.11. stored to his land againe, so ẏ it be brought during the life of the summoners,
viewers, and pernors, or any of them: for if it bee not brought vntill all the
summoners, viewers, and pernors be dead, it will not lye, for after the death
of them the tenant shall not haue a writ of Deceit; for proces shalbe awarded
against the summoners, viewers, and pernors to appeare in Court, and by the
examination of them it is to be tried whether the tenant was summoned, or
50.Ed.3.16. not: for the summons must be made by two summoners at the least, and two
5.H.6.1. viewers. And if any of them did not their duty, then the writ was not execu-
Fitz.Deceit ted as it ought to haue béene, and therefore the plaintife in the writ of Deceit
48. Fitz.Deceit ought to be restored. But the K. shall haue the issues of the land in the meane
32.33.34.46 time. And if the demaundant, who did recouer by the shirifes false returne, do
make a feoffement of the land, then the writ of Deceit must be brought against
the demaundant, the feoffée, and the shirife: and if the demaundant that doth
8.E.3.6. recouer, & the shirife also, be both dead, yet the writ of Deceit may be brought
10.Ed.3.43. against the heirs of the demaundant, and the tenant of the land, if the summo-
ners, viewers, and pernors be liuing. And if a man do lose his land by default
Fit.Nat.Br. in a Præcipe quod reddat, whereby he was not summoned, and then dieth, his
98. heire may haue a writ of Deceit as well as his auncestor, and shall haue resti-
Fitz.Deceit tution: and the vouchée may haue a writ of Deceit, where he doth lose by de- The vouchée.
43.80. fault, if he were not summoned.

7 And so it is, if a man sue a Scire facias against another, to haue execution Deceit to auoid a recouerie vpon a Scire facias.
of a fine, if the shirife returne the tenant of the land summoned by two sum-
moners, whereas he was not summoned, by which returne the demaundant
shall recouer, and haue execution of the land, if the tenant do not appeare, and
the tenant shall lose the land: in this case the tenant may haue a writ of De-
ceit against the shirife, and the demaundant that did recouer, and him that is
then

Deceit to auoid a recouery of debt.
Where executors shall haue a writ of Deceit.
Annuity.

then tenant of the land, and shalbe restored to his former possession. And the like law is, if a man sue a Scire facias vpon a Recognizance against another 17.Ed.3.12.
for a debt before recouered, if the shirife returne the defendant summoned, whereas he was not summoned, by reason whereof the defendant hath execution awarded against him of the debt, then the defendant may haue a writ of Deceit against him that had the execution, and the shirife, and the shirife shall be punished for his false returne, and the party who did recouer, shall make restitution of that which he recouered: and if the defendant die, his executors may haue a writ of Deceit, and be restored, if the deceit be proued, and that the Testator was not garnished, whereupon the garnishers shal be examined. And so it is, if a man recouer in a writ of Annuity, and after doth sue a Scire Fitz.Deceit 42.
facias, and recouereth by default of garnishment, the defendant may haue a writ of Deceit: For by the statute of Anno 2. Ed.3. a writ of Deceit holdeth St.2.E.3.17.
place, and is maintenable as well in place of garnishment, which toucheth plea of land where such garnishment is giuen, as in case of Summons in a plea of land: for in all the cases aforesaid a Deceit was wrought by the shirife to the Court and the party grieued by his false returne: and the Law hath ordained, That euery of those deceits shal be reformed by the writ of Deceit. And a recouerie and iudgement had, made, and giuen, to the intent to defraud and frustrate the true meaning of a statute, shalbe void, as amongst others it appeareth by the statute of Anno 43 Eliz. whereby it was ordained, That all St.43.Eli.9.
iudgements which shalbe had, for the intent to haue & enioy any lease of a benefice with cure, or any bonds, contracts, promises, & couenants made for any person to enioy the same, contrary to the statute of An.13.El.20.& An.14.El. 11. or any of them, shalbe void, in such sort as bands & couenāts are appointed to be void, which are made void for that purpose: for that the suits whereupon the same iudgements be giued, were commenced & prosecuted vpon collusion & fraud, to defeat and make frustrate the true intent and meaning of the said statutes, or of one of them.

A iudgement to defraud the meaning of a statute.

Deceit vpon recouery in a Quare impedit
Deceit vpon a recouery in Wast

8 If any person do recouer against another in a Quare impedit by default 27.H.6.5.
of the defendant, whereas he was not summoned, then the same defendant Fitz.Deceit
may haue a writ of Deceit, and the Summoners, and the pledges vpon the 57.
attachment, and the mainpernors vpon the distresse shall be examined, and if 19. Eliz.
the deceit be found, the first iudgement shalbe reuersed, and there shalbe a writ Dyer 353.
awarded to the Bishop, to remoue the Clerke that was in the Church. And so it is, if any person do bring an action of Wast against another, & the plain- 29.Ed.3.42.
tife doe recouer against the defendant by default, whereupon a writ is awar- 48.Ed.3.20.
ded to the shirife to inquire of the wast, whereas the defendant was not sum- Fitz.Deceit
moned, the defendant may haue a writ of Deceit against him that recouered 30.
in the same action of Wast, and he shall suppose that hee was not summoned, attached, nor distrained: and proces shalbe awarded against the summoners, the pledges, and the mainpernors, who shalbe seuerally examined, and if they all did not their duty according to the Law, the plaintife in the writ of Deceit shal recouer, and be restored to that which before he lost in the action of Wast.

Deceit vpon a recouery by a Præcipe in capite.

9 And the like law is, if any person doe recouer land against another by a 17.Ed.3.31.
Præcipe in capite, where the same land is not holden of the King in chiefe, but 36.
of a meane lord by other seruices, and where the demaundant had no licence of the chiefe lord to sue at the common place: then the chiefe lord may haue a writ

of

of Deceit against him that recouered the same land, wherein he shall recouer his dammages, & the demandant shal be imprisoned for the deceit, and also the lord shal retaine his seigniory in the same land: But the recouery shal remain in force, and he that did recouer, shall also hold of the K. in chiefe, by the way of estoppell. And this writ of Deceit is maintenable in this case, by force of the
3.24. stat. of Magna Charta, whereby it is ordained, That the writ which is called Præcipe in capite shalbe granted to no man, wherby any freeman may lose his Court.

Where a good title shalbe impaired by a couenous recouery.

10 Couin is accounted so professed an enemy to iustice, & therefore is so hated by the law, that she adiudgeth that bad and vnlawful which is mixed with couin, though before of it selfe it were good & lawful: as if the issue in taile, who
44. Ass. p. 28 hath good cause to bring a Formedon in discender vpon a discontinuance made
41. Ass. p. 28 of certaine lands by one of his auncestors, be of couin, that a stranger shall disseise the tenant of the land, against which stranger he doth bring his action, & doth recouer this land, and hath execution: in this case he shall not be remitted to his former estate, though his title be good, but shall be adiudged in possession
44. Ed. 3. 46. by disseisin, in respect of the couin. And so it is, if a woman that hath good cause
15. E. 4. 4. to be indowed of her late husbands lands, will be of couin that a stranger shall
7. H. 7. 11 disseise the tenant of the land whereof she is indowable, against which stranger
Co. lib. 5. 31 she will bring a writ of Dower, and recouer, & hath execution, she shalbe adiudged in possession against the disseisee but as a disseisor, in respect of her couin, though she had good title to be indowed. And so couin mingling together vertue & vice, persuadeth the law to reiect & condemne a lawfull title, which is vnlawfully atchieued.

Warranties deuised by fraud.

11 As the law doth both condemne & reiect fines and recoueries, which bee practised or put in execution by fraud or deceit, so doth she renounce and make frustrate all sorts of warranties that be deuised or contriued vpon collusion or couin to defeat or defraud others of their iust & lawfull titles: for though warranties be much fauored in the law, for that they be meanes to establish the title of those who be tenants of land in possession, but yet if any of thē be vndertaken, performed, or mixed with fraud, then it doth not only lose his fauor, but
Co. lib. 5. 79 also his force in law. As if land be giuen to the father for the terme of his life,
50. Ed. 3. 12. the remainder to his sonne & heire apparant in taile, and the father by couin &
43. E. 3. 7. agreement betweene him and another (to barre his sonne by a collaterall warranty of his remainder) will make a lease of the same land to that other person, who will make a feoffement in fee to a third person of the same land, to whom the father will release with warranty: and thē the father dieth, & the warranty doth discend vpon his sonne being of full age: yet this warranty wil not barre the sonne of this land: for the feoffement of the lessee for yeeres was a disseisin, and the father was partaker of the offence, an actor, & agreeing thereunto: and though the release with warranty was made after the disseisin, yet seeing the disseisin was made to that end, the law doth adiudge the whole fact frō the beginning to be fraudulent, the warranty to begin by disseisin, & so all that assurance to be void against the heire in taile. And in like sort, other warranties that do commence by disseisin, be contriued to deceiue & defeat the right heirs of their iust and lawfull titles.

Deceit by getting of a Protection.

20. H. 6. 10. 12 If one do bring a Præcipe quod reddat against two other men, and they
Regist. f. 113 do purchase a protectiō for one of thē, suggesting ŷ he is to go beyond ŷ sea in ŷ
44. Ed. 3. 4. kings

kings seruice, whereas he doth not so, but remaineth still in England, and so hath done euer sithence his protection purchased, by which meanes the demaundant is delayed of his suit; in this case the same demaundant may haue a writ of Deceit against the said tenants for this deceit and delay, and shall recouer his dammages.

Deceit by purchasing a writ to charge another.

13 Whereas according to the course of the Chauncery, the king is to haue of euery person, who doth bring against another an action of Debt of the summe of fortie pounds, or more, vj. s. viij. d. for a fine, and for an hundred markes, vj. s. viij. d. and so for euery hundred markes vj. s. viij. d. and for euery Præcipe quod reddat brought of land, to the yearely value of fiue markes, vj. s. viij. d. and so according to that rate (vnlesse it be a writ of right patent.) If any other person doe purchase a writ in the Chauncerie in my name, without my priuitie, whereby I shall be charged to pay to the king for a fine any of the summes aforesaid, I may haue an action of Deceit against him, and recouer my dammages, for this writ was obtained to put me to charges, and thereby to deceiue me of so much. Fit. Nat. Br. 96.

Deceit for purchasing a writ in anothers name.

14 If A. being patron of a Benefice, when the Church is void do present his Clerke to the Ordinary, and B. doth disturbe him, whereupon C. doth purchase a Quare impedit against B. in the name of A. returnable in the common pleas, A. not knowing thereof, and after doth cause the writ to be abated, or A. to be nonsuit in that writ: in this case A. may haue a writ of Deceit against the same C. and recouer his dammages. And if B. doe procure C. to sue an action against A. whereby A. is vexed, A. may haue a writ of Deceit against B. Fitz. Na. Br. 96. Regist. f. 112. 7. H. 6. 45. Fitz. Na. Br. 98.

Deceit for procuring of a suit.

Deceit by acknowledging of a statute.

15 If A. and B. doe come before the Mayor of the Staple, or before any other Mayor of any Citie, Borough, or Towne, hauing authoritie to take acknowledgement of debts, and there A. doth acknowledge a statute to B. of an hundred pounds, or &c. in the name of C. and doth report himselfe to be C. where he is not so, wherupon C. is troubled, and this statute extended against him, then the same C. may haue a writ of Deceit against the said A. and B. and shall recouer his dammages. And so it is, if another man will leuie a fine of my land in my name, or confesse an action brought against me in my name, or will enter into a voucher in my name, and confesse the demaundants action, or will acknowledge a Recognizance, or statute Marchant, or other matter of Record in my name, I haue no other remedie but by an action of Deceit. But it is otherwise, if he seale and deliuer an obligation in my name: for I may plead that it is not my deed, which I cannot doe against a Record. Fitz. Na. Br. 105 & 100. Regist. f. 115 19. H. 6. 44. Regist. f. 113

Deceit by doing of a iudiciall act in anothers name.

Deceit by forging of a resignation.

16 If a Notarie, and other persons doe by agreement counterfeit the seale of any Parson or Vicar, and forge letters of resignation of his Parsonage or Vicarage, in the name of the same Parson or Vicar, by which meanes he is remoued from the possession of the same Parsonage or Vicarage, he may haue a writ of Deceit against the same forgers. Fitz. Na. Br. 99. Regist. f. 114

17 If

20.H.6.36. 21.H.7.41. 16.Ed.4.9. 17 If a man doe bargaine with another to enfeoffe him of certaine lands within twenty daies, or &c. and after he doth enfeoffe a stranger of the same land, then he with whom the bargaine was made, and was deceiued therein, may haue a writ of Deceit against him that so bargained and defeated him thereof. And so it is, if a man doe compound with another to purchase a manor, or certaine land for him, and hee doth buy it for himselfe, the partie may haue an action of Deceit against the same purchasor. And in all cases, where a man doth promise to doe a thing, and he doth it falsely, a writ of Deceit is maintainable against him: as if a man doe promise to assure land to another, and after he doth graunt a Rent charge, or a common out of it, or doth make a Lease for life or yeares of it, and then doth assure it to the bargainee, this is deceit, and a writ of Deceit is maintenable against him for it, for though he hath assured the land, he hath not assured it cleere and discharged, according to his bargaine, but hath deceiued the purchasor therein. Deceit by assuring of land to one man, which was bargained to another.

11.E.4.6. 18 If a man doe sell a piece of cloth to another, and warrant it to be fortie elles long, and it is not so long, the buyer may haue a writ of Deceit against the seller of the same cloth, by force of his warranty, although the warranty be by word onely, without writing, so that it be at the time of the bargaine made. 6. Ed. 6. Dyer 76. But if the warranty be at another time after the bargaine made, then the buyer must haue some writing to testifie this warranty, or otherwise hee shall not haue a writ of Deceit against the seller. Deceit vpon a warranty.

9.Ed.4.13. Fit.Nat.Br. 98. 19 If an action of Debt bee brought against two as executors, whereas one of them was neuer executor nor administrator, and if he which is executor do make default, & he who was not executor doe appeare, & confesse the action, he that was named executor may haue against the other an action of Deceit: for he hath vndertaken to plead a plea to the action of debt, which he could not doe, and that also to the deceit and hurt of another. Deceit by confession of an action brought against executors.

36.H.8.7. 20 If a man doe marry a wife possessed of goods, those goods be the husbands, to giue and dispose at his pleasure during the mariage betweene them. But, if after they be diuorced, the wife shall haue her goods againe, vnlesse the husband hath giuen or sold them before the Diuorce, for in that case the wife is without remedie. And yet if the husband doe alien those goods by couin, to the intent to defraud and defeat his wife of them, and after they be diuorced, then shee may auerre the couin, and recouer the goods from the alienee. Couin by aliening of his wiues goods.

35.H.6.5. Co.lib.3.78 83.li.5.83. 21 Though buying of goods in an open market doth worke an alteration of the property of the same goods, and doth bind the Title as well of all strangers as of the owner (if the goods be sold in such a shop or place as is commonly vsed for the selling of goods of the same kind or nature) yet if one man do steale, purloine, or iniuriously take away another mans goods, and then by couin betweene him and a third person doth sell the same goods in an open & vsual place 7.H.7.12 of sale, in an open market or faire, to ye third person, who at the time of buying Sale of goods in opē market by couin.

of

of the same goods, did know that the seller came not lawfully by them, or that they were not his goods, this is a void sale. And in respect of this Couin, the first and right owner of these goods may lawfully take and carrie them away, notwithstanding the said sale in open market.

Fraudulent assurances to defeat the discontinuee in tayle.

22 If the father being tenant in tayle of certaine lands, will make a feoffement thereof to another with warrantie, and so discontinue the estate taile, hauing assets of other lands in fee simple, to leaue to discend to his son and heire, and then within few dayes before his death will alien the same fee simple land to his sonne and heire, and to his heires, upon couin, and to the intent that the same fee simple land should not be pleaded to come by discent from the sayd father to his sonne, nor adiudged as Assets by discent in his hands: yet this couin being found by verdict in a writ of Formedon brought against him by the heire of the land entailed, shall giue the discontinuee aduantage to plead, that the same heire had assets by discent in fee simple left him by his said father: for that the law doth adiudge this alienation made by the father to the sonne a little before his death, by couin to defraud the discontinuee of his lawfull plea, to be as no alienatiō, but that the father dyed seised of the same fee simple land, and that it came to his sonne and heire by discent. M.34.E.3. Fitz Garrantie 88.

Fraudulent conueyance to defeat a Lord of his wardship.

23 Because Lords of Mannors, lands and tenements, haue as great right to enioy the wardship of the bodies and lands of their wards, as they haue to their other inheritances, lands, and goods, and it is as great an iniury to deceiue them thereof by couin and collusion, as to defeat and defraud them of their other lawfull titles: therefore by a statute made at Marlebridge anno 52.H.3. it was enacted, That if any man do enfeoffe his eldest sonne or heire, being within age of his inheritance, that therby the Lord might lose his wardship, yet notwithstanding such feoffement, the chiefe Lord shall haue his wardship. St.52.H.3.6. And by the said statute it was further ordained, That if any persons meaning to demise their lands for terme of certaine yeares (that they might thereby defeat the Lords of the fee of their wardships) will faine false feoffements, containing, that they are satisfied of the whole seruice due unto them, untill a certaine terme, and that such feoffees are bound to pay at the said term a great summe, to the value of the same lands, or much aboue, so that after the said terme the land shall reuert to them or their heires, for that no man wil desire to hold the same of so great a price, yet by such fraud no chiefe Lord shall loose his wardship. And if the chiefe Lords do by iudgement of the Court recouer their wardships, yet the feoffees shall haue their action reserued, to recouer their terme or fee, when the heires shall come to their lawfull age. And for the further preuention of couin in auoiding of wardships, by one other stat. made anno 34.H.8. it was ordained, That if any person or persons hauing estate of inheritance of or in any Mannors, lands, tenements, or hereditaments, holdē of the king by Knights seruice, in chief, or otherwise of the king by Knights seruice, or of any other person or persons by Knights seruice, haue giuen at any time since the 20. day of July anno 32.H.8. & anno Dom. 1540. or hereafter shall giue, will, deuise, or assigne by will or other act executed in his life, his mannors, lands, tenements, or hereditaments, or any of them by fraud or couin to any other person or persons, for terme of yeares, life, or liues, with one remainder ouer in fee, or with diuers remainders ouer for terme of yeares, St.34.H.8.5.

life,

life or liues, with one Remainder ouer in fee simple to any person or persons, or to his or their right heires: Or at any time since the said 20. day of July, hath conueyed, or hereafter shall conuey, or make by couin (contrarie to ye true intent of the Act prouided 34. H.8. for the making of Wils) any estates, conditions, mesnalties, tenures, or conueyāces, to the intent to defraud or deceiue the King of his Prerogatiue, primer seisin, liuerie, reliefe, wardships, mariages, or rights; or any other Lords of their wardships, reliefes, heriots, or other profits which should or ought to accrue, growe or come vnto them, or any of them, by or after the death of his or their tenant, by force and according to the Statutes made 32. H.8.1. & 34. H.8.5. and the same estates, and other conueyances being found by office to be so made by couin, fraud, or deceit, contrary to the true intent of the said Acts: Then the king shal haue as wel the wardship of the bodie, and custodie of the lands &c. as liuery, primer seisin, reliefe and other profits, which should or ought to appertaine to him, according to the true meaning of the said acts, as though no such estates or conueyances by couin had neuer beene had or made, vntill the said office be lawfully vndone by trauerse or otherwise. And the other Lord and Lords of whom any such lands &c. shalbe holden by Knights seruice, as is aforesaid, shall haue their remedy in such cases, for his or their wardships of bodies, and lands, by writ of right of ward, and shall distraine and make auowrie or cognisance by themselues or their bailifes for their reliefes, heriots, and other profits, which should haue beene to them due, by or after the death of their tenant, as if no such estate or conueyance had beene had or made: Sauing the right and title of the donees, feoffees, leasees, and deuisees thereof against the said deuisor and his heyres, after the interest and title of the King or other Lord therein ended.

24 If the father doe make a feoffment of his lands holden by Knights seruice, to his eldest sonne, then by the foresaid Statute of Marlebridge the Lord of whom the same lands be holden is in possibilitie to haue the wardship of the said sonne, if the father die, his said sonne being within age. But if the same sonne doe after make a feoffment of the same land to an other bona fide, and after the father doth die, leauing his sonne within age, there this possibilitie is destroyed: for that the stranger who had no notice of this fraud, hath purchased the land bona fide, and therefore shall sustaine no preiudice by it. And yet in that case, if the sonne had made the Feoffment after the fathers death, this alienation had not depriued the Lord of his wardship, which was once lawfully deuolued vnto him.

Fitz. Collusion 29. 33. H.6 14. Co. li. 1. 122.

He that is not partie to a fraud shall sustaine no losse.

Co. li. 2. 94.

25 And it is a deceit, collusion, and defrauding of the lawe and a great disheritance, and preiudice to the Lords of the Fee of whome any lands bee holden, to giue the same lands in Mortmaine, or to doe any Act, or procure any thing to be done, whereby they may come into Mortmaine, contrarie to the statutes of Magna Charta, 7. Ed. 1. 13. Ed. 1. 15. R. 2. and 23. H. 8. for the Lordes doe loose the wardships, mariages, reliefes, and other seruices of their Tenants by that meanes. And therefore by the Statute of West. 2. it was enacted, That if any religious or Ecclesiasticall person doe impleade an other, by a Reall action of land, and the Tenant will make default after default, whereby hee ought to loose the land. Then hee which doth recouer, shall not haue Execution of the same Land recouered, vntill

St. 13. E. 1. 31.

he hath sued forth the kings writ of Qualc ius directed to the Eschcatoz of the same countie, to make enquirie by a Jurie, what right hee that recouered the land hath to the same: And if he hath right, iudgement shalbe giuen for him, & he shall haue execution of the same land: And if it be found, y he hath no right to recouer by his said action, but that the lands were lost by collusion betwéen him, and the tenant of the land, then the land shall accrue to the next Lord of the fee, if hée demaund it within a yéere next after the Enquest taken: And if he doth not demaund it within a yeare, it shall accrue to the next Lord aboue, if he demaund it within halfe a yeare after the same: And so euery Lord after the next Lord immediat shall haue halfe a yeare to demaund it successiuely, vntill it come to the King, to whom through the default of other Lords the land shall accrue: For this recouerie of land by default, by a compact and couin before agreed vpon, betwéene the demaundant being a religious or Ecclesiasticall person, and the tenant, is to defraud the intent and meaning of the Statutes of Magna Charta, and an. 7. Ed. 1. whereby it was ordained, That if any religious person, or other whatsoeuer, will buy or sel any lands or tenements, or wil receiue the same by colour of any gift, or lease, or by reason of any other title whatsoeuer, or will by other practise or deuise procure the same to himselfe, whereby such lands or tenements may come into mortmayne, he shall forfeite the same lands. And by the equitie of the foresaid Statute of Westminster 2. if any Ecclesiastical person doe recouer land against another by reddition, confession, or action tried, yet the collusion shalbe inquired of, for that the same recouerie may be by collusion before had betweene the demaundant and the tenant. And because that by feoffments, fines, recoueries, and other assurances made of trust of lands to the vse of parish Churches, Chappels, Guildes, Fraternities &c. there groweth to the King, and other Lords, and subiects of the Realme, the like losses, & inconueniences, and is as much preiudiciall to them, as doth and is where lands be aliened in mortmaine: Therefore for the eschuing and auoydance of them, by a Statute made an. 23. H. 8. it was enacted, That all feoffments, fines, recoueries, wills, and other estates deuised, or in any wise made of trust, of any mannors lands, tenements or hereditaments, to the vse of any parish churches, chappels, churchwardes, Guildes, fraternities, or brotherhoods erected or made of deuotion, or by common assent of the people, without any corporation: Or that the Feoffees, Conisees, Recouerées, or other persons, and their heires thereof scised, shall take, leuie, or perceiue, or cause to be taken &c. the issues and profites thereof, and the same to dispose, or otherwise imploy, or suffer or cause to be paid, disposed, or imploied to any of the foresaid vses, or to any of the like vses (aboue the terme of 20. yeares next after the first making and beginning of any such vses) shalbe vtterly voide. But for the preuenting of collusion and fraud which might bee deuised for the further establishing or corroboration of such vses, by the said Statute of an. 23. H. 8. it was moreouer prouided, That if any person or persons in defraud of the said Statute, doth bind, or ordaine any of their heirs or successors, or any other persons, that they shall suffer such vses, intents or purposes to continue, contrarie to the said Statute, vpon paine of losse of any other lands, or of any other thing: or doe deuise by any colour, craft, or meanes any thing to make such vses declared contrarie to the meaning of the said Act to continue for any longer time then is aboue limitted for the same: Then euerie such penaltie, craft, colour, and euery other thing that is made or deuised in defraud of the said act, shalbe voide: for the said Statute shalbe interpreted as beneficiallie as may be to the destruction, or vtter auoyding of the vses aboue remembred, and of all other like, other then such as are before expressed.

Deceit and Collusion to bring land into mortmaine.

St. 9. H. 3. 37
St. 7. Ed. 1.

3. Ed. 4. 14.

Lands assured in Mortmaine to churches, chappels, Guilds, &c.

St. 23. H. 8. 10.

Collaterall conueyaunces to defraud the assurance to Churches.

Not-

Notwithstanding the foresaid Statute of An 23.H.8. it is lawfull for any person at this day to giue his lands, tenements, or hereditaments to any person or persons, & to his or their heirs, for to find a preacher, for the maintenãce of a Schoole, for the reliefe of maihemed souldiers, for the sustentation of poore people, for the reparation of churches, highwayes, bridges, cawseis, for the discharge of ỹ poore inhabitants of a towne of cõmon charges, for to make a stock for poore labourers in husbandrie, & poore apprentices, for the mariage of poore maids, or for such other charitable vses: for the said stat. was made onely to restraine the assuring of lands to superstitious vses, and not to charitable vses. And in this case it shalbe expedient that the feoffor which doth assure his land to any of the vses aforesaid, doe reserue to himselfe some annuall rent, or take some money of the feoffées at the first, for then the feoffement or assurance shal be good to the feoffées, and their heires, though the vse be vnlawfull. And it appeareth by the stat. made an. 43. El. that they be accounted good and charitable vses, & no superstitious vses, to giue lands, tenements, rents, annuities, profits, hereditaments, goods, chattels, money, and stocks of money for the reliefe of aged, impotent, and poore people: or for the maintenance of sicke and maihemed souldiers, & mariners, schooles of learning, frée schooles, & schollers in Vniuersities: or for repaire of bridges, ports, hauens, cawseys, churches, sea-bãks, & high waies: or for education or preferment of orphans: or for, or toward reliefe, stocke, or maintenance for houses of correction: or for mariage of poore maids: or for supportation, helpe, & ayd of yong trades-men, handicrafts-men, and persons decaied: or for reliefe or redemption of prisoners or captiues: or for aid or ease of any poore inhabitants concerning paiment of fiftéens, setting out of souldiers, and other taxes. For the said Stat. of 43. El. doth giue authoritie to the L. Chauncelor, the L. Kéeper &c. & to the Chauncelor of the Duchie, to award commissions from time to time into all or any parts of this Realme to certaine persons, to enquire of al & singular such gifts, assignments, & appointments, and of the abuses, breaches of the truce, negligences, misimployments, not imploying, concealing, defrauding, misconuerting, or misgouernment of any lands, tenements, rents, &c. goods, chattels, money &c. heretofore giuen or assigned, or which hereafter shalbe giuen, limited, or assigned to or for any the charitable or godly vses before rehearsed: And after such enquiry, hearing, and examining thereof, to set downe such orders, iudgements, and decrées, as the same lands, tenements, rents, goods, money &c. may be duly and faithfully imployed to and for such of the charitable vses and intents aforesaid respectiuely, for which they were giuen or appointed by the donors and founders thereof.

Co. lib. 1. 26 — To what vses lands may be giuen.

Stat. 43. El. 4.

26 Because when tenants for terme of life, tenants in dower, or by the curtesie of England, or tenants after possibilitie of issue extinct were impleaded, they would often be of couin with the demandants, that the tenemẽts demanded should be recouered against them, & they would not pray in ayde, nor vouch to warrantie them in the reuersiõ, but plead in chiefe such a plea wherby they knew the tenements should be lost: for the preuention and eschewing of which couin, by a stat. made an. 13. R. 2. it was ordained, That if any such tenant be impleaded, and he in the reuersion come into the Court, and prayeth to be receiued to defend his right at the day that the tenant doth plead to ỹ action, or before, he shalbe receiued to plead in chiefe to the action, without taking delay by voucher, ayd-prayer, nonage, or other delay whatsoeuer; so that after such receipt, he shal haue no delay by protection, essoine of the Kings seruice, or common Essoine, but the sute shalbe hastened as much as it may be by the lawe: And dayes of grace shalbe giuen by discretion of the Iudges betwixt the

St. 13. R. 2. 16.

Couin by a particular tenant to defraud him in the reuersion.

the demaundant and him which is receiued, and not the common daies giuen in pleas of land (except the demaundant will thereunto assent) to the intent the demaundant shal not be too much delaied which must plead with two aduersaries: And he in the Reuersion which praieth to be receiued shall finde sureties for the issues of the Land, aswel where the receite is counter-pleaded, as where it is grauted. And by the Statute of Westminster 2 it was established: That if by default, or yeelding of such tenant in dower, or &c. iudgement shalbe giuen, then the heyres, or they which haue the reuersion shal recouer after the death of such tenants by a writ of Entrie ad communem legem. And by the same Statute of Westminster 2. it is also ordained, That if in an Action, brought against the husband and the wife of lands which bee the right of the wife, the husband will absent himselfe, and will not defend his wiues right, or will against his wiues consent yeeld the land: If the wife wil come before iudgement, and be ready to answere to the demaundant and to defend her right, she shalbe thereunto admitted. And for the further auoiding of Couin in Recoueries suffred by particular tenants, by the Statute of Anno 14. Eliz. it was enacted, That all recoueries to be had or prosecuted by agreement of the parties, or by Couin, against any tenants by the Curtesie of England, Tenants in taile after possibilitie of issue extinct, or otherwise onely for the terme of life, or liues, or of estates determinable vpon life, or liues, of any lands, Tenements, or hereditaments, whereof the same particular Tenant is or shalbe seised of any such particular estate, as is aforesaid, or against any other with Voucher ouer of any such particular Tenant, or of any hauing or that had right or title to any such particular estate, or tenancie as is aforesaid, shal as against such person or persons to whom any reuersion, or remainder thereof, by force of any Conueyance or deuise before that time had or made, shall, ought, or lawfully may appertaine, and against their heyres and successors be vtterly voide. Prouided alwaies that this Act shall not extend to any person or persons that shall by good title recouer any lands, tenemēts, or hereditaments, without fraud or Couin, by reason of any former right or title: But al & euery such recouerie and recoueries vpon former rights and titles shall stand and be in like force, as they were before the making of this Acte. And in all and euerie recouerie and recoueries to be had or prosecuted of any lands, tenements or hereditaments by the assent and agreement of any person, or persons, to whom any reuersion or remainder thereof then shall or ought to appertaine (so that the same assent and agréement doe appeare of record in any of the Kings Courts) shall stand in like strength, and of like effect against such person and persons that shal so assent and agree, their heyres, & successors, as they were before the making of this act.

Stat. West. 2. 13. Ed. 1. 3

The wiues receit vpon the husbands default.

Stat. 14. El. 8.

Recoueries against particular tenants by Couin to defraud him in the reuersion.

27 And for that Couin and fraud should be restrained and punished when it shall be put in practise, or intended by those in reuersion to defeate their Lessees of their termes for yeares, as it was by the aforesaid Statutes, when it was executed by particular Tenants, to the preiudice or disheritance of them in the Reuersion: Therefore by a Statute made Anno 21. H. 8. it was enacted, That if any persons doe make leases of their lands, tenements, or other hereditaments by Indentures, or without writing to other persons, for terme of yeares, if after the same Lessors, their heires or assignes do cause or suffer recoueries to be had against them in the Kings, or any other Lordes Court, vpon fained and vntrue title, by craft and Couin to put the said Termors from their Termes: all such Termor shall and may falsifie for his terme only

Couin by him in the reuersion to defeate his Lessee for yeeres.

Stat. 21. H. 8. 15

Stat. 6. E. 1. 11.

only such recouerie, in such wise and forme, as a tenant of freehold shall & may doe by the course of the cōmon law, where such tenant was neither priuie, nor party to such recouerie. And the same Termors their Executors & assignees, notwithstanding such recouerie so had, shall enioy, retaine, and hold their said termes, according to their said leases, against all such recouerors, their heyres, and assignees. And the said recouerers, their heyres, and assignees after such recouerie so had, shal haue like remedy against the said termors, their Executors and assignees by auowrie, or action of debt for the rents and seruices reserued vpon the same leases, being due after the same recoueries, & also like actions against them for waste done after the same recoueries so had, in like manner and forme, as the said Lessors should or might haue had, if the same recoueries had neuer beene had. No manner of Statute of the Staple, statute marchant, nor execution by Elegit, shalbe auoided by meanes of any such feyned recouerie, but all persons hauing any lands, tenements or other hereditaments in execution, or being intituled to haue execution of any lands or tenements by any such meanes, shal haue like remedie to auoide and falsifie ỹ same recouerie, as before is prouided for the lessee for terme of yeares. Couin to auoide a Statute or recognisance.

28 There haue beene many lawes and Statutes deuised from age to age, to restraine and punish seueral sorts of deceits, Couins, collusions and frauds, but most to encounter and checke fraudulent deeds cōtriued of malice or guile, to defeate, delay or hinder others of their lands, leases, goods, cattels, debts, &c. as it appeareth by the statute made A. 50. Ed. 3. 1. R. 2. 2. R. 2. 3. H. 7. 13. El. & 27. El. But as deceit and fraud increased in this realme, so new penalties, and greater punishments were inuented from time to time to inflict vpon the transgressors therin. And because fained, couenous, and fraudulent Feoffmēts, gifts, graunts, alienations, conueyances, bonds, sutes, iudgements, & executions of lands and tenements, goods and cattels being deuised of Couin & guile, to defraud creditors, and others of their iust and lawful actions, dets &c. be not only to the let of the due course and execution of law, & iustice, but also to the ouerthrow of all true and plaine dealing, bargaining, and cheuisance betweene man and man, without the which no common weale, or ciuill societie can bee maintained or continued: Therefore by a Statute made A. 13. El. it was enacted; That all and euery Feoffment, gift, graunt, bargaine, alienation, and conueyaunce of lands, tenements, hereditaments, goods & cattels, or of any of them; or of any lease, rent, common or other profite or charge out of the same lands, hereditaments, goods, &c. or any of them by writing or otherwise; And all and euery bond, sute, iudgement, and execution at any time had or made, sithence the beginning of Queen Elizabeths raigne, or at any time hereafter to be had or made, which haue beene, and are deuised, & contriued of malice, fraud, couin, collusion, or guile, to the intent, &c. to delay, hinder, or defraud creditors, & others of their iust & lawfull actions, sutes, debts, accompts, damages, penalties, forfeitures, hariots, mortuaries, or reliefes, shalbe taken & deemed onely as against ỹ person, his heires, executors, successors, or assignes whose actions, sutes, debts, accoũts &c. by such guileful, couenous, or fraudulēt deeds, deuises, practises as is aforesaid, are, shall, or mought be in any wise disturbed, hindered, delaied, or defrauded, to be cleerly void & of none effect, any colour, fayned cōsideration, expressing of vse, or any other matter to ỹ cōtrary notwithstanding: And al & euery ỹ parties to such fained, or fraudulēt feoffment, gift, graunt, alienation, bargaine, conueyance, bond, sute, iudgement, execution, &c. or being priuie and knowing of the same, or any of them, which shall willingly and wittingly, put in vre, auowe, maintaine, iustifie or defend the same or any of them, as true, simple, and done or made bona fide, and vpon good con-

Stat. 50 Ed. 3. 6. 1. R. 2. 9. 2. R. 2. 3. 3. H. 7. 4. 13. El. 5. 27. El. 4.

Stat. 13. El. 5 Stat 29. El. 5.

Fraudulent deeds to auoide other mens debts and duties.

Parties to fraudulent deedes.

consideration, or shall alien, or assigne any the lands, tenements, goods, leases, &c. to them conueied, or any part thereof, shall forfeit to the Queene &c. and the partie grieued by such fraudulent feoffement, gift, bond, suit, &c. one yeares value of the said lands &c. leases, rents, or other profits, and the whole value of the said goods and cattels, and so much money as shall be contained in such couenous and fained bond, to bée recouered by A. I. B. P. &c. wherein no W. E. P. &c. And béeing thereof lawfully conuicted, shall suffer imprisonment one halfe yeare, without Baile or Mainprise. But common Recoueries had against Tenant in taile, or other tenant of the fréehold of lands, the Reuersion or Remainder, or right of Reuersion or Remainder whereof then shall bée in any other person, shall as touching such person, and his heires, which hath the Reuersion or Remainder thereof, be of like force, and none other, as the same should haue béene if this Act had not béene made: And no estate or conueyance, by reason whereof any person shall vse any voucher in any writ of Formedon, shall bée made void by this Act: But euery such voucher in any writ of Formedon, shall be of like force, as if this act had not béene made. Prouided alwaies that this Statute shall not extend to any estate or interest in lands, leases, goods, &c. lawfully assured vpon good consideration, and bona fide, to any person or persons, bodies politique or corporat, not hauing at the time of such conueyance &c. any knowledge of such fraud or collusion, as is aforesaid.

Common recoueries.

Voucher in Formedon.

Lands or goods assured bona fide, and vpon good cōsideration.

Fraudulent déeds to auoid forfeitures.

29 If a man to preuent a forfeiture for a felonie, or vpon an outlarie, will make a gift of all his goods, and after is attainted of felonie, or outlawed, these goods shall be forfeited, notwithstanding this gift: for this word forfeitures specified in the foresaid Statute of Anno 13. El. shall not be intended onely of the forfeiture of an obligation, Recognisance, or such like, but also of euery thing which by the Law may be forfeited to the King, or to a Subiect. And the same Act of Anno 13. El. shall not extend onely to creditors, but also to all others, who haue cause of Action, or suit, or to haue any penaltie or forfeiture. And if a man do bind himselfe and his heirs to pay to another a certaine sūme of money at a day assigned, and before the day doth come of paiment, the obligor dieth, leauing to his sonne and heire sufficient land to pay the same debt, & the heire doth enter and alien the same land before the obligée doth commence his suit vpon the said obligatiō: If vpon the suit of the same obligation ẏ heire do plead nothing but discent, and vpon the trial of that issue, the foresaid alienation be found by the Iurie to be made by fraud to deceiue the said creditor of his debt, or that be pleaded, the said alienation shalbe void by the foresaid statute of 13. El. and the plaintife shall recouer.

Co.li.3.82.

St.13.El.5.

Co.li.5.60.

A déed of gift must be vpon good consideration, and bona fide.

30 In the said Statute of Anno 13. El. there is one Prouiso, That the said Act shall not extend to any estate or interest in lands, tenements, or hereditaments, leases, rents, commons, profits, goods, or cattels, which is, or hereafter shall be lawfully had, made, conueyed, or assured vpon good consideration, & bona fide to any person or persons, or bodies politique or corporat, not hauing at the time of such conueyance or assurance to them made any manner of notice or knowledge of such couin, fraud, or collusion. By which Prouiso it appeareth, that the gift which is within the compasse of the same Prouiso, must be both vpon good consideration, and also bona fide. And therefore, whereas A. did owe to B. CC. l. and to L. a hundred pounds, payable by two seuerall obligations, L. brought an Action of debt against A. vpon his said

St.13.El.5.

Co.li.3.80.

obli-

obligation of a hundred pound; during which sute A. being possessed of goods and cattells, to the valew of two hundred pounds, in secret made a generall deede of gift by writing, of all his goodes and cattells, Realls and Personalls whatsoeuer to B. in satisfaction of his debt, and notwithstanding A. continued in possession of the same goods, and sold some of them, and did share and brand the sheepe with his owne brand: and after L. had iudgement to recouer against A. and had a Fieri facias directed to the Shiriffe of the Countie where A. dwelt, who by force of the Writ came to make execution of the same goodes; but B. resisted him by force, clayming those to be his goodes, in respect of his said deede of gift, and reported that it was a good deed of gift, and made vpon lawfull consideration: But in the Starrechamber this was adiudged a fraudulent deede, and within the statute of 13. Eliz. for this deed of gift had all the badges and markes of fraud: for it was generall, and without any exception of his apparrell, bedding, or any other necessary thing: and the owner continued in possession of all the goods, and vsed them as his owne: and the deede of gift was made in secret, and not sealed, deliuered, nor published amongst his neighbours: And it was made whilest the sute was depending betweene L. and A. And heere was a trust betweene the Donor of these goods and the Donee, for the Donor possessed the goodes, and vsed them as his owne; and fraude is alwayes shaddowed with trust, and trust is the couer of fraud: and the writing purported, that the deede was made honestly, truely, and Bona fide, which be not accustomed words in a deede of gift; and vnusuall termes in any Instrument doe breed suspition. And though this was a true debt due to B. and the consideration was good, yet this was not within the before specified Prouiso, for that the deede of gift was not made also Bona fide; for no deede shall be adiudged to be made Bona fide according to the said Prouiso, which is accompanied with any trust: and the words of the Prouiso be in the copulatiue, vpon good consideration and Bona fide: So that good consideration will not serue, vnles the gift be also Bona fide, viz. to the intent, that the Donee shall haue, carry away, and enioy to his owne vse the possession of the same goodes, without any trust expressed, or implied.

Infallible markes of a fraudulent deede of gift.

And therefore whosoeuer will make a deede of gift of goods to an other in satisfaction of his debt, or for any other reasonable cause, and will eschew therein the suspition and question of fraude, or of a fraudulent gift, it is expedient for him to make the same deede openly, and before his neighbors, or some men of credite in those partes where he doth liue, and not in any secret place, or before witnesses of small credite, or vnknowne in that Countrie; and further, that the goods which shall be aliened by that deede of gift be set downe in particular, and praised to the vttermost value by indifferent persons, or seene that they be of the same valew, and that the partie to whom the gift is made doe presently take them into his owne possession, and carry them away: for to leaue them in the Donors possession is an vndoubted argument of trust: which trust is a principall vaile of fraude and deceit: for though betweene the Donor and the Donee this trust hath a pleasing & goodly shew of confidence, and faithfull, and true dealing: yet betweene the same Donor and his Creditors, it is meere fraude and deceit: for the Donor maketh his deede of gift of trust, hoping the Donee will not deceiue him, who by the selfe same deede meaneth to deceiue others.

How a deed of gift may be made without fraude.

But as a deede of gift must be made Bona fide, viz. without any trust, so must it be made vpon good consideration, viz. vpon valuable consideration: For if a man being in debt to diuers persons, will make a deede of gift of his goods to his sonne, his nephew, or neare kinsman in

A deed of gift must bee made vpon valuable consideration.

in blood, and deliuer him possession thereof, and the Donee doth take and carrie away the goods, and imployeth them to his owne use; In this case the deede is made bona fide, for that the Donee hath taken and carried away the goods, and it is made upon good consideration, viz. consideration of Nature, and blood, but it is not made upon valuable consideration, for money paid, or wares delivered, according to the intent and meaning of the Prouiso aforesayd: And further, though heere is no trust expressed, by the Donor in the Donee, yet the Lawe doth intend that there is a trust implied betweene the Donor and his sonne, nephew, or neare kinsman, to whome hee hath made this deede of gift, and therefore accompteth it voyde against Creditors, &c.

31 Forasmuch as diuers persons after conueiances obtained, and purchases made of lands, tenements, leases, estates, and hereditaments for mony, or other good considerations, may receiue great preiudice by reason of fraudulent and couenous conueiances, estates, gifts, graunts, charges, and limitations of uses before made, of, in, or out of lands so purchased: which saide gifts, graunts, &c. are or shall be meant by the parties that so make the same to be fraudulent and couenous, of purpose, and intent, to deceiue such as shall purchase the same: or else, by the secret intent of the parties, the same be to their owne proper use, and at their free disposition, coloured neuerthelesse by a fained countenance and shew of wordes and sentences, as though the same were made bona fide, for good causes, and upon iust and lawfull considerations: For the remedie of which inconueniences, and for the auoiding of such fraudulent, fained, and couenous conueiances, gifts, graunts, charges, uses, and estates, and for the maintenance of iust and upright dealing in purchasing of lands, &c. by a Statute made Anno 27. Elizab. it was ordained, That all and euery conueiance, graunt, charge, lease, estate, incombrance, and limitation of use, or uses, of, in, or out of any lands, tenements, or other hereditaments whatsoeuer, had, or made at any time heeretofore sithence the beginning of the Queenes raigne that now is, or heereafter to be had or made, for the intent, and of purpose to defraud and deceiue such person or persons, bodies politike, or corporat, as haue purchased, or shall afterwards purchase in fee simple, fee taile, for life, liues, or yeares, the same lands, tenements, and hereditaments, or any part or parcell thereof, so formerly conueyed, granted, leased, charged, incombred, or limited in use; or to defraud and deceiue such as haue, or shall purchase any rent, profit or commoditie, in, or out of the same, or any part thereof, shall be deemed and taken only as against that person and persons, bodies politike, and corporat, his and their heires, successors, executors, administrators, and assignes, and against all and euery other person and persons lawfully hauing and claiming, by, from, or under them, or any of them, which haue purchased, or shal hereafter so purchase for mony, or other good consideration, the same lands, tenements, or hereditaments, or any part or parcell thereof, or any rent, profit or commoditie, in, or out of the same, to be utterly voide, frustrate, and of none effect: Any pretence, colour, fained consideration, or expressing of any use or uses to the contrary notwithstanding.

A — Fraudulent assurances to deceiue purchasors.

St. 27. Eli. 4. St. 39. Eli. 18.

B — Parties to fraudulent conueiances, which doe auow the same.

All & euery the parties to such fained, couenous, & fraudulent gifts, grants, leases, charges, or conueiances before expressed, or being priuie, & knowing of ye same, or any of thẽ, which shal wittingly put in ure, auow, maintain, iustifie, or defend the same, or any of thẽ, as true, simple, & done, had or made bona fide, St. 27. Eli. 4.

or upon

vpon good consideration, to the disturbance, or hinderance of the said purchaser or purchasers, leasees, or grauntees, or of or to the disturbance or hinderance of their heires, successors, executors, administrators, or assignes, or such as haue, or lawfully claime any thing by, from, or vnder them, or any of them, shall incurre the penaltie and forfeiture, of one yeares valew of the said lands, tenements, and hereditaments so purchased or charged: The one moitie whereof to be to the Queene, her heires, and successors, and the other moitie to the partie or parties grieued, by such fained and fraudulent gift, graunt, lease, conueiance, incombrance, or limitation of vse, to be recouered in any of the Q. Courts of Record by action of debt. B.P. or I. wherein no E.P. or W. &c. And also being thereof lawfully conuicted, shall suffer imprisonment for one halfe yeare without baile or mainprise.

St.27. El.4. This Act, or any thing therein contained, shall not extend, or be construed to impeach, defeate, make voide, or frustrate any conueiance, assignement of lease, assurance, grant, charge, lease, estate, interest or limitation of vse or vses, of, in, to, or out of any lands, tenements, or hereditaments, heretofore at any time had or made, or hereafter to be had or made vpon, or for good consideration, and Bona fide, to any person or persons, bodies politike or corporate: any thing before mentioned to the contrary hereof notwithstanding. C. Conueiances made vpon good consideration, and Bona fide.

St.27.El.4. If any person or persons haue heretofore sithence the beginning of the Q. raigne that now is, made, or hereafter shall make any conueiance, gift, grant, demise, charge, limitation of vse or vses, or assurance of, in, or out of any lands, tenements, or hereditaments, with any clause, prouision, article, or condition of reuocation, determination, or alteration, at his or their will or pleasure of such conueiance, assurance, grants, limitations of vses or estates, of, in, or out of the said lands, tenements, or hereditaments, or of, in, or out of any part or parcell of them, contained or mentioned in any writing, deede, or indenture of such assurance, conueiance, grant, or gift, and after such conueiance, grant, gift, demise, charge, limitation of vses or assurance, so made or had, shal or doe bargaine, sell, demise, grant, conuey, or charge the same lands, tenements, or hereditaments, or any parcel thereof, to any person or persons, bodies politike, or corporate for money or other good consideration paid or giuen, the said first conueiance, assurance, gift, grant, demise, charge or limitation not by him or them reuoked, made voyde, or altered, according to the power and authoritie reserued, or expressed vnto him or them, in and by the said secret conueiance, assurance, gift, or grant: Then the said former conueiance, assurance, gift, demise, and grant, as touching the said lands, tenements, and hereditaments so after bargained, sold, conueied, demised, or charged, against the said bargainees, vendees, lessees, grauntees and euery of them, their heirs, successors, executors, administrators, and assignes, and against all and euery person and persons which haue, shall, or may lawfully claime any thing, by, from, vnder them or any of them, shall be deemed, taken, and adiudged to be voide, frustrate, and of none effect by vertue and force of this present Act. D. Conueiances with condition of reuocation or alteration.

St.27.El.4. Prouided neuerthelesse, that no lawfull morgage, made or to be made Bona fide, and without fraud or couin vpon good consideration, shall be impeached or impaired by force of this Act, but shall stand in the like force and effect, as the same should haue done, if this act had neuer beene had or made: Anie thing, &c. E. Morgages.

This

F

Assurances of lands defeated before the Statute.

This Act, nor any thing therin contained, shall extend or be construed to make good any purchase, grant, lease, charge, or profit, of, in, or out of any lāds, tenements, or hereditaments, heretofore made void, defeated, or undone, by reason of any former conueiance, graunt, or assurance, so as the partie or parties, or their heirs or assignes, which haue so defeated, or made void the same, were in actuall possession, the first day of this present Parliament, of, or in the said lands, tenements, or hereditaments, whereof, or out of which any such purchase, graunt, lease, charge, or profite was made. Neither this Act, nor any thing therein contained, shall extend in any sort, to restraine or impaire the iurisdiction, power, or authoritie of the Court of Starrechamber. St.27.Eli.4.

The authority of the court of Starre-chamber.

A purchasor doth know before of a fraudulent deede.

32 If a man seised of land in fee, do make a fraudulent conueiance thereof, to the intent to deceiue and defraud purchasors, contrary to the said Statute of Anno 27. Eliz. and doth continue in possession of it, and taketh the profite of it, and doth after enter into communication with a stranger for the sale of it to him: and by chaunce the same stranger hath knowledge of the same fraudulent assurance, and notwithstanding he doth bargaine with the same party for his land, doth conclude with him, and taketh his assurance from him: in this case, the same purchaser, shal auoide this former fraudulent cōueiance, made by the seller of this land, though hee had notice thereof before: for the said Act of Anno 27. Elizab. by expresse words doth make the fraudulent conueiance voide touching the purchasor: and seeing it is within the expresse purview of the same Statute, it is to be so taken and construed in repressing of fraud, and it is not the purchasors knowledge thereof, that doth make the fraudulent conueiance good which the said statute hath made voide. Co.li.5.60.

The father maketh a fraudulent lease, and the sonne selleth the land.

33 If the father doe make a lease for yeares of his land by couin, to defraud others to whom he will demise, or sell the same land, (as all fraudulent leases shall be intended to be made to that end) and before he doth sell or demise the same land, he dieth, and his sonne and next heire knowing, or not knowing of the said lease, doth sell the same land for good consideration: Then the purchasor shall auoide this lease by force of the forelaide Statute of Anno 27. Elizab. for seeing the Lawe doth presume that euery fraudulent lease is made generally to defeate purchasors, lessees, &c. within this generality euerie particular purchasor, farmor, lessee, &c. is included. And it is not materiall, though he who sold the land, did not make the former fraudulent lease, estate, or incombrance: but if the estate be fraudulent, the purchasor shall auoide it, whosoeuer selleth the land. Co.li.6.72.

A womans iointure made by fraud.

34 And the same Lawe is, if a man doe conuey land to the vse of his wife, for her iointure, by deceit and couin to defraud a purchasor to whom he intendeth to sell the same land: in this case, if the same fraud be proued by euidence, or confessed by pleading, the purchasor shall auoide the said wiues estate. Co.li.6.73

Fraudulent deeds to defeat successors of dilapidations.

35 Because diuers Ecclesiasticall persons being possessed of mansion houses, and other buildings belonging to their Ecclesiasticall Benefices, or liuings, did suffer the same for want of due reparations partly to decay, and partly to fall downe, conuerting the timber, lead, and stone to their owne vses, and also made deedes of gift, and colourable alienations, and other conueiances of like effect of their goods and cattels in their life time, of purpose

after

after their deaths, to defraud their successours of such iust Actions and remedies, as otherwise they might and should haue had against the executours, or administratours of their goodes, by the Lawes Ecclesiasticall of this Realme: for the redresse whereof by a Statute made Anno 13. Elizab.
St.13.El.10 it was enacted, That if any Archbishop, Bishop, Deane, Archdeacon, Prouost, Treasurer, Chancellor, Chaunter, Prebendarie, or any other hauing any dignitie or office in any Cathedrall, or Collegiat Church within this Realme, or any Parson, Vicar, or other Incumbent, of any Ecclesiasticall liuing, whereunto doe belong any houses or buildings, which by lawe or custome hee is bound to maintaine in reparation, doe suffer any of his saide houses or buildings to fall downe, or runne in decay, and after doe make any deede of gift, alienation, or other conueyance of his moueable goodes or cattells in his life time, to the intent after his death to defeate his successors of such iust Actions and Remedies, as otherwise they might haue had for the same, against their executours, or the administratours of their goods: Then the Successours of him which shall make such deede, &c. shall and may commence sute, and haue such remedy in any Court Ecclesiasticall within this Realme, competent for the matter, against him or them to whom such deed of gift, or alienation shall be so made, for the amending and reparation of such Dilapidations, or iust recompence for the same, as hath hapned by his fact or default, in such sort as he might, should, or ought lawfully to haue, if he or they to whom such deed of gift were made, were executor of him that made such deede, &c. or administrator of his goods, &c.

St.1.Iac.25

Fraudulent deedes to defeate successors of dilapidations.

36 For the auoiding and preuenting of couin or collusion in suing of Actions popular, which haue bin ordained from time to time to restraine and punish seuerall sorts of offenders: and to the intent that the penalties of those Statutes might indeede be imposed vpon the transgressors thereof, and the same offences might not be shadowed, and the meaning of the makers of those Statutes might not be deluded by the couenous, deceitfull, and fraudulent sutes of the same offendors friendes, whose practises haue beene to couer, and not to punish the same offences: by a Statute made Anno 11.
St.11.H.7.20. H.7. it was established, That if an Action popular be sued against any man by collusion, and the plaintife in the same doe recouer against the defendant, or be barred; any other person may after sue against the same defendant another Action popular, with good faith, and shall in the same recouer and haue execution, if the Recouerie or barre in the first Action be found to be by couin. And the defendant being attainted of Couin, shall haue two yeares imprisonment, by processe of Capias and Vtlarie, to be sued within the yeare after iudgement giuen, or at any time after, vntill the defendant be had and imprisoned, and that aswell at the Kings suite, as at euery other persons, that will sue in that behalfe. And no release of any common person, made to any partie before or after an Action popular or inditment hanging, shall be auaileable to let or surcease the said Action, inditment, processe, or execution. Prouided alwaies, that no plaintife or plaintifes be in any wise receiued to auerre any couin in any action popular, where the point of the same Action, or else collusion haue beene once tried, or lawfully found, with, or against the plaintife by triall of twelue men, and not otherwise.

An Action popular sued by Collusion.

No couin shal be auerred where there hath beene triall by verdict.

St.13.Eli.7. 37 By the Statute made Anno 13. Elizab. intituled, An Act touching

Fraudulent possessing of Bonkerupts lands, goods, or debts.

orders for Bankerupts, amongst other things it is enacted, That if at anie time before, or after that any such person (viz. a Bankerupt) departeth the Realme, or shall keepe his house, or otherwise absent himselfe, or take Sanctuarie, or suffer himselfe to be arrested, outlawed, or yeelde his body to prison, any person doe fraudulently by couin claime, demaund, recouer, possesse, or detaine any debts, dueties, goods, cattels, lands, or tenements, by writing, trust, or otherwise, which were or shall be due, or appertaine to any such offendor, other than such as hee can, and doth proue to be due by right and conscience, for money paid, wares deliuered, or other iust consideration, to the iust valew thereof before the Commissioners thereunto authorized, or the more part of them, and the same to proceed (bona fide) without fraud or couin: Then euery such person so craftily demaunding, claiming, hauing, or possessing any such debt, shall forfeit double as much as he shall so claime, demaund, detaine, or possesse, which said forfeiture shall be recouered, leuied, and imployed for the payment of the Creditors debts.

38 Forasmuch as it was oftentimes put in vre to the defrauding of Creditors, that such persons as were to haue the administration of the goods of others dying intestate committed vnto them, if they require it, would not accept the same, but suffer, or procure the administration to be graunted to some stranger of meane estate, and not of kinne to the intestate, from whom themselues, or others by their meanes did take deedes of gift, and authorities by letter of Atturney, whereby they obtained the estate of the intestate into their handes, and yet stood not subiect to pay any debts owing by the said intestate, and so the creditor for lacke of knowledge of the place of habitation of the Administrator could not arrest him, nor sue him: and if they fortuned to finde him out, yet for lacke of abilitie in him to satisfie of his owne goods the valew of that hee had conueied away of the intestates goods, or released of his debts, by way of wasting, the creditors could not haue or recouer their iust and due debts: For reformation whereof by a Statute made

Fraudulent administratiō of intestates goods.

Anno 43. Elizab. it was ordained, That euery person and persons that hereafter shall obtaine, receiue, or haue any goods or debts of any person dying intestate, or a release, or other discharge of any debt or duety that belonged to the intestate vpon any fraud as is aforesaid, or without such valuable consideration, as shall amount to the valew of the same goods and debts, or neere thereabouts (except it be, in, or towards satisfaction of some iust and principall debt of the valew of the same goods or debts to him owing by the intestate at the time of his decease) shall be charged and chargeable as Executor of his owne wrong, and so farre onely as all such goods and debts comming to his hands, or whereof he is released or discharged by such Administrator will satisfie, deducting neuerthelesse to and for himselfe allowance of all iust, due, and principall debt vpon good consideration, without fraud, owing to him by the intestate at the time of his decease, and of all other payments made by him, which lawfull Executors or Administrators, may, and ought to haue and pay by the Lawes and Statutes of this Realme. St. 43. El. 8.

Allowance of iust debts and other lawfull payments.

39 By a Statute not imprinted, made Anno 27. H. 8. it was enacted, That all craftie and fraudulent Recoueries, feoffements, estates, giftes, grants, and leases, and euery of them made by any of the chiefe gouernours of such religious houses, as were giuen to the King by that Statute (viz. of such as had not in lands aboue two hundred pounds by the yeare) vnder their St. 27. H. 8.

Fraudulent conueiances of Abbey lāds

Couent

couent seales, within one yeare next before the making of the said act, should be vtterly void. And by a like statute made Anno 31. H. 8. it was ordayned, That all leases of lands, tenements, or other hereditaments not vsually let, leases of lands &c. in reuersion, leases of lands &c. not reseruing the old and accustomed rent, sales of wood, assurances of lands of the kings gift, or auncient foundation, without the kings licence made by any abbots, or gouernours of any Monasteries or other religious houses (which were before the making of the said act dissolued) within one yeare before the comming to the K. hands of the same Monasteries, religious houses &c. (or which after that should bee dissolued, or come to the kings hands, should be vtterly void: for the same leases, sales of wood, and assurances were intended to be made by fraud to deceiue the king of certaine commodities which the makers of that statute did meane and intend to giue him.

St. 31. H. 8. 13

40 Where maidens and women children of noblemen, gentlemen, and others, as well such as were heires apparant to their auncestors, as others, hauing left vnto thē by their father, or other auncestor & friends, lands, tenemēts & hereditaments, or other great substance in goods & cattels moueable, for and to the intent to aduaunce them in marriage somewhat like, according to their degrees, and as might be most for their surety & comfort, as wel for themselues as of all other their friends & kinsfolks, were oftimes vnawares to their said friends or kinsfolkes, by flattery, trifling gifts, faire promises (and other such deceitfull & fraudulent practises) of many vnthrifty & light persons, & therunto by the intreaty of lewd persons & others that for rewards bought and sold the said children, secretly allured, and won to contract matrimonie with the said vnthrifty & light persons, and thereupon either with sleight or force oft times were taken & conueyed away from their said parents, friends, or kinsfolkes, to the displeasure of God, disparagement of the said children, & continuall heauinesse of all their friends. For the redresse and preuention whereof, by a statute made Anno 4. & 5. P. & M. it was enacted, That it shall not be lawfull to any person or persons to take or conuey away, or cause to be taken or conueyed away any maid or woman child vnmaried, being within the age of xvi. yeares, out of, or from the possession, custodie, or gouernance, and against the will of the father of such maid or woman child, or of such person or persons to whom the father of such maid or woman child, by his last Will, or by any other act in his life time, shall assigne, bequeath, giue, or graunt the order, keeping, education, or gouernance of such maid or woman child: except such taking & conueying away as shalbe had, made, or done by or for such persō or persons as without fraud or couin then shalbe the master or mistresse, or the gardian in socage, or gardian in chiualry of or to such maid or woman child.

A

St. 4. & 5. P. & M. 8.

Deceitfull conueying a maid inheritable vnder xvi. yeares of age.

If any person or persons aboue the age of xiiii. yeares shal vnlawfully take or conuey, or cause to be taken or conueied any maid or woman child vnmaried, being within the age of xvi. yeares, out of, or from the possession, & against the will of the father or mother of such child, or out of, or from the possession of such person or persons as then shall haue by any lawfull wayes or meanes the order, keeping, or education, or gouernance of any such maid or woman child, then euery such person & persons so offending being thereof lawfully attainted or conuicted by the due course of the law of this realme (other then such of whō

St. 4. & 5. P. & M. 8.

B

The forf. for taking away a maid vnder 16 yeares of age.

such person taken away shall hold any lands or tenements by knights seruice) shalbe 2. yeeres imprisoned of his or their bodies without baile or mainprise, or els shall pay such fine for his or their said offence to the Q. and party grieued, as shalbe assessed by the Q. counsell in the starre chamber at Westminster.

C
Taking away & deflouring, or cōtracting matrimony with a woman &c.

If any such person or persons shall so take away, or cause to be taken away as is aforesaid, and deflowre any such maid or woman child as is aforesaid: Or shall against the will, or vnknowing of, or to the father of such maid or woman child, if the father be in life, or of or to the mother of such maid or woman child (hauing the custody & gouernance of such child, if the father be dead) by secret letters, messages, or otherwise, contract matrimony with any such maiden or woman child (except such contracts of matrimony as shalbe made by the cōsent of such person or persons as by the title of wardship shall then haue or be intituled to haue the mariage of such maid or woman child) then euery such person or persons so offending, being thereof lawfully conuicted, as is aforesaid, shall suffer imprisonment of his or their bodies by the space of fiue yeares, without baile or maineprise, or els shall pay such fine for his or their offence to the Queene and party grieued, as shalbe assessed by the Queenes Counsell in the Starre-Chamber. St. 4 & 5. P. & M. 8.

D
Who may hear and determine these offences.

The Queenes Counsell of the Starre-chamber by bill of complaint or information, and Justices of Assise by inquisition or indictment, haue authority to heare and determine the said offences, vpon euery which indictments and inquisitions such processe shall be awarded, as vpon an indictment of Trespas at the common law. St. 4 & 5. P. & M. 8.

E
A woman consenting to an vnlawfull contract.

If any woman child, or maiden, being aboue the age of xij. yeres and vnder xvj. doe at any time cōsent to such person that so shall make any contract of matrimonie, contrary to the forme and effect of this statute: then the next of her kinne, to whom the inheritance should returne or come after her decease, shall from the time of such assent, haue and enioy all such lands, tenements, and hereditamēts, as she had in possession, reuersion, or remainder, at the time of such assent, during the life of such person that so shall contract matrimony: and after the decease of such person so cōtracting matrimony, thē the said lands shall discend, reuert, remaine, and come to such person or persons, as they should haue done in case this act had neuer been made, other then to him onely that so shall contract matrimony. St. 4 & 5. P. & M. 8.

F
Orphans.

But this act shall not extend to take away or diminish any liberty, custome, or authority, cōcerning any orphans within the City of London, or any other City, Borough, or Towne, where Orphans are commonly vsed to be prouided for, either by grant, or by custome: But the Lord Maior of the city of London, and the Aldermen of the same, and euery other head Officer of any other Citie &c. where such Orphans be prouided for, shall and may haue & take like rule, order, keeping, and charge of such Orphans, and of all their lands, tenements, goods, & cattels, as heretofore they vsed, or lawfully might haue had & vsed, if this act had not bin made. St. 4 & 5. P. & M. 8.

G

There was grandmother a widdow, mother a widdow, & ij. daughters, the grandmother being seised of certain land in fee holden in socage, did by her last wil in writing bequeath ẏ same to the said ij. daughters, & to ẏ heirs of their ij. bodies Co. li. 3. 37.

bodies begotten, by euen portions, equally to be diuided, the remainder to the mother, being her sole daughter and heire apparant & her heires: and after the mother maried a second husband, and then the grandmother dyed, after whose death both the said daughters entred into the said lands so deuised vnto them: and then the yonger daughter being betwéene the age of xiiij. and xvj. yeares, and liuing in house with her father in law and mother, of her owne will and forwardnesse, and with the consent and agréement of her father in law, departed foorth of his house in a morning, and the same day in another place maried a husband: In this case it was adiudged, that the said yonger daughter had forfeited her moitie or halfe part of the said lands so deuised vnto her, by her contracting of Matrimonie, and that her said mother should take the benefit of the said forfeiture; for the mother had the custodie and gouernement of the said daughter at the time of the said contract, by the special words and prouision of the said statute, which gouernment was annexed to the person of the mother Iure naturæ, and was not transferred to her second husband by her mariage, as her lands and goods were, and so her husbands consent was not materiall, nor that consent which the meaning of the makers of that statute did respect and prouide for. And though the daughter was forth of her mothers house at the time of the contract of mariage, yet in the iudgement of law the mother had then the custodie of her, which was inseperable from her person. (The daughters forfeiture for mariage without her mothers consent.)

(St. 4. & 5. P. & M. 8.) And séeing the foresaid stat. of 4. & 5. P. & M. doth giue the forf. to the next of the kin to whom the inheritance should discend or come after her decease, during the life of such person that so shall contract matrimonie, therefore the partie must be of the blood, & next of ye blood to whom the inheritance vpō such forf. shal discend or come, which is the mother, & not the eldest sister (for administration may be grāted of ye goods of the son, or of the daughter, dying intestat, to the father or mother, as to the next of the blood of the party deceased, according to the stat. of an. 21. H. 8. 5.) And further, though the elder sister be of kin to the yonger, yet in this case if the yonger haue any issue, her land should discend to her issue; and if she haue no issue, it should remaine to her mother: for that the elder and yonger sisters were tenants in common in taile, though they neuer made partitiō indéed, the remainder therof to their mother in fée, by force of the said deuise of their grandmother, who by her will meant and ordained, that the land should bee diuided, and that one of them should not enioy the whole as suruiuor to the other.

41 Hauing written of deceits and frauds practised or performed by some particular persons to others, as by the tenant to his Lord, the debtor to the creditor, the seller to the purchaser, the lessor to the lessée, &c. I am now to expresse and discouer some other guiles, frauds, and falshoods, which the offendors therin do endeuor to put in vse or practise, not onely against any one, two, or more speciall persons (as in the cases aforesaid) but against euery person that shall put them in trust, or otherwise shall haue occasion to vse them, or theirs, which our stat. lawes haue accused, and condemned to be offences, and haue inflicted vpon the transgressors thereof seuerall punishments. As, by the stat. of Anno (Seuerall deceits prohibited by seuerall Statutes.)

(St. 9. H. 5. 8.) 9. H. 5. falsifiers and counterfeiters of deceitfull and vntrue weights, being attainted thereof, shalbe taken by Iust. of peace, Sherifes, Eschetors, & other cōmissioners, & kept in prison without mainprise, vntill they haue made fine and ransome according to the Iust. discretion. (Counterfeiting of weights deceitfull.)

(St. 23. H. 8. 4) By the stat. of An. 23. H. 8. If any diminish a barrell, a kilderkin, or firkin, to the deceit or hurt of another, by taking out the head or any staffe, he shal forf. iij. iiij. d. and be punished by the discretion (Deceit by diminishing of a vessell.)

Deceitfull things vpon fustian.

cretion of the chiefe officer, before whom the offence shall be presented, and the vessell shall be burned. By the stat. of An. 11. H. 7. If any denizen or forreiner shall vse yrons or other deceitfull thing vpon fustians vnshorne, to breake off the nap and cotton of the same, but onely the broad sheeres, he shall forfeit for euerie offence twentie shillings to the king and him that will sue. By the statute of Anno 18. El. If any Goldsmith doe make any Goldsmithes worke, or plate, which shall be touched, marked, or allowed for good by the Wardens or Masters of that Mysterie, and that in the same there shall be found any falshood or deceit, then the sayd Wardens and Corporation shall forfeit the value of the thing exchanged or sold, to the king and the partie grieued. By the Statute of Anno 1. Eliz. If any do cast, or cause to be cast, any peece of linnen cloth ouer a peece of timber, and doth by any deuice, racke, draw, and stretch the same of length and bredth, and then doth beat it, and cast deceitfull liquors mingled with chalke or other things, vpon it: or doth vse any other deceitfull thing, wherby it shalbe the worse, for the vse thereof, then he shal forf. the same to the K. and him that will sue for it, be one moneth imprisoned at the least, and pay such fine as shall be assessed by the Justices before whom he is condemned. By the Statute of Anno 19. H. 7. If any person vsing buying and selling of Pewter or Brasse, doe occupie any false or deceitfull beames or weights, of the sayd wares, hee shall forfeit xx. s. to the King and the partie that will sue. And if hee be not able to pay so much, he shall be put in the stockes vntill the next Market day, and then set on the Pillorie all the Market time. By the Statute of Anno 23. H. 8. No person shall wind, or cause to be wound, any fleece of wooll, not beeing sufficiently washed, nor put in a fleece any clay, lead, stones, sand, tailes, deceitfull lockes, cot, calles, cumber, lambes wooll, nor any other thing whereby the fleece may be the more weightie, to the deceit and losse of the buyer, vpon paine to forfeit for euery fleece vj. pence, to the king and finder and prouer of the same deceit. By the Statute of Anno 8. H. 6. If any wooll packer doe make any other but good and due packing, hee that feeleth himselfe grieued thereby, shall haue his action of Trespasse and deceit at the Common law against him. And if any stranger doe force, clacke, or beard any wooll, hee shall forfeit the same, or the value thereof, and bee imprisoned. By the Statute of Anno 23. Eliz. Euery person which in the making and melting of waxe or hony, shall vse any deceit by mingling the same with rosin, tallow, turpentine, or any other deceitfull thing, to the intent to sell, or offer the same to bee sold, shall forfeit the same mingled waxe or hony. And if it be sold before the corruption shalbe found, then he shal forf. ij. s. for euery pound to the K. & the party deceiued, if he will sue. By the stat. of An. 11. H. 7. & An. 5. E. 6. If any person shal make to the intent to sell, or offer to sell, any featherbed, boulster, or pillow, except the same be stuffed with drie pulled feathers, or cleane downe onely, without mingling of scalded feathers, fen-downe, thistle down, sands, lime, grauel, haire, or any other deceitfull or corrupt stuffe: or shal make to the intent to sell, or offer to put to sale, any quilt, mattrice, or cushions, which shall bee stuffed with any other thing than feathers, wooll, or flockes alone, hee shall forfeit the same so sold, or offered to be sold, to the K. and him that will sue. By the stat. of Anno 1. Iac. If any forreiner, denizen, or Englishman, shall bring, or cause to be brought into this realm, out of any forreine dominion beyond the sea, any deceitful hops mixed with powder, dust, sand, or other soile whatsoeuer, he shal forf. the same hops. And if any Brewer of ale or beere, which shall buy the same brought from beyond the seas, or growing within this realme, shall spend the same about ẏ brewing of ale or beer to be sold, being corrupt or mixt with powder, dust, or any soil whatsouer, he shal forf. ẏ same, or the value therof to the K.

Marginal notes (left): Deceit in goldsmithes worke. — Deceitfull vsing of linnen cloth. — Deceits in weights or beames for pewter or brasse. — Deceit in winding of wooll. — Deceit in packing of wooll. — Deceit in vsing of waxe or hony. — Deceit in Vpholsters. — Bringing in deceitful hops.

Marginal notes (right): Sat. 11. H. 7. 27. — Sta. 18. El. 14. — St. 1. El. 12. — St. 19. H. 7. 6. 4. H. 8. 7. — St. 23. H. 8. 17. — St. 8. H. 6. 22. — St. 23. El. 8. — St. 11. H. 7. 19. 5. E. 6. 23. — St. 1. Iac. 18.

and him that will seise or sue for the same. For the auoiding of great deceits committed in selling of sundry sorts of corrupt and mingled spices, drugges,
St.1.Iac.19. wares, and other marchandizes garbleable, by a statute made Anno 1. Iac. Deceit in spices & drugs.
it was ordained, That all spices, wares, drugges, and other marchandizes garbleable, shall for the fees vsually allowed in that behalfe, be sufficiently garbled and diuided, and after sealed by the garbler, his deputy or seruant, before the same be sold, & shall not after be mixed with any garble, vpon paine of the forf. of the same, or the value thereof, to the King and him that will sue for the Deceit in same. And because in seuerall ages there haue bin diuers & many deceits and Woollen cloth frauds practised & put in vre in the spinning, carding, & dying of wooll & wollen yarne, & in the making, weauing, fulling, watering, tucking, milling, rowing, dying, thicking, folding, pressing, tacking, mingling, tentering, straining, stretching, measuring, searching, marking, & sealing of wollen cloth, & in ye length, bredth, & weight thereof, to the preiudice & hinderance of the buiers or wearers of the same: for the preuention & restraint whereof, by the statutes made Ann 2.E.3.14. 3.R.2.2. 13.R.2.11. 4.H.4.6. 7.H.4.10. 13.H.4.4. 6.H.8.9. 25.H.8.18. 27.H.8.12. 3.Ed.6.2. 5.Ed.6.6. 4.& 5.P.& M.5. 8.El.12. 23.El.9. 27.El.18. 35.El.10. 39.El.20. 43.El.10. 3.Iac.16. it was ordained & enacted, how the wooll prouided for the making of cloth to be sold, shal be spun, carded, & dyed, and of what length, bredth, & weight seuerall sorts of clothes wrought in seuerall counties, cities, townes, and parts of the realm made to be put to sale, shall and ought to be, and how & in what maner & sort the same seueral clothes shall be made, wouen, fulled, watered, tucked, milled, rowed, dyed, thicked, folded, pressed, tacked, mingled, tentered, strained, stretched, measured, searched, marked, & sealed, & seueral penalties be inflicted vpon the transgressors therin, if any of the same be omitted, or otherwise vsed then they ought to be. Euery of which to set downe particularly, or so much thereof as at this present are reputed in force, would require a large discourse or whole Treatise by it self. And the which I do the rather refraine to set downe & expresse, because it is doubtfull and disputable, whether any branch or article in either of the foresaid statutes or any other statute doe repeale, diminish, or alter the force of any other former statute or braunch of statute. And therefore consider of three seuerall branches of repeale in the before mentioned statutes of Anno 5.Ed.6.6. 8.El. 12. & 43.El.10. Et quære.

42 As the gouernors of this state haue bin prouident from time to time to preuent & punish deceits and frauds, when they were practised towards mens lands, leases, annuities, rents, debts, or other goods, cattels, or rights, so haue they taken care, that mans health shalbe preserued, & their bodies defended frō feeding vpon deceitful & corrupt victuall, & haue ordained laws to punish those who in steed of good, deceiued men with bad, corrupt, & vnwholsome viands: as it appeareth by ye stat. made An.51.H.3.& An.51.E.1. wherby it is ordained,
St.51.H.3.3 That a butcher ye selleth swines flesh measled, or flesh dead of the morion, after Deceit by selling of vnholesome victuals.
St.51.Ed.1. ye he shalbe conuict therof, for the first time shalbe grieuously amerced, ye second time he shalbe adiudged to ye pillory, ye third time he shalbe imprisoned, & make fine, & the fourth time he shall forsweare the towne. And in this manner shal it be done of all that offēd in like case, as of cookes that seeth flesh or fish any waies that is not holesome for mans body, or after that they haue kept it so long, that it looseth the naturall holesomenesse, then seeth it againe, and sell it. And in like
St.39.El.10 sort, by one other statute made An.39.El. it was enacted, That if any alien or stranger born, or any denizen or naturall born subiect of this realme shal bring into any hauen, port, creeke, or town of this realme any salt fish or salt herrings which shal not be good, sweet, seasonable, & meet for mās meat, & shal offer ye same

to be sold, and shall be warned by any officer of such Port &c. where the same shalbe offered to be sold, that the same be not seasonable, nor meat for mans meat: Then if he or they shall after that offer any of the said vnseasonable fish to be sold to any person within this Realme: or being an alien borne, and no denizen, shall not depart with the same from the said Hauen, Port, or Towne so soone as conueniencie will serue: Then all and euery person, owners therof, shall forfeit to the Quéen all the said vnseasonable fish, vnméet for mans meat, as is aforesaid. And by a statute made Anno 4. Ed. 3. it was established, That St. 4. E. 3. 12 assay shall be made of wines twice euery yeare, once at Easter, and another time at Michaelmas, and more oft if néed be, by the lords of the Townes, and their Baylifes, and also by the Mayors and Baylifes of the same townes: and all wines that be found corrupt shal be powred out, and the vessels broken.

Extor-

Extortion, Exaction.

1 Extortion is a wrong done by an Officer, as Ordinarie, Archdeacon, Officiall, Maior, Bailiffe, Shirife, Escheator, Coroner, Vndershirife, Auditor, Receiuer, Clerke, or other Officer, or by any other by colour of an office, in taking of an excessiue reward or fee, and more then the law doth allow him, for execution of his said office: which offence in some degrees is worse then the priuy picking of a mans purse in secret, and the transgressor in a sort may be compared to the Freebooter, which with drawne sword and with menacing words assaulteth the trauailer by the way, who casteth down his purse to him for feare of further hurt: And so is the poore sutor many times inforced to doe to the Officer, when of necessitie he must vse his helpe. It is a thing most odious and offensiue to the iustice and peace of the Realme, and to all the members thereof, that those men who be specially made choice of, and principally selected to serue their prince and countrey, and to further the execution of iustice in their offices and places, and be sufficiently rewarded with conuenient stipends for their paines therein, should in contempt of the law assesse their owne fees, in a sort put their hands in other mens purses, and there take what they will, and thereby doe wrong, vnder the colour and shadow of iustice. What is Extortion.

Exaction is a wrong done by an officer, or by one pretending to haue authoritie, in demaunding and taking reward or fee for that matter, cause, or thing, which the law doth allow no fee at all. And as our common & statute lawes haue declared, which offences or acts they doe condemne and adiudge as Extortions and Exactions, so haue they prescribed in most cases seuerall penalties to be inflicted vpon the seuerall transgressors therein, leauing the residue to be punished at the kings pleasure, or by the discretion of such of his Iudges, Iustices, or others by his commission authorized, before whom the effendors shall be thereof conuicted. And further, our said statute lawes haue set downe for the most part, what fees or duties the sutor ought to pay to the officer, & the officer is to demaund of him; to the intent that the one shall not be ignorant what to offer, nor the other what to require; and to the end, that the Law hauing written it in a sort in the officers forehead what his duty is, he may blush when he looketh in the sutors face, and demaundeth more. What is Exaction.

2 I will begin with an Exaction, that no former generation did tast of, heare

heare of, or feare, but it hath sprung up of later yeares, & bin greatly exclaimed of, and condemned in this our present age (which is taking of money, or some other reward for a Report or Certificat) wherein the offendor most commonly doth a double iniury, and to two seuerall persons, viz. first to him whose mony, fee, or other reward he taketh for the fauourable making of that report in his behalfe, whereas the law doth allow him none for reporting, but otherwise bountifully rewardeth him for that and all such other paines, and next and chiefely to him, in preiudice of whom, or whose case he maketh that report. He doth not now indifferently respect the cause in question, but bendeth his eye vpō the reward which he hath receiued, and deuiseth to accomplish the request of the one, and yet to yeeld to the other not the effect, but some colour of iustice. The King at his coronation doth promise to all his subiects, Quod nulli vendemus, nulli negabimus, aut differemus iusticiam: whereupon the whole realme did take it vnkindly at their hands, who being the kings Substitutes in place of iustice, and receiuing but a small particle of his authoritie, would doe then all the said offences at once, and sell, denie, and deferre iustice to some of the kings subiects, & certifie that for good which was bad, or that for iustice which was meere iniurie: Or if they did make report and certificat of that which was iust and true, would sell it, and take money or other reward for it, which the king himselfe vpon his oath refuseth to doe. And therefore, because all exactions, extortions, and corruptions be odious as well in this, as in all other well gouerned Commonweales, and to the intent to preuent the like enormities in this and other ages, by a statute made Anno 1. Iacob. it was enacted, That no person to whom any order or cause shalbe committed, or referred, by any of the Kings Iudges, or Courts at Westminster, or any other Court, directly or indirectly, or by any act, shift, colour, or deuice, haue, take, or receiue any money, fee, reward, couenant, obligation, promise, agreement, or any other thing, for his report or certificat, by writing, or otherwise, vpon paine of forfeiture of one hundred pounds for euery such report or certificat, and to be depriued of his office and place in the same Court: The one moitie to be to the king, his heires &c. the other moitie to the party grieued, which will sue for the same at any time during the said suit, or within one yeare after the same cause discontinued or decreed: and in his default of such suit, to him or them that will sue for the same by originall writ, B. P. or I. in the Kings Court of Starre-chamber, or in any of his Courts of Record at Westminster: in which suit by B. P. or I. no W. E. P. S. P. or any other delay shall be admitted. Prouided neuerthelesse, That it shalbe lawfull for the Clerke to take for his paines for writing of euery such report or certificat twelue pence for the first side, and two pence for euery side after, and no more, vpon paine to forfeit tenne shillings for euery penny taken, ouer and aboue the said summes to be had and recouered as aforesaid.

Mag. Chart. St. 9. H. 3. 29

St. 1. Iac. 10

Exaction by taking of reward for a report.

The Clerkes duty.

3 For that the kings of this Realme haue allowed to their Officers from time to time sufficient Salaries to maintaine them, according to their estates and degrees, to the intent that they should not otherwise extort any thing from their subiects, but such fees & duties, as the auncient customes, laws, or statutes of the realme did allow them. Therfore by the statute of West. 1. it was ordained, That if any shirife, coroner, or other officer of the kings do take any thing to execute his office, but only that which the king alloweth him, he shal render double to the party, and shalbe punished at the kings pleasure.

Extortion in the shirife, coroner, & other officers.

St. 3. E. 1. 26

4 To

St.3.E.1.29 4 To preuent extortion in certaine Officers of the Judges, by the same stat. of West. 1. it was enacted, That if the Serieant, Crier, or Marshall of any Justice, do wrongfully take mony of any which doth recouer land, obtaine his suit, leuie a fine, or prosecute any suit touching any plea of the Crowne, he shal be punished at the kings pleasure, and yeeld treble damages to the party grieued. And if hee be a Serieant of fee, his Office shalbe seised into the K. hands. 19.Ass.p.13 But in an attaint, if the plaintife be nonsuit, euery of the petit Jurie shall pay xij. d. to the Marshall, and be discharged. Extortion in a Serieant, Crier, or Marshall, of a Judge.

5 To eschew extortion which in some cases before had been committed by some Coroners, first by the stat. of anno 3.E.1. and after that by the stat. of anno 1.H.8. it was established, That a Coroner vpon request made to him to come, and inquire vpon the view of any person slaine, drowned, or otherwise dead by misaduenture, the same Coroner shall doe his office diligently, vpon the view of the bodie of euerie such person or persons, without taking any thing therefore, vpon paine to euery Coroner that will not endeuor himselfe to doe his Office, as is aforesaid: or that hee taketh any thing for doing of his Office vpon euerie person dead by misaduenture, for euerie time fortie shillings. And vpon the said statute of Anno 3.Ed.1. two Coroners were indicted of Extortion, for that they had taken of some of the K. people, halfe a mark at seuerall times, contrarie to the foresaid stat. and their othes, and therefore they paid a fine to the King. Extortion in a Coroner. St.1.E.1.10. St.1.H.8.7 27.Ass.p.14

6 Because the Sherife of euerie Countie is a great and necessarie Officer in the Commonweale, and vsed as a speciall instrument to the furtherance of iustice, in all suits pursued at the common law, and his seruice is imployed in the beginning, prosecuting, and ending of the most of them: therefore as the law hath allwayes had a speciall regard of him, and foreseene that he shall be a man of wisedome, of worth, of credit, countenance, and ability, and that he shall be allowed a conuenient stipend, and salary for his pains in most cases: so doth she carrie a vigilant and watchfull eye vpon him, and his inferiour Officers, or Substitutes, knowing what grieuous oppressions might ensue, if she should leaue a man of his authoritie, and necessarie imployment, at libertie to diue at his pleasure into other mens purses, and to take what hee would; and therefore she hath restrained him, his Undersherife, Bailife of Franchise, and other Bailife within certaine lists, and assigned them what they shall take for Arrests, Attachements, Mainprises, letting to Baile, and seruing of Executions, which if any of them do exceed, he shall forfeit the penalties hereafter expressed, and be adiudged an extortioner: As appeareth by the stat. of An. 23.H.6. whereby it was ordained, That no Sherife, Undersherife, Bailife of Franchise, nor any other Bailif, by occasion, or vnder colour of his Office, shall take any other thing, by themselues, or by any other person to their vse, or to their profit, of any person by any of them arrested, or attached, nor of any other for them, for the omitting of any arrest or attachement to bee made by their bodies, or of any person by any of them by force or colour of their office arrested or attached, for fine, fee, mainprise, letting to bayle, or for shewing any ease or fauour to any such person so arrested, for their reward or profit, but such as followeth, viz. The Sherife xx.d. the Bailife which maketh the arrest or attachement iiij. d. the Gaoler (if the prisoner be comitted to his ward) Extortion in Sherifes, Undersherifes Bailifes. St.23.H.6.10. The fees of the Sherife for arrests, &c.

The Sherifes duetie for the making of a copie of a Panel

ward) iiij.d. The Sherife, Undersherife, Sherifes Clerke, Steward, or Bailif of Franchise, seruant to the Bailife, or Coroner, shall not take by colour of his office, by himselfe, nor by any other person to his vse, any thing of any person, for making of any returne or panell, and for the copie of a panell iiij.d. No Sherife, nor none of the officers aforesaid, shall take, or cause to be taken or made any obligation by colour of their office, but onely to themselues, of any person, nor by any person which shall be in their ward by course of the law, but in the name of their office, and vpon condition written, that the said prisoners shall appeare at the day of the said writs, bils, or warrants, and in such places as the said writs, bils, or warrants shall require. And if any of the said Sherifes, or other officers aforesaid, take any Obligation in any other forme, by colour of their offices, it shall be void. And he shall take no more for making of any such obligation, warrant, or precept by him to be made, but iiij.d. And all Sherifes, Undersherifes, Clerks, Bailifes, Gaolers, Coroners, Stewards, Bailifes of Franchises, or any other Officers or Ministers, which doe contrarie to the foresaid ordinances, in any point of the same, shall lose to the partie in this behalfe endammaged or grieued, his treble dammages, and shal forfeit xl.l. at euery time that any do the contrarie in any point of the same, whereof the king shall haue the one halfe, to be imployed onely to the vse of his house, & the party that will sue, the other. But the Warden of the Fleet, and of the K. palace at West. shall not be preiudiced by this ordinance, in his dutie of his office.

The Sherifes, &c. forfeiture for extortion.

The warden of the Fleete.

Extortion in a Sherife for sparing of a Juror.

7 To the intent that the Sherife nor any of his officers should take any reward, for the sparing to returne any Juror, and by that meanes commit extortion, by a stat. made anno 27. El. it was prouided, That if any Sherife, Undersherife, Sherifes deputie, Sherife or Undersherifes Clerke, or any Bailife of Franchise, shall receiue, haue, or take, by himselfe, or any other, any summe of money, reward, or other profit, directly or indirectly, or do take any promise, make any agreement, or assent to haue any summe of money, reward, or other profit, directly or indirectly, of any person or persons, for the sparing, not warning, or not returning of any person to be sworn as a Juror, for ÿ tryal of any issue ioyned in any of the courts of the K. Bench, Common Pleas, and Exchequer, or before any Justice: then euery Sherife &c. so offending, shal forfeit for euery such offence v.l. to the K. and J. to be recouered in any Court of Record by A.B.P.J.&c. wherein no W.E.P.&c. St.27.El.6.

How much Sherifes may take for seruing of an execution.

8 And for that our later age thought it as expedient to preuent extortion or oppression in Sherifes and other their Officers in seruing of executions, as the former age did in making of arrests or attachements, &c. and to the intent that the Sherife and his Officers might know what to demaund and take for the seruing of an execution, without danger of extortion, and that the sutor might be ascertained what to offer and pay therefore, without any scruple of receiuing iniurie, by a statute made An. 29. Eliz. or rather An. 28. Eliz. St.29.El.4.
it was enacted, That it shal not be lawful, to, or for any Sherif, Under-sherife, St.28.El.4.
Bialife of Franchises, or liberties, nor for any of their, or either of their officers, ministers, seruants, Balifes or Deputies, nor for any of them, by reason or colour of their or either of their offices, to haue, receiue, or take of any person or persons whatsoeuer, directly or indirectly, for the seruing and executing of any extent or execution vpon the body, lands, goods or chattels of any person or persons whatsoeuer, more or other consideration or recompence, than in this Act is and shall be limited, which shall be lawfull to bee had, receiued,

and

and taken, viz. twelue pence of and for euery 20. shillings, where the summe exceedeth not an hundred pounds, and sixe pence of and for euery 20. shillings, being ouer & aboue the said summe of an hundred pounds, that he or they shall so leuy, or extend and deliuer in execution, or take the body in execution for, by vertue and force of any such extent or execution whatsoeuer, vpon paine & penaltie, that all and euery Shirife, Undershirife, Baylife of Franchises &c. which at any time shall directly or indirectly doe the contrary, shall lose to the party grieued his treble dammages, & shall forf. xl.l. of lawful English money for euery time that he, they, or any of them shall do the contrary, to the Q. & I. to be recouered by A. S. B. or I. wherein no W. E. P. Prouided alwaies, that this act shall not extend to any fees to be taken or had for any execution within any city or towne corporat. Execution within cities or townes corporat.

St. 2. H. 4. 8 9 By the stat. of An. 2. H. 4. it was established, That the Chirographer of the common place, nor his fermor, deputy, or lieutenant, shall not take any more then iiij. s. for any fine leuied in the same court. And if the fermor, deputy, or lieutenant do take any more, he shall forf. his office, be excluded the same court, suffer one yeeres imprisonment, & pay to the party grieued his treble damages: and the party grieued shall haue his suit before the same Iustices. Extortion in the chirographer of the common place

Sta. 33. H. 8. 39. 10 By the stat. of Ann. 33. H. 8. it was enacted, That if any auditor of the Exchequer, Duchy of Lancaster, & court of Wards and Liueries, or any of his clerkes, or any other, to their or any of their vse, shall take for the inrolment of any letters patents, decrees of the same courts, grants, or indentures of leases, or for the allowance of the same, aboue 3. s. 4. d. he so offēding shal forf. 6. s. 8. d for euery peny that he taketh aboue the foresaid summe, to the K. & I. &c. to be recouered by A. I. wherein no W. E. P. &c. And if any person doe offer to any such auditor any such letters patents, decrees, or leases, to be inrolled, hee shall inroll the same, or as much thereof as shall appertaine to his office. Extortion in auditors, or their clerkes.

St. 33. H. 8. 39. 11 By the same stat. of An. 33. H. 8. it was moreouer ordained, That euery receiuer of the Exchequer, Duchy of Lancaster, & court of Wards & Liueries, which shall pay to any person an annuity, pention, or other rent, shall (if the same person will vpon the receit thereof deliuer vnto him a sufficient acquittance, sealed & signed, testifying the same receit) receiue the same, without taking any reward therefore, vpon paine to forf. for euery penny or pennyworth receiued, 6. s. 8. d. And if the party do not deliuer such a sufficient acquittance, but that the receiuer or his clerke doth make the same, he shall haue therefore 4. d. and if he take aboue 4. d. he shall forf. for euery penny or pennyworth so taken, 6. s. 8. d. And if any Treasurer, Receiuer, or Minister accomptant, or their deputies, which shall pay to any person any fee, annuity, pention, dutie, warrant, or rent, do retaine, receiue, or take of the party to whom he shal pay ẏ same, in way of reward, or otherwise, aboue 4. d. for euery l. that he shal pay, he shal forf. 6. s. 8. d. for euery penny or pennyworth that he shall receiue ouer, to the party grieued, to be recouered by A. B. or P. wherein no W. E. or P. &c. Extortion in the kings receiuers. Extortion in them who doe pay fees, pentions, &c.

12 By the stat. of An. 26. H. 8. it was ordained, That if any Officer of the exchequer do take of any archbishop, bishop, or other persō hauing charge with the Extortion in officers of the Exchequer.

the collection and payment of the Tenth of Spirituall promotions, any reward for making his account or Quietus est in the same Exchequer, or for any thing concerning the Tenth, he shall forfeit his office, and make fine at the kings pleasure.

Extortion in a clerke of the signet or priuy seale.

13 By the statute of Anno 27.H.8.it was established, That all and euery Clerke, and Clerkes of the Signet, and priuie Seale, shall haue and take for his or their writing of a warrant vpon a Bill for Tales of reward, twelue pence: for the writing of a warrant for the gift of euery office, twenty pence: for the writing of a warrant for a pention, annuitie, or wages, twenty pence: for the writing of a warrant for a speciall Liuery, or other perpetuity, sixe shillings eight pence: for the writing of a warrant vpon euery bill for a Conge deslier, royall assent, restitution of Temporalties, Donatiues, Aduocations, Presentations, or other Ecclesiasticall matter, three shillings foure pence: for the writing of euery warrant vpon a Placard, Licence, Pardon, or Shirifes reward, two shillings: for the writing of euery warrant vpon a denizen, three shillings foure pence: for the writing of a warrant for the keeping of an ideot, twenty pence: for the writing of a warrant for the keeping of a Ward, three shillings foure pence. And no Clerke or Clerkes of the Signet or priuy Seale aforesaid, shall take for the writing of any manner warrant aboue specified, more large and ample fees then is before prescribed, vpon paine of ten pounds to be forfeited to the K. & I. to be recouered by B.A.P.I. in any of the kings Courts, wherein no E.P.W. shalbe admitted. St.27.H.8.11

Extortion by officers of the faculties.

14 To the intent that the Clerke of the Faculties, and his inferior officers and clerks might content themselues with their fees & duties assigned, & extort no more, by the statute of Anno 25.H.8.it was enacted, That such as shall exact or receiue of any sutor more for a dispensation, faculty, or licence, then is contained in the two bookes of one tenor of Taxes, shall forfeit tenne times so much as he shall so extortiously receiue & exact, to the K. his heires & successors, & the party that will sue, to be recouered by A.B.P. wherein no E.W.P. shal be admitted. St.25.H.8. 21.

Extortion vpon prentices & freemen.

15 Because no Extortion should bee committed vpon apprentices when they begin or end their termes, by the stat. of Anno 22.H.8.& Anno 28.H.8. it was established, That no Masters, Wardens, or Fellowships of crafts, nor any of them, shall take of any apprentice, or other person, for the entry of the said prentice into their said Fellowship, aboue the summe of ij.s. vj.d. nor for his entry when his yeares or terme is expired, aboue iij.s.iiij.d. vpon paine to forf. for euery time that they or any of them shall offēd contrary to this act, xl.l. to the K. and the I.&c. to be recouered by A.I.&c. wherein no P.E.&c. St.22.H.8.8 St.22.H.8.5

The fees of the officers of the court of wards.

16 Because the makers of our lawes were willing to giue forewarning to the officers of the Court of Wards to eschew extortion, therefore by the stat. of An.32.H.8.it was enacted, That the master & officers of the Court of wards & liueries shal take for the fees of all proces at the suit of the parties, vnder ỹ priuy seale of the same court, ij.s.vj.d.& for the fees of al cōmissions directed out at the suit of the parties ij.s.vj.d.& for recording of all apparāces iiij.d.& no more. St.32.H.8. 46.

17 By

St.26.H.8.3 17 By the statute of Anno 26.H.8. it was prouided to auoide Extortion in the officers of the first fruits, That no person shall compell an other to pay for any writing obligatorie to be made for the paiment of the first fruits of Ecclesiasticall liuings to the King, aboue eight pence, nor for any acquitance for the receit thereof, aboue foure pence. The fees for obligations for first fruits.

18 For that Eschetors should know what is their duetie for the finding of offices, and for the execution of Writs, to the intent that they might thereby the easlier shunne the danger of Extortion, if they will: by a statute made Anno 33. H.8. it was enacted, That if any Escheator doth take aboue the summe of xv. shillings for the finding of an office of any lands, tenements, or hereditaments, not exceeding the cleere yearely valew of fiue pound, viz. for the Escheators fee vi.s viii.d: for the writing of the office iii.s iiii.d: for the charges of the Iurie iii.s, and for the officers that shall receiue the said office in any court of Record ii.s, he shall forfeit for euery time so offending, v.l. to the K. and I. to be recouered by A.I. wherein no W.E.P.&c. And by the statute of Anno 23.H.6. it was ordained, That if an Escheator do take priuily, or openly, by himselfe, or any other, aboue the summe of xl.s, for the execution of any Writ in one countie, he shall forfeit for euery offence forty pounds, whereof one halfe shall be to the King, and the other to him that will sue. Extortion by Eschetors. St.33.H.8. 22. St.23.H.6. 17.

19 To preuent Exactions by the officers of the Admiralty vpon those who trauaile into other Countries, for the getting of fish, by a Statute made Anno 2.Ed.6. it was ordained, That if the Admirall, or any officer, or minister of the Admiraltie shall exact, receiue, or take by himselfe, his seruant, or deputie, of any merchant, or fisherman, any summe of mony, doles or shares of fish, or any other reward, or benefite, for any licence to passe this Realme into Island, New-found-land, Ireland, or other places commodious for the getting of fish, or for any other respect concerning the said voiages: hee shall forfeit for the first offence treble the summe, or valew of the reward so taken, to the King and him that will sue for the same, to be recouered by A.I. &c. wherein no W.E.P. &c. And for the second offence, shall loose his office, and make fine at the Kings pleasure. Exactions vpon them who trauaile for fish. St.2.Ed.6.6

20 To the intent that the Marshall of the Marshalsey of the Court of the Kings house may take such fees in open Court as were wont to be taken in the time of King Edward the third, and none other, and may thereby omit to commit Extortion: by a Statute made Anno 2.H.4. it was declared, That the said Marshall may take the fees heereafter following, viz. of euery person which commeth by Capias to the said Court iiii.d, and if he be let to mainprise vntill his day ii.d more. And of euery person being defendant which is impleaded of Trespas, and findeth two Mainpernors to keepe his day vntill the end of the plea ii.d. And of euery person committed to prison by iudgement of the steward, in what soeuer maner the same be, iiii.d, and of euery person deliuered of felony iiii.d, and of euery felon let to mainprise by the Court, iiii.d. But if the Marshall, or any of his officers vnder him, doe take any other fees, than are before declared, the said Marshall and euery of his officers, shall lose their offices, and also pay to the partie greeued treble dammages, for the which the said party shall haue his sute before the Steward of the said Court for the time being. A seruitor of bills, which beareth a staffe of the The fees of the Marshall of the K. house. St.2.H.4. 23. A Seruitor of bills in the Marshals Court.

the Court, shall take for euery mile from the said Court vntill the same place, where he shall do his seruice, j.d, and for xij. miles xij.d, & to serue a Venire facias, or a Distringas out of the same court the double. And if any Seruitor of Bills do the contrary, he shall be imprisoned, and make fine to the K. after the discretion of the Steward of the same court, and also be forejudged and banished the same court. All which articles the steward at his comming into the country hath authoritie to proclaime, and put in execution.

21 And for that the kings of this realme haue from time to time bestowed vpon such as they assigned to be muster masters, or captains in times of wars liberall and bountifull stipends, and allowances, the rather, to the intent they should not exact, or make a pray, of such as should be, or then were souldiers: Therfore to preuent such like exaction, by a statute made Añ 4.& 5. P. & M. St.4.& 5.P. & M,3.

Muster masters exacting mony to spare souldiers.

it was ordained, That if any person which shall be commanded by the Q. her heirs or successors, by commission, leters, or otherwise authorized, to leuy muster, or to make men to serue in her warres, or otherwise for the defence of this Realme, do by any meane exact, lenie, receiue, or take, or cause to be taken any mony, or other reward, or thing whatsoeuer, of any persõ for seruice in wars, or that shalbe appointed, named, or mustred to serue in any such seruice, or for the sparing, or discharging of such person from the said seruice, then he shall forfeit ten times so much, as he shall receiue, exact, or take, to the Q. & I. to be recouered by A.I. &c. wherein no W.E.P. If any captaine, petit captaine, or other hauing charge of men, shall for any aduantage or gaine by him to be receiued, discharge, or licence any of the men, or souldiers appointed to serue in the warres vnder his rule, or order, to depart from the said seruice: or shal not pay vnto his souldiers, & to euery of thẽ their full & whole wages, conduct, and coat mony, within x. daies next after he shal haue receiued the same: then the party offending in giuing such licence, or discharge, shall forfeit for euery such offence x. times the value of the thing so receiued, to the Q. & I. to be recouered by A.I. wherin no W.E.P. &c. And also he shal pay vnto euery such souldier from whom he shall with-hold any such wages, conduct, or coat money, treble the summe so with-holden.

Exacting by captaines of their souldiers

22 Because Scauage, otherwise called Shewage was many times wrõgfully, and extortiously taken by Magistrates of cities and corporat townes, of merchants that transported or brought their marchandizes thither: therefore by a statute made Anno 19.H.7. it was prouided, That if any maior, shirife, bailife, or other officer, in any city, borough, or towne within this realme, doe distraine, take, or leuie any custome called Scauage or Shewage of any merchant denizen, or of any other the K. subiects denizens, for any merchandize to the K. before truly customed, that is brought by land or water to be vttered in any citie, borough, or towne in this land: or if any maior, shirife, bailife, or other officer in any city, borough, or towne for non paiment of the said scauage, let or disturbe any merchants, or any other persons denizens, to sel and vtter their merchandize by them brought into any city, borough, or towne; then he which offendeth shal forfet for euery offence xx.l. to the K. & the party grieued, or any other that wil first sue by A. of debt in any shire, wherein no W.E.P. shalbe allowed. But the maior, shirifes, & cõmunalty of London and euery of them shall haue such summes of mony for scauage of euery person denizen, as of right they ought to haue.

Extortion by taking of scauage of merchants.

St.19.H.7.8

23 Euery of the chiefe Iustices of the Kings Bench and Common Pleas, and the maior of the Staple at Westminster, and the Recorder of the Citie of London,

London, before whom any obligation being of the nature and force of a Statute Staple shall be recognized, according to the statute of An 23. H.8. shal take for every such Recognisance iij.s iiij.d, & the clarke that shall write, make and inroll the same iij.s iiij.d, and for the certificat of every one such obligation xx.d. And if any of the said Justices, Maior, Recorder, or Clarke take of any of the K. subiects above the summe or summes to them limited by this statute, then the same offendor shal forfeit for every time so offending, xl.l to the K. and I. to be recovered by A.I. wherein no W.E.P.&c. And by the Stat. of An 27. Eli. it was further ordained, That no Clarke of the same Recognisances shall or may take, for, or in respect of any search to be made for, or concerning any statute Merchant, or of the Staple, brought unto him to be entred, above ij.d for one yeers search, & so after the rate of ij.d for every yeere, & not above, upon paine to forfeit & lose to the partie or parties grieved twentie times as much as he shal take, contrary to the true meaning of this Act: to be recovered in any of the K. courts of Record, by action of debt B.P.I. wherein no W.E.P.

St.23.H.8.6 — The Justices & Clarks fee upon every Recognisance

St.27. Eli.4. — The Clarkes fee for search.

24 Because it is well perceived, that learned and expert Atturnies be necessarie members in our State, and great meanes to further iustice, and to bring sutes to their expected ends, and that they must therefore disburse money for learned councell, for processe, for pleading, for copies, and many other things, and after receive the same againe, with their owne fees, and salarie for their paines of their Clients: Therefore the Law (as a provident mistris) taking care that Atturnies and Sollicitors, shal not in any secret maner commit extortion, by charging their Clients with excessive fees, & unnecessary demaunds, by a statute made An 3. Iac. procured it to be established, That no Atturney, Sollicitor, or servant to any, shalbe allowed from his Client, or master, of, or for any fee given to any Serieant, or Councellor at law, or of or for any sum or sums of mony, given for copies to any clarke or clarkes, or officers in any court of Record at Westm. unles he have a ticket subscribed with the hand & name of the same Serieant, or Councellor, clarke, clarks, or officers aforesaid, testifying how much he hath received for his fee, or given or paid for copies, & at what time, & how often. And all Atturnies and Sollicitors shall give a true Bill unto their masters, or clients, or their assignees, of all other charges, concerning the suits which they have for them, subscribed with his owne hand, & name, before such time, as they or any of them shall charge their clients with any the same fees or charges: And if the atturney or sollicitor doe or shall willingly delay his clients suits, to worke his owne gaine, or demand by his bil any other sums of mony, or allowance upon his accompt of any mony which he hath not laid out or disbursed: then in every such case the partie grieved shall have his action against such atturney, or sollicitor, and recover therein costs and treble dammages: And the said atturney & sollicitor shall be discharged from thenceforth from being an atturney or sollicitor any more.

St.3. Iac.7. — Meanes for Atturnies to avoide the suspition of extortion.

An Atturney delaying of a suite, or demanding more than is due.

25 For that the Stewards of Leets and court Barons, did of late yeares get into their owne hands, and in their owne names, or into the hands of some of their friends to their use, the profits and perquisites of the said Leets, and court Barons, whereby many sutors to the same Courts were iniustly vexed, and by grievous fines and amerciaments, unduely punished, and much extortion was done unto the Tenants and Inhabitants where such Stewards were, to make and obtaine an undue & extraordinary gaine to them-

 selves:

A preuention of extortion in Stewards of Courts.

St.1.Iac.5.

selues: for the restraining whereof, by a statute made Anno 1. Iac. it was established, That no Steward, deputie Steward, or vnder Steward of any court Leete, or court Baron, shall directly, or indirectly in his owne name, or in the name of any other, take, receiue, or make benefite to his owne vse, in money, goods, or any other thing, to the valew of twelue pence, or more, by vertue or colour of any demise or graunt, hereafter to be made, of any of the profites, or perquisites, or amerciaments of any such Courts, whereof they are Steward, which rightfully shall belong to the Lords of the same: vpon paine that euery Steward offending contrary to the Tenour of this Act, shall for euery such offence forfeit tenne pounds, and to be disabled euer after to be Steward of such Court, or of any other: The one moitie of which forfeiture shall be to the K. &c. and the other to any party that will sue, to be recouered in any of the Kings Courts of Record, by A.B.P.I. &c. wherein no E.P. or other dilatorie plea shall be allowed.

Extortion in Gaugeors, Searchers, and Packers of fish.

St.11.H.7. 23.

26 To the intent that Gaugeors, and Searchers of barrells of fish should know what was due vnto them for their paines, and take no more, nor commit extortion, by a statute made Anno 11.H.7. it was enacted, That euery Gaugeor, Packer, and Searcher shall take no more for gauging of a barrell of salmon, herring, fish, eeles, halfe barrell, and firkin, than for euery peece a farthing, and for his labour for searching and packing, if neede be, of a barrell of salmon from head to head a peny, and for boning, naping, and packing of a barrel of fish, if need be, a peny, and for searching and for packing of a barrell of herring, if need be, two pence: and for searching and packing of euerie barrell of eeles ij.d: and so in halfe barrels, and firkins of herrings, and eeles, they shal take according to the former rate. And if any Gaugeor, Searcher, or Packer do the contrary, he shall loose his office, and also be imprisoned forty dayes. But the said Searcher, or Packer shall receiue nothing of the said fees by colour of their office, but onely for such Buts, Barrels, halfe Barrels, and Firkins, as by them shall be sufficiently searched and packed, and were not sufficiently packed before.

A preuention of extortion in Ordinaries and their officers.

St.31.Ed.3. 4.

St.3.H.5.8.

St.21.H.8.5

27 In the raignes of K. Edward the third, and K. Henry the fift, the Commons seuerall times complained in parliament of diuers extortions committed by Ordinaries, and their officers, in probat of Testaments, making of Inuentories, and giuing of Acquitances, as it doth appeare by the statute of Anno 31.Ed.3. and Anno 3.H.5. But because the former of those statutes inflicted no condigne punishment vpon the offendors therein, and the later is expired; and also, for that the same extortions enormity did encrease: Therfore for the redresse of the same, by a Statute made Anno 21.H.8. it was established, That nothing shall be demaunded, receiued, or taken by any Bishop, Ordinarie, Archdeacon, Chancellor, Commissarie, Officiall, nor any other person or persons whatsoeuer, hauing authoritie to take, or receiue probation, insinuation, or approbation of Testament, or Testaments, by him, or themselues, nor by his, or their Registers, Scribes, Praisors, Summoners, Apparitors, or by any other of their Ministers, for the probation of any Testament, or for writing, sealing, praising, registring, fines, making of inuentories, giuing of Acquitances, or for any cause concerning the same, where the goods of the Testator of the said Testament, or person so dying doe not amount cleerly ouer & aboue the value of C.s. sterling: except only to the scribe to haue for the writing of the probat of the Testament of him deceased, vj.d.

The Ordinaries duty for probat of Testaments.

The goods not amounting to C.s.

And

And for the commission of administration of the goods of any man deceasing intestate, not being aboue the like valew of C. s. cleere vj. d. And when the goods of the Testator do amount ouer and aboue the cleere valew of C. s, and do not exceed the summe of fortie pounds sterling; Then no Bishop, Ordinarie, nor other person or persons whatsoeuer, hauing authoritie to take probation of any Testament, by himselfe, or any of his ministers, for the probation, insinuation, and approbation of any testament or testaments, or for the registring, sealing, writing, praising, making of Inuentories, giuing of acquitances, fines, or any other things concerning the same, shall take, or cause to be taken of any person or persons, onely three shillings six pence, and not aboue, whereof to the Ordinarie for him and his ministers, two shillings six pence, and to the scribe the xij. d residue, for registring of the same. And where the goods of the Testator doe amount aboue the cleere valew of fortie pounds sterling: then the Ordinarie by himselfe, nor any of his Ministers for the probation of any testament, or for the registring, sealing, &c. or for any thing concerning the same probat, shall take of any person but onely fiue shillings, and not aboue, whereof to be to the saide Ordinarie for him and his ministers, two shillings six pence, and not aboue, and two shillings six pence residue to be to the scribe for the registring of the same: Or else the scribe to be at his libertie to refuse the two shillings six pence, and to haue for the writing of euery tenne lines of the said testament a penny (whereof euery line to containe in length tenne inches.) And euery such Bishop, Ordinarie, or other person, hauing authority to take the probation of any testament, their Registers, Scribes, and Ministers, shall approue, insinuate, seale, and register the said Testaments, and deliuer the same sealed with the seale of their office, to the executor or executors named in such testaments for the summes aboue said, and in manner and forme aboue rehearsed with conuenient speede, without any frustratorie delay. If any person die intestate, or the executors named in any such testament, refuse to proue the said testament: Then the Ordinarie, or other person or persons, hauing authoritie to take probat of testaments, shall graunt the administration of the goods of the testator, or person deceased, to the widdow of the same person, or to the next of his kinne, or both, as by the discretion of the same Ordinarie shall be thought good, taking surety for the true administration of the same goods, & taking nothing for the said administration granted, vnles the goods of the person so deceased amount aboue the value or summe of C. s. And in case the goods of the person so deceased amount aboue the value of C. s, and not aboue xl. l. then hee & his officers shall take only ij. s vj. d, & not aboue. And in case any person or persons at any time require a copie or copies of a testament proued, or inuentorie made; then the said ordinarie, &c. or his ministers shal from time to time with conuenient speed, without frustratory delay, deliuer, or cause to be deliuered, a true copie, or copies of the same vnto the said person or persons demanding the same, taking for the search, & for the making of the copie of either of ye said testamēt or inuentorie, but only such fee, as is before rehearsed for ye registring of the said testament; or else the scribe or register to be at his libertie to demand, haue, & take for euery x. lines thereof, being of the proportion before rehersed, j. d. But where any persons hauing authority to take probat of testamēts haue vsed to take lesse sums of mony than abouesaid, for ye probat of testamēts, or cōmissiō of administratiōs, or other cause concerning ye same, they shal take such sums for ye same, as they before ye making of this act vsed to take, & not aboue. Euery Bish. ordinary, archdeacō, chācelor, cōmissary, official, & other persō & persons,

The goods not amounting to xl. l.

The goods exceeding xl. l.

An administration granted.

The fees for copies.

hauing authoritie to take probat of Testaments, their Registers, Scribes, Praisors, Summoners, Apparitors, and all other their Ministers whatsoeuer they be, that shall doe, or attempt, or cause to be done, or attempted against this Act, in any thing, shall forfeit for euery time so offending, to the partie grieued in that behalfe, so much money as he shall take contrary to this Act, and ouer that shall forfeit to the King and the party grieued ten pounds to be recouered by A. I. B. &c. wherein no W.E.P. And euery of the same Bishops, and other persons, which shall incurre the danger of such penalty, shall be charged onely for himselfe, and none of them shal be chargeable to the penalty for others offences.

The forfeiture of the offendor

28 Shortly after the making of the foresaide Statute of Anno 21.H.8. the grand Councell of the Realme being as carefull that Ordinaries, or their Officers, should no more commit extortion in sealing of Citations, than they might in prouing of Willes, granting of Administrations, or such like, did therefore by a statute made Anno 23.H.8. ordaine, That if any Archbishop, Bishop, Ordinarie, Officiall, Commissarie, or other person hauing spirituall iurisdiction, or any substitute, or minister of his, doe aske, demand, take, or receiue, more than three pence for the seale of a Citation, hee shall pay to the partie, of whom he doth demand, take, or receiue the same, double damages, and costs, and shal forfeit for euery offence tenne pounds to the king, and I. to be recouered by A.I. wherein no W.E.P. &c.

Extortion is an Ordinary for the Seale of a Citation.

St.23.H.8.9

29 Because in former times it was vncertaine, and by this meanes, oft times great question did grow, what, and how much Parsons, Vicars, or other spirituall men, or their farmors ought to take for Mortuaries, or Corse Presents, after the death of their Parishioners: Therefore, to the intent that the same should be limited in certaintie, and not be excessiue, nor any Extortion, Exaction, or other wrong committed in the taking, or receiuing of them, by a Statute made Anno 21.H.8. it was established, That no Parson, Vicar, Curate, or parish Priest, nor any other spirituall person, nor their farmers, Baylifes, or Lessees, shall haue, take, receiue, or demaund of any person or persons within this Realme, for any person or persons dying within the same, any maner of Mortuarie or Corse present, nor any money, or other thing for the same, more than is heereafter expressed: Nor shall conuent, or call any person before any Iudge spirituall, for the recouerie of any such Mortuaries, or any other thing for the same, more than is heereafter expressed: vpon paine to forfeit for euerie time so demaunding, receiuing, taking, conuenting, or calling any such person or persons before any spirituall Iudge, so much in valew, as they shall take aboue the summe limited by this Act, and ouer that, fortie shillings to the partie grieued, contrary to this Act: for the which the partie grieued shal haue an action of debt by W.B.P. or I. in any of the K. Courts, wherein no W.E.P. &c. But it is lawfull for any spiritual person to take any summe of mony, or other thing, which by any person dying shalbe giuen & bequeathed to him, or to the high altar of the Church.

Mortuaries.

St.21.H.8.6

The penaltie for extorting for a Mortuarie.

A Legacie giuen to a spirituall person.

No Mortuary or Corse present shall be giuen or demaunded of any person, but in such place onely where Mortuaries haue beene vsed to be paied and giuen: Nor any person shall paie Mortuaries in more places than one, that is to say, in the place of his most dwelling and habitation, and there but one Mortuarie.

St.21.H.8.6.

B.

But one Mortuarie for any person.

No

St.21.H.8.6 No Mortuarie shalbe taken, or demaunded of any person whatsoeuer he be, which at the time of his death hath in moueable goods vnder the value of ten markes. No parson, curat, or other spirituall person, nor any of their farmors, bailifes or lessees, shall for any person dying, or dead, and being at the time of his death of the value in moueable goods of ten markes or more, aboue his debts paied, and vnder the summe of thirtie pounds, take for a mortuarie aboue three shillings foure pence in the whole: And for a person being at ỹ time of his death of the value of thirtie pounds aboue his debts paied in moueable goods and vnder the value of fortie pounds, there shall no more be taken for a mortuarie then sixe shillings eight pence: And for a person hauing at the time of his death of the value in moueable goods of fortie pounds or aboue, to any summe, there shall no more be taken, paied, or demaunded for a Mortuarie, then ten shillings in the whole.

C The parsons dutie for all Mortuaries.

St.21.H.8.6 No Parson, Vicar, Curat &c. or other, shall take, demaund, or aske any Mortuarie, or other thing by way of mortuarie, for any woman being couert baron, nor for any childe, nor for any person not keeping house, nor for any waifaring man, or other that maketh not residence in the place where they shall happen to die: But the mortuaries of such wayfaring persons shalbe answerable (in places where mortuaries haue beene accustomed to be paied, and in maner, forme, and rate aboue mentioned and none otherwise) in the places where such wayfaring persons, at the time of their death had their most habitation, house, and dwelling place, and no where else.

D. Who shall pay no Mortuaries.

St.21.H.8.6 No mortuaries, or Corse presents, nor any summe of money for them, shalbe demaunded, or had in the parts of Wales, nor in the Marches of the same, nor in the towne of Barwicke, or the Marches of the same, but onely in such places where Mortuaries haue beene accustomed to be paid: Neither shal any Mortuaries, nor Corse presents, nor any thing for them be demaunded, or had in those places, but only after the order, and manner aboue specified, and none otherwise, nor for any other person then is aboue limitted. But it is lawfull to the Bishop of Bangor, Landaffe, S. Dauid, and S. Asse, and likewise to the Archdeacon of Chester, to take such mortuaries of the priests within their Diocesses, & iurisdictions, as heretofore haue beene accustomed.

E. Mortuaries in Wales, Barwicke, and the Marches.

St.21.H.8.6 No person shalbe compelled in such places (where mortuaries haue beene accustomed to be taken of lesse value then is aforesaid) to pay any other mortuaries, or more for any mortuarie, then hath beene accustomed: Nor any mortuarie shalbe demaunded taken or had in such place, of any person or persons exempt by this Act, nor contrarie to this Act.

F. Mortuaries of lesse value by custome.

30 There be certaine other extortions, or exactions in spirituall, Ecclesiasticall, or Scholasticall causes, which antiquitie did not know, or dreame of, and therefore neither made Statutes, or ordained any temporall lawes against them; but the same, hauing great societie and intermixture with Simonie, and being sprung out of a spurce of the roote of Auarice, are so secretly put in practise, that humane pollicie only, will be hardly able to know them, and

lesse to represse them; for in most cases the offendors therein do wittingly enter into corrupt, and wilfull periurie, and vpon premeditate consideration doe violate their oathes solemnly and aduisedly taken, when they doe first enter into their owne vocations and degrees: It is a foule and odious fact, and hatefull in the eies, eares, and hearts of all good persons, that a man to whom the law hath giuen no profit, interest, or right, in the tythes, glebe, or other fruits of a Benefice, but onely a bare and naked authoritie to present, collate, or admit a worthy, meet, and fit man to the same, should for a lease, annuitie, money, or other reward, present, collate, or admit a man, be he worthy or vnworthy, to the same: Or that a man who doth: or ought to come to a benefice with cure of soules freely, should for any money, pension, or other consideration, corruptly resigne or exchange the same: Or that a man in whom the law hath reposed a speciall trust, to make choice of ministers, and preachers, according to their vertue, learning, and worth, should admit them for money, or other reward: Or that they who haue but onely the nomination, or presentation, of a fellow, scholler, or other person, to any place in a colledge, schoole, or other societie, should take money or other reward for their voices or assents in such election: Or that he who hath place in such a societie should take reward for the resigning, or leauing of it, as if the same places and liuings were their owne lawfull freehold, and they authorised to make sale thereof: The which grieuous and irreligious enormities, the high court of Parliament assembled Anno 31. El. did there indeauour and shew their good meaning to reforme, by an Act wherein it was agreed, That if any person or persons, bodies politique or corporat, shall, or doe, for any summe of money, reward, gift, or profit directly, or indirectly, or for or by reason of any promise, agreement, graunt, bond, couenant, or other assurance, directly or indirectly, present, or collate any person to any Benefice with cure of Soules, dignitie, prebend, or liuing Ecclesiasticall: Or giue or bestowe the same, for, or in respect of any such corrupt cause or consideration: Then euery such presentation, collation, gift, and bestowing, and euery admission, institution, inuesture, and induction thereupon shall be vtterly void, and of none effect in law. And it shall and may be lawfull, to, and for the Queene, her heires and successors, to present, collate vnto, or giue, or bestowe euery such Benefice, dignitie, prebend, and liuing Ecclesiasticall, for that one time, or turne onely. And all and euery person or persons, bodies politique and corporat, that from henceforth shall giue or take, any such summe of money, reward, gift, or benefit, directly or indirectly: Or that shall take or make any such promise, graunt, bond, couenant, or other assurance, shall forfeit the double value of one yeares profit of euery such benefice, dignitie, &c. to the Queene and I. to be recouered by A. B. I. wherein no W. E. P. And the person so corruptly taking, procuring, seeking, or accepting any such Benefice, dignitie, prebend, or liuing, shall thereupon, and from thenceforth bee adiudged a disabled person in law, to haue or enioy the same Benefice, &c.

St. 31. El. 6.

Exaction for presenting or collating to a Benefice.

The penaltie of the corrupt taker of a Benefice.

31 And by the same Stat. of an 31. El. it was further established, That if any person shall for any summe of money, reward, gift, or profit whatsoeuer, directly, or indirectly, (other then for vsuall and lawfull fees) or for, or by reasō of any promise, agreemēt, grāt, couenāt, bond, or other assurance, of, or for any sūme of money, reward, gift, or profit whatsoeuer, directly or indirectly admit, institute,

Stat. 31. El. 6

Exaction for admitting to a Benefice.

institute, install, induct, inuest, or place any person, in, or to any benefice with cure of soules, dignitie, prebend, or other liuing Ecclesiasticall: then euery such person so offending shall forfeit the double value of one yeares profit of euery such Benefice &c. to the Q. and I. to be recouered by A.B.I. wherein no W. E.P. And thereupon immediately from and after the inuesting, installation, or Induction thereof had, the same Benefice, dignitie &c. shalbe eftsoons meerely void. And the patron, or person to whom the Aduowson, gift, presentation, or collation shall by law appertaine, shall and may by vertue of this Act, present, or collate vnto, giue, and dispose of the same Benefice, dignitie, &c. in such sort to all intents, as if the partie so admitted, installed, inuested, inducted, or placed, had béene, or were naturally dead. But no title to conferre, or present by lapse, shall accrue vpon any voydance mentioned in this act, but after sixe moneths next after notice giuen of such voydance by the Ordinarie to the Patron. Notice of Lapse.

St. 31. El. 6. 32 By the Statute of Ann 31. El. it was moreouer ordained, That if an Incumbent of any Benefice with cure of soules doe, or shall corruptly resigne or exchange the same: Or corruptly take, for, or in respect of the resigning, or exchanging of the same, directly or indirectly, any pension, summe of money, or benefit whatsoeuer; Then aswell the giuer, as the taker, of any such pension, summe of money, or other benefit corruptly, shall loose double the value of the summe so giuen, taken, or had, to the Q. and I. to bee recouered by A.P.I. wherein no W.E.P. But this Act shall not take away, or restraine any penaltie prescribed by the Ecclesiastical law, for any offence in this Act mentioned, but the same shall remaine in force, and be put in execution, as before &c. Exaction for resigning or exchanging of a Benefice. Penalties by the Ecclesiasticall law.

Stat. 31. El. 6 33 By the foresaid Statute of Anno 31. El. it was also enacted, That if any person or persons whatsoeuer, shall, or doe receiue or take any money, fée, reward, or other profit directly, or indirectly: Or shall take any promise, couenant, bond, agréement, or other assurance, to receiue, or haue any money, fée, reward, or any other profit directly, or indirectly, either to him, or themselues, or to any other of their or any of their friends (all ordinarie and lawful fées onely except) for, or to procure the ordaining, or making of any minister, or giuing any Orders, or licence, or licences to preach: Then euery person and persons so offending, shall for euery such offence forfeit x.l. & the partie so corruptly made minister, or taking Orders x.l. to the Q. & I. to be recouered by A.P.I. wherein no W.E.P. And if at any time within vij. yeares next after such corrupt entring into the ministerie, or receiuing of Orders, he shall accept, or take any Benefice, liuing, or promotion Ecclesiasticall, then immediatly from, and after the induction, inuesting, or installation thereof, or thereinto had, the same Benefice, liuing, &c. shalbe eftsoones meerely void. And the patron, or person, to whom the aduowson, gift, presentation, or collation, shall by law appertaine, shall, and may (by vertue of this Act) present, or collate vnto, giue, and dispose of the same benefice, liuing, &c. in such sort to all intents, as if the partie so inducted, inuested, or installed, had béene, or were naturally dead: Any law, ordinance, qualification, and dispensation to the contrary notwithstanding. Exaction for making of ministers, or giuing licence to preach.

Stat. 31. El. 6 34 By the same statute of an 31. El. for the causes before rehearsed, it was also prouided, That if any person or persons, bodies politique, or corporat, which

which haue election, presentation, or nomination of any fellow, scholler, or any other person, to haue roome or place in any Churches collegiat, Colledges, Schooles, Hospitals, Halles, or Societies, shall haue, receiue, or take, any money, fee, reward, or any other profit, directly or indirectly, either to him, or themselues, or to any other of their, or either of their friends, for his or their voice, or voices, assent or assents, or consent in electing, choosing, presenting, or nominating of any officer, fellow, scholler, or other person to haue any roome or place in any of the said Churches, Colledges, Halles, Schooles, Hospitals, or Societies: then and from thenceforth, the place, roome, or office, which such person so offending shal then haue in ẏ said churches, colledges, &c. shalbe void. And then as well the Queene, her heires, and successors, & euery other person & persons, or their heires, or successors, to whom the presentation, gift, donation, election, or disposition shall of right belong, of any such of the said roomes or places of ẏ said person offending, as is aforesaid, shal or may at their pleasure, elect, presẽt, nominate, place, or appoint any other person or persons, in ẏ roome, office, or place of such person or persons so offending, as if ẏ said person or persons were naturally dead.

Exaction for a voice in electing of a fellow or scholler

35 For some reason before alledged, it was lastly ordained by ẏ said stat. of añ 31. El. That if any fellow, officer, or scholler of any of the said churches, colledges, schooles, halls, hospitals, or societies, or other persons hauing roome or place in any of the same, shal at any time hereafter directly or indirely take, or receiue, or by any way, deuise, or meanes, contract, or agree to haue, or receiue any money, reward, or profit whatsoeuer, for the leauing or resigning vp of the same his roome, or place, for any other to be placed in the same: then euery person so taking, or contracting, or agreeing to take, or haue any thing for the same, shall forfeit double the summe of money, or value of the thing so receiued and taken, or agreed to be receiued or taken. And euery person, by whom, or for whom, any money, gift, or reward as aforesaid shalbe giuen, or agreed to be paid, shalbe vncapable of that place, or roome, for that time, or turne, & shall not be, nor had, nor taken to be a lawfull fellow, scholler, or officer, of any the churches, colledges, halls, hospitals, schooles, or societies, or to haue such roome or place there: But they to whom it shall appertaine at any time thereafter, shall and may elect, choose, present, and nominate any other person fit to be elected, presented, or nominated into the said roome, or fellowship, as if the said person, by, or for whom any such money, gift, or reward shall be giuen, or agreed to be paid, were dead, or had resigned, and left the same. And to the intent that euery person that is or may be subiect to the said penalties, may take notice thereof, by the said statute it was also ordained, That at euery election of fellowes, schollers, and officers, this Act, and the Statutes of the same places, concerning such election, shalbe publikely read: vpon paine ẏ euery person in whom the default shalbe, shal forfeit xl. li. to him that will sue, and to the same colledge, societie, &c.

Exaction by taking money to resigne a place.

St. 31. El. 6.

This Stat. shall be read at euery election.

36 If any person doe leuie and receiue money of certaine other persons, which they ought to pay in discharge of a fifteene, due by a towne to the king, and he doth not pay the same money to the king, he may be indited of extortion, and the matter beeing found accordingly, the offendor shall be distrained to pay the same money to the people of the said towne, toward their discharge of the said fifteene.

Extortion by gathering others money.

27. Ass. p. 15

48.Ed.3.8. 37 If a man be amerced in a Court Baron for a trespasse done to the Lord of the Manor, and the amerciament is affeired in the Lords court, this is extortion in the Lord: But if the Lord doe accept the amerciament, that is a sufficient satisfaction for the trespasse, and a good barre in an action of trespasse brought by the Lord against the offendor. Extortion for amerciament in a court baron.

38 But though extortion and exaction be prohibited by the lawes & Stat. before specified, as things offensiue to the lawes and iustice of the Realm; yet the same law doth allow to each officer and other person, to haue a reasonable consideration and satisfaction for his paines, according to his countenance, degree, and calling, and the paines and seruice which he shall doe and imploy in y furtherance or execution of iustice: as the L. Chancellor, and they which write to the great seale are not to make writs without their fees: and if a prisoner be discharged of his imprisonment by the court, paying his fees, the Marshall of y Kings Bench, the Sherife of the countie, nor any Gaoler or keeper of prison, ought to detaine him in prison, for meat, drinke, or other thing which he hath bought, but for his fees onely. But if a man be committed to prison for suspitiō of felonie, and after he is acquitted thereof, and discharged by the court paying his fees: the Sherife or Gaoler may take of him barre-fees, and this is no extortion, but iustifiable: for this money is not taken cōtrarie to the foresaid Stat. of an 23. H.6. which prohibiteth the sherife to take money for shewing ease or fauour to any person arrested. For this barre-fee is money which the court frō one age to another, hath in discretion assigned the prisoner so discharged to pay to the Sherife, or Gaoler for his great paines and charge, for the safe keeping of the prisoners, for attending vpon them, and for conueying of them safely to the barre, and from it, to the prison. If a man bee committed to prison for two seuerall felonies, and after he is discharged by the court paying his fees, he shal pay but one fee, for the Gaolers attendance was but vpon one person. And if the Sherife or Gaoler take from a prisoner in his custodie, the money in his purse, or any garment that he hath, this is no extortion, but a trespasse, for the recouerie whereof the prisoner may haue an Action of trespasse against the same Sherife or Gaoler, and recouer the value thereof in dammages. And if a man indited and arraigned of felonie, doth plead and shew forth the Kings pardon of the same felonie, which is allowed by the court, whereupon hee doth pay and giue his fees of gloues to the Iustices, and other officers of the court, this is no extortion, but an aunciēt fee, and lawfully due vnto them. If the Iustices in an especiall Assise doe take their lawfull fees, this is no extortion: for they are not bound to sit vnlesse they haue them.

Margin notes: No extortion to take lawful fees. — 34.H.6.38. 8.Ed.4.18. — 21.H.7.16. — Taking of barre-fees no extortion. — 26.Ass.p.47. — 4.Ed.4.10. — No extortion for gloues giuen vpon the allowance of pardon. — 34.H.6.38.

34.H.6.42. 39 If a man that is attainted of trespasse, doe come into the court, where he was attainted, and prayeth to make his fine to the King, and offereth pledges for his fine, if the Warden of the Fleet, or other Keeper of a prison do take any fees of him, it is extortion, seeing hee came in gratis, and out of ward, and yeelded himselfe to the court. But if there be proces awarded against him for his said fine, and he be taken thereby, then he shall pay his fees to the warden or Keeper &c. and it is no extortion to take them, for that he came in by compulsion, and not willingly. Extortion in taking fees of him that doth appeare gratis

St.27.H.8.26. 40 After that by the Stat. of an 27. H.8. it was enacted, That the Kings country countrie or dominion of Wales, should be incorporatd, united, and annexed to and with the Realme of England, and that all persons borne and to be borne in the said Principalitie and dominion of Wales should haue, enioy, and inherit all and singular freedomes, liberties, rights, priuiledges, and laws within this Realme, and al other the kings dominions, as other the Kings subiects borne within the same, haue, enioy, and inherit. And that the lawes, ordinances and statutes of this Realme of England for euer, and none other, shall bée vsed and executed in the said dominion of Wales, and euery part thereof, in like manner, forme, and order, as they be in this Realme. And that the said dominion of Wales was by the said Statute of 27. H. 8. and by the statute of an 34. H. 8. diuided into xij. shires, and a President and Councel established there and in the Marches of the same, with all officers, clerkes, and incidents to the same. And that there should be Iustices of Assise and Gaole deliuerie there, which should kéepe Sessions in euery of the said shires twice in the yeare, and a Marshall, and a Crier in euery circuit. And that there should be original and iudiciall seales, for the sealing of Writs and Proces in the said shires: And ÿ there should bee foure Prenotaries in Wales, and also certaine Iustices of Peace and Quorum, and a Custos Rotulorum, Bailifs of Hundreds, Sherifs, Escheators, Coronors, & Constables of Hundreds in euery of ÿ said xij. shires. Then to preuent and auoyd extortion of the foresaid Officers in Wales, and to the intent that the said Officers might know what money to demand, and euery sutor what to paie for all Proces originall and iudiciall, declarations, pleadings, &c. by ÿ said Stat. of an 34. H. 8. it was particularly expressed how much should bee paied for the writing and sealing of originall and iudiciall Writs and proces, and what Prenotaries shal take for their fées, what euery Marshall and Crier of the Iustices shall haue, and what fées the said Sherifes and Coroners shall take, in many, diuers, and seuerall cases. But after, in and by the said Stat. of an 34. H. 8. it was further ordained, That in all and euery Writs originall or iudiciall, or other Proces, pleas, or writings which bée not expressed in the said ordinance, the fées thereof, as well for the seales as writing, shalbe rated by the said President, Councell, and Iustices, or thrée of thē, whereof the said President to be one, by their discretion from time to time, as the case shall require. And they shall haue full power from time to time, to assesse and appoint what fee the said Sherifes, Escheators, and Coroners, and their ministers, Prenotaries and their clerkes, and other ministers of iustice in the said shire, shall haue of the kings subiects for any maner writs, plaints, pleas, proces, returnes, or any other matter or thing, concerning or belonging to the execution of their offices and roomes, and to augment or diminish any fée or fées aboue declared, as shalbe thought by their discretions to be conuenient and méet for the common wealth of the kings subiects of those partes of Wales.

The fées expressed to preuent extortion in Wales.

Oppresion.

Oppresion.

1 Oppression is a grieuance done by one man or more to the hurt or preiudice of others, without any warrant of law, or colour of iustice: or it is a burden or charge which one man doth impose on another, more than the law doth lay vpon him, and is for the most part wrought by the superior in countenance, abilitie, or office, to the inferior in the same: for the oppressor sicuti Nimroth robustus venator, & tanquam Leo subuersor in domo sua, is alwayes offering hard measure to them who are to deale with him, vntill they be able and willing to resist him. The fraudulent deceiuor yeeldeth a man something for his money, or at the least giueth a faire colour so to do. The extortioner is most times an officer, and doth take paines, and is worthy of his due reward, & so is tollerable, vntill he wresteth more than his desert. But the oppressor grapleth for what he can get, and returneth nothing, and wresteth to reap that which he hath not sowen, and to gather fruit where he hath not grafted: the marke he roueth at, is his priuat profit, & respecteth not how many, and how much he in that cause hurteth, so that his owne purse be filled, or his will be accomplished. As, euerie disseisor who doth vnlawfully expell and put another man out of his freehold, may aptly be termed an oppressor, for hee doth not put in practise that iniurie couertly and secretly, by fraud and collusion vnder hand, as the deceiuor & extortioner do, but by plain and open wrong, and doth stand in the face of al his beholders, and commonly iustifieth that which he hath done. And therfore as the said disseisin and oppression is manifest, so hath the stat. of West. 2. appointed a speedie and manifest remedie to the disseisee to redresse and reforme the same, which is by an Assise of Nouel diss. to the end, that as he was newly and lately disseised so he might be quickly and speedily restored. And because the law doth adiudge a man oppressed and iniured, who is disseised of estouers of wood, or of profit to be taken in wood, nuts, acorns, and of other fruit to be gathered: or of a corrody of deliuering corne, and other victuals and necessaries to bee receiued yearely in a place certaine: or of toll, tonnage, passage, pontage, pawnage, or such like things to be taken in places certain: or of the keeping of woods, forrests, parks, chases, warreines, gates, and other bailiwikes and offices in fee: or of common of pasture, turbaries, fishing, and such like, which a man hath belonging to his freehold, or without his freehold by speciall deed, at the least for terme of life: or when one man doth pasture anothers seuerall: or when tenant for yeares, or garden of a tenement doth alien the same in fee, whereby the freehold is transferred to the feoffee: therefore in all the cases aforesaid, that said stat. of West. 2.

What oppression is.

Oppression by disseisin.

Of what things one may be disseised.

St. 13. E. 1. 25.

doth

doth giue to the party ſo oppreſſed and diſſeiſed, his remedie to recouer the ſame by the ſaid Aſſ. of nouel diſſ. in which the writ ſhal be De libero tenemento. If tenant by Elegit be put out of the tenement which he hath in execution: or tenant by Statute marchant be put out of the land which he hath in execution: or tenant by Stat. ſtaple be put out of the land which he hath in execution: or tenant by Recogniſance in the nature of a Statute ſtaple, his executors, adminiſtrators, or aſſignes, or any of them be diſſeiſed, or put out of the land which he or they haue in executiõ, he or they ſo diſſeiſed, or put out, may haue & maintaine an Aſſiſe, for it is to him or them a diſſeiſin & an oppreſſion. If any perſon who hath an eſtate of inheritance or freehold, in any parſonage, vicarage, portion, pention, tithes, oblations, or other Eccleſiaſticall profit, made temporall, be deforced, kept, or put from the ſame, this is a diſſeiſin and oppreſſion, & the party ſo wronged may haue an Aſſiſe to recouer the ſame. And if any Eſcheator, Sherife, or other of the K. Bailifes, ſhall by colour of his office (without ſpeciall warrant or certaine authoritie which belongeth to his office) diſſeiſe any man of his freehold, or of any thing which belongeth to his freehold, this is an oppreſſion, and the diſſeiſee may at his choyce either haue an Aſſiſe, and recouer double dammages, and the defendant ſhal be amerced, or elſe the K. vpon complaint ſhall redreſſe the matter. If lands be graunted by the Kings Patent, without any title found by Enqueſt, or where the Kings entrie is not giuen by the law, and if any be put out or diſſeiſed of his freehold thereby, this is an oppreſſion: And the partie put out, ſhal haue a ſpeciall Aſſiſe againſt the kings Patentee, and recouer treble dammages.

St. 13. E. 1. 25. St. 13. E. 1. St. 27. E. 3. 9. St. 23. H. 8. 9. St. 32. H. 8. 7. St. 3. E. 1. 24. St. 1. H. 4. 8.

Oppreſſion by approuement of common.

2 If the Lord of a Mannor (wherein he hath certaine freehold tenants, and certaine neighbours) do approue ſome part of the waſts, woods, or paſtures of the ſame Mannor, not leauing to his ſaid tenants and neighbours ſufficient common of paſture vnto their tenements, or not ſufficient and conuenient ingreſſe and regreſſe to the ſame, this is an oppreſſion of the ſame tenants, and a diſſeiſin of their common. And the ſayd tenants and neighbours (or any of them) may by force of the Statutes of Merton, and Weſt. 2. bring an Aſſiſe of Common of paſture againſt the Lord who doth ſo approue and oppreſſe. And if it be found by the Jurie, that their ingreſſe and regreſſe were any thing hindered by the deforceors, or that they had not ſufficient paſture, then they ſhall recouer their ſeiſin by the view of the Jurors: ſo that by their diſcretion and othe they ſhall haue ſufficient paſture, ingreſſe and regreſſe, and the diſſeiſors ſhall be amerced, and render dammages, which dammages (by force of the ſtatute of Anno 3. Ed. 6.) ſhall be trebled by the iudgement of the Court where ſuch Aſſiſe and iudgement ſhall be had. And ſo it is if the Lord of a Manor doth ſurcharge the common with ſo many cattell, as that his freeholders or neighbours cannot haue ſufficient common for their cattell, as they had wont to haue, or as they ought to haue belonging to their tenements, this is an oppreſſion and diſſeiſin of their common, and any of them may bring an Aſſiſe of Common of paſture againſt the ſaid Lord, and recouer his common, and his dammages. But if there be two Lords of two ſeuerall Mannors, which haue two waſts adioyning parcell of their mannors, lying together without incloſure or ſeperation, and yet the bounds of each mannor is well knowne by certaine meers and marks, in which waſts the tenants of the one mannor and of the other haue reciprocally had and vſed common by cauſe of vicinage: In this caſe one of thoſe Lords may incloſe againſt the other, & by that meanes vtterly take

Oppreſſion by ſurcharge of common.

Incloſure of common by cauſe of vicinage, is no oppreſſion.

St. 20. H. 3. 4. St. 13. E. 1. 46. St. 3. E. 6. 3. Fitz. Admeſ. 11. Common 29. Co. li. 4. 38. 13. H. 7. 14. M. 14. Eliz. Dyer 316.

take away his common by cauſe of vicinage from him, though it hath beene otherwiſe vſed time out of the remembrance of man. And this common per cauſe de vicinage, is rather an excuſe of a Treſpaſſe when the cattell of the tenant of one Mannor do ſtray into the waſts of the other Mannor, than any certaine inheritance: for the tenants of one Mannor may not put their cattell into the waſt of the other Mannor, but they may come thither onely by eſcape, and this incloſure is onely to preuent the eſcape of the cattell, which is a lawfull act, and no oppreſſion: For in the caſe aforeſaid, where the waſts of both the Mannors be adioyning together, and that the one of them hath common with the other by cauſe of vicinage, and that the one village hath an hundred acres of common, and the other but fiftie acres of common: in this caſe the inhabitants of the village which hath but fiftie acres of common can put no more cattell into their ſayd common of fiftie acres, than it will maintaine, without hauing reſpect to the common in the ſaid hundred acres, for if they do, it is an oppreſſion and wrong, nec e conuerſo: for the originall cauſe of this common by cauſe of vicinage, was not for profit, but for preuenting of ſuits in a Champion countrey, in reſpect of reciprocall eſcapes from one towne to another.

Co.li.7.5.

Commoners ſhall charge common acording to the quantity thereof.

3 It appeareth by the preamble of the ſtatute of Marlebridge, that they who tooke diſtreſſes of their tenants, or neighbours, for rents ſuppoſed to bee due to them, or for any treſpaſſes done to them, and after did driue the ſame diſtreſſes forth of the countie where they were taken, to be impownded in another countie, were accounted to do it to oppreſſe them whoſe cattell they ſo did diſtrain and impownd, and the ſame was alſo adiudged an act done againſt the peace: whereupon, for the eſchewing of ſuch oppreſſions, by the ſame ſtatute, and alſo by the ſtatute of Weſt. 1. it was ordained, That no man ſhall cauſe a diſtreſſe to be driuen forth of the Countie wherein it was taken. And for the auoiding of the like oppreſſions, vexations, and troubles, by a ſtatute made Anno 1. & 2. P. & M. it was enacted, That whoſoeuer ſhall driue any diſtreſſe out of the Hundred, Rape, Wapentake, or Lath where it was taken (except it be to a pownd ouert within the ſame ſhire, being not aboue three miles diſtant from the place where it is taken) or ſhall impownd in ſeuerall places, goods diſtrained for any cauſe at one time, whereby the owner ſhall be conſtrained to ſue ſeuerall Repleuies for the deliuerie of the ſame diſtreſſes, ſhall forfeit to the partie grieued for euerie ſuch offence fiue pounds, and treble dammages. And whoſoeuer doth take for keeping in pownd, pondage, or the impownding of a whole diſtreſſe, aboue iiij. d. or doth take ſo much where leſſe hath vſually been taken, ſhall forfeit to the partie grieued fiue pounds, and ſo much as hee taketh ouer the ſaid iiij. pence. And becauſe the law hath deuiſed, that one neighbour may diſtraine the goods of another for his debt, duetie, or dammages ſuſtained, and that the ſame diſtreſſe ſhall be reaſonable, according to the quantitie of the ſayd ſuppoſed debt, or dammages, and that then the ſame diſtreſſe ſhall bee put in a pownd ouert ſub cuſtodia legis, vntill it bee decided whether the ſame was taken vpon iuſt cauſe or not: and not to the end that one neighbour ſhould by diſtraining vniuſtly oppreſſe another, or demaund of him that which is not due, or put him to further charge or trouble than the neceſſitie of that cauſe, for the recouerie of his owne debt or damages required: therefore by the before mentioned ſtatute of Marlebridge, it was further

St. 25. H. 3. 4
St. 3. E. 1. 16.
St. 1. & 2. P. & M. 12.

Oppreſſion by diſtreſſes.

Pondage money.

established, That if one neighbour take a distresse of another (whereby he hath receiued lesse) without award of the Kings Court, he shall make fine according to the quantitie of the trespas: and neuerthelesse sufficient amends shalbe to them which haue receiued losse by such distresse: Or if one do distrain another to come to his Court which is not of his fee, or vpon whom hee hath no iurisdiction by reason of his Hundred or Bailiwike, or doe take a distresse without his fee, or the place where he hath iurisdiction or bailiwike, hee shall make fine according to the quantitie of his offence. Or if one do take any vnreasonable & excessiue distresses, which is grieuous, and more than the quantitie of the debt or damages, this is an oppression, an he shall be amerced: As a man auowed the distraining of 200. sheepe and 16. beasts for ij. pence rent, and he was amerced therefore: for all that he tooke aboue vj. sheepe, were adiudged an oppression, and so vnlawful. But if a man distraine for homage, the distresse cannot be too excessiue, how many beasts soeuer he doth take, for that homage is not valuable, though for rent, fealtie, and other seruices, it may be excessiue. And in like sort, if the Lord of a Mannor, or any other, who hath rent issuing forth of certaine land, do distraine the tenant of the same land diuers times for rent, or seruices, where none is behind vnpaid, this is an oppression of the same tenant who is distrained: for in this case the partie who claimeth this rent, cannot distraine for rent, seeing none was due to him, but his distresse is onely taken to vexe the tenant of the land, and so to oppresse him. And therefore the sayd tenant may haue an Assise of Souent foits distresse against the same Lord, and recouer dammages of him according to the losse he hath receiued by the same distresses, viz. for not plowing, or for not manuring his land, or for taking no profit thereby. But it is otherwise, if the same seuerall distresses were taken for homage. And so it is, if a man do distraine for rent, or seruices, or for any other thing, and depending a suit betweene the parties for the same rent, seruice, or other thing, he who did distrain doth distrain again for the same rent, seruice, or thing, for ẏ which he did distrain before, the beasts or goods of him whose hee did first distraine, this is an oppression of him whose goods be twice distrained: For the redresse whereof hee may haue a writ of Recaption against him who so did distraine his goods twice for one cause, whereby hee shall recouer dammages for his second distresse: And also hee that did take the same distresse, shall make fine to the King for his oppression and wrong, though the first distresse were lawfully taken, yea and though the rent or seruice for the which he did distraine, were behind, vnpayed, or vndone, seeing by the first distresse (the cause being proued true and lawfull, hee might haue had returne of the goods or cattell which hee did distraine) vntill hee had beene satisfied of the rent, seruice, or thing, for the which hee did distraine. But a man may distraine the cattell of him who bee eating of his corne or grasse, or doing any other hurt in his ground, so often as he shall find them doing hurt therein, and it is no oppression or wrong so to do: for he doth not distraine twice for one cause, as in the former case, but distraineth seuerall times for seuerall new offences.

Margin notes: Distraining out of his fee. — Excessiue distresse. — 41.Ed.3.26 — 29.Ed.3.23. — 28.Ass.p.50 — 42.Ed.3.26. — Co. li. 4. 8. — Fitz.Na.Br. 178. — Oppression by often distresse. — 27.Ass.p.51 — 28.Ass.p.50 — Lib.int.82. — Co.li.4.8. — Seuerall distresses for one thing. — Fit.Nat.Br. 71. — A writ of Recaption. — 47.Ed.3.7 — Distresses for damages feasant.

4 And euerie Trespasse which the law doth interpret to bee iniuriously committed vi & armis, may also fitly be termed an oppression: for it is done vpon the offendors owne wrong, without warrant of law: As if one person doe enter vpon anothers land, & expell him out of the possession therof, whereas St.5.R.2.5

his

Fitz.Tresp. 13.45.234 20.H.6.22. 9.Ed.4.28. 9.H.6.64. 21.H.6.5 21.Ed.4.18. 9.Ed.4.29. 10.Ed.4.4. 21.Ed.4.4. 1.H.7.10. 37.H.6.36. 21.H.7.13. 11.H.4.64. 20.H.6.14. 3.H.6.12. 10.H.6.16. 43.Ed.3.13. 4.Ed.3.48 47.Ed.3.22 43.Ed.3.35 1.H.5.1.

Oppression by Trespasses.

his entry is not giuen by the law, or doth enter with strong hand, or multitude of people, and not in peaceable manner, this is an oppression. And so it is, if one person doe pull downe, breake, or impaire anothers house, or any part thereof: Or if one person doe fell, cut downe, or carrie away the Tymber, Trees, or Wood of another: Or if one person doe fell, cut, tread downe, or carrie away the corne or grasse of another: Or if one person doe with his cattell depasture, feed, or eat the corne, grasse, or hay of another: Or if one person doe take and carrie away the money, plate, iewels, houshold-stuffe, cattell, corne, hay, or any kind of goods of anothers: Or if one person doe plough, till, eyre, or digge the ground or soyle of another: Or if one person doe mayme, imprison, wound, or beat another, or doth mayme, wound, or beat the seruant of another, whereby he looseth his seruice: Or if one person doe hunt, chase, or hawke in the free Warren of another, or doe take, kill, or destroy his game there: Or if one person doe fish in the Pond, Poole, Mildam, Stew, or other seuerall fishing of another: Or if one person doe breake the doue-house of another, or destroy the flight of the doues of another: Or if one person doe digge the Myne of Tinne, Lead, Stone, Coale, Grauell, Sand, Marle, Chalke, &c. of another: Or if one person doe pull vp & take away the meerestones which by consent haue been set betweene his own ground and anothers: In all and euerie of which cases, the partie grieued may pursue an Action of Trespasse against the offendor, and declare that hee committed any of the said offences, vi & armis, wherein (if the defendant be attainted) hee shall pay to the plaintife his dammages sustained, and to the King a fine, for that he hath done an oppression to one of his subiects, and made an offence to the law.

Fit.Nat.Br. 183. 4.Ass.p.3. 18.Ed.3.22. 21.Ed.3.2 Co.li.5. 101. Li.Int.406. 46.Ed.3.23. 7.Ed.3.56. 27.Ed.3.88. 12.H.4.3. 8.Ed.4.5. 48.Ed.3.27 8.Eliz. Dyer 250. 14.Eliz. Dyer 319. 4.Ed.3.36 5.Ed.3.43. 4.Ass.p.3.

Oppression by Nusances.

5 Euerie Nusance which one person doth to the land of another, wherein the owner hath an estate for the terme of life, in tayle, or in fee simple, may also bee accounted an oppression: for those Nusances be put in practise by the offendors onely will, and by his owne open, playne, and manifest wrong, to the disheritance of another, or to the preiudice of his Freehold, without any warrant of law, or colour of iustice: As if one person doe build or leuie a house, a wall, a shead, a leantor, a chimney, a gutter, or other structarie, in his owne ground, to the offence of anothers freehold, or to the drowning or rotting of his house, or to the stopping of his light, or way thereunto, this is an oppression. And if one person doe leuie, rayse, abate, or pull downe a Damme, Poole, Pond, or Ditch, to the hurt of anothers Freehold, that is an oppression. And if one person doe stoppe, straiten, or turne an auncient water-course, to the hurt of anothers Freehold, or in such sort as it doth drowne the ground or soyle of another, that is an oppression. And if one person do stoppe, streiten, or greatly impaire anothers highway, which hee hath belonging to his Freehold, that is an oppression. If one person doe conuey water to his house or ground, by a pipe of lead, timber, or vault of stone, and another person will make another pype out of that pype, to take away part of the same water, that is an oppression of him that made the first pype. And if one doe erect a lime-kill neere vnto anothers dwelling house, the smoake and heat whereof, when it is set on fire, doth annoy the inhabitant of the said house and his familie, or doth scorch or dry vp the fruit trees in his orchard, that is an oppression. And if one person hath the freehold of a seueral fishing in a riuer, pond,

poole, moat, mill damme, or other water, and another person will build a dye-house adioyning, or neere vnto it, and then will powre out, or cause to run from thence, corrupt ashes, dung, slime, filth, or other annoyances, into the said seuerall fishing place, to the distruction of the fish there, whereby the owner doth loose the benefit of his seuerall fishing, that is an oppression of him. And if one person will erect or settle vp a Faire or Market, to the preiudice or hinderance of anothers Faire or Market, that is an oppression of him who had the first Faire or Market. And if one person do lay timber, faggots, stones, lime, sand, grauell, dung, or any other thing, vpon or against the house of another, which do rot, putrifie, corrupt, or impaire the walls, timber, or other part of the same house, or any corrupt, noisome, or stinking thing, the sauor or smell whereof is offensiue to the inhabitant of the same house and his familie, that is an oppression of the same inhabitant: In which foresaid cases the parties grieued by the said Nusances, and oppressions, may in some cases haue their remedies by Assise of Nusance brought in the Common Pleas, in some other cases, by writs of Nusance called Vicountiels, tryed in the Countie before the Sherife, in some other cases, by the writ of Quod permittat, in some other cases by action vpon the case: and in most of the sayd cases, the sayd parties grieued by the sayd Nusances, may take away, pull downe, and remoue the same Nusances, as their seuerall estates will enable them, or their seuerall cases doe require.

Lib. int. 406. Fit. Nat. Br. 184. Register. 197. 199. Li. Int. 407. Co. li. 5. 101.

The remedies for oppression by Nusances.

Oppression by Rescous.

6 Euerie Rescous that is vnlawfully made of cattel or other goods distrained, is an oppression; for the offendor doth a wrong of his owne authoritie, to the preiudice of another, in contempt of the iustice of the Realme, without any warrant or colour of law: Seeing when the partie grieued by himselfe, or some other, doth distraine within his fee, for his rent or seruices behind, for dammages which hee hath sustained, for amerciaments, a rent charge, or for some other cause which hee taketh to bee lawfull, the cattell or other goods of him who he doth conceiue deteineth his due rent, or seruice from him, or whose cattell haue eaten or spoyled his corne, or grasse, or otherwise haue trespassed in his ground, and doth in quiet and peaceable manner driue them towards the pownd, there to remaine as a pledge sub custodia legis, vntill the law hath decided whether there was iust cause of distresse or not, the owner of the same cattell, or some other in his behalfe, will by force and strong hand, make Rescous of this cattell, and take them from him who distrayned them, and so will not submit himselfe to the censure of the law, nor tarrie vntill it be discussed by the ordinarie course of iustice, whether the party that distrained had lawfull cause so to doe or not, but will be his owne iudge, and take the authoritie of reuenge to himselfe: which is an oppression of him whose rent or seruices were due, and vnpayd, or whose corne or grasse was eaten, &c. and who was also forcibly depriued of the ordinarie remedie which the law did assigne him for the recouerie of his owne duetie. And moreouer it is a contempt of the law which the same offendor doth refuse to be iudged by: and therefore in this case the partie grieued may pursue against the offendor a writ of Rescous for this Rescous made, and oppression done vnto him, and thereby recouer his dammages: and also the King shall haue a fine of him, for this contempt of his law, and his peace broken, and the offendor shall be imprisoned vntill hee hath paid the same.

44. Ed. 3. 20. 40. Ed. 3. 32. 17. Ed. 3. 43. 18. Ed. 3. 30. 2. H. 4. 15. 7. H. 6. 1. 22. H. 6. 54. Fitz. Na. Br. 101. Li. Int. 527.

Euery

7 Euery Encrochment which one perſon doth make vpon anothers land, ground couered with water, rent, or ſeruice, is alſo an Oppreſſion: for they be done and put in practiſe by the offendors own open, plaine, & manifeſt wrong, without any warrant or colour of the law. As, it is an oppreſſion for one perſon by ploughing, earing, ditching, hedging, remouing of Méereſtones or land markes, to get away the ground or ſoyle of another: and ſo it is for one perſon to draw away or alter an auncient Riuer, Broke, or Streame of another perſons out of the old and wonted courſe: and ſo it is, if there be lord and tenant, and the tenant doth hold his land of his lord by fealty & fiue ſhillings of yearely rent, and of late yeares the lord hath had ſeiſin of more rent of the tenant by the tenants owne payment without cohertion of Diſtreſſe, if in this caſe the lord will diſtraine his tenants Cattell for that ſurpluſage of rent, that is an oppreſſion, and for the redreſſe thereof the ſame tenant may purſue againſt his lord a Writ of Ne iniuſte vexes, grounded vpon a braunch of the ſtatute of Magna Charta, thereby commaunding the Lord, that he ſhall not oppreſſe nor vniuſtly vexe his tenant for more rent or ſeruices then hée ought to pay or doe: Or otherwiſe the tenant may auoid this ſurpluſage of rent in an Aſſiſe, Writ of Reſcous, or Ceſſauit brought againſt him by his lord: but in a Repleuin he cannot auoid his lord of this rent newly incroched, ſéeing the ſame lord hath had ſeiſin thereof: and ſo it is, if the lord of a Manor, which is auncient demeſne, will encroch vpon his tenants, and diſtraine them or any of them that hold their lands by Charter fréely, to doe other ſeruices or cuſtomes to the ſame lord then they ought to doe, or that their auncestors were accuſtomed to do, this is an oppreſſion of the ſame tenants: and for the redreſſe thereof, all the tenants of the ſaid auncient demeſne Manor may haue againſt their ſaid lord the kings writ of Monſtrauerunt directed to the ſaid lord, commaunding him thereby, that hée ſhall not require nor cauſe to bée required of his ſaid tenants more ſeruices or cuſtomes then they ought to doe, or had wont to doe. And if after the ſaid writ directed, he will diſtraine the goods of them or any of them againe, to doe more ſeruices then they ought to doe: Then the ſame tenants, or ſuch, or ſo many of them as bee ſo diſtrained may procure an attachment againſt their ſaid lord, returnable in the K. Bench or common place, for this oppreſſion and contempt, wherin euery of the ſame tenants ſhall recouer his dammages ſeuerally, according to his loſſe.

Oppreſſion by incrochments.

22. Aſſ. p. 93

St. 9. H. 3. 10

12. E. 4. 7.
28. Aſſ. p. 33
5. Ed. 4. 82.

40. Ed. 3. 44.
49. Ed. 3. 22.
39. E. 3. 6.

Fitz. Na. Br. 14.

Fitz. Na. Br. 15.

8 Euery exceſſiue amerciament which one perſon doth take of another, is alſo to be accounted an oppreſſion of the party ſo amerced: for by the Statutes of Magna Charta & Weſt. 1. it is ordained, That no Citie, Borough, Towne, or man ſhall be amerced but for a reaſonable cauſe, and according to the quantitie of his offence: and euery fréeman ſhall bée amerced ſauing his fréehold, a marchant ſauing his marchandize, and euery other mans villaine (beſides the kings) ſauing his villaine tenure: and the ſame amerciaments ſhall bee aſſeſſed by the oath of honeſt and lawfull men of the ſame vicenage. So that if one perſon doe take a much greater amerciament of another then the quantitie of his offence doth require in a Court Baron, or other Court which is not of record, or doe take that amerciament of his owne authoritie, without being before aſſeſſed by others vpon their oathes, and ſo maketh himſelfe iudge in his owne cauſe, this is an oppreſſion

Oppreſſion by exceſſiue amerciament.

St. 9. H. 3. 14
3. Ed. 1. 6.

of the party amerced: for the redreſſe whereof the party grieued may procure to be directed to the lord of the said Manor, or to his Baylife, a Writ of Moderata misericordia (which was founded vpon the said stat. of Magna Charta) commaunding them thereby, that they shall take a moderat and indifferent amerciament of the same person, according to the quantity of his offence. And if the lord or his baylife will not then cease to distraine for the said excessiue amerciament, the partie so oppreſſed may haue against the offendor an attachment, directed to the Shirife of that Countie where the same Distresse is taken, to attach him to appeare in the kings Court, and to answere his said offence. Fitz.Na.Br. 75.

Oppreſſion by committing of wast.

9 The Wast and Estrepement which one person hauing a particular estate in another persons land, doth make or commit to the disheritance of him in the reuersion or remainder of the same land, without his consent, may also be accounted an oppreſſion of him in whom the said inheritance is: for when one person doth lease, or otherwise conuey his land to another, for the terme of life, liues, or yeares, he doth in effect but lend the same land to the sayd particular tenant for the terme betwéene them agréed vpon, expecting to haue the same againe at the end of the terme, in as good plight, and in such sort, as it was when he first did deliuer and lend it. And therefore if the particular tenant, during the continuance of his estate, doe commit any wast in the same land, he cannot deliuer it againe at the end of his terme in such plight and sort, as at the first he did receiue and borrow it: but by the wast the perpetuall profit of the land is impaired, and therefore of so much in value, hée in the reuersion or remainder is disherited. And for the preuention thereof, by the statute of Marlebridge it was ordained, That Farmors during their termes shall not make wast, sale, or exile of houses, woods, or men, nor of any thing belonging to the Tenements which they haue in farme, without they haue speciall graunt in writing, making mention of a couenant, that they may doe it. And to the intent that condigne punishment might bée prouided and inflicted vpon such as should be transgreſſors and oppreſſors in these cases of Wast, by the statute of Glocester it was enacted, That a man shall haue an action of Wast in the Chauncerie against him which is tenant by the courtesie of England, or otherwise tenant for terme of life, or for terme of yeares, or against a woman which holdeth in Dower: and he which shall bée attainted of Wast, shall forfeit the thing wasted, and besides shall pay treble so much as the Wast shall be taxed: and after by the statute of Westminster the second, the same was in a sort confirmed, and the said action of Wast was againe giuen against the foresaid tenants by the courtesie, in dower, for terme of life, or yeares, and also ordained to extend against Gardens. And by the same statute, the proces to be vsed in the said action of Wast was aſſigned to be Summons, Attachment, and Distreſſe, and if the party defendant doe not appeare at the distreſſe, then a writ shall be awarded to the Shirife, to inquire of the wast by the oathes of twelue men. And because diuers persons did let their lands to others, sometime for terme of life, or anothers life, and sometime for terme of yeares, and after the said tenants did graunt their estates which they had in the same Lands and Tenements to others, to the intent that they in the reuersion, viz. their leſſors, their heires or aſſignées should not take knowledge of their names, and yet the first leſſées did con-

St.52.H.3. 24.

The tenants fort. which cōmitteth wast.

St.6.Ed.1.5

St.13.E.1.14

continually occupie the ſaid Lands, and toke the profites to their owne vſe, and in the ſaid Lands and Tenements did commit waſt and deſtruction to the diſheritance of them in the reuerſion. For the reſtraint and puniſhment of which ſaid offence, being both an oppreſſion, and alſo a
St.11.H.6.5 fraud and deceit, by a Statute made Anno 11. H. 6. it was ordayned,
Fit.N.B.59 That they in the reuerſion in ſuch caſe may haue and maintaine a writ of Waſt againſt the ſaid Tenants for terme of life, anothers life, or for yeares, and ſo recouer againſt them the place waſted, and their treble dammages, for the waſt ſo by them done, as they ought to haue done for the waſt done by them, before the ſaid Graunt and Leaſe of their eſtate. Prouided, That this Ordinance ſhall not hold place, but where the firſt Tenants, before the Graunt and Leaſe of their eſtates in the manner and forme abouesaid, were puniſhable of waſt: and alſo, where after the ſaid Graunt and Leaſe the ſaid firſt Tenants of the ſaid Landes and Tenements do take the profits at the time of the waſt done to their owne proper vſe. And though the wordes of the ſaid Statute doe giue an A termor alieneth his eſtate, occupieth the land, & cōmitteth waſt.
Co.li.5.77. action of Waſt in the caſe aforeſaid but onely to him in the reuerſion, yet he in the remainder alſo (being in the like miſchiefe) ſhall or may take the benefit thereof, and maintaine an action of Waſt in this caſe againſt his particular Tenant for life, or yeares, if eyther of them doe commit waſt to his diſheritance. And whatſoeuer the intent of the Grauntor is, in the caſe aforeſaid, yet if the Grauntée doe aſſigne his Leaſe, take the profits thereof, and commit Waſt, he is puniſhable according to the ſayd Statute, for his intent ſhall not be iſſuable, nam exitus acta probat, viz. the taking of the profites doe ſufficiently expreſſe his intent: and euery aſſignée of the firſt Tenant, mediat or immediat, is within the compaſſe of this Statute: for the Statute was made to ſuppreſſe Fraud, Waſt, and Oppreſſion. And ſo was the Statute of Weſtminſter the ſecond, béeing made and prouided to reſtraine Waſt and Oppreſſion committed by one Tenant in common to the preiudice and diſheritance of another: by which
St.13.E.1.22 it was ordayned, That whereas two or more doe hold Wood, Turbarie, Fiſhing, or ſuch like things in common, wherein none knoweth his owne ſeuerall, and one of them doth commit Waſt againſt the will of the other, an action of Waſt may lye: and when it is come vnto iudgement, the defendant ſhall chuſe eyther to take his part in a place certaine, by the aſſignement of the Shirife, and by the view and oath of his neighbours ſworne and tryed for the ſame intent, or els he ſhall grant to take Waſt cōmitted by a tenant in common.
3.E.1.Waſt 25. nothing from thenceforth in the ſame Wood, Turbarie, and ſuch other, but as his parteners will take: And if he doe chuſe to take his part in a place
50.Ed.3.3. certaine, the place waſted ſhall be aſſigned for his part, according as it was before he committed the Waſt. And becauſe the before rehearſed ſtatute of Marlebridge doth expreſſe in generall termes, in what thinges Waſt may be committed, as in Houſes, Woods, and Men: and the words of the writ of Waſt in the Regiſter be, Quare fecit vaſtum, venditionem, ſeu deſtructionem de terris, domibus, Boſcis, & Gardinis: and the foreſaid Statutes of Anno 6. Edw.1. 13. Edw.1. and 11. H.6. doe declare, who are forbidden to doe that Waſt: and ſéeing Waſt in Lands, Houſes, Woods, or &c. is a great wrong and oppreſſion to him or them in reuerſion or remainder of the ſame, therefore I will ſomewhat particularly

ex-

explaine, which the Law doth construe and expound to be Wasts, prohi-
bited and punishable by the foresaid Statutes, or either of them, to the
intent, that both he that hath the inheritance, and also the particular Te-
nant, may know what is due to either of them, in respect of their seve-
rall estates, and what to take, and what to leave. And to begin with the
Wast in land. words of the Writ touching Wast in Land: If one person doe demise or
convey to another for the terme of yeares, life, or &c. Land, where there 22.H.6.18
is included in the bowels of the earth Tynne, Yron, Lead, Coale, 2.H.7.14
Stone, Gravell, Morter, Sand, Chalke, or Marle, if the Myne or 17.E.3.7.
Pit thereof be not open, when the Lessees estate or terme doth begin, the 9.Ed.4.35.
said Tenant may not open the ground, make a new Myne, and take the Co.li.5.11.
same Coale, Stone, Gravell, or &c. for if he doe, it is Wast of the land, Fit.Nat.Br.
and he in the reversion or remainder may punish him therefore by an acti- 149.
on of Wast: For whereas there was assured to the Tenant but Vestu- Lib.int.616
ram terræ, and the annuall profit of the Land, hee hath digged and carri-
ed away the Land it selfe, and impaired the inheritance thereof for ever.
But if there bee a Myne or Pit open in any part of the ground so demi-
sed or assured, at the time of the Lease or assurance thereof, or at the
time when the estate of the Tenant did begin, then the Tenant may
digge there, and take and carry away so much of the Coale, Stone, Gra-
vell, as shall be necessarily used or imployed for or towards the repaire or
maintenance of the House, Land, or other commodities therewith demised,
and it is no Wast. But if he do give, sell, or otherwise dispose the same 41.E.3.Wast
to any other person, place, or use (saving as is aforesaid) then for so much 82.
as he shall so mis-imploy, it is Wast. If one person doe lease or assure his
Land to another, and all the Mynes or Pits therein, for yeares, life, or &c. the Co.li.5.11.
Lessee may open and digge the ground for Coale, Morter, Stone, &c. and
take and carry away the same, though there was not any Myne open at the
time of the Lease or estate made: For by the assurance it doth appeare, that
the Lessor was contented that wast should be made in any part of the ground
leased, by myning or digging: and in this case the Lessee may sell or other-
wise dispose the same Coale, Stone, Marle, or &c. at his pleasure, for it is 17.Ed.3.7
as much as if the Lease or assurance had beene made to the Tenant, without
impeachment of any manner of Wast to be committed by Mynes, Pits,
or diggings. If the Tenant for yeares, life, or &c. doe eyre, plough up,
and convert into Tillage or Wood ground an auncient and usuall mowen 15.H.3.
Meddow, it is Wast: and so it is, if he doe drowne or suffer to bee drow- Wast 131.
ned continually a Meddow or other ground demised: for it is not lawfull 46.Ed.3.
for a particular Tenant to convert ground to any other use then hee recei- Wast 91.
ved it, as to turne Meddow into arable, arable into Wood, Wood into 29.H.8.
Pasture or Meddow, arable or Wood into Pooles or Ponds, for thereby Dyer 37.
he doth wrong to the inheritance for his owne profit. And likewise it is wast
if the Tenant doe suffer the Bankes of the Sea or of a River to be usually
overflowne, and to decay, whereby a Meddow, a Pasture, or other ground 20.H.6.1.
which he holdeth for life or yeares, that before was fruitfull, shall become
rushie, sedgie, or otherwise barren. But if he suffer ground set with Saf-
fron to decay, or Land, Meddow, or Pasture to grow full of Bushes or 10.H.7.2
Thornes, or to lye fresh, and not manured, it is no Wast, but evill Fit.N.B.59
husbandrie. If the owner of a Poole or Pond stored with fish, doe assure 2.H.6.10.
the

the same for yeares, life, or &c. and the tenant letteth forth the water, or
otherwise fisheth the same, and taketh forth the fish, or part thereof, and
7.H.3.Wast yet leaueth it as sufficiently stored at the end of his terme, as at the be-
141. ginning thereof he found it, this is no Wast. But if hee doe let forth
5.R.2. the water of the said poole, or &c. and suffer the same to lye continually dry, or
Wast 97. doe destroy by other meanes the fish therein, and doe not repaire it, and leaue
Ed.1.Wast. it as well and sufficiently stored with fish, as he receiued it, by the view and
128. iudgement of the countrey, then it is wast, and hee may bee punished there-
fore by an action of Wast. And the same Law is, if one doe assure to another
for terme of yeares, or life, a Parke stored with Deere, and the tenant de-
stroyeth all the Deere, and doth not store the same againe with as many be-
fore the end of his terme, this is Wast. If the tenant for terme of life,
yeares, or &c. of a seuerall Pasture or Close inclosed with a Wall, Pale, or
12.H.8.1. Quick-set hedge, doe suffer the same to decay, it is wast: for by the decay of
the Wall, Pale, or Quick-set hedge he hath made it no pasture, but layed it
in common. As concerning wast in houses, it is wast, and an oppression of Wast in houses.
him or them in reuersion or remainder, if the tenant for terme of yeares, life,
34.E.3. or &c. doe willingly pull downe, or negligently suffer to decay a dwelling
Wast.145. house, or any Hall, Parlour, Chamber, Buttery, Kitchin, Brew-house,
3.H.6.53. 4.Ed.3. Bake-house, Day-house, Doue-house, Barne, Stable, Ore-house, Kill-house,
Wast.22. Myll, Cottage, or any other House, Cullice, Leantor, Edifice, or Building,
21.H.6.46. being of the value of three shillings foure pence, which being couered, and in
38.E.3.7. good repaire, was standing and beeing vpon the ground, when the same tenant
46.E.3. Wast 90. did or lawfully might haue entred vpon the lands demised, in respect of his
17.E.3.7. Lease, or other estate to him assured thereof. And also it is wast, if any of the
41.Ed.3.22. particular tenants aforesaid doe during his estate build any new House,
17.Ed.2. Flore, or Partition vpon any land demised or conueyed vnto him, and after
Wast 118. hee or his assignees doe pull downe the same againe, or suffer the same to fall
into ruine and decay: for that the House, Flore, or Partition being builded,
was once parcell of the inheritance of the Lessor, and therefore beeing a-
gaine pulled downe, or decayed, it is to his disheritance. But if the Les-
49.Ed.3.1. sor doe build a house vpon the ground so demised or assured, during the e-
state of the particular Tenant therein, and the Tenant doe pull it downe,
or suffer it to decay, it is no Wast, for it was not parcell of the thing
demised, neyther was there any couenant in Law, that it should bee repai-
red. And it is Wast, if any of the Houses, Edifices, or Buildings a-
19.Ed.3. foresaid bee willingly or negligently burned, pulled, or throwne downe by
Wast 30. the Tenant thereof, or by any of his Family, or Neighbours, or by any
20.Ed.3. other person whatsoeuer (so that it bee not by the kings enemies, Thun-
Wast 32. der, Lightening, extreame Wind, or Tempest, in which cases it is no
44.E.3.34. Wast punishable by the Law, seeing they were burned or throwne downe
43.Ed.3.6. by the power and hand of God.) But it is otherwise, if it bee burned or o-
28.H.8. Dyer 33. uerthrowne by Rebels, or others, against whom the Tenant may haue
33.H.6.1 his remedie and recompence by the Law: For in that case it is punishable
by action of Wast, if it bee not repayred againe within conuenient time.
44.E.3.44. If a Tenant for life, yeares, or &c. doe suffer a Pale, or a wall of Stone,
10.H.7.5. 29.H.8. Bricke, Timber, or Mudde, which is couered with Slate, Tyle, Timber, or
Dyer 36. Thatch, to decay, or lye vncouered, it is Wast: But if any House, Pale, or
21.H.6.2 Wall were ruinous, or vncouered, at the time when the estate of the sayd
Fit.N.B.59. 40.Ass.p.22 Tenant begun, and after did decay and fall downe, then the tenant is not
charge-

chargeable therefore in an Action of Waſt, for hée is bound to kéepe them in none other repaire then he found them. If the tenant for yeares, or life, or &c. doe take away a partition, or a loft in a houſe, whereby hée doth make two chambers, or other two roomes, or more, but one, it is waſt: for the tenant muſt maintaine the houſe, and leaue it in ſuch ſort as it was demiſed vnto him, and not tranſpoſe or alter any part thereof otherwiſe then hée receiued it. And in like ſort it is Waſt, if the ſaid tenant doe take away a Furnace, a Bench, a Table fixed in the ground, a Doore, or a Window from a houſe, which were there at the time when his eſtate began: for they bée made parcell of the inheritance of the houſe, and were demiſed with it, and cannot bée ſeuered from it, but by him who hath the inheritance thereof. And yet if the ſame were ſet there by the termor, then hée may take them away againe at any time during his terme, but not after his terme expired. And it is Waſt, if the Tenant doe take away the glaſſe of the windowes of a houſe: for whether the leſſor or the leſſée did ſet vp the ſame glaſſe, and whether it bée ſet vp with nayles, lyme, or otherwiſe, the termor ought not to take it away, for without the glaſſe it is not a perfect houſe. The ſame Law is of Wainſcot, whether it bée affixed to the houſe by the leſſor, or by the leſſée, or whether it bée faſtened by great nayles or ſmall nayles, or by ſcrewes or yrons put through the poſtes or wals, or by any other meanes, yet if it bée taken away, it is Waſt, and the Tenant of the houſe ſhall bée puniſhed for it by action of Waſt: for it is made parcell of the houſe, as ſéeling and plaſtering of a houſe is: For the ſayd Furnace, Bench, Table, Doore, Glaſſe, and Wainſcot are made parcell of the inheritance of the houſe, as the Wals, Beames, and Tranſomes bée, and they ſhall diſcend to the heire of the houſe, and not accrue to the executors: Neither ſhall they bée forfeited by Vtlarie, nor attached in an Aſſiſe, as Chattels may. But if in any of the caſes aforeſaid the Tenant doe repaire the houſe or thing waſted, and make it ſo long, ſo broad, ſo high, and in ſuch and ſo good ſort, as it was when his eſtate did begin, before any action of Waſt ſhall bée brought againſt him therefore, then no action of Waſt is maintenable againſt him for that cauſe. Notwithſtanding, if any houſe, wall couered, or &c. were ruinous at the time of the beginning of the Tenants eſtate, and after the Tenant doe pull it downe, and build it againe, though it bée not ſo large as it was before, yet is it no Waſt, neither is the Tenant puniſhable therefore by an action of Waſt, for that he had not béen puniſhable therefore, if hée had ſuffered it wholly to decay, and not haue builded againe any part thereof. If Waſt bée committed in ſeuerall principall parts of a houſe, he in the reuerſion or remainder thereof may by an action of Waſt recouer the whole houſe for this diſperſed Waſt. As in like caſe, if Timber Trées of Oake, Aſh, or Elme bée felled in ſeuerall parts of a Wood or Cloſe, hée in the reuerſion or remainder may by an action of Waſt recouer againſt the Tenant the whole Wood, or Cloſe, for this diſperſed Waſt. To procéede according to the wordes of the Writ, with Waſt in Woods: If the Leſſée for yeares, Leſſée for life, Tenant in Dower, or &c. doe ſell or fell Oakes, Aſhes, or Elmes, béeing of twenty yeares growth, and aboue the value of thrée ſhillings foure pence, this is Waſt, and puniſhable by an Action of Waſt: For thoſe Trées, of that age, will endure long, bée méete for Building, and bée parcell of the inheri-

Marginal notes: 10.H.7.5. 42.E.3.6. 21.H.6.26 20.H.7.13. Co.li.4.63. 20.H.7.13. 21.H.7.26. 20.E.3. Waſt 32. 22.H.6.58. 28.H.6.2. 38.Aſſ.p.1 42.Ed.3.22. 22.H.6.18 21.Ed.4.39. 4.Ed.3.32. 8.Ed.2. Waſt 112. 12.Ed.3. Waſt 108. 127. Waſt in Woods. Plo.Com. 470. 3.E.6.Dyer 65. 7.H.6.40 21.H.6.46 14.H.4.12.

inheritance of him in the reuerſion or remainder, and notwithſtanding the
27.H.6. Waſt.8. ſaid leaſe, or any other particular eſtate for life aſſured, the ſame trees be the
29.H.8. leaſſors, and not the leaſſees, though the leaſſor cannot fell them, or graunt,
Dyer 36. or ſell them to any other without conſent of the tenant, for that the ſaid
Co.li.4.64 tenant hath the loppe and maſte of them, and ſhade for his cattell. And likewiſe, if the boughes or braunches of any of the ſame trees, beeing of the ſaid age of twentie yeares bee cut downe by the tenant, the ſame is alſo waſt, for they in like ſort may ſerue for building. But if a houſe with certaine ground be aſſured to a tenant for terme of yeares, life, or &c. where-
7.H.6.40. upon Oake, Aſh, or Elme aboue twentie yeares of age be growing, if the
41.Ed.3. ſame houſe doe fall in decay during the ſaid terme, the ſaid tenant of his
Waſt.82. owne authoritie, without the aſſignement of the Leaſſor, may fell ſufficient of the ſaid Oake, Aſhe, or Elme, to repaire the ſame houſe: for the Law hath ordained, that one commoditie or parcell of the farme demiſed ſhall help to maintaine the other. And ſo the tenant if hee will may fell timber to repaire the houſe, though the ſame were in decay at the time of his entrie:
12.H.8.1. Notwithſtanding, if hee bee ſo diſpoſed, hee may permit the ſame houſe
7.H.6.40. which he ſo found in decay, to bee vtterly ruinated and fall downe; for hee
29.H.8. need not keepe the houſe in other repaire than he receiued it. But if the te-
Dyer 36. nant doe giue or ſell any timber, or fell more for any of the vſes aforeſaid, than
49.E.3.1.
42.Ed.3.22. is neceſſarie and ſufficient, or doe fell any timber to build a newe houſe,
11.H.4.31. where there was none vpon the ground before, then he may bee puniſhed
9.H.4. therefore by an Action of waſt. And the ſame Law is of a Copieholder, who
Waſt.59. can fell no timber but to repaire his houſes which hee holdeth by copie of
9.H.6.66. Court Roll. The felling of Maples, Sallowes, Willowes, Hornebeams,
46.E.3.17. Crabtrees, Haſils, Thornes, or ſuch like is no waſt, for that they will not continue long, nor ſerue for building: And therefore they are accounted ſeaſonable wood, and are lawfully to bee felled by the termor, and to bee
12.H.8.1. ſpent vpon the ſame ground for houſe-bot, plough-bot, hedge-bot, fold-bote, or fire-bote, which the Law doth allowe to the termor for yeares or life. And the tenant may fell Oakes, Aſhes, or Elmes for any of the pur-
21.H.6.46. poſes aforeſaid, if there be no vnderwood growing vpon the ſame ground to be imployed to thoſe vſes. By the cuſtome of ſome countrie, where wood is plentifull, Oakes, Aſhes, and Elmes, vnder twentie yeares groweth
11.H.6.1. be called vnderwood, or ſeaſonable wood, and may be felled by the termor for
Lib.Intr. 617. any of the vſes aforeſaid, and ſo may wrangles aboue twentie yeares growth, which are neuer like to proue timber, or meete for building: but in ſome other countries where wood is ſcant, it is otherwiſe. Felling of ſeaſonable
40.E.3.25. wood, which is vſed to bee cut euery ſeauen, tenne, fifteene, or twenty yeares,
Fitz.N.B. is no waſt: Neither is it waſt for the tenant to fell and take dotards, or to
59. take windfalles wherein there is no timber; for they bee the tenants to vſe
7.H.6.40. and ſpend as is aforeſaid: But windfalles wherein there is any timber bee
Co.li.4.64. the Leaſſors. And ſo is the timber of a houſe, which doth decay and fall
Fit.N.B.59 downe during the terme, the Leaſſors, vnleſſe the tenant will reedifie the
29.Ed.3.33. ſame houſe, and imploy the ſaid timber in the building thereof againe. Though the felling of Willowes, or other ſuch like ſeaſonable wood, bee of it ſelfe no waſt, yet if Willowes or any of the trees aforeſaid doe growe with-
40.E.3.15.
12.H.8.1. in the viewe or ſcite of a Mannor houſe to defend the houſe from tempeſts
10.H.7.5. and ſtormes, or neere vnto the banks of a Riuer, to defend the Banke, then the felling of them is waſt: and the tenant of the land is puniſhable

for the same by an action of Wast. If a tenant for yeares, life, or &c. doe fell Okes, Ashes, or Elmes, and after he hath felled them, he doth suffer cattell to come into the same ground, which doe croppe and spoyle the sprouts or newe springs growing out of the rootes of the same trees, then this is a newe, and another Wast, and punishable by the same Action of Wast that the Trees bee, or by another, in which Action hee in the Reversion or Remainder shall recover treble dammages: first for the Trees felled, and also treble dammages for the springs spoiled, though hee can but once recover the place wasted. If the Termor doe fell greene wood to burne, where hee hath dead wood sufficient, it is Wast. But the felling of dead wood which will beare no leaves in Summer is no Wast; neither is the pulling downe of a hedge Wast, or of a Pale or Wall that is uncovered Wast. And the foresaid Writ of Wast proceedeth further to punish wast in Gardens: Therefore if the Termor doe fell and destroy Appletrees or Peartrees growing, dispersed in severall places of the ground demised unto him, it is no Wast; for hee may fell them, and take them to burne as seasonable wood: But if he fell a whole Garden or Orchard of Appletrees or Peartrees, or any great number therein, it is wast; for the wordes of the Writ of Wast doe expresse so much, which be, Non liceat alicui vastum, vendicionem, seu destructionem facere in terris, domibus, Boscis, seu Gardinis. And if any Appletrees, or Peartrees be throwne downe by the winde in an Orchard or Garden, and they doe leane upon some of their boughes, and the spurres or rootes of them continuing fast in the ground, doe so cherrish the trees that they doe beare fruit, it is wast to fell and carrie them away. And to make an end of this Braunch with the wordes of the foresaid Statute of Marlebridge, touching exile of men: If the tenant for yeares, life, or &c. of a Mannor doe so vexe the villeins regardant of the same Mannor by Distresses, Fines, Amerciaments, or otherwise, that the same villeins doe depart from their Tenements, this is to the disheritance of him in the Reversion or Remainder, and therefore punishable by an Action of Wast. But if the Termor of a Mannor during his estate doe enfraunchise a villeine regardant to a Mannor, this is no Wast punishable by the Lawe; for after the particular estate ended, he in the Reversion or Remainder may seize the same villeine againe cum tota sequela sua. If the tenant for yeares, life, or &c. of a Mannor or other land, wherein there bee cottages, or small Tenements, doe demise the same Cottages, or &c. to severall Tenants, and they doe die of the Plague, and the same Leassee can get none other tenants to inhabit the same Cottages or &c. whereby they doe decay, and fall downe, the Leassee is not punishable therefore by an Action of Wast; for that the wast which ensued by the death of those Cotiees or inferiour tenants came by the visitation and hand of God, and not by any default of the Termor, and therefore the said Termor doing his endeavour to reforme the defect, and to provide other tenants, and beeing not able to performe it, could not redresse the same.

Margin notes: Wast in gardens. — Wast in men. — 20.Ed.3. Wast.32. 9.H.6.66. 11.H.6.1. 22.H.6.12. 4.H.3. Wast.140. — 20.E.3. Wast.32. 7.H.6.40. 22.H.6.24. — 10.H.7.5. 21.H.6.46. — 44.E.3.44. — 29.H.8. Dyer 37. Fit.N.B.55 Fitz. Wast. 2.113.118. 130.131. 2.H.6.11. — 44.E.3.21. Fitz. Wast. 104.105.

10 When one person doth bargain, covenant, or conclude with another for any paiment, matter, cause, or thing to be performed, & is once fully satisfied therof by money, wares, or other means, according to the true intent of the same agreement: if the same

same partie doe after sue or attempt by course of Law to obtaine a new,
or other satisfaction for the same contract; this a plaine and manifest wrong
and oppression, for the said partie doth in a sort endeauour to bee twice
satisfied for one debt or dutie. And likewise, it is an oppression and
wrong, if one person doe endeauour to lay a burden or charge vpon o-
thers, which the Lawe of the Realme will not impose vpon them, or
which himselfe alone, or himselfe with others ought to sustaine: or when
one person shall imprison or restraine another of his libertie, who by law
ought to bee free. As if one person bee bound to another by Statute mar-
chant, or Statute-Staple for the paiment of a summe of money, where-
of there is a defeasaunce that if the Conusor doe pay to the Conusee a
46.Ed.3.4. lesse summe of money at a day prefixed, or diuers summes at seuerall
47.Ed.3.26. daies, or doe performe certaine couenants or agreements in the said de-
20.E.3. feasaunce, or in certaine Indentures made betweene them specified, and
Fi.N.B.105 the conusor doth pay the said summe or seuerall summes of money, or
doth performe all the couenants in the said Indenture specified, according
to the purport of the said defeasaunce: and that notwithstanding the
Conusee doth sue execution of the said Statute against the Conusor, this
is a manifest wrong and oppression pretended to the Conusor: Where-
fore the Conusor for his reliefe may haue an Audita querela directed out
of the Chauncerie to the Iustices of the Kings Bench, or Common Oppressions redressed by an Audita querela.
Place, comprehending the whole matter, and charging them to call be-
fore them the parties, Plaintife and Defendant, and to doe them iu-
stice, according to the Law and Custome of the Realme, which is either
to graunt a Supersedeas to stay the Execution, or to set the bodie of the
Conusor at libertie, if hee be taken and imprisoned therefore, and to dis-
charge his lands and goods of execution, if the suggestion of the plaintife
in the said writ be proued to bee true. And if the Conusee in the case a-
foresaid doe take away the defeasaunce or Indenture from the Conusor,
47.Ed.3.26 and after extend the same Statute against him, this is likewise an op-
Fi.N.B.103 pression, and to bee redressed by an Audita querela. And in like sort if the
Conusee after the said Statute acknowledged, doe make a Release or Ac-
quitance of the same to the Conusor, and then doe sue execution of the
47.E.3.3. said Statute against the same Conusor, or any feoffee of any part of his
45.E.3.17. land, this is a great iniurie and oppression, and therefore in this case the
3.H.4.12. said Conusor or his feoffee is to bee relieued by an Audita querela. If a Sta-
31.E.3. tute be made & acknowledged by one person to another, and then committed
in ouell maine to a straunger to bee deliuered to the Conusee vpon certaine
12.H.4.13. conditions performed, and after the same stranger doe deliuer the said Sta-
43.E.3.17. tute to the Conusee before the conditions performed, whereupon he doth sue
execution thereof against the Conusor, this is a great wrong and oppres-
sion of the Conusor, and therefore hee may haue an Audita querela vpon this
matter in fact, stay the the execution, and thereby redresse this iniury. If one
person be bound to another by Statute or Recognisance for the paiment
45.E.3.17. of a summe of money, and after the Conusor doth make seuerall feoffe-
47.E.3.3. ments of seuerall parcels of his land to diuers persons, and then the Sta-
9.H.4.5. tute or Recognisance is forfeited, and the Conusee doth sue execution thereof
13.H.7.22. against one of those feoffees onely, this is a wrong and oppression of him,
16.El.Dyer 332. for that al the land of the conusor which he had at the time of the said stat. or re-

cogniſance acknowledged, or at any time after, ought to be charged and extended for the paiment of this debt, to the intent the money might be the ſooner paid, and the execution more ſpeedily diſcharged: And therefore ẏ ſame feoffée, whoſe land is ſo extended may haue an Audita querela, or a Scire facias, as the caſe requireth, to defeat the execution againſt him, (and thereby hee ſhalbe reſtored to all the meane profits) and to compell the conuſée to ſue execution of all the land which was the conuſors at the time of the ſaid Statute or Recogniſance acknowledged, or at any time after; and ſo the land of euery terre-tenant ſhall bee equally charged, and each perſon contributorie to the ſame extent, in reſpect of his land. If the conuſor after a Statute or Recogniſance acknowledged doe make many feoffements of ſeuerall parcels of his land to diuers perſons, and then all, or any of thoſe feoffées lands bee extended by force of the ſame Statute &c. the partie or parties grieued by the ſame extent, may procure an Audita querela to cauſe the lands of the conuſor to bée likewiſe extended: for hée or they be wronged and oppreſſed by the ſaid conuſors former Act and meanes. But on the other ſide, if the land remaining in the hands of the conuſor bée extended by the conuſée, by force of the ſaid Statute or Recogniſance, the conuſor cannot maintaine an Audita querela againſt his feoffées, or any of them, to cauſe their lands to be extended: for hée is not vexed or oppreſſed by the ſame extent by any of their meanes, nor for any of their debts, but for his owne debt, though in the caſe before rehearſed they bee troubled and oppreſſed for his debt: for when any perſon doth become bound by Statute or Recogniſance to another, and after alieneth his land, or any part thereof to a ſtranger, the body of the conuſor remaineth debtor to the conuſee in reſpect of his acknowledgement and confeſſion of the ſame, made of record before a competent Judge or officer thereunto lawfully aſſigned, and the debt is his, and the burden thereof is his, and the land is onely chargeable in reſpect that it was in his hands at the time of the Statute or Recogniſance acknowledged, or after, and ſo the conuſors perſon, and the land in his hands is onely chargeable in that caſe. As in like caſe, if a man doe become bound by Statute or Recogniſance to another, and after the conuſée doth purchaſe parcell of the land of the conuſor, and then the Statute is forfeited, the conuſée may extend the Statute, take and impriſon the bodie of the conuſor, and haue the reſidue of his land deliuered to him in execution, and the conuſor ſhall haue no remedie by Audita querela againſt the conuſée, for that the conuſor is not wronged or oppreſſed by this extent, ſeeing hée himſelfe is the onely debtor of the conuſée, and his body, lands, and goods, are liable to the payment of this debt, and not the lands in the hands of the conuſee. And ſo it is if a man bée bound by Statute or Recogniſance to another, and after the conuſée doe purchaſſe parcell of the land of the conuſor, and a ſtranger purchaſeth another parcell of land of him, and then the Statute is forfeited, and the conuſée doth ſue execution of the land of that ſtranger the other purchaſer: that is a wrong and oppreſſion, and therefore the ſaid ſtraunger may ſue an Audita querela againſt the ſaid conuſée, and thereby diſcharge his land of execution: for that the ſaid conuſée hath diſcharged this land by his own Act, viz. by purchaſing of parcell of the land charged: for by the Statute or Recogniſance acknowledged, the whole land was charged, and by purchaſing of parcell by the conuſée, hée hath diſcharged the whole, ſa-

Co.li.3.14. 23.Ed.3. Execution 127. 9.H.4.5. 23.Ed.3. Fitz.Execution.127. 45.Ed.3.22. 11.H.7.4. 13.H.7.22. 45.Ed.3.22. 2.El.Dyer 193. Plo.Com. 72. 11.H.7.4. 13.H.7.22. Fitz.N.B. 105.

uing

uing that which remaineth in the hands of the Conusor. If an Infant within the age of one and twentie yeares be bound by Statute or Recognisance, and the Conusor will extend the same, the Infant may pursue an Audita querela to auoid the same, either during his minoritie, if by inspection the Court shall adiudge him within age, or after he shall accomplish his full age: for it was a wrong and oppression practised by the Conusee to abuse the tender age of the Infant, and to urge a Statute of him before the Law did enable him to acknowledge it. And the like Law is, if one person will acknowledge to another a Statute by Dures of imprisonment, and then the Conusee doe sue execution of the same, the Conusor may prosecute an Audita querela and auoyd the Statute: for in this case the Conusee hath done to the Conusor a double wrong and oppression: viz. first, to imprison him, and thereby to exact a Statute of him, and then contrarie to the warrant of the Law to extend the same against him. And as in the cases aforesaid, so likewise in all other cases where any person hath iust and lawfull cause to seeke and haue reliefe by an Audita querela, in the same cases either he is, or is offered to bee oppressed and wronged: And in all the same cases the oppressor endeauoureth to make the Lawe his colour and instrument to abuse him.

6.Ed.3.39. 13.Ed.3. Au.qu.26. Fi.N.B.104

Fi.N.B.104 20.Ed.3. Au.qu.27.

11 Forestallers, Ingrossers, and Regrators deserue to bee reckoned amongest the number of Oppressors of the common good, and publike wealth of the Realme, for they doe endeauour to inrich themselues by the impouerishment of others, and respect not how many doe lose, so they may gaine. They haue beene exclaimed upon, and condemned in Parliament from one generation to another, as appeareth by the Statutes of Anno 51.H.3. Anno 34.Ed.1. Anno 25.Ed.3. Anno 27.Ed.3. Anno 28.Ed.3. Anno 31.Ed.3. Anno 42.Ed.3. Anno 2.R.2. Anno 6.R.2. Anno 14.R.2. Anno 25.H.8. Anno 5.Ed.6. & Anno 5.El. but amongst the others specially forestallers, for by the foresaid Statute of Anno 34.Ed.1. it was ordained, That no forestaller shall be suffered to dwell in any towne: for hee is a manifest oppressor of the poore, and a decayer of the rich, a publike enemy of the countrey, a Canker, a Moth, and a gnawing worme that daily wasteth the common wealth: And the acte and name of a Forestaller was so odious in that time, that it was mooued in Parliament to haue had it established by Law, That a Forestaller should bee baited out of the town where he dwelt by dogges, and whipped forth with whippes. But because in time it grewe in question who was to be accounted a Forestaller, who an Ingrosser, and who a Regrator, and what punishment former lawes had inflicted upon them; therefore to the intent that they and their offences might more certainely be laid open to the knowledge of the whole Realme, and condigne punishment prouided for them, by a Statute made Anno 5.& 6.E.6. it was established, That whatsoeuer person or persons shall buy or cause to be bought any marchandise, victuall, or other thing comming by land, or water towards any faire, or market, to be sold in the same, or cõming toward any citty, port, hauen, creeke, or rode of this realm, or Wales, from any part beyond ye sea to be sold: or make any bargain, cõtract, or promise for the hauing or buying of the same, or any part thereof so comming as aforesaid, before the same marchandise, victuals, or other things shall be in the market, faire, citie, port,

St.34.Ed.1.

Oppression by forestallers ingrossers, regrators.

St.5.and 6. Ed.6.14. — A. Who is a forestaller.

Hauen, Creeke, or Rode, readie to be sold: Or shall make any motion by word, letter, message, or otherwise, to any person or persons for the inhaunsing of the price, or deere selling of any of the things aboue mentioned: Or else disswade, moue, or stirre any person comming to the Market or Faire, to forbeare to bring any of the things aboue mentioned to any Faire or market, citie, port, &c. to be sold as aforesaid, shalbe adiudged a forestaller. But by the statute of an 13. El. it is ordained, That the said Statute of an 5. & 6. Ed. 6. shall not extend to any wines, oyles, sugars, spices, currans, or other forraine victuals, brought from beyond the sea (fish and salt onely except.) St. 13. El. 25.

B. who is a regrator.

Whatsoeuer person or persons shall by any meanes regrate, obtaine, or get into his or their hands, or possession, in any faire or market, any corne, wine, fish, butter, cheese, candles, tallow, sheepe, lambes, calues, swine, pigges, geese, capons, hennes, chickins, pigeons, conies, or other dead victuall whatsoeuer, that shalbe brought to any faire or market within this realme, or Wales, to be sold, and doe sell the same againe in any faire or market holden or kept in the same place, or in any other faire or market within iiij. miles thereof, shalbe reputed and taken for a regrator, or regrators. St. 5. and 6. Ed. 6. 14.

C. who is an ingrosser.

Whatsoeuer person or persons that shall ingrosse, or get into his or their hands by buying, cōtracting, or promise taking, (other than by demise, grant, or lease of land or tythe) any corne growing in the fields, or any other corne or graine, butter, cheese, fish, or other dead victuals whatsoeuer, within the realm of England, to the intent to sell the same againe, shalbe reputed and taken an vnlawfull engrosser or engrossers. St. 5. and 6. Ed. 6. 14.

D. The punishment of forestallers, regrators, and ingrossers.

If any person or persons shall offend in any of the things before recited, and being thereof duely conuicted or attainted by the lawes of this realme, or after the forme hereafter mentioned, he or they shall for his or their first offence, haue or suffer imprisonment by the space of two moneths without baile or mainprise, and shall also lose and forfeit the value of the goods, cattels, and victuall, so by him or them bought or had. And if any person lawfully conuicted or attainted, of or for any the offences abouesaid, be thereof eftsones lawfully conuicted or attainted, then euery person or persons so offending, shall haue & suffer for his said second offence, imprisonment by the space of one halfe yeare, without baile or maineprise, and shall lose the double value of all the goods, cattels, and victuall, so by him bought or had as is aforesaid. And if any person being lawfully twice conuicted or attainted, of or for any of the said offences, shal eftsones offend the third time, and be thereof lawfully conuicted or attainted, then euery such person for the third offence, shalbe set on the pillorie in the citty, towne, or place where he shall then dwell, and inhabit, and lose and forfeit all the goods and cattel, that he or they haue to their owne vse, and also be committed to prison, there to remaine during the kings pleasure. St. 5. and 6. Ed. 6. 14.

E. Cases where in regrating or ingrossing be tollerable.

Prouided alwaies, that the buying of any such barley, bigge, or oates, as any person or persons (not forestalling) shall conuert into mault, or oatmeale, in his or their owne house or houses, or shall so be conuerted indeed: or the buying of any such thing, by any such Fishmonger, Butcher, or Poulter, as concerne his or their owne facultie, craft, or mystery (otherwise than by forestalling) which shall sell the same againe vpon reasonable prices by retaile: or the taking of any cattell, corne, graine, butter, cheese, or any St. 5. and 6. Ed. 6. 14.

other thing aboue mentioned, reserued (without fraud or couin) upon any lease for terme of life or liues, yeare, or yeares, heretofore made, or hereafter to be made: or the buying of any wine or other dead victuall aboue mentioned, being apt and meete for mans sustenance by any Inholder or other victualler, to sell the same by retaile within his house, or to any of his neighbours for their sustenance, for reasonable prices: or the buying of anie dried or salted fish, herring, or sprats (not forestalled) and solde for reasonable prices: or the buying of any corne, fish, butter, or cheese, by any such Badger, lader, kidder, or carier as shall be assigned, and allowed to that office, or doing by three Iustices of Peace of the Countie where the said badger, lader, kidder, or carier shall dwell, which shall sell and deliuer in open faire or market, or to any other victualler, or to any other person or persons for the prouision of his or their house or houses, all such corne, graine, butter, and cheese, as any such person shall buy or cause to be bought (and that within one moneth next after he shall so buy any such corne, graine, butter or cheese) so that the same shall be bought without forestalling: or else that any such common prouision made, or hereafter to be made without fraud or couin, by any person or persons, of any of the things abouesaid, for any citie, borough or towne corporat, or for the prouision or victualling of any ship, castle, or fort within the kings dominions without forestalling, which shall be imployed onely to that use and purpose: or the buying and prouision of any of the victualls aboue mentioned, necessary for the furniture and prouision of the inhabitants, or of the towne of Barwicke, Holy Iland, or the Marches of England against Scotland, which without fraud or couin shall be transported and conueied, as soone as winde and weather may serue to such of the places aforesaid, for the which the same shall be so prouided, shall not be in any wise deemed, adiudged or taken any offence contrarie to this Act.

F

Buying of corne for the change of seede.

St.5.& 6. Ed.6.14.

If any person or persons hauing sufficient corne and graine for the prouision of his or their owne house or houses, and sowing of their grounds for one yeare, doe buy any corne in any faire or market, for the change of his or their seede, and do not bring to the same faire or market the same day so much corne as he shall fortune to buy for his seede, and sell the same if he can, as the price of corne then goeth in the said market or faire: then euery such person or persons so buying corne for seede, shall forfeit and lose the double valew of the corne so bought.

G

Buying and selling of cattell aliue.

St.5.& 6. Ed.6.14.

If any person or persons shal buy any manner of oxen, ronts, stieres, kine, heifers, calues, sheepe, lambs, goats, or kids liuing, and sell the same againe aliue, vnlesse he or they do keepe and feede the same by the space of fiue weeks, in his or their owne houses, ground, farme ground, or else in such ground or grounds where he or they haue the herbage or common of pasture, by graunt or prescription, then euery person and persons so buying and selling againe shall lose the double valew of the cattell, or things so bought and sold againe. The moitie of all which forfeitures afore rehearsed shall be to the King, and the other moitie to him or them that will sue in any of the Kings Courts of Record by B.P.A. or I. &c. in the which no W.E.P. &c.

H

The authoritie of Iustices of peace.

St.5.& 6. Ed.6.14.

The Iustices of peace in euery County within this Realme or Wales, at their quarter Sessions, shall haue full power and authoritie by vertue of this Act, to inquire, heare, and determine all and euery the defaults and offences,

committed

committed or done contrary to this Act within the County where any such Sessions shall be kept, by Inquisition, presentment, bill, or information before them exhibited, by examination of two lawfull witnesses, or by any of the same waies or meanes, by the discretion of the said Justices, and to make processe thereupon, as though they were indicted before them by Inquisition, or by verdict of twelue men, or more, and upon the conuiction of the offendor, by information or sute of any other than the King, to make extracts of the one moity of the forfeitures to be leuied to the Kings vse, as they vse to doe of other fines, issues, and amerciaments growen in the Sessions of peace, and to award execution of the other moity for the complainant or informer against the offendor by Fieri facias, or Capias, as the Kings Justices at Westminster may doe, and vse to doe. And if any such conuiction or attainder, shall héereafter happen to be at the Kings sute onely, then the whole forfeitures to be extracted, and leuied to the Kings vse onely. Whatsoeuer person shall at anie time héereafter be punished by vertue of this Act, for any thing mentioned in this Act, then the same person shall not otherwise be vexed, troubled, sued, or put to any paine or punishment for that one thing, wherefore hée or they shall haue béene so punished.

But once punished for one offence.

I Prouided alwaies, that it shalbe lawfull to euery person or persons which shalbe assigned and allowed by thrée Justices of the peace of the county where he shall dwell, thereunto, to buy (otherwise than by forestalling) corne, graine, or cattell, to be transported or carried by water from any port, or place within the said Realme, or Wales, vnto any other port, or place within the saide Realme, or Dominions, if he or they shall without fraud or couin, shippe or imbarke the same within fortie dayes next after he or they shall haue bought the same, or taken couenant, or promise for the buying thereof, and with such expedition and diligence as winde and weather shall serue to carrie and transport the same to such port or place, as his or their cockets shall declare, and there doe dis-barke, vnlade, and sell the same, and doe bring a true certificat thereof, from one Justice of peace of the County, or maior, or bailife of the towne corporat where the same shall be vnladen, and also of the Customer of the port where such vnlading shal be, of the place, and day, where the saide corne or cattell shall be disbarked, vnladen, and solde to be directed vnto the Customer and Comptroller of the port where the same was imbarked. St.5.& 6.E. 6.14.

Transporting allowed by Justices of peace.

K At all times when wheate shall be commonly at the price of sixe shillings eight pence the quarter, or vnder, mault and barley at thrée shillings foure pence the quarter, or vnder, otes, or otes maulted, at the price of two shillings the quarter, pease or beanes at the price of foure shillings the quarter, or vnder, and rie or mescelin at the price of fiue shillings the quarter, or vnder, (all which quarters shall be intended to be of London measure) then it shall be lawfull to euery person and persons (not forestalling) to buy, ingrosse, and kéepe in his or their grainers, or houses such corne of the kindes aforesaide, as without fraud or couin shal be bought, at, or vnder the prices before expressed, any thing in this Act to the contrary notwithstanding. Prouided alwaies, that this Act, or any thing therein contained, extend not to charge any person or persons for any the offences aboue mentioned, vnlesse he or they be sued for the same within two yeares next after such offence done or committed. St.5.& 6.E. 6.14.

when corne may be ingrossed.

within what time the sute shalbe commenced.

Prouided

5.& 6.Ed.6. 14. Prouided alwayes, that it ſhall be lawfull to euery of the kings ſubiects, now dwelling & inhabiting, or that hereafter ſhal dwel and inhabite within one mile of the maine Sea to buy all manner of fiſh freſh and ſalted (not foreſtalling the ſame) & to ſel the ſame againe at reaſonable prices, this Act, or any thing therein contained to the contrarie in any wiſe notwithſtanding. Prouided alſo, that it ſhall be lawfull to all and euery perſon and perſons knowne to be a common Drouer or Drouers being licenced, or authorized, and allowed in writing by three Iuſtices of peace, whereof one to be of the Quorum of the Countie or Counties where the ſame Drouer or Drouers ſhall be moſt abiding and dwelling, to buy cattell in ſuch Shires and Counties where Drouers haue beene wont in times paſt accuſtomably to buy cattell, at their free liberties and pleaſures, and to ſell the ſame as is aforeſaid at reaſonable priſes, in common faires and markets diſtant from the place or places, where he or they ſhall buy the ſame, fortie miles at the leaſt, ſo that the ſame cattell be not bought by the way of foreſtalling. Prouided alwaies, that ſuch licence of the Iuſtices of the Peace ſhall not endure aboue one yeare, vnleſſe the ſame be yearely renewed by ſo many Iuſtices as is aforeſaid.

L Buying and ſelling of fiſh neere the ſea.

Drouers licen ed may buy and ſell cattle.

The continuance of a licence.

St. 5. El. 12. 12 Becauſe ſince the making of the foreſaid Statute of An. 5. & 6. Ed. 6. diuers perſons by their owne ſute, were licenced to become drouers of cattel, badgers, laders, kidders, cariers, buiers, or tranſporters of corne, graine, butter and cheeſe, thereby to liue eaſily, and to leaue their honeſt labour in huſbandry, or manuall occupations, and alſo to inhaunce the prices of corne, graine, and other victualls; by which meanes they oppreſſed the commonwealth, only to procure vnto themſelues both wealth, and eaſe: for the redreſſe whereof by a Statute made Anno 5. Eliz. it was enacted, That if anie licence ſhall be made to any badger, lader, kidder, or carier of corne, drouer of cattell, buyer or tranſporter of corne and graine, butter or cheeſe, otherwiſe than in the generall and open Quarter Seſſions of the peace holden in the ſhire where the partie admitted doth, and by the ſpace of three yeares before the Teſte of his Licence hath dwelled: Or other than to ſuch perſon as is or hath beene married, is a houſholder, no houſhold ſeruant or retainer, & thirtie yeeres of age at the leaſt: Or to haue continuance for more than one yeere: or which beareth not date the day and place where the Seſſions be holden: Or is not ſigned and ſealed with the handes and ſeales of three Iuſtices of peace being preſent at the ſame Seſſions at the leaſt, whereof one to be of the Quorum, the ſame Licence ſhall be voide: And the party which taketh the ſame, ſhall forfeit fiue pounds. And no perſon ſhall vpon the paine of the forfeiture of fiue pounds by the authoritie of ſuch Licence buy any corne out of open faire or market, to ſell the ſame againe, except he be thereunto ſpecially licenced by expreſſe words in his licence. The moitie of which forfeitures ſhall be to the Q. her heires and ſucceſſors, and the other moitie to him or them that will ſue for the ſame in any of the Q. Courts of Record by B. P. A. or I. wherein no W. E. P. &c. But this Act ſhall not extend to preiudice the liberties of any citie, or towne corporat, but euery of them, may lawfully aſſigne and licence Purueiors for the prouiſion of the ſame citie, or towne, as they might haue done before. Neither ſhall this Act be preiudiciall to the Inhabitants within the Counties of Weſtmerland, Comberland, Lancaſter, Cheſter, Yorke, or any of them, but they may doe as they haue vſed to doe: And the Iuſtices of peace in euery Countie within this Realme, or Wales, ſhall haue authoritie to inquire, heare, and determine all offences committed

Oppreſſion by badgers, kidders, laders, cariers.

Obſeruations neceſſarie in all licences.

committed contrary to this statute by inquisition, presentment, bill, or information before them exhibited, and by examination of two lawfull witnesses, and to make processe thereupon as though they were indited by inquisition or verdict &c.

Oppression of Printers and Stationers.

13 Though by the Statute of Anno 1.R.3. licence was giuen to aliens and strangers to bring bookes into this Realme, and to sell and retaile them at their liberties, for that there were then few Printers, or skilfull binders of bookes within this Realme: But seeing since there haue beene and are many expert and cunning Printers, and skilfull binders of bookes within this Realme, who haue wholly addicted themselues to the saide trades, and made it their whole or chiefe liuing: and therefore to bring into this Realme anie printed bookes bound; or for any stranger to bring bookes into this Realme, to be by them sold by retaile were a great oppression and preiudice to the Stationers, and also the same bookes would be so much the dearer, and so hurtfull to others, who should buy those of them: Therefore by a Statute made Anno 25.H.8. it was ordained, That if any person resiant or inhabitant within this realme shal buy to sell againe any printed bookes brought from any parts out of the Kings obedience, ready bound in boords, leather, or parchment, hee shall forfeit for euery booke bound out of the Kings obeisance, and brought into this Realme, and bought by any person within the same to sell againe, vj.s viij.d to the King, and the party that wil seise, or sue for the same in any of the Kings courts of Record by B.P.I.&c. wherein no W.E.P.&c. And if anie person inhabitant or resiant within this realme, shall buy within this realme of any stranger borne out of the kings obeisance (other than of denizens) any printed bookes brought from any parts beyond the sea (except only in grosse, and not by retaile) he shal forfeit for euery booke so bought by retaile vj.s viij.d to the King, and the party that wil seise or sue for the same in any of the kings courts of Record, by B.P. or I.&c. wherein no W.E.P.&c. The said forfeitures to be alwaies leuied of the buyers of such books contrarie to this statute. For that it was then thought expedient, that Printers and sellers of printed bookes, should as well be restrained from the oppression of others, by making excessiue prices, in sale or binding of their bookes, as it was by the said statute prouided that they should not be oppressed by others: Therefore by the before rehearsed statute of Anno 25.H.8. it was further established, That if any Printers or sellers of printed bookes, inhabiting within this Realme, do at any time in such wise inhance or increase the prices of any such printed books, in sale, or binding, at too high and vnreasonable prices, in such wise as complaint thereof be made to the King, or vnto the Lord Chancellor, Lord Treasurer, or any of the chiefe Iustices of the one Bench, or of the other: Then the same Lords, or two of any of them, shall haue authoritie to enquire thereof, as well by the othes of twelue honest and discreete persons, as otherwise by due examinations by their discretions: and after the same inhauncing and increasing of the prices of the said bookes and binding shal be so found by the said twelue men, or otherwise by the examination of the saide Lord Chancellor, Lord Treasurer, and Iustices or two of them: Then the same Lords, or two of them at the least, shall haue power to redresse such inhancing of the prices of printed bookes from time to time by their discretions, and to limite the prices as well of the bookes, as for the binding of them. And ouer that, the offender or offenders being conuict by examination of the saide Lordes, or two of them, or otherwise shall forfeit for euery booke by them solde, whereof the

St.1.Ri.3.9.

Oppression by Printers or Stationers.

St.25.H.8.15.

St.25.H.8.15.

the price ſhall be enhaunced for the booke and binding thereof thrée ſhillings foure pence to the King and party grieued, that will complaine vpon the ſame in manner and forme aforeſaid.

St.5.Ri.2.2. 14 It appeareth by the preamble of the ſtatute of Añ 5.R.2. that the carying of gold or ſiluer in money, veſſell, plate or iewells forth of the Realme, was then accounted a great miſchiefe, oppreſſion and deſtruction of this land, which the policie of this State hath before, and ſince, by ſeueral Statutes endeuoured to reſtraine: As appeareth by the ſtatutes of Año. Ed.3. Anno 5. R.2. Anno 2.H.4. Anno 2.H.6. Anno 17.Ed.4. Anno 4.H.7. and Anno 19.H.7. Whereupon by the ſaide ſtatute of Añ 9.Ed.3. & Anno 5.R.2. it was eſtabliſhed, That whoſoeuer doth ſend, or carrie out of the Realme of England, any gold, or ſiluer in mony, bullion, plate, or veſſell, without the Kings licence, (ſauing for his reaſonable expences Anno 2.H.4.) ſhall forfeit the valew of the ſumme carried forth: And he which is vpon his paſſage in any ſhippe or veſſell, for to goe out of any port, hauen, or créeke, ſhall immediatly confeſſe and declare after warning vnto him giuen by the Kings ſearcher what gold or ſiluer in coine or maſſe he hath with him for his expences, or elſe that mony ſo concealed ſhall be alſo forfeited to the King: But by the ſtatute of Anno 2.H.6. Raunſoms for fines of Engliſh priſoners taken beyond the Sea, and the mony that ſouldiers ſhall carrie with them for their reaſonable coſts be excepted, ſo that the ſame be not done without the Kings licence, And alſo by the ſame ſtatute is excepted mony for things bought in Scotland to be brought to the parts adioyning. And by the ſaide Statute of Anno 19.H.7. it was ordained, That no perſon ſhall carry or conuey, nor cauſe to be carried out of this Realme, any bullion, plate, or coine of golde or ſiluer into Ireland aboue the ſumme of vi.s viij.d, nor conuey any ſuch bullion into any ſhip or boate, vpon paine of forfeiture of the ſame, and of impriſonment and fine at the Kings pleaſure.

Oppreſſion by tranſporting of gold and ſiluer.

St.9.Ed.3.1

St.5 R.2.2

St.2.H.4.5.

St.2.H.6.6.

St.19.H.7.5

15 Becauſe there is no mine of copper mettall within this realme, where ſufficient copper may be gotten, for the vſe of the King and his people: and for that ſeuerall other mettalls be mixed therewith, of which diuers veſſells and inſtruments be made: And therefore the tranſporting thereof beyond the ſea, was found by experience to be a great hinderance, and oppreſſion to the workers thereof, and alſo to all thoſe that ſhould haue the vſe and occupation of the ſame; which were in effect all ſorts of houſekéepers, wherefore for the reſtraint of the tranſportation of the ſame, firſt one ſtatute was made Anno 21.H.8. And after another Anno 33.H.8. And laſtly, a third Anno 2.Ed.6. By which two laſt Statutes it was enacted, That no perſons ſhall carry or conuey, or ſhip, to the intent to carry or conuey, any braſſe, copper, latten, bel mettall, pan mettall, or ſhroffe mettall, whether it be cléere or mixed (tinne and lead onely excepted) into any part beyond the ſea, or into any outward dominion, vpon paine to forfeit the double value thereof, and x.l. for euery thouſand weight of the ſame mettall ſo carried or ſhipped, to the intent to be caried, to the King, and him that will ſue for the ſame in any of the Kings courts, by A.B.P. or I. wherein no W.E.P. &c.

Oppreſſion by tranſporting copper, braſſe &c.

St.21.H.8.10.

St.33.H.8.7

St.2.E.6.37

16 For that a great nūber of perſons occupying the trade & faculty of pewterers within this Realme were decayed and oppreſſed in eſtate, by reaſon that much ware made of tinne was brought out of other countries into this Realme, and becauſe ſtrangers did learne the occupation of Pewterers in this

Oppression of pewterers.

this Realme, and then did depart the Realme, and taught it to the people of forraine Nations: and for that sometime Englishmen borne would trauaile into other countries, and teach the same to forrainers: for the restraint whereof by a Statute made Anno 25. H.8. it was ordained, That no person inhabiting within this Realme, shall buy, or take by exchange for other wares any wares made out of this Realme of tinne, or mixt with tinne, as platters, dishes, sawcers, pots, basons, ewers, flaggons, goblets, saltsellers, spoones, or any other wares made of tin or pewter whatsoeuer it be, vpon paine of forfeiture of the same wares, in whose hands soeuer it may be found, or taken, to the vse of the King, and the finders thereof, and also lawfull currant mony of this Realme, to the valew thereof. And further, that no stranger borne out of this Realme shall vse the said craft of Pewterers, nor worke any manner of vessell, or other ware aforesaid to be made of tinne or pewter within any part of this Realme, vpon paine of forfeiture of tenne pounds to the vse of the K. and I. to be recouered by A.I. wherein no W.E.P. and also vpon paine of forfeiture of the same pewter or tinne so wrought, in whose handes soeuer it be found, or taken: and no persons borne within this Realme, occupying the said craft of Pewterers, shall resort into any strange countries, there to teach or exercise the said craft of pewterers, vpon paine to lose the priuiledge and benefit of an English man.

St.25.H.8.9 *St.33.H.8.4*

A pewterer shall not goe to dwell in an other realme.

17 Because complaint was made in Parliament, that Linnen Drapers, Wollen Drapers, Haberdashers, Grocers, and Mercers dwelling in the Country out of cities, boroughs, towne corporat, and market townes, did not only occupie the art and mysterie of the said Sciences in the places where they dwelt, but also came vnto the said cities, boroughes, townes corporat, and market townes, and there sold their wares, and tooke away the reliefe of the inhabitants of the said cities, market townes &c. to the great decay, oppression and vtter vndoing of the inhabitants of the same: For the reformation whereof, by a Statute made Anno 1. & 2. P. & M. it was enacted, That no person dwelling in the Countrie any where within England, out of any cities, boroughs, townes corporat, or market townes, shall sell, or cause to be sold by retaile, any wollen cloth, linnen cloth, Haberdash wares, Grocerie wares, or Mercerie wares, at, or within any of the said cities, boroughs, townes corporat, or market townes, or within the suburbs, or liberties thereof (except it be in open faires) vpon paine of forfeiture for euery time so offending the summe of vj.s viij.d, and the whole wares so sold, profered, and offered to be sold, contrarie to the intent of this Act, whereof one moitie shall be to the King, and the other moitie to him or them that will seise or sue for the same, in any of the Kings Courts of Record by A.B.P.I. or otherwise, wherein no W.E.P. &c. But this shall not be hurtfull to any persons that bring any of the said wares, to any of the said cities, market townes, &c. to be sold by whole sale, in grosse, and not by retaile, but euery of them may lawfully sell the same by whole sale, in grosse, and not by retaile, as they might haue done before. Neither shall this Act extend to any persons that dwell in the Country out of any of the said cities, boroughs, &c. but euery of them at any time when he shal be free of any of the guildes or liberties of any of the said cities, market townes &c. and dwell within any of them, shall or may sell, or cause to be solde any of the wares aforesaid by retaile: Neither shall this Act be preiudiciall to the priuiledges of the vniuersities of Oxford & Cambridge, or either of them. And it shall be lawfull to all persons to sell, or cause to be

Oppression of inhabitants of market townes.

St.1.& 2.P. & M.7.

sold

sold by retaile, or otherwise, all linnen or wollen cloth of their owne making, in euery Citie, Borough, Towne corporat, and Market Towne, as freely as they might haue done before. *Cloth of their own making.*

St.25.H.8. 13 — 18 It appeareth by the words of the stat. of An.25.H.8. That for one man to get and take into his hands diuers farmes, which were ordained & prouided habitations and liuings for diuers men: Or for one man to get into his possession many pastures or walkes for sheepe, by the occupying whereof seueral persons before had liued, was accounted a most grieuous & heinous oppression, & to tend to the high displeasure of almighty God, to the decay of hospitalitie, to the diminishing of the kings people, to the let of cloth making, whereby many poore people did liue, and to turne & incline to the vtter desolation & destruction of this realme: for the redresse whereof, by the same statute it was ordained, That no person or persons shal receiue or take in farme, for terme of yeres, life, or at will, by indenture, copy of Court Roll, or otherwise, any more houses or tenements of husbandry, whereunto any lands are belonging in town, village, hamlet, or tything within this realme, aboue the number of two such holds or tenements: and no manner of person shall haue or occupie any such holds so newly taken, to the number of two, as is before expressed, except he or they be dwelling within the same parishes where such holds be, vpon paine of forf. for euery weeke that he or they shall haue, occupy, or take any profits of such holds 3.s.4.d. whereof the one moity shalbe to the king, & the other to the party that wil sue for the same in any of the K. Courts by A.B.P.I. or otherwise within one yeere next after such offence cōmitted. *Oppression by taking of seuerall farmes.* St.4.H.7.16 — And by the stat. of An.4.H.7. it was established, That if any person doe take any seuerall farmes more then one, of any manors, lands, tenemēts, parsonages, or tythes within the isle of Wight, whereof the farme of them altogether shal exceed the summe of x. markes, the lessee shall forf. to the king for euery such taking xl.l. *Taking of farmes in the isle of Wight.*

St.25.H.8. 13 — 19 And for the reasons last specified, the said stat. of an.25.H.8. did also ordaine, That no person shall keepe, occupy, or haue in his possession in his owne proper lands, nor in the grounds of any other which he shall haue or occupy in farme, nor otherwise haue of his owne proper cattell, in vse, possession, or property, by any manner of meanes or couin, aboue the number of two thousand sheepe at one time, within any parts of this realme, of all sorts & kinds (alwais accounting 6. score to the hundred, and 10. such hundreds to the thousand) vpon paine to forf. for euery sheepe that any person shall haue or keepe, aboue the number limitted by this act, 3.s.4.d. to the king and such as will sue for the same by A.B.P.I. in any court of Record, wherein no W.E.P. &c. So that the suit be commenced for the king within three yeeres, & for a subiect within one yeere next after the offence committed. But lambes vnder the age of one whole yeere, and as much as shal be from the time of the falling of them vnto the feast of the Natiuity of S. Iohn Baptist shal not be taken for sheepe prohibited by this statute. *A — Oppression by keeping of many sheepe.* *Lambes.*

St.25.H.8. 13 — If any person hauing sheepe of his owne, happen to be made executor or administrator to any person which had sheep at his death, or happen to be maried to any person which shall haue sheepe at the time of the marriage, by reason whereof the said person shall by such meanes haue aboue the number of 200, *B. — Sheepe comming by executorship or mariage.*

then he shall lose no penalty for hauing aboue the number of 2000. sheepe, by such meanes, so that within one yeare next after such aduancement, he do put to sale, or otherwise dispose so many of the said sheepe, so to him aduanced, or els of his owne sheepe that he had before, so that aboue one yeere he shall not keepe, haue, or occupy by any such means, or otherwise by any fraud, any more number of them, then is before limitted, vpon paine before rehearsed.

C Sheepe giuen by will to a child within age.

If any person by his last Will giue to any child within age any number of sheepe, & appoint them by his last will to be kept by his executors, or by any other person, vntill the foresaid child shall come to a certaine age limitted by his last will: then after the death of the Testator, the said sheepe so being in possession of the executors, or of any other person to the vse of any such child within age, for the time ÿ he shall be limitted to haue the said sheepe, by the will of the Testator, shal not be accounted against the said executors, nor any person hauing the sheepe for the intent aforesaid, any of the number of the said sheep prohibited by this act. St.25.H.8.13.

D Sheepe kept vpon inheritance or freehold.

Euery person being the kings temporall subiect, or borne vnder his obeysance, which shall haue or be seised of inheritance, in possession, or in vse, or that shall haue a iointure in vse, or in possession, or shalbe tenant in dower, or by the courtesie of, or in any manors, lands, tenements, pastures, feedings, or liberty of foldage, within any part of this realme of England, Wales, or the Marches of the same, may haue, keepe, & maintain vpō the same, his own demesn lands, & all other his pastures, feedings, & fold courses, which he so hath, as many his own sheepe & lambs, in number to his own proper behoofe, as he lawfully might haue had & kept vpon the same at any time before the making of this act. 25.H.8.13

E He that keepeth his number vpon his inheritance, shall not keepe vpon a farme.

In case any such person hauing any such estate in vse, or in possession, of, or in any lands, tenements, pastures, feedings, or liberties of fold courses, do keep vpon the same the number of 2000. sheepe, or aboue, then he shall not in any wise keepe or haue any sheepe aboue the number of 2000. vpon any lands, pastures, or feedings, which he shal haue in farme, or otherwise, vpon pain of forf. for euery sheepe, besides the said number of 2000. 3.s.4.d. 25.H.8.13

F Sheepe kept vpon demesns and farmes.

In case the said demesne lands, tenements, pastures, feedings, & liberties of fold courses of any person before rehersed, suffice not for the feeding, pasturing, & keeping of 2000. sheepe, then any such person may haue or feed vpon the said demesn lands, & vpon his farme holds (which he lawfully may haue, to the said number of 2000. sheepe, & not aboue) vpon paine of forf. for euery sheepe aboue that number 3.s.4.d. 25.H.8.13

G Sheepe kept for the maintenance of a mans house.

It shalbe lawfull to euery person keeping a houshold, to haue frō time to time such conuenient number of sheepe, aboue the number expressed in this act, as shalbe necessary for the only expences of his houshold, to be prouided, kept, and fed, in and vpon his own lands, or other lands, such as he lawfully can prouide for, in farme, or otherwise, so that he at no time shall haue for the expence of his houshold, or by colour of the same, aboue the number to him limitted by this act, any number of sheepe moe then shall suffice for the onely expences of his 25.H.8.13

house-

houſehold for one yeare, without fraud or couin. And it is lawfull for all ſpirituall perſons to keepe ſuch and as many ſheepe vpon their owne lands, and after ſuch manner, and none otherwiſe, as they might haue done before the making of this act.

Spirituall perſons.

A

20 As it is a thing farre vnfit, and not conſorting with their function, that ſpirituall perſons, who ought to liue of the altar, and to be chiefely imployed & deuoted to the ſeruice of God, the adminiſtration of his ſacraments, preaching of his Word, & inſtruction of his people, ſhould buſie themſelues with taking of farmes, buying & ſelling for gaine in faires & markets, occupying of Parſonages or Vicarages by farme, or with the vſing or keeping of Tanne houſes or Brewhouſes: So it is an oppreſſion and meanes of impoueriſhment of other temporall perſons, who do chiefely or partly liue by the ſame trades: and therefore by a ſtat. made An. 21. H. 8. it was enacted, That no ſpirituall perſon ſhall take to farme to himſelfe, or to any perſon to his vſe, of the leaſe or grant of ye K. or any other perſon or perſons, by letters patents, indentures, writings, by word, or otherwiſe by any manner of means, any manors, lands, tenements, or other hereditaments, for terme of life, yeares, or at will, vpon paine to forf. for euery moneth that he or they to his vſe doe occupy ſuch farme, by reaſon of ſuch graunt or leaſe, x. l. to the king and him that will ſue, to be recouered in any of the kings Courts by A. B. P. I. wherein no W. E. P. And that no ſpirituall perſon, of what eſtate or degree ſoeuer he be, ſhall by himſelfe, or any other for him, to his vſe, bargaine, and buy to ſell againe for gaine, in any markets, faires, or other places, any manner of Cattell, Corne, Lead, Tin, Hides, Leather, Tallow, Fiſh, Woll, Wood, or any manner of victuall or marchandize, of what kind ſoeuer they be, vpon paine to forfeit treble the value of the things ſo bought to ſell againe to the king and him that will ſue, to be recouered in any of the kings Courts by A. B. P. I. wherein no W. E. P. But a ſpirituall perſon, who without fraud buyeth any horſes, cattell, goods, &c. with only intent at the buying thereof to imploy the ſame to the neceſſary apparrell of himſelfe, his ſeruants, or houſhold, or for the only occupying or manuring of his glebe or demeſne lands annexed to his church, or for the neceſſary expences of his houſehold, and after the buying or exerciſing thereof, miſliketh the ſame, that they ſhould not be good, profitable, and conuenient for the purpoſes abouesaid, for the which they were bought, then he may lawfully bargain, and put them away. And alſo other ſpirituall perſons, not hauing ſufficient glebe or demeſne lands in their owne hands in the right of their churches, houſes &c. for paſturing of cattell, or increaſe of corne for the only expences of their houſeholds, or for their cariages and iourneyes, may take in farme other lands, and buy and ſell corne and cattell for the only maintenance, tillage, and paſturage of ſuch farmes, ſo that the increaſe thereof be alwaies imployed to the onely expences in their houſholds, and not to buy and ſell againe for any other commoditie, but onely the ouerplus of ſuch corne and cattell aboue the expences of their houſholds, if any ſuch ſhall happen to be bred and increaſed therof, without fraud or couin.

St. 21. H. 8. 13

Oppreſſion by ſpirituall perſons in taking of farmes.

Oppreſſion by the in buying and ſelling.

B

And for the cauſes aforeſaid, by the ſaid ſtatute of An. 21. H. 8. it was moreouer ordained, That no ſpirituall perſon, beneficed with cure, ſhall haue or occupy by himſelf, or any other to his vſe, any Parſonage or Vicarage in farme, of

St. 21. H. 8. 13

Oppreſſion by them in farming of parſonages &c.

of the leaſe or graunt of any other perſon, or take any rent or profit out of any ſuch farme, vpon pain to forf.xl.s.euery weeke ỳ he or any to his vſe ſhall occupy any ſuch farme, & alſo ſhall forf. ten times the value of ſuch profite or rent which he ſhall take out of any ſuch farme, to the K. & I. to be recouered by A.I. P.&c.wherein no W.E.P.&c. And moreouer, no ſpirituall perſon ſhall haue, vſe, or keepe by himſelfe, or any other to his vſe or cõmodity, any Tan-houſe, to be occupied to his vſe or cõmodity, or any Brewhouſe, to any other intent, then only to be ſpent and occupied in his own houſe, vpon paine to forfeit for euery month ſo vſing or occupying any of the ſaid miſteries, x.l. to the K. and I. to be recouered by A.P.I. wherein no W.E.P.&c.

Oppreſſion by keeping a Tanne-houſe, or Brewhouſe

Oppreſſion by taking of exceſſiue toll.

21 Becauſe complaint was made in parliament, that ſome did oppreſſe the people, by taking exceſſiue & outragious toll in market townes, therfore by the ſtat.of Weſt.1. it was enacted, That if any do take outragious toll contrary to the cuſtome of the realme in a market towne, which is the K.towne, and let to fee farme, the K. ſhal ſeiſe the franchiſe of the market into his owne hands: & if it be anothers towne, & ỳ be done by the lord of the towne, the K. ſhal do in like ſort: and if it be done by a bailife or other mean officer, without ỳ cõmandemẽt of his lord, he ſhal reſtore to ỳ plaintife for his outragious taking ſo much as he hath receiued of him, if he hath caried away ỳ toll, & ſhalbe impriſoned xl.daies. St.3.E.1.30.

No oppreſſion ſhalbe done to ſtrangers.

22 The gouernors of this realme hauing from time to time a ſpecial regard that reciprocall courteſie & fauor might be performed to all ſtrangers & aliens, that did come into this realme to marchandize, or to any other good intent, and that Ius gentium might be yeelded vnto them, haue made many good laws and ſtatutes to protect & defend them from oppreſſions & wrongs. As K.Henry the third ordained by the ſtat. of Magna Charta, That all marchants (if they were not lawfully prohibited before) ſhall haue their ſafe & ſure cõduct to depart forth of the realme, & to come into England, & to tarry, & go through England, aſwel by land as by water, to buy or ſell without any manner of euill tols, according to the ancient & lawful cuſtomes (ſauing in time of warre.) And if they be of a country in warre with vs, they ſhalbe attached without hurt of their bodies or goods, vntill it be knowne to vs, or our chiefe iuſtice, how the marchants of our land be vſed in ỳ country wherwith we haue war: and if our marchãts be wel vſed there, theirs ſhalbe ſo likewiſe with vs. And by the ſtat.of an.9.E.3.it was enacted, That all marchant ſtrangers & denizens, & all other ỳ will buy and ſel corne, wines, auer de pois, fleſh, fiſh, & all other liuings, & vitual, wools, clothes & all other things vendible, frõ whence ſoeuer they come, at what place ſoeuer it be, city, borough, towne, port of the ſea, fayre, market, or elſewhere, within the realme, within franchiſe, or without, may freely ſel them to what perſon it ſhal pleaſe thẽ, aſwel forreins as denizens, in groſſe, at retaile, or by parcels, at their wils to all people ỳ will buy the ſame (except to the enemies of the K. and his realme) notwithſtanding any charter, vſage, or cuſtome. And if any diſturbance be done to any marchant ſtranger, or denizen, or to any other, for ỳ ſale of ſuch things in any city, borough, towne, port of the ſea, or other place which hath franchiſe, & the maiors & bailifes, or other, which haue ỳ rule of ſuch franchiſe, being required by ſuch marchants, or other, thereof to prouide remedy, & do not, & thereof be attainted, the franchiſe ſhalbe ſeiſed into the K. hands: and neuertheles, they which haue done ſuch diſturbance, ſhal reſtore to ỳ ſaid marchant his double damages, which he hath therby ſuſtained. And if ſuch diſturbance or interruption be done in ſuch places or townes where no franchiſe is,

St.9.H.3.30

St.9.E.3.1.
St.25.E.3.2

and

and the lord, if he be preſent, or his baylife, conſtable, or other ruler of the ſaid townes and places (in the abſence of the lord) being therein required to doe right, and do not, & thereof be attainted, they ſhal yéeld to the plaintife dammages, as aforeſaid, & the diſturbers in the one caſe, & in the other, as well within the Franchiſes as without, if they be attainted, ſhall haue one yéers impriſonment, and be ranſomed at the kings pleaſure: No alien or denizen vpon the foreſaid paine ſhalbe troubled, but he may fréely buy ſuch things aforeſaid in the ſaid places, & carry them where it pleaſeth him, to his owne vſe, or to the profit of the king or the realme, ſauing that ſuch Marchants aliens ſhall carry

St.6.R.2.10 no wine out of the ſame realme. And by the ſtat. of Ann.6.R.2. it was eſtabliſhed, That all aliens being in friendſhip with the king and the realme, & comming into any cities or townes within the realme, with fiſh, or other victuals, and there tarrying, & returning againe to their owne countries, ſhall be vnder the kings protection: and it ſhall be lawfull to euery of them to cut their fiſh & victuals in pieces, & by retaile or in groſſe to ſell the ſame. And by the ſtat. of an

St.14.H.6.6 14.H.6. it was prouided, That if any man diſturbe any alien to ſell his fiſh in forme aforeſaid, he ſhall forf. x.l. to the K. & him that will ſue. And beſides, the ſtat. of an.31.E.3.10, an.7.R.2.11. an.11.R.2.7. & an.16.R.2.1. were made & prouided to giue liberty, protection, & ſafety to aliens & ſtrangers, & to defend them from wrongs and oppreſſions.

St.23.El.5. 23 It appeareth by the preamble of the ſtat. of A.23.Eliz. that by the erection of ſundry yron mils in diuers places of this realme, not far diſtant from the city of London, & from the downes & ſea coaſts of Suſſex, the neceſſary prouiſion of wood, as well timber fit for building, & other vſes, as alſo all other ſellable woods ſeruing for fuell, doth daily decay, & become ſcant, to the great dammage & oppreſſion of the city of London, & the ſuburbes of the ſame, & of al other perſons, hauing occaſion daily to reſort thither from all the parts of this realm: for the remedy whereof, by the ſame ſtatute it was enacted, That no perſon or perſons ſhal conuert or imploy, or cauſe to be conuerted or imploied to coale or fuell, for the making of yron or yron mettall, in any yron mils, furnace, or hāmer, any maner of wood, or vnderwood, now growing, or which hereafter ſhall grow within the cōpaſſe of 22. miles, from and about the city of London, or the ſuburbes of the ſame, or within 22. miles of the riuer of Thames, from Dorcheſter in the coūty of Oxford downward the ſame riuer of Thames, or within foure miles of the foot of the hils called the Downes, betwixt Arundell and Pemſey in the county of Suſſex, or within foure miles of any of the towns of Winchelſey and Rie, or within two miles of the towne of Pemſey, or within two miles of the towne of Haſtings in the ſaid County, vpon paine to forfeit for euery load of Wood ſo to be imploied, or conuerted into coale or other fuell, for the making of yron or yron mettall in any yron mill, furnace, or hammer, as aforeſaid, xl.s. to the Qu. and I. to be recouered by A.B.P.I. wherein no W.E.P.I. &c. But this Act ſhall not extend to any Woods growing, or to grow in any ſuch parts of the Wields of Surrey, Suſſex, or Kent, within the ſaid 22. miles of the ſaid Citie of London, and the riuer of Thames, as is diſtant aboue 18. miles from the Citie of London, and 8. miles from the ſayd

St.23.El.5 riuer of Thames. And by the ſame ſtatute it was moreouer ordained, That no new yron works ſhalbe erected within 22. miles of the ſaid city of London, nor within 14. miles of the foreſaid riuer of Thames, nor within 4. miles of the Downs aforeſaid, or of ý ſaid towns of Pēſey, Winchelſey, Haſtings, or Rie,

Oppreſſion by making of yron workes.

Oppreſſion by new yron workes

 vpon

vpon paine of an hundred pounds to be likewise recouered and emploied, as is aforesaid. But this act shal not extend to any woods or vnderwoods of Christopher Darrell, growing or which shall grow in the parish of Newdigate. And for the causes and reasons aforesaid, by one other stat. made An. 27. El. it was further enacted, That no person or persons shall make, erect, build, or new set vp, at, or in any place within the counties of Sussex, Surry, or Kent, or any of them, any manner of yron mils, furnace, finary, or bloomary, for the making or working of any maner of yron, or yron mettall, other then either vpon such old & former baies or pennes, whereupon hath lately bin, or at the time of the new erection, shalbe then standing some yron mils, furnace, or hammer, or els in and vpon such lands, as ẏ party or parties so erecting any such intẽded new worke, shall continually furnish the same with sufficient supply of his or their owne wood, standing and growing vpon his or their owne soile or land, being to him or them in fee simple, fee taile, or for terme of life or liues, without impeachmẽt of wast at the least, and not otherwise: Nor shal conuert or imploy, or cause to be conuerted to coales or other fuel for the making or working of yron or yron mettall in or about any yron mils, furnaces, hammers, finary, forge, or blomarie the body or bodies of any sound timber tree or trees, apt for the making of good & sufficient cleft wares, or sawing timber of Oke, Ash, or Elme, growing of the breadth or bignesse of one foot square at the stub, or any part of the same body or bodies of any such tree or trees, vpon paine of forfeiture for euery yron mill, furnace, forge, finarie, or bloomarie made, erected, builded, or set vp, contrary to the tenor and true meaning of this act, three hundred pounds: and for euery body of such timber tree so imploied or conuerted to coales or fuell, for the making or working of yron, as is aforesaid, xl. s. to the Q. and J. to be recouered by A. B. P. or J. wherein no W. E. P. &c. Prouided alwaies, that it shall and may be lawfull to & for the owners of such trees, the bodies whereof haue beene or shalbe from time to time conuerted and imployed to or for any maner of tinber or cleft ware within the wields of Sussex, Surrey, or Kent, or any of them (the same not being within 18. miles of the city of London, or 8. myles of the riuer of Thames, or 4. myles of the townes of Rye & Winchelsey, or within 3. myles of Hastings, or within 4. myles of the foot of the Hils, called the Downes betweene Arundel & Pemsey, in the county of Sussex aforesaid, or any of thẽ) to imploy the tops and offals of all such trees to or for coales, or other fuell, seruing to or for yron works at their owne wils and pleasures: This statute or any other notwithstanding. St. 27. El. 1

Oppression by Brewers.

24 If any Ale or Beere brewer do sell or take for any barrell, kilderkin, or firkin of ale or beere, aboue such prices as shalbe assessed by the Iust. of peace of the shire, or by the mayor, shirife, or head officer of the city, borough, or towne corporat, where the said brewer doth dwell, this is an oppression of al those that do buy the same ale & beere: and therefore by the stat. of An. 23. H. 8. the offendor shall forfeit for euery barrell so sold, 6. s. for euery kilderkin 3. s. 4. d. for euery firkin 2. s. for euery lesse vessell xij. d. and for a greater then a barrell, x. s. to the K. and I. And if any Brewer which breweth beere or ale to sell, shal by himselfe, or any other to his vse, occupy the mysterie of Coopers, or make any barrels, kilderkins, firkins, or other vessell of wood, wherein to put his beere or ale, this is an oppression of Coopers, and by the said stat. of An. 23. H. 8. the offendor shal forf. for euery vessell to the K. and I. 3. s. 4. d. But a brewer may keepe a Cooper to bind, hoope, pinne, and amend his vessels. St. 23. H. 8. 4 St. 23. H. 8. 4

Oppression of Coopers by Brewers.

25 It is an oppression to many thousand woollen cardmakers & cardwier-drawers of this realme, who do liue by the same trade, to haue cards for wooll brought out of forraine regions into this Realme, & here sold to the hinderance of the sale of their like wares. And therefore if any person shall bring or send, or cause to be brought or sent any such cards for wooll to be bartered or sold in St.39.El.14 St.1.Iac.25 England or Wales, by the stat. of An.39.El. he shall forf. them or the very value of them to the K. and him that will seise or sue for the same. Oppression by bringing in of woollen cards.

26 If any person shall erect a new weare along the sea shore, or in any hauen, harbour, or creeke, or within 5. miles of the mouth of any hauen or creeke, or shall willingly take, destroy, or spoile any spawne, fry, or brood of any Sea fish, in any weare, or other engins or deuice whatsoeuer, this is an oppression to all those that liue by or vse fishing in those parts, and a hinderance to the cõ- St.3.Iac.11 monwealth. And therefore by the stat. of An.3.Iac. the offendor shal forfeit for euery time so erecting, setting vp, taking, or destroying of fish, x.l. to the king & I. And if any person shall fish with any drawnet or dagnet vnder three ynches meash, viz. one ynch and a halfe from knot to knot (except for the taking of Smoulds in Norfolke only) or with any net with canuas, or other engine or deuice, wherby the spawne, fry, or brood of sea fish may be destroied, this is also an oppression to all those that liue by, or vse fishing, & a hinderance to the commonwealth: and therefore the offendor shall forf. such net, & for euery time so doing, x.s. whereof the one halfe to him that will sue, and the other halfe to the poore of the city, towne, parish, or liberty, where the offence shal be committed. Oppression by erecting of weares. Oppression by destroying of fish. Oppression by nets.

27 For that buying, selling, and regrating of wood by greedy and couetous persons, is a meane to make the same deerer, and is a great oppression & hurt to St.7.E.6.7. the commonwealth, therefore it is ordained by the stat. of An.7.Ed.6. That if any person shall buy any fuell, coales, or wood, but onely such as will burne or consume the same, or such persons as shall sell the same again by retaile to such as shall burne or consume the same for their owne occupying, without fraud or couin, or wharfingers or bargemen, he shall forf. to the K. & I. the treble value of the same wood, coales, or fuell, as shalbe otherwise bought for lucre & gaine. Oppression by buying & selling of fuell.

St.25.H.8.2 28 If any person shall carrie and conuey, or cause to bee carried and conueyed, any victuals necessarie for mens sustenance to any parts beyond the Sea (vnlesse it be by licence vnder the Kings great seale) sauing for the victualling of Mariners and Marchants of Shippes passing the Sea, and sauing barrelled butter, and meale, to be carried to the parts of Ireland, as hath bin accustomed, this is a meane to enhaunce the prices of victuals within this Realme, an so an oppression to the inhabitants of the Realme. And therefore by the Statute of Anno 25.H.8. the partie offending shall forfeit the value of the thing carried to the K. and I. Oppression by transporting of victuals.

St.37.H.8.9 St.13.El.8 St.39.El.18. 29 By the Statute of Anno 37. H. 8. and confirmed and explaned by the Statute of Anno 13.El. it is ordained to be vnlawfull vsurie and an oppression, if any man do sell any marchandises or wares to another, and buy the same againe within three months for a lesse price, knowing them to be the same that he sold: And so it is if any person by any bargaine, loane, exchange, or shift of Oppression by vsurie.

any

any wares, or other things, ſhall take in gaines for the forbearing of his money or other thing one whole yeare, aboue x.l. in the 100.l. And ſo it is, if any perſon ſhall take aboue x.l. for the forbearing of 100.l. for a yeare, vpon ſale or morgage of lands, of the profites of the ſame lands: and in the caſes aforeſaid the offendor ſhall forfeit for euery ſuch offence the treble value of the wares, marchandizes, and other things ſo bargained, ſold, changed, &c. and the treble value of the iſſues and profits of the ſaid lands ſo taken, by bargaine, ſale, or morgage to the K. and I. and ſhall ſuffer impriſonment, & make fine at the kings pleaſure. And all bands, contracts, and aſſurances collaterall made for payment of any principall, or money to be lent, or couenant to bee performed, for any vſurie in lending or doing of any thing, vpon, or by which loane there ſhalbe reſerued or taken aboue the rate of x.l. for the 100.l. for one yeare, ſhall be vtterly void: and he that doth take, or couenant, or reſerue to take x.l. for the forbearance of 100.l. for one yeare, and ſo after that rate, or any ſumme vnder x.l. ſhal forf. only that x.l. or other leſſe ſumme which he doth ſo take, or couenant or reſerue to take (though it be but a penny, or leſſe then a penny) to the K. and I. &c. If A. doe lend to B. 100.l. and do bargaine & agrée with him, that if I.S. do liue one whole yéere next comming, that then B. ſhal pay him xx.l. for the loane of his 100.l. for a yéere, and if I.S. doe die within the yeere, that then B. ſhall pay him but his 100.l. again, this is an oppreſſion of B. and an vſurious bargaine, and A. is to be puniſhed according to the foreſaid ſtat. of 37.H.8. For as he made & reſerued the intereſt of xx.l. payable, if I.S. ſhould liue one yéere, ſo he might as lawfully haue put in the liues of xx. other perſons, and ſo deluded the true meaning of the makers of the ſaid Statute. And in like ſort, if A. do lend to B. 100.l. for a yéere, & do bargaine with B. that if I.S. ſhall liue vntill the end of that yéere, then B. ſhal pay him xx.l. for the intereſt or loane of his 100.l. for that yéere, and if the ſame I.S. doe die within the ſaid yéere, that then B. ſhall repay to A. but lxxx.l. of his principall money, this is an vſurious contract, and an oppreſſion, & to be puniſhed according to the ſaid ſtatute: for in both the foreſaid caſes there was but a ſhaddow deuiſed by the lender, to protect him from the penalty of that ſtatute, which at the time of his loane he meant to offend. And therefore the ſtat. of 13. Eliz. 8. hath wel prouided, that the ſame ſtat. of 37.H.8. ſhalbe moſt largely & ſtrongly cõſtrued for the repreſſing of vſurie, and againſt all perſons that ſhal offend againſt the true meaning of the ſaid ſtatute, by any way or deuice, directly or indirectly.

Fraudulent ſhadowing of vſurious bargaines. — Co.li.5.70.

30 It is an oppreſſion, and manifeſt and palpable iniury, if any perſon do wilfully, maliciouſly, and vnlawfully cut or cauſe to be cut out the head or pipe of any conduit of any other perſons: Or burne or cauſe to be burned any wain or cart laden with coales, or any other goods, or any heape of wood of any other perſons prepared & felled for making of coales, billet, or Tallwood: Or to cut or cauſe to bee cut out the tongue of any tame beaſt, being aliue, of any other perſons: Or to cut, or cauſe to be cut off, the eare or eares of any of the kings ſubiects, otherwiſe then by authoritie of Law, chance-medley, ſudden affray, or aduenture: Or to barke any Appletrées, Peaaretrées, or other fruit trées of any other perſons: in all which caſes, by force of the ſtatute of Ann. 37.H.8. the offendor ſhall forfeit to the party grieued treble dammages, to be recouered by action of Treſpas at the common law, and to the king 10.l. for a fine.

Oppreſſion by cutting out the head or pipe of a conduit.
Oppreſſion by burning a cart laden.
Oppreſſion by cutting off eares.
Oppreſſion by barking of trées.
St.37.H.8.6

Oppression by hawking or hunting in corn growing.

31 It is an oppression, and a resolued intent to do hurt & wrong to others, if any person shall hawke or hunt with his spaniels in any ground (except his owne) where corne or graine shall then grow, at such time as any eared or codded corne or graine shalbe standing and growing vpon the same, or before such time as such corne or graine shalbe shocked, cocked, hiled, or copped: in which cases the stat. made an. 23. El. hath ordained, That the offendor shall forf. for euery time that he shall so hawke or hunt, without consent of the owner of the corne, to such person as shalbe owner of the eared or codded corne, xl. s.

St. 23. El. 10.

Oppression by taking of fish.

32 If any person shal by day or night vnlawfully, without authority, break, cut downe, cut out, or destroy the head or dam of any pond, poole, moat, stagn, stewe, or seuerall pit, wherein fish shal be put, or stored by the owner thereof: Or shall wrongfully fish in any of the said seuerall ponds &c. to the intent to destroy, kill, take, or steale away any of the same fish, against the will of the owner or possessor thereof, not hauing lawfull authority so to do, this is an oppression to the said owner or possessor: and therefore by the stat. of an 5. El. it is enacted, That the offendor being lawfully conuict of any of the said offences, at the suit of the K. or the party grieued, shall pay to the party grieued his treble damages, suffer imprisonment 3. moneths, & find sufficient surety for his good abearing for the space of 7. yeeres, or els remain in prisō without baile or mainprise, vntill he hath found such surety. And it shalbe lawfull for the party grieued to take his further remedy against the offēdor for his losse & damages, and vpon satisfaction or confession of the dammages, to release the offendor of the suretiship and good abearing at any time within vij. yeares.

St. 5. El. 21

Oppression by decaying of townes & houses of husbandry.

33 I will draw toward an end of this title of Oppression, with one of the greatest and most durable of all oppressions, viz. with oppression by pulling downe of Towns, houses of Husbandry, and decaying of Tillage. When the realme ceased to be oppressed by the long & tedious ciuile warres, which before were many yeeres continued betweene the ij. houses of Yorke and Lancaster, and that K. Edward the fourth had ouerthrowne Q. Margaret & Prince Edward her sonne at Tewksbury field, & setled the title of the Crowne, & planted peace in the Realme, then some men of stirring spirits diuerting their bloudy humors to couetous humors, pulled downe townes, & laid wast houses of husbandry, thrusting forth of dores men, women, & children, & conuerting the same to their owne priuat vses: which offence then daily increasing (though it were but in Cunabilis, being about 120. yeres sithence) was so bewailed, exclaimed of, & cried out vpon in open parliament, that the same may in a sort be resēbled to the pitifull lamentation which the prophet Ieremy (sitting downe weeping) made, after ẏ temple of God & the city of Hierusalē were destroyed, & ẏ priests, Leuits, & Elders slaine by Nabuchadnezzar K. of Babilon: Or the same may be cōpared to those wofull miseries & calamities which ẏ prophet Esay foretold should after fall vpō the said great city of Babilon: for as it appeareth by ẏ stat. of an. 4. H. 7. 12. & 19. & 7. H. 8. 1. it was then holden, That by the desolation & pulling downe of houses and townes, and laying to pasture land, which customably hath beene manured & occupied with tillage, idlenesse (the ground and beginning of all mischiefes) doth increase: men, women, and children, that were dayly occupied, and liued by the sowing of Corne, and breeding of Cattell, and other increase, were diminished: husbandry, the greatest commodity of this Realme for sustenance, was decaied, Churches were destroyed, the

Threnæ Ierem.

Esay 13.

St. 4. H. 7. 12
St. 7. H. 8. 1.

seruice

seruice of God was withdrawne, Christian people there buried are not praied for, the Patrons and Curats were wronged, Cities and market townes were brought to great ruine and decay, necessaries for mans sustenance were made scarce and deare, the people of the realme were sore minished, the power & defence therof was feebled & decayed, to the high displeasure of God, & against his lawes, and to the subuersion of the Commonwealth, & desolation of the same. Which grieuous & dolefull mone made, and enormities so displaied, the grand counsell of this realme hauing commiseration vpon, did indeuor to reforme at seuerall parliaments: as appeareth by the stat. of An. 4. H. 7. 12. & 19. Ann. 7. H. 8. 1. An. 27. H. 8. 22. An. 5. E. 6. 6. An. 2. & 3. P. & M. 8. & An. 5. El. 2. which said stat. were all after repealed by a stat. made an. 39. El. And then by the same St. 39. El. 1
stat. it was enacted, That euery house that now hath (viz. 24. die Octob. an. 39 Reg. El. & An. Do. 1597.) or heretofore had 20. acres of arable land, meddow, and pasture, or more thereunto belonging, and so occupied or letten to farme by the space of 3. yeeres together, at any time sithence the beginning of the Qu. raigne that now is (& which is not or hath not bin the castle or dwelling house of any nobleman or gentleman, nor the chiefe mansion house of any manor) is and shal be adiudged a house of husbandry for euer: and all acres spoken of in this statute, shalbe adiudged acres according to the Statute or Ordinance de terris mensurandis.

which is an house of husbandry.

which is an acre of land.

The forf. for not building a house of husbandry.

And euery person & persons, bodies politique and corporat, which shall offend in not building, erecting, repairing, continuing or maintaining of houses of husbandry, according to the purport & true meaning of ẏ said statute, shall, for euery house that shal not be erected, builded, repaired, continued or maintained in necessary reparations tenantable, according to the intent of the same act, by the space of one yeere, forf. x. l. and so yeerely x. l. vntill ẏ same shalbe sufficiẽtly erected, continued, repaired &c. and for euery acre of land, meddow, or pasture, which shal not be laid vnto, or let with such houses of husbandry, when the same shalbe demised, shal forf. for euery yeere that he or they shal so offend, the summe of x. s. as long & as often as such acre shall not in those respects be ordered & vsed according to the intent of this act: of which forf. the K. shal haue one part, the poore of the parish where the offence was committed the second part, and he that will sue in any of the K. courts of record at Westminster the third: and if none will sue, thẽ the K. shal haue also that third part. But no offendor shall be impeached or sued by vertue of this act, except the suit be brought and commenced by the party for the king & himselfe, within 2. yeares of the same offence done: but where the suit shalbe prosecuted for the K. only &c. then within 3. yeeres after the offence done.

within what time the suit shalbe presẽted

Oppression by decay of Tillage.

34 By the stat. of an. 39. El. 2. it was ordained, That all lands and grounds St. 39. El. 2
which now are vsed in tillage, or for tillage, hauing bin tillable lands, fields or grounds, such as next before the first day of this parliament haue beene by the space of 12. yeres together at the least vsed in tillage, or for tillage, according to the nature of the soile, & course of husbandry vsed in that part of the countrey, shall not be cõuerted to any sheepe pasture, or to the grazing or fatting of cattel by the occupiers or possessors thereof, but shall according to the nature of that soile, & course of husbandry vsed in ẏ part of the country continue to be vsed in tillage, and for tillage for corne & graine, & not for wood. And if any person, body politique or corporat shal offend against ẏ premisses, thẽ the offẽdor shal forf. for euery acre not restored or not cõtinued, as is aforesaid, x. s. for euery yere ẏ he or they so offẽd, to be diuided into 3. parts, & then to be distributed as is aforesaid, so ẏ the suit be cõmenced or prosecuted wᵗin ẏ time or times before mentioned. I haue for some special causes herein set down but only the effectes & penalties

men-

mentioned in the two last specified stat. of an. 39. El. 1. & 2. omitting purposely the exceptions, reseruations, prouisoes, and some other matters in the same.

Wherefore the two last stat. bee not set down at large

35 As Menaces, Assaults, Batteries, Imprisonments, Maihems, Riots, Routs, vnlawful assemblies, Forgeries, Periuries, Maintenances, Deceits, Extortions, Oppressions, & all other the crimes before mentioned, haue from one age to another bin noted & accused as maladies in the common wealth, and adiudged & condemned as professed enemies to the peace of the realme, and by seuerall lawes & statutes diuers penalties haue bin imposed vpō the transgressors thereof, in a measure certaine, & within some limits: So the prouidence of our forefathers sounding déeper into the corruptiō of mans nature, & foreséeing that sometime his cholerike passions, & turbulent spirit, sometime the gall and bitternes of his heart, sometime his couetous & insatiable affections, & eftsoons his secret desires & deuices of reuenge, doe carry him headlong into exorbitant & vnusuall designments & practises, be they neuer so contrary to the Lawes of God, of Nature, & Reason, & in seueral degrées further thē our said lawmakers did then either fore-thinke, feare, or by particular words restraine: & knowing also, that the subtiltie of the Serpent (and of men of the serpents nature) doth excéed the other beasts of the field: haue therefore erected & established the most honorable Court of Starre-chamber, to the intent that the wisedome of that Court, authorized partly by the K. prerogatiue, & partly by seuerall lawes & statutes of the realme, might search forth the serpents subtilty, and vtterly crush & dash the same: and séeing ẏ dead letter of each law doth ordaine in most cases but one kind of punishment for one sort of offence, & the circumspection of the makers of that law (were they neuer so wise or experiēced) could not foresée all the circumstances which in time might ensue in the maner of transgressing of that law: Therfore the lords & others of that high Court, being now the speaking law, & representing the persons of the dead lawmakers, & carefull expositors of their meanings, by their graue foresights & déep considerations do looke into those offēces which be cōmitted contrary to the same lawes, do search into euery quarter, corner, & circumstance therof, & do pierce through the very bowels & intrailes of them, and the transgressors thereof: as what persons, of what estate, degrée, ability, function, or calling cōmitted the offēce, to whom, in what manner, in what place, at what time, before whom, with what number, & for what cause the same was done, & then do inflict punishmēt vpon the transgressors thereof, first according to the lawes & statutes therfore prouided, & then do qualifie or aggrauate the same, according to the circumstances. As it is a Riot punishable by the stat. of An. 13. H. 4. & Ann. 2. H. 5. if thrée persons, or more, do assemble together, and beat or mayme a man, pull downe his house, pale, or ditch wrongfully &c. so if a great number of meane persons, of small ability or credit, shall assault a péere of the realme, or a Knight, or Esquire, that is Custos Rotulorum of the shire, or a Justice of peace and Quorum in his country, shall strip and whip him, shall pull downe his house to the ground, shall set him in the stockes, or on the pillory, shall beat his wife and children, kill his cattell, and spoyle his corne before his face, and shall vse other acts and wordes of infamie and disgrace vnto him, and only for that he did cause some lawfull punishment to be inflicted vpon certaine of them for their crimes: notwithstanding all these or such like misdemeanors, be neither Treason nor Felony by the Law, but a Riot; and yet in respect of the basenesse of the parties which committed this wrong, of the cause for the which they put it in practise, of the worthinesse of the person, and of his place, vpon whom it was executed, of the barbarous course taken in the performance therof, of the perillous exāple giuen

All the former offences punishable in the Star-chāber.

St. 13. H. 4. 7
St. 2. H. 5. 8

giuen to other malefactors, these riotors deserue to bée censured with a much sharper punishment then the former. For as there be no bounds obserued by lewd and wicked persons of their outrages, so be there no certaine means or limits assigned of their punishments; but the said most honourable Court of estate may draw forth his Maiesties sword of iustice, and first punish the said offences according to the particuler lawes and statutes prouided therfore, and then euery person transgressing by himselfe, according to the circumstance of his demerits: as partly may appeare by the statute of anno 3.H.7. which ex- St.3.H.7.1.
presseth some parts of the authority giuen to the Lords of the said Court, and more by a branch of the statute of Magna Charta, whereby it is enacted, That St.9.H.3.14
euery fréeman shall be amerced, viz. punished for reasonable cause, & according to the quantity of his offence. And further, by the statute of Anno 33.H.8. St.33.H.8.1
which giueth the lords of the said Court of Starre-chamber authority to punish those, who by counterfeit letters or tokens shall get other mens goods into their hands, by imprisonment, setting vpon the pillory, or other corporall paine whatsoeuer (except death.)

Trea-

Treasons.

1 Crimen lesæ Maiestatis, in our English tongue called Treason, is a great offence done to ye Maiestie of gouernement and the peace of the land, which the wisdome of this Realme hath from age to age so much hated and abhorred, that they haue persecuted those that were guiltie therin, with most violent and vntimely death, and with extreame and seuere tortures: they haue ordained, that an offendor therein shall be hanged, and cut downe aliue, that his bowels shall bee cut off, and burned in his sight, that his head shall bee seuered from his bodie, that his quarters shall bee diuided asunder, and disposed at the Kings pleasure, and made food for the birds of the aire, or the beasts of the field, and that his wife and children shall be thrust out of his house and liuings, that his seed and blood shall be corrupted, that his lands and goods shall be confiscated, and (as by the statute of 29. H.6.1. it is ordained of the Traitor Iohn Cade) he shall be called a false Traytor for euer. And as our respectiue and considerat forefathers haue deuised to yeeld vnto those grieuous offendors Legem talionis, and to teare their bodies, lands, and goods, who doe practise to rent and pull asunder this Maiestie of gouernement, by destroying the head, or such as are like to be the principall succeeding members thereof, or by diuiding the bodie into parts, or by weakning the force and strength thereof, or by subuerting the chiefe Magistrats of iustice, or by counterfeiting, stainìng, or blemishing of the peculiar and royall Ensignes, Cognisances, and Sinewes thereof: so haue they beene carefull and prouident, that there should be no greater number of those dreadfull, sharpe, and bitter lawes, than vrgent necessitie, for the preseruation of that Maiestie of gouernment required. And because it was in former times greatly doubted, and ofttimes called in question amongst the Sages of the Realme, and learned in the lawes, which offences were by the common law high Treason, and which not, and which were petit Treason, and which not, and seuerall men were of seuerall opinions therein, and to the intent that al future ages might know, and be more vigilant to eschew the penalties thereof, King Edward the third at his Parliament begun at Westminster the thirteenth day of Ianuarie, in the 25. yere of his raign, at the request of his Lords, and petition of his Commons, made a declaration thereof in manner as hereafter followeth, viz. It is high Treason where a man doth compasse, or imagin the death of our Soueraigne Lord the King, or of our Ladie the Queene his wife, or of their eldest sonne and heire, or if a man doth deflower the Kings wife, or the Kings eldest daughter, being vnmaried, or the kings eldest sonne

Marginal notes: What is Treason. — St.25.E.3.2 — High treason.

and heires wife: or if a man doe leuie warre against our Lord the king in his Realme, or be adherent to the kings enemies in his Realme, giuing to them aid and comfort in his Realme, or else where, and thereof be probably attainted of open deed, by people of their owne condition: And if a man do counterfeit the Kings great Seale, or his priuie Seale, or his money (which offences Bracton doth terme Crimen falsi) And if a man bring false money into this Realme, counterfeit to the money of England, knowing the money to be false, to marchandise, or make paiment, in deceit of our Lord the King, and his people: And if a man kill the Chauncellor, Treasurer, or the Kings Iustice of the one Bench or the other, Iustices of Eire, and of Assises, and all other Iustices assigned to heare and determine, beeing in their places doing their Offices. And it is to bee vnderstood, that in the cases aforesaid it ought to bee adiudged Treason, which extendeth to our Lord the King and his royall Maiestie. And of such Treason the forfeiture of the escheat doth appertaine to our Lord the King, as well of the lands and tenements holden of others, as of himselfe. And moreouer there is another manner of Treason, that is to say, When a seruant killeth his Master, or a wife her husband: or when a secular or religious man killeth his Prelat, to whom he oweth faith and obedience. And such manner of Treason giueth the escheats to euery Lord of his owne fee. And because many other cases of like Treason may happen in time to come, which a man cannot thinke of, nor declare at this present: It is accorded, that if any other case supposed to be treason, that is not before specified, doth happen of new before Iustices, the Iustices shall stay without proceeding to iudgement of Treason, vntill the case be declared and shewed before the King and his Parliament, whether it ought to be adiudged Treason, or other Felonie. And in case any man of this Realme doe ride armed, openly or secretly, with people armed, against another, for to kill or rob him, or to take and detaine him vntill he hath made fine and ransome to be deliuered, it is not the King or his Counsels wil, that in such case it shall be adiudged Treason, but it shall be adiudged Felonie or Trespasse, according to the law of the land in auncient time vsed, and according as the case doth require. And if in such case, or any like, the Iustices haue adiudged it Treason before this time, and thereby the offendors lands and tenements haue come into the kings hands as forfeit, the chiefe Lords of the fee shal haue their Escheats of those tenements which be holden of them, whether the same tenements be in the hands of the King, or of any other, by gift, or in other manner (sauing to our Lord the King the yeare and wast, and the forfeiture of the chattels which doe belong vnto him in the cases aforesaid.) And in such cases writs of Scire facias shal be awarded against the tenants of the land, without any other originall, and without allowing the kings protection in the same suit. And touching those lands which be in the kings hands, there shalbe writs granted to the Sherifes of the Counties where the lands be, to deliuer them out of the kings hands without delay.

Bracton de Corona, cap. 3.

Petit treason.

2 By which statute it doth appeare that there be two sorts of Treason by the auncient common lawes of this Realme, viz. High Treason, and Petit Treason; High Treason when any of the grieuous offences aforesaid be done, or attempted to the vniuersall and generall Maiestie of gouernment, that is to say, to the bodie of the whole Commonwealth, or to the King, the head, ruler, and directer thereof, in his person, wife, issues, or authoritie. Petit Treason is when the bloudie and grieuous offence of wilfull murder is done and committed

High treason.

Petit treason.

mitted by an inferiour person, and one in subiection to another, that hath a dominion, or a kind of Maiestie in gouernmẽt ouer the same partie. And though sithence the before mentioned Statute of 25.Ed.3. diuers other offences haue béene made Treason by the Statutes of 21.R.2. 3.H.5. 4.H.5. 8.H.6. 14.H.6. 20.H.6. 4.H.7. 22.H.8. 26.H.8. 27.H.8. 28.H.8. 31.H.8. 32.H.8. 33.H.8. 35.H.8. & 1.Ed.6. yet euerie of the succéeding ages were soone wearie of the sayd new Treasons, and thought that the grieuous paines and most hainous punishments of them were too heauy and vnsupportable for the Subiects of this Realme to endure. As the Lords and Commons in the Parliament holden Anno 4.H.4.10. did complaine, that diuers paines were ordained to be Treason by the statute of 21.R.2. insomuch that no man did know how he ought to behaue himselfe, to doe, to speake, or say, for doubt of such paines: and thereupon it was enacted, That in no time to come any treason shall bée adiudged otherwise, than was ordained by the Statute of 25.Ed. 3. And long time after, the makers of the statute of Anno 1.Mar. considering and rehearsing, that the state of euerie King, Ruler, and Gouernour of any Realme, Dominion, or Comminaltie, consisteth more assured by the loue and fauour of the subiects towards their Gouernour, than in the dread and feare of lawes made with rigorous paynes, and extreame punishment: and that lawes iustly made for the preseruation of the Commonwealth, without extreame punishment or great penaltie, are more often obeyed and kept, than lawes and statutes made with great and extreame punishments; and in speciall such lawes and statutes so made, whereby not only the ignorant, vnlearned, and rude people, but also learned and expert persons minding honestie, are often trapped and snared, yea many times for words only, without any other fact or déed done or perpetrated: and therefore to the intent that the seueritie of such like extreame, dangerous, and perillous laws might be abolished, and adnulled, by the said statute of Anno 1.M.Parl.1. it was ordained, That from thenceforth none act, déed, or offence, being by act of Parliament or stat. made Treason, Petit Treason, or Misprisiõ of Treasõ, by words, writing, ciphering déeds, or otherwise whatsoeuer, shalbe taken, had, déemed, or adiudged to bée High treason, Petit treason, or Misprisiõ of treason, but only such as be declared & expressed to be high Treason, Petit treason, or Misprision of Treason, in or by the stat. of 25.E.3. concerning Treason, or the declarations of Treasons, and none other: Nor that any paines of death, penalty, or forfeiture in any wise ensue, or be to any offendor or offendors, for the doing or committing of any Treason, Petit Treason, or Misprision of Treason, other than such as bée in the said stat. of 25.E.3 ordained and prouided. By force of which stat. made Anno 1.M. the subiects of this Realme were eased and vnburdened of al acts, déeds, and offences, made or declared to be treason, by the space of two hundred and more years before: Or as it may more aptly be said of all offences made Treason by any stat. or act of parliament whatsoeuer. But sithence the stat. of repeale made Anno 1.M. there haue béen diuers other offences made or declared to be treason by the stat. of An. 1.M.6. 1.&2.P.& M.11. 5.El.11. 18. El.1. 5.El.1. 13.El.2. 23.El.1. 27.El.2. & 3.Iac.4. whereof the first foure were but as an addition, augmentation, enlargement, or exposition of the before specified Treasons ordained by the common law, or declared by the foresaid stat. of 25.E.3. All which said last mentioned Treasons I will set downe and expresse verbatim, after I haue somewhat more particularly expressed how the Sages and Iudges of this Realme haue construed and expounded seueral

St.4.H.4.10

St.1.M.

A repeale of former treasons.

Offences made treason by Statutes.

branches of the said statute of explanation made Anno 25. Ed. 3.

3 The foresaid statute of 25. Ed. 3. doth confirme it to be high treason, for any person to compasse or imagine the death of our Soueraigne Lord the K. the Quéen, &c. by which words it doth approue what a great regard and reuerend respect the common law hath alwayes had to the person of the K. which it hath endeuored religiously & carefully to preserue, as a thing consecrated by almightie God, and by him ordained, to be the head, health, & wealth of the kingdome, and therefore it hath ingrafted a déepe and setled feare in the hearts of all sorts of subiects, to offer violence or force vnto it, vnder the paine of high treason; insomuch as if he that is non compos mentis do kil, or attempt to kill the K. it shal be adiudged in him high treason, though if he do cōmit petit treason, homicide, or larceny, it shall not be imputed vnto him as felonie, for that hee knew not what he did, neither had he malice prepenced, nor a felonious intent. And this law doth not only restrain al persons from laying violent hands vpon the person of the K. but also by preuention it doth inhibit them so much as to compasse or imagin, or to deuise or thinke in their hearts to cut off by violent or vntimely death, the life of the K. Qu. &c. for the only compassing or imagination, without bringing it to effect, is High treason, because that compassing and imagination doth procéed from false and traiterous hearts, and out of cruell, bloudy, and murdering minds. But séeing compassing & imagination is a secret thing lying hidden in the breast of man, and cannot bee knowne but by an open fact or déed, it is requisit to haue some thing or means to notifie the same to others, before it can be discouered and punished: and therfore if it be vttered by words it is a sufficient signification therof. If two, thrée, or more, doe conspire to commit High treason, as to compasse or imagin the kings death, or to leuie warre, and some of them after do commit and execute it, this is High treason in them all by the common law.

Leges Aluredi cap. 4. Co. li. 4. 124

Compassing or imagining the death of the K. &c.

Bracton de Corona, cap. 3.

19. H. 6. 47. 13. H. 8. 13. Co. li. 1. 28.

Conspiracy by diuers, executed by some of them.

P. 1. M. Dyer 98. Co. li. 1. 28.

4 And because by the said statute of 25. E. 3. it is declared to be High treason, to leuie warre against the king in his Realme, or to be adherent to his enemies, aiding them in his Realme, or elsewhere: therefore if a subiect borne of this Realme being beyond the seas, doth practise with a prince or gouernor of another countrey to inuade this Realme with great power, and doe declare, where, how, and by what meanes the inuasion may best bee made, it is High treason: for an inuasian with great power cannot be, but of likelyhood it will tend to the destruction or great perill of the K. and hurt to the Realme: & moreouer the said offendor hath manifested himselfe to be adherent to the K. enemy and to aid him with his counsell, though not in the Realme, yet elsewhere. And this offence shalbe tryed in the K. Bence, or elsewhere, before such commissioners, and in such countie, as the king by commission shal appoint, according to the stat. of 35. H. 8. 2. If a man do confederat with others to destroy the king, subuert the realme, and to aduance a rebell to be king, and doe indeuor by such friends & meanes as he can to put the same in practise, this is high treason, and he shall suffer death, and forfeit, as in case of High treason. And if a man accōpanied with a conuenient number of persons, do ride towards the king, to help him in his wars, & another doth encounter him, and kill him, this is high treason, for he doth leuie warre against the king, who doth incounter in fight such as

Leuying of warr, or adhering to the K. enemies.

13. Eliz. Dyer 298.

The tryall of his offence.

Co. li. 1. 28

21. Ed. 3. 23.

as be assisting to the king in his wars, and he is adherent, and giueth comfort
to the K. enemies, who in open field giueth battell to the K. friends, for taking
he K. part. Before the foresaid stat. of 25. E. 3. it was adiudged Treason to kill
22. Ass. p. 49 the K. messenger, who was sent to execute his commandement.

5 And though the words of the foresaid stat. of 25. E. 3. be, That it is High Counterfeiting the kings Seale.
Treason for a man to counterfeit the K. great seale, or his priuie seale, yet the
2. H. 4. 26. law doth construe it a counterfeiting of the great seal, to take the ware printed
40. Ass. p. 33 with the great seale, to affixe it to a writing made in the K. name, and to vse it
as the kings commission, to gather money of the kings people, though this is
not making or counterfeiting of a new seale, but the abusing of an old seale, to
remoue it from one Patent to another, and thereby to abuse the K. prerogatiue
and authoritie, and to exact money of his subiects. And so though the letter of
A. 37. H. 8. the law be not infringed, yet the meaning of the law, which is the essence and
Brooke substance of the law, is broken; wherefore the offendor shalbe punished in this
Treason 3 case as a traitor: And yet when a Chaplein had affixed an old seale of the kings
to a Patent of Non-residence, it was adiudged but Misprision of treason, and
not High treason. And notwithstanding that in the foresaid stat. of 25. Ed. 3. Consenters & aiders to treason.
there is no mention made of any consenters or aiders to this counterfeiting,
yet the consenters and aiders be taken to be within the purview of this stat.
19. H. 6. 47. for in that they be aiders and consenters to a treason, they be offendors, and in
treason all the offendors be principals, and none accessarie, and therefore they
be principall traitors in this fact.

6 And whereas it appeareth by the foresaid stat. of Anno 25. E. 3. that if a Counterfeiting, but not vttering of false money.
6. H. 7. 13. 1. R. 3. 1. man do counterfeit or forge the K. money, it shall be Treason; the meaning of
the said law is, that the counterfeiting or forging of the sayd money, shall bee
construed and expounded Treason, although the offendor doth not vtter the
same in paiment: for the K. by his prerogatiue royall, hath the onely authority
to coyne money, and to make the price or value of the quantitie thereof, and to
3. H. 7. 10. set a seale therupon. But if false mony be made within the Realm, in Ireland,
11. Eliz. or any the Dominions thereof, and another knowing thereof doth vtter it in
Dyer 266. paiment, he committeth not high treason, but misprision of treason. And the
receiuing, helping, and comforting of him which hath coyned money of false
mettall like to the money of England, knowing him to haue coyned it, is but
misprision of treason. A woman that did coine money before the foresaid stat. of
23. Ass. p. 2 25. E. 3. was adiudged a traitor, and burned for the same, which doth proue,
that the said offence, amongst the others before rehearsed, was high treason by
the common law, and not newly ordained by that stat. If he which doth coine He who coineth money by warrant doth abuse it.
3. H. 7. 10. money by the kings warrant in the tower of London, or elsewhere, maketh it
lesse in weight by much than the old and antient ordinance, or coyneth false
mettal, it is high treason in him: But yet they which do vtter it in paiment to
the K. subiects within the Realme be not traitors, for it is in them onely Misprision of Treason.

7 And whereas the words of the foresaid stat. of 25. E. 3. be, That there is Petit treason.
another manner of Treason, when a seruant killeth his Master, &c. although
there be therein no mention made of the Mistresse; yet if a man or woman ser-

A seruant killeth his Master or Mistresse. — 19.H.6.47. 12.Ass.p.30

uant do kill his or her Mistresse or Dame, it is Petit treason, and within the purview and meaning of the said stat. though it be not within the letter thereof, and it was Petit Treason by the common law: for the seruant is retained to serue as well the one as the other, and to be obedient as well to the one as to the other, and one of them hath affiance in the seruant as wel as the other. And if a seruant kill his Master after he is out of seruice, if it be upon a premeditat malice conceiued against him during the time that he was in seruice, it is petit Treason: for the execution of the fact doth respect and looke backe to the originall cause, which was the malice the seruant conceiued against his Master when he was his seruant. If a seruant do procure one to kill his Master, who doth kill him in the seruants presence, this is petit Treason in the seruant: but if he do kill him in the seruants absence, then is it not petit Treason in the seruant, but he is accessory to murder. A woman seruant conspired with a stranger to rob her Mistresse, and at a time appointed in the night she did let him into the house, and led him to the bed with a candle, where her Mistresse lay sleeping, & the same stranger killed her Mistresse in her bed, the seruant saying or doing nothing, but holding the candle: in this case the seruant committed petit Treason, and was adiudged a principall therein, though the partie who did the bloudy fact, was but a murderer. If a wife and a seruant do conspire to kill the husband, and appoint a time and place for it, and the seruant killeth the husbād in the wiues absence, this is petit Treason in them both, though the wife bée absent: and yet the law is otherwise if he be not a seruant, but a stranger: for if a woman procure a strāger to kil her husband, which he doth in her absence, she shalbe hanged and not burned, for that the principall offendor was a murderer, and not a Traitor, as the seruant was in the former case. And so abettors and procurers, be within this part of the stat. touching petit Treason, although they are not expresly named within the letter of the statute.

Margin: 33.Ass.p.7 — Co.li.1.99. — 40.Ass.p.25 — 2.& 3.P.& M.Dy.128 — *The wife conspireth with another to kill her husband.* — P.16.Eliz. Dyer 332. — 4.Ass.p.25. — *Abettors and procurers in petit Treason*

The son killeth father or mother. — 21.Ed.3.17.

8 Some do affirme it to be petit Treason in the sonne, or daughter, to kill the father or mother, and some others doe not thinke it to bée so, unlesse the father or mother doe at the same time giue meat and drinke to that sonne or daughter which doth kill him, or her, as to a seruant, and so, that the Treason should be in respect of the duetie of seruice broken, and not of duetie of nature violated.

Breaking of prison. — 1.H.6.5.

9 It is Petit Treason if a man outlawed of felonie, and imprisoned in the K. Bench, be attainted for breaking of prison, and letting at libertie such persons as were there imprisoned for Treason, and the offendor shalbe drawn and hanged. And it hath béene adiudged petit Treason in some age, and felony in another age, for one of the inditors to discouer the K. counsell and his fellowes: but sithence it hath béene taken onely as finable to the King.

An Inditor doth discouer counsell. — 27.Ass.p.68 — S.Felonie &c.15.

Treasons by Statutes.

10 Besides the before mentioned offences which be explained to be Treasons by the common lawes of this realme, and besides all the offences aforesaid, which were made Treason by the seuerall stat. before rehearsed, and after repealed by the foresaid stat. of An. 1. M. there haue béen sithence that time seuerall other offences made high Treason by seueral stat. which I wil set down in order as they were made, and, as néere as I can gather, expresse the causes

why

why they were made. For as much as by the lawes of this Realme small and no due and condigne punishment was before prouided for such euill disposed persons, as should counterfeit or forge such kind of gold or siluer of other realms, as is not the proper coine of this realm, and yet permitted by the Queens consent, and heretofore suffered by her progenitors to be currant in paiment within this realme: nor for such persons as should counterfeit the Queens signe manuall, her priuie signet, or her priuie seale, therfore by a stat. made An. 1. M. 6. it was enacted, That if any person or persons shall hereafter falsly forge or counterfeit any such kind of gold or siluer, as is not the proper coine of this realme, and is or shalbe currant within this realme by the consent of the Q. her heires or successors: or if any person or persons at any time hereafter, doe falsly forge or counterfeit the Qu. signe manuall, priuie signet, or priuie seale, that then euery such offence shalbe deemed & adiudged high treason, & the offendors therein, their counsellors, procurers, aiders, and abettors, being conuict according to the lawes of this realme, of any the said offences, shall be likewise deemed and adiudged Traitors against the Qu. her heires and successors, and the realme, and shall suffer and haue such paines of death, forf. of lands, goods, and cattels, and lose the priuiledge of all Sanctuarie, as in case of high Treason is vsed and ordained.

St. 1. M. 6.

Forging the coins of other realms currāt in this realme

Forging the Kings signet Manuall, &c.

11 Where sundrie coynes of gold and siluer of other realms, not being the proper coine of this realme of England, and by the sufferance of the K. and Q. be currant in paiment within this realm, many euil disposed persons for their owne corrupt lucre, did bring into this realme from the parts beyond the sea, great quantitie of forged and counterfeit money, like to the said coine of other forreine realmes, and did vtter the same by marchandises, and otherwise, to diuers subiects of this realme, to their great damage, for that there was not any sufficient law then prouided, for the condigne punishment of the offendors in that behalfe, therfore by a stat. made An. 1. & 2. P. & M. it was established, That if any person or persons shal bring from the parts beyōd the sea into this realme, or into any of the dominions of the same, any such false and counterfeit coine of money being currant within this realme, as is aforesaid, knowing the same coine or mony to be false & counterfeit, to the intent to vtter or make paiment with the same within this realme, or any the dominions of the same, by marchandizing, or otherwise, then all & euery such person or persons so offending, as is aforesaid, their counsellors, procurers, aiders, and abettors, in that behalfe, shalbe deemed and adiudged to be offendors in high Treason, and shall suffer (after lawfull conuiction or attainder thereof) such paines of death, losse and forf. of lands, goods, and cattels, as other offendors shall do in cases of high Treason. And all & euery person and persons, that shalbe accused or impeached of any of the offences contained and prouided for in this stat. or of any other offence or offences, cōcerning the impairing, coūterfeiting, or forging of any coin currant within this realme, shal and may be indicted, conuicted, or attainted by such like euidence, & in such manner and forme, as hath beene vsed within this realme at any time before Anno 1. Ed. 6. Any Statute, custome, law, &c. notwithstanding.

St. 1. & 2. P. & M. 11.

Bringing in of counterfeit money.

By what euidence an offendor shalbe indicted or attainted.

12 Because diuers false and euill disposed persons, for wicked lucre & gains sake, did diminish impaire, and falsifie the money and coynes currant within this

Clipping, washing, rounding or filing of money. this Realme, by clipping, washing, rounding, and filing therof, to the dishonor of the Quéene, and losse of the subiects of this Realme: for the remedy wherof by a stat. made An. 5. El. it was enacted, That clipping, washing, rounding, or filing for wicked lucre or gaines sake, of any the proper monies or coynes of this realme, or the dominions therof, or of the monies or coines of any other realme, allowed and suffered to be currant within this realme, or the dominions thereof, at this present, or that hereafter at any time shalbe the lawful monies or coines of this realme, or the dominions thereof, or of any other realme, and by proclamation allowed and suffered to bee currant here, by the Qu. her heires or successors, shalbe taken and adiudged by vertue of this act to be treason: and the offendors therein, their counsellors, consenters, and aiders, shalbe taken, déemed, and adiudged as offendors in Treason: and being thereof lawfully conuicted or attainted, according to the due order of the law, shall suffer death, and lose & forf. all his and their goods and cattels, and also shall lose and forf. all his and their lands and tenements, during his and their naturall life or liues onely. St. 5. El. 11.

To whom the forfeiture shall accrue. And euery person which hath any lawfull grant to haue and enioy the forf. of lands, goods, or cattels of offendors, and men attainted of high treason, within any Manor, Lordship, Towne, Parish, Hundred, or other precinct within this realme of England or Wales, shall & may at all times hereafter, haue like libertie, to take, seise, & enioy all such forf. of lands, tenements, goods, and cattels, as shall come or grow within their liberties, by force of the attainder of any person or persons, for & vpon any offence and offences made treason by this act, as they or any of them should, ought, or might by vertue of any good and lawfull grant to them or any of them heretofore had or made.

No corruptiō of blood, or forf. of dower. Prouided alwayes, and be it enacted, That this act, nor any attainder or attainders of any person or persons, for any offence or offences made treason by this act, shall extend or be expounded, to make any corruption of blood to any the heire or heirs of any such offendor or offendors, or to make the wife of any such offendor to lose or forf. her dower, of, or in any lands, tenements, or hereditaments, or her title, action, or interest in the same: Any thing in this act contained, or attainder &c. notwithstanding.

Tryall of a Peere. If any of the Lords of the Parliament, or Péere of the realme, shalbe indicted of any offence made treason by this act, then they shall haue their triall by their Péeres, as heretofore hath béene vsed in cases of High Treason. By a stat. made An. 3. H. 5. it was ordained, That clipping, washing or filing of the money of the land, shold be adiudged treason, but that stat. was repealed by the before rehearsed stat. of An. 1. M. as is aforesaid. St. 3. H. 5. 6

13 For that diuers euill disposed persons knowing that the said act of an. 5. El. 11. being penall, ought to be expounded strictly according to the words therof, & the like offences not by any equitie to receiue the like punishment, did sithence the making of the said stat. practise for gaines sake, other vndue means, to falsifie, impaire, diminish, and lighten as wel the proper mony of this realm, as also of other realms, allowed to be currant within this realm and the dominions thereof by the Qu. proclamation, to the great losse and deceit of the Q. and her subiects: for the redresse whereof by a Statute made Anno 18. Eliz. it was established, That if any person or persons shall for wicked lucre or gaines sake, by any act, waies, or means whatsoeuer, impaire, diminish, falsifie, scale, or lighten the proper monies or coynes of this Realme, or any the Dominions thereof, or the monies or coines of any other Realmes, allowed and suffered to bée currant, at the time of the offence committed, within this Realme of Eng- St. 18. El. 1.

Diminishing, scaling, or lightning of money.

England, or any the Dominions of the same, by the proclamation of the Qu. her heires or successors, it shall be taken, deemed, and adiudged to be Treason: and the offendors therein, their counsellors, consentors, and aydors, shall bee likewise deemed and adiudged as offendors in treason, and being thereof lawfully conuict or attainted, according to the due course of the lawes of this realm, shall suffer death, & lose and forf. all their goods and cattels, to the Queene, her heires and successors, and shall lose and forfeit to the Queene, her heires and successors, all their lands, tenements, and hereditaments, during his or their naturall life or liues onely. Prouided alwayes, that this Act, nor any attainder or attainders, for any offence or offences made treason by this Act, shall in any wise extend, or be iudged, or expounded, to make any corruption of blood to any the heire or heires of such offendor or offendors, or to make the wife of any such offendor to lose or forfeit the dower of, or in any lands, tenements, or hereditaments, or her title, action, or interest to the same, Any thing in this Act contained, or any attainder hereafter to be had &c. notwithstanding. If any Lord of the Parliament, or Peere of this Realme, shalbe indicted of any offence made treason by this Act, then euery of them shall haue his tryall by his Peers, as hath been heretofore vsed in cases of High Treason.

No corruptiō of blood, nor forf. of dower.

Tryall of a Peere.

14 For preseruation of the Queenes Highnesse, her heirs and successors, and the dignitie of the imperiall Crowne of this realme, and for auoiding of such hurts, perils, dishonors, and inconueniences, as haue before time fallen as well to the Qu. noble progenitors, Kings of this realme, as for the whole estate thereof, by meanes of iurisdiction and power of the Sea of Rome, vniustly claimed and vsurped within this realme, and the dominions thereof, and also of the daungers by the fautors of the said vsurped power, growne to licentious boldnesse, and maruellous outrage, by a stat. made An. 5. El. it was ordained, That if any person or persons, dwelling, inhabitāt, or resiant within this realme, or within any other the Qu. dominions, seigniories, or countries, or in the Marches of the same, or elsewhere, within or vnder her obedience & power, of what estate, dignitie, preheminence, order, degree, or condition soeuer hee or they be, shall by writing, ciphering, printing, preaching, or teaching, deed, or acts, aduisedly and wittingly, hold, or stand with, to extoll, set forth, maintaine, or defend the iurisdiction, or power of the Bishop of Rome, or of his Sea, heretofore claimed, vsed, or vsurped within this realm, or in any dominion or countrey, being, of, within, or vnder the Queenes power or obedience: Or by any speech, open deed, or act, aduisedly and wittingly, attribute any such manner of iurisdiction, authority, or preheminence, to the said Sea of Rome, or to any Bishop of the same Sea for the time being, within this Realme, or in any the Q. dominions or countries, then euerie such person or persons so doing or offending, their abettors, procurers, & counsellors, and also their aidors, assistants, and maintainors, vpon purpose, and to the intent to set forth, further, and extoll the said vsurped power, authoritie, or iurisdiction of any of the sayd Bishop or Bishops of Rome, and euerie of them, beeing thereof lawfully indicted or presented, within one yeare next after such offences by him or them committed, and beeing lawfully conuicted, or attainted at any time after, according to the lawes of this Realme, for euerie such default and offence, shall incurre the daunger, penalties, paynes, and forfeitures ordayned and prouided by the Statute of Prouision and Præmunire, made Anno 16. R. 2. And for stronger defence and maintenance of the sayd

St. 5. El. 1.

Maintaining the authoritie of the Bishop of Rome.

The penaltie for the first offence.

St. 16. R. 2. 5

said Act, it was further established by authoritie of the said Parliament, That if any such offendor or offendors, as is aforesaid, by writing, cyphering, printing, preaching, or teaching, déed, or act, aduisedly, and wittingly, doe hold or stand with, to extoll, set forth, maintaine, or defend the authority, iurisdiction, or power, of the Bishop of Rome, or of his Sea heretofore claimed, vsed, or vsurped within this Realme, or in any Dominion or Countrey being of, within, or vnder the Quéenes power or obedience: Or by any spéech, open déed, or act, aduisedly and wittingly, attribute any such manner of iurisdiction, authoritie, or preheminence to the sayd Sea of Rome, or to any Bishop of the same Sea for the time being, within this Realme, or in any the Quéenes Dominions or Countries, or bée to any such offendor or offendors abetting, procuring, or counselling, or ayding, assisting or comforting, vpon purpose, and to the intent to set forth, further, and extoll the sayd vsurped power, authoritie, or iurisdiction, after such conuiction and attainder, as is aforesayd, doe eftsoones commit or doe the sayd offences, or any of them, in maner and forme aforesaid, and bée thereof duely conuicted and attainted, as is aforesayd, then euery such offendor and offendors, for the same second offence and offences, shall forfeit, lose, and suffer such like and the same paines, forfeitures, iudgement, and execution, as is vsed in case of High Treason. Prouided alwayes, that this act nor any thing therein contained, nor any attainder to bee had by force of this Act, shall not extend to make any corruption of bloud, the disheriting of any heire, forfeiture of dower, nor to the preiudice of the right or title of any person or persons, other than the right & title of the offendor or offendors, during his, her, or their naturall liues onely. And it shall and may be lawfull, to euerie person and persons, to whom the right or interest of any lands, tenements, or hereditaments, after the death of such offendor or offendors, should or might haue appertained, if no such attainder had béene, to enter into the same, without any Ouster le mayne to be sued, in such sort as hee or they might haue done if this act had neuer béene made. Prouided, that charitable giuing of reasonable almes to any of the offendor or offendors aboue specified, without fraud or couin, shall not be taken and interpreted to be any such abetment, procuring, counselling, aiding, assisting, or comforting, as thereby the giuer of such almes shall incurre any paine, penaltie, or forfeiture appointed in this Act. Prouided also, that if any Péere of this realme shal offend contrarie to this Act, or any branch or article thereof, in all such cases they shalbe tried by their Péers, in such maner and forme as in other cases of treason they haue vsed to be tried, & by none other meanes. No person or persons shall be indicted for assisting, aiding, maintaining, comforting, or abetting of any person or persons, for any the said offences, in extolling, setting forth, or defending of the vsurped power and authoritie of the Bishop of Rome, vnlesse he or they be lawfully accused by such good and sufficient testimony and proofe, as by the Jury by whom he shalbe indicted, shalbe thought good, lawfull, and sufficient to proue him or them guiltie of the said offences.

The second offence Treason.

No corruptiō of bloud, nor fort. of dower.

Giuing of almes to an offendor.

15 To the intent that all vsurped & forein power & authoritie spiritual and tēporal, may for euer be cléerly extinguished & neuer to be vsed or obeied within this realm, or any other the Q. dominions, by a stat. made an. 1. El. 1. it was ordained, That no forein prince, person, prelat, state, or potentat, spiritual or temporall, shall at any time after the last day of this Session of Parliament, vse, enioy, or exercise any manner of power, iurisdiction, superioritie, authoritie, St. 1. El. 1.

prehemi-

preheminence or priuiledge Spirituall or Ecclesiasticall within this Realme, or any other the Queenes Dominions or Countries that now be, or hereafter shall be: But from henceforth the same shall bee cleerely abolished out of this Realme, and all other the Queenes Dominions for euer: any statute, ordinance, custome, &c. notwithstanding. And for the better obseruation and maintanance of the said statute, it was then further enacted, That all and euery Archbishop, Bishop, and all and euerie other Ecclesiasticall person, and other Ecclesiasticall Officer and Minister, of what estate, dignitie, preheminence, or degree soeuer he or they be, or shall be, and all and euerie temporall Iudge, Iustice, Maior, and other lay and temporall Officer and Minister, and euery other person hauing the Queenes fees or wages within this Realme, or any of her Dominions, shall make, take, and receiue a corporall othe vpon the Euangelists, before such person or persons as shall please the Queene, her heires or successors to assigne and name, to accept and take the same othe. And euery person that at any time shalbe preferred, promoted, or collated to any Archbishopricke or Bishopricke, or to any other Ecclesiasticall benefice, promotion, dignitie, office, or ministrie, or that shall be by the Queene, her heirs or successors preferred to any temporall or lay office, ministrie, or seruice, within any her Dominions, before he shall take vpon him to receiue, vse, exercise, supplie, or occupie any such Archbishopricke, Bishopricke, promotion, dignitie, office, &c. shall receiue the same othe before such persons as shal haue authoritie to admit any such person to any such office, &c. or else before such person or persons as by the Queene &c. vnder the great Seale, shall be assigned to minister the sayd othe. And euerie person temporall suing liuerie, or Ouster le maine out of the hands of the Queene, her heires or successors, before his liuerie or Ouster le maine sued forth, and allowed: And euerie temporall person doing any homage to the Queene, her heires and successors: or that shall bee receiued into seruice with her, &c. shall take the foresaid corporall othe before the Lord Chancellor, or Keeper of the great Seale, or before such person or persons, as by the Queene &c. shalbe appointed to receiue the same. And euery person taking orders, and euery other person which shalbe preferred to any degree of learning, in any Vniuersitie within this Realme, or dominions, before he shall receiue such orders, or be preferred to such degree of learning, shall take the foresayd othe before his Ordinary, Commissary, Chancellor, or Vicechancellor, or their sufficient deputie in the said Vniuersitie. And by another stat. made an. 5. Eliz. it was further enacted, That all other persons which haue taken or shall take orders, commonly called Ordines sacros, or Ecclesiasticall orders, or haue been or shalbe promoted, preferred, or admitted to any degree of learning in any Vniuersitie within this Realme, or dominions to the same belonging: And all Schoolmasters, and publique and priuat teachers of children, as also all maner of person and persons that haue taken, or hereafter shal take any degree of learning, in, or at the common laws of this realm, as well vtter-barresters, benchers, readers, ancients in any house or houses of court, and al principal Treasurers, and such as be of the grand companie in euery Inne of Chancerie, & all Atturneies, Prothonotories and Philozers, towards the laws of this realme: And all manner of Sherifes, Escheators, and Feodaries, and all other person and persons, which haue taken, or shall take vpon him or them, or haue been, or shall be admitteed to any Ministrie or Office, in, at, or belonging to the common law, or any other law or lawes, of, to, or for the execution of them, or any of them, vsed or allowed, or at any time hereafter to be vsed or allowed within this Realme, or any the Dominions or Countries belonging, or which hereafter

Abolishing of foreine authoritie.

Who shal take the othe for the Queenes supreame gouernment.

St. 5. El. 1.

hereafter shall happen to belong to the Crowne, or dignitie of the same. And all other Officers or Ministers of or towards any Court whatsoeuer, and euerie of them, shall take and pronounce a corporall othe vpon the Euangelists, before hee or they shall bee admitted, allowed, or suffered to take vpon him or them, to vse, exercise, supply, or occupie any such vocation, office, degree, ministrie, roome, or seruice, as is aforesaid, and that in the open Court whereunto hee doth or shall serue and belong. And if he or they doe not, or shal not serue or belong to any ordinarie or open Court, then hee or they shall take and pronounce the othe aforesaid, in an opē place before a conuenient assembly to witnesse the same, and before such person or persons, as haue, or shall haue authoritie by common vse, or otherwise, to admit or call any such person or persons, as is aforesaid, to any such Vocation, Office, Ministrie, roome, or seruice, or else before such person or persons, as by the Queene, her heires or successors, by commission vnder the great Seale of England, shall be named or assigned to accept and take the same, according to the tenor, effect, and forme hereafter following, viz. I A.B. doe vtterly testifie and declare in my conscience, that the Queenes Highnesse is the onely supreame gouernour of this Realme, and of all other her Highnesse Dominions and Countries, as well in all Spirituall or Ecclesiasticall things, or causes, as temporall: And that no forreine Prince, Person, Prelate, State, or Potentate, hath, or ought to haue any iurisdiction, power, superioritie, preheminence, or authoritie Ecclesiasticall or Spirituall, within this Realme: And therefore I doe vtterly renounce and forsake all forreine iurisdictions, powers, superiorities, and authorities, and doe promise, that from henceforth I shall beare faith and true allegiance to the Queens Highnesse, her heirs & lawful successours, and to my power shall assist and defend all iurisdictions, priuiledges, preheminences, and authorities graunted or belonging to the Queenes Highnesse, her heires and successors, or vnited and annexed to the imperiall Crowne of this Realme: So helpe me God, and by the contents of this booke. And by the foresayd Statute of Anno 5. Elizab. 1. it was further enacted, That euerie Archbishop and Bishop within this Realme, and the Dominions of the same, shall haue authoritie to tender or minister the othe aforesaid, to euerie or any Spirituall or Ecclesiasticall person, within their proper Diocesse, as well in places and iurisdictions exempt, as not exempt. And that the Lord Chauncelor, or Keeper of the great Seale of England for the time beeing, shall and may at all times hereafter, by vertue of this Act, without further warrant, make and direct Commission and Commissions vnder the great Seale of England, to any person or persons, giuing them thereby authoritie to tender and minister the othe aforesaid, to such person or persons, as by the foresaid Commission or Commissions, the sayd Commissioners shall bee authorised to tender the sayd othe vnto. And moreouer it was enacted, That if any person or persons appointed or compellable by this Act, or by the foresaid Act made Anno 1. Eliz. to take the sayd othe: or if any person or persons, to whom the sayd othe by any Commission or Commissions shall be limited or appointed to be tendered, refuse to take, or pronounce the said othe, in manner and forme aforesaid, that then the partie so refusing, and being thereof lawfully indicted, or presented, within one yeare next after such refusall, and conuicted or attainted at any time after, according to the lawes of this Realme, shall suffer and incurre the daungers, penalties, paines, and forfeitures, ordained and appointed by the Statute of Prouision and Præmunire, made An. 16. R. 2. And also if any of the persons aboue named, and appointed by this Act, to take the othe aforesaid, St. 16. R. 2. 5.

The Othe.

A Bishop may tender the Othe.

The L. Chācellor may grant commissions to tender the Othe.

The penaltie for the first refusall of the Othe.

saide doe after the space of thrée moneths next after the first tender thereof, the second time refuse to take, and pronounce, or doe not take and pronounce the same in forme aforesaide to be tendered: That then euerie such offendor and offendors for the same second offence and offences shall forfeit, lose, and suffer such like, and the same paines, forfeiture, iudgement, and execution as is vsed in cases of high treason: But no attainder by force of this Act shall extend to make any corruption of blood, the dis-heriting of any heire, forfeiture of dower, nor to the preiudice of the right or title of any person, other than of the offendor during his, her, or their naturall liues onely, &c. But forasmuch as the Quéene is otherwise sufficiently assured of the faith and loyaltie of the Temporall Lordes of her high Court of Parliament: Therefore this Act shall not extend to compell any temporall Lord, of, or aboue the degrée of a Baron of this Realme, to take or pronounce the Othe aforesaide, nor to incurre anie penaltie limited by this Acte, for not taking, or refusing the same. Prouided alwayes, that no person shall be compelled by vertue of this Acte to take the Othe aboue mentioned, at, or vpon the second time of offering the same, according to the forme appointed by this Statute, except the same person hath béene, is, or shall bée, an Ecclesiasticall person, that had, hath, or shall haue in the time of one of the Raignes of the Quéenes father, brother, or sister, or in the time of the Quéenes Maiestie, her heires, or successors charge, care, or office in the Church: Or such person or persons as had, hath, or héereafter shall haue any office or ministerie in any Ecclesiasticall Court of this Realme, vnder any Archbishop, or Bishop in any the times or raignes aforesaide: Or such person or persons as shall wilfully refuse to obserue the orders and rites for diuine seruice, that bée authorized to be vsed and obserued in the Church of England, after that he or they shalbe publikely by the Ordinary or some of his Officers for Ecclesiasticall causes admonished to kéepe and obserue the same: Or such as shall openly and aduisedly depraue by wordes, writings, or any other open fact, any of the rites and ceremonies at anie time vsed, and authorized to be vsed in the Church of England: Or that shall say or heare priuate Masse prohibited by the Lawes of the Realme: And all such persons shall be compellable to take the Othe vpon the second tender or offer of the same, and incurre the penalties for not taking the saide Othe, and none other.

The second refusall of the Othe high Treason.

No corruption of blood or forfeiture of dower.

Temporall Lords discharged of the Othe.

Who only shal take the Othe vpon the second tender.

16 Because diuers seditious and euill disposed people haue lately procured and obtained to themselues from the Bishoppe of Rome, and his Sée diuers Bulles and Writings, the effect whereof hath béene, and is, to absolue, and reconcile all those that will be contented to forsake their due obedience to the Quéene, and to yéelde and submit themselues to the vnlawfull and vsurped authoritie of the saide Bishoppe and his Sée: and by colour of the saide Bulles and Writings, haue by their lewd practises, and perswasions so farre wrought, that sundry simple and ignorant persons haue béene contented to be reconciled to the saide vsurped authoritie, and and to take Absolution at the handes of the aforesaide subtile practisers, whereby there hath growen disobedience in many, to absent themselues

X from

from diuine seruice, and thought themselues discharged from all allegeance to her Maiestie, whereby vnnaturall Rebellion hath ensued. For redresse whereof, and to preuent great inconueniences that might ensue, by a Statute made Anno 13. Elizab. 2. it was enacted, That if any person or persons shall vse or put in vre in any place within this Realme, or any the Queenes dominions, any bull, writing, or instrument written, or printed, of absolution, or reconciliation, obtained from the Bishop of Rome, or any his successors, or from any other person or persons authorized, or claiming authoritie, by, or from the said Bishoppe his predecessors or successors, or See of Rome: Or if any person or persons shall take vpon him or them by colour of any such bull, writing instrument, or authoritie, to absolue or reconcile any person or persons, or to graunt or promise to any person or persons within the Realme or any other the Queenes Dominions any such absolution or reconciliation, by any speach, preaching, teaching, writing, or any other open deede: Or if any person or persons within this Realme, or any the Queenes Dominions shall willingly receiue and take any such absolution or reconciliation: Or else, if any person or persons haue obtained or gotten since the last day of the Parliament holden Anno 1. Elizab. or shall obtaine, or get from the said Bishop of Rome, or any his successors, or See of Rome, any manner of bull, writing, or instrument written, or printed, containing any thing, matter, or cause whatsoeuer: or shall publish, or by any waies or meanes put in vre any such bull, writing, or instrument: Then all and euery such Act and Acts, offence and offences shall be deemed and adiudged to be high treason, and the offendor and offendors therein, their procurers, abettors and councellors to the fact, and committing of the saide offence or offences shall be deemed and adiudged high traitors, to the King, and the Realme, and being thereof lawfully indicted and attainted according to the course of the Lawes of this Realme, shall suffer death, and forfeit all their lands, hereditaments, &c. and cattells as in cases of high treason, by the Lawes of this Realme ought to be lost and forfeited, &c. All and euery ayders, comforters, or maintainers of any of the saide offendor or offendors, after the committing of any of the saide actes, or offences, to the intent to set forth, vpholde, or allow the doing or execution of the saide vsurped power, iurisdiction, or authoritie concerning the premisses, or any part thereof, shall incurre the paines and penalties contained in the Statute of Premunire made Anno 16. Ri. 2.

Giuing or taking absolution by any bulles from Rome. St. 13. El. 2.

Obtaining of bulles from Rome.

The forfeitures of Ayders, Maintainors, &c. after the offence. St. 16. R. 2. 5

17 Because diuerse persons euill affected had practised contrarie to the meaning of the foresaide Statute of 13. Elizab. 2. by other meanes than by Bulles, or Instruments written or printed, to withdrawe seuerall of the Queenes subiects from their naturall obedience to her Maiestie to obey the vsurped authoritie of the Bishop of Rome, and in respect of the same to perswade great numbers to withdrawe their due obedience to her Maiesties Lawes established for the due seruice of God: For reformation whereof, and to declare the true meaning of the same Lawe by a Statute made Anno 23. Elizab. 1. it was declared and enacted, That all persons whatsoeuer, which haue or shall haue, or shall pretend to haue power, or shall by any wayes or meanes put in practise to absolue, perswade, or withdrawe any of the Queenes subiects, or any within her Realmes or Dominions from their naturall obedience to her Maiestie, or to withdrawe them

Perswading to the Romish religion. St. 23. Eli. 1

them for that intent from the Religion now by her Highnesse authoritie established within her Highnesse Dominions, to the Romish Religion, or moue them, or any of them to promise any obedience to anie pretended authoritie of the Sea of Rome, or of anie other Prince, State, or Potentate to be had or vsed within her Dominions, or shall doe anie ouert Act to that intent or purpose, and euerie of them shall be to all intents adiudged to be traitours: and being thereof lawfully conuicted, shall haue iudgement, suffer, and forfeit, as in case of high Treason: And if any person shall by any meanes be willingly absolued, or withdrawen as aforesaide, or willingly be reconciled, or shall promise anie obedience to any such pretended authoritie, Prince, State, or Potentate, as is aforesaide: Then euerie such person and persons their Procurers and councellors thereunto, being thereof lawfully conuicted shall be taken, tried and iudged, and shall suffer and forfeit as in cases of high Treason. Being perswaded to the Romish Religion.

And for the further confirmation and explanation of the saide Statute of Anno 23. Elizab. 1. and for a more augmentation thereof in some sort, St.3.Iac.4 there was an other Statute made Anno 3. Iacob. 4. whereby it was enacted, That if any person or persons shall either vpon the Seas, or beyond the Seas, or in any other place within the Dominions of the King, his heires, or successours, put in practise to absolue, perswade, or withdrawe any of the Subiects of the King, his heires, or successours of this Realme of England, from their naturall obedience to his Maiestie, his heires or successours: Or to reconcile them to the Pope or Sea of Rome; or to moue them or any of them to promise obedience to anie pretended Authoritie of the Sea of Rome, or to any other Prince, State, or Potentate: Then euery such person and persons their Procurors, Aidors, Councellors, and Maintainors knowing the same, shall be to all intents adiudged Traitours, and being conuicted shall haue iudgement, suffer, and forfeit as in case of high Treason. Practising to absolue or reconcile to the Romish Religion.

And if any such person as is aforesaide, either vpon the Seas or beyond the Seas, or in anie other place within the Dominions of the King, his heires, or successours shall be willingly absolued, or withdrawen as aforesaide; or willingly reconciled, or shall promise obedience to anie such pretended authoritie, Prince, State, or Potentate, as is aforesaide: Euery such person and persons, their Procurers, Councellours, Aidors, and Maintainours, knowing the same, shall be to all intents adiudged Traitours, and being conuict, shall haue iudgement, suffer, and forfeit as in case of high Treason. Absolued or reconciled.

But this Clause touching Reconciliation shall not extend to anie person which shall bee reconciled to the Pope or Sea of Rome, that shall returne into this Realme, and within sixe daies after his returne, before the Bishoppe of the Diocesse, or two Iustices of the Peace of the Countie where hee shall arriue, shall submit himselfe to the King and his lawes, and take the othe of Supremacie, ordained Anno 1. Eliz. 1. and the othe set downe in this Act. A reconciled person submitteth.

18 Whereas diuerse persons, called or professed Iesuites, Seminarie priests, and other priests made beyond the Sea, according to the order of the Romish Church, haue come, and beene sent into this Realme, of purpose, not onely to withdraw the Queenes subiects from their due obedience

to her Maiestie, but also to moue sedition, rebellion, and open hostilitie within her Highnesse Dominions: For reformation whereof, by a Statute made Anno 27. Elizab. it was enacted, That it shall not be lawfull, to, or for any Jesuite, Seminarie Priest, or other such Priest, Deacon, or other Religious or Ecclesiasticall person whatsoeuer, being borne within this Realme, or any of the Dominions thereof, and heretofore (since 24. Iun. Anno 1. reginæ Eliza.) made, ordained, or professed, or hereafter to be made, ordained, or professed by any authoritie or iurisdiction deriued, challenged, or pretended from the Sea of Rome, by, or of what name, title, or degree soeuer the same shall be called or knowen, to come into, be, or remaine in any part of this Realme, or any Dominions thereof, other than in such cases, and vpon such speciall occasions onely, and for such time onely, as is expressed in this Act (viz. if he be so weake and infirme of body, that he cannot passe out of this Realme:) And if he doe, then euery such offence shall be adiudged high Treason: And euery person so offending shall for his offence be adiudged a Traitor, and shall suffer, lose, and forfeit as in case of high Treason.

Jesuites and Priests shall not come into this Realme.

St. 27. E. 2.

19 By a Statute made Anno 27. Elizab. it was established, That if any the Queenes subiects (not being a Jesuite, Seminarie Priest, or other Priest, Deacon, or Religious or Ecclesiasticall person) as is before mentioned, now being, or which hereafter shall be of, or brought vp in any Colledge of Jesuites, or Seminaries, already erected or ordained, or hereafter to be erected or ordained in any parts beyond the Seas, or out of this realme, in any forraine parts, shall not within sixe moneths next after Proclamation in that behalfe to be made within the citie of London, vnder the great Seale of England returne into this Realme, and thereupon within two dayes next after such returne before the Bishop of the Diocesse, or two Justices of peace of the County where he shall arriue, submit himselfe to her Maiestie and her Lawes, and take the Othe set forth Anno 1. Elizab. 1. Then euery such person which shall otherwise returne, come into, or be in this Realme, or any other the Dominions thereof, for such offence of returning, or being in this realme, or &c. without submission as is aforesaid, shall be adiudged a Traitor, and suffer, and lose, and forfeit as in case of high Treason.

St. 27. El. 2.

Seminarie persons shall retire into England.

20 Hauing treated of Treasons generally, and first shewed which be high Treasons, and which petit Treasons by the common lawe, and which be made treasons by Statutes: It resteth that I declare what is Misprision of treason; how many sortes thereof there be, and what is the penaltie, or punishment of the offendors therein. Misprision of treason, or felony, is most properly when any person doth vnderstand or know that another person hath committed treason or felony, and he will not disclose it to the King, or his Councell, or to some Magistrate, that it may be repressed and punished, but doth conceale it. Bracton writeth, That if any man doth know another to be guilty of a treason, or to be vehemently suspected thereof, he ought presently, and without any delay, come to the King if he can, or send to him if he be not able to come, or to some other neere about the King, and to declare euery thing in order: he ought not tarrie in one place two daies or two nights before

What misprision of treason is.

Bracton de Corona cap. 3

before he doth see the Kings person, neither must he attend any other busines, be it of neuer so great importance, for hee is scarcely allowed to looke backe, because if he doe delay, and conceale the matter for a time, he shall be accounted a manifest deceiuer of the King, and as consenting and agreeing to the offence, whether the partie which is accused be his familiar friend or a stranger: and if he would after accuse the offendor, he shall not be heard, vnlesse he can proue, that he was hindered vpon good cause. And to the intent it might be certainely knowen what misprision of treason is, the Statutes of 5. & 6. Ed. 6. and 1. & 2. Ph. & M. haue defined it in this manner, viz. concealement, or keeping secret of any high treason shalbe deemed and taken only misprision of treason, the offendors heerein to forfeit, and suffer as in cases of misprision of treason, as theretofore hath beene vsed: And in all cases of misprision of treason, the offendor shall forfeit to the King his goodes, and his lands during this life, and he shall be imprisoned during his life. And euery treason or felony doth include Misprision, so that where any person hath committed treason or felony, the King, if hee will, may cause the offendor to be indicted, and arraigned, but of misprision. But some other offences, partly by the common Lawe, and partly by Statute be misprision of treason, besides concealement or keeping secret of treason, which be heereafter expressed.

St. 5. E. 6. 11 1. & 2. P. & M. 10.

The forfeture

2. R. 3. 10.

21 By reason that diuers euill disposed persons, as well without this Realme, as within were boldened to counterfait and forge such kinde of golde and siluer, and vtter the same in the Realme, as is not the proper coine of this Realme, nor currant in paiment in this Realme, because before there was no condigne punishment prouided for such offences: For the redresse whereof, by a Statute made Anno 14. Elizab. 3. it was enacted, That if any person or persons shall heereafter falsely forge, or counterfait any such coine of golde or siluer, as is not the proper coine of this Realme, nor permitted to be currant within this Realme: Then euery such offence shall be deemed and adiudged Misprision of high Treason: And the offendors therein, their procurors, aiders, and abettors, being conuicted according to the Lawes of this Realme of such offences, shall be imprisoned and forfeit such Landes, goodes, and Chattells, as in cases of Misprision of treason, for concealement of treason. S. Br. 6.

St. 14. El. 3

Counterfaiting of money not currant.

22 By the Statute made Anno 23. Elizab. 1. it is enacted and declared, That all and euerie person and persons that shall wittingly bee Aidors or Maintainors of such persons as shall offend in perswading or reconciling to the Romish Religion, or being reconciled thereunto, or in any of the same offences, knowing the same, or which shall conceale any of the saide offences, and shall not within twentie daies at the furthest after such persons knowledge of such offence disclose the same to some Iustice of Peace, or other higher officer, shall be taken, tried, and iudged, and shall suffer, and forfeit as offendors in misprision of Treason. S. Br. 17.

St. 23. Eli. 1

Aiding of perswaders to Romish religion.

Concealing of reconciliation offered.

23 By the Statute made Anno 13. Elizab. 2. it was ordained, That if any person or persons to whom anie absolution, reconciliation, bull, writing, or instrument obtained from the Bishop of Rome, or any of his successors, or from any other claiming authoritie, from, or by them, shall be offered, moued, or perswaded to be vsed, put in vre, or executed, shall conceale the same offer, motion, or perswasion, and not disclose and signifie the same by writing, or otherwise, within sixe weekes then next following, to some of the Queenes priuie Councell, or to the president or vicepresident established in the North, or the Marches of Wales for the time being: Then the same person or persons so concealing, shall incurre the penaltie and forfeit of misprision of high Treason. But no person or persons shall be troubled, in, or for misprision of high Treason, for any offence made Treason by this Act, other than such as by this Act before are declared to be in case of misprision of high Treason. S.Br.16. St.13.Eli.2.

Recording an indictment not found.

24 If a Justice of Peace doe inroll a bill of indictment not found by the Countrey, amongst other indictments which be found; This is a great misprision, and fineable, and he shall lose his office. 2.R.3.10.

Drawing a sword to strike a Justice.

25 If one draw his sword to strike a Justice assigned, sitting in place of Judgement, this is misprision of Treason, and the offender being indicted, and found guiltie thereof, shall haue iudgement to forfeit his landes and chattels, & to haue his right hand cut off, & to be perpetually imprisoned: for that the Justice assigned by the Kings Commission to execute iustice, sitteth in the place and stead of the King, and so the offender opposeth himselfe against the King, and the office of iustice. Mi.22.Ed.3 13.

Striking a Juror in a Justices presence.

26 If in the presence of a Justice assigned, one doe strike a Juror that is returned vpon an Enquest: this is misprision of Treason, and the offender being indicted thereof, shall haue iudgement to lose his lands and goods to the King, to haue his right hand stricken off, and to be committed to perpetuall prison. M.19.Ed.3. Fitz.Iudgement.174.

Striking in Westminster Hall.

27 And the same Law is, if one strike another in Westminster Hall during the time that the Kings Courts be sitting there, and be indicted thereof; this is misprision of Treason, and an indignitie offered to the Magistrates, and place of iustice: Therefore in this case the offender shall haue iudgement to haue his right hand cut off, to lose his lands, and goods, and to be perpetually imprisoned. Fitz. Cor. 280. M.2.& 3. P.& M. Dy.188.

Rescuing a prisoner arrested by a Judge.

28 If one of the Kings Justices assigned, doe arrest any person which hath made a fray before him, and a stranger will rescue the prisoner, whereby he doth escape, this is misprision of Treason, and in this case, as well the prisoner, as he that made the rescous, shall forfeit to the King his landes and goods, and be imprisoned during their liues: Because the attachment of such a Justice, is the Kings owne attachment in the construction of Lawe. M.22.Ed.3. 13.

29 Because striking in the Kings pallace, or where he shall remaine in person, is a kinde of disgrace offered vnto, or contempt had of the maiestie of the King, who is the head of the common wealth, and the chiefe preseruer of

of peace therein, and therefore it is to be accounted a great Misprision, and worthy of seuere punishment: wherefore for the preuention thereof, by a Statute made Anno 33. H.8.12. it was established, That if any person or persons shall malitiously strike any other person, whereby blood shall be shedde in any of the Kings houses, or Palaces, or any other house wherein the king, his heires, or successors, shall bee at that time abiding in his royall person, viz. within any edifices, courts, places, gardens, orchards, or houses within the Porters ward of any of the houses aboue rehearsed, or within any Gardens, priuie walkes, orchards, tilt-yards, wood-yards, tennice-plaies, cockefights, bowling alleyes neere adioyning to the said houses, and being part of the same, or within two hundred foot of the Standard of any outward gate, or gates of any of the said houses, commonly vsed for passage from any of the houses &c. and shalbe thereof indicted, arraigned, and attainted, according to the forme of the said Statute, he so offending, shall haue his right hand cut off, bee imprisoned during his life, and make fine to the King at his pleasure. But this Act and the paines and forfeitures before rehearsed shall not extend to any Noble man, nor other person, that shall strike his seruant within the said Palaces, or Houses, or the limits of the same, with his hand or fist, or any small staffe or sticke, for correction for any offence committed: Nor to any of the Kings officers, that in execution of his office, shall strike any person with his hand, fist, or small staffe, sticke, or tipstaffe: Nor to any other person that in doing seruice at any triumph, or any other time of seruice by the Kings, or any of his Councel, or other his head officers commandement, shal for the execution of his said seruice strike any person w^t his hand, fist, smal staffe, or stick, or any tipstaffe within the same palace, house, &c. although by reason of ye same stroke or strokes, there happen to bee any blood-shed of such person as shalbe so stricken, except the person so stricken die of the same stroke within one yeare next after.

St. 33. H.8. 12.

Shedding of blood within the kings palace.

And so it is to be noted by the foresaid Statute of 33. H.8. and the foure cases next precedent, that striking in the Kings Palace, or House where himselfe doth make his abode is not so penall, as striking, or drawing a weapon to strike is, where he is but represented by others in time and place of Justice; for the law doth inflict a more seuere punishment vpon him who striketh, or draweth his weapon to strike, in place & time of execution of Justice, than it doth to him who offereth the like violence in the house, and at the time where the kings owne person is remaining: In which case the offendor receiueth no punishment at all for striking, or drawing of his weapons to strike, vnlesse blood be shed thereby. Which lawes doe proceed of the great care and reuerend respect that is had of Justice, and of peace ensuing thereof.

30 For as much as some doubts and questions were moued, that certaine kinds of Treasons, Misprisions, and concealements of Treasons, committed out of this Realme, could not by the common lawes of this Realme be enquired of, heard, and determined within this Realme of England: for a plaine declaration whereof, by a Statute made Anno 35. H.8. it was enacted, That all manner of offences being alreadie made or declared, or hereafter to bee made or declared to be Treasons, Misprisions of Treasons, or concealements of Treasons, and done, perpetrated, or committed by any person or persons out

St. 35. H.8. 2. 26. H. 8. 13. 5. Ed.6.11.

Trial of treasons committed out of the Realme.

out of this Realme of England, shalbe enquired of, heard, and determined before the Kings Justices of his Bench, for pleas to be holden before himselfe, by good and lawfull men of the same Shire, where the said Bench shall sit, and bee kept: or else before such Commissioners, and in such Shire of the Realme, as shall be assigned by the Kings Commission, and by good and lawfull men of the same Shire, in like manner and forme to all intents, as if such treasons &c. had béene committed in the same Shire, where they shall be so inquired of, heard, and determined as is aforesaid. And if any Péere of this Realme shall be indicted of any such Treasons &c. then he shall haue his triall by his Péeres, &c. Which foresaid Statute of Anno 35. H. 8. remaineth in force notwithstanding the Statute of Anno 1. & 2. P. & M. 10. By which it is ordered, That all Trials had, awarded, or made for any Treason, shall bee had and used onely according to the course of the common lawes of this Realme, and not otherwise. h. 13. El. Dyer. 298.

Outlawrie of offendors in Treason beeing beyond Sea.

31 By a branch of a Statute made Anno 26. H. 8. it was ordained, That all Proces of Outlawrie to be made within this Realme, against any offendors in Treason, being resiant or inhabiting out of this Realme, or beyond ÿ Sea, at the time of the Outlawrie pronounced, shalbe as good and effectuall in the law to all intents, as if any such offendors had béene resiant within this Realme, at the time of such Proces awarded, & Outlawrie pronounced. And after by a Statute made Anno 5. E. 6. it was conditioned and prouided, That if the partie so outlawed shall within one yeare after the said Outlawrie pronounced, or iudgement giuen thereupon, yéeld himselfe to the chiefe Justice of England for the time beeing, and offer to trauerse the said indictment, or Appel, whereupon the said Outlawrie shalbe pronounced: then he shalbe receiued to the said trauerse, & being thereupon found not guiltie by verdict of xij. men, he shalbe cleerely discharged of the said Outlawrie, and of all penalties and forfeitures by reason of the same; as though no such Outlawrie had bin made. And it is to be noted, that the foresaid two Statutes doe extend to offendors in any manner of Treasons by ÿ Common law, or Statute, and not to those onely which were declared to be Treasons by the Statute of 25. Edw. 3. St. 5. E. 6. 11. h. 12. El. Dyer 287.

32 For the spéedie triall and punishment of such persons, as shall commit any manner of Treasons within the Principalitie of Wales, and the Marches of the same, or elsewhere within the Kings dominions, where his originall Writs in the Chauncerie of England commonly runne not, by a Statute made Anno 32. H. 8. it was enacted, That all such Treasons and Misprisions of Treasons as is aforesaid, shall be presented, and tried by the oathes of twelue men, inhabiting within any such Shires, and before such commissioners, as the King from time to time in such cases shall assigne and appoint by his Commission, or Commissions of Oyer & Determiner, in like manner & forme, as if such Treasons, or misprisions of treasons had bin done and committed within such of the said Shires, into the which the said Commissions of Oyer and Determiner shall bée directed, as is aforesaid: And all Presentments, Trials, Processes, Judgements, Executions, and forfeitures hereafter to be had, made, or done by vertue of such Commissions, shalbe good and effectuall in the law, to all purposes. St. 32. H. 8. 4.

Triall of treasons committed in Wales.

Any

Any graunt, custome, or vsage, to the cōtrarie notwithstanding &c. After that, by the Statute made an̄ 1. & 2. P. & M. it was enacted, That all trials hereafter to be had, awarded, or made for any Treason, shalbe had and vsed onely according to the due Order and Course of the common law of this Realme, & not otherwise. Quære whether this Statute of 1. & 2. P. & M. doth repell or take away the force of the before rehearsed Statute of 32. H. 8.

St. 1. & 2. P. & M. 10.

33 By a statute made an̄ 33. H. 8. it was established, That if any person or persons shalbe attainted of high Treason by the course of the common laws or statutes of this Realme, in euery such case, euery such attainder by the cōmon law shalbe of as good strēgth, value, force, & effect, as if it had bin done by authoritie of Parliament. And the king, his heires, and successors shall haue as much aduantage by such attainder, as well of vses, rights, entries, conditions, and possessions, reuersions, remainders, and all other things, as if it had béene done and declared by authoritie of Parliament, and shalbe deemed and adiudged in actuall and reall possession of the lands, tenements, hereditaments, vses, goods, chattels, and all other things of the offendors so attainted, which his Highnesse ought lawfully to haue, and which they so béing attainted, ought or might lawfully lose and forfeit, if the attainder had béene done by the authoritie of Parliament, without any office or inquisition to be found of the same: Any Law, Statute, &c. notwithstanding. Sauing to all and euery person and persons, and bodies politique, and their heires, assignes, and successors, and euery of them, (other than such person and persons which shall be attainted of high Treason, and their heires and assignes, and euery of them, and all and euery other person and persons claiming by them, or any of them, or to the vses of any of them, after the said Treasons committed) all such right, title, vse, possession, entrie, reuersions, remainders, interests, conditions, fees, offices, rents, annuities, commons, leases, and all other commodities, profits, and hereditaments whatsoeuer, they, or any of them, should, might, or ought to haue had, if this Act had neuer bin made.

St. 33. H. 8. 20.

The force of attainder of treason by the common law.

34 Because through corruption, or negligent kéeping, the Records of attainders of Treasons happen to be many times impaired, blemished, or otherwise to be defectiue; therefore by a Statute made an̄ 29. El. it was ordained, That no Record of attainder that now is, of any person or persons, of or for any high Treason, where the partie so attainted, is, or hath béene executed for ẏ same Treason, shall by the heire or heires, of any such person, or by any other whatsoeuer, clayming in, by, from, or vnder any such heire, or heirs, be in any wise hereafter reuersed, vndone, auoyded, or impeached by any plea, or for any error whatsoeuer. But this Act shall not extend to any Record of attainder of or for any treason vpon which any writ of Error is now depending, or which Record is already reuersed, repealed, or vndone, by or for any error, matter, plea, or cause whatsoeuer, but the same shall be and remaine as vnto, and against that partie at whose suit the same writ of Error is depending, or at whose pursuit the same Record hath bin reuersed, repealed, or vndone, & his, & their heires and assignes onely, as if this Act had neuer beene had, or made: Any thing in this Act &c.

St. 29. El. 2.

No record of attainder shall be reuersed when the offendor is executed.

35 If an offence be murder, or other felonie by the common lawe, and after the same offence shalbe made treason by a Statute, Then it is not punishable

M. 33. H. 8. Dyer 50.

Felony made treason by Statute.

shable as murder and felonie, but as Treason: And no appeale will lie thereof, and the Kings pardon of all Treasons will discharge the offendor therein.

An English traitor subiect to another prince.

36 If an English man borne beeing indicted of high Treason, will upon his arraignment plead, that he will not answer to the said indictment, for that he is a subiect and seruant to a forraine Prince, and not subiect to the King of England: in this case the Court will record a Nihil dicit, and he shall haue such iudgement as is used in cases of Attainder of Treason. P. 13. El. Dyer 300.

An alien borne committeth treason.

37 If an alien borne doe commit high Treason in England in the time of peace, betwéen England and that Nation where the same alien was borne, he shalbe indicted and arraigned of high treason, and shall haue iudgement according to his desert. But if it were in the time of warre betwéene England and that nation where the said alien was borne, then the alien shall be ransomed, and not arraigned. P. 3. & 4. P. & M. Dyer 140. H. 33. H. 6. 1

Ioyning the kings armes with his owne.

38 An Earle of this Realme was attainted of high treason, for ioyning the Armes of England before the Conquest, and the Armes since, to his owne Armes, & for some other offences: Quære within which words of the first rehearsed Statute of 25. E. 3. or of any other Statute at the time of his arraignment in force, that offence was comprised and made Treason. S. Triall by Peeres. 2. An. 38. H. 8. Bro. Treason 2.

Homicide.

Homicide.

Homicide is a word compound, and is derived of these two words, viz. hominis & cedium, and the most apt and proper definition thereof is, when one man or moe men doe kill another man: for if a man be killed by a dogge, a beast, or other thing, it is not properly termed homicide. The said homicide may be committed by severall meanes, viz. by iustice, as when a Iudge doth command or pronounce his sentence, that a man attainted by course of law shal be put to death: By necessitie, as when one man killeth an other with griefe and sorrowe of minde, thereby to deliver himselfe, or that which is his, or some other persons, or things which he is bound to defend from further perill, which he or they cannot otherwise escape: By mischance, as when a man casteth a stone at a bird, or a beast, or is in lopping or felling of a trée, and another man passing by is slaine therewith, without the foreknowledge and against the will of him who did the déede: By will, as when one man hath a will to fight with another, and then doth kill him, or some other that is in his company, and doth take his part in that combate: But of this Homicide by will there bée two sortes, whereof the one is called Murder, and that is, when one man upon malice prepenced, and forethought, doth feloniously kill an other. And the other is called Manslaughter, or Chance medley, and that is, when two men fight together upon a suddaine heat of blood, without any malice precedent, and one of them doth kill the other.

Bracton de corona.

Homicide by iustice.

Homicide by necessitie.

By mischance.

By will.

By murder.

By manslaughter.

2 If a man be adiudged by the court to be hanged, and the Sherife is commanded by the Iudge to doe execution in that manner, and he doth it accordingly; this is Homicide by iustice. But if the Sherife do behead him, or cause him to be beheaded, or by any other meanes to be put to death, than according to the Iudgement, this is no Homicide by iustice, but felonie in the Sherife, for that he hath not observed the order of the Law, viz. the iudgement in putting the offendor to death. And the same law is, if one which is not Sherife, or other officer thereunto lawfully deputed, will put to death an offendor that is condemned to die upon his owne authoritie: for that is no Homicide by iustice, but felonie in him who beeing not the Kings officer thereunto assigned, hath killed one of the Kings Subiects, without warrant of his law. And therefore if the Iudge himselfe who gave iudgement of death against an offendor, shall after put the same offendor to death, it is not iustifiable, but beeing indi-

Homicide by iustice.

M. 35. H. 6. 18.

The order of law, not observed in execution of Iustice.

sed and arraigned thereof, he must plead not guiltie. And in this case the wife may haue an Appell of the death of her husband so put to death, against the said Sherife or other person, though the heire cannot haue an Appell of ẏ death of his father so executed, because his blood is corrupted by the Attainder. 35.H.6.57.

No man may kill him that is outlawed of felony, or attainted in a Præmunire.

3 If a man be attainted of felonie by Outlawrie, it is Homicide by iustice for the Iudge before whom he is brought, to command him to be put to death, and for the sherife to see executiõ done of him, according to the iudgement, viz. to hang him: But it is felonie and not Homicide by iustice, for any other man of his owne authoritie to kill him. And for as much as it was doubtfull whether by the lawes of this realme there was any punishment for such as kill, or slea any person or persons attainted in, or vpon any Præmunire. Therefore by a Statute made añ 5. El. 1. it was enacted, That it shall not be lawfull to any person or persons to slea or kil any person or persons in any manner attainted, or hereafter to be attainted of, in, or vpon any Præmunire by pretence, reason, or authoritie or force of any word, or words, thing or things contained or specified in any Statute or Law of Prouision and Præmunire, or in any of them: Any Law, Statute, Opinion, or Exposition to the contrarie notwithstanding: So that to kill any person attainted vpon a Premunire is felonie, and not Homicide by iustice. 2. Ass. p. 3. 27. Ass. p. 4. 35. H. 6. 58. St. 5. El. 1.

Killing a felon that will not be arrested.

4 A shirife, a bayly, or any other which hath warrant to arrest a man indicted of Felony, may well iustifie the killing of him, if he wil not suffer himselfe to be arrested, but that he doth stand at his defence, in such manner, that the officer and his assistants cannot arrest him without killing of him. And in this case the officer shalbe discharged without the kings pardon: for this is homicide by iustice done vpon him, who refuseth to yeeld vnto, and submit himselfe to the iustice of the Law. And euery person, as well he that hath no warrant, as he that hath, may apprehend a Felon: and if he wil not yeeld to be arrested, but stand to his defence, or flie, the pursuer may kill him without blame, the arrest being for Felony, and therein he shall commit homicide by iustice. And by the statute of Anno 1. M. it is established, That if any persons, aboue the number of two, shall vnlawfully assemble together, to the intent with force & armes to doe, practise, or put in vre any of the things in the said statute mentioned, then it shall be lawfull to euery Iustice of peace, and to euery Shirife, Mayor, Bailife, and other head officer of any Citie, or Towne corporat, or to any other hauing the Kings commission, or letters, to raise & assemble ẏ Kings subiects in maner of warre to be arraied in such great number as he or they shall thinke meet or able, to the intent by violence of strength to suppresse and take the said persons so vnlawfully assembled. And if the said persons so vnlawfully assembled, or any of thẽ shall fortune to be slaine, maihemed, or hurt, in, or about the repressing or taking of them, then euery such Iustice, mayor, sherife, &c. and euery other person hauing authoritie as is aforesaid, and euery person and persons by him or them assembled, shalbe free, discharged, and vnpunished, as well against the King, as against all and euery other person and persons, of, for, or concerning such killing, maiheming, hurting, &c. for it is homicide by iustice done and committed by persons lawfully authorised, vpon such riotous and rebellious persons which after Proclamation made will not depart, and seuer themselues asunder, and submit and yeeld themselues obedient to the law of the Realme. S. Riots 37. 22. Ass. p. 45 Fi. Cor. 261 St. 1. M. 1.

Killing of such as be vnlawfully assembled.

5 As

5 As any man may iustifie the killing of another before arrest, if he wil not yeeld, so may he doe after arrest, if there be any ineuitable necessitie therein: as if an offendor be arrested for felony, and when he is in leading towards the Gaole he breaketh from those that doe conduct him, and flieth away, and his conductors doe pursue him so, that they cannot apprehend and take him againe without killing of him: In this case, if they doe kill him, this is homicide by iustice, and iustifiable, for that the offendors would not yeeld to the triall & iustice of the law. But if he which killed the offendor, procured the matter which is iustifiable for the cause aforesaid, to be found before himselfe, in respect of some iurisdiction which he hath to enquire of felonies, he shall not bee discharged vpon such an inditment found, vntill he be arraigned thereof, and the matter also found by verdict, because he himselfe was Judge. But the law is otherwise if it were found before other commissioners.

22. Ass p. 55 Fitz. Cor. 288.

Fi. Cor. 318

Killing him that is carrying to the Gaole.

6 As a man may kill an offendor before arrest, or after arrest if he will not yeeld, so in some case a man may kil him that is vnder arrest, & in prison: As a Gaoler came in the night with a Lanthorne in his hand to see his prisoners, who before his comming had broken their yrons, and stood all ready to kil him, and did beat and euill intreat him, and he hauing a hatchet in his hand, therewith slew two of them, and escaped from the residue: This was adiudged to be well done, and to deserue no punishment, for this was by the Gaoler homicide done by iustice, to kill them who attempted to kill him, and who indeauoured to escape the triall and iustice of the law.

22. Ass. p 55

Killing a prisoner attempting to escape.

St. 24. H. 8. 5

7 It appeareth by the Statute of an̄ 24. H. 8. 5. That it is homicide iustifiable, if a man doe kill an offendor which attempteth feloniously to robbe, or murder him, in, or neere any high way, cart way, horse way, or foot way, or in his mansion house, or to kill him which attempteth burglarie to breake his dwelling house in the night, and that the same shalbe by verdict so found and tried; for he shall neither lose lands, goods, or cattels for the death of any such euill disposed person, but shalbe fully discharged as if he were acquit thereof.

22. Ass p. 55 26. As p. 23 & 32 Co. l. 5. f. 91 Fi. Cor 303 & 305.

Killing him that attempteth robbery or burglary.

8 To the intent that Trespassors in forrests, chases, parkes, and warrens, may more charily eschew, and feare to enter and trespasse in the same, by a Statute made an̄ 21. E. 1. it was ordained, That if any forrester, parke-keeper, or warreiner shall find any offendors within his Bailiwicke there wandring and doing hurt, which after Huy & Crie leuied to keep the peace, and obey the law, will not yeeld themselues to the Forrester &c. but will flie & defend themselues by violence, Then though the Forresters, Park-keepers, and Warreiners, & any other comming in their companie to keep the Kings peace, endeauouring to arrest such offendors, doe kil any of the same offendors, he shal neither suffer death, nor sustaine any other trouble or punishment therefore: But if any of the said Forresters, Parke-keepers, or Warriners, or any other by reason of contention, despite, or hatred, will lay to any mans charge passing through his Bailiwicke, that hee came thither to doe hurt, whereas hee did not, neither was found wandring or offending, and so kill him, and thereof be conuicted, he shalbe punished for his death, as he ought to be for the death of another being in the Kings peace. And by this meanes the Forrester doth commit

Stat. 21. E. 1.

Killing of an offendor in a Parke, warren, or forrest.

mit homicide by iustice upon the offendor, because he will not submit himselfe, and yeeld to be iustified by the law.

9 If the king have an auntient Chace, whereof the Lieutenants, or Keepers have used time out of ỹ remembrance of man, as well by night as by day to hunt in the Manor of Dale adioyning to the said Chace such deare as do straie out of the same Chace into the said Manor, as in the purlewe of the said chace, but yet divided from the same with hedge and ditch. And, after the same Manor of Dale doth come unto the Kings hands, and the King doth grant the same Manor to another and his heires, and further doth grant unto the same person free Warreine in all his demesne lands of the said Manor, which free Warreine hath bin before confirmed by divers auncient Charters with these words, viz. Ita quod nullus intret in Warrennam illam ad fugandum sine licentia & voluntate of the grauntee of the said Manor. In this case, notwithstanding the unitie of the possession of the Chace, and the Manor of D. in the king, and notwithstanding the Kings grant of the manor, and the confirmation of the warreine with the generall words of the Prohibition aforesaid (which doe onely extend to the Subiect) the kings libertie of the purlewe doth remain unextinguished. And therefore if one of the Kings Keepers of the said Chace shall come into the said Manor of D being purliew to fetch in his straied deere, it is not lawfull for the Lord of the said manor of D. or for any of his servants to kill him after huy and crie made to keep the peace, and obey the law, and if he doe, it is not iustifiable by the foresaid Statute of 21. Ed. 1. for he cannot commit homicide by iustice, nor iustifie the killing of him in his Warreine, who hath in a sort, and to some purpose, interest, to come into ỹ said ground to fetch forth his straied deere. M. 15. & 16 El. Dyer. 327.

Unity of possession in a chace, and a manor adioyning, having free warrein.

10 If in Appell of murder, burglarie, or other felonie, the defendant doe, plead not guiltie, ready to defend it by his body, and the Appellant and Appellee doe ioyne in the combat, and one of them doe kill another in battell: This is Homicide by iustice, and not punishable: for as the law of the Realme doth allow triall by battel in that case, so doth it ratifie and confirme the event and successe thereof to be iustifiable. And the law (depending upon the iudgement of God, who giveth victory according to the truth) hath assigned either of thē to doe execution of iustice upon the other, as it hath assigned the Sherife to do execution of iustice upon him that after verdict, confession, or outlawrie is condemned to die. 37 H. 6. 21.

One killing another in combat.

11 Homicide upon necessitie, as before is said, is when one man killeth an other with griefe of mind, and sorrow of heart, and beeing enforced unto it, therby to deliver himselfe, or that which is his, or some other persons that he is bound to defend from further perill, which otherwise cannot be avoyded, and this homicide is by law iustifiable. As if one or divers persons come to a mans house to burne his house, but he or they doe not burne it, if the owner of the house or any of his servants doe shoote forth of the house, and kill the offendors or any of them, this is homicide by necessitie in defence of his house, and not felony. And in like sort if one or more come to a mans house to rob him, and the owner or any of his servants, or company being with him in the house doe kill the offendors, or any of them, this is homicide by necessitie in defence of his goods, and thereby iustifiable: for a servant 26. Ass p. 23 Co. L. 5. 91. Lex Alured.

Homicide upon necessitie.

Homicide in defence of his house from burning.

Homicide in defence of a man from robbery.

seruant may iustifie the killing of an other in defence of his masters person,
21.H.7.39. or house, if the offence can not be otherwise auoided. And he may iustifie the
26.Ass.p.23 killing of him who robbed and killed his Master, so that he doe it presently. And if one doe attempt to robbe an other being out of his house, and pursueth
26.Ass.p.32. him to that end, the true man may kill the offendor, and shall be discharged thereof, without any forfeiture or suing of the Kings pardon. And so shall be in the other former cases, where anie doe attempt to burne, or robbe a mans house: for a mans house is his Castle, out of which the Lawe will not
21.H.7.39. compell him to flie.

12 Forasmuch as it was in question, and doubt, if any euill disposed person or persons, doe attempt feloniously to robbe or murder any person or persons, in, or nigh any common high way, cart way, horse way, or foote way, or in their mansion, messuages, or dwelling places: Or that feloniously do attempt to breake any dwelling house in the night time, should happen being in their such felonious intent, to be slaine by him, or them whom the said euill doers should so attempt to robbe, or murder, or by any person or persons being in the dwelling house which the same euill doers shall attempt burglarily to breake by night, if the saide person so happening in such cases to slay any person so attempting to commit such murder, or burglarie, should for the death of such euill disposed person forfeit and lose his goods and cattells for the same, as any other person should doe, that by chaunce medley should happen to kill any other person in his or their defence: for the declaration of
St.24.H.8.5 which ambiguitie and doubt by a Statute made Anno 24.H.8. it was enacted, That if any person or persons shall be indicted or appealed for the death of any such euill disposed person or persons, attempting to murder, robbe, or burglarily to breake mansion houses as is aforesaide, that the person or persons so indicted, or appealed thereof, and of the same by verdict so found and tried, shall not forfeit or lose any lands, tenements, goods, or cattells, for the death of any such euill disposed person in such manner slaine, but shall be thereof, and for the same fully acquited and discharged, in like maner as the same person or persons should be, if he or they were lawfully acquited of the death of the said euill disposed person or persons. No forfeiture for homicide vpon necessitie.

13 But if one man doe come in the day time to an other mans house, and
Fi.Cor.305 doth make an assault vpon him in his owne house, and doth fight with him, if the owner of the house doe slay the assailant in his owne defence, the owner of the house shall forfeit his goods, and be driuen to sue for the Kings pardon, except that it be proued and found, that the assailant came also to robbe the other in his house. Killing another in his owne defence in his owne house.

14 Homicide in a mans owne defence, ought to be so great, and vpon such necessitie, that it must be esteemed to be ineuitable, or otherwise it will not excuse: for heere the killer of the man hath not to doe with a felon, as in some of the former cases, but with a lawfull and true man. And it is not materiall whether the person that did kill, or the person which was slaine did beginne the fray, but the whole matter will consist vpon the ineuitable necessity, without the which the killing is by no meanes excusable. And therefore the true definition of Homicide in his owne defence is, when the assailant doth make a
Fi.Cor.284 286.287. 297. fray, or offer force to the defendant, and doth strike him, & the defendant doth flee so farre as he can for sauing of his life, so that he is come to a straite, beyond Necessitie ineuitable is requisite in homicide in his owne defence. The definition of homicide in his owne defence.

the which he cannot flie, and the Assailant doth continue his assault; whereupon the defendant doth strike the assailant, and doth kill him, this is homicide in his owne defence. For if the defendant could haue auoyded the assailant, and did not, but when the assailant did strike him, he did strike him againe and killed him, this is felonie in the defendant. And though the defendant doth giue to the assailant diuers wounds, yet that is not materiall, if he flie to a straite before he doth giue him the mortall wound: for the Law doth allowe that iustifiable, which a man doth in defence of his owne person. And yet in the case aforesaid, if the defendant vpon malice prepenced, doth strike another and thē flie to a wall or straite, and the other doth pursue and strike him, and the defendant who fled doth kill the pursuer, this is murder and not homicide in his owne defence: for the malice prepenced was the ground and beginner of this homicide, and not necessitie ineuitable. 43.Ass.p.31 Fi.Cor.387

where in homicide in his owne defence goods shall be forfeit, and where not.

15 One man did strike another to the ground, and then drewe his knife to kill him, and the defendant lying vpon the ground drew his knife, and the assailant was so hastie to kill the defendant, that he did fall vpon the defendāts knife, and so was slaine: In this case the defendant was not adiudged guiltie of the assailants death, neither did he forfeit his goods, for the assailant in a maner killed himselfe. But if one man doe strike another, and the defendant doth flie to a straite, and there seeing and perceiuing that the assailant would kill him, holdeth a pitchforke betweene the assailant and him, and the assailant is so fierce that he runneth vpon the pitchforke, and is slaine: In this case the defendant shal be forced to purchase his pardon, and shal forfeit his goods, for here he did not lie vpon the ground, but stood vpon his feet, and so might haue made some other defence for his safety, that the other in the case aforesaid lying vpon the ground could not doe. 44.Ass.p.17 Fi.Cor.286 287.

Killing of a man in his owne defence found by verdict.

16 When a man is indicted and arraigned of murder or manslaughter, it is not a sufficient verdict for the Iurie to say, that the prisoner killed the dead man in his owne defence; but they must shew specially how: And though it be specially found vpon the indictment, yet the prisoner shall not bee discharged, vntill he hath purchased his Charter of pardon; for that it is a confession by implication of the indictment: Or otherwise he shall wholly estrange himselfe from the fact, and plead not guiltie. And this is done to the intent to induce a forfeiture of his goods, which be forfeit for the said offence: for the better corroboration and establishment whereof, the Statute of Anno 6. E.1. made at Glocester was ordained, by which it is enacted, That no writ shalbe awarded out of the Chauncerie touching the death of a man, to enquire if a man killed another by misaduenture, or in his own defence, or in other manner, without felonie: but the prisoner shall remaine in the Gaole vntill the comming of the Iustices in Eire, or assigned to deliuer the Gaole, and thē he shal put himselfe vpon the countrie before them of good and euill: And if it be found by the countrey that he did it in his owne defence, or by misaduenture, the Iustices shal giue intelligence thereof to the King, & the king shall giue him pardon, if he please. And so note, that thogh by this Stat. the life of a man is meant to be pardoned, who doth kill another by misfortune, or in his own defence (for the which by the common law he should haue bin hanged) yet his goods do remain forfeit to ẏ K. as they were at ẏ common law, Et ipse in misericordia dn̄i regis. 43.Ass p.31 26.H.8.11. St.6.E.1.9 21.E.3.17

why the goods shalbe forfeited.

17 Wherein

17 Whereas the foresaid Statute of Anno 6.Ed.1. hath ordained, That the prisoner shall put himselfe upon the Enquest of good & euill, that is to be intended, when he is indited of murder, or homicide, & not where in the inditement the speciall matter is found: for to such an indictment of murder or homicide, he must plead not guiltie, because it is no plea to plead the special matter, viz. that he killed the dead man in his owne defence, for then it should be as a iustification of the offence, whereas this kind of homicide is in no manner iustifiable: wherefore he must plead not guiltie, and then the special matter being found by verdict, shall giue him aduantage.

The prisoner indited must put himselfe upon the countrey.

4.H.7.2. Kel.fol.53. 26.H.8.5.

18 He that is in this manner charged for the killing of a man in his owne defence, shal not be discharged thereof, until he hath obtained the Kings pardō, or be acquit thereof, and then his discharge shalbe in this manner, viz. if he desire to purchase his pardon, he shall first be let to mainprise, & then shall sue to haue the Record certified by the Iustices before whom he was arraigned to ỳ Chauncellor of England, who shal make him a charter of pardō, without speaking to the king: for the giuing of intelligence to the King, wherof the foresaid Statute of Gloucester maketh mentiō, is intended to certifie him in ỳ Chancerie: for that in law the King is alwaies said to be present in the Chancery, to giue eare to euery of his Subiects petitions.

How he shall be discharged who killeth a man in his own defence.

Fi.Cor. 116 361. Fi.N.B. 246.

19 Homicide by misaduenture is when any person without any euil intent doth a thing that is lawfull, or which is not prohibited by the law, & yet another is slaine, or commeth to his death thereby: as if a man casteth a stone at a bird, or a beast, & another man or woman passing by the way is stricken thereby, & dieth: Or if one man be in felling of a trée, and the same trée, or some arme or bough thereof falleth upon another person, & killeth him: Or if one do shoote an arrow at a Butte, or other marke, and another passing that way is killed therwith; Or if one man do let a stone or a péece of timber fal frō a house, or out of a window, and another passing that way is killed by it, this manner of killing is homicide by misaduenture, for the which he that doth kill shal haue his pardon of course, as it doth appeare by the before rehearsed stat. of Gloucester, and also he shall forfeit his good, as in the foresaid case of killing of a man in his owne defence. But in this case it is to be considered, whether he that committed this homicide by Misaduenture was then busied in a thing that was lawfull, or unlawfull, for if he were doing of a lawfull act, as if the Schoolemaster do in reasonable manner beat his Scholler for correction onely, or the master his seruant, and after the Scholler or Seruant dieth: Or two men doe by consent wrestle one with another, and one giueth the other a fal and hurteth him, whereby he dieth: Or one doth play with the other at hand sword by consent, and one of them giueth the other a blowe, or thrust, whereby he dieth: or if a mā do cast wood, stone, or other thing from a cart, a house, or from a window, houel, or ricke, & another is oppressed therewith, and dieth: Or if a man béeing in due and conuenient time doing any thing that might bréed danger to passengers thereby, doe crie out with so loud and audible voice to giue warning therof, that any other which trauelleth that way may heare and flie the perill, and yet one carelesse and nrt respectiue of his life and safetie is oppressed therewith and dieth: Or where two men doe run at Tilt, Iust, or fight at Barriers together by the Kings commandement, and one of them doth kill another, in these cases & the like the offēces shalbe adiudged as homicide by misaduēture. But if a mā being in doing of an unlawful act, as casting of stones into a high

Homicide by misaduenture.

What is homicide by misaduenture.

Fi.Cor. 302 354. St.6.Ed.1.9.

Kel fol.108 136.

P.11.H.7 33.

way where men doe vsually passe, or shooting of arrowes into a Market, or other place, whither men doe vsually resort, or fighting at Barriers, or running at Tilt, or Iustes with others without the kings commandement, whereby a man is slaine: in these last specified cases it is felonie at the least, viz. manslaughter, if it be not murder; for the offendor beeing doing of an vnlawfull act by his owne will, the law will construe his meaning and will therein by the successe of the act. As if two men be fighting together, and a third man commeth to part them, & he is slaine, by one of those two without any malice prepenced, or euill intent in him that slue him: this is murder in him that killed him, and not Homicide by misaduenture, because they both that fought together were doing of an vnlawfull act. And if they both that did fight together, came thither with malice prepenced, one intending to kill the other, then is it murder in them both.

P.11.H.7.23

Fitz.Cor. 262.

22.Ass.p.71

2.& 3.P.M. Dyer 128.

The like order in misaduenture as in his owne defence.

20 The same order shalbe obserued in the pleading, verdict, forfeiture, and pardon of one which killeth another by misaduenture, as shalbe of him who slayeth another in his owne defence: And the before rehearsed Statute of Gloucester shall extend as well to the one as to the other.

St.6.Ed.1.9

Homicide by murder or manslaughter

what is murder.

what is manslaughter.

21 Homicide by murder is when one man vpon malice prepenced doth kil another feloniously. And because it should be certainly knowne to all persons, which offences should be adiudged murder, by a Statute made at Marlbridge Anno 52.H.3. it was ordained, That murder from henceforth shall not be iudged before the Kings Iustices, where it is foūd missfortune onely; but murder shalbe intended vpon them which bee feloniously slaine, viz. with a premeditate and malitious mind. And some doe define murder to be a secret killing of one man by another, none being present, nor none knowing thereof. But if one man kill another vpon malice prepenced, the law doth not respect whether he doe kill him secretly, or openly, or whether he that was slaine be an English man, or other countrie man, so that he liued vnder the Kings protection: Neither doth the law regard who gaue the first blow, for though he that was slaine did strike the first blowe, yet if he were slaine vpon malice prepenced, it shalbe adiudged murder in him that killed him. And manslaughter, otherwise called Chance medley, is when two doe fight together vpon the suddaine, without any malice precedent, and one of them doth kill the other; in which case the offendor shall haue his Clergie.

St.52.H.3. 26.

Pl.com.261

Pl.com.261

The name of murder.

Murder more grieuous than felonie.

22 The name of murder is an old and auncient terme, and it is the rather continued to make a difference betwæn Homicide committed by Chance medley, and Homicide committed by malice prepenced. And therefore if a man be indicted of murder, a pardon of al felonies wil not excuse & discharge him; as it appeareth by the Statute of an̄ 13.R.2. which hath ordained, That no charter of pardon shalbe allowed before any Iustice for murder, for the death of a man slaine by a wait, assault, or malice prepenced, Treason, or Rape of a woman, vnlesse the same murder &c. be specified in the same Charter: For murder is a more grieuous and hatefull offence in the hearts, and eares of men, than other felonies be. And yet if a Commission be granted to certaine persons to enquire of all felonies, they may thereby take indictments of murder, though a pardon of

St.13.R.2.1 Stat.2.

S.Pardon.9

Kel.fol.91.

of all felonies will not auaile him, who hath committed murder; but that is in respect of the Statute aforesaid.

St.1.E.6.12 23 By a Statute made Anno 1.Ed.6. it was ordained, That all wilful killing by poysoning of any person or persons that at any time hereafter shall be committed or done, shall be adiudged and taken wilfull murder, of malice prepenced: and that the offendors therein, their aydors, abettors, procurers, and councellours shall suffer death, and forfeit in every behalfe, as in other cases of wilfull murder of malice prepenced. Wilfull poysoning.

24 To the end that stabbing, and killing men on the sodaine, done by many inhumane and wicked persons, in the time of their rage, drunkennes, hidden displeasure, or other passion of minde, may be from henceforth restrained through feare of due punishment to be inflicted on such cruell and bloodie malefactors, who heretofore haue béene thereunto imboldened, by presuming on the benefite of Clergie: St.1.Iac.8. Therefore by a Statute made Anno 1.Iac. it was enacted, That if any person or persons shall stabbe, or thrust anie person or persons, that hath not then a weapon drawen, or hath not then first stricken the partie which shall so stabbe or thrust, so as the person or persons so stabbed or thrust shall die within the space of sixe moneths then next following (although it cannot be proued that the same was done of malice forethought) yet the party so offending, and being therof conuicted by verdict of xii. men, confession, or otherwise, according to the lawes of this realme, shall be excluded from the benefite of his or their Cleargie, and suffer death, as in case of wilfull murder. Prouided alwaies, that this Act shall not extend to any person or persons, which shall kil any person or persons, se defendendo, or by misfortune, or in any other manner than as is aforesaide: nor shall extend to any person or persons, that in kéeping and preseruing the peace, shall chaunce to commit manslaughter, so as the said manslaughter be not committed wittingly, willingly, and of purpose, under colour or pretence of kéeping of the peace; nor shall extend to any person or persons, which in chastising his childe or seruant, shall besides his or their intents or purpose, chance to commit manslaughter. Stabbing to death wilfull murder.

Co.l.4.40.

25 If upon a fray made, the Constable with others to assist him, do come to part the fray, and to preserue the peace, and in doing of his office, the Constable, or any of his assistants shal be slaine, this is wilfull murder in him that slew him, although the murderer did not know the party whom hée killed, and although the fray was on the sodaine: Because the Constable and his assistants came by authoritie, warrant, and commaund of the Lawe to kéepe the peace, and auoide the danger which might ensue by the breach thereof: And therefore the Lawe doth adiudge this murder, and that the murderer had a prepenced malice in him, to oppose himselfe against the Lawe and the iustice of the Realme. And if the Shiriffe or any of his Bayliffes, or Officers be killed in the execution of the Kings Processe, or in doing their office, this is murder. And it is murder, if a watchman be killed in watching, and doing of his office; for in those cases the Lawe doth construe the offence, not onely as done to the person that is slaine, but to the office of execution of iustice, Constable or other is slaine in parting of a fray. The Shiriffe or his officer is slaine in execution of Processe.

stice, or the keeping of the peace, which the law had imposed upon him that was slaine, and so the offender by killing of this man, hath done as much as in him lieth, to restraine the execution of iustice, or to hinder the preseruation of the peace.

Murder and manslaughter committed in the death of one man.

26 If a man goe with malice prepenced to fight with an other, and to kill him, and a third person séeing them fighting, goeth on the suddaine without malice, to take the part of him that went with his malice, and to fight for him, and then they two strike and kill the man that was by them assaulted: This is wilfull murder in the first man which went with the malice prepenced to kill, and but manslaughter, and no murder in the other who went to take his friends part, and had no malice prepenced to kill. As if the master vpon malice prepenced doth lie in the way to assault and kill a man, and taketh some of his seruants with him that hee doth not acquaint with this malitious intention, and the master doth assault the same person who he did lie in waight for, and doth fight with him, and the seruants doe take their masters part, and also fight with the partie assaulted, and they altogether doe kill him; This is willfull murder in the master, and but manslaughter in the seruants, for that in them there was no malice prepenced towardes the partie slaine. But if the master had made his seruants priuie to his intention, and they had gone with him and killed the other, it should haue beene adiudged murder in the seruants also. Plo. Com. 100.

A man bearing malice to one doth kill an other.

27 If a man vpon malice prepenced do lie in waight to kill an other man, and doth méet him, assaile, and fight with him, & a third man being in the companie of him that is assailed doth fight, and defend him. In this case if the first man that made the assault doe kill the third man, who tooke part and defended the second man that was assailed, it is in him wilfull murder, though at the first he did beare no malice to him that hee killed, neyther knew him. But when the first man did beare malice to the second man that hee first assaulted, and ment to haue killed him, and to haue put his intended malitious purpose in execution against him, and slew one other who resisted his purpose: the law doth construe it that he caried a malicious and reuenging mind against all those that did resist his wicked purpose. And therefore as he slew one in the defence of an other, so is his malicious and murdering minde, and intention expounded to be transferred from the one to the other: and he shalbe adiudged a murderer, as if he had killed the first man. And the same lawe is, if one man doe lie in waight in a place to kill an other man, and a stranger doth come to the same place, and he that doth lie and waite to kill, mistaking the man, doth kill that straunger, thinking he had bin the same person which he did meane to kill: This killing shalbe adiudged wilfull murder, for it is grounded vpon malice prepenced, though it were not executed vpon him to whom he did beare the malice. And therefore it shalbe adiudged the like offence, as if hee had slaine the same person that hee meant to haue killed. And so it is, if a man vpon malice prepenced doe shote at one man with intent to kill him, and his arrow or pellet doth kill an other man to whom he did beare no malice, this shalbe adiudged murder in him, for in his act doing Plo. Com. 101.

he

he intended murder: and seeing he directed his arrow to kill one man, and that slew another, the offence shall be accounted in equall degree, as if had killed him whom he meant to haue slaine, for the end of the fact shall be iudged by the beginning thereof, and the later part shall taste of the first, and the first part, which was the shooting of the arrow or pellet, was grounded vpon malice prepenced, and a murdering minde, and so the offence in Lawe shall be iudged wilfull murder.

Plow.com. 474 — 28 The husband did giue to his wife a rosted apple, wherein hee had put poison, with intent to poison and kill her; and the wife not knowing the intent of her husband, nor that the apple was poisoned, deliuered the same apple in the presence of her husband to a yong childe of their owne to eate, who did eate of it, and died thereof within few daies after: This was adiudged wilfull murder in the husband, for that he deliuered the poisoned apple, with intent to kill one person, and seeing by his act death did ensue, although it was to another person than he meant to kill, yet it shall be adiudged murder in him, for he was the originall founder, and only cause of this death: and this murder should be vnpunished, if he should not be punished therefore; for the wife which deliuered the poisoned apple to her owne childe, could not be guiltie of any offence, for that she was ignorant of the mischiefe pretended. But if one doe lay rats-bane, or other venomed thing in a house or place, with intent to kill rattes, mice, or other vermine, and a man or woman doth eate of it, and dieth thereof; this is no murder or other felony in him that laied it, for that he had no intent to hurt any man or woman. — Giuing poison to one, & another taketh it, & dieth

M.2.El.Di. 186 — 29 An adouterer and a harlot being by him begotten with childe, did agree, that after the womans deliuery, the childe should be killed, whereupon the mother, after her deliuerie, perswaded the Midwife to kill the childe, who did it accordingly, viz. she cut the throat of it: In this case the mother and midwife were adiudged principall murderers, and the adouterer, who was accessarie before the birth of the childe, and the murder done, was adiudged to continue accessarie after the murder done, and to suffer death without the benefit of his Clergie. — Two agreeing vppon a murder, and one of them doth it.

Fitz.Cor. 383 — 30 If a man intending the death of another, doth beate him so greeuously that he doth leaue him by all the beholders iudgement thought to be dead, and then doth flie away, and after the other doth reuiue, and liue; this is not felony in him that did that violence, though it doth plainely appeare that hee had a meaning to kill him: for it is not felony, except the partie stricken be indeede killed, and die within a yeere and a day after the stripes giuen. But on the other side, if one man doe strike another, with intent onely to beate him, yet if hee die of this battery within a yeare and a day after, it is felonie in him that did strike him. For though, as Bracton affirmeth, the old Lawe of this Realme did hold, Quod in maleficijs spectatur voluntas & non exitus, & nihil interest, vtrùm quis occidat, an causam mortis præbeat: But now we say, Lex antiqua mutatur, and doe affirme, Quod exitus in maleficijs spectatur, & non voluntas duntaxat. — Meaning without act is not homicide. — Act without meaning is homicide.

Co.l.4. 40. — 31 A man brought drinke to another that was mingled with poison, and aduised him to drinke it, telling him that it would be a meane to procure him to get a childe of his wife; by reason of which perswasion, he to whom that poisoned — Homicide by giuing poisoned drinke to another.

poisoned drinke was brought, did receiue it, & after drunke it in the absence of him who brought it vnto him, and shortly after died: In this case hee that brought the drinke was adiudged a principall murderer, though he was not present at the time of the receipt of the drinke: or otherwise he shoulde haue beene guiltie of that horrible offence, and yet haue escaped vnpunished, for there was none in this case to whom hee could be accessarie. And so note this for a speciall case where a felonie is committed, and neither principall nor accessarie be present at it.

Many doe attempt an vnlawfull acte and one of them committeth homicide.

32 If seuerall persons assemble together to doe a disseisin, to breake a house, or commit any vnlawfull act, and one of them killeth a man, he & all the other shalbe adiudged principall fellons, because they all came to doe an euill acte, though not that act, as if they all had come to haue killed or robbed one man, and after they killed, or robbed an other.

Fitz.Cor. 350.
11.H.4. 13.

Homicide by carying abroad.

33 A man was indicted that he did feloniously carry his owne father being sicke against his will in a frostie and colde time from one towne to an other, whereof he died; and this was adiudged felony in him: for in this case the sonne had a meaning that his fathers life should be shortened, and he brought to his death.

2.Ed.3.18

A man dieth in the handes of a Phisition or Surgion.

34 If a phisition or surgion hath a man in his cure, who dieth being in his cure, or at any time after: this is not felony in the same phisition or surgion, bicause he did not any thing to his patient with a felonious intent, but against his will. And moreouer it is not to be discerned whether the man came to his death by any willfull default in the said Phisition, or Surgion, or by his former infirmitie, or other cause.

Fit.cor.163

Homicide vpon the euill wordes of an other.

35 Anno.3.Ed.3.Itin.North. it was presented that through the euill wordes of a woman, two men did fall out, and fought, and one of them killed an other: and this was adiudged felony in the woman. But it must be intended that the woman by her words did perswade, councel, or aduise them, or one of them to fight with the other, and so was accessarie before the felonie committed.

Fit.cor.331

Homicide by a franticke man.

36 A man that is franticke though he kill an other man, cannot commit murder, for he hath not a felonious intent, nor doth carrie within him malice prepenced to any, neyther doth know what he doth. And therefore he is not to be arraigned for the killing of a man in his Lunacie, though after hee doth recouer his memorie, neither shall he be inforced to sue for his pardon. And the same law is of a man that is deafe and dumbe, who can not commit murder, for he hath not a felonious intent, neither doth he know what hee doth. And therefore if he kill a man he shall not be arraigned thereof, nor driuen to sue for his pardon. But if a man that is drunke, doe in his drunkennes kill an other man, it is felony, and he shalbe hanged therefore, for it is voluntarie ignorance in him to be drunke.

M.21.H.7. 13.
Fitz.forf.33
Fi.Dower 183.
Fitz.N.b. 202.d
Fitz.cor.193 351.
Co.l.4.42
26.Ass.p.27
Plow.com. 19.
Co.l.4.125

Homicide by an Infant.

37 An Infant of the age of twelue yeares, or aboue may commit murder, and so may an Infant of the age of eight, or nine yeares if it may appeare (by hiding of the person slaine, or by any other act) that the aboundance

3.H.7.2.& 12.
12.Ass.p.30

of

of his malice doth exceede the tendernes of his yeeres. But if an enfant of tender and yonger yeeres doe kill a man, this is no felonie, because he wanteth
Pl.com.19. discretion and understanding, and the Lawe will impute it to the ignorance which commeth to him by nature.

Fit.cor.311. 38 If a man hath a beast that is accustomed to doe hurt, and the owner knowing thereof, doth not tie him, or otherwise keepe him fast shut up, but suffer him to goe at libertie, and after that beast killeth a man: this is felony in the owner, for by his sufferance of the beast to goe at libertie, the owner doth seeme to haue a will to kill: or that hee used this beast as an instrument wherewith to kill. And this was a Lawe ordained by Alured king of the West Saxons. Alured. Homicide by a beast.

Fit.cor.263 22.Ass.p.94 39 To make it Homicide, it is requisite that the partie killed be in Esse, viz. in rerum natura: for if a man kill an infant in his mothers wombe, this is no felonie, neither shall he forfeit any thing for it, and that for two causes, the one, because the thing had no name of Baptisme, the other, for that it is hard to iudge if the infant died of that batterie or not, or upon some other cause. Wherefore a man being indicted in the Kings Bench, for that he did beate a woman great with childe with two children, so that one of the children died presently, and the other was borne, baptised, and had a name of Baptisme giuen, and within two daies after that childe also died by the hurt it receiued by the foresaid beating: this was adiudged no felonie, for the reasons aforesaide: But if a woman being deliuered of a childe, doth presently kill it before it be baptized, this is felony in her, though the childe had no name of Baptisme, because the childe was in rerum natura before it was killed, and it is knowen by whom, and what meanes that childe came to his death. Ass 3.Ass. pl.2. M.1.E.3.24 Fit.cor.418 M.2.El.Di.186. In homicide the party killed must be in Esse.

Fit.cor.303 40 If a man doe beate, or otherwise hurt another, whereby hee dieth, it is requisite to make it Homicide, that the partie doe die within a yeere and a day next after the batterie, or hurt done: Or else the Lawe will not adiudge it homicide, or that the partie stricken did die of that beating or hurt. And the same Lawe is, if poison be giuen by one man to an other, whereby hee dieth, the Lawe will not construe it to be murder, unlesse the partie doe die within a yeere and a day next after the poison receiued. In homicide, the party must die within a yeare and a day.

41 As a man may commit felonie in killing of an other, so he may commit felonie in killing of himselfe, and then the Law doth aptly call him felo de se: for though Homicide is most fitly and commonly termed where one man doth kill an other, yet the same phrase may in good congruitie of speach be well applied to one that killeth himselfe, for there is an Agent and a Patient, a killer, and one slaine, and both in one and the selfe same person. And though there may be many causes why a man may kill himselfe, as there be many and seuerall humours, opinions, distractions, and fantasies in men, yet most commonly he becommeth felo de se, & feloniously killeth himselfe, who being guilty of any grieuous crime is apprehended for ye same, or vehemently suspected, Bracton de coro.ca.31. Homicide by felo de se.

suspected, or accused thereof, or being wearie of his life, for extreamitie of paine or pouertie, as being not able to kill his enemie, or to be reuenged of him according to his desire, doth therefore kill himselfe, &c. Which felon of himselfe shall forfeit to the King, his goodes, chattells, reall and personall, and debts, but not his lands: for the Lawe doth so greatly fauour inheritance, that it shall not escheate without attainder indeede: Neither shall his wife forfeit her dower, nor his blood shall be corrupt. And the reason why the King shall haue the goodes, chattels, and debts of felo de se forfeited vnto him, is, for that the King hath lost a subiect, and the same subiect hath broken the Kings peace, in killing of himselfe, and giuen an euill example to his people, and hath fled from, and escaped the triall of the Lawe, and he himselfe was the cause why he could not be tried by the Lawe. But the goodes of felo de se be not forfeited vntill his death be presented and found of Record: And therefore those goods cannot be claimed by prescription. And if felo de se be cast into the Sea, or a great River, or so secretly buried that the Coroner cannot haue the sight of his body, and by that meanes can not enquire thereof: Then all such Iustices of Peace, and Oier and Determiner which haue authoritie to enquire of felonies, shall enquire thereof.

Plow.com. 260.261. Fitz.Cor. 362.301. 426.

The cause of the forfeiture of felo de se.

Co.l.5.110.

An Enfant or Lunatike killeth himselfe.

42 If an Enfant, furious, or frantike man doe drowne, or otherwise kill himselfe, hee shall not forfeit his goodes, &c. because he wanteth reason and iudgement. And if a man that is lunatike doe strike himselfe with his knife, or other weapon, and after doth recouer, and notwithstanding dieth of the same stroke that himselfe did giue within one yeere and a day after the stroke giuen, yet he shall not be adiudged felo de se, nor forfeit his goods, or any thing therefore: for the Lawe doth respect what he was at the beginning when hee gaue himselfe the stroke, which was the cause of his death, and not what he was when he died. For if a man that is frantike from day to day doe kill himselfe, he shall not forfeit his goods. But the Lawe is otherwise if a man doe kill himselfe who is frantike but at certaine times, viz. per lucida internalla.

Bracton de coron.ca 31 21.H.7.31 Fitz.cor. 244. Co.li.1.99. Plow.com. 260.

Fitz.coron 324.

Killing of himselfe in the stead of an other.

43 If a man doe strike an other to the ground, and then draweth his knife to kill him, and the defendant lying vpon the ground draweth his knife to defend himselfe, and the assailant is so hastie to kill the defendant that hee falleth vpon the defendants knife, and so is slaine: In this case the assailant is felo de se: for he had an intention to kill, though not himselfe, yet the defendant. And so as the death intended by him, was by his hast transferred from the defendant to himselfe, so is the name of a murderer transfered to felo de se.

H.44.Ed.3 44.

44 If a lease of lands be made to the husband, and the wife for the terme of certaine yeares, and the husband goeth into the water and drowneth himselfe in this case, after the death of the husband shalbe found by the Coroner vpon the sight of the dead body, and the title of this land shalbe likewise found by an inquisition taken before commissioners authorised thereunto, the foresaid lease and whole terme of yeeres shalbe forfeited to the King, and the wife shall haue no part thereof: for this forfeiture shall haue relation to the husbands

Plow. com. 258.

Forfeiture of lease made to felo de se and his wife.

bands going into the water, whereupon the drowning did ensue, at the which of going into the water hee had the whole interest of the lease in him so to dispose, that hee might haue aliened the whole interest thereof from his wife: and this going into the water, wherupon this drowning and death did ensue, was a forfeiture or alienation in law of the terme, and was as much in construction of the law, as if hee had then aliened the whole terme to the King. And the finding of the death of this man before the Coroner, vpon the sight of the bodie, and the finding of the title of this lease before Commissioners, bee equiualent to a iudgement that might haue beene giuen against him in his life time, for murder of another person: And if this man had beene outlawed, or otherwise attainted of Felonie in his life time, this lease should haue beene forfeited to the King, and the wife should haue had no part thereof.

P.16.E.4.7 P.9.Eliz. Dyer 262. 45 If one which is felo de se, hath a debt due to him vpon a contract, and not by specialtie, hee shall not forfeit the debt to the King amongst his other goods and chattels, for that the sayd debtor shall bee rebutted of his law against the King. No forfeiture of a debt vpon a simple contract.

Pl.Com. 260.262. 46 If a villeine doe giue himselfe a deadly wound, and after the Lord of the same villeine doth seise his goods, and then this villeine doth dye within a yeare and a day after the wound giuen, and so becommeth felo de se, and after the whole matter is found before the Coroner, those goods of the villeines shal bee forfeit to the King, and the King shall haue them out of the Lords possession: for the forfeiture shall haue relation to the wound which the villeine gaue himselfe, and that was before the Lords seisure of his goods. For if a man doth giue himselfe a deadly wound, and dyeth thereof within a yere and a day after, all the goods, cattels, and debts which hee had at the time of the blow giuen, or at any time after, shall bee forfeited to the King, and in his life time hee hath no authoritie to dispose of them after the wound was giuen. A villeine felo de se, and then his Lord seiseth his goods

4.& 5.P.& M.Dy.160 47 A man was bound with two Suerties, for the payment of twentie pounds at two seuerall dayes, and the principall debtor, for the securitie of his Suerties, by his Indenture did sell vnto his sayd two Suerties, twentie oxen for twentie pounds, with a Prouiso in the Indenture, That if hee did discharge or saue them harmelesse of the sayd Obligation of twentie pounds, that then the said sale of the twentie oxen should bee void. And it was agreed betweene them, that the principall debtor should haue the occupation and vse of the said twentie oxen, at the will of the said Suerties, and to bee vsed as his owne. And after one day of paiment due to the Oblige, and no money payd by the seller or principall debtor, and before the second paiment was due, the seller killed himselfe, and became felo de se, hauing those twentie Oxen in his possession, and the Suerties seised the beasts as their owne: And notwithstanding the propertie was in them, by the not performance of the condition, yet it was adiudged that the Aulmoner should haue the beasts, or the money which they were sold for, and then hee should discharge the Suerties against the Creditor. And so the Aulmoner was awarded to One mortgaged his goods and then became felo de se.

haue in these beasts the best estate of the seller, and the same that the Debtor might haue had, if hee had payed the debt at the due times which were agreed vpon.

Homicide by casualtie.

48 Though Homicide is most vsually knowne and termed by the killing of one man, or woman, or more, by another man or woman, or more, yet hominis cedium, whereof the same word Homicide is deriued, may bée done by some other casualtie; though when a man is slayne by some other mischaunce than by the hand or meanes of another man, as by the fall of a pit of earth, or stone, or a trée, or killed by a Beare, or Bull, or such like, it is not aptly nor vsually sayd, that Homicide is committed, but that such a man is slaine.

A Deodand.

49 When a man commeth to his death by the meanes of any thing that falleth vpon him, or by the meanes of a hurt which himselfe receiueth in falling from some other thing, without the procurement of another man, that thing which is the cause of his death, shall bee forfeited to the King, taken for a Deodand, and distributed in almes. And it is not materiall whether the thing that killed the man was mouing or not, at that time when it killed him: for though it were not mouing, yet it shall bée taken and accounted as a Deodand, as well as if it were mouing, because all things mouing with the thing which was the cause of the mans death, shall bée forfeited, in like sort as the principall thing, according to the old rule, Omnia quæ mouent ad mortem sunt Deodanda. And yet those goods which bée forfeited as Deodand, bée not forfeited vntill the matter be found of Record, and therefore they cannot be claimed by prescription. And the same Jurie which doth find the death of the man, must also find and appraise the Deodand.

Fitz.Cor. 403. M.6.E.6. Dyer 77. Co.li.5.110

A trée and the bough of another trée do kil a man.

50 If a man do fell a trée, and that trée falleth vpon the bough of another trée, which bough falleth vpon a man and killeth him: in this case both the bough that killed the man, and also the trée which did fall vpon that bough, shal be Deodand: for they both did moue vnto, and were the cause of his death.

Fitz.Cor. 398.

Falling off a cart, or from a cart.

51 If a man do ride in a cart, and the same cart falleth vpon him, and killeth him, as well the same cart as the horses that drew the cart, shall be Deodands. And in like sort, if a man bee in a cart, and by the stirring of the horses which drew the cart, or any of them, he is cast out of the cart, and dyeth thereof, as well the horses which drew the cart, as also the cart, shall be Deodands: for the horses and cart béeing fastened together, bée all the cause of the mans death.

Fitz.Cor. 388. Fitz.Cor. 397. Pl.Com. 323.

Falling from a cart laden.

Falling from cart that is in lading.

52 If a man fall from a cart laden with Corne, Hay, Wood, &c. and the wheele of the cart breaketh his necke, backe, or &c. whereby hée dieth, as wel the Corne, Hay, Wood, or &c. as the cart, shalbe Deodands. But if a man do fall from a cart as he is lading of Corne, Hay, Wood, &c. by the stirring of the horses, and thereby breaketh his necke, backe, or &c. whereby he dyeth, the cart

Fitz.Cor. 326. Fi.Cor.326

and

and hoꝛses shalbe Deodands, but not the coꝛne &c. foꝛ that the coꝛne &c. were not the cause of his death. If a man that doth dꝛiue a cart, doe clime vpon one of the wheeles of the cart, to gather apples, plums, oꝛ &c. and doe fall from that wheele, and bꝛeaketh his necke, back, oꝛ &c. whereof he dieth, if it be pꝛoued that neither the hoꝛses noꝛ cart did stirre, then the wheele of the cart onely shall be a Deodand, and not the hoꝛses, noꝛ the residue of the cart, foꝛ that none of them did moue to the carters death. Fitz. Cor. 409.

Fitz. Cor. 401. Fitz. Cor. 398. Pl. Com. 260.

53 If a man ride into the water, to water a hoꝛse, and then falleth from the hoꝛse, and is dꝛowned, the hoꝛse shalbe a Deodand. And if a hoꝛse, bull, boare, &c. do strike a man, and after he dyeth of that blow, the hoꝛse, bull, boare, &c. shalbe a Deodand. And if the owner of the hoꝛse that did giue the same moꝛtall blow, doe alien the hoꝛse to another betweene the time of the stroke giuen, and the death of the man, yet the King may seise that hoꝛse as foꝛf. foꝛ a Deodand: foꝛ the foꝛfeiture shall haue relation from the stroke giuen, which was the cause of the mans death.

Falling from a hoꝛse into the water. A hoꝛse killeth a man. From what time a Deodand shal haue relation.

Fitz. Cor. 405. Fitz. Forf. 20.

54 If a beame whereupon a bell in a Church doth hang, doe fall vpon a man, and kill him, as well the beame as the bell shall be Deodands, notwithstanding that they were befoꝛe the goods of the Church, and in a soꝛt Deo datum. But if a man be digging in a pit, mine, oꝛ quarrey of stone, marle, grauel, sand, coale, oꝛ turfe, and a great heap of earth do fall vpon him, and kill him, the same heape of earth onely shall be foꝛf. to the K. and not the whole pit, mine, oꝛ quarrey.

A beame of a bell of a church.

Fi. Cor. 389 Kel. fol. 68

55 If a man do fall from a bꝛidge into the water, and is carried by the foꝛce of the streame vnder the wheele of a mill, and thereby is slain, the wheele of the mill only shalbe a Deodand. If timber, boꝛds, wainscot, oꝛ other goods, do fall vpon a man, and oppꝛesse him to death, the same shalbe a Deodand.

The wheele of a mill.

Fitz. Cor. 314.

56 If a man falleth from his hoꝛse, and bꝛeaketh his head, necke, back, &c. against a trunck, peece of timber, oꝛ any other thing, whereby he dieth, the hoꝛse onely shall bee a Deodand, and not the trunck, timber, oꝛ &c. because it did not moue.

Falling from a hoꝛse against a trunke.

Fitz. Cor. 348.

57 If a man fall from a ricke oꝛ houell of coꝛne, hay, oꝛ &c. whereby hee is killed, the same houell oꝛ ricke shall be foꝛfeit to the king as a Deodand. And so Deodands may be of some things that a man doth moue vnto, oꝛ from them, as well as of those things which moue to a man to kill him.

Falling from a houel oꝛ rick

58 If a man do fall from a ship that is sailing, and dye thereof, neither the marchandise, noꝛ any other thing in the ship is the cause of his death, but onely the ship, and therefoꝛe the ship only shalbe a Deodand. And that ship must be vpon the fresh water, foꝛ if it be vpon the salt water, and one doe fall from it, then it shalbe no Deodand. Bracton. Britton.

Falling from a ship.

within the age of xiiij. yeares.

59 If he that doth come to his death by any casualtie, be within the age of xiiij. yeares, nothing shalbe forf. to the king as a Deodand for him, for the form of the Presentment is A. filius B. vltra ætatem quatuor decem annorum: sed quære. Fitz. Cor. 389.

The Sherife shalbe charged with the Deodand.

60 The Sherife of that countie where a Deodand shall be found to bee, shall be charged with the price of euerie Deodand, and shal answer for it, and he shall leuie the value thereof of the same towne where it falleth, notwithstanding it was not committed to them to keepe: And therefore when such a mischance is found, the presenters thereof must also find & appraise the Deodand. Fitz. Cor. 298.

A man found dead in the field.

61 If a man be found dead in the field, his apparell, and the money which he hath about him, shalbe giuen to a Church, and shalbe distributed to the poore &c. and it shall not be taken as a Deodand, for it doth varie from the nature of a Deodand, being no cause of his death. But that distribution shall bee in case where the same man is vnknowne, for if he be knowne, his money, apparell, and other things about him, shalbe deliuered to his executors, or administrators, or to the Ordinarie. Fitz. Indict. 27.

Felonies by the Common Law: Larcenie, Theft.

1 Larcenie is a fraudulent taking away of another mãs goods, aboue the value of twelue pence, with intent to steale them, without the knowledge of him whose the goods be: For if the goods do not exceed the value of twelue pence, it is not felonie, but petit Larcenie, for the which the offendor shalbe imprisoned, or otherwise punished by the discretion of the Justices before whom hee is arraigned, and also shall forfeit his goods, but he shal not be put to death. And this intent of stealing to make it Larcenie, ought to bee at the time when the partie doth first come to the possession of the goods, for if the partie doth come lawfully to the possession of the goods, though hee hath an euill intent after, to conuert them to his owne vse, it is not felonie in him: As if a man doth deliuer goods to another, who after doth conuert them to his owne vse, it is not felonie in him, for no felonie is intended to be done but with violence, and vi & armis, & contra pacem, which cannot be supposed in this case, seeing they were deliuered vnto him by the owner of them, and so hee came lawfully to them.

17.H.8.22. Fitz.Cor. 430.451. 27.H.8.22. 13.Ed.4.9.

What is Larcenie. Petit larcenie. The intent of the stealing must be at the time of the receit of the goods.

2 If any person at seuerall times doe steale seuerall parcels of goods, which parcels being put together, do amount aboue the value of xij.d. it is felonie, and the offendor shall be hanged. And if two, three, or more together, doe steale goods to the value of twelue pence, this is felonie in them all, for the felonie in them is seuerall, though the stealing be ioint.

Fitz.Cor. 415. Fitz.Cor. 404.

Stealing goods at seuerall times, aboue the value of xij.d. Felonie in seuerall persons.

3 If any person be indicted for stealing of goods aboue the value of twelue pence, and arraigned thereupon, yet the Jurie that passeth vpon his arraignement, may giue a speciall verdict, and say, that the goods did not exceed the value of eight pence, or ten pence, &c. and then that offence shall be taken for petit Larcenie onely, and the offendor shall be punished by imprisonment or &c. according to the Justices discretion.

Fitz.Cor. 451. 28.Ass.p.14 22.Ass.p.39

The Jurie may find an vnder value of the goods.

Taking away a Tauerners plate.

4 If a Tauerner doe set a peece of siluer plate before his guest to drinke in, and that guest carrieth away the peece of plate, this is felonie in him: for he had not the possession of the same peece of plate, but the vse thereof onely to drinke in for that time: And the offendor did fraudulently take the plate away, with intent to steale it, without the knowledge of the owner thereof. A man beeing lodged in an Inne, did rise in the night, and carrie linnen and other goods of the Inne keepers, out of his chamber where hee was lodged, into the hall, with intent to steale them, and then went to the stable to seeke his horse, and the Ostler tooke him therewith, this was adiudged felonie, and yet the goods were not carried out of the house of the owner of them, but taken out of the place where he had assigned thẽ to be. And so it is if a man do take vp another mans horse in his close, with intent to steale him, and the owner, or some other, doth apprehend the partie with the horse, before hee is gone out of the close, this is felonie.

P.13.Ed.4.9 27.Ass.p.39

A seruant hauing the vse of his masters goods, doth steale them.

5 If a man commit money to his seruant to keepe, or plate to his Butler, or vessell to his Cooke, to be vsed in his house, or a horse to his Horsekeeper, to be kept and dressed, or sheepe to his Shepheard, to be followed and pastured, and the seruant who hath the same thus committed vnto him, doth goe away with them, this is felonie by the common law in that seruant: for these goods were alwayes in the Masters possession, and kept and vsed to the Masters benefit. But if a man deliuer a horse to his seruant, to ride to the Market, or money to carrie to a Faire, or to pay to another, or to buy cattell, or other things, and the seruant doth go away therewith, this is not felony: for the Master deliuered the same to his seruant, and therefore he came lawfully by the possession of it. See Felonie by stat. 12.

21.H.4.14. 3.H.7.12. 13.Ed.4.10.

One hauing the key of a chamber, doth steale the goods.

6 If a man deliuer to his seruant, or another, the key of his chamber doore, and he to whome the key is deliuered taketh away the goods in the chamber, aboue the value of xij. d. this is felonie in him: for the goods were not deliuered, but did alwayes remaine in the possession of the owner of them.

13.Ed.4.9

A bargaine with a carrier and not a deliuerie of goods.

7 If a man do bargaine with a carrier, or other, to carry certaine bales of wares, or other goods to a place prefixed, and he taketh them, and carrieth them to another place, and openeth the bales, and taketh forth the goods within them feloniously, and conuerteth them to his owne vse, this is felony in him: for that this is more than a deliuerie, viz. it is a bargaine, so that he receiueth thẽ by the bargaine agreed vpon, and not by the deliuerie, the which bargaine he hath not performed, but hath taken the goods of his own wrong: and in this case the propertie of these goods did alwayes remaine in the first owner or deliuerer.

13.Ed.4.9.

A carrier stealeth the goods committed.

8 If one man do deliuer goods to another to carrie to a place appointed, and he doth carrie them thither, and then he doth take and steale them away, this is felonie in him: for the priuitie of the bailement, and the carriers possession was determined, when he had carried them to the place appointed, and therefore what he did after, was feloniously done, and of his owne wrong.

13.Ed.4.10.

13.E.4.9 9 If one man doe deliuer a Tunne of Wine to another, to carry to a place agréed vpon, if the Carrier sell or giue away the same whole Tunne of wine, it is no Felony, for it was deliuered vnto him: but if he take out twenty gallons, or other quantitie aboue the value of twelue pence, or &c. then it is Felony. A Carrier stealing part of his charge.

7.H.6.45 13.E.4 10 5.H.7.18 10 If a man deliuer goods to another man to kéepe, & after the owner who deliuered them, doth take them away feloniously, to the intent to recouer damages against the party to whom they were deliuered by an actiõ of Detinue, this is Felony in him that deliuered those goods, & yet the property of the goods was alwaies in him that did steale them. Felony for taking of his owne goods.

7.Ed.4.14 9.Ed.4.33 11 It is felony to steale the goods of a Church or Chappell, or the goods of a Deane & Chapter, Colledge, or other corporation, or the goods of a corporation during the time of the vacation of the gouernour thereof: and the indictment shalbe, Quod bona domus & ecclesiæ, &c. The goods of a Church or Corporation.

27.Ass.p.40 12 If a wife doe steale goods by the compulsion of her husband, this is not felony in her: and likewise it is, if she do it by the commaundement of her husband: and if the husband and wife together do steale goods, this shalbe takẽ the only act of the husband, and not felony in the wife: But a woman alone by her selfe, her husband not being priuy thereunto, may commit felony, and may be principall or accessary: as if a married wife steale goods, or receiue Felons or stolne goods into her house, knowing them so to be, or lock them vp in her chest or closet, her husband not knowing thereof: Or if her husband as soone as he knoweth thereof, refuseth her company, and his own house, and maketh his abode elsewhere, in which case the wiues offence shal not be imputed to her husband; or otherwise the law will impute the fault to him, and not to her: for if the husband do commit felony, and the wife knowing thereof, do receiue him, and kéepe him company, she is not therby accessary to the felony: for a wife cãnot be accessary to her husband, for that by the law of God she ought not to discouer him or his counsell: which law was first established by Inas, King of the West Saxons. As the husband & wife stealing together the goods of another, the whole offence shalbe imputed to the husband, & it shal be adiudged no felony in the wife: so if the wife doe take the goods of her husband, the law wil not construe them to be stolne, nor charge her with felony therefore: for at the time of the solemnization of their mariage in the face of the Church, her husband endowed her with all his wordly goods, & so gaue her a kind of interest in them. And if the wife doe take her husbands goods, and giue them to another, this is not felony in him to whõ she did giue them: but if a man do take away another mans wife and the husbands goods against the husbands will, this is felony, S. Felony by stat. 31. That it is felony in the wife to send any mony, victual, &c. to her husband, being assembled with others in rebellious manner contrary to the stat. of An. 1. M. 12.

Fit. cor. 160. Fit. cor. 383. Britton. Bracton, de coron, c. 32. Inæ leges 58. Fit. cor. 455. Bro. cor. 242.

In what case a married wife may commit felony, in what not. Canuti lex 74. Inæ lex. A woman taking her husbands goods.

Fi.N.B.102 Bracton. 35.H.6.11 13 If an infant aboue the age of xij. yeares doe take any goods of another mans, aboue the value of xij. d. with intent to steale them, it is felony in him: and some do affirme, that if an infant of any age do take the goods of another, In what case an infant may commit felony.

and

and that the Iustices before whom he is arraigned doe thinke that hee did it with a felonious intent, and had discretion to vnderstand what he did, and the offence, and the perill thereof, that then it is felony in him. And yet Inas king of the West Saxons ordained, That a child of tenne yeares of age should bee condemned for Felony. But an Ideot or Lunaticke cannot commit Felony by the stealing of the goods of another, for that neither of them doth know what he doth. Lex 7. Co.li.4.124

An Ideot or Lunaticke cannot cōmit Felony

Burning of a house or barne Felony.

14 Burning of a house willingly, and feloniously done, is Felonie by the common Law. For the statute of West. 1. hath ordained, That they which be taken for the burning of a house feloniously done, be not repleuisable. And if one do burne a barne feloniously in the night, which is adioining to a dwelling house, it is felony by the common law. St.3.E.3.15. 11.H.7.1

Felony in inditors to discouer their counsell.

15 If an inditor, which (with others) hath indicted other persons of Felony, do therin discouer the kings counsell, contrary to his oath, in publishing to others, that he and his companions haue indicted such and such persons, this discouery is felony. S. Treason 9. 27.Ass.p.63 Fit. cor.272

Rescuing of a prisoner felony

16 If an offendor be arrested or imprisoned for felony, or attainted of felony, and a stranger will take him out of the possession of him that did arrest him or keepe him in prison, or will take a felon attainted and condemned to die out of the possession of the Shirife, or his Officers, whereby he escapeth, this rescous is felony, as well in him that made the rescous, as in him that is rescued. And if a stranger do rescue one that is indicted of felony he may be indicted and arraigned thereof presently, before the principall felony be tried, & if he be found guilty, he shalbe perpetually imprisoned, or otherwise punished at the K. pleasure, but shall not be hanged, because the principall felon is not tried. S. Breaking of Prison 5.10. 1.H.7.6 1.E.3.17.

Wilfull escape is felony.

17 When a man doth arrest another for felony, or any other crime, & after let him go at liberty whither he will, this letting him at liberty is a wilfull escape: and if the arrest of him that escaped, was for felony, it shall be adiudged felony in him that did let him escape: and if it were for treason, then it shall be adiudged treason: and if but for trespas, it shalbe adiudged trespas. 9.H.4.1

Goods stolne from him that hath the custody of them.

18 If a man do deliuer cloth to a tailor to make him a garment, & a felon doth steale that cloth out of the possession of the taylor, the offendor may be indited for the stealing of that cloth of the goods of the taylor, for the taylor had possession of the cloth, and property also against all others, sauing against him that deliuered it vnto him. Kel.fol.70.

Goods stolne from a felon

19 If a Felon do steale another mans horse, beast, or other goods, & another Felon doth steale the same frō him, the owner of the same horse, beast, or other goods, may haue an appeale against the first or second Felon at his own choice, for the property of the goods did alwaies remain in him: for no felon can by the Law clayme property in any stolne goods. 13.Ed.4.3. 4 H.7.5

20 Larcenie

22.Ass.p.95
18.Ed.4.8.
18.H.8.2
St.3.E.1.20.

Of what things Larcenie may be committed, of what not.

20 Larceny cannot be committed by taking of sauage beasts found in their wildnesse, as Deere, Pigeons, Hawks, nor by taking of doues found out of a douecoat, nor by taking of fish in a riuer: for such taking is not the stealing of the goods of another, seeing that they be no mans goods, neither can any person claime propertie in them: neither can felonie bee committed in the taking of Apes, Hounds, Thrushes, Squirels, or such domesticall things, kept only for pleasure, and that but of some speciall persons, and profitable to none. Neither is the taking of Pheasants, Partridges, or Conies, being fowles, and things of warrein felony. But it is felonie, if a man do take out of another mans douecoat, yong pigeons, which can neither go nor flie, for that the propertie of them is alwayes in him who is owner of the douecoat. And likewise it is felonie to take yong Goshawks, or yong Herons breeding in a parke, or seueral ground, which can neither go nor flie out of their nests: Or to take fish out of a pond, or trunk, or to take Swannes, Peacocks, Turkies, Capons, Geese, or Ducks: Or to take a Stag, Hind, Bucke, or Doe which is marked, and domesticall, and made tame by the owners diligence. And by the stat. of West. 1. it is felonie to take a tame beast, or other thing in a parke, by maner of robberie. And it is felonie to kill sheepe, and take their skinnes, or to pull wooll from sheeps backs. So that in all the cases aforesaid, the thing so taken or stolne do exceed the value of twelue pence.

12.Ass.p.32
18.H.8.2
Fit. cor.256
10.E.4.15.
Bracton, de coroñ, c.3
22.Ass.p.99
Fit.cor.265

Felony must be of personall goods, & not of things reall.
The lead of a house.
A lease for yeares
A ward.
writings.
Treasure troue.
Wrecke of the sea.
Waife.
Strey.

21 The taking away of another mans goods, to make it felonie, must be of personall things, for if it be of things reall, it is not felonie: As if one cut down a tree of another mans, and carrieth it away, or cutteth the corne, or pulleth the apples of another, and carrieth them away, or hideth them, it is no felonie, because the tree &c. was parcell of the owners inheritance, and not of his personall goods. But it is otherwise, if the owner do cut downe the tree, corne, &c. and another carrieth it away, then he committeth felonie. And likewise if one doe take and carry away the lead which couereth a church, or any mans house, it is no felonie, for it is parcell of the church, or house, and of the inheritance, and no personall goods. And so it is if an Indenture or deed poll, purporting a lease for terme of yeares, or a ward bee taken, and carried away, it is no felonie: for a lease for the terme of yeares, is a chattell reall, and so is a ward, and not a chattell personall. And the same law is, if a writing, or boxe of writings, for if it bee imbeciled & carried away, it is no felonie, because they cannot be valued: and moreouer, for that they concerne inheritance, chattels reals, or things in action: & the taking and carying away of Treasure troue, Wrecke of the sea, Waife or Stray, is not felony, for that the owner of them is vnknowne, and it is vncertaine whose they be, though Bracton termeth the taking away of Treasure troue, *Quasi crimen furti*. But the offendor who taketh them away shalbe punished by fine and imprisonment: and if a lord doe secretly take away his villaines goods, this is no felony in him, for he may seise and take them away all openly when he will.

Bro.cor.202

A felony made by statute, and after repealed.

22 If an offence be made felony by statute, and then one doth commit the same offence, and before he is arraigned thereof, that statute is repealed, by the repeale of the stat. the felony is extinct, and the offendor shall not be arraigned thereof, nor punished by force of that statute for that fact.

Thiefe-boot.

23 Thiefe-boot is not when a man doth take his owne goods again, which were feloniously stolne from him: but Thiefe-boot is properly when a man doth take goods of a felon to fauour him, the punishment of which Thiefe-boot is not as for a felony committed, but only to be ransomed and imprisoned.

42. Ass. p. 5. Fit. cor. 353

Felony committed in one kings raigne, punished in another.

24 A man committeth Felony in the time of one king, may be arraigned for it after in the raigne and time of another king: for the same Law and forme of gouernment, to the which the offence is done, remaineth, though the king dyeth.

1. Ed. 3. 3 Bro. Cor. 177.

Stolne goods caried into seuerall counties.

25 If a Felon steale a Horse, Beast, Sheepe, or other goods in one countie, and doth carry them into another countie, it is felony in euery countie whether he doth carry or driue those goods: and the offendor may be indicted or appealed in any of those counties, be arraigned, and haue his iudgement there. And if a felon doe steale goods, commit murther, or doe any other felonie in one countie, and then flie into another countie, and is taken there, he shalbe imprisoned in the Gaole of the countie where he is taken, and after shall be remoued by the kings Writ into the Gaole of the countie where hee committed the felony.

Bro. cor. 170 4. H. 7. 5 7. H. 4. 44 13. Ed. 4. 9.

In what gaole a felon shalbe imprisoned.

Breaking a house to take a felon.

26 A man may breake a house to apprehend a felon, or him that is suspected of felony, for it is for the Commonwealth: and the king hath a kind of interest in felony, viz. to cause it to be punished: and where the king hath an interest, that writ or act is a Non omittas propter aliquam libertatem: and so the liberty of a house will not defend him who hath cōmitted, or is suspected to haue committed felony against the K. But if it were for debt, or trespas, it were otherwise, for that is only the interest of one particular person.

13. E. 4. 9.

What is Robberie.

27 Robbery in Latin called Rapina, is in his naturall signification, when one man taketh any thing from the person of another against his will feloniously, although the thing taken be but to the value of a penny, for the which the offendor shalbe hanged. And yet in some case it may be robbery, notwithstanding the party doth not take it from the person of the owner. As if a felon doe take any of the goods of another openly in the place where the owner is present, against his will, this is robbery, though the offendor doe not take it from the person of the owner: for he doth it with that violent force, that the owner dareth not, or is not able to resist him. As if one doe threaten another presently to deliuer his purse, or otherwise that he will kill him, by force of which threats he doth deliuer his purse, this is robberie, as well as if the felon had taken the purse from the person of the owner by violence, or strong hand: Or if one or more doe take vp a horse out of the pasture of the owner, or driue cattell out of his ground, the owner standing by and looking on the Felon at the same time, this is robbery, so that the felon doth make an assault vpon the owner, or do put him in feare. But if a felon do take money from the person of a man in the high way, and not put his person in feare, it is no robberie, but only felony, for the which the offendor shall haue his clergy.

22. Ass. p. 39 Fit. cor. 115 5. El. Dyer 224.

Robberie by threatening.

Taking a mans money, but not putting him in feare.

44.E.3.14 4.H.4.3 28 If two, thrée, or more, do by force take a man, and by threats compell him to sweare to bring them a certaine summe of money, menacing him, that they will kill him if he doe it not, by force wherof he doth bring them the same summe of money, this is robbery, for that he did first sweare, and after bring the money against his will: and yet by this enforced oath he was not bound to bring them the said money, for that the oath was taken for feare of death, and so against his will. And likewise, if felons come to a mans house in the night to rob him, and the possessor of the house fearing that they will enter his house and rob him, doth cast out unto them mony, or plate, which the felons do take, and then depart, this is robbery, for it is in construction of the law taken from the person of a man, and for feare. Robberie by taking an oth to bring mony. Robbery in taking money giuen.

9.E.4.26. 29 If one lye in the high way to rob passengers, and draweth his sword against a man that travelleth the same way, and commaundeth him to deliuer his purse, whereupon the same party encountreth him, & is to strong for him, and apprehendeth him, or leuieth Huy and Cry, and the offendor is thereby taken, yet this is no Robberie, nor Felony, for there was no act done, though there was an intent and will to robbe, Quia voluntas non reputabitur pro facto. Robbery in will, but not in déed.

30 Burglary is, when one or more persons do in the time of peace breake a house, a Church, a Wall, a Tower, or Gatehouse in the night, with a felonious intent to robbe, kill a man, or commit some other Felonie, for the Fit. cor.264 which Burglarie the offendor shalbe hanged, though he take nothing away. 22.Ass.p.95 But that breaking of the house must bée to commit some Felonie: For if the offendor be indicted for the breaking of a house to beat some person, that 13.H.4.8 is but Trespas, but if it be to kill another, then it is Felony. And if a man bée indicted for the breaking of a Close, to kill or robbe another, it is not Burglarie. What is Burglary

1.M.Dy.99. 31 If a man doe breake a house, and doe not enter into it, then it is no Burglarie: for a man was indicted, Quod burglariter fregit ecclesiam in nocte & intrauit, ad deprædandum bona parochianorum in eadem existent' sed nihil abstulit: and this was adiudged Burglary, for that the party indicted did enter. Breaking a house, but not entring.

32 Burglary cannot be committed in the day, but in the night: for all the St.39.El.15. indictments of Burglary be Noctanter fregit: for though by the statute of 39. Eliz. the benefit of Clergie is taken away from any person, conuicted for the felonious taking away in the day time of any money or goods, of the value of fiue shillings, or upwards, in any dwelling house or out-house, although no person shalbe in the same at the time of the said felony committed, and so that offence is made as penall as Burglary, by the losse of the benefite of Clergie, yet is it not Burglary, for it may be committed in the day time, & the penaltie of losing of his Clergy is not inflicted, unlesse the money or goods taken away be of the value of fiue shillings, or upwards. No Burglary in the day.

33 If

Breaking a dwelling house where no person is

33 If a man hath a mansion house, and he and his family doth upon some cause goe forth of the house, and in the meane time one doth come, and breake the house in the night, to commit felony, this is Burglary: For although the owner, nor any of his family were in the house, yet it is his mansion house: for the words of an appeale or inditment of Burglarie be, Domum mansionalem ipsius A.B. fregit. And in like sort, if a man have two houses, and doth inhabite sometime in one of them, and some other time in another, and hath a familie or servants in them both, and in the night, when the servants be out of the house, felons doe breake the house, this is Burglarie, for that the house is broken. Co.li.4.40.

Felonies by Statute.

And now hauing expressed which bee felonies by the common Law, it resteth that I declare which be felonies by Statute, with the reasons and causes why the same statutes were made, so farre as I may be warranted by the same statutes. And as in Treasons I began with those Treasons which did concerne the K. and his chiefe magistrates of iustice: So in reporting of such lawes and statutes as haue beene made for the supply of some defects at the common Law, I will begin with a statute which indeuoreth to restraine such as practise or confederat to destroy the king, or his chiefe officers attending on his person or estate.

1 For as much as by quarrels made to such as haue beene in great authority, office, and of counsell with the kings of this Realme, hath ensued the destruction of the kings, and thereby the vndoing of this Realme: so as it hath appeared euidently, when compassing of the death of such as were of the kings true subiects was had, the destruction of the prince was imagined thereby, and for the most part it hath growne, and beene occasioned by enuie & mallice of the kings owne houshold seruants. And for that by the lawes of this land, if actuall deeds were not had, there was no remedy for such false compassings, imaginations, and confederacies had against any lord, or any of the kings Councell, or any of the kings great Officers in his houshold, or Steward, Treasurer, Controller, and so great inconueniences did ensue, because such vngodly demeanor was not straitly punished, before that an actuall deed was done: for the remedy whereof, by a statute made An. 3. H. 7. 14. it was ordai- Conspiring to destroy the king, or any lord &c.
St. 3. H. 7. 14. ned, That the Steward, Treasurer, and Controller of the kings house for the time being, or one of them, shall haue full authority and power to enquire by xij. sad men and discreet persons of the Checke Roll of the kings honourable houshold, if any seruant, admitted to be his seruant sworne, and his name put into the Checke Roll of houshold, whatsoeuer he be, seruing in any maner office or roome, reputed, had, and taken vnder the estate of a lord, make any confederacies, compassings, conspiracies, or imaginations, with any person or persons to destroy or murder the king, or any lord of this realme, or any other person sworne to the kings Councell, Steward, Treasurer, Controller of the kings house: that if it be found afore the said steward for the time being by the said xij. men, that any such of the kings seruants, as is abouesaid, hath confede-

red, compassed, conspired, or imagined, as abouesaid, that he so found by the inquiry, be put thereupon to answere. And the Steward, Treasurer, and Controller, or two of them haue power to determine the same matter according to the law. And if he be put in triall, that then it be tried by other xij. sad men of the same houshold. And that such misdoers haue no challenge but for mallice. And if such misdoers be found guilty by confession, or otherwise, that the said offence be iudged felony, and they to haue iudgement and execution as felons attainted ought to haue by the common law.

Challenge.

Rauishment of a woman

2 For that vnlawfull and forcible violence, and also detestable aduowtrie were committed in the rauishment of women, therefore by the stat. of West. 2. it was enacted, That if any man from henceforth rauish any woman maried, maid, or other woman, where she doth not consent neither before nor after, he shall haue iudgement of life & of member: and likewise where a man rauisheth a woman married, lady, damsell, or other with force, although she consent afterward, he shal haue such iudgement as before is said, if he be attainted at the K. suit: for the K. shall haue the suit. St. 13. E. 1. 34

Abusing a woman vnder x. yeres of age

3 By a stat. made An. 18. El. it was ordained, That if any person shall vnlawfully & carnally know & abuse any woman child vnder the age of x. yeares, every such vnlawfull & carnall knowledge shalbe felony, & the offendor thereof being duly conuicted, shall suffer as a felon, without allowance of clergy. St. 18. El. 6

The forf. for consenting to a rape.

4 By a statute made An. 6. R. 2. 6. it was ordained, That wheresoeuer and whensoeuer ladies daughters, and other women be rauished, and after such rape do consent to such rauishers, that as wel the rauishers as they that be rauished, & euery of them, be frō henceforth disabled, & by the same déed vnabled to haue or challenge heritage, dower, or ioint feoffemēt after the death of their husbands, and auncestors: and that incontinently in this case the next of the blood of those rauishers, or of them that be rauished, to whom such heritage, dower, or ioint feoffemēt ought to reuert, remaine, or fall after the death of the rauisher, or of her that is so rauished, shall haue title incontinently, that is to say, after the rape to enter vpon the rauisher, or her that is rauished, and their assignes, and land tenants, in the same heritage, dower, or ioynt feoffement, and the same to hold in a state of heritage: and that the husbands of such women, if they haue husbands, or if they haue no husbands in life, that then the fathers or other next of their bloud haue from henceforth the suit to pursue, and may sue against the same offendors and rauishors in this behalfe. And to haue them thereof conuict of life and of member, although the same women after such rape do consent to the said rauishers. And further it is accorded, that the def. in this case shall not be receiued to wage battell, but that the truth of the matter be thereof tried by inquisition of the countrey, sauing alwayes to our soueraign lord the K. and to other lords of the said realme, al their eschets of the said rauishers, if peraduenture they be thereof conuict. St. 6. R. 2. 6.

D

A woman rauished conceiued with child

By the opinion of Britton, if a woman at the time of the supposed rape doe conceiue with child by the rauisher, this is no rape, because a woman cannot conceiue Britton.

conceiue with child, if she doe not consent.

Bracton. It is a good plea in an appeale of Rape, to say, that before the rauishment supposed, he kept and used the plaintife as a Concubine: Or to plead, that though he lay with her, yet he did not carnally know her, for that is the force of the declaration in an appeale of Rape. E A Concubine.

T.9.E.4.26 If a man shalbe charged with a Rape by the way of inditemēt, or otherwise, he ought to be charged expressely by this word (Rapuit) and not by any other words, notwithstanding they doe amount to as much as this word (Rapuit) doth; as carnaliter cognouit, or such like. S. Appeales 81.85. F This word (Rapuit) necessary in an indictment.

St.3.H.7.2 5 By a statute made Anno 3.H.7. it is ordained, That if any person or persons shall take any maid, widdow, or wife, which hath any lands or goods, or is heire apparant to her auncestor against her will vnlawfully, such taking, procuring, and abbetting to the same, and also receiuing wittingly the same woman so taken against her will, and knowing the same, shal be felony: and such misdoers, takers, and procurers to the same, and receiuers, knowing the offence in forme aforesaid, shalbe reputed and iudged as principal felons. But this act doth not extend to any person taking any woman, onely clayming her as his ward or bondwoman. And by a statute made An.39.El. it was enacted, That all and euery such person & persons as shall be conuicted or attainted for any offence made felony by the said act of 3.H.7. or which shalbe indicted or arraigned, of, or for any such offence, and stand mute, or make no direct answer, or challenge peremptorily aboue the number of twenty, shal in euery such case lose his and their benefit of clergy, and shall suffer paines of death without clergy: any former law &c. notwithstanding. Prouided alwaies, That this act shall not extend to take away the benefit of Clergy, but onely from such person and persons as hereafter shalbe principals, or procurers, or accessaries before such offence committed. Taking a woman against her will. St.39.El.9. No Clergy allowed.

St.8.El.3. 6 By a statute made Anñ 8.El. it was enacted, That no person or persons shall bring, deliuer, send, receiue, or take, or procure to bee brought, deliuered, sent, or receiued into any shippe, or bottome, any Rammes, Sheepe, or Lambes, or any other kind of Sheepe, being aliue, to be conueyed out of any of the Queenes dominions, vpon paine, that euery such person, his aidors, abbettors, procurors, and comforters shall for his first offence forfeit all his goods for euer to the Queene and Informer, that will sue for them in any Court of Record, wherein no W.E.P. &c. And further, euery such offendor shall suffer imprisonment one whole yeare, without baile or mainprise, and at the yeares end shall in some market Towne, in the fulnesse of the Market, on the Market day, haue his left hand cut off, and that to be nailed vpon the openest place of such Market. And euery person eftsones offending against this statute, shalbe iudged a felon, and shal suffer death as in cases of felony. But this act shall not extend to any corruption of blood, or be preiudiciall to any women claiming dower by or from any such offendor. And the Iustices of Oyer & Determiner, Iust. of Gaole deliuery, and I. of P. in euery Countie Transporting of sheepe. The second offence felony.

and Shire within this Realme of England and Wales, and other the Ma. Dominions, shall haue full power and authoritie by vertue of this Act to enquire of euery offendor and offendors, contrary to the forme and effect of this act: and to heare and determine euery offence and offences committed & done contrary to the forme and effect of the same, according to the course of the laws of this Realme.

7 For as much as diuers euill disposed persons, being married, did run out of one countrey into another, or into places where they were not knowne, and there became to be maried, hauing another husband or wife liuing, to the great dishonor of God, & vtter vndoing of diuers honest mens children, and others: therfore by a stat. made an̄ 1. Iac. it was enacted, That if any person or persons within his Ma. dominiōs of England & Wales, being maried, or which hereafter shall marry, do marry any person or persons, the former husband or wife being aliue, that then euery such offence shalbe felony, and the party & parties so offending shall receiue such & the like proceeding, triall, and execution in such county, where such person or persons shalbe apprehended, as if the offence had bin committed in such county where such person or persons shal be takē or apprehended. Prouided alwaies, that this act shall not extend to any person or persons, whose husband or wife shalbe continually remaining beyond the seas by the space of 7. yeeres together, or whose husband or wife shall absent him or her selfe the one from the other by the space of 7. yeares together, in any parts within his Ma. Dominions, the one of thē not knowing the other to be liuing within that time. Prouided also, that this act shall not extend to any person or persons that are or shalbe at the time of such mariage diuorced by any sentence had or hereafter to be had in the Ecclesiasticall Court, or to any person or persons, where the former mariage hath bin or hereafter shalbe by sentence in the Ecclesiasticall court declared to be void, and of no effect: Nor to any person or persons, for, or by reason of any former mariage had or made, or hereafter to be had or made within age of consent. Prouided also, that no attainder for this offence made felony by this act, shall make or worke any corruption of blood, losse of dower, or disinherison of heire or heires.

Felony in marying vntill the former husband or wife be dead.

St. 1. Iac. 11

No corruptiō of blood, or disheritance

8 By the stat. made an̄ 1. Iac. it was ordained, That if any person or persons infected with ẏ plague shalbe by the Maior, Bailifes, Constables, or other head officers of any City, Borough, Town corporat, priuiledged place, or Market Towne, or by any I. of Peace, Constable, Headborough, or other officer of the county (if any such infection be out of any City, Borough, Towne corporate, priuiledged place, or market towne) commaunded or appointed to keepe his or their house, for auoiding of further infection, & shall notwithstanding contrary to such commandement wilfully & contemptuously goe abroad, & shall conuerse in company, hauing any infectious sore vpon him vncured, then such person & persons shalbe taken & adiudged a felon, and suffer death as in case of Felony. But if such person shall not haue such sore found about him, thē for his said offence to be punished as a vagabond should or ought to be by the stat. made 39. El. 4. for the punishment of vagabonds, and further to be bound to his or their good behauior for one yeere: but no attainder of felony by vertue of this act shal extend to any attainder or corruption of blood, or forf. of any goods, chattels, lands, tenements, or hereditaments.

Infected with the plague.

St. 1. Iac. 31

No corruptiō of blood, or forfeiture.

9 By

St.35.El.1 St.2.Iac.25 9 By the stat. made An 35. El. it was ordained, That if any such offendor, which by the tenor & effect of the said act (intituled an act to retaine the Queens subiects in due obedience) is to be abiured, shal refuse to make such abiuration, as by the said stat. is appointed: Or after such abiuration shall not goe to such hauen, and within such time as is appointed, and from thence depart forth of the realme, according to the said statute: Or after his departure shall returne and come againe into any of the Q. Realmes or Dominions, without her speciall licence in that behalfe first had and obtained: Then in euery such case the person so offending shall be adiudged a felon, & suffer as in case of felony, without benefit of clergy. Prouided, that the wife of such offendor, by force of this act, shal not lose her dower: nor that any corruption of blood shal grow, or be by reason of any offence mentioned in this act. But the heire of such offendor by force of this act, shall and may after the death of euery such offendor haue and enioy the lands, tenements, and hereditaments of such offendor, as if this act had not bin made. Prouided, that no Popish Recusant or feme couert shall be bound to abiure by vertue of this act. Abiuration by a Recusant.

St.35.El.2. 10 By a stat. made an. 35. El. it was enacted, That any such offendor, which by the tenor & intent of the act made to restrain Popish Recusants to some certaine place of abode, is to be abiured, shal refuse to make such abiuration, or after such abiuration made shal not go to such hauen, and within such time as is appointed, and from thence depart out of the realme according to this act: Or after such his departure shall returne or come againe into any of her maiesties realmes or dominions, without her maiesties speciall licence, in that behalfe first had and obtained: then in euery such case the person so offending shall be adiudged a felon, and shall suffer and lose as in case of felony, without benefit of Clergy. Abiuration of a Recusant.

St.25.H.8.6 St.5.Eli.17. 11 By a stat. ordained an 25. H. 8. and made perpetuall an. 5. El. it was enacted, That the detestable & abominable vice of Buggery committed with mankind, or beast, shalbe adiudged felony, and such order & forme of proces therein shalbe vsed against the offendors as in cases of felony at the common law. And the offendors being thereof conuict by verdict, confession, or outlary, shal suffer such pains of death, & losses, & penalties of goods, cattels, debts, lands, tenemēts and hereditaments, as felons be accustomed to do according to the order of the common law of this Realme. And no person offending in such offence, shall be admitted to his Clergy. And I. of Peace shall haue authority within ÿ limits of their iurisdiction and commission to heare and determine the same, as they haue in cases of other felonies. Buggery No clergy

St.21.H.8.7 St.5.El.10. 12 By a statute prouided An. 21. H. 8. and made perpetuall An 5. El. it was established, That all and singular seruants, to whom any caskets, iewels, money, goods, or cattels, by his or their master or mistresse, shall be deliuered to keepe: if any such seruant or seruants withdraw him or them from their said master or mistresse, & go away with the said caskets, iewels, mony, or cattels, or any part thereof, to the intent to steale the same, & defraud his or their said master or mistresse thereof, contrary to the trust & confidence in him or thē put by his or their master or mistresse; or els being in the seruice of his said master Seruants imbesiling their masters goods.

 or

or mistresse, without assent or commaundement of his master or mistresse hee imbesill the same caskets, iewels, money, goods, or cattels, or any part thereof, or otherwise conuert the same to his owne vse, with like purpose to steale it: if the said caskets, iewels, money, goods, or cattels that any such seruant shall go away with, or which he shall imbesill with purpose to steale it, as is aforesaid, be of the value of forty shillings, or aboue: then the same false fraudulent and vntrue act shalbe from henceforth deemed and adiudged felony, and he or they so offending shalbe punished as other felons be punished for felonies cōmitted by the course of the common law. Prouided allwaies, that this act, or any thing therein contained, shall not in any wise extend, or be preiudiciall to any apprē-tice or apprētices, nor to any person being within the age of xviij. yeeres, going away with his or their masters goods, or iewels, or otherwise, conuerting the same to his or their owne vses, during the time of their apprentiship, or being within the said age of xviij. yeares, but that euery apprentice or apprentices, such person or persons being within the said age, doing or offending contrarie to this act, shalbe and stand in like case, as they and euery of them were before the making of this act.

B

Receiuing money vpon an obligation.

If a man do deliuer an obligation to his seruant to receiue xx.l. and the seruant doth receiue the money of the obligor, and thē goeth away with the same, or doth conuert it to his owne vse, this is not felony within the compasse of the foresaid stat. of 21. H.8. for the master did not deliuer any goods to his seruant in this case, but an obligation, which is not valuable, but a thing in action: and moreouer, the money was not deliuered to the seruant by the hands of his master, but by the obligor. But if one of a mans seruants doth deliuer to another of his seruants goods of the masters, being aboue the value of 40.s. and he doth go away with it, or conuert it to his owne vse, this is felony. M.25.H.8. Dyer 5.

C

Receiuing money for wares.

If a man do deliuer to his apprentice wares or marchandises, to sell at a faire, or a market, and he selleth them, and receiueth the mony, and then goeth away with the mony, or conuerteth it to his own vse, this is not felony by the stat. of 21. H.8. for he had not the mony by the deliuery of his master, neyther went he away with the thing that was deliuered vnto him. M.25.H.8. Dyer 5.

Seruants imbesilling their masters goods after his death

13 By the stat. of An̄ 31. H.6. it was ordained, That executors shall haue a writ out of the Chancery, by the aduice of the Chauncelor, two chiefe Iustices, and the chiefe Baron of the Exchequer, with two proclamations, returnable in the K. Bench against such houshold seruants of the Testator, as haue spoiled or eloigned the goods of their master, after ỹ death of the Testator. And if the writ be returned serued, & the defendants make default, they shall be attainted of felony: and if they appeare, they shalbe cōmitted to prison, there to remaine at the discretion of the Iustices, vntill the defendants do answer vnto the said executors in such actions which the said executors will declare against them, or any of them, by bill or writ, for the riot, taking, and spoiling aforesaid, and that the same actions be determined, so that such actions be pursued with effect, and not slackly to retaine the same persons in prison. And if the same persons be enlarged out of prison by the said Iustices, then they shal find sufficient sureties to the executors by recognizance to keepe such daies as they shal haue assigned by the Court. And if the keeper of the prison, whereunto they St.31.H.6.1.

shalbe

shalbe committed, doe let them go at large, without order of the Justices, then the said keeper shall forfeit xl. li. to the executors. No protection shall lye in any action upon this statute.

St.14.E.3.10 14 By the stat. of An 14. E. 3. it was accorded, That shirifes shalbhaue the keeping of gaoles, as they had wont to haue, and put in such keepers for whom they will answer. And if any keeper of prison or under keeper shall by too great dures of imprisonment and paine cause any prisoner which he hath in his custody, to become an approuer against his will, and is thereof attainted, he shall be adiudged a felon. Enforcing a prisoner to become an approuer.

St.5.El.20. 15 By the stat. of an 5. El. it was enacted, that euery person & persons which shalbe seene or found within this realme of England or Wales, in any company of vagabonds, commonly called, or calling themselues Egyptians, or counterfeiting, transforming, or disguising themselues by their apparell, speech, or other behauiour, like unto such vagabonds, commonly called, or calling themselues Egyptians, & so shall or doe remaine & continue in the same by the space of one moneth: then the same person or persons shall be deemed & iudged a felon and felons, and shall suffer paines of death, losse of lands & goods, as in cases of felony by the order of the common lawes of this realme, and shall upon triall of them, or any of them, be tried in the countrey, and by the inhabitants of the county, or place, where he or they shall be apprehended, or taken, and not per medietatem linguæ, and shall loose the priuiledge and benefit of Sanctuary and Clergy. Prouided, That this act shall not in any wise extend to any child or children, being within the age of 14. yeares. Egyptians. Triall. No Clergy. xiiij. yeares.

St.8.H.6.12. 16 By the stat. made An. 8. H. 6. it was ordained, That if any Record, or parcell of the same, Writ, Returne, Pannell, Proces, Warrant of Atturney in the Courts of Chauncery, Exchequer, the one Bench, or the other, or the Treasury, be willingly stolne, taken away, withdrawne, or auoided by any Clerke, or other person, by cause whereof any iudgement be reuersed, such stealer, taker away, withdrawer, or auoider, their procurors, counsellors, & abbettors, being thereof indicted, and by proces thereupon made, therof duly conuict by their owne confession, or by enquest to be taken of lawfull men (whereof the one halfe shalbe of the men of any court of the same courts, and the other halfe of other) shalbe iudged for felons, and shall incurre the paine of felony. And the Judges of the said Courts, of the one Bench, or of the other, haue power to heare and determine such defaults before them, and thereof to make due punishment, as is aforesaid. Imbesilling of Records.

2.R.3.10 Br. Cor.173 If a Judge doe file an indictment with other indictments, which was not found by the Jury, that did find other indictments: Or if he do imbesill or rase a Record, or such like, this is but misprision in the Judge, but this is felony in another person who is no Judge: and the Judge shalbe indited and arraigned thereof, & shall make a fine, & lose his office for this misprision. And if the steward of a Liberty doth arraigne a man by the colour of Infangtheefe, and doth adiudge him to death, the liberty shall be seised therefore: but no punishment shalbe inflicted upon the steward, for he did it by colour of the liberty, and so no felony: and if a man do sue another by an action of debt to ẏ exigent, whereupon he is outlawed, & another mã doth rase ẏ originall, & the 3. capias, & the exigent, The penalties of Judges or officers abusing Records.

and

and maketh part in London, and the residue in Middlesex, and doth write in them W. B. for J. B. this is felony by the foresaid statute of 8. H. 6. which is, if a Record in either of the Benches, or in the Exchequer, bee imbesiled, carried away, withdrawne, or avoided, wherby a iudgement shalbe reversed, that then it shalbe inquired by clerkes of those Courts, and others, & it shal be adiudged by the Justices of the same court, and it shall be ordained as felonie: and this rasure doth avoid the whole Record, so that it cannot be redressed by error, & it is a greater offence then if part onely had bin avoided: and all which be agreeing thereunto be felons. 2.R.3.10

Cutting of tongues, putting out of eies.

17 By a stat. made an. 5. H. 4. it was enacted, That the offendors which do cut the tongues, or put out the eies of any of the Kings liege people, and that duely proued, and found that such deed was done of malice pretenced, shall incurre the paine of felony. St. 5. H. 4. 5.

Multiplication.

18 By the stat. made anno 5. H. 4. it was ordained, That none shall use to multiply gold or siluer, nor practise the art of Multiplication: and if any do, he shall incurre the paine of felony in this case. St. 5. H. 4. 4.

Withholding of a hauke.

19 By the Statute made Anno 34. Ed. 3. and 37. Ed. 3. it was enacted, That whosoeuer findeth a Falkon, Tarcelet, Laner, Lanerct, or other Hawke, which the owner thereof hath lost, shall immediately bring the same to the Sherife of the Countie, which shall make proclamation in all the good Townes of the Countie, that he hath such a hawke in his custodie, and if the owner which lost the hawke, or any of his seruants come to challenge it, and prooueth that it is his Maisters, hee shall pay for the costs, and haue it. And if none doe come within foure moneths to challenge it, then the Sherife shall haue the hawke, agreeing with him that tooke it up, if hee be a simple man, and if hee be a Gentleman, and of estate to haue a hawke, then the Sherife shall deliuer him the hawke, taking reasonable allowance for the keeping thereof. And whosoeuer taketh a hawke, and the same concealeth from the owner, or from his falkoners, or taketh away a hawke from the owner, or stealeth a hawke and carrieth it away, not obseruing the foresaid ordinances, and is thereof attainted, shall be used as a felon, which hath stolen a horse or other thing. St. 34. E. 3. 22 St. 37. E. 3. 19

Cōgregatiōs by masons.

20 By a Statute made Anno 3. H. 6. it was ordained, That Congregations and Confederacies shall not be holden by Masons in their generall assemblies. And if any such bee made, they that cause such Chapters, and Congregations to be assembled and holden, if they be thereof conuict, shall be adiudged for felons. And all other Masons that come to such Chapters and Congregations, shall be punished by imprisonment of their bodies, and make fine and ransome at the Kings will. St. 3. H. 6. 1.

A Souldier departing from his captaine.

21 By the statutes of Anno 18. H. 6. Anno 2. E. 6. 2. and Anno 4. & 5. P. & M. it was enacted, That if any Souldier, man of Armes, or Archer, which hath taken parcel of his wages of his captaine, hath mustred, and is entred of record the Kings souldier, doth not passe ẏ sea, or go with his captaine, St. 18. H. 6. 19 St. 2 E. 6. 2. St. 4 & 5. P. & M. 3.

except

(except notorious sicknesse or impediment by Gods visitation doth stay him, which he shal immediatly certifie his captaine, and repay his money) or els being in the enemies countrey in garrison, or elsewhere in the K. seruice, where he is appointed to serue, doth depart without licence of the kings Lieutenant, Deputy, high Admirall, vice-Admiral, Warden, Captaine, or in their absence of their Deputies, then he shall be taken, iudged, and executed as a Felon, without hauing any aduantage of Clergie or Sanctuarie. And Iustices of Peace shall haue authoritie to enquire thereof, and to heare and determine the same, as they do other felonies committed in that Shire where such Souldior shall be taken. And by a braunch of a statute made an̄ 5. Eli. it was ordained,

St.5.El.5. That the foresaid statute of 18. H.6. in all pains, forfeitures, and other things,

2.Iac.25. did, doth, and hereafter shall extend, as well to all and euery mariner and gunner, hauing taken, or which hereafter shall take prest or wages, to serue the king, his heires or successors, to all intents and purposes, as the same did or doth to any souldier. S. the statutes of 7.H.7.1.& 3.H.8.5. made to the like — A Mariner or Gunner.

St.7.H.7.1. effect. Et Quære whether the first stat. which were made for couenant soul-

3.H.8.5 diors, or the later stat. which were ordained for prested Souldiors, bee, or

Co.li.6.27. ought to be put in execution: wherein haue respect to the meaning of the makers of the foresaid stat. of an.5.El.5.

St.27.El.2. 22 By the statute of Anno 27.El.2. it was ordained, That euery person which shall wittingly & willingly receiue, relieue, comfort, aid, or maintain any Iesuit, Seminary priest, or other priest, made out of the realm of England, Deacon, or religious or Ecclesiasticall person, being at liberty, or out of hold, knowing him to be a Iesuit, Seminary priest, or other such priest, Deacon, or religious or ecclesiasticall person, shal for such offence be adiudged a felon, without benefit of clergy, & suffer death, lose, & forf. as one attainted of felony. — Receiuing or relieuing of Iesuits. No Clergy

St.28.E.1.2 23 By the statute made An.28.Ed.1. it was established, That if any make purueyance or prizes without warrant, and do carry them away, against the will of the owner, he shalbe arrested by the town where the prizes were made, and carried to the next Gaole, and if he be therof attainted, he shal be punished as a felon, if the value of the goods do so require. — Purueiance without warrant.

St.25.E.3.15 24 By the Statute of Anno 25.Edw.3. it was ordained, That no Purueyor of the kings shall take any more Sheepe before sheare time, but so many as may reasonably suffice vntill sheare time, and after that time they shall take as many shorne Sheepe, and not other, as may reasonably suffice for the time to come. And if any Taker, Purueyor, or Buyer, take any sheepe with their Wooll betwixt Easter and the Feast of Saint Iohn Baptist, praise them at a small price, and send them to his house to bee shorne to his owne profite, and thereof be attainted at the suit of the king, or the party, he shalbe vsed as a Theefe or a Robber. — Purueying of sheepe.

St.5.Ed.3.2. 25 By the Statutes made Anno 5.Edw.3.10.Edw.3.25.Ed.3.36.Ed.3.

10.Ed.3.1. it was enacted, That the Corne, Cattell, & other victuall, & things which shalbe

25.E.3.1. taken for the kings house, shalbe taken in such place where most plenty is, and

36.Ed.3.2. in — Appraisement of things purueied.

in conuenient time, and no more then is néedfull for that season. And if the purueyor or buyer cannot well agrée with the seller for that which hee shall néed, then the same shall be praised at the very value by the Constables and foure honest men of the Townes where such taking is, thereunto sworne: and the praysers shall not be constrained by menace, threats, duresse, or other villanie, to set any price other then their oathes doe require, but as such things doe commonly goe in the next Markets. And Indentures or Tallies shall be presently made betwixt the purueyors and those from whom the goods bee taken, in the presence of the said Constables, and foure praysers, contayning the quantitie of their takings, the price, and of what persons, and they shal be sealed with the purueyors seales, by which Indentures or Tallies satisfaction shalbe made to them, from whom such goods be taken. And if any Taker or Purueyor do make his prouision in other manner then by foure discréet men of the Towne, or doe not deliuer Tallies or Indentures with his seale, as is beforesaid, he shall be incontinently arrested by the Towne where such purueyance was made, and brought to the next Gaole: and if hee bee thereof attainted, he shall be punished as a felon, if the quantity of the goods doe require.

Taking of cariage.

26 By the Statute of Anno 36. Edw. 3. it was enacted, That if any Taker or Buyer, after Commission to him directed, doth puruey, leuie, or take any carriage in other manner then is comprised in his Commission, it is Felony. St. 36. E. 3. 2

And by the Statute of Anno 36. Edw. 3. it was ordained, That Commissions shall be awarded, to enquire of Purueyors behauior: and if it be found at the king, or parties suit, by euidence of the inditors, or other manner, that the Purueyors haue taken more then they haue deliuered to the kings house, and that they haue not paid for that which they haue taken, it is felony, & they shalbe punished as felons. St. 36. E. 3. 4.

Forging of euidence.

27 By the Statute of Anno 5. Eliz. it was ordained, That it shall be Felony, without benefit of Clergie or Sanctuarie, eftsoones to commit any of the offences prohibited by the said Statute, ordained against the forging of Euidences and Writings, being once before conuicted or condemned of any of the said offences by any of the waies or meanes limitted by the said statute. But there shall be no corruption of blood, or forfeiture of dower, by reason of this felony. S. Forgerie 3. &c. St. 5. El. 14

A Rogue banished.

28 By the Statute of Anno 39. Eliz. it was enacted, That it shall be felony for any Rogue, beeing by the Justices of Peace adiudged incorrigible and dangerous, and therefore banished this Realme by the Justices, in their Quarter Sessions, to return again into any part of this Realme, or Wales, without licence or warrant so to doe, which felony shall be heard and determined in that County of this Realme, or Wales, in which the offendor shall be apprehended. St. 39. El. 4.

And

St.1.Iac.7. And by the statute made Anno 1.Iacob. such Rogues as shall be adiudged (as aforesaid) incorrigible or dangerous, shall also by the iudgement of the same Iustices, or the more part of them then present, in their open Sessions of the Peace, be branded in the left shoulder with an hot burning yron, of the breadth of an English shilling, with a great Romane R. vpon the yron, and the branding vpon the shoulder to bee so thoroughly burnt and set on vpon the skinne and flesh, that the letter R. be séene, and remaine for a perpetuall marke vpon such Rogue, during his or her life, and thereupon bée sent by the same Iustices to the place of his dwelling, if he haue any: if not, then to the place where he last dwelt by the space of a yeare, if that can be knowne by his confession, or otherwise: and if that cannot be knowen, then to the place of his birth, there to be placed in labour, as a true subiect ought to be: and after such punishment of any such Rogue, as aforesaid, if any Rogue so punished shall offend againe in begging or wandering, contrarie to the said stat. of 39. El. 4. or this present act, Then in euery such case the party offending shalbe iudged a felon, & shall suffer as in cases of felony, without benefit of clergie, the same felony to be tried in the countie where any such offendor shalbe taken.

Rogues incorrigible.

Lex Alure. di Regis.

St.1.Iac.12 29 By the statute of Anno 1. Iacob. 12. it was enacted, That if any person or persons shall vse, practise, or exercise any inuocation or coniuration of any euill and wicked spirit, or shall consult, couenant with, entertaine, employ, féed, or reward any euill or wicked spirit, to or for any intent or purpose, or take vp any dead man, woman, or child, out of his, her, or their graue, or any other place, where the dead body resteth, or the skinne, bone, or any other part of any dead person, to bee employed or vsed in any manner of Witchcraft, Sorcerie, Charme, or Enchantment, or shall vse, practise, or exercise any Witchcraft, Enchantment, Charme, or Sorcery, whereby any person shall be killed, destroyed, wasted, consumed, pyned, or lamed in his or her body, or any part thereof: then euery such offendor, or offendors, their aydors, abbettors, and counsellors being of any the said offences duely and lawfully conuicted and attainted, shall suffer paines of death as a felon or felons, and shall lose the priuiledge and benefite of Clergie and Sanctuarie.

Coniuration, witchcraft.

Lex Athelstani 6.

If any person or persons shall take vpon him, or them by witchcraft, inchantment, charme, or sorcerie, to tell, or declare in what place any treasure of gold or siluer, should, or might be found, or had in the earth, or other secret places: Or where goods, or things lost or stollen should be found, or become: Or to the intent to prouoke any person to vnlawfull loue: Or whereby any cattell, or goods of any person shalbe destroyed, wasted, or impaired, or to hurt or destroy any person in his or her bodie, although the same be not effected and done: Then all and euery such person and persons so offending, and beeing thereof lawfully conuicted, shall for the said offence suffer imprisonment by the space of one whole yeare, without baile or mainprise, and once in euery quarter of the said yeare shall in some market towne, vpon the market day, or at such time as any Faire shalbe kept, there stand openly vpon the Pillorie, by the space of sixe houres, and there shall openly confesse, his, or her error or offence.

Finding of treasure.

Declaring where goods lost should be found.

Prouoking to loue.

Destroying of any person or cattell.

If any person or persons being once conuicted of the same offences, as is aforesaid, doe efttsoones perpetrate and commit the like offence, then euery such offendor being of any the said offences the second time lawfully and duly conuicted and attainted, as is aforesaid, shall suffer paines of death, as a felon or felons, and shall lose the benefite and priuiledge of Clergie and Sanctuarie: sauing to the wife of such person as shall offend in any thing contrarie to this Act, her title of Dower, and also to the heire and successor of euery such person, his and their title of inheritance, succession, and other rights, as though no such attainder of the auncestor or predecessor had beene made.

Prouided alwayes, That if the offendor in any the cases aforesaid shall happen to bee a Peere of the Realme, then his triall therein to bee had by his Peeres, as it is vsed in cases of Felony or Treason, and not otherwise.

Hunting with Visors.

30 By a Statute made Anno 1.H.7. it was ordained, That at euery such St.1.H.7.7
time as any information shall be made of any vnlawfull hunting by night, or with painted faces, in Forrest, Parke, or Warren, to any of the Kings Councell, or to any Iustice of Peace of the Countie where such hunting shall be, of any person suspected thereof: It shall bee lawfull to any of the same Councell, or Iustice of Peace, to whom such information shall bee made, to make a Warrant to the Shirife, or to any Constable, Baylife, or other Officer of the same County, to arrest and take the same person, to haue him before the maker of the same Warrant, or any other of the Kings councell, or Iustice of Peace of the same Countie. And the Counsellor or Iustice before whom such person shall bee brought, shall haue power to examine him of the said hunting, and of the doers thereof: and if he conceale the offence, or any offendor, it is felony: and if he confesse the truth, and all that he shall be examined of and knoweth in that behalfe, then the offence of hunting by him done, shall be against the King but trespas fineable, to be assessed at the next generall Sessions by the Iustices there. And if any Rescous or disobedience be made to any person hauing authority to doe execution or iustice by any such warrant, by any person which should be arrested, so that execution of the same warrant be not had, then the same rescous and disobedience shalbe felony: and the same felony shall be enquired of, and determined as other felonies beene.

Rescous.

Twelue or aboue assembled together to change any law.

31 By a Statute made Anno 1. Ma. & 1. Eliz. it was ordained, That St.1.M.12
if any persons, to the number of twelue, or aboue, being assembled together, St.1.El.16
shall intend, goe about, practise, or put in vre, with force of armes, vnlawfully and of their owne authority to alter or change any lawes, made or established for Religion, by authoritie of Parliament, which stand in force; or any other Lawes or Statutes of this Realme, or any of them: the same number being commaunded or required by the Shirife of the Shire, or by any Iustice of Peace of the same Shire, or by the Mayor, Shirife, Iustices of Peace, or Baylifes of any Citie, Borough, or Towne Corporate, where any such assemblies shall be vnlawfully had or made, by proclamation in the Queenes name, to retire and repaire to their owne houses and habitations, or places

from

from whence they came: And they or any of them notwithstanding such proclamation, shall remaine and make their abode, or continue together by the space of one whole houre, after such commaundement or request made by proclamation, or after that shall willingly in forcible and riotous manner, attempt to doe, or put in vre any things aboue specified, then as well euery such abode or continuing together, as euerie such act or offence, that after such commaundement or request by proclamation had or made, shall bee attempted to bee done, practised, or put in vre by any persons being of the number aforesaid, shall be adiudged Felonie in all and singular those persons, that so shall make their abode and continue together, or shall attempt or commit any such act. And the offendors therein shall be adiudged Felons, and shall suffer onely execution of death as in case of Felony.

If any persons to the sayd number of twelue or aboue, shall intend, goe about, practise, or put in vre, in manner and forme aforesayd, to ouerthrow, cut, breake, cast downe, or digge vp the pales, hedges, ditches, or other inclosure of any Parkes or Parke, or other ground inclosed, or the bankes of any Fish Pond, or Poole, or any Conduits for water, Conduit heads, or Conduit pipes hauing course for water, to the intent that the same, or any of them from henceforth should remaine open, not inclosed, or voyd: Or vnlawfully to haue common or way in the sayd Parkes or Parke, or other grounds or ground inclosed, or in any of them, or to destroy in manner and forme aforesayd, the Deere in any Parkes or Parke, or any Warreins or Warrein of Conies, or any Doue-houses, or any Fish in any Fish ponds, or Poole, or to pull, or cut downe any Houses, Barnes, Mills, or Bayes, or to burne any stackes of corne or graine, or to abate or diminish the Rents, or yearely value of any Mannors, Lands, or Tenements, or the price of any victuals, corne, or graine, or any other thing vsuall for the sustenance of men, and bееing required and commaunded by any Iustice of Peace, or by the Sherife of the Countie, or by the Maior, Bailife or Bailifs, or other head Officers of any Citie, or Towne Corporat, where such assembly shall bee had, by Proclamation to bee made in the Queenes name, to retire or returne in peaceable manner to their places and houses from whence they came, and they or any of them (notwithstanding such Proclamation) shall remaine, or make their abode, or continue together by the space of one whole houre, after such commaundement or request made by Proclamation: or after shall in that forcible manner doe, or put in vre any of these things last before mentioned, then as well euerie such abode, or continuing together, as euerie such act, that after such commaundement or request by Proclamation had or made, shall bee done, practised, or put in vre, by any persons, bееing aboue the number of twelue, shall bee adiudged Felonie, and the offendors therein shall be adiudged Felons, and shall suffer onely execution of death, as in case of Felonie.

Practising to destroy parks, ponds, conduits.

If any person or persons, vnlawfully, and without authoritie, by ringing of any Bell or Bells, sounding of any Trumpet, Drumme, Horne, or other instrument whatsoeuer, or by firing of any Beacon, or by malitious speaking or vttering of any words, or making of any outcrye, or by setting

Raising of vnlawful assemblies by some act or words.

up, or casting of any bills or bill, or writing whatsoeuer, or by any other deed or act, shall raise, or cause to bee raysed, or assembled, any persons to the number of twelue, or aboue, to the intent that the same persons should doe or put in vre any of the acts or things abouesaid, and that the persons to the number of twelue, or aboue, so raysed and assembled, after request or commaundement had or giuen, in forme aforesayd, shall make their abode, or continue together, as is aforesayd, or vnlawfully, and in forcible manner perpetrate, doe, commit, or put in vre any of the acts or things abouesayd, then all and singular persons, by whose speaking, deed, act, or any other the meanes aboue specified, any persons to the number of twelue shall bee raysed or assembled, for the doing, committing, or putting in vre any of the acts or things aboue mentioned, shall bee adiudged for his so speaking or doing, a Felon, and shall suffer execution of death as in case of Felonie.

Releeuing them which be assembled.

If any wife, or seruant of any of the same persons, or any other person whatsoeuer, shall willingly and without compulsion, bring, send, deliuer, or conuey, any Money, Harneyes, Artillerie, Weapons, Meat, Bread, Drinke, or other Victuall to any person or persons so being assembled, as is aforesayd, during such time as hee or they shall bee so assembled together in forcible manner, as is aforesaid, then euerie wife, seruant, or other person so bringing or conueying &c. any of the foresayd things, to the same persons so beeing assembled together in forcible manner, or to any of them, and not departing to their houses or dwelling places, vpon request or commaundement made vnto them, as is aforesaid, shalbe adiudged a felon, and shall suffer execution of death as in case of felonie.

Vnlawful assembly by xl. and more.

If any persons to the number of fortie, or more, shall assemble together in forcible manner vnlawfully, and of their owne authoritie, to the intent to execute, doe, or put in vre any of the things aboue specified, or to do other felonious or rebellious act or acts, and so shall continue together by the space of three houres, after Proclamation shall bee made, at, or nigh the place where they shall bee so assembled, or in some Market Towne, thereunto next adioyning, and after notice thereof to them giuen, then euerie person so willingly assembled in forcible maner, and so continuing together by the space of three houres after such Proclamation made, and notice thereof giuen, shalbe adiudged a felon. S. Riots &c. 32. &c.

Wandring souldiers and mariners.

32 By the Statute made Anno 39. Eliz. it was enacted, That all idle and wandring Souldiers, or Mariners, or idle persons, which now are, or hereafter shall bee wandring as Souldiers or Mariners shall settle themselues in some seruice, labour, or other lawfull course of life, without wandring, or otherwise repaire to the places where they were borne, or to their dwelling places, if they haue any, and there remaine, betaking themselues to some lawfull trade or course of life, vpon payne that all persons offending contrarie to this Act, to bee reputed as Felons, and to suffer as in case of Felonie, without any benefit of Cleargie to bee allowed. And euerie idle and wandring Souldier St. 39. El. 17.

Souldier or Mariner, which comming from his Captaine from the Seas, or from beyond the Seas, shall not haue a Testimoniall vnder the hand of some one Iustice of Peace, of, or néere the place where hee landed, setting downe therein the place and time where and when hée landed, and the place of his dwelling, or birth, vnto which he is to passe, as aforesaid, and a conuenient time therein limited for his passage: or hauing such testimoniall, shall wilfully excéed the time therein limited aboue fouretéene dayes: And also as well euerie such idle and wandring Souldier or Mariner, as euerie other idle person wandring as a Souldier or Mariner, which shall at any time hereafter forge or counterfeit any such Testimoniall, or haue with him or them any Forging a Testimoniall. such Testimoniall forged or counterfeited, as aforesayd, knowing the same to bée counterfeited or forged, in all these cases euerie such act or acts to bée Felonie, and the offendors to suffer, as aforesayd, without any benefit of Clergie. It shall and may bée lawfull for the Iustices of Assises, Iustices of Gaole deliuerie, and Iustices of Peace of euerie Countie, and for all Iustices of Peace in Townes Corporat, hauing authoritie to heare and determine Felonies, to heare and determine all such offences in their generall Sessions, and to execute the offendors, which shall bée conuicted before them, as in cases of Felonie is accustomed: Except some honest person, Retaining an offendor into seruice. valued at the last Subsidie next before that time, to tenne pounds in goods, or fortie shillings in lands, or else some honest Freeholder, as by the sayd Iustices shall bee allowed, will bee contented before such Iustices as such person shall bee arraigned of Felonie, to take him or them into his seruice, for one whole yeare then next following, and before the sayd Iustices will bee bound in Recognisaunce of tenne pounds, to bee leuied of his lands, goods, tenements, and cattels, to the vse of the King, if hée kéepe not the sayd person or persons for one whole yeare, and bring him to the next Sessions for the Peace, and Gaole deliuerie next ensuing after the sayd yeare. And if any such person retained depart within the yeare, without the licence of Departing without licéce him that so retained him, then to be indicted, tried, and iudged as a felon, and not to haue the benefit of his Clergie.

St.31.El.4. 33 By a Statute made Anno 31. Elizab. it was established, That if any person or persons, hauing at any time hereafter the charge or custodie of Imbeceling the K. Armor, &c. any Armour, Ordnance, Munition, Shot, Powder, or Habiliments of Warre of the Quéenes, her heires or successors, or of a Victuals prouided for the victualing of any Souldiers, Gunners, Mariners, or Pioners, shall for any lucre or gaine, or wittingly, aduisedly, and of purpose to hinder or impeach her Maiesties seruice, imbecile, purloyne, or conuey away any the same Armour, Ordnance, Munition, Shot, or Powder, Habiliments of Warre, or Victuals, to the value of twentie shillings, at one or seuerall times, then euerie such offence shall bée adiudged Felonie, and the offendor and offendors therein to be tried, procéeded on, and suffer as in case of Felonie. But The suit within a yere after the offence. none shall bée impeached for any offence against this Statute, vnlesse the same impeachment bée prosecuted, or begun within a yeare next after the offence done. And this Act, nor any attainder or attainders of any person or persons, for any offence made felonie by this Act, shall in any wise extend, or bée interpreted to make the offendor or offendors to forfeit any lands, tenements, or hereditaments, any longer than during his or their life or liues, or to make

No corruptiō of blood, or forf. of dower.

Prœfe in discharge of the offendor.

any corruption of blood to any the heire or heires of any such offendor or offendors, or to make the wife of any such offendor to lose or forfeit her dower, or title of dower, of, or in any lands, tenements, or hereditaments, or her action or interest to the same: any thing in this Act &c. notwithstanding. And such person or persons as shall be impeached for any offence made felonie by this Statute, shall by vertue of this Act bee receiued and admitted to make any lawfull prœfe that hee can, by lawfull witnesse, or otherwise, for his discharge and defence in that behalfe: any law, &c. notwithstanding.

Cutting downe of Powdike.

34 By a Statute made Anno 22. H. 8. and reuiued Anno 2. & 3. Ph. & Mar. it was ordained, That euerie peruerse and malitious cutting downe, and breaking vp of any part or parts of the dike called new Powdike in Marshland in the Countie of Norffolke, and the broken dike, otherwise called Oldfield dike by Marshland, in the isle of Ely, in the Countie of Cambridge, or of any other banke béeing parcell of the Kinde, and vttermost part of the causey of Marshland aforesaid, made for the defence and saluation of the sayd countrey of Marshland, at euerie time and times from henceforth committed and done (otherwise than in working of the sayd bankes or dykes, for the fortifying, repayring, and amending of the same) shall bee taken, reputed, and adiudged Felonie: And the offendors and doers of the same, and euerie of them, shall bée adiudged and reputed felons. And the Iustices of Peace of the sayd Counties of Norffolke and Cambridge, within the sayd isle, at euerie of their Sessions within the same isle and Counties to be kept, shall haue power to cause inquirie to bée made of euerie such offence, so at any time in forme aforesayd hereafter to bée done and committed, and to award like Proces against euerie of the sayd offendors, with like iudgement and execution of the same (if they or any of them bée found guiltie by verdict, or otherwise) as the sayd Iustices haue vsed to do vpon other felonies, being felonie by the common law. St. 22. H. 8.

Taking the othe for the Kings title.

35 By a Statute made Anno 3. Iac. 4. it was enacted, That euerie subiect of this Realme, that after the tenth day of Iune next comming, shall goe or passe out of this Realme to serue any forreine Prince, State, or Potentate, or shall after the sayd tenth day of Iune passe ouer the Seas, and there shall voluntarily serue any such forreine Prince, State, or Potentate, not hauing before his or their going or passing, taken the othe (viz. That our Soueraigne Lord King Iames is lawfull and rightfull King of this Realme &c.) before the officer thereunto appointed, shall be a felon. And if any Gentleman, or person of high degrée, or any person or persons which hath borne, or shall beare any office or place of Captaine, Lieutenant, or any other place, charge, or office in Campe, Armie, or Companie of Souldiers, or Conductor of Souldiers, shall after go or passe voluntarily out of this Realme, to serue any such forrein Prince, State, or Potentat, before that he and they shal become bound with two such sureties as shall be allowed of by the officers, by this Act limited to take the said bond, vnto the K. his heires or successors, in the summe of xx. l. of currant English money at the least, with condition to the effect following, he shall be a felon, viz. That if the within bounden &c. shal not at any time thē after be recōciled to the pope or sea of Rome, nor shal enter into St. 3. Iac. 4.

Bound not to be reconciled, nor to make conspiracie.

or

or consent vnto any practise, plot, or conspiracie whatsoeuer, against the Kings Maiestie, his heires and successors, or any of his or their estate and estates, realms and dominions, but shall within cōuenient time after knowledge thereof had, reueale & disclose to the K. Maiestie, his heires and successors, or some of the Lords of his or their priuie Counsell, all such practises, plots, and conspiracies, then the said Obligation to be void.

St. 43. El. 13 36 By the stat. made Anno 43. El. it was ordained, That whosoeuer shall at any time hereafter, without lawfull authoritie, take away any of the K. subiects, against his or their will, or wils, and carrie them out of the counties of Cumberland, Northumberland, Westmerland, and the Bishopricke of Durham, or to any other place within any of the said Counties, or detaine, force, or imprison him, or them, as prisoners, or against his or their wills, to ransome them, or to make a prey or spoyle of his or their person or goods, vpon deadly fewd, or otherwise: Or whosoeuer shalbe priuie, consenting, aiding, or assisting to any such taking, detaining, or carrying away of any such person or persons, as aforesaid: Or whosoeuer shall take, receiue, or carrie, to the vse of himselfe, or wittingly to the vse of any other, any money, corne, cattell, or other consideration, commonly called Blacke mayle, for the protecting or defending of him or them, or his or their lands, tenements, goods, or chattels, from such thefts, spoyles, and robberies, as is aforesaid: Or whosoeuer shall giue any such money, corne, cattel, or other consideration, called Blacke mayle, for such protection as is aforesaid: Or shall wilfully and of malice burne or cause to be burned, or aid, procure, or consent to the burning of any barne or stacke of corne or grain, within any of the said Counties, or places aforesaid, & shalbe of the said seueral offences, or any of them, indicted, & lawfully conuicted, or shall stand mute, or shall challenge peremptorily aboue the number of xx. before the Iust. of Assises, I. of Gaole deliuerie, I. of Oier and Terminer, or I. of peace within any of the said counties, at some of their generall Sessions, within some of the said counties to be holden, shalbe adiudged, reputed, and taken to be as felons, and shall suffer death, without any benefit of Clergie, Sanctuarie, or Abiuration, and shall forfeit as in case of felonie. Forcible carrying any person out of Cumberland, &c.

St. 1. Ed. 2. 37 By the stat. of An. 1. E. 2. it was ordained in this maner, viz. Touching prisoners breaking of prison, the K. doth will and command, that none which from henceforth doth breake prison, shall haue iudgement of life and member for the breaking of prison onely, except the cause for which hee was taken and imprisoned, do require such iudgement, if he should haue been conuicted thereof, according to the law and custom of the Realm, though in times past it hath beene otherwise vsed. Breaking of prison.

Principall and Accessorie.

1 Hauing treated sufficiently of Treasons, Homicides, and other Felonies, and shewed how many of euerie of them there be, I am now to write of those that be culpable therein, and to declare which be the chiefe and most grieuous offendors in those crimes, whō the law doth terme & adiudge Principals, and which be but Abettors, Procurers, and Receiuers, whom the law doth brand & mark with the name of Accessories: and which of those be Accessories before the offence committed, and which after: in what cases one of them shalbe arrested, imprisoned, appealed, indicted, arraigned, or attainted, before the other, and in what not: when the acquital of the one shall discharge the other, and when not: and where the punishment of the one shalbe greater than of the other, and where not. And in this title, to begin with the greatest & highest offence, The law doth hold it a rule infallible, that in High Treason there is no Accessorie, for all the aduisers, counsellors, persuaders, and assistants therein, be Principals, as much as if they were actors or doers: so that whatsoeuer offence doth make a man Accessorie in Felonie, the like maketh him Principall in High Treason. But in Petit Treason there is oftentimes a Principall and an Accessorie, as there is in Homicide, Robberie, and other Felonies.

No accessorie in high treasō.

3.H.7.10.

Accessorie before the offence committed.

2 There be two sorts of Accessories in Felonie, whereof the one is Accessorie before the felonie committed, and the other is Accessorie after the offence done: As if one hire, procure, or commaund another to commit a Felonie, but is not present when the other doth it, this procurer or commaunder is Accessorie before the offence committed: But otherwise it is, if hee bee present at the time of the felonie committed, for in that case he is Principal. And in some case one may be appealed as Principall and Accessorie in one Appeale.

10.Ed.4.14.
4.H.7.18.
7.H.4.27.

Procurement of felonie.

3 If one bee present at the death of a man, and moueth another to strike and kill him, by this meanes hee is principall, though hee did strike no stroke, as well as hee that killed him: For the blowes of him that did strike him, bee in

4.H.7.18.
13.H.7.10.
Plo.Com. 100.

in construction of law the blowes of him which commaunded him, when hée was present, for if the commaunder had sayd nothing, the man slaine had not béene killed.

21.Ed.4.71. 4 If one be present at the killing of a man, and commeth thither for that cause, although he at that time doth not moue another to strike or kill him, neither doth any thing, yet hée shall bée adiudged principall: For when diuers doe come to doe an euill act, and one alone doth it, and the others bée present abetting him, or readie to aid him in the fact, they bée principals to all intents, as fully as hée who did the act: for the presence of the other is a terrour to him that was assaulted, and the occasion that hée durst not defend himselfe; for when one doth sée his enemie and diuers of his companions comming to assault him, and they all doe draw their swords, and doe enuiron him, and one onely doth strike him, so that hée dyeth thereof, the others shall be adiudged as great offendors as hée who did strike him; for if the others had not béene present, peraduenture hée would haue defended himselfe, and haue escaped: for the number of the others that were present, and also readie to strike him, was a great feare vnto him, and an abatement of his courage, and a cause to make him dispaire of his defence, and so the occasion of his death. And though but one man gaue the blow, which was the cause of his death, yet the law will adiudge it the stroke of them all, giuen by the hands of that one man, and to bée in each degrée as penall to them all, as if they all had holden their hands at one time vpon that sword, or staffe, and giuen him his deadly wound.

Coming purposely to a manslaughter.

Bro.Cor. 171. Kel fol.161 Pl.Com.98 13.H.7.10.

Fitz.Cor. 309. 5 If one béeing present at the killing of a man doth nothing, but would haue aided his companion, if the partie that was slaine had made any resistance, hée shall thereby bée adiudged principall: For all those which come in companie in any place where any assembly is gathered, that an euill fact is committed, bée it Homicide, Robberie, or other Trespasse, euery of them shall bée adiudged a principall actor, though they stand by, and doe not hurt: As if one come with others to doe a disseisin, and a man is killed by another, and hée therein did nothing, notwithstanding hée shall bée adiudged principall, though hée came not to any such purpose, because hée came to doe an vnlawfull act.

A will to assist a felon.

Fitz.Cor. 314.350. 433. 11.H.4.13. Fitz.Cor. 314.350.

6 If one chaunce to bée present when another is slayne, or when any other felonie is committed, and doth not come in companie with the felons, neither is of their confederacie, although hée doth not make any resistance, or disturbe the felon, or leuie Huy and Crye, yet he is neither principall nor accessorie: for it is no felonie in him, but finable as a Trespasse. And some do hold, that he shalbe but amerced in that case; and if he be within age, hee shall haue no punishment.

In companie, but not consenting to a felony

Fitz.Cor. 395. 14.H.7.31.

25.Ed.4.44 13.H.7.10. 7 If one man doe hold another in his armes, or doe bind him, vntill a third man hath killed him, hée that did hold the partie slaine in his armes is principall: But that holding in his armes must bee proued to bée done of a wicked and felonious intent; for sometimes a man holdeth his friend in his

Holding a man vntill he be slaine.

Bracton.

armes

armes of a louing mind, to kéepe him from taking or doing of hurt, and vpon no malicious or euill intent.

One thing commanded, & another effected.

8 If one command another to lay hold vpon a third man, and the party commaunded goeth and robbeth him, if the commaunder be absent when this Robberie is done, this is not Felony in him: for the party to whom the commaundement was giuen, excéedeth his commaundement; and also the commaundement might haue béene performed without the Robberie. But otherwise it is, if the commaundement were to beat him, and the party commaunded did kill him in the commaunders absence, in this case he is accessory to the felony, for it is hard to beat a man so, that he shall be sure that he shall not die of that beating. Fitz.Cor. 314.

Councelling to rob one, and another is killed.

9 If A. doe commaund B. to robbe C. and hee attempteth to robbe him, and D. doth defend C. and fighteth with B. that assayleth him, and B. doth kill D. in this case A. shall bee accessorie to this murther, for that B. attempting to robbe C. doth pursue the commaundement of A. and so being in the pursuit of that commaundement, and resisted, another thing doth chaunce, viz. the death of D. therefore A. shall bee partaker of that fact, and of the punishment thereof, for that his commaundement was the cause thereof. Plo.Com. 475.

Commanding to beat one, and hee is killed.

And the same Law is, if A. doe command to beat C. and he doth beat him so, that hee dyeth thereof, A. shall bee accessorie to this murther: For his commaundement was the foundation of this murther, and the murther is the sequele of the commaundement, and if A. be present at this beating, then he shall be adiudged principall. Fitz.Cor. 314.350. Pl.Com. 474.

Commaundement of burning one house and another is burned.

And so it is, if A. doe commaund B. feloniously to burne the house of C. in the night, and he doth it, and the same fire doth also burne the house of D. neighbour to C. in this case A. shall be accessorie as well to the burning of the house of D. as of C. for séeing the burning of the house of D. doth ensue vpon the burning of the house of C. and the first house was burned by the commaundement of A. whereunto A. was accessorie, he must also be accessorie to the burning of the second house, viz. of the house of D. for he that commaundeth an euill and vnlawfull act to be done, shall be adiudged accessorie to all that shall ensue vpon the same euill act, but not to any other distinct thing.

Counsell of one act, and another is done

But it is otherwise, where A. doth commaund B. to burne the house of C. whom hee knoweth, and hee doth burne the house of D. or doth commaund him to steale a Horse, and he stealeth an Oxe: or doth commaund him to steale a white Horse, and hée stealeth a blacke Horse: or doth commaund him to robbe another by the high way of his money, and he doth rob him in his house of his plate; this doth differ from the commaundement of A. and therefore these acts cannot bée drawne within the compasse of his commaundements, and so hée shall bée adiudged no Accessorie to any of the foresaid offences; for these bée other acts and other felonies, and not any of those which A. did commaund or counsell to bée done. Pl.Com. 475.

The felonie commanded, committed in another maner.

And yet if B. shall commit the same felonie which A. doth commaund or counsell to bée done, though he doth it at another day, at another time, with another instrument, or in another sort than A. doth commaund or counsell him to doe it, A. shall bee accessorie thereunto: As, if A. doe counsell B. to kill C. by poysoning of him, and hee doth kill him with his dagger: or doth counsell him to kill C. by the

high

high way, and he killeth him in his house: or doth counsell him to kill him vpon one day, and he killeth him vpon another day; in all these cases and the like A. shall bee accessorie to the murder: for the murder is the substance and principall matter that doth ensue vpon the commandement or counsell of A. which the law doth wholly respect, and not the circumstances, being onely the maner and forme of the facts.

Pl. Com. 476. 10 If A. do commaund or counsel B. to kill C. and before he hath killed him A. doth repent him, and commeth vnto B. and telleth him, that hee is sorie for his wicked counsell, and persuadeth and chargeth B. that he shall not kill C. and yet after that B. doth kill C. in this case A. shall not be adiudged accessorie to the death of C. but it is the onely murder and act of B. because A. did countermaund his first counsell: And the law doth adiudge no man accessorie to a Felonie before the Felonie committed, but him onely whose mind and meaning is, that the Felonie should bee committed at that time that it is done. The felonie commaunded countermaunded.

Pl. Com. 475. 11 If A. doe procure and counsell B. to poyson C. and to that end doth buy some venim or poyson, and delivereth it to B. who tempereth it in an apple, or other thing, and delivereth it to C. with intent to poison him, and C. not knowing the poyson in the apple, nor the intention of the said B. doth giue the sayd apple to E. to eat, who eateth it, and is poysoned therby, and dyeth of the same poyson within few dayes after: In this case notwithstanding this bee wilful murder in B. that deliuered the poysoned apple to C. (though it poysoned not him who hee meant to haue poysoned, but E. a straunger, to whom hee pretended no hurt) yet A. who procured and counselled B. to giue this poyson to C. is not accessorie to the murder of E. for that he neuer persuaded, nor gaue his counsell, that E. should be poisoned, which assent of his the law will neuer straine further than he gaue it. Counselling to poison one, and another is poisoned.

12 As commaundement and ayde is in Murder, and Homicide, so is it in euerie other Felonie, as Rape, Robberie, &c. for in Rape, if one do not commit the act, but aideth and assisteth his companion, hee is principall as well as hee that committeth the fact. And the same law is, if one doe commit a Robberie, and others be in his companie, and do come with him for that purpose, they bee all principals. Commanding or aiding to Rape or Robberie. Fitz. Cor. 314. 350.

13 Accessorie after the offence is he, who knowing that another hath committed a felonie, doth receiue him, ayd him, or comfort him: As if one do receiue a felon (before he is attainted of felonie) knowing of the felonie which he hath committed, or doth fauour him, or ayd him with money, meat, drinke, or lodging, by that meanes he shalbe adiudged accessorie. But this difference is to be taken of aid, or counsell: for if he aid him by his good word, or suit for his deliuerance, or do send a letter for his enlargement, this doth not make him accessorie to the felonie. Accessorie after the offence committed. 26. Ass. p. 47. What act of the accessorie maketh him a felon, what not.

Receit of a felon attainted in the same Countie.

14 If one receiue a felon that is attainted of Felonie by verdict or confession in the same Countie where the receiuer is commorant or dwelling, and doth ayd him, he is accessorie to the Felonie, though he doth not know that the other hath committed Felonie, because hee is a Felon by matter of record, whereof euerie straunger dwelling or commorant in the same Countie is to take notice. And it is Felonie, if one be indicted of the receit of another that is Outlawed of Felonie in the same Countie where the receiuer dwelleth: for that the offendor is attainted of Felonie in that Countie by matter of record. S. Indictments 34. Fi. Cor. 377 Bracton.

Receit of a felon attainted in another Countie.

15 If one be attainted of Felonie by verdict, confession, or outlawry in one Countie, and another doth receiue him, and aid him in another Countie, he is not accessorie to the Felonie, vnlesse he doth know of the Felonie: because hee cannot take knowledge of an act done in another Countie, though it be by matter of record. S. Indictments. 34. Fi. Cor. 377

Indictment of an accessorie in one County to an offence done in another.

16 Because that Theeues and Robbers that had robbed or stollen in one Countie, would conuey their spoile, or part thereof so robbed and stollen, vnto some of their adherents in another countie, where the principall offence was not committed; who knowing of such felonie, willingly and by couin did receiue the same: in which case, though the principall felon were attainted in one countie, the accessorie escaped, by reason that he was accessorie in another Countie, and that the Jurors of the same countie by the common law could take no knowledge of the principall felonie ne attainder in the first countie, and so such accessories escaped thereof vnpunished: For the remedie whereof, by a Statute made Anno 2. & 3. E. 6. it was ordained, That where any murder or felonie shall be committed in one countie, and another person or moe shall be accessorie to the same in another countie, Then an Inditement found or taken against such accessorie and accessories, vpon the circumstance of such matter, (before the Justices of Peace, or other Justices or commissioners, to enquire of felonies in the countie, where such offences of accessorie shalbe committed) shalbe as good in the law, as if the said principall offence had bin committed within the same coũtie where the same indictment against such accessorie shalbe found. And the Justices of Gaole deliuerie, or Oyer & Terminer, or two of them, of, or in such countie, where the offence of any such accessorie shalbe committed or done (vpon suit to them made) shall write to the Custos Rotulorum, or Keepers of the Records, where such principall shalbe attainted or conuict, to certifie them, whether such principall be attainted or conuicted, or otherwise discharged of such principall felonie, who vpon such writing shall make sufficient Certificat in writing vnder their Seale or seales to the said Justices, whether such principall bee attainted, conuicted, or otherwise discharged, or not. And after that they doe certifie, that such principall is attainted, conuicted, or otherwise discharged of such offence, Then the said Justices &c. shall proceed vpon euery such accessorie in the Countie where he became accessorie, in such manner and forme, as if both the said principall offence and accessorie had beene committed in the same Countie where the offence of accessorie was committed, and euery such accessorie and other offendors aboue expressed, shall answer vpon their Arraignments, and receiue such Triall, Judgement, order, and execution,

Triall of an accessorie in one County, to an offence done in another.

St. 2. & 3. E. 6. 24.

and

and suffer such forfeitures as is used in other cases of Felonie.

27. Ass. p. 69. 25. Ed. 3. 39. 9. H. 4. 1.

Receiuing of stolne goods.

17 If one receiue goods stollen, or any parcell thereof, yet hee shall not bee accessorie to the felonie, if he do not receiue the Felon himselfe. But if he doe receiue the goods stollen, and also the Felon, he shallbe accessorie to the felonie, so that the same Felon be before accessorie of the same felonie. S. Indict. 34.

Fitz. Cor. 427.

Receiuing the Felon.

18 If a Felon doth flie, and come to his friends house, and his friend doth shut the doore, and the countrey which pursueth him, doe thinke that the Felon doth continue in the house, whereas he escapeth: in this case the friend shall bee adiudged accessorie to this felonie, for that his friend did ayd and releeue him, and endeuoured to defend him from the iustice of the law. S. Escape 2.

26. Ass. p. 52.

Accessorie to an accessorie.

19 And also a man may be accessorie to an accessorie: as if one doe receiue him who is accessorie to a felonie, by this meanes he himselfe shall be accessorie to this accessorie, because that first accessorie is a felon.

1. H. 7. 6.

Rescue of a Felon.

20 If one doe rescue him that is arrested, conuicted, or attainted of felonie, hee is a principall Felon, and not an Accessorie: and the reason is, for that this is a new felonie by it selfe, though it doth depend upon the former felonie.

A wife no Accessorie to her husband.
A maried wife a principall Felon.

St. 1. M. 12. St. 1. El. 16.

21 A woman couert cannot bee accessorie in felonie to her husband, for that by the lawes of God shee ought not discouer his counsell: But by force of a Statute made Anno 1. Mar. a wife shall be a principall Felon, if shee doe send, deliuer, or conuey any reliefe to her husband, which amongst others, to the number of twelue, or aboue, shall bee assembled, practise, and put in ure any of the offences prohibited by the said stat. prouided against Rebellious and unlawfull assemblies, Anno 1. M. 12. S. Felonies by statute 31.

Accessorie to offences made felony by stat.

19. H. 8. 47. St. 25. E. 3. 2.

22 If an offence be made felonie by statute, although the same statute doth not expresly make mention of abettors, procurers, councellors, and receiuers, yet they shall be taken within the compasse of the same statute, as the consenter and aider to the counterfeiting of the great Seale, priuie Seale, or the Kings money, is Treason: and yet the words of the statute bee, If any doe counterfeit &c. which the other doth not, because hee was but consenting and ayding thereunto.

St. 13. E. 1. 34. 11. H. 4. 13. Fitz. Cor. 228. Br. Appeale 32.

Rape.

23 In Rape, if one doe commit the fact, and another doth ayde and assist him therein, hee is thereby a rauisher, as well as his companion which committed the Rape: and yet the words of the statute of Westminst. 2. be, If a man doe rauish a woman: for the assistant was the cause of the offence, without whom peraduenture the Rape had not been done. And he is principal, because

because hee was present when the fact was done, and therefore as much guiltie as hee which did the fact. And yet in the foresayd case, if two bee indicted for committing of a Rape, one for doing the fact, and the other for ayding and assisting him, whereby they both be principals: if hee that was indicted for ayding and assisting, bee first arraigned, and by one Enquest found guiltie, and after he that was indicted for doing the act is arraigned, and by another Enquest is acquite: In this case iudgement shall not bee giuen against him who was found guiltie of ayding and assisting, because he cannot be guiltie but in respect that the principall actor was guiltie: and hee beeing found not guiltie of doing the fact, the other could not be ayding and assisting to a thing which was not done: And seeing both the verdicts cannot bee true, but one of them must needs be false, the Iudges ought to giue more credit to the verdict which acquited him who was charged with doing of the fact, than to the other: For the Enquest which acquited him that was charged with the fact, was charged vpon the principall poynt, viz. if the supposed rauisher committed the rape or not, and the other Enquest was not so fully charged vpon the principall poynt, but onely whether hee that was indicted of ayding and assisting, bee guiltie of the Felonie whereof hee is impeached, viz. of the ayding and assisting. Plo.Com. 97.

Imbecilling of Records.

24 By the Statute of Anno 8.H.6.12. it was ordained, That if any record, or parcell of the same, writ, returne, panell, proces, or warrant of Atturney in the Chauncerie, &c. bee willingly stolne, taken away, withdrawne, or auoyded by any Clerke &c. such stealer, taker away, withdrawer, and auoyder, their procurers, counsellors, and abettors, beeing thereof indicted, &c. shalbe adiudged felons. S. Felonies by statute 16. St.8.H.6.12.

Rebellious assemblies.

25 By the stat. of an.1.M.12.1.El.16. it is enacted, That if any wife or seruãt (of any of the persons being in rebellious manner vnlawfully assembled, contrarie to the ordinance of the same statute) or any other person whatsoeuer, shall willingly and without compulsion, bring, send, deliuer, or conuey any money, harneyes, artillerie, weapon, meat, drinke, or other victual, to any person or persons so beeing assembled, during such time as hee or they shalbe so assembled, or be together, then euery wife, seruant, or other person, so bringing or conueying any of the foresaid things to the same persons so being assembled together in forcible manner, or to any of them, and not departing to their houses vpon request or commaundement made, shalbe adiudged Felons. But no person shalbe put to any losse, forfeiture, paine, or punishment of life, lands, or goods, as accessorie to any person or persons, that shall commit any of the offences contained in this Act, for receiuing, comforting, or aiding of any such offendor after such act committed or done. S. Felonies by Statute 31. Riots &c. St.1.M.12. St.1.El.16.

Coniuration.

26 By the stat. of An.1.Iac. it was ordained, That if any person or persons shal vse, practise, or exercise any inuocation, or coniuratiõ of any euil or wicked spirit, &c. then euery offendor or offendors, their aiders, abettors, and counsellors, being of any of the sayd offences lawfully conuicted and attainted, shall suffer paines of death as a felon or felons, without benefit of Clergie or Sanctuarie. S. Felonies by Stat. 29. St.1.Iac.12.

27 By

St.3.H.7.2 27 By the Statute of An 3.H.7.2. it was prouided, That if any person shal take any maid, widow, or wife, which hath lands or goods, or is heire apparant to her ancestor, against her will, vnlawfully, such taking, procuring, and abetting to the same, and also receiuing wittingly the same woman so taken against her will, and knowing the same, shall be felonie: And such misdoers, takers, and procurers to the same, and receiuers, knowing the saide offence in forme aforesaide, shall be reputed and iudged as principall felons. S.Fel. by Stat.5. Taking a woman against her will.

Br.23,24, 25,26,27. 28 Note that in all the Cases aforesaid touching offences made felonie by Statute, the aidors, abettors, and councellers be made principalles, by the speciall wordes of the same Statutes, and not accessories to the same felonies. Aydors &c. be principals.

27.Ass.p.10 8.H.5.6 2.Ed.3.25 Bro.Coro. 185. 29 If one be acquited of the principall act, hee is acquited of all offences committed as accessorie, before the doing of the principall fact; but not of offences committed as accessorie after the principall fact. A man being indicted as accessorie in murder was acquite by verdict, and after hee was indicted as principall of the same murder, and was found guiltie, and hanged, for though it concerned the same murder, yet it was not the same offence wherof he was first arraigned. Acquitall of the principall is acquitall of accessorie.

Co.l.4.43 30 A. brought an appeale of the murder of B. his brother, against C. as principall, and D. as accessorie before the murder committed, and E. as accessorie after the murder. C. the principall pleaded not guiltie, and by the Jurie was found guiltie of manslaughter, but not of murder, and then praied, and had his Cleargie: In this case, D. which was charged as accessory before the offence committed, was discharged, because he cannot be charged as accessorie before the act of manslaughter committed, for manslaughter doth follow vppon a sodaine debate, or fray, for if it be premeditate, it is murder. And because C. the principall had his Cleargie before iudgement, so that it did not appeare by the iudgement of Lawe, that he was principall, both the accessorie before, and the accessorie after the manslaughter were discharged. And so it is, if the principall vpon his arraignement, doth confesse the felonie, and before iudgement hath his pardon, or cleargie allowed, the accessorie shalbe discharged. S.Br.51. Principall and accessorie in manslaughter.

31 There be two maner of attainders, wherof the one is vpō apparance, that is to say, by confession, verdict, or battell: the other is by default vpon proces of outlarie. And in both cases the principall ought to be attainted before the accessorie: as it doth appeare by these wordes of the Statute of West. 1. viz. No person shalbe outlawed vpon appeale of commaundement, force, aide, or receit, vntill he that is appealed of the fact be attainted: and one lawe shalbe kept thorow the whole realme: But he that will appeale shall not let to attach his appeale at the next County, aswel against the accessorie, as against the principall; and yet the Exigent shall stay vntill the principall be attainted, by outlawrie or otherwise. And to the like effect be these wordes of the Statute of Officium Coronatoris, If any be appealed of an act done as principal, they that be appealed as accessorie shall be attached, and surely kept vntill the principall be attached. St.Ed.1.14. St.3.Ed.1. Two attainders. The principall shalbe attainted before the accessorie.

Appeales cōmenced by writ or Bill.

32 The foresaide Statute of Westm. 1. is to be intended of appeales commenced by Bill, but not of appeales commenced by Writ: for of appeales commenced by writ, there doth not appeare any to be accessorie, untill the count be made, which is not made untill there be an apparance of the accessorie. And therefore in that case where the appeale is commenced by writ, if the plaintife will pray an Exigent against them all, he is thereby concluded to count against any of them as accessories: for if he should so doe, he ought not to haue had the Exigent against them untill the principall had béene outlawed, and therefore therein he is concluded. 43.Ed.3.18. 7.H.4.27.

Principall shal be attainted before the Exigent against the accessorie.

33 Where the wordes of the foresaide Statute of Westminster be. That he which is appealed of the fact shall be attainted before the accessorie be outlawed: If at the time that the accessorie is come to the Exigent the principall doth appeare, and so the processe is determined against him: Notwithstanding, because he is not as yet attainted, the Exigent shall not be awarded against the accessorie, untill the principall be attainted. And this is to be intended where the accessorie doth not appeare, but maketh default. S. Triall by the Country 8. 7.H.4.36.

The principall maketh default, and the accessorie appeareth.

34 If Processe be awarded against the principall and accessorie, and the principall maketh default, and the accessorie doth appeare; in this case the accessorie shall answer: But if he pleade to an issue, processe shall not be awarded against the Enquest, untill the principall doe appére, or be attainted by proces, viz. be outlawed. And yet this processe against the Enquest shal not cease unlesse the accessorie will: for if the accessorie will request to haue processe against the Enquest before the principall be attainted, he shall haue it, for that it is preiudiciall to none but to the accessorie himselfe: and whether he be attainted or acquited, it is góod. And he shall not be arraigned againe, for the taking of the Enquest is not erronious. 9.H.4.2. 7.H.4.36. Fitz. Cor. 12. 8.H.5.6.

The accessorie wageth battell.

35 If processe be awarded against the principall and the accessorie, and the principall maketh default, and the accessorie doth appeare, if the accessorie will wage battell with the appellant before the principall doth appére; he may: for he may waiue the benefit which the Lawe doth giue him, if he will. Fitz. Cor. 12.

Accessorie pleadeth in abatement of the writ.

36 If the principall doe make default, and the accessorie doe appeare and pleade, then if the plea which the accessorie pleadeth be a plea in abatement of the whole writ, the principall shall take aduantage thereof, notwithstanding his absence: So that the Exigent which is to be awarded against the principall shall be stayed, untill it be knowen whether the whole writ shall abate, or not. 9.H.4.2.

Both the principal and accessory doe appeere.

37 If both the principal and the accessorie do appeare, then the principall shall answer first, and the accessorie after: for the principall may pleade such a plea, that the accessorie shall not be put to answer untill the principalls plea be tried. And that is in case where the principall doth not pleade directly to the felony, but some other plea; as if hée do pleade that he himselfe was at an other

9.H.7.19. other time attainted of the same felony, &c. And the appellant doth take issue thereupon, viz. not comprised, &c. In this case the accessorie shall not be put to answer untill this issue be tried. Where the principalls plea shal be tried before the accessories answer.

38 And so it is if both the principall and accessorie doe appeare, and the principall doth pleade a plea in abatement of the whole writ of Appeale, then the accessorie shall not be put to answer untill this plea be tried. The principall pleadeth in abatement of the writ.

Fit. Cor. 10 39 If the principall and accessorie doe both appeere, and the principall doth pleade to the felonie, viz. not guiltie, then the accessorie shall presently after that plea pleaded, pleade also. And if they be at issue, one Venire facias shall be awarded for them both: But if at the day of the Venire facias returned, or at the time of the apparance of the Enquest, the principall being in the meane time let to mainprise, doth make default, and not appeere, the Enquest shall not be taken against the accessorie. The principal pleadeth not guiltie.

2. & 3. P. & M. Di. 120 40 If there be divers principalls, and one accessorie, or more: and processe is awarded against all the principals, and the accessorie, and some or one of the principalls doe appeere, and some not, and also the accessorie doth appeere: in this Case processe shall not be awarded against the Enquest for the triall of the accessorie, untill all the principalls doe appeare, or be attainted by outlawrie: viz. if he be indicted or appealed as accessorie to them all. But it is otherwise if he be indicted or appealed onely as accessorie to some of those principalls: for there it is sufficient to have that principall, or those principalls onely to appeare, or to be attainted by Outlawrie, to whom he is appealed or indicted as accessorie, without having regard to the residue. Several principalls, and one accessorie

40. Ass. p. 25
7. H. 4. 36
Plo. com. 99

41 To have Processe awarded against the Enquest for the triall of the accessorie, it is requisite, that the attainder of the principall be in the same sute, in the which he and the accessorie be sued: for if he be attainted in another sute, that shall not enforce the accessorie to proceede with his Enquest untill the principall which is sued with him doth appeere, or be attainted by processe of outlawrie, &c. As in appeale of homicide against the principall and accessorie, and the principall before that time is attainted of the death of the same man upon an indictment at the Kings sute. And the accessory shall pleade for his owne discharge the acquitall of the principall in an other sute; so that it be an acquitall for that offence, for the which he is charged as accessorie. The attainder must be in the same sute.

7. H. 4. 36

7. H. 4. 27 42 If the principall be attainted of the death of a man, and then dieth, and the Justices before whom the accessorie is sued have the record of the same attainder before them, then they may proceede against the accessorie, otherwise not: for it doth by the Record appeere unto them, that hee which was appealed of the fact, is by Lawe attainted of felonie, according to the foresaid Statute of Westminster 1. though he was not executed therefore. The principall attainted and dieth.

The principall standeth mute.

43 And though the Lawe be, that an Enquest shall not procéede against the accessorie to trie him untill the principall doe appeare, or be attainted by outlawrie, yet if the principall doe appeare, and will say nothing, but stand mute, the accessorie shall be arraigned. Sed quære; for the principall is not attainted of felonie. Fit. Cor. 58

Error in the Attainder of the principall.

44 If the Attainder of the principall be erronious, yet the accessorie shall be arraigned: for the accessory shall take no aduantage of any errour committed in the attainder of the principall. 2.R.3.21.

An abiured accessorie returneth.

45 If one do abiure as accessory, and after doth returne againe, the principall not being attainted, the accessorie shall be hanged: for that he hath confessed the felonie before the Coroner, and did returne without the Kings pardon or licence. Fi. Cor. 124

The accessory tried upon his owne request.

46 If the accessory of his owne desire wil wage battel before the principal be attainted, and be subdued therein: or will desire to haue an Enquest to try him before the principall be attainted, and be found guiltie therefore: In both these Cases he shall be hanged, though by the Lawe he was not compellable to either of the said trialles, untill the principall had béene attainted; for hée hath aduentured his life, in hope to gaine his libertie. Fit. Cor. 12

The principall found not guiltie.

47 If the principall be found not guilty by verdict, the accessorie shall be discharged thereby: for where there is no déede, there can no force, ayde, or commaundement hurt, in that the intended iniury tooke no effect. So that the acquitall of the principall is in Lawe the acquitall of the accessorie. Bracton.

The principall dieth in prison before attainder.

48 If the principall can not be tried (as if he die in prison before he be attainted of the felonie) the accessorie shall be thereby discharged: for there can none be found accessorie to a felonie, where there is none attainted to commit the same felonie. But otherwise it is if the principall be attainted of the felonie, and dieth, there the accessorie shall be arraigned, and hanged, if he be found guiltie. Co.l. 4. 43

The principall attainted of an other felonie.

49 If the principall be attainted of another felonie, and hanged, before he is attainted of this felonie, whereof he and the accessorie be indicted, the accessorie to this felonie shall be discharged thereby. And the same Lawe is, if hée be attainted of the first felonie, though he be not hanged: because in that case after attainder, he shall not answer to other felonies, but onely to robberie and treason, Fi. Cor. 378.

The principall slew the partie in his owne defence.

50 If it be found by verdict that the principall slew him, of whose death he is arraigned, in his owne defence, the accessory shalbe therby discharged: And yet the principall shall be enforced to purchase his pardon: But this pardon prooueth not, that he is guilty in other maner, than in his owne defence. Notwithstanding in an other pardon it is otherwise; for if a principall pleade his pardon to a felony generally, without any special matter found, which should cause the Fi. Cor. 116

2.Ed.3.27 Fi.Cor.260 3.Ass.p.14 41.Ass.p.16 the pardon, and is by that discharged; yet that will not discharge the Accessorie, but he shall be hanged if he be found guiltie of the felonie: for by that pardon the felony is confessed, of the which felonie, he praieth to be discharged by the Kings fauour, and not by the benefit of lawe, as he doth in the other case.

3.H.7.12 10.H.4.5 13.Ed.4.3 Bro.Cor. 184 51 And in the like case, and vpon the same reason, if the principall and accessorie be arraigned of felonie, and both be found guilty, and the principall doth pray, and hath the benefit of his clergie; yet the accessorie shalbe hanged: for by the praying of his clergie, the felonie is confessed, and the principall in this case is not saued by his innocencie, but by a priuiledge in Lawe, which the accessorie, being no clarke, cannot take the benefit of: But it is otherwise, if there be principall and accessorie, and the principall is pardoned, or hath his Clergie before iudgement, the accessorie shall not be arraigned: for where there is no fact, there is no force, and where there is no principall, there can be no accessorie, and no man can be accompted principall, before it be so proued and adiudged by the Lawe, and that must be by a iudgement vpon a verdict, confession, or outlawrie: and it is not sufficient that indeed there be a principall, vntil that appeereth by a iudgemēt in Law. And the acceptance of pardon, or the praying of his clergy is an argumēt, but no iudgement in law, that he is guiltie. But if the principal after attainder be pardoned, or hath his clergie alowed, the accessory shalbe arraigned (and hanged if he be found guiltie) for it doth appeare iudicially, that he was principall. The principall hath his clergie. Co.l.4.43 The principall is pardoned, or hath his clergie before iudgemēt

41.Ass.p.24 52 The acquitall of the principall is the acquitall of the accessorie (as is aforesaide) if it be not in an appeale, where the accessorie is to recouer dammages: for if he will recouer dammages, he must be tried, notwithstanding the acquitall of the principall. But some doe thinke, that he shall recouer dammages by the acquitall of the principall without being further tried: or otherwise it would ensue, that the Court should admit an accessorie, where there had beene no principall, which were inconuenient. In appeale the acquitall of the principall is not the acquitall of the accessorie.

Breaking of Prison, and Rescous.

By the common Law of this Realme, if a man had béen imprisoned, and broken the prison, hée should haue béene hanged, for what cause soeuer he had béene imprisoned, yea although it had béene but for trespasse. Which great enormitie was redressed by the statute of Anno 1. Ed. 2. intituled, De frangentibus prisonam; the wordes whereof be these. Touching prisoners breaking of prison, our Lord the King doth will and commaund, that none which from henceforth doe breake prison, shall haue iudgement of life, and member, for the breaking of prison onely, except the cause for the which he was taken and imprisoned doth require such iudgement, if hée should haue béene conuicted thereof according to the lawe and custome of the Realme, though in times past it hath béene otherwise vsed. And therefore it is to be considered, who is a prisoner, and what is breaking of prison, according to the meaning of the foresaide Statute. Euery person who is vnder arrest for felony, is a prisoner, aswel being out of the Gaole, as within: So that if hée be but in the Stockes in the stréete, or out of the Stockes in the possession of any that hath arrested him, and doth make an escape; that is a breaking of prison in the prisoner: for imprisonment is none other, but a restraint of libertie.

Margin notes: St. 1. Ed. 2. — Who is a prisoner. — 1. Ed. 3. 17. 1. M. Di. 99

2 Though the letter of the stat. of An 1. Ed. 2. be touching prisoners breaking of prison, yet if a stranger do breake the prison, he is within the compasse of this statute, for that by the common lawe this was a breaking of prison in a stranger, and felonie in him at that time, and is felonie also at this time in the prisoner, that escapeth by force of such breaking of prison by a stranger, although before the said Statute it was not felony in the prisoner.

Margin notes: A stranger breaketh prison. — 1. H. 7. 6. 25. Ed. 3. 42. 1. Ed. 3. 17.

3 If a Gaoler, or any other which kéepeth a prisoner vnder arrest doe let him goe at libertie, this is not felonie in the prisoner, because it was no breaking of prison in the Gaoler: But all the felonie in this case resteth in him who did let the prisoner escape, and that is by a voluntary escape, and not by breaking of prison: which is felony in him that suffered him to escape.

Margin note: Letting a prisoner escape.

4 If

2.Ed.3.1 — *Negligent escape*

4 If by the negligence of the Gaoler, or any other which hath the prisoner under arrest, the prisoner doe escape: this is felonie in the prisoner that doth escape, for that the prisoner in making of escape did breake the prison: but it is not felonie in him out of whose custodie he did escape.

1.H.7.6. — *Rescuing of a prisoner.*

5 To breake prison is intended aswell of a Rescous made of a prisoner, as of breaking of prison: As if a prisoner be under arrest for felony, and a stranger will feloniously take him out of the possession of him that hath arrested him, this Rescous is a breaking of prison, and is felonie, as wel in the partie which escapeth, as in him that made the Rescous, and so was it by the common law.

Fi.Cor.333 — *Disturbing of arrest.*

6 If a stranger disturbe the arresting of a felon, that manner of Rescous is not felonie; for the letting of a felon escape, which is not arrested for felony, is not felonie: but if the felon had béene taken, and arrested, and after rescued, this had béene felonie.

2.Ed.3.1. 1.H.7.6. St.25.E.3.4 St.28.E.3.3 St.42.E.3.2. — *The Sherife returneth a Rescous.*

7 If the Sherife returne a Rescous of a felon taken out of his possession, or doe returne an escape, that the prisoner escaped from him; this wil not serue as an indictment to put the partie to answer thereunto, for that it is contrarie to the Statutes of 25. Ed. 3. 28. Ed. 3. & 42. Ed. 3. which haue ordained, That none shall be imprisoned, or put out of his fréehold, without an indictment or presentment before Justices, or some matter of Record, or by due Proces, or by writ originall, which the Sherifes returne is not. S. Indictments 19.

2.Ed.3.1. Britton. — *Whose the prison broken must be.*

8 It is no difference whose prison the offendor doth breake, viz. whether it be the Kings prison, the Lords of a fraunchise, or any other persons: for whose soeuer it be, the offendor is within the compasse of this statute, though it was otherwise before the Statute, viz. it was not felonie, unlesse he had broken the Kings prison.

St.1.E.2. 22.Ed.3.13 — *Attachment for trespasse.* — *A Justice sitting in iudgement arresteth an offendor*

9 If one be attached & taken for trespasse, and he which is attached doth escape, or is rescued by a stranger, this is no felonie, but trespas: for that ẏ Statute saith: Except the cause for the which he is taken and imprisoned doth require such iudgement. But yet the fine shalbe according to the qualitie of the person to whom the rescous is made, & according to the time and place, whē, & where it is done. And therfore if a Justice assigned shall arrest a man that maketh a fraie before him, and a stranger doth rescue him, by force whereof the prisoner escapeth: in this case as wel the prisoner, as he that made the rescous, shalbe disherited, and shal suffer perpetuall imprisonment: for that the attachment of such a Justice, was the attachment of the King himselfe in the iudgement of the law. But if such a Justice make an arrest when he is out of his place, then such an arrest and escape is but fineable, nor of any other effect, but as if the Sherife, or some other officer had made the arrest.

1.H.7.6.

10 If a mā be rescued at ẏ gallows, or as he is in going to executiō, this is within

Rescous after iudgement.

within the compasse of this Statute: for the words of the Statute shalbe intẽded aswell in the preter tence, as in the present tence: viz. as well of iudgemẽt giuen, as of iudgement to be giuen; for the cause for the which he was taken and imprisoned did require such iudgement.

The imprisonment and not the attainder respected.

11 It is not material whether the prisoner which did escape, was, or should haue béene attainted of the felonie, for the which he was imprisoned, so that he were in prison for felonie, at the time of breaking of prisõ: for a stranger which did rescue one that was indited of felonie, was indited, arraigned, and found guiltie thereof presently, before the principall felonie tried. 1.Ed.3.17.

Imprisoned for Treason

12 If a man imprisoned for felonie, doth breake the prison, and let escape a prisoner that is in prison for treason, this is petit treason in him that did breake the prison. 1.H.6.5. S.Treason 9.

Disobeying of a warrant.

13 By a Statute made añ 1.H.7. it is ordained, That it shalbe felony for any person which should bee arrested, to disobey, or make rescue to any person hauing warrant to arrest a hunter in the night in any forrest, parke, &c. or with painted faces &c. so that execution of the same warrant be not had. S. Felonies by Statute 30. St.1.H.7.7.

Confession before a Coroner.

14 The confession of breaking of prison before the Coroner is an attainder in it selfe, without any more; if the cause of the imprisonment be for felonie. 25.E.3.42. Fitz.Cor. 243.435.

Opening the prison, but not escaping.

15 If a man come to a prison, and setteth open the prison doore, & persuadeth the prisoners which be in the Gaole, to come forth of prison, & to depart, yet if the prisoners doe not come forth, and escape, this is no felony in him or them: but if any of the prisoners doe escape, then is it felonie in him or them that did escape, and in him also that set open the doore. And a man is alwaies said to bée in prison, so long as he is within sight of the Gaoler, or of hym that hath him in custodie, though he doe escape, or breake away. Kel.fol.87 30.H.8. Dyer 44.

Escape.

Ins lex 36. There be two kinds of escape, viz. voluntarie, and negligent: Voluntarie escape is when one doth arrest another for felonie, or other offence, and after letteth him goe at libertie whither he will; this letting him goe at libertie is a voluntarie escape. And if the arrest of him wh did escape, was for felonie, it shalbe adiudged felony in him wh did let him escape: And if it were for treason, then it shalbe adiudged treason. But it is not materiall whether he that escaped, was arrested by him that set him at libertie, or by some other, so that he were arrested: for without arrest it shall not be accounted an escape. If a felon be in a house, and another not seeing him being in ẏ street, doth call to him, and telleth him, that he doth attach him, but doth not arrest his person, this is no arrest. Voluntarie escape.

17. Ass. p. 9

9. H. 4. 1. 2 If a man receiue a felon, knowing of the felonie which he hath committed, and willingly suffer him to escape, this suffering the felons escape, is not felonie in him that receiued the offendor, because he did not arrest him. S. Principall &c. 17. & 18. Escape of an offendor not arrested.

11. H. 4. 4. 3 Also such an escape is not felonie, if it were not felonie at the time of the escape made: for notwithstanding that the first act, for the which the partie was arrested, is after become felonie, yet that shall not make the escape felony, which was not felonie at the time of the escape. As if A. doe strike B. whereupon the Constables doe arrest A. and willingly suffer him to escape, and after B. dieth of that stroake, this is not felonie; for that B. beeing liuing at the time of the arrest, and escape of A, it was then no felonie in A. But yet in this case, the partie which arrested the offendor, shall pay to the King a fine to the value of his goods, because the escape was voluntarie, and vpon an hainous offence before committed: for the law hath alwaies so much endeauoured to represse and punish felons, that if one man doe kill another, and a third man is present at the same time, but of no confederacie with the manqueller, yet if he beeing of full age, doe not his best endeauour to apprehend the same felon, he shalbe imprisoned vntill he hath made fine to the king therefore. Felonie at the time of the escape.

Fi. Cor. 293 331. 395.

4 Neg-

Negligent escape. 4 Negligent escape is, when one is arrested for felonie, and after doth escape against the will of him that arrested him, and is not freshly pursued, and taken againe, before the pursuer shall lose the sight of him: this shalbe adiudged a negligent escape, notwithstanding that he out of whose possession hee escaped, did take him againe after he lost the sight of him. Fi.Cor. 236 400.

Killing him that escapeth. 5 It is a negligent escape, if the pursuer doe kill the partie which escaped in the pursuit of him, as he is carrying him to the Gaole, though he did neuer lose the sight of him: for by this meanes the partie that escaped cannot bee attainted of felonie, and so the king shall lose his Escheates. Fit. cor. 328 346

Taking againe the partie escaping. 6 Upon fresh suit the Gaoler may take againe the prisoner which escaped seauen yeares after the escape made, notwithstanding that in the meane time he lose the sight of him: but that will not discharge the Gaoler of his fine for the same escape. And if the sherife be in carrying one that is condemned to die, to ye place of execution, and the prisoner be rescued, and taken from him by force, & the Sherife doth againe take away the prisoner from those that did rescue him, and hang him: this shall not be adiudged an escape in the Sherife. 13.E.4.9. 14.H.7.1 Fi.N.B.130 6.H.7.12

Licence to go to another towne. 7 If a Gaoler licence his prisoner to goe to another towne, and to come againe, this is a negligent escape, because the prisoner in this case was found out of the bounds of the prison. Fitz.Cor. 242.

License to go into the same towne. 8 If a Gaoler giue leaue to his prisoner to goe into the same towne, and to come againe, and he wandreth into another town out of his prescribed limits, and is there found wandring with an intent to escape, this is a negligent escape in the Gaoler. Fi.Cor.431

Mainprise. 9 If one which by the law is not maineprnable, be let to maineprise, that shalbe adiudged a negligent escape in him who did let him to mainprise. 25.Ed.3.39

Petit larceny. 10 As an escape may be of one that is imprisoned or arrested for felonie: so it may be of him, that is arrested, or in prison for petit Larcenie: But not of any that is arrested or imprisoned for trespasse. Fi.Cor.430 431

Escape by returne of Cepi Corpus. 11 A Capias was awarded to the Sherife to arrest one of felonie, and hee thereupon did returne Cepi Corpus, and at the day had not the bodie: upon this matter of Record, it was adiudged an escape in the Sherife: and he was amerced a hundred shillings. 40.Ass.p.43

12 If an offendor be in prison at the suit of one man, and then at anothers, or of diuers men, and he doth escape: this shalbe adiudged but one escape, and the Gaoler shalbe charged but with one escape. But if one that is arrested for felonie 26.Ass.p.51

Fi.Cor.422 felonie doe escape, and flie to the Church, and after escapeth out of the Church, these shalbe adiudged two escapes; viz one from the prison, and another from the Church. And the Gaoler, or other who suffereth him to escape shalbe charged with the first of those Escapes, and the towne wherein the Church is with the last of them. Double escape

St.3.H.7.1. 4.El.Dyer.110. Fitz.Cor.238.293. 13 There be certaine cases wherein an escape shall be adiudged, though there was no arrest before: as if one be murdred or slaine in a towne in ẏ day time, and the murderer doe escape without bẹing taken or arrested by those of the towne: in this case those of the towne shalbe charged with this escape, that is to say, they shalbe amerced for it, and though the escape be at the euening. Escape without arrest.

St.13.Ed.1.1.2. And by the Statute of Winchester, viz. of 13.Ed.1. If a man be robbed, and the felon doth escape, and be not taken within fixe moneth, the towne or hundred shall answer the partie robbed that made huy and crie, for the robberie, and the dammages.

Fi.Cor.302 14 If one doe kill another by misaduenture, or in his own defence, and doe escape: the towne where he was slaine shalbe amerced for it, though the offendor was not arrested: for the people of the town doe see a man slaine, but they are not to iudge, whether it be felonie or not; and therefore they ought to haue apprehended the manqueller. Who shalbe charged with an escape.

15 As the law is of a towne not walled in, or inclosed, touching a murder committed in the day; so is it of a citie or towne inclosed, of a murder committed in the night: for if in a towne inclosed one be murdered, be it done by day or night: if in that case the murderer doe escape, the towne or citie inclosed shalbe amerced: because the citie or towne inclosed ought by the Statute of Winchester to be kept fast locked, from the Sunne setting, to the Sunne rising. Escape in a towne walled Fi.Cor.299.

Fi.Cor.352.415. 16 If a felon doe flie to a Church, and before abiuration he doth escape: in this case the towne where the Church is, shalbe charged with this escape: viz. they shalbe amerced for it. But this must be before abiuration, for if hee doe escape after abiuration, the towne shall not be charged therewith, for that by the abiuration, he is in law attainted. Flying to a Church and escaping.

17 And so it is, if a felon take a Church, which by the law cannot make abiuration: in this case, if he flie from thence, the towne shall not be charged with an escape: As if a man that is adiudged to be hanged, doth escape from the sherife, when he is in carrying him to the gallowes, and doth take a Church, and then escape: the towne where the Church is, shall not be amerced for this escape; for that in this case, he cannot make an abiuration, which is an attainder in it selfe, beeing attainted before. Escaping by making abiuration. 27.Ass.p.54 Fi.Cor.313 335 9.E.4.28.

18 And so it is to be noted, that a city, borough, or town may be charged wt the escape of an offendor, which hath committed murder, or homicide, thogh he Escape before or after arrest

were

were not arrested: But one, two, or more priuat persons cannot be charged with the escape of an offendor, untill he be arrested.

Where the Sherife, and where the towne charged.

19 If the Sherifes bailife doe arrest one for felonie in a town, and do carry him towards the prison, and certaine persons of the towne doe go with the bailife to assist him, & the felon escapeth by the way, the sherife shalbe charged with the escape: but it shalbe otherwise, if the felon be committed to the people of the towne to carrie to prison; for in that case, if the prisoner doe escape, the towne shalbe charged therewith. Fi.Cor.328. 337.

The hundred charged with escape.

20 One was arrested for felonie, and led to the hundred court, and then he was persuaded to goe abroad, and seeke his warrant, viz. one that should warrant him those goods, which he was charged to steale, and he went, and fled to the Church, and abiured: In this case the whole hundred was charged with ye escape, and the partie who gaue him the counsell, and leaue, paid a great ransome to the king, and the felons goods were forfeited to the King. Fi.Cor.316

Escape of one imprisoned for a time.

21 One that hath committed petit larcenie is adiudged to be imprisoned by the space of a moneth for his punishment, and then beeing kept in prison after the moneth, he breaketh prison, and escapeth: the keeper of the prison shalbe charged with this escape. But if one that is arraigned of felonie, bee adiudged to be acquit, viz. that he shalbe discharged, paying his fees: By this hee shalbe out of prison touching the felonie, and the Gaoler shall not be charged, if hee doe escape; for the prisoner in the first case was by iudgement committed to prison, and in the last, adiudged to be acquit of imprisonment, paying &c. 27 Ass.p.27 Fi.Cor.430 21.H.7.17

Where the towne, hundred, or countie shalbe charged with escape.

22 If one be slaine in the day time in a towne, and the murderer escape without beeing taken, the towne shalbe charged with the escape: And if the partie be killed out of any towne, then the Hundred shalbe charged therwith: Or if the towne be not sufficient to answer the amerciament for the escape, then the Hundred shalbe charged therewith: And for the disabilitie of the hundred, the whole countie shalbe charged with the escape. And the same law is of Abiuration, where the Church is in a field out of any towne. Fitz.Cor. 238.293. Fi.Cor.425 316.

The Gaoler will not receiue a prisoner.

23 If the Constable doe arrest a felon, and carrie him to the Gaole of the same countie, and the Gaoler will not receiue him, the Constable ought not to let him goe, but the towne where the Constable dwelleth shalbe charged with the keeping of him, untill the next Gaole deliuerie. 10.H.4.7.

Prisoner by matter of record.

24 The law hath two seuerall respects to two sorts of prisoners, whereof the one is prisoner by matter of Record, and the other by matter in deed. A prisoner by matter of Record is, when one that is present in Court, is committed to prison by the Court. In this case, if the keeper of the prison hath not this prisoner alwaies readie, when the Court will send for him, or else doe shewe a reasonable cause why he cannot haue him, the Court will iudge this an escape Fi.Cor.466

by

by the Keeper without further inquirie. But if the Keeper of the prison bee in
39.H.6.33. this case examined by the court of his prisoner, and he will say nothing, the
Court will adiudge it a voluntarie escape.

Fi.Cor. 352 25 If it be found in the Coroners Roll, that one did flie to the Church, and no abiuration is found in the same Roll: in this case, the court will adiudge an escape upon the whole towne without further presentment. Escape by a towne. And if a man be
Fi.Cor. 346 apprehended for felonie in a towne, and carried towards the Gaole by certain of the same towne, and if he doe resist them, whereupon they doe kill him: in this case it shalbe adiudged an escape upon that town; for in that hee was not safely carried to the Gaole, & attainted of felonie, ye king doth loose his escheats. A man killed beeing in carrying to the Gaole.

26 When the Deciners doe present that a felon is apprehended for felony, and deliuered to the Sherife, it will be adiudged an escape, if they doe not declare to which Sherife he is deliuered, and name him, so that his rolls may bee searched and seene, whether the prisoner came within the charge of the Sherife: Escape by the Sherife.
Fi.Cor. 345. and if it be not found, how he came out of the Sherifs ward, according to the law of the Realme, an escape shalbe adiudged upon the Sherife.

39.H.6.33. 27 It is used in the Kings Bench, to send a Coroner once or twice euery Terme to the Marshalsey, to see all the prisoners that be committed to ye marshall by matter of Record: and if any of them be wanting, & cannot be found there, to set his name in a booke, and to informe the Iustices thereof: and then the Court will examine the Marshall thereof, and if he cannot sufficiently excuse himselfe, the Court will record escapes upon him for euery of them. A Coroner sent to the Marshalsey to enquire &c.

21.Ass.p.12. 28 And touching those which bee prisoners of Record, the Keeper of the prison cannot trauerse the escape; but confesse, and auoyd it: as in alleadging that the prison was burnt, or broken by the Kings enemies: or by saying, that he which is supposed to be escaped, is not the same prisoner which was committed to him. Confessing & auoiding of an escape.

29 Prisoner by matter in fait, is where one is prisoner by arrest onely, whether it be by the Sherife, the Constable, or any other, and he doth escape: there the Escape shall bee presented before he shall aunswer unto it. Prisoner by matter in fait, viz. by arrest. And this presentment ought to be before the Iustices of the Kings Bench, the Iustices in Eire, or some other Iustices that haue authoritie to enquire thereof: As it appeareth by the Statute of Westminster 1. the words whereof be these: Before whom an escape shall be presented.
St.3.E.1.4. It is ordained, that nothing shall be demanded, nor taken, nor leuied by the Sherife, nor by any other, for the escape of any theefe or felon, untill it shalbe adiudged by the Iustices in Eire. And he that shall doe otherwise, shall restore
St.31.E.3.14. to him that paid it, so much as he hath receiued, and to the King as much. And likewise by the Statute of 31.Ed.3. it is prouided, That the Escape of felons and Clerkes conuict, shall bee adiudged by the Iustices, and by their viewe leuied. And though the foresaid Statute of Westminster

the first, doth not make mention of any but of Justices in Eire, yet it doth also extend to the Justices of the Kings Bench: because the Kings Bench is in Eire, and higher then an Eire, for if the Justices in Eire doe sit in a Countie, and the Justices of the Kings Bench come thither, the Eire shall cease. 21.As.p.12. 27.As.p.1.

Ju. of peace and Coroner shall enquire of escapes.

30 And by the Statute of 1. R. 3. Justices of Peace may enquire of all manner of Escapes, of every person arrested and imprisoned for felonie. And by the Statute of 3. H. 7. They may enquire of the escape of any that hath committed murder, and make certificat thereof into the Kings Bench. And also by the said Statute of 3. H. 7. the Coroner upon the viewe of the dead body, may enquire of the escape of the murderer: for if he doe commit the murder in the day, and escape, the towne shalbe amerced. And also the Coroner shall deliver his Inquisition therof to the Justices at the next Gaole deliverie of the same Countie. St.1.R.3.3. St.3.H.7.1.

Traverse to a presentment of an escape.

31 Upon an escape, for the which no fine is to be paied, but an Amerciament, he or they which be charged therewith, shal have no Traverse to the presentment thereof: Quia de minimis non curat lex. Fi.Cor.291 328.346.

Escapes inquirable in Leetes and Turnes.

32 Although Escapes of felons be at this day inquirable in Léetes, and Sherifes Turnes, yet it shall not be levied, untill it be adiudged before the Justices: for that should bee contrarie to the foresaid Statute of Westminster 1.

The penalties of escapes

33 The penaltie of him, which doth voluntarily suffer one arrested for felonie to escape, is the forfeiture of all that he hath, because it is felonie. The penaltie of him which doth suffer a negligent escape of a felon, is to pay a fine. The penaltie for the escape of him which was never arrested, is but an amerciament. And if any doe suffer him that is attainted of felonie, negligently to escape, he shall pay to the King for a fine an hundred pounds. And if the partie escaping were but indicted, and not attainted, then he shall paie to the King for a fine a hundred shillings. If one which is not indicted, nor taken with the manner, nor apprehended at the suit of the partie, but onely taken by a straunger for suspition of felonie, do escape, there shal no penaltie nor punishment follow thereof. But yet if after the same escape, he that did escape, shalbe indicted of felonie, or make his abiuration, then he that suffered him to escape, shall pay a fine to the King. 42.As.p.5. 44.As.p.12. 42.As.p.5. 43.E.3.36

Where a man arrested may be set at libertie, without further triall: where not.

34 If a man be arrested of felonie by the Constable, or some other man, and after he that made the arrest hath intelligence, that there is no such felony committed: in this case, he may set the partie arrested at libertie, and hée shall not be charged with an escape: for there can be no felon where there is no felonie committed. But if a man be slaine, and one is arrested for the same felonie, or for the suspition thereof, although that he who made the arrest, Kel.fo.34

doth

44.Aſ.p,12. doth after vnderſtand, that the partie arreſted, is not guiltie of that offence, or that the party was arreſted vpon malice, yet he may not ſet the partie arreſted at libertie, for he muſt be deliuered by a courſe of lawe, and not by any mans diſcretion: for as the law hath taken knowledge, that a man was arreſted of felonie, ſo muſt it take knowledge how he is diſcharged thereof. And the ſame law is, if a man be arreſted for any other felonie committed, and after ſet at libertie by the partie, that arreſted him, or any other &c.

Purſuit by Huy and Crie.

FOr the preuention of felons, and felonies by watch and ward, and to the intent that they which ſhall commit any Homicides, Burglaries, Robberies, or other felonies may be apprehended, and iuſtified by the Law: Or if they eſcape, and flie away, that they may be purſued and taken by Huy and Crie, and committed to priſon: and to the end that due puniſhment may be inflicted vpon thoſe that do not purſue, or doe conceale, or not attach felons, a Statute was made at Weſtminſter Anno 3. Ed. 1. by the which it was ordained, That all men generally ſhalbe readie at the commandement and ſummons of the Sheri'fes, and at the crie of the Countrie to purſue and arreſt felons when neede ſhall be, as well within Fraunchiſes as without; & they that wil not, and thereof be attainted, ſhal make a grieuous fine to the King. And if default be found in the Lord of a Franchiſe, the King ſhall ſeize the Fraunchiſe into his hands: And if default be in the bailiſe, he ſhall be one yeare impriſoned, and after make a grieuous fine: and if he haue not whereof, he ſhall haue two yeares impriſonment. And if the Sherife, Coroner, or any Bailife, within ſuch franchiſe or without, for reward or intreatie, or any affinitie, doe conceale, conſent or procure to conceale the felonies done in their liberties, or otherwiſe will not attach or arreſt ſuch felons (whereas they may) or otherwiſe will not doe their offices, for the fauour that they beare to ſuch offendors, and be thereof attained, they ſhalbe one yeare impriſoned, and make a grieuous fine; and if they haue not whereof to make fine, they ſhall be thrée yeares impriſoned. And by a Braunch of an other Statute made the ſame Anno 3. Ed. 1. intituled Officium Coronatoris, it was enacted, That vpon all Homicides, Burglaries, men ſlaine, or put in great danger, huy and crie ſhall be leuied, and euery man ſhall follow the huy and crie, and the offendors ſteps if it may be: and whoſoeuer doth not, and is thereupon conuicted, ſhall be attached to appeare before the Iuſtices of Gaole deliuerie.

All men ſhall purſue the huy and crie. — *St. 3. E. 1. 9.*

Concealemēt or not attachment of felons — *St. 3. Ed. 1.*

2 After, by another Statute made at Wincheſter Anno 13. Ed. 1. it was prouided, That immediately after any felonies and robberies be committed, freſh ſuit ſhall be made from towne to towne, and from countrie to countrie, and Enqueſts ſhall be taken, if néed be, by him that is chiefe Lord of the town, and after in hundreds, franchiſes, and in the countie, & ſometime in two, thrée,

Freſhſuit and inquirie after felons. — *St. 13. E. 1. 1*

or

or foure counties, in case where felonies be committed in the Marches of the Shire, so that offendors may be attainted, and suffer punishment. And if the countrie will not answer for the bodies of such offendors, the people dwelling in euery such countrie shall answer for the robberies done, & the dammages: so that the whole hundred where the robberie shall be done, with the franchises which be within the same hundreds shall answer for the robberies done. And if the robberie be done in the diuision of two hūdreds, then both the hundreds, together with the franchises within the precinct of them shall answer. And the countrie shall haue no longer time after the robberie and felonie committed, than halfe a yeare, within the which halfe yeare they must agree for ẏ robberie, or else they shalbe answerable for the bodies of the offendors. After, by a Statute made an̄ 28.E.3.11. it is established, That the countrie shal haue no longer terme after the robberie or felonie committed, than fourtie daies, within which it behoueth them to make gree of the robberie or offence, or that they answer the bodies of the offendors. And whereas the said Stat. of Winchester hath ordained, That immediately after any felonies and robberies be committed, fresh suit shalbe made from towne to towne, and from countrie to countrie: Though the said Stat. doth not make mention in what place, or at what time the robberie shalbe done, for the which the countrie shall answer, if they doe not pursue and apprehend the felons: yet the sages of the law respecting the reason and ground of that Stat. doe resolue, that the robberie which ẏ countrie must answer for, is to be committed in an open place, which the cōtrey may take knowledge of by themselues, without huy and cry, or other notice giuen to them: for if a man be robbed in his house in the night, or day, and the felons escape, the hundred where the house is shall not be charged therewith, for euery mans house is his castle, which he must defend at his owne perill, and if a man be robbed in his house it shalbe accounted his owne follie that he did defend it no better. And other men may not enter into that house for the safeguard thereof, as they may enter into the common field. And also the robberie which the countrie must answer for, is to be committed in the day time, and not in the night, viz. at such times and seasons as be méet for men to trauel in, and not at such a time which is ordained for men to rest in. And therefore if a man be robbed in the morning before day, the countrie shall not be charged therewith: but if it be during the day light, though the sunne be set, the countrie shalbe charged therewith: for whosoeuer doth trauel during the day light, is in the guard and protection of the lawe: and if any doe iourney by night, he doth it at his owne perill.

[Margin notes: The penaltie of the countrie if a felon bee not taken. — St. 28.E.3.11 — Co.li.7.6. — The place & time of the robberie committed.]

St.13.E.1.4 3 For the more suretie of the countrie, and spéedier detecting of offendors, by the said Statute of Winchester it was enacted, That in great townes beeing walled, the gates shalbe shut from the sunne setting vntill the sunne rising: and no man shall lodge in the Suburbs, or any place out of the town, frō nine of the clocke vntil day, vnlesse his Host will answer for him. And the bailifs of townes euery weeke, or at the least euery fifteenth day, shall make enquirie of all persons beeing lodged in the Suburbes, or in forraine places of the townes, and if they find any that hath receiued any suspitious persons, not kéeping the Kings peace, the baylifs shall execute right and iustice therein.

[Margin note: Warding of walled towns.]

St.13.E.1.4. 4 And by the said statute of Winchester it was moreouer ordained, That in

When the night watch shall begin and end.

in all townes watch shall be kept, as in times past it hath beene used, That is to say, from the feast of the Ascension untill Michaelmas, in every citie sixe men shall watch at every gate, in every Borough twelue men, in every town sixe or foure, according to the number of the inhabitants of the towne, and they shall watch the towne at night from the sunne setting to the sunne rising. And if any stranger doe passe by them, he shall be arrested untill the morning, and if no suspition be found, he shall goe quit: and if they find cause of suspition, they shall forthwith deliuer him to the Shirife, and the Shirife shall receiue him without hurt, untill he be acquited in due manner. And if he will not obey the arrest, they shall leuie Huy and Cry upon him, and such as keepe the Towne, shall follow with Huy and Cry with all the Towne and Townes neere, and from Towne to Towne, untill he be taken and deliuered to the Shirife, as is beforesaid: and for the arrestments of such strangers none shall be punished. And by the Statute of Anno 5. H. 4. Justices of Peace haue power to make inquisition in their Sessions from time to time, and to punish them which be found in default, after the tenour of the foresaid statute of Winchester. St. 5. H. 4. 3

Resisting of arrest.

Enlarging of high waies.

5 And for the more speedie apprehension of felons, and that they may haue the lesse meanes to escape, when they haue robbed, or otherwise offended, by the said statute of Winchester it is further established, That the highwaies leading from one Market towne to another shalbe enlarged there where any wood, hedges, or ditches be, so that there shalbe no ditch, wood, or bush where he that doth lewdly may escape, within two hundred foot of the high way on the one side, and two hundred foot on the other (but this Statute extendeth not to Ashes or great Trees.) And if any robberies be done by default of breaking downe ditches, underwood, and bushes, the Lord shall answer therefore: and if it be a murder, the Lord shalbe punished at the Kings pleasure. And if the Lord be not able to cut downe the underwood, the Countrie shall helpe him. And within the kings demesne woods in forrests and without, the waies shal be enlarged as before is said. And if any Parke be neere unto the high way, the Lord thereof shall diminish it by the space of two hundred foot from the high way, or els make such a wall, ditch, or hedge, that offendors cannot goe forward or backeward to any hurt. St. 13. E. 1. 5.

6 Because it is very hard, and extreame to many persons, for that by the foresaid Statutes of 13. Ed. 1. & 28. E. 3. 11. they do remaine charged with the penalties therein contained, notwithstanding their unabilitie to satisfie the same, and though they do as much as in reason might be required in pursuing such malefactors & offendors, whereby both large scope of negligence is giuen to the inhabitants & resiants in other hundreds & counties, not to prosecute the huy & crie made, followed, & brought unto them, by reason they are not chargeable for any portion of the goods robbed, nor with any dammages in that behalfe giuen: & also great incouragement & imboldening is likewise giuen to ye offendors to commit daily more felonies and robberies, seeing it is in a maner impossible for the inhabitants and resiants of the said hundred and franchise wherein the robberie is committed to apprehend them, without the ayde of other hundreds and counties adioyning. And for that also the partie robbed hauing remedie by the foresaid statutes for the recouering of his goods robbed

and

and dammages against the Hundred wherein the robberie was committed, is many times negligent and carelesse in prosecuting and pursuing the saide malefactors and offendors. For the qualifying of all which extreamities by a statute made Anno 27. Eliz. it was ordained, That the inhabitants and resiants of every, or any such Hundred (with the franchises within the precinct thereof) wherein negligence, fault, or defect of pursute and fresh sute after huy and crie made shall happen to be, shall answer and satisfie the one moitie or halfe of all and every summe and summes of money and dammages, as shall by force and vertue of the saide Statutes (viz. of 13. Ed. 1. and 28. Ed. 3.) or either of them be recovered or had against, or of the same Hundred, with the franchises therein, in which any robberie or felonie shall at any time hereafter be committed or done. And the same moitie shall and may at any time hereafter be recovered by action of debt, bill, plaint, or information in any of the Queenes Courts of Record at Westminster, by, and in the name of the Clerke of the Peace for the time being, of, or in every such Countie within this Realme where any such robberie and recoverie by the party or parties robbed shalbe, without naming the Christian name or the surname of the saide Clerke of the Peace. Which moitie so recovered, shall be to the only use and behoofe of the inhabitants of the said Hundred, where any such robberie or felonie shall be committed or done.

St. 27. El. 13 (margin)

The Hundred charged wher fresh sute shall cease. (margin)

The Clerke of the Peace shall prosecute the sute. (margin)

St. 27. El. 13 — 7 If any Clerke of the Peace, of, or in any Countie within this Realme, shall at any time hereafter commence, or preferre any such sute, action, or information, and shall after the same so sued, commenced, or preferred, happen to die, or to be remooved out of his office before recoverie and execution had, yet no such action, sute, bill, plaint, or information sued, commenced, or preferred, shall by such displacing, or death, be abated, discontinued, or ended. But it shall and may be lawfull, to, and for the Clerke for the Peace next succeeding in the saide Countie, to prosecute, pursue, and follow all, and every such action, bill, plaint, sute, and information for the causes aforesaid, so hanging and depending, in such maner and forme, to all intents and purposes, as that Clerke of the Peace might have done, which first commenced or preferred the said sute, bill, plaint, or information.

The Clerke of the Peace doth die, or is remooved. (margin)

8 Although the whole Hundred where such robberies and felonies are committed, with the liberties within the precincts thereof, are by the said two former statutes charged with the answering to the partie robbed his dammages, yet neverthelesse the recoverie and execution by and for the partie or parties robbed is had against one or a very few persons of the saide inhabitants, and he and they so charged, have not heretofore by Lawe had any meane or way to have any contribution, of, or from the residue of the saide Hundred where the said robbery is committed, to the great impoverishment of them against whom such recoverie or execution is had: for the remedy whereof by the saide statute of Añ 27. Eliz. it was enacted, That after execution of dammages by the partie or parties so robbed, had, it shall and may be lawfull (upon complaint made by the partie or parties so charged) to, and for two Justices of the Peace, whereof one to be of the Quorum, of the same Countie, inhabiting within the saide Hundred, or neare unto the same, where anie such execution shall be had, to assesse and taxe ratably, and proportionably, according

St. 27. El. 13 (margin)

A remedy for an equall contribution.

according to their discretions all and euerie the Townes, Parishes, Villages, and Hamlets, as well of the saide Hundred where any such robberies shall be committed, as of the Liberties within the saide Hundred, to, and towards an equall contribution to be had and made for the reliefe of the saide inhabitant or inhabitants, against whom the partie or parties robbed before that time had his or their execution. And that after such taxation made, the Constables, Constable, Headboroughs, or Headborough of euerie such Towne, Parish, Village, and Hamlet, shall by vertue of this Act haue full power and authoritie within their seuerall limites, ratably and proportionably, to taxe and assesse according to their abilities, euerie inhabitant and dweller in euerie such Towne, Parish, Village, and Hamlet, for, and towardes the paiment of such taxation and assessement, as shall be so made vpon euery such Towne, Parish, Village, and Hamlet, as aforesaide, by the saide Justices. And if any Inhabitant of any such Towne, Parish, Village, or Hamlet, shall obstinately refuse and denie to pay the saide Taxation and assessement so by the said Constables, Constable, Headboroughs, or Headborough taxed & assessed: then it shall and may be lawfull, to, and for the said constables, & headboroughs, & euery of the within their seuerall limits & iurisdictions, to distraine all and euery person and persons so refusing and denying, by his & their goods and chattels, & the same distresse to sell, and the mony therof comming to retaine to the vse aforesaid. And if the goods or chattells so distrained and solde, shall be of more value, than the said Taxation shall come vnto, then the residue of the said money ouer and aboue the saide Taxation, shall be deliuered vnto the said person or persons so distrained.

Deliuering the contribute money.

9 All and euery the saide Constables and Headboroughs, after that they haue within their seuerall limites and iurisdictions leuied and collected their said rates and summes of mony so taxed, shall within ten dates after such collection, pay and deliuer the same ouer vnto the said Justices of Peace, or one of them, to the vse and behoofe of the saide Inhabitant or Inhabitants, for whom such rate, taxation, or assessement shall be had or made, as aforesaide: Which money so paied, shal by the Justices or Justice so receiuing the same, be deliuered ouer (vpon request made) vnto the saide Inhabitant or Inhabitants, to whose vse the same shall be collected. St.27.El.13

Leuying of contribution.

10 And the like taxation, assessement, leuying by distresse, and payment, as aforesaide, shall be had and done within euerie Hundred where default or negligence of pursute and fresh sute shall be, for, and to the benefite of all and euery Inhabitant or Inhabitants of the same Hundred, where such default shall be, that shall at any time heereafter by vertue of this Act, haue any dammages or money leuied of them, for, or to the paiment of the one moitie or halfe of the mony recouered against the said Hundred, where any robberie shall be hereafter committed. St.27.El.13

No penaltie where any of the offenders be apprehended.

11 Prouided, that where any robberie is, or shal be hereafter committed by two or a greater number of malefactors, and that it happen any one of the said offenders to be apprehended by pursute to be made according to the saide former mentioned Lawes and Statutes, according to this present Act, that then, and in such case, no hundred or franchise shall in any wise incurre, or fall into the penaltie, losse, or forfeiture mentioned either in this present Act, or in any the saide former statutes, although the residue of the saide malefactors St.27.El.13

shall

shall happen to escape, and not to be apprehended: Any thing in this statute, or in the said former statutes to the contrary notwithstanding. Which saide Braunch doth in some sort qualifie part of the foresaid statute of Winchester: for by the saide statute, the Country must agrée for the saide robberie within halfe a yéere, or else they shall be answerable for the bodies of the saide offendors, which is of all the offendors. But by this statute it is sufficient if they take any of the offendors, although not all.

Co.l.7.fol.7

St.27.Eli.13 12 Prouided also, That no person or persons héereafter robbed shall take any benefite by vertue of any the saide former Statutes to charge any Hundred where any such robberie shall be committed, except hée or they so robbed shal commence his or their sute or action, within one yéere next after such robberie so to be committed.

Within what time the sute shal be commenced.

St.27.Eli.13 13 No huy and crie, or pursute héereafter to be done or made by the Country, or inhabitants of any Hundred shall be allowed and taken to be a lawful huy and crie, or pursute, vpon, or after any of the saide felons, or offendors, except the same huy and crie and pursute be done and made by horsemen and footmen: Any vsage, or custome to the contrary notwithstanding.

In what maner huy and crie shalbe made.

St.27.El.13 14 No person or persons that shal hereafter happen to be robbed, shal haue or maintaine any action, or take any benefite by vertue of the saide two mentioned Statutes, or either of them, except the saide person or persons so robbed, shall with as much conuenient spéede as may be, giue notice and intelligence of the same felonie or robberie so committed vnto some of the inhabitants of some Towne, Village, or Hamlet neare vnto the place where any such robberie shall be committed: Nor shall bring or haue any action vpon, or by vertue of any the statutes aforesaide, except hée or they shall first within twentie dayes next before such action to be brought, be examined vpon his or their corporall Othe to be taken before some one Justice of the Peace of the Countie where the robberie was committed, inhabiting within the said Hundred where the robberie was committed, or neare vnto the same, whether hée or they doe knowe the parties that committed the said robberie, or any of them. And if vpon such examination it be confessed, that he or they doe know the parties that committed the saide robberie, or anie of them, then he or they so confessing, shall before the saide action be commenced, or brought, enter into sufficient bond by Recognisance before the saide Justice, before whome the saide examination is had, effectually to prosecute the same person and persons so knowen to haue committed the saide robbery, by inditment, or otherwise, according to the due course of the Lawes of this Realme.

Notice must be giuen of the robberie.

The party robbed examined & bound to prosecute the offenders.

15 Because the inhabitants of the Hundred of Benherst in the countie of Berke consisting onely vpon fiue small villages, and thrée hamlets, and hauing in it two great road waies of thrée miles in length at the least, through the Thicket, haue béene ouercharged by seuerall Braunches of the said Statute of Anno 27. Eli.13. In reformation thereof, by a Statute made an

39. El.

39. Elizab. it was enacted, That the inhabitants of the Hundred of Benherst, alias Beinersh, within the Countie of Berke, shall and may to their owne proper use, in the name of the Clerke of the Peace of the said Countie of Berke, recouer, haue, and leuie all such summes of money, costs, and dammages as hereafter shall be recouered, or leuied, of, or against them by the foresaide Statutes, or any of them, against the inhabitants and resiants of euery, or any such Hundred, with the franchises within the precincts thereof, wherein negligence, fault, or defect of such pursute, and fresh sute (as by the said Statute of 27. Elizab. is appointed to be made) shall happen to be, after notice giuen, or huy and crie brought to the saide inhabitants or resiants, or any of them, of, or upon any robberies which shall be at any time hereafter done within the saide Hundred of Beinersh. And this present Act shal giue as full power and authoritie in all respects to the inhabitants of the saide Hundred of Benherst (in the name of the Clerke of the Peace of the saide Countie) for recouerie, hauing, and leuying of all the saide money, costs, and dammages as aforesaide, as the aforesaide Statute of 27. Elizab. gaue or intended to giue for the recouerie of a moitie, or one halfe thereof. Prouided alwaies, that no such remedie, or recouerie shall be had by this Statute, for all, or the whole summe or summes of money, and dammages aforesaide, but onely in these two Cases, viz. The one, where no such notice or intelligence (as by the said Statute of 27. Elizab. was appointed to be giuen of euery, or any Robberie) shall be giuen to the inhabitants of the saide hundred of Benherst alias Beinersh: The other where the inhabitants of the same Hundred (after such notice of any Robberie to them, or some of them giuen, or after huy and crie for the same to them brought) shall make, or cause to be made fresh sute, and pursute after the offenders with horsemen and footmen, according to the saide Statute of 27. Elizab. and where neuerthelesse the offenders, or any, or one of them shall not be apprehended within fortie daies after the Robberie committed. St. 39. E. 25

A remedy for the inhabitāts of Benherst in Barkshire.

In what cases onely the recouerie shall be had.

16 Two ioynt owners of a summe of mony, which were robbed by felons unknowen at A. in the Hundred of B. in the countie of C. brought their action against the inhabitants of the said Hundred of B. and declared, that wheras huy and crie was leuied by them, and notice there giuen, and the felons were not apprehēded, nor descried, nor amends made within the six months, according to the statute of Winchester: whereunto the defendants, viz. the inhabitants of the saide Hundred of B. pleaded in barre of the action, that immediately upon the huy and crie leuied, they made fresh sute from the said Towne of A. where the robbery was committed thorow their other townes unto the towne of D. which is next adioyning to the said Hundred, and there huy and crie was giuen to the inhabitants of the saide Hundred. But this maner of pursute was adiudged no excuse, according to the meaning of the said statute of Winchester, without apprehending, or answering of the robbers, or descrying of their names, that they might be indicted and outlawed. And in this case the plaintifes may ioyne in action, because they were ioynt owners of the money: But if the summes of money had béene seuerall, and they had seuerall properties in them, they would not haue ioyned in Action. P. 24. El. Dy. 370.

Pursute will not serue without apprehension of the felons, or descryingthē.

Arresting of him that is pursued by huy and crie.

17 If a man be driuing of cattell, and be pursued by huy and crie, the Shirifes Bailiffe, or any other, may arrest him and the cattell supposed to be stolen, 29. Ed. 3. 39.

ſtolen, and commit them to the Towne where they be apprehended to anſwer to the King, according to the Lawe, though the man arreſted be not of euill name, ſuſpicious, nor a ſtranger in thoſe partes, nor indited. For the Lawe doth giue that credite to huy and crie, that euerie man is a ſufficient Bailiffe and officer to apprehend him that is purſued by huy and crie, and taken with the thing ſuppoſed to be ſtollen. And therefore if one man doe leuie huy and crie vpon an other without cauſe, both the one partie and the other ſhall be attached to anſwer it, as diſturbers of the Peace.

Appeales.

Appeales.

When a murder, manslaughter, rape, burglarie, robberie, or other felonie is committed, and that the offendor (be he principall or accessorie) is apprehended by huy and crie, or by any other meanes, and so by imprisonment or mainprise brought to his answer: Or otherwise if he flee and escape, when he is so discouered and knowen, that Processe may be awarded against him by name, to take him, and bring him into the Kings court to his answer: Then either the partie most interessed or grieued by the same murder or felonie, is to prosecute sute against the saide offendor by Appeale, and thereby to seeke reuenge against him for the wrong done to himselfe, or his auncestor; or else the offendor is to be indited at the Kings sute, whose peace hee hath broken, and whose lawe he hath offended, and who hath a speciall interest in all manner of treasons and felonies to punish them, to weede them out of his kingdomes and dominions, and to defend his subiects from them. And therefore I am to expresse in this Chapter, and the next, what an Appeale of felonie is, and what an Inditement is, by whom, for whom, and against whom, and in what cases they are to be begunne, prosecuted, and maintained, what defences or pleas are to be made or pleaded by the supposed offendors vnto them, and what counterpleas may be obiected against the same plees. An Appeale is a plaint of one person made against another, with an intent to attaint him of felonie, by a course of Lawe prouided therefore; which appeale may be brought against a woman couert without her husband, against an infant, and all others that can commit felonie: and a woman may haue an appeale for the death of her husband (because the husband and wife be one flesh) but of the death of none other, by force of the Statute of Magna Charta, which hath ordained, That none shall be taken, or imprisoned by the appeale of any woman for the death of any other, than of her husband. And therefore if a woman doe bring an appeale of the death of her father, and the Defendant would admit it, yet the Court will abate it, because it is contrary to the said Statute.

Appeale of death.

Appeale by a woman of the death of her husband.

St.9.H.3.34

10.Ed.4.7. Plow.Com. fol.85.

Appellāt conueieth his title by a woman.

2 As a woman shall haue no Appeale of the death of any other, but of her husband; No more shall any cosin of him that was slaine, who maketh his conuei-

conueiance in kinred by a woman, haue any appeale of the death of him that is killed; notwithstanding he be issue male, and not female; and notwithstanding that the woman by whom he maketh his conueiance, died in the life time of him, of whose death the appeale is commenced. As if a man haue issue one onely daughter, who marrieth a husband, hath issue a sonne, and dieth, and after the father of that woman is slaine. In this case the sonne of the woman shall not haue an appeale of the death of his saide grandfather, though hee be his next heire at the common lawe, and inheritable to his land; because his mother was foreclosed of it by the foresaid statute of Magna Charta, and so likewise he which hath none other title thereunto, but that which he deriueth from his saide mother. But if he that was slaine, haue none heire on the fathers side, then the uncle or next of kinne on the mothers side, shall haue the appeale, yea though he doe conuey his title thereunto by a woman.

Appellant conueyeth his title by a woman.

20.H.6.46 Fi. Cor. 385 17.Ed.4.1. Fi. Cor. 384 17.Ed.4.1

3 By the auntient lawe of this Realme, a woman could not haue an appeale of the death of her husband, unlesse her said husband were slaine betwene her armes, within the yere and day before: Neither could shee, or any other haue an appeale, unlesse she or he were present at the death of the partie slaine, and see it. But that Lawe was altered by the Statute of Gloucester, whereby it was ordained, That no Appeale shall be abated, so soone as they haue beene heeretofore: But if the appellant in an appeale doe declare the deede, the yeare, the day, the houre, the time of the King, and the Towne where the deede was done, and with what weapon hee was slaine, the appeale shall stand in effect. And the appeale shall not be abated for default of fresh sute, where a man doth sue within the yeare, and the day, after the deede done.

St.6.Ed.1.9

The declaration in appeale of murder.

4 If a woman will haue an appeale of the death of her husband, it is requisite, that shee be not onely his wife indeede, viz. de facto, but also lawfully, and in right, viz. de iure: for neuer accoupled in lawfull marriage, is a good plea, to barre her of her appeale. And it shall be tried by the Bishop, whether she be his lawfull wife, or not.

50.Ed.3.15. 28.Ed.3.91. 27.Ass.p.3.

The woman must be the deads lawfull wife.

5 It is requisite, that a woman who will maintaine an appeale of the death of her husband, shall liue sole, and unmarried: for by her second marriage, her appeale is extinct, though her second husband doe die, within a yeare and day after the death of her first husband. And if a woman doe bring an appeale of the death of her husband, and hanging the Writ, shee doth marry an other husband, her appeale shall abate for euer.

20.H.6.46. 12.El.Dyer.296.

The woman must liue unmarried.

6 If a woman doe bring an appeale of the death of her husband, and doe pursue the Defendant untill Judgement: And then after iudgement, and before

11.H.4.46.

A woman marrieth betweene iudgemēt & executiō

before execution, shée marrieth an other husband : In this case, shée shall not obtaine execution, viz. the Defendant shall not be hanged at her sute: for shée hath willingly lost the name of her first husband, before shée hath obtained the effect of her sute, and the reuenge which shée brought her appeale for.

Where appeale lieth, but no dower.

7 There be some Cases, where a woman shall haue an appeale of the death of her husband, though she be not endowable of the possession of the same husband : As where her husband is attainted of treason, and after one doth kill him, his wife shall haue an appeale, and yet she shall haue no dower. 27.Ass.p.41 35.H.6.58 And in like sort, if a woman doe elope from her husband, and after one doth kill him, she may maintaine an appeale against the offendour, but no writ of dower against his heire. And many other Cases there be, where a man was so seised of his lands, that his wife is not thereof endowable by the Lawe: And yet if hée be slaine, she may maintaine an appeale against the manqueller.

Where the wife may haue appeale, none other shall.

8 Where a woman may haue an appeale of the death of her husband, none other shall haue it during her life, nor after her death, though the wife 20.H.6.47 Kel.fol.120 doe die within the yeare and day after the death of her husband, and before the appeale commenced; for that the appeale was once out of the blood, it shall not be restored to his blood againe. If the husband be killed by his wife, his sonne shall haue an appeale. And yet if in that case the King doe pardon the 33.H.8. Dyer 50 wife all treasons, the sonne shall be barred of his appeale. 18.Ed.4.1.

The husband killed by his wife.

Appeale of death by the heire.

9 If he that was slaine, had no wife liuing, at the time he was killed, then his next heire by the common Lawe, if he be male, shall haue the appeale. But if hée which bringeth the appeale be the next heire male to him that was slaine, yet if there be another liuing, which is his heire by the common Lawe, though not his heire male, his appeale shall abate. As if he that was slaine had issue a daughter, and no sonne, his brother cannot maintaine 27.Ass.p.25. an appeale against the offendor, though hée be his next heire male, because Fi.Cor.384 he is not next heire by the common Lawe to him that was slaine, but his daughter is. And by the same reason, a Bastard, nor the youngest sonne, which doth inherite lands in Borough English, shall not maintaine an appeale, because neither of them is heire by the common Lawe. It was a custome in olde time, if one were found guiltie in an appeale of murder, that his wife, and all the nearest of his kinne, which was murdered, should 11.H.4.11. drawe the felon who committed the murder, by a long rope, to the place Plo.com. 306 of execution.

A Bastard.

Heire in Borough English.

The maner of a murderers death.

An appeale dieth with the Appellant, or by his nonsuite &c.

10 This appeale of the death of the auncester is so tied and affixed to the next heire male at the Common Lawe of him that was slaine, that if it be once attached by him, although that hée die, hanging the suite, or be non-suite therein, or doe discontinue the suite, and that within the yéere, 38.H.6.13. yet the appeale is extinct for euer : because it is but a personall action, and 9.H.7.5. not auncestrell, (for he that was slaine could not haue maintained it:) and 16.H.7.15. therefore

therefore being but personall, it doth die with the person of the appellant. But it is otherwise, if the appeale were not attached by the heire, during
11.H.4.11. his life, but that hee died before hee brought his appeale, or died in the life
20.H.6.46 of his auncester that was killed: In that case, hee which is next heire male liuing, shall haue the appeale.

9.H.7.5. Stamf.fo.59 11 If the eldest sonne, before the appeale commenced, and within the yeare, doth release the appeale, and then dieth, the second sonne and euery other which claimeth as heire to the partie slaine, shall bee barred thereby. The heire doth release, and die.

16.H.7.15. 38.H.6.13. 12 If the eldest sonne doe bring an appeale, and hath iudgement, and before execution of the offendor dieth, his heire shall not haue execution: for if he should, he is to haue it as heire to him that recouered, and not as heire to the partie slaine: which cannot be, for hee that demaundeth reuenge of his auncestors death, must make himselfe immediate heire to the same auncestor which was slaine, or otherwise his sute shall not be allowed, which the heire of the eldest sonne in this case cannot doe. Recouery and death before execution.

13 If the eldest sonne, after the title of appeale accrued vnto him, or during the life of his auncester that was slaine, doe disable himselfe by attainder of felonie, or by being a Monke, a Priest, or mayhemed by the Defendant, or by any other cause: So that by such disabilitie hee cannot haue an appeale, yet the second sonne shall not haue it. The eldest sonne disabling himselfe.
Fitz.Cor. 235.322.

14 If the eldest sonne doth kill his father, or his mother, the second sonne shall haue an appeale against him. And if there be three brethren, and the middlemost killeth the elder brother, the youngest brother shall haue an appeale against him: And yet in the foresaide cases, hee that bringeth the appeale, is not heire to him that is slaine. And if the husband doe kill his wife, his sonne shall haue an appeale against him. Killing father, mother, brother, or wife.
Fi.Cor.459. 18.Ed.4.1. 33.H.8. Dyer 50.

1.H.4.6. Littl. vill. 15 If the Lord doe kill his Villaine, the heire of him that was slaine, may haue an appeale against his Lord, notwithstanding that the Plaintife in the appeale is villaine to the Defendant: for the villaines heire doth not sue for the recouerie of lands, goods, or liberty from the Lord, but onely for a lawfull reuenge of his auncesters death. And if the villaines heire should not haue an appeale in this case, the said offence should remaine vnpunished by appeale: for none other may pursue it. The Lord killeth his villaine.

41.Ass.p.14. 45.Ed.3.25 27.Ed.3.83. Kel.fol.120 32.Ass.p.8. 16 An Infant within the age of twenty and one yeares, may haue an appeale of the death of his auncester, (and in like sort hee may haue any maner of appeale:) But notwithstanding, the plea shall remaine to be tried, vntill he come to his full age of one and twentie yeares, for that in this case the Defendant cannot wage battell against him: Attamen quære. An Infant.

A man of 70. yeares of age. 17 A man of the age of thrée score and tenne yeares may haue an appeale of the death of his auncestour, (and in like sort may haue any manner of appeale:) and yet being of that age, hée shall put the Defendant from waging of battell with him. Fi.Cor. 385

Disabilities to bring an appeale. 18 If the Plaintife which ought to sue the Appeale be attainted of treason, or felonie, or a Monke, or a Priest, or mayhemed by the Defendant, he shall not haue an appeale. Fi.Cor. 322

Disabilities in the appellant. 19 A man that is not of perfect memorie, or that is deafe and dumbe, or a Lazar, or a foole naturall, shall not haue an appeale of death, nor any other appeale. For battell cannot be waged against any of them, euery of them being vnperfect to performe the same. Britton.

Pleading that the appellant hath an elder brother. 20 If one brother doe bring an appeale of the death of his auncestor, it is no plea for the appellée to say, that the said auncestor, at the time of his death, and after the Writ purchased, had an elder brother named B. to whom the appeale is giuen, and not to him that is plaintife: for it may be, that the same B. was his brother of the halfe bloud. And therefore the surest way is to begin his plea with the father of him that was slaine, as to say, that such a man tooke to his wife such a woman, and had issue betwéene them B. their eldest sonne, and hee which was slaine their second sonne, and the appellant their youngest sonne, and that he which was slaine died, liuing B. their eldest sonne. 7.Ed.4.15

The appellāt in appeale of death may sue by atturney. 21 For that by the common Lawe, hée that will sue an appeale, must sue it in proper person, which sute is long, and costly, and maketh the partie appellant wearie to sue: For the reformation whereof it was ordained by the Statute of Anno 3. H.7. That the Appellant in any appeale of murder, or death of a man (where battaile by the course of the common Lawe lieth not;) may make his atturney, and appeare by the same, in the saide appeale, after it is commenced, to the end and Execution of the same. St.3.H.7.1

Who shall maintaine an appeale of robberie. 22 As concerning an appeale of Robberie, who shall maintaine it, and for what causes, it is to bée obserued, That hée from whom the goods be taken, may haue the same appeale: As the Seruant shall haue an Appeale of Robberie, if the goods of his Masters bée taken out of his custodie and possession, and yet hée had onely the possession, but no propertie in the goods robbed. A Carrier. And so it is, if a Stranger bee commaunded to carrie another mans goods, and as hée is in carrying of them, hée is robbed of them, and they taken from him: In this case the same Stranger may haue an Appeale of Robberie against those Robbers, because hee standeth charged to him, who commaunded him to carry the same goods. Fi.Cor.100 2.Ed.4.15.

23 A wo-

Fi.Cor.357 23 A woman may haue an appeale of robberie: and so may an infant: Likewise Executors may haue an appeale of Robberie, of a Robberie of the Testators goods done to themselues, but not done to their Testator: for if a man be robbed, and after maketh his Executors, and die, the Executors shall not haue an appeale of Robberie; for an appeale, being a personall action, dieth with the partie, and shall not accrew to his Executors. A woman. An Infant. Executors.

Fit.Cor.17. 24 A Villaine shall not haue an appeale of robberie, against his Lord, for any goods robbed, or taken from him by his said Lord: Because all the goods of the Villaine be the Lords at his pleasure. Lord. Villaine.

17.Ed.3.13 25 One may haue an appeale of robberie for the King, or the Queene; as of any iewelles, plate, or other goodes of the Kings or Queenes robbed or taken from him. And a man may be indicted of felonie, for the stealing of goods of another, that was attainted of Treason, which goods by the said attainder were forfeited to the King. Appeale for the King or Queene. Stealing the goods of a mã attainted of treason.

11.H.4.40.

26 There be some Cases, where one may haue an appeale of robberie, though the robberie was not done to him, but to another: as if there be two marchants, or other tradesmen, that doe merchandize, or occupie their goods in common, and one of them is robbed, and slaine: In this case, the other merchant or tradesman, may haue an appeale of robberie against the Robbers. And in like sort, if one doe steale my goods from me, and another doth steale them from him: In this case I may haue an appeale against the second felon, because by the first taking, the propertie was not out of me, for a felon doth not claime any propertie in the thing stolen; in such sort as hee doth, who taketh a thing as a trespassor. An appeale of robbery done to an other.

Fi.Cor.392

4.H.7.5.
13.Ed.4.3.

27 Touching an appeale of rape, and who by the Lawe shall maintaine the same, it is to be noted, That if a woman sole, be rauished, she may haue an appeale of rape. But if a woman married be rauished, she cannot haue an appeale without her husband. Appeale of rape.

8.H.4.21.1

28 If a woman couert be rauished, and after she doth consent to the rauisher, her husband onely shall haue an appeale of rape, by the Statute of Anno 6. Ric.2. the words whereof be these: It is ordained, that wheresoeuer, and whensoeuer any Ladies, Noblemens daughters, or other women be rauished, and after the same rape committed, doe consent to the rauishers, as well the rauishers, as they that be rauished, and euerie of them, shal be disabled, and be disabled ipso facto to haue or challenge all manner of inheritance, dower, or ioint feoffment after the death of their husbands, and auncestors. And the husbands of such women (if they haue husbands) or if they haue no husbandes liuing, then their Fathers, or other their next kinsmen in blood, shall haue the sute to prosecute, and may pursue against the same offendours, and rauishers in this behalfe; and to conuict them of felonie, though the same woman after the Rape, doe consent to the Rauishers. An appeale where a woman rauished consenteth.

St.6.R.2.6

uishers. And in this case the Defendant shall not wage battell, but the truth of the matter shalbe tried by the Countrie. S.Felonies by Statute 4.

A lawfull husband.

29 The wordes of this Statute be: That the husbands of such women &c. which is to be intended, of her lawfull husband, That is to say, that her husband in right and possession, shall haue the Appeale: for neuer accoupled in lawfull marriage, is a good plea in barre against him. And in like sort it is 11.H.4.14. if the appeale be brought by the husband and wife, because the appeale is in the right; and so hee must be her lawfull and rightfull husband, that must maintaine the appeale alone, or iointly with his wife.

where the father or kinsman shal haue an appeale of rape.

30 This Statute of 6.Ric.2. doth giue the appeale for default of the husband to the father, or to some other their next kinsman in blood; and so by the expresse words of this Statute, an appeale of rape is giuen to the father: and yet hee shall not haue an appeale, of the death of his sonne, or daughter. And where the said statute doth giue the appeale for default of the husband, to the father, or &c. That is to be intended, where the woman doth consent to the rauisher: for otherwise the woman shall haue an appeale vpon the statute of St.13.E.1.34 Westminster 2.

A Lord rauisheth his niece

31 If a Lord doe rauish his Niece, she shall not haue an appeale of Rape Fit.Cor.17 against him: But the King shall punish him by indictment.

Pledges in rape.

32 It appeareth by the statute intituled Officium Coronatoris, That if St.3.Ed.1. any be appealed of rape, hee shall be attached by foure or sixe pledges, if the appeale be fresh, and the signe of truth apparant, by effusion of blood, or an open outcrie leuied. But if it be without any manifest token, or outcrie, two pledges shall suffice.

within what time an appeale shalbe commenced.

33 The before mentioned Statute of Glocester hath ordained, That an St.6.Ed.1.9 appeale shall not be abated, for default of fresh sute, where a man doth sue, within a yeere and a day, after the deede done. These words of the Statute be generall, not making mention more, of an appeale of death, than of an appeale of any other felonie: But yet conferring them, with the other words in the statute, they may be intended specialy to extend to an appeale of death, and to none other appeale: for if a man that is robbed doth make fresh sute, 7.H.4.44. and doe his endeuour to apprehend the felon, and vse all his diligence to find him, although he doe not commence his appeale, two or three yeares after the robberie committed, yet he may then well pursue it. And so in appeale of robberie, fresh sute shall be decided by the discretion of the Iustices. But H.22.Ed.4 39. in an appeale of death, it is a good plea for the Defendant to pleade, that he of whose death, this appeale is pursued, died aboue a yeare and a day, before the said appeale commenced.

34 The words of the foresaid Statute of Glocester be, That a man shall St.6.Ed.1.9

pursue

pursue his Appeale, within a yeare and day, after the déed done. And therefore if one man doe strike another vpon one day, and he dieth of the same stroake certaine daies after, the Appeale shalbe commenced within the yeare and day after the death, and not within the yeare and day after the stroake giuen: for there was no felonie committed, vntill the man was dead. But yet if one mã doe giue to another a mortall wound in Februarie, and the king doth in April next giue pardon to the offendor of all felonies before that time committed, and the partie stricken doth die of the same wound in May following; this pardon shall discharge the offendor, because the wound giuen by the offendor was the cause of the felonie, the which wound was the offence towards the King, and that the king hath pardoned, and so thereby the death of the partie, and all other things depending vpon the same offence be pardoned.

Co.l.4.42 — From what time the yeare shal haue relation, touching an appeale.

Plo.com. f.401 — How the K. pardon shal haue relation.

35 Where the words of the Statute of Gloucester be, That a man shall pursue his Appeale within a year and a day after the deed done: Those words (viz. the déed done) shalbe intended of the felonie whereupon the appeale is commenced: for if one be accessorie to another a yeare after the homicide or murder committed, an appeale shalbe pursued against him, and yet it is not within the yeare and day after the homicide or murder committed. S.Br.52.

St.6.E.1.9. — 26.Ass.p.52 — The yere shall haue relation to that offẽce.

36 It appeareth by Britton, and also by the Statute of Westminster 1. that an appeale of Rape ought to be commenced within fourtie daies after the fact done: But then Rape was but a trespasse, which after by the Statute of Westminster 2. was made felonie. In which Statute of Westminster 2. there is no time limited, within the which a woman shalbe compellable to pursue her Appeale of Rape. And therefore it séemeth she is at libertie to bring it when she will, so that it be within a reasonable time.

St.3.E.1.13 — St.13.E.1.34. — Within what time an appeal of rape shalbe commenced.

37 An appeale ought to be brought in the Countie where the felonie was committed, as if it be murder or homicide, where the same murder or homicide was done: But if a man be striken in one county, and then goeth into another countie, and there dieth of the same wound, by the common law an appeale may be commenced either in the countie where the stroake was giuen, or in the countie where the partie stricken did after die, and the trial thereof shal be by the Jurors of both the counties, viz. as well of the countie where he was stricken, as of the countie where he died. And so it was at the plaintiffes pleasure to bring his appeale in which of those two coũties he would. But since by the Statutes of Anno 2. & 3. E.6. it is ordained, That where any person shalbe feloniously stricken, or poisoned in one countie, and die of the same stroake or poysoning in another countie, then an inditment thereof found by Jurors of the countie where the death shall happen (whether it be found before the Coroner, vpon the sight of such dead bodie: or before the Justices of peace, or other Justices or Commissioners, which shall haue authoritie to enquire of such offences) shalbe as good in law, as if the stroake or poysoning had béene committed in the same countie, where the partie shall die, or where such inditement shalbe found. And such party, to whom appeale of murder shal be giuen by the law, may commence, take, and sue Appeale of murder in the same countie where the partie so feloniously stricken or poysoned shall die, as well

18.Ed.3.32 — 3.H.7.12. 4.H.7.18. — St.2.& 3. E.6.24. — In what countie an appeale shalbe brought. — A man stricken in one countie dieth in another.

well against the principal and principals, as against euery accessorie to the same offences, in whatsoeuer countie or place the accessorie shalbe guiltie to the same. And the Justices before whom any such appeale shall be commenced, sued, and taken within the yeare and day, after such murder & manslaughter committed, shall procéede against euery such accessorie, in the same countie, where such appeale shalbe so taken, in like manner and forme, as if the same offence of accessorie, had béene committed in the same countie, where such appeale shalbe so taken, as well by the triall of the Jurors of the countie, where such appeale shalbe taken, vpon the plea of not guiltie, pleaded by such offendor, as otherwise. But note that no Appeale is giuen by this Statute, nor remedie prouided against accessories in a forreine countie, of other felonies (sauing for murder or manslaughter) but the same is left to the common law. Stamford.

Accessories in other offences sauing murder.

In what countie an appeale of Rape shall be brought.

38 An appeale of Rape ought to be brought in the countie where the Rauishment was done. And therefore if a man doe take a woman against her will in one countie, and then carrie her into another countie, and there doe rauish her, the appeale shalbe onely commenced in the countie where the rauishment was committed. And though shee doe declare of the taking of her in another countie, yet it shalbe tried onely in the countie where the appeale is brought: for the declaring of taking of her in another countie, was but surplusage, and néeded not to haue béene inserted, which doth not cause her count to abate. And in this case the woman appellant shall recouer nothing but the defendants death for the felonie, which she shall obtaine in respect of his rauishment of her in the countie, wherunto he forcibly carried her, wherein only the felonie was committed. 3.H.7.12.

Appeale of Robberie.

39 By the same reason if a man doe take another by force in one countie, and then carrie him into another countie, and there robbe him, or kill him: an appeale of felonie shalbe commenced onely in the countie where the robberie or murder was done: for the taking, and carrying him away out of the first countie was but trespasse, and there was no felonie committed, vntill the robberie or murder was committed. 3.H.7.12.

Threatning in one county to bring money into another.

40 If one man doe threaten another in one countie that he will kill him if he doe not bring him a summe of money into another countie such a day: In this case, if he that is threatened, doe in respect of that menace, carrie, and pay the said summe of money to him that threatened him, according to his promise in the said other countie: this is robberie, though the partie néeded not to haue paid the said money according to his promise, for that his said promise was by menace, and not voluntarie, nor vpon cause. And there is reason that the appeale of robberie shalbe commenced in the countie where the money was paid, and not in the countie where the menace was made: for the effect and successe of the matter maketh it felonie, which is the paiment of the money; and not the first cause, which was the threatening. 44.E.3.14 4.H.4.3.

Goods robbed caried into diuers counties

41 If a felon commit a robberie in one countie, and then carrie the goods stolen into diuers other counties, hee that is robbed may haue his appeale of felonie 7.H.4.44 4.H.7.5.

in which of those Counties he will: for the felon committeth felonie in euerie of the Counties, whither he carrieth any of the goods: And in which of those Counties the partie robbed doth commence his Appeale of Felony, there it shal be tried: for the propertie of those goods was alwayes in the first and right owner of them. But he that is robbed may commence his Appeale of Robberie onely in that Countie where hee was robbed, for there is no robberie done but in that Countie onely. But if a man being in one Countie, doe procure another man to commit a robberie in another Countie, which he doth accordingly: in this case the partie robbed shall haue his Appeale of Robberie against the said procurer, as accessorie to this felonie, in the Countie where the procurement was, and not where the robberie was committed; for there was his felonie committed, where he did persuade and procure the robberie to be done.

Co.li.7.2. 26.Ass.p.32. 29.H.8. Dyer 40

42 He that may pursue an Appeale, is at his choyce, whether he will haue it by writ, or by bill. If he pursue it by bill, then he must find to the Sherife in the full Countie, two sufficient pledges, being of the Countie where the felonie was committed, and distrainable within the sayd Countie, that hee shall prosecute his Appeale according to the law of the Realme, and he shalbe thereunto receiued. And then the Coroner shall enter his Appeale, and the names of his pledges: and after the Baily of the place where the felonie was committed, shall be commaunded, that he shall bring the bodies of those that be appealed, to the next Countie Court, to answer to the plaintife. And if the Baily doe answer at the second Countie Court, that he cannot find them, then it shall bee ordained, that they which be principall Appellees of the fact, shall bee solemnly commaunded to yeeld to the Kings peace, and to appeare, and stand to the answer of such a felonie, whereof they be appealed: And so they shall be demanded from Countie to Countie, untill they do appeare, or bee Outlawed. And yet because the Statute of Magna Charta hath ordayned, That no Sherife, Constable, Escheator, Coroner, or other Bailiffe of the Kings, shall hold plea of the Crowne, It is agreed for law, that upon an Appeale commenced before the Sherife and the Coroners, although they may award proces against the Appellees until the Exigent, yet they cannot award the Exigent against the Appellee, if he do not appear: neither if he do appear, they can cause him to answer, but onely they may commit him to prison, and that by force of the sayd statute of Magna Charta.

Before whõe an appeale shalbe broght. Britton. 22.Ass.p.97. St.9.H.3.17

43 When an appeale is commenced before the Sherife and the Coroners in the countie, it may be remooued into the Kings bench by a Certiorari, which must be awarded out of the Chauncerie, or out of the Kings bench, and is to be directed to the Sherife and the Coroners: which prooueth that an appeale is begunne, and of Record, as well before the Sherife, as before the Coroners: according to the Statute of West. 1. which hath ordained, That the Coroners shall lawfully attach, and represent the pleas of the Crowne, and that the Sherife shall haue counter-rolles with the Coroners, as well of appeals as of Enquests, of Attachments, or other things that doe belong unto this office. And therefore a Certiorari to remooue an appeale directed to the sherife onely is voyd: and an appeale of murder may be commenced, as well before the Sherife, as before the Coroners, as it is prooued by these words of the Statute of 3. H. 7. viz. The wife or heire of the person slaine, or murdered, as case shal require,

Remoouing an appeale out of the countie. St.3.E.1.10 4.H..15 St.3.H.7.1

quire, may commence their appeale in proper person, at any time within the yeare after the felonie done, before the Shirife and Coroners of the Countie, where the said felonie and murder was done, or before the King in his Bench, or Justices of Gaole deliuerie.

An appeale before Justices of Gaole deliuerie.

44 An appeale by Bill may be commenced before Justices of Gaole deliuerie: but then the Appellee at the time of the Appeale begun against him, must be prisoner in the same Gaole, whereof those Justices are to make deliuerie, or else such an appeale is not to be receiued: Or otherwise one of them at the least, against whom and others the said appeale is entred, ought to be prisoner in the same Gaole, and if not, the same appeale is void. Yet an approuer may appeale others that are not in prison, but at large: which is by force of the statute of 28. Ed. 1. de Appellatis. And when an appeale is commenced before Justices of Gaole deliuerie against diuers, whereof there is but one in prison before them, this appeale ought to be remooued into the Kings bench by a Certiorari, and from thence proces shall be awarded against them which be at large. And Justices of Assise may hold plea of appeales of robberie, by the commission of Gaole deliuerie.

13.H.4.10. 9.H.4.2. 5. Approuers 19. St. 28. E. 1. 9.H.4.2. Anno 1 M. Dyer 99.

An appeale before Ju. of Assise.

An appeale before the J. of the Kings Bench.

45 As well as Justices of Gaole deliuerie, and the Sherife and Coroners haue authoritie to receiue an appeale by Bill, in like sort Justices of the kings bench haue power to accept an appeale by Bill: for they be the soueraigne coroners of the Realme. 17.Ed.3.13

Appeale against one Bayled.

46 If one be in prison for felonie in the Kings bench, or before the Justices of Gaole deliuerie, and after let to baile, yet an appeale by bill may be commẽced against him, for he is a prisoner notwithstanding that bailement: for they which tooke him in baile, be his guardians, and shall be charged if he escape: & some doe affirme that they may imprison him; and some do hold, that they shall be hanged for him. And vpon his bailement he shall find sureties to answer to all persons. But an appeale is not to be pursued against him, who is let at libertie by mainprise: for that he is not in ward.

21.H.7.33. 32.H.6.4. 9.Ed.4.2. 39.H.6.27.

No appeale against him that is let by mainprise.

No appeale before Justices of peace.

47 Some doe affirme that an appeale may be commenced before Justices of peace, for they haue authoritie by their commission, and by the Statute of 18. Ed. 3. 2. to heare and determine felonies. But others doe hold, that they must onely procéed vpon inditment found by a Jurie before them, and not vpon an appeale prosecuted at the suit of the partie grieued: for the words of their commission be, Ad inquirendum per Sacramentum proborum & legalium hominum de comitatu prædicto, per quos rei veritas melius sciri poterit, de omnibus & omnimodis felonijs &c. Et ad omnia & singula felonias &c. indictamẽta prædicta, cæteraque omnia & singula premissa, secundum leges & statuta regni nostri Angliæ (prout in huiusmodi casu fieri consueuit aut debuit,) audiendum & terminandum. By which words it is to be inferred, that they shall enquire and punish at the Kings suit vpon inditment, and not at the parties suit by appeale, such felonies as shall bee committed within their Jurisdiction. 44.E.3.44.

48 If

48 If one of the Kings subiects doe kill another of his subiects in a forrain Realm, the wife or next heire of him that was slain, as the case requireth, may haue an appeale of the same death in England, before the Constable & Marshall of England, by force of the Statute of 1. H. 4. which doth ordaine, That all appeales of things committed within the Realme, shall be tried and determined by the lawes of the Realme; and of things committed out of the realme, before the Constable and Marshall of England for the time being. And no appeales from henceforth shalbe made or pursued in Parliament.

St. 1. H. 4. 14

An appeale before the Constable and Marshall.

No appeale in Parliamēt.

49 It doth appeare by Bracton and Britton, that one might haue had in former ages, one appeale against the principall, and another against the Accessories: but since that law is changed, viz. The appellant shall haue but one appeale, in the which he must comprehend as well the principals as the accessories, vnlesse it be in speciall cases: and that is confirmed by the Stat. of West. 1. which doth ordaine, That no person shall be outlawed vpon appeale of commandement, force, aide, or receit, vntill the principall be attainted. But the appellant shall not let to attach his appeale at the next countie, as well against the accessorie, as against the principall: But the Exigent against the accessorie shall staie vntill the principall be attainted, by outlawrie or otherwise.

Bracton. Britton. Co. li. 4. 47. St. 3. E. 1. 14

Where there shalbe diuers appeales for one felonie, and where not.

50 In an appeale against two, if one doe appeare, and the other make default, yet the plaintife shall count against them both: and the same law which compelleth the appellant to count at one time against them both, doth enforce him to sue his appeale against them both: for if an appellant doe bring an appeale against one person, and the appellée is attainted and hanged at his suit, and after he will bring an other appeale against one, or two others, for the same offence, he shall take no benefit by his suit, for he should haue ioyned thē all in his first appeale. And the same law is, if the first appellée had béene acquited, or that the appellant had bin Non-suit after apparance.

9. H. 4. 1. Co. l. 4. 47 47. E. 3. 16.

One onely appeale for one felonie.

51 It séemeth that in some cases at this day, one may haue diuers appeals for one felonie: as if one in one countie doe procure another to robbe a man in another countie: In this case, the partie robbed shall haue one appeale against the principall in one countie, and another against the accessorie in another countie: or otherwise he should be without his remedie against the accessorie by Appeale. But by the Statute of Anno 2. & 3. E. 6. if one in one countie doe procure another to kill a man in another countie, hee to whom the appeale of murder is giuen, shall commence his appeale in the countie where the partie shall die. S. Br. 37.

St. 2. & 3. E. 6. 24.

where diuers appeales for one felonie.

52 And so it is, if the Appellant doe commence his appeale against the principall within a yeare and a day after the felonie committed, and after the said appeale commenced, another will receiue the same felon: In this case the appellant may pursue another appeale against the said accessorie, for these two be seuerall felonies, which began at seuerall times. S. Br. 35.

26. Ass. p. 52 Co. li. 4. 48.

Two appeals founded vpon one felonie.

53 If

Robbery of severall parcels of goods.

53 If a man be robbed of two severall parcels of goods at one time, he cannot haue two severall appeales for them, and put parcel of the goods robbed in one appeale, and parcel in another: but he must commence one appeale for the whole, or for parcel. And if he doe bring his appeale but for parcell, he shal lose the residue of the goods robbed, and the king shall haue them, for he cannot enlarge his appeale. Fit.Cor.100

Where one shall answer to divers appeales or inditements.

54 If one man robbe severall men, every of the persons robbed may haue an appeale against the felon. And although he be attainted at the suit of one of them, yet he shalbe tried at the suit of the others, upon their appeales, if it be so that they haue commenced their appeales before the said attainder. And if he be found culpable at their severall suits, and that they haue made fresh suite, they shall haue their goods againe which were taken from them by robbery, as well as he shall, at whose suit he was first attainted. And those last Enquests shalbe taken at the suit of the parties, and not be adiudged Enquests of office. But if the other who haue cause of appeale, doe not commence their appeales, untill the appellee be attainted, at the suit of the first appellant, and that in the same countie where they ought to haue prosecuted their appeals, after such attainder, they shal not be received to commence them. But yet, if after such first attainder the king will graunt to the partie attainted his pardon, then he shal answer to the said appeales so commenced against him after his Attainder: yea and for the Kings advantage, a man attainted of felonie, shall answer to an offence committed before any pardon was graunted unto him. As, a man being attainted of felonie, shalbe put to answer to a treason before committed, because in that case the King is to haue the Escheat. But in an appeale of murder, or rape, the lawe doth differ from the before mentioned case of appeale of robberie: for if in appeale of murder or rape, the offendor bee attainted at the first appellants suit, hee shall not be put to answer to other appeales brought after for murder or rape, though they were commenced before the appellees attainder: seeing the appellants are not to haue any restitution of goods, or other benefit thereby, but only the attainder of the appellee, which is already attainted at the first appellants suit, and so to be hanged therefore.

4 Ed.4.11. 7.H.4.31. Fi.Cor.379 4 Ed.4.11 Fi.Cor.227 M.10.H.4. 1.H.6.5.

Answer to divers inditements.

55 As severall persons upon their severall appeales commenced shall haue restitution of their goods stollen or robbed from them by one man; so by the statute of an 21.H.8. a man shall haue restitution of his goods robbed or taken from him, upon the inditment and arraignement of the offendor, and evidēce given against him, by the partie robbed, or owner of the goods, or by some other by his procurement. Therefore if one man doe robbe or steale goods from three men severally, and he is indited of the robbing or stealing from one of them, & arraigned thereupon: In this case, though the other two would give evidence against the offendor, yet they shall not haue restitution of their goods by the intention or meaning of that stat. for the felon is not attainted of any other robberie or felonie, sauing of that whereof he is indited. But if he be indited of all the three robberies or felonies severally, and arraigned upon one of them, and found guiltie by the evidence given by one of the parties robbed or &c. yet hee shalbe after arraigned upon the other two inditements, to the intent that hee may be also found guiltie by the evidence of the other two persons robbed or &c. & that they may haue their goods stollen againe, according to the meaning of the foresaid statute. S. Restitution 4.

St.21.H.8.11

56 Whereas

56 Whereas by the common laws of this Realme, and also by the stat. pro Clero, made an. 25. E. 3. no clerke arraigned of felony before a secular Judge, which was demanded by the Ordinarie of the place, should be remanded to the gaole, but ought presently to be arraigned of all his offences, or otherwise deliuered to the Ordinary: But because diuers persons did ofttimes commit and do sundrie detestable murders, haynous robberies, and felonies, and other capitall offences, for the which clergie is not allowable by the laws and statutes of this realm; and after the same offences so done, either did fly out of the countie, or other parts of this realme, into the parts beyond the seas, or kéepe themselues secret in other places, whereby they were not knowne for a great time, and after did cōmit some other felony, for the which they might haue their clergie, and being arraigned of the same, had their clergie to them allowed, & thereupon were committed to the custodie of the Ordinarie, according to the law and custome of this realme, the former offence, wherein clergie was not grantable, being then not knowne, and so by that meanes could not after be impeached for the said other horrible and great offences, by the law and custome of this realme, to the great encouraging of offendors, vsing such practises of foreknowledge and set purpose, for the discharge of the same: Therefore for the reformation of the premisses, by the stat. of an. 8. Eliz. it was enacted, That euery person which shall vpon his arraignement for any felonie, bee admitted to his clergy by the lawes of this realme, & shall before the same admission haue committed any other offence, whereupon clergie by the laws & stat. is not allowable, and not being thereof before indicted & acquited, conuicted or attainted, or pardoned, shall & may be indicted or appealed for the same, and thereupon ordered and vsed in all things according to the lawes, in such maner, as though no such admission of clergie had béene.

St. 25. E. 3. 5 — He that is allowed his clergie shall answer to former offences.

St. 8. El. 4. — Appeale of former offences.

57 And after, viz. an. 18. Eliz. a more generall stat. was made, That all and euerie person & persons which shall hereafter be admitted to haue the benefit of his or their clergie, shal notwithstanding his or their admission to the same, bée put to answer to all other felonies, whereof he or they shalbe hereafter indicted, or appealed, and not being thereof before acquited, attainted, conuicted, or pardoned, & shal in such maner and forme be arraigned, tried, adiudged, and suffer such execution for the same, as he or they should haue done, if as clerk or clerks conuict, they had bin deliuered to the Ordinary, & there had made his and their purgation.

St. 18. El. 6. — A Clerke shal answer to former offences.

S. Indict. 52.

58 If a man cōmence his Appeale of death before the Coroner in the county, presently the Serieant of the county shalbe commanded, that hee bring the bodies of the apellées to the next countie, to answer the plaintife. And if the said Serieant do answer at the second county, that he cannot find them, thē an Exigent shalbe awarded against the principals. But the Exigent touching the accessories shall stay, vntill the principals be outlawed. And so it appeareth by Britton, & some other authoritie, that an Exigent shalbe awarded in Appeale of death cōmenced before the coroner in the coūty, after the first Capias returned.

Britton. — The proces in Appeale.

Proces vpon Appeal before the Coroner.

22. Ass. p. 81. Fi. Cor. 234. Fitz. Proces 226.

59 But in an Appeale or Indictment of robbery, or other felony, there shal be two Capias awarded before the Exigent. And the same is confirmed by these words of the stat. de proditionibus, made 25. E. 3. viz. It is agréed, that after any man be indicted of feloni, ebefore the Just. to heare and determine, in their

Fitz. Proces 226. Fitz. Cor. 184. St. 25. Ed. 3. 14. — Proces vpon an Appeale or Indictment of felonie.

Sessions, the Sherife shalbe commanded to attach his body, by a writ or precept called Capias. And if the Sherife returne in the said precept, that the body is not found, another writ or precept of Capias shall incontinently be awarded, returnable thrée wéekes after, and in the same writ or precept it shall bée comprised, that the Sherife shall cause to be seised all his chattels, and safely kéepe them untill the day of the writ or precept returned. And if the Sherife returne, that the body is not found, and the indictée commeth not, the Exigent shalbe awarded, and the chattels shalbe forfeited, as the law of the crown commaundeth. But if he come and yéeld himselfe, or be taken by the Sherife, or other minister, before the returne of the second Capias, then the goods and chattels shall be saued. This statute doth not make mention of the death of a man, nor of robberie, but of felonie generally, which includeth all. And yet some doe affirme, that it was intended to be made onely for robberie and larcenie; but it is prouided for those which be indicted before Just. to heare and determine, and not for those against whom an Appeale is commenced before the Coroner: and it was rather ordained to seise the felons goods upon the second Capias, than to giue proces. S. Forf. 44. Fitz. Proces 226.

Proces against indictées in another county.

60 And because some persons appealed or indicted of diuers felonies in one countie, or outlawed in the same countie, were dwelling or receiued in another county, whereby such felonious persons indicted and outlawed, haue béen incouraged in their mischiefe, for that they might not be attached in another countie: for the redresse whereof, by a stat. made anno 5. E. 3. it was ordained, That the Just. assigned to heare and determine such felonies, shall direct their writ to all the counties of England, where néed shall be, to take such persons indicted. St. 5. E. 3. 11.

61 Because diuers persons for their singular reuenge, and not of right, malitiously, of their subtill imagination, haue caused and procured, falsly to indict and appeale seuerall of the Kings subiects, of diuers treasons, felonies, and trespasses, before J. of peace and other commissioners, & other Just. hauing authoritie to take indictments or appeals, in diuers forreine counties, liberties, and franchises of England, wherein the said liege people neither bee, nor euer were conuersant or dwelling: By force of which appeales and indictments, and the processes therupon made in the said counties, franchises, and liberties, the said persons so indicted haue béen put in Exigent, and after outlawed, and therupon their goods and chattels, lands and tenements haue bin forf. and they in great perill of their liues, whereas the said persons so indicted, appealed, or put in Exigent, or outlawed, had neuer knowledge of such indictmẽts, appeals, Exigents, or Outlawries: For the preuention whereof, it was ordained by the stat. of an. 8. H. 6. That upon euery indictment or appeale, by the which any of K. liege people dwelling in other counties than there where the indictment or appeale shalbe taken, of treason, felony, & trespas, before J. of peace, or any other hauing power to take such indictments or appeales, or other Commissioners or Justices in any county, franchise, or libertie, within England, before any Exigent awarded, upon any indictment or appeale to be taken in forme aforesaid, immediatly after the first writ of Capias, upon euery such indictment, or appeale, awarded and returned, another writ of Capias shalbe awarded, directed to the Sherife of the county, whereof he which is indicted is or was supposed to be conuersant by the same indictment, returnable before the same Justices St. 8. H. 6. 10

Appeale of indictments of persons dwelling in forrein Counties.

stices or Commissioners, before whom he is indicted or appealed, at a certaine day, containing the space of iij. moneths, from the date of the said last writ: by the which writ of second Capias, it shalbe contained & commanded to the same Sherife, to take the body of him which is so indicted or appealed, if he may bee found within his bailiwike: & if he cannot be found within his bailiwike, that the Sherife shall make proclamation in two counties, before the returne of the same writ, that he which is so indicted or appealed, shal appeare before the same Iust. or Commissioners, in the countie, liberty, or franchise where he is so indicted or appealed, at the day contained in the said last writ of Capias, to answer to the K. or to the party, of the felony, treason, or trespas, whereof he is indicted or appealed: After which second writ of Capias so serued and returned, if hee which is so indicted or appealed, doth not come at the day of the said writ of Capias returned, the Exigent shalbe awarded against such indictees or appellees, and euery of them. And if any Exigent be awarded vpon any such indictment, or appeale, against the foresaid forme, or any outlawrie therupon pronounced, the sayd Exigent and the Outlawrie thereupon pronounced, and euery of them shall bee void. And the partie against whom such Exigent is awarded, or outlawrie pronounced, against the foresaid forme, shall not bee endamaged in his life, lands, goods, &c. And euery one which is indicted or appealed in forme aforesaid, after he is acquited by verdict, in forme of law, may haue an action vpon the case, against euery procurer of such indictments or appeales: in which actiō there shalbe like proces as in an action of trespas vi & armis. And if the said procurers be attainted, the plaintife shall recouer treble damages. But this stat. extendeth not to indictments or appeals taken in the countie of Chester: Nor to any indictment or appeale of felonie or treason, taken of any of the K. liege people, which at the time of the same felonie or treason supposed, is, and was conuersant within the countie, whereof the indictment or appeale maketh mention, but the like proces shalbe made against such indicted or appealed person as hath beene vsed.

62 And because after the making of the sayd Statute of Anno 8. H. 6. some intending to defraud the sayd Statute, did sue to remoue such appeales and indictments, out of the hands of the Iustices or Commissioners aforesayd, into the Kings bench, and elsewhere, by Certiorari, or otherwise, vnknowne to the partie so indicted, and therupon sued the proces vsed at the common law before the making of the said Statute, in the Kings Bench, and elsewhere, after the remouing therof, to the great impouerishment of diuers the kings subiects: Therefore by the Statute made Anno 10. H. 6. it was enacted, That if any such indictments taken before any Iustices of peace, or any other hauing power to take such indictments or appeales, or other Iustices or Commissioners, in any county, franchise, or libertie of England, shalbe remoued into the Kings Bench, or elsewhere, by Certiorari, or otherwise, then after such remouing, before any Exigent awarded vpō any such indictment or appeal, in forme aforesaid taken, immediatly after the first writ of Capias, vpon euery such indictment or appeale awarded and returned, another writ of Capias shall bee awarded, directed to the Sherife of the countie, wherof he that is indicted or appealed, is, or was supposed to be conuersant, by the same indictment or appeale returnable in the K. Bench, at a certaine day, contayning the space of three moneths, from the date of the said last writ of Capias, according to the maner and forme that the I. of peace and others ought to haue done before such remouing.

St. 10. H. 6. 6

Proces vpon an indictment or appeale remoued into the K. bench.

And if any Exigent be awarded upon any such indictment or appeale after such remouing, against the forme aforesaid, or any outlawrie thereupon pronounced, as wel the same Exigent as the outlawrie, and euery of them, shalbe void.

In the Appeale he must be supposed to be of a forrein County.

63 The foresaid stat. of 8. H. 6. doth not take place, but where by the Appeal or by the Indictment it is precisely supposed, that the defendant was dwelling in a forrein county: for if he be supposed to be dwelling there by an Alias dict', it is out of the compasse of the stat. As in an appeal or indictment in the county of Middlesex against A. B. in comitatu tuo yeoman, alias dictum A. B. de C. in comitatu Sussex yeoman: Because that which is supposed by the Alias dict' is not trauersable, nor materiall. And likewise it is in an appeale or indictment against J. of S. in comitatu H. nuper de L. in comitatu K. nuper de R. in com T. St. 8. H. 6. 10. 1. E. 4. 1.

An appellée dwelling in no place certaine.

64 If a man be appealed to be dwelling in no place certaine the day of the Appeale commenced, but in this maner, viz. nuper de S. in comitat L. and nuper de B. in comit T. then proces shalbe awarded into all the counties whereof he is so supposed to be of late dwelling. Fitz. Proces 192.

Proces into a County Palantine.

65 The foresaid stat. of 8. H. 6. hath ordained, That after the first Capias, another Capias shalbe awarded to the Sherife of the county whereof he which is so indicted is, or was supposed to be dwelling by the same indictment. And therefore if an appeale or indictment be exhibited against one in the countie of M. naming him of D. in the county of Chester, or of some other place, which is a countie Palantine: In this case, no proces can be awarded upon this Stat. which may be directed to the Sherife, according to the words of the Statute. But proces shalbe awarded upon this statute to the prince, or his lieutenant: for it is in like mischiefe, and the statute is generall in all the Realme, which doth bind as well those which be of a Countie Palantine, as others. But if they of the Countie Palantine will not serue, and returne the writ directed to them upon this statute, then without further delay the Exigent shall be awarded, otherwise the party should be infinitly delaied. St. 8. H. 6. 10. 19. H. 6. 2. 31. H. 6. 11.

Proces against principal & accessory.

66 The foresaid Proces specified in the before rehearsed stat. of 8. H. 6. shal extend as well to accessories, as to principals, sauing that the Exigent as to the accessories, shall be staied untill the principals be outlawed: And that by the Statute of West. 1. the words whereof be these. Because men haue used in some counties to outlaw such persons as be appealed of commandement, force, aide, or escape, within the same terme that they do outlaw him which is appealed of the fact, it is ordained, that none shalbe outlawed for an appeale of commandement, force, ayd, or receit, untill he that is appealed of the déed be attainted, so that one law shalbe thereof through the whole Realme. But the appellant shall not let to attach his appeale at the next countie against them, as well as against the appellées of the déed. But the Exigent against the Accessorie shal stay untill the appellée of the déed be attainted by outlawrie, or otherwise. And Britton doth affirme, That as sone as the principals be outlawed, the Exigent shalbe awarded against the accessories. St. 3. E. 1. 14. Britton.

67 The

St.3.E.1.14 67 The before rehearsed statute of West.1. seemeth onely to extend to Appeales commenced by bill: for in an Appeale commenced by writ, it appeareth not untill the declaration made thereupon, that there bee any accessories in the Appeale, but, for any thing contained in the writ, all doe appeare to be princi- 43.Ed.3.17. pals, and for that cause the Exigent is awarded against them all at one time. And therefore the plaintife must be aduised, how he doth pray the Exigent, and against whom: for if he do pray the Exigent against them all, he is therby concluded after to count against any of them as accessories: for the law intendeth that he must take knowledge which were accessories, and which not. And therefore in that case he should haue staid the demaunding of the Exigent against them, untill the principals had beene attainted. And that is the difference betweene the principals and the accessories, as touching the time of the awarding of the Exigent. The stat. of W.1. extendeth onely to Appeals commenced by bill.

68 If an Appeale be brought against diuers, and one doth appeare & plead, yet proces shall be continued against the residue. But if hee which appeareth doth plead in abatement of the Appeale, or matter in barre, which proueth that the Appeale doth not lye: in those cases the court shall stay the awarding of the Exigent against the others, untill the court be aduised whether the Appeal wil lye or not: for if the Appeale do abate, it doth abate against them all, as well 9.H.4.2. principals as accessories. In Appeale one doth appeare, and another makes default.

69 The proces to remoue an Appeale out of the countie, or from the Iustices of gaole deliuerie, is a Certiorari awarded out of the Chauncery, or the K. 10.H.4.4. Bench, and it may be sued as well by the def. as the plaintife: which Certiorari must agree with the Appeale or the Indictment that is to be remoued: for if the 3.Ass.p.3. Appeale or Indictment be of two horses, and the Certiorari is but of one, this is no good writ. Proces to remoue an Appeale.

4.H.6.15. Register. Ind.fo.76. 70 If an Appeale be attached within the countie, before the Sherife & the Coroners, the Certiorari must be directed to them both, viz. as wel to the sherif as to the coroners, for a Certiorari directed to the sherife onely, is void. Certiorari into the Countie.

71 After an Appeale is remoued, the parties be without day before the sherife & the coroners. And therefore if the plaintif do not proceed with his Appeale in the K. Bench, yet he shal not be nonsuit therby, untill a Scire fac' be awarded against him, and that he be thereupon returned warned, and doth make default: for if a Nihil be returned upon him, an Alias shalbe awarded against him before he shalbe nonsuit: upon which writ, if at another time a Nihil be retur- 48.E.3.32. ned, another Scire fac' shalbe awarded, returnable at a certaine day, and in the meane time the appellee shalbe let to mainprise. Proces against the pl'. after an Appeal remoued.

72 After an Appeale is remoued, if the plaintif pursue his Appeale, he need not sue a Scir fac' against the def. if he do make default, but a Capias & Exigent. And if the defendant doth appeare and plead, and after at another day maketh default (either because he is escaped out of prison, or being let to mainprise doth not appeare) yet the Enquest shall not bee taken in his default, nor in any case of Felonie. But Proces shall bee awarded against him ad audiendum Proces against the def. after an Appeale remoued.

Iudicium, in such maner, that if he come not at the beginning by the Exigent, then Exegi de nouo shalbe awarded, by the which the Sherife shalbe commanded to take him, if &c. to heare his iudgement. And if not &c. that he be outlawed. But if he do not come at the first by Capias, then a Capias de nouo shall be awarded, and after the Exigent, or another Capias, according to the nature of the offence, whereupon the appeale is grounded. 26. Ass. p. 13 25 Ass. p. 51 Fitz. Exigent 10.

Proces against one that by the Sherifes returne is escaped.

73 A woman brought an Appeale against another of the death of her husband: upon proces awarded against the appellée the Sherife returned Cepi corpus, and at the day had not the bodie, whereupon he was amerced, and also was commanded to bring the body, and so twice or thrice, and did nothing: wherupon the plaintife praied an Exigent, affirming that the prisoner escaped, as the Sherife was carrying him to the gaole: But the Iustices would not award the Exigent against one, which appeared to them to bee in prison: And therefore they sent to the Sherife to haue the body, & if he returned this escape, then the plaintife should haue his request, and not otherwise. 30. Ass. p. 23

Proces with a prouiso for the appellée.

74 In an Appeale, if the parties be at issue, and the plaintife will not sue forth proces against the Enquest, in that case the defendant may sue forth proces with a prouiso, as well as he may in other actions: which writ when it is returned serued, the plaintife may pray a Tales, notwithstanding that the Venire fac' was pursued by the defendant, and shall haue it by common course, whether the defendant do agrée therunto or not. 15. H. 7. 9.

Proces to remoue prisoners or records.

75 By the Statute of Anno 1. & 2. P. & M. it is ordained, That no writs of Habeas corpus, or Certiorari shalbe granted to remoue any prisoner out of any gaole, or to remoue any Recognisance, except the same writs be signed with the proper hands of the chiefe Iust. or in his absence, of one of the Iust. of the court, out of the which the same writs shalbe awarded or made, upon pain that he which writeth any such writs, not being signed as aforesaid, shall forfeit to the K. for euery such writ v. l. St. 1. & 2. P. & M. 13.

How the appellée shall be led to the bar.

76 He that is appealed or indicted of felonie, and imprisoned for the same, when he commeth before the Iustices to the place of iudgement, to answer for the same felonie, shall come bare headed, lose, at libertie, without any yrons or bonds (sauing with shackles about his legs, for feare of escaping) so that no paine shall take away or weaken his reason to defend himselfe, nor constraine him to make any other aunswer, but such as best standeth with his owne frée will. Bracton de Corona, cap. 18. Britton.

Count in Appeale.

An Appeale of Murder.

77 When the Appellée is at the barre to answer to the Appellant, the Appellant must count or declare against the Appellée, the which count doth varie according to the varietie of Appeales; for some be of death, some of rape, some of robberie, and some other of other felonies. The forme of Appeale of Murder is in this manner: A. hic instantèr appellat B. de morte C. fratris sui, de eo quod cum prædictus C. fuit in pace Dei, & Domini Regis apud D. tali die, hora, & anno,

anno, ibi venit B. vt felo domini regis in assultu præmeditato, vi & armis &c. & in ipsum C. felonicé adtunc & ibidem insultum fecit, & cum quodam gladio precij xij. d'. quem ipse in manu sua dextra adtunc & ibidem tenuit, prædictum C. super caput suum percussit, et vnam plagam mortalem, in longitudine duorum pollicium, in anteriore parte capitis sui, vsque ad cerebrum, eidem C. adtunc & ibidem felonice dedit: de qua quidem plaga prædictus C. per tres dies proxime sequentes languebat, & tunc ibidem obijt: vel immediate ibidem obijt. Et sic ibidem B. vt felo domini Regis prædictum C. felonice interfecit, & murdrauerit, contra pacem dicti domini Regis, coronam, & dignitatem suas, & quod hoc fecit nequiter, & vt felo, contra pacem Dei & Domini Regis, prædictus A. offert hoc dirationare, prout curia Domini Regis hic consideraverit. And so it appeareth, that the auncient Law in diuers points touching Ap-
St.6.Ed.1.9. peales is chaunged by the statute of Glouceſter Ann. 6. Ed. 1. which hath ordained, That if the appellant in appeale doe declare the deed, the yeare, the day, the houre, the time of the king, and the Towne where the deed was done, and with what weapon he was slaine, the appeale shalbe of force. This statute maketh the yeare, the day, the houre, the time of the king, and the towne,
Bracton. things materiall; and that upon good cause: For if the appellee can proove by certain demonstration, and the testimonie of credible persons, that he was the same day in another place, so that by no meanes it can be presumed, that he was present the same day at the committing of that fact, in respect of the great distance of the place, then the appellants suit shall faile. And the same reason is of the houre: if for he that is supposed to kill the man, was twenty myles from that place where the deed was done, the same houre wherein that murther was committed, hee cannot bee guiltie of that fact, and yet it may be he was there sometimes the same day, but not that houre: But a man is not of necessitie compellable at this day by the common law, to put into his declara-
Stamf. tion the houre: which declaration by the common law any man may yet make, notwithstanding the foresaid stat. of Glouceſter, because the same statute doth not forbid it, for it is in the affirmatiue.

The yeare, day, houre, time of the king, and the towne materiall.

Where the houre may be left out.

78 The plaintife is to make speciall care, that he put into his declaration the place where the fact was done, for the said statute of Glouceſter doth speci-
21.E.4.25. ally commaund it by expresse words. And therefore if an appeale be brought against diuers, naming them of seuerall Townes, or Villages, and after in his Count he will say, at the place aforesaid, this is not good, for no man can tell to which of the places aforesaid, to referre it: and seeing there be diuers of them in number, he ought to expresse the place by name, or otherwise it is not good. If a man be stricken mortally in one place, whereof he dieth shortly after in a-
Co.lib.4.42 nother place, the appellant must count in his appeale, that the def. did commit the murther in the place where the party died, and not in the county, towne, or place, where the stroke was giuen.

The place where the fact was done.

44.E.3.38 79 There be diuers other formes of declarations in appeales of death: as in appeale of death against three as principall, and the appellant doth count, that such a day and such an houre one of them did strike her husband (of whose death she doth bring the appeale) in the necke, whereof he died: and the same houre another did strike him to the heart: so that if he had not died of the first blow, he would haue died of the second: and that the third did strike him in ano-

Count in appeale of death against three as principals.

another part of his body, and so count seuerally against them, that euery of them gaue him a mortall wound, and shew the manner of the wound, according to the fact: for the statute of Glocester doth ordaine, That he shall count of the fact, and according to the difference of the fact the count in an appeale shall differ, for of necessity the fact must be declared as it was done, or as the law doth expound it to be done. And therefore, if two be present at the death of a man, and one doth not strike him, but commandeth the other to strike him, in regard whereof he doth kill him, in this case, in an appeale against them, the appellant shall count, that either of them did strike him mortally: and in like sort, in an appeale of Rape against two, where one was present, & did abbet the other to rauish the woman, in that case the count shalbe, that they both did rauish her, for in that one there was the rauishment of them both.

The fact must be declared.

21.E.4.71. 4.H.7.18 11.H.4.13 Fit. cor.228

Count in appeale of Robbery.

80 In an appeale of death, as cousin and heire, the appellant must shew in his count, how he is cousin: and in appeale of Robbery, he must expresse the things robbed: as whether they were his owne goods, or another mans: and if it were in money, he must shew how much, and what kind of money: if it were bullion, the value: if it were coyned, the quality and the price: if it were a garment, the colour, and the price: if it were Cloth, the colour, price, and number of elles: if it were Cattell, the kind, the colour, and price: and in an appeale of Rape, he must count of the tearing of garments, and sheading of bloud.

45.E.3.25 27.Ass.p.25 Bracton.

Wherein appeale of Rape the stat. must be rehearsed in the count.

81 There be two appeales of Rape, one vpon the stat. of West.2. which maketh it felony to rauish a maried wife, maid, or other woman: and another vpon the stat. of 6.R.2. which giueth the forfeiture, where the woman rauished doth consent, and assigneth who shall prosecute the suit against the rauishers. In an appeale brought vpon the stat. of Westm.2. the appellant need not rehearse the statute. But otherwise it is in an appeale brought vpon the stat. of 6.R.2. for there he must rehearse the statute in his count: and if in appeale of Rape brought vpon the said stat. of 6.R.2. the plaintife doe count, that the defendant did rauish his wife, contrary to the forme of the said statute, hee shall not need to alledge, that his wife did consent to the rauisher: for that is implied in those words, contra formam statuti, which words be in the declaration: and although there be not in the declaration these words, viz. carnaliter cognouit, yet if there be these words, viz. felonice rapuit, they doe imply the other words: for it can be no felony, if there be not carnall knowledge: and so it is to be noted, that in felony a count may be by implication. S. Felonies by Statute 2.

St.13.E.1.34 St.6.R.2.6 11.H.4.13 14.El.Dyer 311.

Defence in appeale.

82 The defence which the appellee is to make in an appeale is, viz. That he doth defend all maner of Appeals, Awaights, Assaults, Pretences, & whatsoeuer is against the peace of the King, his Crowne, and Dignitie, and to say, that he is not guilty. Bracton writeth, That he which is appelled of the dead, doth come and defend all manner of felony, and that the peace of the king is not broken, & whatsoeuer is against the K. peace, and the death, & whatsoeuer is obiected against him: and that he doth put himselfe vpon the countrey, of good and euill, that he is not guilty thereof, if he do chuse the country: Or that he

44.E.3.38. Bracton.

he is ready to defend himselfe by his body against the appellant, as the kings court shall consider: for if he will simply say, that he will defend himselfe as the kings court shall consider, vnlesse he will say more he shal not be defended: for the kings court must not instruct him, in what manner he ought to defend himselfe: and if he doe say, that he is ready to defend himselfe either by his body, or by the countrey, as the kings court shall consider, he seemeth thereby to take from himselfe election: And the kings court ought not to compell him to the one, more then to the other, nor to inforce him how he shall defend himselfe, seeing he hath free choice: and therefore he must hold him to one of them: But if he make his election to be tried by the countrey, it shall not be in his choice what countrey he will take.

Fi.Cor.121 83 A writ of Appeale shall abate for false Latine, or for lacke of forme: as in a writ of Appeale this word Habeas did want, and therfore the appeale abated, without amendment. In an appeale brought against a principall and accessorie of the death of A.B. of C. in the County of D. the accessory pleaded, that there was no such A. B. at the time of the writ brought, neither was there euer any such, as the writ supposeth, and demaunded iudgement of the writ: and this was adiudged a good plea, in abatement of the writ, if there were no such A.B. in the said County of D. though there was one at that time of the name of A.B. in another County: Or if the said A. B. dyed before this appeale commenced. Pleas to the writ in appeal

18.El. Dyer 348.

84 In an appeale of Rape the writ shall be, ad respondendum appellanti secundum formam statuti, quare vxorem suam rapuit, and not vnde eum appellat secundum formam statuti: because the statute doth not giue the appeale: for the appeale was at the common Law: but hee ought to answere according to the Statute, to this intent, that he shall not wage battaile: for the Statute sayth, Ad duellum vadiandum minimè recipiatur. And though in his writ of appeale of Rape, he doth not vse these words felonice Rapuit, yet is the writ good, notwithstanding that, for in this word Rapuit, felony is implied. If in an appeale of Rape the writ hath not this word Rapuit, it shal abate, although it hath words amounting to the same effect, as carnaliter cognouit, & such like. S.Felony by Statute 4. The forme of the writ of appeale of Rape.

St.6.R.2.6

3.Eli.Dyer 202. Rapuit materiall.

85 One shall not haue diuers writs of Appeale, depending at one time against another, of one felony. But yet before the writ be abated, it is requisite, that the court be satisfied, that both those writs were pursued by the plaintife, which must be proued by some act that the plaintife hath done, as if he hath appeared to them both, and counted vpon them: for notwithstanding, that one of them hath bin deliuered of record to the shirife to serue, yet seeing that may bee done by a stranger, as well as by the plaintife, it shall be no conclusion to the plaintife to say, that the said writ so deliuered of record, was not his sute. And the like law is, if an appeale by bill be commenced in the county before the shirife and the Coroners, and is remoued out of the county into a court of record, and there depending, the plaintife doth purchase another appeale by writ, this appeale by writ shal abate. But it is otherwise, if ẏ appeal by writ be purchased before Not two appeales for one offence against one person.

7.H.7.6 Co.li.4.47.

4.H.6.15.

before the appeale by bill remoued out of the county: for there the Court ought to send for the appeale in the county, without abating the appeale, which is cõmenced by writ: and this is more worthy, and of an higher nature, then is the appeale by bill commenced in the county, which is but as a plaint, untill after it be remoued: for it is a common course in the K. Bench, when an appeale is depending there by Writ, to send for the appeale cõmenced by bill in the county: and yet if the appellant be nonsute in his appeale depending in the county, his Writ shall abate. 10.H.4.4.

Pleading of one in appeale against two

86 In an appeale brought against two, one of them may plead, that his companion, that was named with him in the Writ, died at such a place, before the Writ purchased: Or that there was none such in Rerum natura, as the other which was named with him in the Writ, the day of the Writ purchased: for if he that doth appeare, should not plead these pleas, there is none to plead them: and in the foresaid cases, and in all other cases of appeales against seuerall persons, if the appeale doth abate against one of them, it doth abate against them all. 21.E.4.71. 7.H.4.27. 9.H.4.2.

The plaintife misnamed.

87 In an appeale, if the def. do plead, that the plaintife is misnamed, if the plaintife will confesse it, the couin shalbe examined, viz. whether he doth it by couin betwéene him and the plaintife, or not. But if it be proued true, that the plaintife is misnamed, the appeale shall abate. 9.H.5.2.

Two or thrée pleas to the writ.

88 In an appeale the defendant may haue two or thrée pleas to the writ, as the tenant shal haue in an assise: But he must take care, that one of them be not contrary to the other.

Barres in appeale.

89 To make a barre in appeale, is to run ouer the foresaid title to whom appeales be giuen, and according thereunto to frame his plea in barre: for if an appeale be commenced by one that hath no title to maintaine it, that is good matter to plead in barre against the appellant. As, if a woman doe bring an appeale of the death of her husband, it is a good plea to plead, that after the death of her husband she hath married another husband: Or that shee was neuer accoupled in lawfull marriage to him, of whose death shee doth bring the appeale. 28.E.3.9. 27.Ass p.3 50.Ed.3.15.

Appeale of death brought by the wife.

Barres in appeale of death by the heire

90 If an appeale of death be brought by the heire, it is a good plea to plead, that he which is dead, hath a wife liuing, to whom the appeale is giuen: or that the plaintife who supposeth himselfe to be heire, is not next heire to him that was slaine, but that he hath an elder brother, or that he is a bastard: or to plead, that the plaintife in this appeale of death hath surceased his time, for that the appeale was not brought within the yeare and day after the death of him, who is supposed to be killed: or to say, that he of whose death this appeal is brought is liuing at such a place: or to bring the party supposed to bee slaine, into the court, that he may be séene, and knowne to be liuing. 20.H.6.47. Kel.fol.120 Fi.Cor.384 27.Ass.p.25 8.H.4.18

Fi.Cor.17 91 In an appeale of Robbery it is a good plea to plead, that the plaintife is his villaine. And in appeale of Rape brought by the husband and wife, it is a good plea to plead, neuer accoupled in lawfull marriage, or to plead villenage in the plaintife. In an appeale of Robberie it is no good plea for the defendant to plead in barre, that the appellant brought an action of Trespas against him for the same goods caried away, and recouered: for the appeale of Robbery is of a higher nature, and concerneth the life of a man. Robbery Rape.

11.H.4.14

Co.lib.4.43

2.R.3.14

92 There be some other pleas in barre in an appeale, which bee generall, and will serue for all manner of appeales of Felony: as to plead, that the plaintife is attainted of Treason or Felony: Or that he is a Monke, a Priest, not of perfect memorie, dumbe, deafe, a lazar, a naturall foole, or that he is maymed by another, and not by the defendant. But if the plaintifes attainder bee but by Outlawrie, which is erronious, then his attainder is no barre but for the time, viz. vntill he hath reuersed the Vtlary. S. Approuers 10.14. Generall pleas in barre in appeale.

Fi.Cor.322

Fit.Vtlarie 47.

93 It is a good plea in barre in an appeale, to say that the plaintife at another time brought an appeale of the same felony against the defendant, in the which he was Nonsute, or made a Retrarit: Or that the plaintife did at another time pursue an appeale of the same felony against another, who was attainted or acquit at his sute. If a man be indicted of Manslaughter, and vpon his arraignment he confesseth the felony, and prayeth, and hath his Clergy: If after an appeale of murther be brought against the said offendor, of the murther of the same man, it is a good plea for him to plead, that he was at another time conuict of the same felony. And the same law is, if one bring an appeale of Murther against another, and the defendant pleadeth not guilty, and is found guilty of manslaughter, and hath his Clergy, if after he be indicted & arraigned of the same offence, and he doth plead the former conuiction, it is a good plea in barre. S. Indictments 47. The plaintife brought another appeale.

9.H.4.2.

47.Ed.3.16.

Co.li.4.40.45.

Fit.Cor.98. 94 It is a good plea in barre in an appeale for the defendant to plead, that the plaintife made vnto him a Release of the same offence: for it will not serue to plead a Release made to any other, sauing to himselfe, though the other to whom the Release is made, be named with him in the appeale. And in like sort, though the plaintife made a Retrarit against one of them, this shall not barre him against them both, but the appeale shall stand good against the other. The plaintifs release in barre.

95 And when the defendant hath pleaded any of the foresaid pleas, yet (in fauor of life) the law doth permit him to plead ouer to the felony (viz. not guilty) and his plea by that means shall not be adiudged double, vnlesse it be in the case of a release: for there he shall not be allowed to plead ouer to the felony, because it is contrary to his foresaid plea: Neither shall he plead ouer to the felony, when the defendant in an appeale of Robbery doth plead Villenage in the plaintife, for if hee should plead ouer to the felony, the plaintife by that meanes should bee infranchised. But if the Villenage be found against the defendant, hee shall haue this plea of not guiltie, as well as hee shall haue Pleading not guilty after other pleas.

22.E.4.39.

28.E.3.91.

18.E.3.32

haue, when he pleadeth any of the foresaid barres, without concluding ouer to the felony: yet notwithstanding if the barre be foūd against him, he may plead ouer to the felony, viz. not guilty, sauing in pleading of a release, for by that plea he confesseth the felony by implication.

Where the K. may prosecute an appeale begun by another.

96 If the appellant do surcease to prosecute his appeale against the defendant, the king may pursue it: for the appellant may by seuerall meanes leaue off, and omit to prosecute his appeale, as by Nonsute, Release, Retrarit, or a woman by taking a husband during the sute of Appeale: and because in all those cases the sute doth cease by the act of the party plaintife, therfore in which of them soeuer it doth cease, after declaration in the appeale, the defēdant shall not go at liberty, but shalbe arraigned at the kings sute, vpon the same declaration, for that it doth appeare by the declaration there is a felony committed, and the yeare, day, and place, where and when the said felony was committed, and the same is not yet tried, and the law will not allow such great offences, whereof she taketh notice, to be concealed, and remaine vnpunished. And the same law is, if the appellants appeale doe cease by the act of God, as if the appellant doe die: Or if it cease by the act of the Law, as if the appellant be hanged: Or if the appellant do take the priuiledge of his Clergy, in which cases the defendant likewise shalbe arraigned at the K. sute. But in euery arraignment, which is to be at the K. sute, vpon an appeale begun by an appellant, the declaration in the same appeale must be once good and true: for if it were neuer good, and abated for that cause, the appellée shall not be arraigned at the kings sute, notwithstanding the abatement be after declaration. And therefore if the appeale be abated by misnaming of the defendant, he shall not be arraigned at the kings sute: Or if it be abated by misnaming of the plaintife, or of the towne, or for want of a materiall word. And so it is, if the defendant in an appeale doe plead, that the plaintife is outlawed, or is attainted of Treason or Felony, or otherwise is disabled to maintaine an appeale: as if a woman doe bring an appeale of the death of her husband, and the defendant doth plead, that she and her said husband were neuer accoupled in lawfull marriage, or that she hath married another husband: Or that the appeale was not cōmenced within the yeare & day, after the offence committed: Or that the appellant hath an elder brother liuing, to whom the appeale is giuen, & not to the plaintife. And all those matters which shalbe a barre to the plaintife to bring the appeale, shall also be a barre to the K. to take any aduātage against ỳ appellée vpō the same appeal: for in all these cases it may appeare, ỳ the appeale was cōmenced without cause, & grounded vpon false & insufficient matter. And the king shall be in no better condition than the appellant, for the defendant is arraigned vpon the declaration of the appellant: and yet it is otherwise, where the Appeale was at the first grounded vpon sufficient and true matter. But in all the cases aforesaid, though the king can take no aduantage of the Appeale against the defendant, yet he may compel him to answer to an inditment of the same felonie: for that by these pleas the defendant is not discharged of the felonie, though he be discharged of the Appeale. S. Approuers 15.17.18.19.

3.H.6. Fi. Cor. 3

21.E.3.18.

Fi. Cor. 369

Fit. cor. 121

4.H.6. 16

17. Ass. p. 26
11. Ass. p. 27
18. E. 3. 35
Fi. Cor. 3

Fit. cor. 384. 387.

No appeale of Treason.

97 If an act which was murder, felony, or other offence, by the cōmon law, be after made treason by stat. & then one doth offend in the same, no Appeal wil lye against him therefore, for that no Appeale will lye of High or Petit Treason. And therefore whereas wilfull poysoning was wilfull murder by the com-

common law, and after by the stat. of 22. H. 8. 9. the same was made high treason, and ordained, that the offendor therein should be boyled to death: (which stat. was sithence repealed by the stat. of 1. Ed. 6. 12. & 1. M.) yet during the said stat. of 22. H. 8. in force, the sonne and heire of a man poysoned, brought an appeale against a woman for poysoning her husband, and because the offence was then high Treason, and no appeale will lye of Treason, the appeale was adiudged not maintenable. And yet by the ancient lawes of this realme (as Bracton affirmeth) the accusor might haue pursued an appeale of high Treason against the defendant or party accused, and the defendant might haue thereunto pleaded not guilty, and waged battell with the accusor: But that Law is sithence altered.

M. 33. H. 8. Dyer 50.

Bracton, de coron. c. 3

Gg In-

Indictments.

What an Indictment is.

1 AN Indictment of Treason, Felony, Trespas, or other offence, is an inquisition taken, and made by twelue men at the least, thereunto sworne, whereby they doe find and present, that such a person, of such a name, and sirname, dwelling in such a place of such a County, and of such a degree, hath committed such a Treason, Murther, Rape, Burglarie, Robberie, Felony, Trespas, or other offence, at such a place, vpon such a day, and in such a manner, against the Kings peace, his Crowne, and Dignitie, and contrary to the Lawes of this realme: and so it is an accusation by the Jury of the offendor, and an information of the Court, from whence they receiue their charge, of his offence, and of all such necessary circumstances thereof, and in such certaintie, that thereupon the same Court may procéed to the triall or arraignement of the party accused, if he be present, or otherwise may award Proces against him to appeare, and to make answere thereunto, if he be absent. And because this Indictment and accusation doth sometime concerne the life or member of man, sometime his liberty, sometime his fame and credite, sometime his Lands and Tenements, and some other time his Goods & Cattels: Therefore the Law hath a speciall regard, that the procéedings therein may be effected with all sinceritie and vpright dealing, and doth carry a vigilant and watchfull eye, not onely vpon the Jurors which are returned and sworne in those Enquests, that they may be men of integritie, sufficiencie, and indifferencie, but also vpon Shirifes, and Baylifes of Liberties, who haue authoritie to returne the same Jurors: for she hath prouided by seuerall Statutes,
That they shall take no Indictments by Commissions procured at their owne St.28.E.3.9
sute, but in their Turnes: That they shall hold their Turnes, and take In-
dictments but in conuenient and vsuall times: That they shall take Indict- St.31.E.3.14
ments by twelue men at the least, and then by Roll indented: That they shal St.13.E.1.13
take their Indictments by men of good name, & credit, and sufficient of estate: St.1.E.3.16
That they shall bring their Indictments and Presentments found and made St.1.R.3.4
in their Turnes to the Justices of Peace of the same Countie, that they may St.1.E.4.3.
award Proces against those that be indicted, and set fines vpon them: That

Jurors

St.11.H.4.9 Jurors impanelled to make inquiries, shall be lawfully returned by shirifes, or baylifes of Franchises, without the denomination of any other person:
St.3.H.8.12 That Panels returned by the Shirife to make inquiries, may be reformed
St.3.H.7.1 by the Justices: and that one Enquest may be impanelled and charged to inquire of concealements of offences made by another Enquest: So that the Law hath provided, that Indictments may be found by men of worth, and upon iust causes. And as touching Commissions, because in times past Shirifes of divers Counties, by vertue of Commissions & generall Writs graunted unto them at their owne sute, for their priuat gaine, did take divers Enquests to indict people at their owne pleasures, and then tooke fines and ransomes of them to their owne uses, and after set at libertie the parties, and never brought the same persons so indicted before the Kings Justices, to be delivered there, according to the forme of Law: It was therefore by a Statute
St.28.E.3.9 made Anno 28. Ed. 3. ordained, That all such Commissions & Writs should be from thenceforth repealed, and that none such should be at any time after graunted. By force of which Statute the Shirife is restrained to make any inquirie by Writ or Commission: But yet by vertue of his office he may at this day make inquirie in his Turne of Felonies, obseruing such orders as by the statutes hereafter limitted be expressed.

Commissions to shirifes to take indictments.

The shirife may inquire of Felonies

St.9.H.3.36 2 Whereas by the statute of Magna Charta, it was ordayned, That no Shirife or his Baylife shall hold his Turne by Hundreds but twice in the yeare, in a due and accustomed place, that is to say, once after Easter, and another time after the Feast of Saint Michael. And because some Shirifes did hold their Turnes in Lent, when men should attend their deuotion, and other workes of charitie: and sometimes after the Gule of August, when most men be occupied in felling and carrying in their corne, contrarie to the
St.31.E.3.14 foresaid statute of Magna Charta, therefore by a statute made Anno 31. E. 3. it was enacted, That euery Shirife should hold his Turne yerely once within a moneth after Easter, and at another time within a moneth after the feast of Saint Michael: and if they hold their Turne in any other manner, that then they shall lose their Turne for that time. And so, if any man be indi-
38.H.6.7. 6.H.7.2 cted of Felony or other offence in the Shirifes Turne after the moneth of Easter, and Saint Michael, the Indictment shall be void, because it is against the forme of this statute: for the words of the statute be, they shall lose their Turne for this time, which is as much, as if it had been said, their Turne holden at this time is void. And by this statute it doth appeare when the Turne shalbe holden to make a good Indictment.

When the shirife shall hold his Turne.

An indictment found in an unlawful time

3 Because Shirifes did faine diuers times certaine persons to be indicted before them in their Turnes of Felonies, and other Trespasses, and did apprehend certaine persons that were not culpable, nor lawfully indicted, and imprisoned them, to the intent to exact money from them, whereas they were not lawfully indicted by twelue men: For the preuention whereof, by the
St.13.E.1.13 statute of Westm. 2. made Anno 13. Ed. 1. it was prouided, That Shirifes in their Turnes, and in other places where they haue authoritie to inquire of Trespasses by the Kings Precept, or by their Office, shall cause inquisitions to be made of malefactors by twelue lawfull men at the least, which

Shirifes shall inquire by xii. lawfull men at the least.

 shall

shall put their seales to such inquisitions. And the said Shirifes shall apprehend those which shall be found culpable by such inquisitions, and imprison them, as they haue vsed to doe. And if they doe imprison any other but such as be indicted by the inquisitions aforesaid, they which be imprisoned shal haue their action of false imprisonment against the Shirife, as they might haue against any other person that should imprison them without warrant: and what is said of the Shirife, shall bee obserued of euery Baylife of Libertie.

4 Because the said Inquisitions taken by the Shirife should not bee concealed, imbesilled, or mistaken, but that the truth of them should bee shewed to the Iustices, when they come to deliuer the Gaole, Therefore by the Statute of Anno 1. Edw. 3. it was established, That Shirifes and Baylifes of Franchises, and all others who take Indictments at their Turnes, or elsewhere that Indictments should be made, shall take those Indictments by Roll indented, whereof one part shall remaine with the Indictors, and the other with him that doth take the Enquest: So that the Indictments shall not bee imbesilled, and that one of the Enquest may shew one part of the Indenture to the Iustices, when they shall come to make deliuerance. This Statute by generall words doth extend to Stewards in Leetes, and all others.

Indictments by roll indented before the Shirife.

St.1.E.3.16.

5 For that great inconueniences and Periuries were in seuerall Counties of this Realme, by false verdicts giuen in inquisitions and inquiries before Shirifes in their Turnes, by persons of no substance, nor behauiour, nor fearing God, nor respecting the world: by which meanes many persons of seuerall parts of this Realme, by the inticement and persuasion of their enemies, were wrongfully indicted: and some others, which ought to haue beene indicted by such procurement, were spared: For the auoiding whereof, by a Statute made Anno 1. R. 3. it was enacted, That no Bayly, or other Officer shall returne in any pannell any such person in any Countie within this Realme of England, to be taken or put in or vpon any such inquirie in any of the said Turnes, but such as be of good name and fame, and haue lands and tenements of freehold within the same County, to the yearely value of twenty shillings at the least, or otherwise Lands and Tenements, holden by the custome of the Manor, commonly called Copyhold, within the said Counties, to the yearely value of six and twenty shillings eight pence at the least. And if any Bayly or other Officer within the said Counties shall returne or impannell any person contrary to this ordinance, he shall lose for euery person so impanelled or returned, not being of the sufficiencie aforesaid, so often as he shall offend, forty shillings, and the shirife other forty shillings, whereof the one halfe shalbe to the King, and the other to such as will sue for the same. And euery person that will sue for himselfe, shall haue seuerall actions of Debt at the common Law, as well against the Shirife, as against the Bayly. And like and the same Proces shalbe had and vsed in those actions, as be had and vsed in other actions at the common Law, and no Protection or Essoine shalbe allowed therein: and euery such Indictment otherwise taken before

Of what sufficiency Iurors returned in the Shirifes Turne, shalbe.

St.1.R.3.4.

before the Shirife in his Turne, shall be void: which foresaid statutes were made, to auoid the corrupt and euill demeanor of Shirifes and other officers, which take Inditments in shirifes Turnes and Leets.

6 Because diuers persons were greatly vexed and troubled by the inordinat and immeasurable Inditments and Presentments, as well of Felonie and Trespasses, as of other things which were taken and used before shirifes, their Undershirifes, Clerkes, Baylifes, and other Ministers at their Turnes or Law-daies holden before them seuerally in their Counties: Which inditments and Presentments were often affirmed by Iurors, hauing no conscience, nor freehold, and small wealth, and sometime by the meniall seruants and Baylifes of the said Shirifes or Undershirifes. By reason of which Inditments and Presentments many people were attached, arrested, and put in prison by the said Shirifes, their Undershirifes, Clerkes, Baylifes, and Ministers, and then they were constrained to pay unto them great fines and ransomes, to deliuer them out of prison: and also the said Inditments and Presentments were imbesilled, withholden, and concealed. And further, the said Shirifes and other Officers had amongst themselues the awarding of Proces upon such Inditments when they were found, and the assessing of fines: So that all the corrupt misdemeanors sought to be reformed by the before specified statutes, were little or nothing amended. And therefore for the St.1.E.4.3. reformation of the enormities aforesaid, by a statute made Anno 1. Ed. 4. it was ordained, That upon all Inditments and Presentments which shall bee taken before any of the Shirifes of Counties for the time beeing, their Undershirifes, Clerkes, Baylifes, or Ministers at their Turnes, or Law-daies, they nor any of them shall haue power or authority to arrest, attach, or put in prison, or to leuy any fines or amerciaments of any person or persons so indicted or presented by reason or colour of any such Inditment or Presentment taken before them, or any of them, or to leuy or take of any such person or persons so indicted or presented, any fine or ransome. But the said Shirifes, Undershirifes, Baylifes, or Ministers shall bring, present, and deliuer all such Inditments and Presentments taken before them, or any of them in their Turnes, or Law-daies, to the Iustices of the Peace, at their next Session of the Peace, which shalbe holden in the County or Counties where such inditments and presentments shalbe taken. And if any of the said Shirifes, Undershirifes, Clerkes, Baylifes, or Ministers doe not bring, deliuer, or present all such inditments or presentments so taken before them and euery of them in their Turnes, or Law-daies, as is aforesaid, to such Sessions of the peace, before the said Iustices: then the said Shirifes, Undershirifes, Clerkes, Baylifes, and their Ministers, and euery of them which shall faile of the bringing, deliuering, or presenting of such Inditments or Presentments, shal forfeit to the king forty pounds, so often as they or any of them shall doe the contrarie. And the said Iustices of peace shal haue power and authority to award proces upon such Inditments and Presentments as the Law doth require, and in such like manner, as if the said Inditments and Presentments had bin taken before the said Iustices of Peace in the same County or Counties: and also to arraigne and deliuer all person and persons so indicted and presented, before the said Shirifes, Undershirife, their Clerkes, Baylifes, or Ministers, or any of

Inditments taken in ye shirifes Turne shalbe deliuered to the Iu. of peace.

Proces upon Inditments awarded by I. of peace

of them in their Turnes or Lawdaies, and to set such fine upon every person or persons indicted or presented of Trespas, as it shall seeme good to their discretions. And the Estreats of the same fines and amerciaments shall be inrolled, and by Indenture delivered to the said Shirifes, Undershirifs, Clerks, or Ministers, or to some of them, to the use and profit of him which was shirife of the County at the time of the taking of such indictments or presentments. And if any of the said Shirifes, Undershirifes, Clerkes, Bailifes, or ministers shall cause to be arrested, attached, or put in prison, or shall cause to be raised or taken any fine or ransome, or leuy any amerciament of any person or persons so indicted or presented, by reason or colour of any such indictment or presentment before him taken at his foresaid Turne, or Law-day, before they haue proces from the said Justices of Peace, or Estreats deliuered out of the said indictments or presentments so brought, deliuered, or presented unto them: then the shirifes which doe so shall forfeit an hundred pounds, whereof the one moitie shalbe imployed towards the expences of the kings house, and the other to the party or parties that shalbe endamaged: And he or they shal haue an action of Debt at the common law, and like proces as is used in an action of Debt at the common law, wherein the defendants shal not be essoined, wage their law, nor haue any protection. But this Ordinance shall not extend or be preiudiciall to the shirifes of the city of London, touching indictments or presentments to be taken before them in the said city: Neither shall this ordinance extend or be preiudiciall to any person or persons that haue graunt of any fines, or other amerciaments by any letters patents of the king, or of any of his progenitors or predecessors, bearing date before the x. day of December next after the beginning of this Parliament, being An. Dom. 1461.

Indictments in London,

B

This statute doth giue authority to Justices of peace to award proces upon all indictments taken in the shirifes Turne, when they be brought and deliuered unto them: But yet it is alwaies intended, That those Indictments shalbe lawfull, and containe matter whereof the Shirife hath iurisdiction in his Turne, and power to make inquirie: For if the Shirife in his Turne will make inquiry of the statute of Liueries, or indict one who did feloniously rauish a woman, or such other matters, which be not inquirable in the shirifes Turne, although he wil bring the indictments before the Ju. of peace, and deliuer them according to the foresaid stat. of 1. Ed. 4. yet they ought not to award proces upon them, for they were taken coram non iudice, and so void.

The shirife inquiring of things not inquirable in his Turne.

4. E. 4. 31. 8. E. 4. 5.

7 And for that Enquests were sometimes taken, without being duly returned by the shirife, of such persons as were outlawed before Justices of Record, and of some such as were fled to sanctuary for Felony or Treason to haue refuge, by whom sometimes not only offendors were indicted, but also seueral of the kings liege people not guilty, by the conspiracie, abbetment, and false practise of others, for their owne speciall aduantage and priuat gaine: for the auoiding whereof there was a statute made Anno 11. H. 4. which doth enact, That no indictment shalbe made by any such persons, but by enquests of the kings liege people, as it hath bin used in the time of the kings progenitors, duly returned by shirifes, or bailifes of Franchises, without any maner of denomination St. 11. H. 4. 9

mination before made to the said shirife, or bailifes of Franchises, by any person of the names of those who shal be impanelled by him, unlesse it be by the officers of the said shirifes, or bailifes of Franchises, knowne or sworne thereunto, and other ministers to whom it appertaineth by the law of England to make the same. And if any indictment be made in any point to the contrary, the same shalbe void, reuoked, and of no force. Jurors in indictments shal be returned by the shirife without denomination

According to this statute, some haue béen discharged of their Indictments, because certaine of the Indictors were before that outlawed of Felony. This B.
11.H.4.40. statute of Anno 11.H.4. is altered by the next statute of Anno 3. H. 8. for
St.3.H.8.12. so much onely as doth concerne denomination to be made by the Justices, for the reformation of Panels returned before them by the Shirifes, when the said Justices will haue the same Panels reformed: But for all the residue it continueth in force.

8 The whole authority of returning of Enquests to make Indictments, without the denomination of any person before made, béeing by force of the foresaid statute of 11.H.4. in shirifes and bailifes of Franchises, seuerall great extortions and oppressions were done in diuers Counties of this Realme by subtilty and untrue demeanor of shirifes and their ministers to many persons by making and returning at euery Sessions holden within the said Counties for the body of the shire, names of such persons, as for the singular gaine of the said shirifes and bailifes would be wilfully forsworne, by the sinister labour of the said shirifes and their ministers: By reason whereof, by their couin and falsehood, many true and substantiall persons were diuers times wrongfully indicted of Murthers, Felonies, and other misbehauiours, to the utter losse of their liues, goods, and lands: and sometime also by the labor of the said shirifs great Felonies and Murthers were concealed, and not presented by the said persons, partially returned by the same shirifs, or their ministers, to the intent to compell the offendors to make fines, and giue rewards to the said Shirifes and their ministers: For the preuention of which enormities, by a stat. made
St.3.H.8.12 Anno 3.H.8. it was established, That all panels to be returned, which bée not at the suit of any party, that shall be made and put in by euery shirife and their ministers before any J. of Gaole deliuery, or J. of Peace (whereof one to be of the Quorum) in their open Sessions to inquire for the king, shalbe reformed by putting to and taking out of the names of the persons which so be impanelled by euery shirife and their ministers, by the discretion of the same Justices before whom such panels shall be returned. And the same Justice and Justices shall commaund euery shirife, and their ministers in his absence, to put other persons in the same panels by their discretions. And the same panels so reformed by the said Justices, be good and lawfull. And if any shirife, or any of their ministers at any time do not returne the same panels so reformed, then euery such shirife or minister so offending for euery such offence shall forfeit xx.li. the one halfe to the king, and the other to him or them that will sue for the same by action of Debt at the common law, or Bill &c. wherein no W. E. or P. shalbe allowed: and the kings pardon shall be no barre against the party or parties that shall sue the same. Panels for indictments reformed by the Justices.

9 It

9 It is to be thought, that by force of the statutes before rehearsed sufficient, honest, and indifferent Jurors were returned by the shirifes of Counties, or that the Panels by them returned were reformed by the Justices; so that if any defect were committed in Indictments, or in concealing of offences, or offendors, then the same was in the Jury, which were charged for the body of the Shire to make inquirie: for the searching forth of the truth whereof, and for the punishment of the said offendors according to their demerites, by a statute made Anno 3.H.7. it was ordained, That the Justices of peace of St.3.H.7.1 every Shire of this Realme, for the time being, may doe to take by their discretion an enquest, whereof every man shall have Landes and Tenements to the yearely value of forty shillings at the least, to inquire of the concealements of other Enquests taken before them, and before other, of such matters and offences as are to bee inquired and presented before Justices of Peace, whereof complaint shall be made, by Bill, or Bils, as well within Franchise, as without: and if any such concealement be found of any Enquest had or made within the yeare after the same concealement, every person of the same Enquest shall bee amerced for the same concealements, by the discretion of the same Justices of Peace, the said amerciaments to bee assessed in plene Sessions.

Enquest to inquire of concealments.

10 For as much as severall persons upon great grounds of vehement suspitions, as well of high Treasons, petit Treasons, and misprision of Treason, as of Murthers, were many times sent for from divers Shires and places of this Realme, and other the Kings Dominions, to the Kings great charges, to be examined before the Kings Councell upon their offences, to the intent that conviction or declaration of such persons should speedily ensue, as the merits of their cases should require: And albeit that after great travaile taken in the examination of such persons, it appeared to the said Councell, by confession, witnesse, or vehement suspect, that such persons were rather guilty of such offences whereof they were examined, then otherwise, yet neverthelesse, such offendors so examined by the course of the common Lawes of this Realme, must be indicted within the Shires or places where they committed their offences, and also tried by the inhabitants and freeholders of such Shires and places, although by their confessions, or by sufficient witnes their offences were certainely knowne to the Kings Councell: By reason whereof, besides the travaile of the Kings Counsell, the King was often put to great charges, in remaunding such persons to the countries where they offended, there to bee indicted and tried of their offences. And sometimes the inhabitants and freeholders of the Shires or places where such offences were done, were compelled to appeare out of their shires or places for such causes, to their great charges, for the triall or declaration of such offences. And sometime by occasion of the charges for remaunding such offendors to be indicted and tryed by the course of the common Law, such offendors did lye still in prison, and were forgotten: whereby many times, by the helpe of their confederats, they escaped unpunished, to the great courage and evill example of evill doers. For the reformation whereof, by a statute made Anno 33.H.8. it was enacted, St.33.H.8. That if any person or persons, being examined before the Kings Coun- 23. cell, or three of them, upon any manner of Treasons, misprision of Treasons,

or

or Murthers, doe confesse any such offences, or that the said Councell, or thrée of them upon such examination shall thinke any person so examined to be vehemently suspected of any Treason, misprision of Treason, or Murther: then in euery such case, by the Kings commaundement, his Maiesties Commission of Oyer and Terminer under his great Seale shal be made by the Chancellor of England to such persons, and to such Shires and places as shall bée named and appointed by the Kings Highnesse, for the spéedie triall, conuiction, or deliuerance of such offendors: Which Commissioners shall haue authoritie to inquire, heare, and determine all such Treasons, misprisions of Treasons, and Murthers, within the Shires and places limitted by their Commission, by such good and lawfull persons as shalbe returned before them by the Shirife, or his ministers, or any other, hauing power to returne Writs and Proces, for that purpose, in whatsoeuer other Shire or place, within the Kings Dominions, or without, such offences of Treasons, misprisions of Treasons, or Murthers so examined, were done or committed: and that in such cases no challenge for the Shire or Hundred shall bee allowed. After which Statute there was a Statute made Anno 1. & 2. Ph. & Ma. whereby it was ordained, That trials to be hereafter had, awarded, or made for any Treason, shalbe had and used only according to the due order and course of the common lawes of this Realme, and not otherwise.

Indictments and trials where the king will.

St. 1. & 2. P. & M. 10.

Triall of Treason.

12. El. Dyer fol. 286

B

The foresaid stat. of 33. H. 8. is repealed by the said stat. of 1. & 2. Ph. & M. touching the indictment and triall of Traitors: for they are to be indicted and tried in the county where the offence was committed, or by fréeholders of that county, according to the course of the common law, notwithstanding that they haue confessed their offences before iij. of the K. Councell. But for the triall of Murther the said stat. of 33. H. 8. doth continue in force.

11 For as much as some doubts and questions were moued, whether certaine kinds of Treasons, misprisions and concealements of Treasons committed out of the Realme of England, and other the Kings dominions, can or may by the common lawes of this Realme be inquired of, heard, and determined within the Realme of England: Therefore for a plaine order, remedy, and declaration therein to be had, by a statute made Ann 35. H. 8. it was enacted, That all manner of offences being already made, or declared, or hereafter to be made, or declared by any of the Lawes and Statutes of this realme to be Treasons, misprisions of Treasons, or concealements of Treasons, and done, perpetrated, or committed, or hereafter to be done, perpetrated, or committed by any person or persons out of this Realme of England, shall be from henceforth inquired of, heard, and determined before the kings Justices of his Bench, for pleas to be holden before himselfe, by good and lawfull men of the same shire, where the said Bench shall sit, and be kept: Or els before such commissioners, and in such shire of the realme as shalbe assigned by the kings commission, and by good and lawfull men of the same shire, in like manner & forme, to all intents and purposes, as if such treasons, misprisions of treasons, or concealements of treasons had bin done & committed within the same shire, where they shalbe inquired of, heard, and determined, as is aforesaid. But if any péere of

Indictments and trials of Treasons cōmitted out of this Realme

St. 35. H. 8. 2

of this Realme shall be indicted of any such Treasons, or &c. he shall haue his triall by his Peeres.

B If any subiect of this Realme being beyond the sea, doth practise with the Prince or Gouernour of another countrey to inuade this Realme of England with a great power, and in his practise doth declare by what meanes, how, and in what place the same may be done; and though there be no such inuasion, yet this practise is high Treason: for an inuasion with power may tend to the destruction or great perill of the person of the King. And this offence shall bee tryed according to the foresaid Statute of 35. H. 8. which Statute doth remaine in force, and is not repealed by the before rehearsed Statute of 1.& 2. Ph. & Ma. 10.

Treason practised beyond the sea.

13.El. Dyer 298.

Indictment in the County of Lancaster of a forraine.

12 For the conseruation, tranquillity, and peace of the Kings liege people as well within the County Palantine of Lancaster, as of other his liege people out of the said County, within the Realme of England, by a statute made Anno 33.H.6. it was established, That euery Indictment to be taken before any of the Kings Iustices in the County Palantine of Lancaster, or before any Shirife in his Turne in the said County, whereby any person or persons be supposed by the same Indictment to be, or to haue beene inhabiting or conuersant out of the said Countie, and within any other Countie within England, shall be taken by verdict of twelue men, whereof euery of them, or some other to their vse, shall haue Lands and Tenements to the yearely value of an hundred shillings, and no proces shall be made out of such Indictment, before it be duly examined before the Iustices within the sayd County, whether the said Indictors and euery of them, at the time of such Indictment taken, had lands and tenemēts within the said County of Lancaster, to the yearely value of an hundred shillings, aboue all charges. And if it be found, that euery of the said indictors at the time of the said Indictment taken had not lands &c. to the said yearely value of 100. shillings, then the Indictment, as to such persons so indicted, supposed by the said Indictment to be inhabiting or conuersant out of the said County of Lancaster, shalbe void.

St.33.H.6.a

Indictment in a forraine County of a Lancashire man.

13 And by the same statute of Anñ 33.H.6. it was likewise enacted, That euery Indictment from henceforth to be taken within any County of the said Realme, and out of the said County of Lancaster, before any Iustice, or the shirife in his Turne, whereby any person or persons supposed by the same indictment to be, or to haue bin conuersant or inhabiting within the said county of Lancaster, and without such county where such indictment shall happen to be taken, shalbe taken by verdict of twelue men, whereof euery of thē, or some other person or persons to their owne vses, shall haue lands and tenements to the value of 100. shillings. And that no proces be made out of any such indictments, before it be duly examined and inquired before the K. Iustices, hauing power to award any proces vpon such indictments, whether the said indictors and euery of them, at the time of such indictments taken, or any other person

St.33.H.6.a

or persons to their use, had any Lands or Tenements, to the yearely value of an hundred shillings within the same Countie aboue all charges, where such Indictments happen to be taken. And if it be found before the King, or any of his Iustices, that the said Indictors, or any of them, had not at the time of such Indictment taken, nor that none other to their use had Lands and Tenements to the yearely value of an hundred shillings, that then the said Indictment, as to any such person or persons supposed by the said Indictment to be, or to haue bin inhabitants or conuersant within the said County of Lancaster, shalbe void, and of none effect.

14 Though by the rules of the common Law euery offendor shall be tried in that County wherein he is indicted, and he shall be both indicted and tried in the County where he doth commit the offence whereof he is so indicted: yet for the preseruation of mans life, and condignely to punish such persons as unlawfully and wilfully murther, slay, or destroy men, and to preuent the practise of those Theeues and Robbers, that doe steale or robbe in one Countie, and conuey their spoyle or part thereof to some of their adherents knowing thereof in another Countie, by a Statute made Anno 2. & 3. Edw. 6. it was enacted, That where any person or persons shall be feloniously stricken, or poysoned in one County, and dye of the same stroake or poysoning in another County, that then an Indictment found by Iurors of the County where the death shall happen (whether it shall be found before the Coroner upon the sight of any such dead body, or before the Iustices of Peace, or any other Iustices, or Commissioners, which shall haue authoritie to enquire of such offences) shall bee as good, and effectuall in Law, as if the stroake or poysoning had beene done or committed in the same Countie where the party shall dye, or where such Indictment shall bee so found. And by the same Statute it was further ordayned, That where any Murther or Felony shall bee committed and done in one County, and another person or moe shall bee accessarie or accessaries in any manner wise to any such Murther or Felony in any other County, that then an Indictment found or taken against such accessarie or accessaries, upon the circumstance of such matter before the Iustices of Peace, or other Iustices or Commissioners, to inquire of felonies in the County where such offences of accessarie or accessaries in any manner of wise shall bee committed or done, shall bee as good and effectuall in the Law, as if the principall offence had beene committed or done within the same County where the same Indictment against such accessary shalbe found.

St. 2. & 3. Ed. 6. 14.

A man stricke or poysoned in one county, dieth in another.

Indictment of an accessary in one county, to an offēce done in another.

6. H. 7. 10 / 7. H. 7. 8 — Before which Statute made, the manner was, to carry the body of the offendor to the County where the first offence was committed, and there to indict and try him. B

Fi. Cor. 33 — A man was indicted in the County of Middlesex, for that hee in the same County procured another man to kill a third man in the Countie of Essex, by force whereof hee did kill him accordingly. This was a good and sufficient Indictment: for hee was indicted in the county where he committed his offence, viz. the procurement. And if a man being in one county, doth procure another to kill a third person in another coūty,

Kel. fol. 67.

where-

whereby he doth kill him accordingly, in this case a Jury of the county where the murther was committed, may indict this procuror as accessory, for that this murther was begun by his procurement.

Insidiatores viarum depopulatores agrorum.

15 By the Statute of Anno 4. H. 4. it was ordained, That the words Insidiatorum viarum, & Depopulatores agrorum shall not be from henceforth used, or put in Indictments, Arraignements, Appeales, nor other impeachments: Nor that by force of any such word, or terme, any of the kings people shall be arraigned, appealed, impeached, nor grieued before any secular Judge. But the Justices may take and receiue before them Indictments, Arraignements, and Appeales of Felony, containing in them the effect of the said words and termes, if any shalbe hereafter indicted, arraigned, or appealed before them of any such Felonies. And if in time to come any Clerkes shall be indicted, arraigned, or appealed, and their indiments, arraignements, or appeales doe purport the effect of the said wordes, or other wordes of the like effect; notwithstanding, they shall enioy the priuiledge of their Clergie. St.4.H.4.2.

Words not necessarie in Indictments.

16 By a Statute made Anno 37. H. 8. the words vi & armis, viz. cum baculis, cultellis, arcubus, & sagittis, or such other like (before time commonly used and comprised in all Indictments and inquisitions of Treason, Murther, Felony, Trespas, and other offences) shall not of necessitie bée put or comprised in any Inquisition, or Indictment: Nor the party being indicted of any offence, shall take aduantage by Writ of Error, Plea, or otherwise, to auoid any such Inquisition or Indictment, for that the said wordes or any of them shall not bée put in the said Inquisition or Indictment: But the said Inquisitions or Indictments lacking the foresaid words, or any of them, shall bée taken to all intents as good and effectuall in Law, as if the said words were in them. St.37.H.8.8

No more shall be in an indictment then is true.

17 By these two last Statutes it doth appeare, that the Realme was offended because Indictments were stuffed with more words then the offence required, and that of purpose to aggrauate the offence more then it was grieuous in it selfe. For the circumstances of euery offence doe augment, or diminish it, according to the qualities thereof. And therefore it is requisite that there shall be no further circumstance put in Indictments, more then the fact, sauing that which is true, least Periurie should ensue, and Justice bée subuerted thereby: for such words be not words of forme, but as materiall and necessarie, as Proditorié, or Felonicé, which ought to be put in euery Indictment of Treason, or Felony, or otherwise the Indictment is not good, for they doe expresse the intent wherewith the fact was committed, which maketh the offence to bee knowne. As, one was indicted, That he tooke his father being sicke, & carried him against his will from towne to towne in a great frost, whereof he died: and for that this word Felonicé was not in the indictment, it was adiudged void. And if one be indicted of murther, St.4.H.4.2. St.37.H.8.8 Fi.Indict.3.

Felonice omitted in an indictment of felony.

or

1.M.Di.99. or manslaughter, there must be of necessitie in the indictment a stroke supposed viz. tali die & anno felonicè & ex malitia præcogitata interfecit & murdrauit, &c. without saying percussit. And if a man be indicted of Piracy, there ought to be in the indictment not only this word felonicè, but also this word piraticè. Piracie in an indictment. Stamf. 114.

18.E.3.32. Fitz.Cor. 122. 13.Ass.p.6 Fitz.Indict. 31. 18 In an action of trespas brought for the taking away of a mans wife, and the goods of the husband, the def. pleaded not guiltie, and was found by verdict guiltie: in this case the same verdict shall serue as an indictment for the K. and the def. shalbe thereupon arraigned of felony. And in like sort, in an action of trespas brought for the taking away of his goods, the defendant pleaded not guiltie, and it was found by verdict, that the defendant with other his companions did steale those goods from the plaintife: whereupon the defendant was awarded presently to answer to the felony at the K. suit. But it was then affirmed, that if the enquest had passed in any other place sauing the K. Bench, nothing ought to haue beene done touching the felony, untill the Eyre of the Iustices. Where a verdict shalbe an indictment.

1.H.7.6. 19 If the Sherife returne a Rescous made unto him of one which hee did arrest for felony, and was taken out of his possession: In this case notwithstanding this return be matter of record, yet it is not sufficiēt to serue as an indictment against him that made the Rescous. And the same law is, if the Sherife returne, that the party arrested did escape from him. And the reason of the difference betweene the two former cases & these, is, for that in the first cases there is a verdict of twelue men, which will alwaies serue for the King, if they conteine matter that will intitle him. For the King is euer present in court, and if the parties in pleading, or the Iurie in their verdict, do disclose any matter which shall intitle the King, the court shall adiudge for the King, though he be none of the parties to the action. But in the other case of the Sherifes returne, it is not so: for the Sherifes returne will rather attaint him, than put him to answer, for that it is a common rule, that against the Sherifes returne there is no Trauerse, nor answer. S. Breaking of prison 7. The Sherifs returne no indictment. 2.E.3.1.

25.E.3.43. 8.H.5.8. 2.H.7.7. 3.H.7.5. 5.E.6.Di.69 20 An Indictment which is uncertaine is not good, and therefore to make a good Indictment, it is necessarie to put in the yeare, day, and place, when, and where the felonie was committed: And it ought to bee such a day as is not doubtfull, nor uncertaine: for if it be so, it is as much as if no day had bin put in. And therefore if a man be indicted, that hee committed felonie in the Feast of Saint Paul, without addition, and there be two Feastes of Saint Paul in the yeare, this is an uncertaine indictment, and so void. A man was indicted, for that the first day of May, and the fourth day of May, at Dale hee did beat and wound I. S. and then and there did take and steale from him feloniously, a white horse: and this was adiudged a void indictment, for it is uncertaine whither these words adtunc & ibidem shall haue relation, for a felony can be committed but at one time and place. The yere, day, and place, necessarie in an indictment. Certaintie in the day. 2.H.7.7.

8.E.4.3. 21 An Indictment ought to be certaine not onely in the day, but also in the matter. As if one be indicted for apprehending of a man for suspition of felony, and Indictment certaine in the matter.

and that he did after voluntarily and feloniously let him go at libertie, and the inditment doth not shew in certaintie for suspition of what felony he was taken, this is a void inditment.

Inditments certain in the persons received.

22 If a man be indicted as accessory to foure men, in this maner, viz. that he knowing those foure to haue committed felony, did receiue them feloniously at D. and the inditment doth not shew which of them he receiued, this inditment is void for the incertaintie: for the inditment should haue bin, that he did receiue them all foure by name, or thrée, two, or one of them by name. 30.H.6.2.

Inditment uncertain at which court.

Inditment uncertaine in the addition.

23 If an inditment be, Ad magnam curiam cum leta tentam tali die & anno extitit præsentatum quod &c. this is a void inditment, for that it is uncertaine to which of those courts a man will refer the presentment, whether to the Léet, or to the Court Baron. And so must the words of an inditment be certaine in euerie addition of the county, towne, place, time, person, mysterie, &c. and in an Aliàs dictus &c. and in the placing thereof. 49.H.6.15. 31.H 8. Dyer 46. 4.& 5. P.& M. Dy. 164. 33.H.8. Dyer 50.

Inditment for making of money.

24 If a man be indicted, that he made C.s. by Alchimy, like the mony of our Soueraigne Lord the K. and it is not alledged in the inditment what mony it was, viz. pence, grotes, or &c. this is a void inditment for the uncertaintie. Fitz. Indict. 10.

A common théefe.

Inditment of the Ordinarie must be certaine.

25 If a man be indicted, that he is a common euill doer, or a common théefe, without shewing specially in what thing, this is a void inditment, because it is uncertaine in what things the transgressor hath offended. By the stat. of anno 25. E.3.9. pro Clero, it is ordained, That no Ordinarie, or any minister of his, shalbe indicted of extortion or oppression generally: but it must be declared and put in certaine in the inditment, in what thing, of what, and in what maner the said Ordinaries or their Ministers haue done extortion and oppression: or otherwise the said Ordinaries and their ministers shal not be impeached by the K. Justices for the said inditment. 22. Ass. p.73. 29. Ass. p.45. St.25.E.3.

The foresaid A. where none is named.

26 If a man be indicted for the stealing of the goods of the foresaid A. where there is no such A. before named in the inditment, this is a void inditment: for that words subsequent cannot haue relation to words precedent, where there be none such. 9.E.4.12.

Inditment for the killing of a man unknowne.

Inditment for stealing the goods of a man unknowne.

27 No man is bound to answer to an appeal of felony touching the death of a man, if the appellant do not name the name of the party that was killed. But a man may be indicted quod interfecit quendam hominem ignotum: for he that is slaine may be so mangled in the face, or was dwelling so far off, that he cannot be knowne by name. And in like sort a man may be indicted for the stealing of the goods of cuiusdam hominis ignoti. And the reason is, for that this inditment is not the suit of the owner of the goods, but is the Kings suit, who is to haue the goods, if no man doe claime them: And it were not expedient that the King should loose the goods, for that the name of the owner is not there knowne, which owner peraduenture for feare wil not claime the goods as 22. Ass p.94. 2.E.3.26. 9.H.6.64. 1. Ass. p.74. Fitz. Indict. 12. 1.M. Di.96. 11. Eliz. Dyer 285.

his

his owne, or who (it may be) is dwelling in another Countie, farre distant from the place where the goods were stollen: so that the country where the goods were stollen, doth neither know his name or sirname. And therefore for the K. aduantage, and for to print a greater terror into the hearts of malefactors, to commit such hainous crimes, such Indictments bee allowed good. And yet a
Fitz. Indict. 27. man being indicted for stealing of the coat of a dead man vnknowne, the Indictment was not allowed: for it was holden, that the executors of the dead shal haue this coat, or the Ordinarie, or else it shalbe deliuered to the church, or otherwise be imployed to charitable vses. Quære differentiam.

28 If a man be indicted Quod bona Capellæ in custodia &c. aut bona domus & ecclesiæ tempore vacationis felonicè furatus est &c. this is a good Indictment: And yet in this case there is no owner here, but because the propertie can be in no other, neither can it be otherwise done, for that cause the Indictment is allowed to be good. The goods of chappell or church.
7.E.4.14. 9.E.4.33.

29 An Indictment the force whereof doth depend vpon an argument, or implication, is not good: As if one be indicted, Quod felonicè abduxit vnum equum, he did feloniously lead away a horse: this is not a good Indictment without saying felonicè cepit & abduxit, viz. that he feloniously tooke and led him away, for it may be that the horse was lent him, & so he led him away, in which case then it is no felonie: and yet in these words felonicè abduxit is implied, that he did steale the horse. An indictmēt depending vpon an argument or implication.
2.Ed.3.1. Fitz. Indict. 8. Co.li.4.42. 44.

18.E.4.10. 30 If an Indictment be, Quod furatus est vnum equum, viz. that hee did steale one horse, and saith not felonicè, this is a void indictment, though felonicè be implied in these words, furatus est. And in like sort it is, if a man be indi-
9.Ed.4.26. cted of a rape, and the indictment is, quod eam carnalitèr cognouit, without vsing the word rapuit, this is no good indictment, and yet carnalitèr cognouit is an argument of a rape, though it may be that he did carnally know her by her
9.Eliz. Dyer 261. owne will and consent, and so not rauish her. And in an indictment of murder, if these words be in the indictment, ex malitia præcogitata, & voluntariè, & fe-
13.Eliz. Dyer 304. lonicè interfecit, & not this word murdrauit, it shall not be adiudged a murder, but homicide. Furatus est without felonicè. Murdrauit.

31 If an indictment of felonie be found before A. B. Iust. of peace, without making mention of any commission that they haue to heare & determine felo-
St.18.E.3.2 nies, this is no good indictment: for by the stat. of an. 18. E. 3. they haue power by commission to heare & determine felonies, and not by vertue of their office only, and yet it is to be implied, that all Iust. of peace by force of their commis-
5.E.6.Di.69 sion, haue authoritie to heare and determine felonies: And they haue authoritie to inquire of murder, for that it is felonie. Indictment before I. of peace.

22.E.4.12 32 If one be indicted vpon the sight of the body before the Maior of London, without adding thereunto this word Coronatore, this is no good indictment: and yet he that is Maior of London is alwayes Coroner, & so by implication it may be taken. But such an indictment is not good, which must haue an argument or implication. Maior of London Coroner.

Indictment of the receit of a felon, as accessorie.

33 If one be indicted as accessorie for the receit of a felon, there must in the indictment mentiō be made of the maner of the felony, & that the party indicted knowing the principal to haue committed such a felony, did feloniously receiue him. But it is otherwise, if a man receiue one attainted of felony in the same county where the felony was committed: for in that case, if he be indicted of the receit of the felon, mention néed not be made of the maner of the felony, because it is sufficient that the party attainted of felony was receiued, though the attainder be erronious: séeing it is not lawfull for any to receiue him, for euery person is bound to take notice of this attainder which is in the same countie where he dwelleth. But it is otherwise, if the attainder were in a forein county, for there none be bound to take knowledge therof but the inhabitants of the same county, and therefore in that case, notwithstanding the attainder, mention ought to be made of the maner of the felony.

Indictment of the receit of one attainted of felonie.

2.H.6.42. 8.E.4.3. Fi.Cor.377

Receit of the goods stolne and felon.

34 It is no good indictment of an accessory, to say, that the said accessory did receiue the goods stoln, without affirming that he receiued the felon also, for he is not accessory to a felony, which doth receiue goods stolne only, except he doth also receiue the felon. S. Principall & Accessorie 14. & 17.

25.Ed.3.39. 27.Ass.p.69 9.H.4.1.

Indictments void to one purpose, will serue to another.

35 Although in the cases aforesaid, the indictments be void touching felony, yet diuers of them shall serue as indictments of trespas, to cause the partie offending to make a fine, & specially such indictments that do not want any certaintie, but only words which make the offence felony. And in those indictmēts which do want certainty, the Iust. may award a Scire fac' against the indictors to amend that which wanteth. And so may the Iust. of the K. Bench, if the indictment be taken in the same county where the said bench is sitting. Or otherwise, if the indictment were taken before the sherife, coroner, or Iust. of peace, the court may direct a writ to the said sherife, coroner, or Iust. of peace, to know if they haue any other indictment before them.

18.E.4.10. 2.H.7.7. 6.H.7.4. 8.H.5.8. 2.E.3.1. & 18.

A prisoner discharged, retained in prison.

36 If the court vpon the arraignmēt of a prisoner, doth discharge him of the indictment, paying his fées, because at that time they do think the indictment to be insufficient, yet if after at another day, or time, they alter their opinion, then they may send to the gaoler, & charge him, that the prisoner shal not depart forth of prison, but stand againe at his deliuerance, notwithstanding their iudgemēt before, if so be that the iudgement be not entered: And this is by the kings prerogatiue, who is partie to the suit.

Fitz.Indict. 27.

The differences betwéen Appeale and Indictment.

37 And séeing I haue treated first of Appeales, & now of Indictments, it is to be considered, what differences there be betwéene them. In an Appeal of the death of a man, the name of him which is dead must be contained, or otherwise it is not good. And therfore there lyeth no Appeale of the death of an infant in his mothers womb, for that infant had neither name nor sirname: and moreouer that maner of killing is no felony. But if one be indicted of the death of a man vnknowne, it is a good indictment: for he that was slaine may be so mangled in the face by the murderer, or some other, or by some other means, that he cannot be knowne. And though in that case no man can be of kin to him who is vtterly vnknowne, by which meane no Appeale can be maintained by any, yet séeing offences must not remaine vnpunished, the offendor in this case shall be indicted: and the enquest which shall passe vpon his arraignment, shall deliuer to the court a name of him that was slain, to the intent, that if the party arraigned, or any other, shall vouch that record, hee shall not depart from thence

No name.

Killing of a mā vnknowne.

22.Ass.p.94 M.2.E.3.26 9.H.6.45. 1.Ass.p.7. 2.Ed.3.26. 11.Eliz. Dyer 285.

without

without a certaine name. In an indictment of treason or felony, the party indicted shall not plead misnaming of his sirname, but he must answer to the indictment, whether he haue one name or other: And yet in an Appeale it is otherwise: But in an Appeale & also in an Indictment, the prisoner may plead misnaming of his name of baptisme, and it being proued, the indictment shalbe quashed. In an indictment the partie indicted may become an approuer, and so cannot an appellée in an appeale. In an appeale the defendant may haue his trial by battel, if he wil, but so he cannot haue which is indicted. A felon may be indicted in the county where he did steal the goods, or in any other county whither he carried them. And in like sort an appeale may be pursued against a felon, in the county where he did first steal the goods, or in any other county whither he carried them.

Margin: 1.H.5.5. 11.H.4.40 11.H.7.5. Fi.Cor. 113 22.Ed.4.19. 4.H.7.5. — Misnaming. Approuer. Triall by battell.

38 It is a good plea in an appeale or indictment of felony, to say, that he was at another time arraigned of the same felony, before such Just. & acquited, and to vouch the record: for he shal not be compelled to haue the record in hand, because his plea is not dilatory, but in bar, and that plea shalbe a good bar (if it bée a lawfull acquitall) for that by the common law a man shall not put his life in ieopardie of triall twice for one and the same felony, sauing in certaine speciall cases. But it ought to be of one offence, or else his plea is to no purpose. And therfore if two men be indicted of felony, as principals, and after by another indictment it is found, that one of them committed the felony, and the other did but feloniously receiue him after the felony committed, & vpon the first indictment they be both arraigned & acquited, and after hée which was indicted as accessorie, is arraigned, and pleadeth, that he was at another time acquited of the same felony: this plea wil not discharge him, because it is not of one offence, but of diuers, for it was done at seueral times. But if he had bin indicted as accessory before the offence committed, this acquitall of him as principall, would haue discharged him of his offence also, for they be in maner one offence, although they be done at seuerall dayes: For when a felony is cōmitted by force of commandement, the commander in that case is party to the principal fact, so is not the other which is accessory after the felony committed. Bracton sayth, that force and commandement be as the foundation of the principall fact, and so annexed and conioyned vn to it, that they cannot be seuered from it: because a wound, a déed, and commandement, do procure one onely fact, and it may bée there should haue béen no wound, except there had béen force, neither wound nor force, vnlesse commandement had gone before, and bidden it to haue béene done. But force and commandement (which in the time of Bracton were but accidents to the fact, and made the offendors therin but accessories) be now the principal fact, if the giuer of that commandement be present when the felony is done. S. Appeales 94.

Margin: Fi.Cor.232 41.Ass.p.9. Co.li.4.45. 8.H.5.6. 27.Ass.p.10 Bro.Cor. 185. 2.E.3.26. Fitz.Cor. 424. Bracton. — Pleading another time acquit of the same felonie. Another offence.

39 If a man be indicted & arraigned of the death of J. Stile, which J. Stile was also knowne by the name of J. Noke, as well as by the name of J. Stile, in this case the def. may plead, that he was at another time indicted & acquited of the death of J. Noke, & auerre, that the said J. Noke & John Stile, were one person, & not diuers, and demand iudgement, if he shalbe put to make answer to that inditmeut: in which case, notwithstanding this variance of names, he shalbe discharged, because he was indicted and acquited of the death of the selfe same man, of whose death he is now againe indicted and arraigned.

Margin: 26.Ass.p.15 11.H.4.41. Fi.Cor.336 — Indictment of the death of a man knowne by two sirnames.

Indicted of the same mans death. 40 If a man be killed two yeares past, and one is indicted and arraigned of his death, and acquited, and after he that was acquited is againe of new indicted and arraigned of the same mans death, supposing that he killed him this present yeare: yet notwithstanding this variance, the party indicted shal shew the truth of the case, and plead his first acquitall for his discharge, and bee discharged: And the reason is, because one man cannot bee twice killed; for the Court in this case doth use to charge the enquest with the time of the death of him who is supposed to be slaine, and also whether there were any other which was killed, as the last indictment doth suppose, or not. 3. Ass.p.15 22. Ass.p.55 Fi. Cor. 336

Indictment in two counties of one offence. 41 If a man be indicted in one county of the death of another, and thereupon arraigned, & after he is indicted in another county of the same parties death, he may plead the same acquitall in bar, for that no mans life shall be twice put in ieopardie of triall for one offence, and one man can be but once slaine. But it is otherwise in an indictment of robberie, for a man may be robbed by one person at severall times, and in several counties, and so the acquitall of one of the same robberies will not serve him for the other. And therfore if one be indicted of robbery in one county, the defendant cannot plead, that he was indicted of the same robberie in another county, and acquited, for no man can be indicted or arraigned for a robbery, but in the coũty where the same robbery was committed: and though the def. doth surmise, that it is but one and the same felony, yet that cannot be tried, for the county where the first indictment was taken, and the county where the last was taken, cannot ioyne to make triall thereof. But some do affirme, that it is a good plea in an Appeale of robbery, for by the Appeale the plaintif is to recover his goods by the common law, and so he is not upon an indictment. 4. H.7.5. A man was indicted in the K. bench of a rape and robbery committed in the county of C. and he pleaded, that he was before indicted of the same rape before the Iust. of Assise in the county of C. and arraigned and acquited of the same fact: And for that it was of the same fact, he was discharged. Indictment of rape. 41. Ass.p.9.

Arraigned upon an insufficient indictment or appeale. 42 It is not a sufficient plea in bar in an Appeale or Indictment of felony, to plead, that he was at another time acquited, if there were not sufficient matter of felony in that apeale or indictment whereof he was acquited: for if there were not sufficient matter of felony in the first appeale or indictment, and the same partie is againe indicted of new, by an indictment which doth comprehend sufficient matter of felony, he shalbe againe arraigned, because in that case he never put his life in ieopardy. For when an offendor is discharged upon an insufficient indictment, the law hath not had his end, neither was the life of the party in the iudgement of law at any time in ieopardie: And the law will not suffer great offences to go unpunished. Co. li. 4. 45. Fitz. Cor. 444.

Acquit upon an erronious appeale. 43 If one be acquited upon an erronious appeale, which acquitall is reversed by errour, he shall now be arraigned at the K. suit, upon an indictment, for that by the reversall he is become in that state, as if he had not béene acquited. But untill that reversal be made, it shalbe a good plea to plead, another time acquit. And it séemeth, that the same is when the errour is in Proces that is not materiall, which the defendant doth appeare and answer to the originall writ. But the def. shal not any more make answer to the appellant, although the first 9. H.5.2. Fitz. Cor. 444.

acqui-

acquitall be reuersed, for so the appellant might delude the court infinitly, and the defendant should neuer be deliuered.

21.H.6.20 — Acquit vpon an Appeale brought by one that hath no right.

44 If one do bring an Appeale, which hath no cause to maintaine the same: As if one which is not the lawfull wife, or the next heire of him that was slain do bring an Appeale, and the defendant doth take no aduantage thereof, but pleadeth not guiltie, and is acquit, yet this acquitall will not serue to barre the lawfull wife, or next heire of the dead, when they shal bring their Appeale, neither in this case the king shalbe barred to arraigne him vpon a indictment, or vpon a new appeale, when the partie plaintife is nonsuit therein.

16.Ed.4.11. 8.H.5.6. — One arraigned vpon an indictment before the parties appeale be determined.

45 If one bee arraigned vpon an Indictment at the Kings suit, and acquited (where, by the order of law, the King ought to haue tarried vntill the Appeale which was depending had been determined) yet this is no errour: but the foresayd plea, viz. another time acquit of the same felonie, shall serue him that doth plead it.

Fitz. Cor. 375. Bracton. — Acquit by battell in an Appeale.

46 If a man be indicted of felony, and arraigned at the Kings suit, it is no plea for him to say, that at another time he was acquited of the same felony in an Appeale, if so be that the same acquitall were not by enquest, but by battell. And the reason is, because tryall by battell lyeth not against the King, and therefore it is not meet that he should be bound by that tryall, whereunto hee neither was, nor could be partie. And yet Bracton sayth, that if the appellee in an Appeale doth make his choyce, to defend himselfe by his bodie, and all things be readie which doe ioyne the Appeale, battell shal be presently waged, and if in that case he that is appealed by diuers, of one fact, and of one wound, doe defend himselfe against one of them, hee shall goe acquit against all the residue of the appellants. And so it is at the Kings suit, for by this meanes he doth purge his innocencie against them all, as much as if hee had put himselfe vpon the countrey, and the countrey had cleerely acquited him. Ideo quære.

A murderer indicted and arraigned at the K. suit.

47 Because, by the common law, within a yeare and a day after any murder or homicide had beene done, the felonie should not haue beene determined at the kings suit, for sauing of the parties Appeale, wherein the partie was ofttimes slow, and also agreed with, and by the end of the yeare all was forgotten: And also for that hee which wil sue an Appeale, must sue it in proper person, which suit is long and costly, and maketh the appellant diuers times weary thereof, which were occasions of murder and manslaughter: for the reformation whereof, by a statute made Anno 3. H. 7. it was enacted, That if any man be slaine, or murdered, and the slaiers, murderers, abettors, maintainers, and comforters of the same bee indicted therefore, the same slayers and murderers, and all other accessories of the same, shalbe arraigned & determined of the same felony & murder at any time at the K. suit, within the yeare after the same felonie & murder done, and not tary the yere & day for any appeal to be taken for the same felony or murder. And if it happē any person so named as principall or accessorie to be acquited of such murder at the Kings suit, within the yeare

St. 3.H.7.1.

and

and day, then the Justices before whom he is acquited, shall not suffer him to go at large, but either shall remit him againe to prison, or else let him to baile after their discretion, till the yeare and day be passed. And if the same Felons, Murderers, and Accessories, or any of them so arraigned, be acquited, or the principall of the sayd felonie, or any of them be attainted, the wife, or next heire to him so slaine, as case shall require, may take their Appeale of the same death and murder, within the yeare and day after the same felonie and murder done, against the said person so arraigned and acquit, and all other their accessories, or against the accessories of the sayd principall, or any of them so attainted, or against the sayd principall so attainted, if they be then liuing, and the benefit of the Clergie thereof before not had. And the appellant shall haue such aduantages, as if the sayd acquitall and attainder had not béene, the acquitall or attainder notwithstanding. The wife or heire of the person so slaine or murdered, as case shall require, may commence their Appeale in proper person, at any time within the yeare after the felonie done, before the Sherif and Coroners of the Countie where the sayd felony and murder was done, or before the King in his Bench, or Justices of gaole deliuerie. And though that by force of the sayd statute of 3.H.7. at another time acquited is no plea in an Appeale of death at this day, yet in an indictment of death, it is a good plea, to plead that he was at another time acquited in an Appeale brought of the same parties death. S. Appeales 93.

Another time acquit, no plea in Appeale, but in Indictment.

48 And so it appeareth, that the before rehearsed enormities that were at the common law, and some others, touching the indicting and arraigning of murderers and manquellers, be remedied by the foresaid statute of 3.H.7. but in other Appeales the rules of the common law doe continue in force: For if a man be indicted of robberie, and hee that was robbed hath an Appeale depending of the same robberie, against the partie indicted, in which Appeale he hath procéeded so farre, that the Just. may perceiue that it is of the same robbery, they ought to surcease to try the Appellée vpon the indictment, vntill the plaintife hath made his declaration: For in an Appeale by writ the robbery cannot be certainly knowen vntil he hath made his declaration, though it be otherwise in an Appeale commenced by bill. 31.H.6.11

No indictmẽt of robbery vntil the Appeal be tryed.

49 Though at another time conuicted or attainted of the same felony, was and is a good plea for him that is the second time, or more often, indicted and arraigned againe vpon the same felony, yet by the common law, if one had béen indicted and arraigned of felonie, and deliuered to the Ordinarie as a Clerke conuict, and before he had made his purgation of the same felony, he had broken the Ordinaries prison, and escaped, he might haue bin another time arraigned vpon the same indictment. And it was no plea for him to plead, that hee was another time conuict of the same felony, and deliuered to the Ordinarie, or that he was a Clerke, and could not answer without his Ordinarie, because hée remained vnpurged of the felonie, and did lose the benefit of his Clergie, by the breaking of prison. And yet at that time, if hee had not broken the Ordinaries prison, but departed by his licence, then at another time conuict shold haue bin a good plea for him vpon his second arraignmẽt. But now sithence by the stat. of an. 18. El. euery person which shalbe admitted to haue the benefit of his clergie, shal not therupõ be deliuered to the Ordinarie, as hath bin accustomed, but after

Another time conuict of the same felonie.

Fitz. Cor. 232.

St. 18. El. 6.

after such clergie allowed, and burning in the hand, shal forthwith be enlarged and deliuered out of prison by the Iust. before whō such clergy shal be granted. Therefore at this day, if one bee conuicted of felonie, and hath the benefit
Co.li.4.40. of his Clergie, and is burned in the hand, if after in any case he shall be indicted
45. and arraigned of the same felonie, it shalbe a good plea for him to plead, that hée was another time conuict of the same felonie (because the life of a man shall not be twice put in ieopardie for one offence) yea though he shall breake the prison, and depart from thence within that time after his conuiction which the Iustices shall thinke conuenient to detaine him in prison for his further correction: for now he is not in prison for felonie, but for correction.

50 It is a good plea for him that is arraigned of felonie, to plead, that he is attainted of felonie, and to demand iudgement, if during this attainder he shal be put to answer to that felony whereof he is attainted, or to any other felonie: for if he should be put to answer, no more could be recouered of him than is re- Another time attainted of felonie.
28.E.3.90 couered, neither can he forf. more than he hath forfeited, hauing forfeited life, lands, goods, and all that he hath: and therefore it should bee to no purpose to trouble him any more. But it is otherwise, where it is to any end or purpose to put him to answer, and plead againe to a new indictment, as in some speciall cases it may be done: As a man attainted of felony, hath also committed treason at the time of the felonie committed: in this case he shal answer to the trea-
1.H.6.5. son for the K. aduantage, notwithstanding his attainder of felony before: because, if he be attainted of treason, the king shall haue the escheat of his lands, of whomsoeuer they be holden: but if the treason were committed after the felony, or at the least after the attainder of felony, then it were otherwise: for then the title which was vested in the chiefe Lord of whom his lands were hol-
4.E.4.11. den, cannot be deuested by a matter accrued, ex post facto. And also where diuers men haue seuerall Appeals of robbery against one man, though he be attainted at the suit of one of them, yet to the intent that euerie of them may recouer his goods which were robbed and taken from him, vpon his fresh suit, hée shalbe againe arraigned at euery of their suits. And it is no plea for him in this case, to plead, that he was another time attainted of felony.

51 In all cases where the defendant would discharge himselfe by pleading that he was attainted of another felony thē this whereof he is now arraigned, it may be replied for the party, or the king, that after the same attainder the K. did pardon him that felony, whereof he saith he was attainted, and his attain- The K. pardō obiected against another time attainted.
6.H.4.6. der thereof, whereby he was restored to the law: and so he ought to answer to all other felonies, notwithstanding they were committed before this whereof he pleadeth that he was attainted: but of that felony whereof he is attainted, he shall not answer any more, after that he hath the K. pardon thereof.

52 A man attainted of felony is he, which vpon his arraignement submitting himselfe to be tried by the country, is found guilty of felony by the verdict of xij. men, or doth confesse the felony in court of Record before the Iudge, vpon his arraignment, or is indicted of felony, and for default of apparance is outlawed, and in any of the said thrée cases hath his iudgement of death. A man conuict of felonie, is he, who being indicted of felonie, vpon his arraignement doth submit himselfe to be tried by the country, and is found guiltie of felonie by the verdict of twelue men, and then before iudgement praieth his clergie, and hath his clergie, and is burned in the hand. This difference there is Who is sayd attainted, and who conuict of felonie.

betwéene

betwéene a man attainted of felonie, and a man cōuicted of felony, as touching their arraignments againe for other offences: for a man attainted of felonie, shall not be arraigned againe of any other offences whatsoeuer, whether clergy were allowable in them or not (vnlesse it be in some speciall cases before declared) because there can no more be recouered of him than is recouered, neither can he forfeit more than he hath forfeited. But because of a clerke conuict, there may be more recouered than is recouered, & he may forf. more than he hath forfeted: therfore by the stat. of An. 8. El. & 18. El. it was ordaind, That euery person which shal vpon his arraignment for any felony be alowed his clergie, shal answer to all former felonies, as though no such admission of clergie had béene. St. 8. El. 4. St. 18. El. 6. S. Appeales 56. 57.

If a man that is indicted of piracie doth stand mute, or wil not answer directly, or &c. whereupon iudgement of paine fort & dure is giuen against him, but hée is not put to execution: and after by a generall pardon by act of parliament, all contempts, pains, and executions, be pardoned (but all piracies bee except) in this case the same party may be indicted and arraigned againe for another robberie vpon the sea, or piracie committed vpon the sea at the same time that hée did the first. 14. El. Dyer. 308.

Mainprise and Bayle.

1 When the defendant in case of felony is taken and arrested, he will ofttimes desire to be let to baile or mainprise: and therefore it is to be considered in what cases the prisoner by the law is mainpernable, and in what not. There be two sorts of offendors in felony, viz: the Principall and the Accessory. The Accessorie is repleuisable by the common law until the Principall be attainted, but not after, as it appeareth by Bracton, Britton, and diuers iudgements. But sithence that time the law hath bin put in vre to the contrary, viz. That after plea pleaded (notwithstanding the principal be attainted) yet the accessorie shalbe let to mainprise, and though it be in appeale of death: And the reason is, because the stat. of W. 1. affirmeth expresly, That they which be indicted of receit of théeues, or felons, or of commandement, or force, or aid of the felony committed, shalbe let out by sufficient suertie: which stat. is expounded so fauorably towards the accessory, that those be vsed to be let to baile which be indicted of abetment, consent, or procuremēt. And yet such accessories be not expresly contained in the said stat. And so the accessorie as well in case of the death of a man, as in other felony, is to bee let to mainprise.

In what case a prisoner is mainpernable in what not.

40.E.3.42 43.Ed.3.17. 27.Ass.p.10 2.& 3.P.& M.Dy. 120 St.3.E. 1.15

The accessory let to mainprise.

Register, fo.270.

2 The principall in case of the death of a man, is not to be let to mainprise, either by the common law, nor by the stat. (but in some speciall cases) for if an appeal of death be commenced, which is not grounded vpon an indictment (but is suggested to be begun vpō malice) and that some others were indicted of the same persons death, yet because the appeale was of the death of a man, and the malice suggested was not confessed of the K. or appellants part, the Iust. wold not let the appellée to mainprise. And so it séemeth, that notwithstanding it bée an appeale of death, yet if there be no indictment to affirme the same appeal, the Iust. vpon the consideration aforesaid, or such like, may let the defendant to mainprise, though he be appealed as principall.

25.E.3.44. 44.E.3.38. 21.E.4.71. 21.Ed.4.25.

The principal in death.

48.E.3.22.

The principal in appeale of death let to mainprise.

2.& 3.P.& M.Dy. 120

3 An Appeale of death was remoued out of the countie into the K. Bench by a Certiorari, & a Scire fac' was sued against the plaintife in the appeal, which was returned Nihil, and so it was returned vpon the Sicut alias. And thereupon the

48.Ed.3.22.

the Iust. considering that it was a mischiefe to the plaintife to loose his suit, and to yeeld damages, whereas he was neuer warned, and peraduenture hath somewhat in another countie: and on the other side it was inconuenient for the appellee to remaine continually in prison: therefore they awarded another Scire fac' against the appellant, returnable at a certaine day, before which day they would bee aduised what was by law to be done, and in the meane time they did let the appellee to mainprise.

The principall in appeale of death let to mainprise.

4 If in an Appeale the def. do plead Excommunication in the plaintife, the appellee shalbe let to mainprise from day to day, vntil the plaintife be absolued, though it be in an Appeale of death: or otherwise the appellee should remain in prison vntill the pl. were assoiled, which peraduenture will neuer be. And in respect of this mischiefe, it was ordained by the stat. of 3. H. 7. That he which is within the yeare acquited of murder at the K. suit, shalbe sent to prison againe, or otherwise let to baile vntill the end of the yere, within which time the partie is to haue an Appeale, if he will.

Excommunication in the plaintife; 3. Ass. p. 12 13. E. 4. 8. St. 3. H. 7. 1.

5 Because Sherifs and others did take & keepe in prison some persons accused of felony, and presently did let out to baile such as were not repleuisable, and kept in prison such as were mainpernable, to the intent to get of the one, and to grieue the other. And forasmuch as it was not before determined, which persons were mainpernable, and which were not, but only they that were taken for the death of a man, by the comandement of the K. or his Iust. or for the forest: therefore by the stat. of W. 1. viz. 3. E. 1. it was ordained, That prisoners which before were outlawed, and they which haue abiured the realm, prouers, and they which be taken with the maner, and such as haue broken the K. prison, theeues openly defamed & knowne, and such as be appealed by prouers, so long as the prouer doth liue, except he be of good fame: and such as be taken for burning of a house feloniously done, or for false mony, or for counterfeiting the Kings Seale: Or persons excommunicat, taken at the Bishops request, or for a manifest offence, or for treason touching the King, shall be in no wise mainpernable by a common writ, nor without writ: But such as be indicted of larceny by enquests taken before Sherifs or Bailifs by their office, or of light suspition, or for petit larceny that amounteth not aboue the value of xij. d. if they were not guiltie of some larceny before, or guiltie of receit of theeues or felons, or of commandement, or force, or of aid in felony done, or guilty of some other trespas, for which one ought not to loose life or member: And a man appealed of an approuer, after the death of the approuer, if he be no common theefe, nor defamed, shalbe let out by sufficient suertie, whereof the Sherife will be answerable, and that without giuing any part of their goods.

Not bailable by the common law. St. 3. E. 1. 15

Who are mainpernable, and who not.

If the Sherife or any other let one go at large by suertie, which is not repleuisable, if he be Sherife, Constable, or any other Bailife of fee, which hath the keeping of prisoners, and is thereof attainted, he shal loose his fee and office for euer. And if the Vndersherife, Constable, or Bailif of such as haue fee for keeping of prisoners, do it contrary to the will of his Master: or any other Bailife being not of fee, they shal haue iij. yeres imprisonment, and make fine at the K. pleasure.

Bailement by the Sherife. St. 3. E. 1. 15

Whosoeuer doth withhold prisoners repleuisable, after they haue offered sufficient suerty, shal pay a grieuous amerciamet to the K. & he that doth take any reward

Withholding of prisoners repleuisable. St. 3. E. 1. 15.

reward for the deliuerance of such, shall pay double to the prisoner, and also a grieuous amerciament to the King.

6 By the foresaid Stat. of West. 1. 15. it doth appeare that in foure cases a man was not mainpernable at the common law, viz. they that were taken for the death of a man, or by the Kings commandement, or of his Iustices, or for the forrest. Touching the death of a man it is intreated of before. And as concerning the Kings commandement, this is intended the Kings commaundement, by his owne mouth, or by his councell which is incorporat to him, & doe speake with the Kings mouth, and by authoritie from him: Or otherwise, if those words should be taken his generall commandement, it may be said that euery Capias in a personall action is the Kings commandement, for it is Precipimus tibi quod capias &c. and yet in that case the defendant is repleuisable by the common law. And as touching the Iustices commandement, this shall be intended their absolute commandement: for if it be their ordinary commandement he is repleuisable by the Sherife, sauing in certain cases prohibited by the statute.

In what cases no mainprise at the common law.

The kings commandement.

The Iustices commandement.

7 Because in times past diuers persons that were indited of felonies, robberies, & larcenies did remoue the same inditements into the K. Bench, & there yeelded themselues prisoners, & were presently bailed by the marshals of the same Bench, and after did lie in wait to kill or misuse their inditors: And also for that certain persons appealed of felonie, after the Exigent awarded, did yeeld themselues in the K. Bench, & then were let to baile by the marshals of the said bench,
St. 5. Ed. 3. 8 for the preuention whereof it was enacted by a statute made an 5. E. 3. That such inditees and appellees shalbe safely and surely kept in prison, according to the charge which the said marshals shal haue of the Iustices. And the marshals of the K. Bench shal not baile any felons, but shal keep them in prison, and shal not suffer them to go wandring abroad by baile, nor without baile. And if any such prisoner be found wandring out of prison by baile, or without baile, & that be proued at the K. suit, or the parties, the marshals which shalbe found guilty thereof, shalbe halfe yeare imprisoned, & ransomed at the Kings pleasure. And the Iustices shal inquire therof when they see cause. And if the marshals suffer the prisoner to escape by their assent, they shalbe at the law as before time they haue bin. And so it appeareth by this Stat. that imprisonment by commandement of a Iustice, was not sufficient to restraine bailement in all cases, where bailement was not prohibited by the law, vntil the foresaid Stat. of an 5. E. 3. was made, and that is to be intended of an ordinarie commandement of a Iu. for if he doe giue an absolute commandement, the prisoner is not baileable: As if the Iustice command one to prison, without shewing cause why he doth so command, or for misdemeanor done in his presence, or for some other cause, which lieth in the discretion of the Iustice more than in his ordinary power.

The marshall of the Kings bench shall baile no prisoner.

A Iustices ordinarie commandement, and absolute.

8 The fourth cause why a man is not repleuisable by the common law, is
St. Char. Forest. 16. the forrest: for whereas by the Statute of Charta foreste, made an 9. H. 3. and confirmed by King E. 1. The king did graunt for him and his heires that of trespasses committed in his Forrests of vert, and venison, that the Forresters in whose Bailiwickes such trespasses should be committed, should present the same trespasses at the next Swanimot, before the Forresters, Verderers, Regardors,

gardors,and Agistors, and other ministers aforesaid, by the oathes as well of Knights,as others,wise,and lawful men,and not suspitious of the parts next adioyning, and néerest where those trespasses shalbe so presented, and where the truth may best and most certainly be inquired of, and the same truth being once found out,those presentments by the common assent and agreement of all the Officers aforesaid,shalbe solemnely written & sealed with their seales. And if any inditement be made in other manner,it shalbe accounted void.And because the chiefe wardens of Forrests did not obserue the said order, but that diuers people were disherited,ransomed,and vndone by the chiefe wardens of the Forrest on this side Trent, and beyond, and by other ministers, against the forme of the foresaid great Charter of the Forrest.Therefore by the Stat.

Punishment for vert or venison.

made an̄ 1.E.3.it was ordained,That no man shalbe taken or imprisoned for St.1.E.3.8 vert or venison,vnlesse he be taken with the maner, or else indited in forme aforesaid.And then the chiefe warden of the Forrest shall let him to mainprise, vntill the Eire of the Forrest, without taking any thing for his deliuerance. And if the said warden will not doe it, there shalbe a writ awarded out of the Chancerie (which was in auncient time ordained for such persons so indited) to let him to mainprise vntill the Eire. And if the said warden after the receit of the same writ wil not deliuer to mainprise such person indited, without delay,then the plaintife shall haue a writ out of the Chancerie, to the Sherife, to attach the said warden to be before the K. at a certaine day, to answer wherefore he hath not repleuied him that was so taken: And the Sherife calling to him the Verderers shall deliuer him which was taken to mainprise in the presence of the Verderers,and shall deliuer the names of the mainpernours to ẏ same Verderors to answer in Eire before the Iustices. And if the chiefe warden shall be thereof attainted, the plaintife shall haue his treble dammage awarded vnto him,and the warden shalbe committed to prison, and ransomed at the Kings pleasure.And by the Statute of an̄ 7.R.2.it was ordained,That St.7.R.2.4 if any officer of the Forrest doth imprison any person,or doth compell any person to make any Obligation,or ransome vnto him, against the ordinance aforesaid,and is thereof attainted, hee shall pay to the partie grieued his double dammages,and make fine to the King.

9 Whereas the before rehearsed stat.of West.1. doth begin with those pri- St.3.E.1.15 soners which before were Outlawed, &c.yet there be some cases wherein such as be outlawed may be let to mainprise: as where in an appeal of robberie or other felonie(being not for the death of a man) the defendant doth come in by Capias vtlagatum,and plead misnaming of himselfe, and hath a Scire facias a- 5.H.7.16. gainst the appellant:In this case he shalbe let to baile. And the same law is,if he which is outlawed for felonie be taken,and brought to the barre, and allea- 19.H.6.2 geth error in the Record,the Court of fauour wil suffer him to find mainprise, and to go and séeke to purchase his writ of Error.

In what cases he that is outlawed may be let to mainprise.

Mainprise during the Prouers life.

10 And ẏ foresaid stat.of West.1.saith further, that they which be appelled St.3.E.1.15 by Prouers shal not be let to mainprise,so long as the Prouers doe liue,if they be not of good fame:& yet in some cases he ẏ is appealed by a prouer shalbe let to mainprise during the Prouers life:as where the Approuer doth waiue his ap- 25.Ed.3.42 peale,and that the defendant is not appealed by another approuer, hee shalbe let to mainprise: for if he bée appealed by another approuer, hée shall not bée

be let to mainprise. And if the Appellée doe vanquish one Approuer in battell, yet if he be appelled by another Approuer, he shall not be let to mainprise.

St.3.E.1.15 11 Whereas by the words of the foresaid Statute of West.1. such as be indited of Larcenie by Enquests taken before Sherifs or bailifes by their office, shalbe let at libertie upon sufficient suretie. Yet it appeareth by the Register, ý they shall not be let to mainprise, if they be not also of good fame. But if they be of good fame, they are to be let to mainprise, notwithstanding they be not indited before Sherifes or Bailifes, but before any other Justice that hath authoritie to heare and determine felonie, and that aswell the principals as the accessories: for the said Stat. of West.1. doth no more restraine the principals, than the accessories, in those cases where the same statute doth not prohibit to let to mainprise. As if a man be indited of Burglarie as principall, yet he may be let to mainprise: And the principall in an appeale of Robberie may be let to mainprise. And in the Register there is a writ de Manucaptione graunted in that case.

Registrum de manucaptione.

Mainprise upon good name.

29.Ass.p.44 Registrum.

The principall in Burglarie or robbery mainpernable.

12 Though it doth not appeare by any words of the foresaid stat. of West. 1. that it doth prohibit the bailement of those which be attainted by verdict: yet it is to be intended, that the same Stat. doth as well prohibit the bailement of those which be attainted by verdict, as it doth of thē who be attainted by Outlawrie: for séeing before the Statute of 18. El. 6. if a clerke conuict had béene deliuered to the Ordinarie, he was not mainpernable, which is a stronger case than a man attainted by verdict. Therefore it is cleare, that a man attainted is not mainpernable: for if a prisoner after that he hath pleaded not guilty, be attainted by verdict, that he killed a man in his owne defence, or by missfortune, yet he shall not be let to mainprise: for it is in the Kings pleasure whether hée will grant him pardon or not. But in that case the Justices commanded the Sherife to put no yrons upon the same prisoner, and to shew him as much fauour as he could. And the Ju. are to certifie the King of the said verdict, who at his pleasure may write to the Sherife to baile the same prisoner. And if a man that is arraigned of homicide doth plead not guiltie, and is found guilty, & doth pray his Clergie, and is repried without iudgement, he is not baileable, for hée is more than vehemently suspected, béeing conuicted of felonie.

15.H.7.9.

No bailement of a prisoner attainted.

25.Ed.3.42 Fi.Cor.354 297.

No bailement of a prisoner conuicted.

2.El.Dyer 179.

St.3.H.7.3. 13 Whereas by the stat. of an̄ 3.H.7. it was enacted, that no prisoner arrested for felony should be let to baile or mainprise by any one Ju. of peace, but by the whole Justices, or at the least by two of them, whereof one to be of the Quorum: Since the making of which statute one Justice of peace in the name of himselfe, and one other of the Justices his companion, not making the said Justice partie nor priuie unto the case wherefore the prisoner should be bailed, hath oft times by sinister labour and meanes set at large the greatest and notablest offendors, such as be not repleuisable by the lawes of this Realme: and yet the rather to hide their affection in that behalfe, haue signified the cause of their apprehension, to bée but onely for suspition of felonie, whereby the said offendors haue escaped unpunished, to the incouragement of théeues, and euil doers: For reformation whereof by a stat. made Anno 1. & 2. P. & M. it was ordained, That no Justice or Justices of Peace shall let to baile or mainprise any such person or persons which for

St.1.&2. P.&M.13

Bailing of offendors by Just. of peace.

any offence, or offences by them or any of them cōmitted, be declared not to bee repleuisable or bailed, or forbiddē to be repleuied or bailed by the stat. of West. 1. made An 3. E. 1. And furthermore, that any person or persons arrested for manslaughter or felonie, or suspition of manslaughter or felonie, being baileable by the law, shal not be let to baile or mainprise by any Ju. of Peace, if it be not in open Sessions, except it be by two Ju. of peace at the least, whereof one to be of the Quorum: and the same Justices to be present together at the time of the said bailement or mainprise, which bailement or mainprise they shall certifie in writing, subscribed or signed with their owne hands at the next generall Gaole deliuerie, to be holden within that countie, where the said person or persons shalbe arrested or suspected. And the said Ju. or one of them beeing of the Quorum, when any such prisoner is brought before them, for any manslaughter or felonie, before any bailement, or mainprise, shall take the examination of the said prisoner, and information of them that bring him, of the fact and circumstances thereof, and the same, or as much thereof as shal be materiall to prooue the felonie, shall put in writing before they make ẏ same bailement: which said examination, together with the said bailement, the said Ju. shall certifie at the next generall Gaole deliuerie to be holden within the limits of their commission. And euerie Coroner vpon any inquisition before him found, wherby any person or persons shal be indited for murder, or mãslaughter, or accessorie or accessories to the same, before the murder or manslaughter committed, shall put in writing ẏ effect of the euidence giuen to ẏ Jury before him, being materiall. And aswel ẏ said Ju. as the said Coroner shall haue authoritie by this act to bind all such by recognizance, or obligation, as do declare any thing materiall to prooue the said murder, or manslaughter, offences, or felonies, or to be accessory or accessories to the same, as is aforesaid, to appeare at the next generall Gaole deliuerie to be holden within the county, city, or town corporat, where the triall thereof shalbe, then, & there, to giue euidence against ẏ partie so indited at the time of his triall, and shal certifie aswel the same euidence, as such bond & bonds in writing, which he shal take together with ẏ inquisition or inditement before him taken & found, at, or before the time of his said triall thereof, to be had or made. And likewise the said Ju. shall certifie all & euery such bond taken before him, in like maner as before is said of bailmēts and examination. And in case any Ju. of peace, or Quorum, or Coroner shal offend in any thing contrarie to ẏ true intent and meaning of this act, then the Ju. of Gaole deliuerie of the shire, citie, towne, or place where such offence shal happen to be committed, vpon due proofe thereof by examination before them, shal for euery such offence, set such fine on euery of the same Ju. of peace, & Coroner, as the same Ju. of Gaole deliuerie shall thinke meet, and shall estreat ẏ same, as other fines, and amerciaments assessed before Justices of Gaole deliuerie ought to be. Prouided alwaies, that Ju. of Peace, and Coroners within the city of London, and the County of Middlesex, & in other Cities, Boroughs, and Townes corporat within this Realme, and Wales, shall within their seuerall iurisdictions haue authority to let to baile felons and prisoners, in such manner & forme as they haue bin heretofore accustomed. This act or any thing therein contained to the contrary notwithstanding. And also shall take examinations & bonds as is aforesaid vpon euery bailement by them or any of them to be made, and shall certifie euery such bailements, bonds & examinations by them, or any of them takē, or made, at the next Gaole deliuery to be holdē within the shire, city, borough, or towne, where their seuerall iurisdictions extēdeth, vpon like paine and forf. as is before limitted in this present act.

The Coroners duty vpon an inquisition found.

Certificat of a bond taken by a Ju. of peace.

S.3.E.1.15. 14 Because Sherifs and others did in times past let to mainprise notorious and knowne theeues, being taken and imprisoned for murder, and other felonies, and such as be not mainpernable, contrarie to the forme of a Statute made touching those which bee repleuisable, and which not, and thereby such malefactors as were not repleuisable were let to mainprise. And for to deliuer them deceitfully before the comming of the Justices in Eire, or other assigned for their deliuerance, they procured and suborned by themselues, and by their friends, Jurors of the countie, & some they threatened: And so partly for feare of the Sherifs and others which did let them to baile, and partly for feare of those felons which were so let to mainprise, many robberies and homicides were hidden and concealed from the Justices of Gaole deliuerie: for the preuention whereof, by a Stat. made an 27. E. 1. intituled the Stat. of fines leuied, it was ordained, That Justices assigned to take assises, in euery countie where they take assises, presently after the assises taken, shall remaine both together if they be Laie. And if one of them be a Clerke, then one of the most discreet knights of that county being associate vnto him, by the kings writ, shall deliuer the Gaole in that countie, aswell within liberties as without, of all the prisoners, according to the vsuall forme of deliuering of Gaoles. And then the same Justices shall inquire which sherifs and others haue let to baile any prisoners that were not repleuisable, or haue offended in any thing contrarie to ye Stat. of West. 1. and to punish and chasten them in euery respect, according to the forme of the said Statute.

An. 27. E. 1. 3.

Bailement of offendors by Sherifes.

St. 4. E. 3. 2 15 And for the causes aforesaid it was ordained by the stat. of an 4. E. 3. that good and discreet persons (other than of the places if they may be found sufficient) shalbe assigned in all the counties of England to take assises, Juries, and certifications, and to deliuer the Gaoles: And the same Justices shall take the assises, Juries, and certifications, & shall deliuer the Gaoles thrice in the yeare at the least, and more often if need be: And there shall be assigned good & lawfull men in euery Countie to keepe the peace, and at the said assignements mention shalbe made that such as shalbe indited or taken by ye said wardens shal not be let to mainprise by the Sherifs, nor by any other, if they be not mainpernable by the law: Nor that such persons indited shalbe deliuered, but according to the course of the common law. And the Justices assigned to deliuer ye gaoles shall haue power to deliuer the Gaoles of those that be indited before the gardeins of the peace: And the same gardeins shall send before the said Just. their inditements. And the same Justices shall haue power to enquire of Sherifes, Gaolers, and others, in whose custodie such persons indited shalbe, if they deliuered or let to mainprise any so indited, which be not mainpernable, & to punish the same Sherifes, Gaolers, and others, if they haue done any thing contrarie to this Statute. This statute of 4. E. 3. doth make no mention that the Justices of Gaole deliuerie shall punish sherifs and others according to ye foresaid statute of West. as the other statute of 27. E. 1. doth, but ordaineth generally that they shalbe punished, without determining in what maner: And yet it is to be intended that they shalbe punished according to the forme of the said Stat. of West. 1. And moreouer the said Justices of Gaole deliuerie may punish them by the common law, for a negligent escape: for it is a negligent escape to let one to mainprise, who by law is not mainpernable. And one Justice did in that case set a fine vpon the Sherife, for the like Bailement, a hundred shillings.

Bailement of offendors by sherifes and others.

Where mainprise is a negligent escape.

25. E. 3. 39.

Imprisonment at the Kings pleasure.

16 In all cases where a statute doth ordaine that an offendors bodie shalbe imprisoned at the Kings pleasure, the prisoner cannot be deliuered or let to mainprise, vntil the King hath signified his pleasure of him. As, if one be imprisoned for going or riding armed, contrary to the Statute of Northampton, made Anno. 2. E. 3. 3. 24. Ed. 3. 42.

The differēce betwéene bailement in felonie, and in a personall action.

17 There is a difference betwéene bailement in felonie, and bailement in a personall action: for in felonie the bailement shall containe a certaine summe of money to be forfeited, if the prisoner doe not appeare at a day prefixed. And in a personall action, it is but fineable. And the bailement in felonie is Ad standum rectum de latrocinio prædicto secundum legem & consuetudinem regni nostri Angliæ, as it doth appeare by the writs of Manucaptione in ẏ register, which doe imply as much as they that haue him to baile, shall not onely cause him to appeare, but also to answer. 21. H. 7. 20.

Mainprise is matter of Record.

18 If one doe find mainprise in Court, it is presently matter of Record, though it be not entered into the Roll vntil the next Terme. 8. Ed. 4. 5.

Confession of the Offence.

When a prisoner is appealed, or indited of treason, or felonie, and brought to the barre to be arraigned thereof, and his initement is read unto him, he is asked by the Court what he will say unto it: Then either hee doth confesse the offence, and the initement to bee true: or he estrangeth himselfe from the offence, and pleadeth, Not guiltie: or else hee doth answer indirectly, and so in effect he standeth mute, and maketh no answer. Of the which later two I will intreate heereafter. An offendour pleadeth one of three pleas.

And therefore beginning with the prisoners Confession of the offence upon his arraignement: That confession may be made in two sorts, and to two severall ends, whereof the one is, he may confesse the offence whereof he is indited openly in the Court before the Judge: and that he hath committed that act whereof he is indited and arraigned, and submit himselfe to the censure and iudgement of the Lawe. Which Confession of the offence by the prisoner himselfe in person, is the most assured answer, and best satisfaction that can be delivered to the Judge to condemne the offendour, and to all the hearers to give approbation thereof: So that the said Confession do procéede fréely, and of his owne good will, without menace, threats, rigor, or other extreamities: For if the Judge doe perceive that the offendors confession doth growe upon either of those extreamities, he ought not to record the confession, but to cause the prisoner pleade to the offence, not guiltie. As, a woman was indited for the felonious stealing of bread to the value of two shillings, and being arraigned thereof, she confessed the felonie, and saide that she did it by the commaundement of her husband, and the Judges for pitie would not record her confession, but caused her to pleade, not guiltie to the felonie: whereupon a Jurie being charged, it was found that she did steale the bread by the compulsion of her husband, against her will, by which meanes she was discharged. And in like sort if the Judges doe perceive that the offendour doth confesse the offence in mistaking of the Lawe, they may shew

Confession in two sorts.

Confession must be free and without menace.

27. Ass. p. 40

shew him that fauour, as not to record his confession, but cause him to pleade to the inditement, not guiltie. As a man being indited of the death of another man, pleaded, that he and one B. hauing a quarrell, and fighting each with the other, the party of whose death he was indited, came betwéene them to part the fray, and he against his will, by misfortune, gaue him a blowe, whereof hée died. For though by the Lawe this was felonie in him being fighting, and intending to hurt or kill B. yet he did mistake the Lawe therein, and did not take it to be so, for that his quarrell was not towardes him which he slue, but to B. who had no hurt. And further, this confession of the Offence is not so penall to the prisoner, (though he doth it fréely, and without menace, or other extreamitie) that he is thereby presently attainted or condemned of that felonie, but in many cases he may be saued from death, the most bitter rigour of the Lawe, by the benefit of his cleargie, or by the Kings pardon. 22.Ass.p.71

He that confesseth doth become an Approuer.

3 The other kinde of confession of felonie that is made by a prisoner at his arraignement, openly in court before the Judge, is when the prisoner doth confesse the inditement to be true, and that he hath committed the offence whereof he is indited, and then doth become an approuer, viz. an accuser of others, who haue committed the same offence whereof he is indicted, or other offences with him, and then doth request the Judge to haue a Coroner assigned vnto him to whome hée may make relation of those offences, and of the whole circumstances thereof.

Confession before the Coroner.

4 There is also a third kinde of confession made by an offendor in felonie, which is not in Court before the Judge, as the other two be, but before the Coroner in a church or priuiledged place, whereupon the offendor by the antient Lawe of this Realme is to make his abiuration out of the Realme: Of which approuing, and abiuration, I will write in the two next chapters.

Appro-

Approuer.

An Approuer is a felon that hath committed a felonie, and after confesseth the same, and then doth appeale and accuse others, who were helpers or coadiutours with him to commit the same felonie: which thing being done, he is thereby called an Approuer, who in latine is termed Probator, for that he must proue that, which is contained in his appeale or accusation. And the proofe must be by battell, or by the verdict of twelue men, at the choice of him who is appealed. And if he doe proue it, the kings of this Realme haue vsed to graunt him pardon of his life, because he doth fight for the peace of the Realme, and doth deliuer the countrie of malefactors: for he is to make couenant or promise to the Judge, who will be sutor to obtaine his pardon, how many offendors he will conuince, and accordingly he is to vanquish them in battell, attaint them by verdict, or cause them to flée, and so by that meanes to become outlawes. But yet he shall be banished the Realme, and not continue therein, though he would finde pledges for his good abearing.

Who is an Approuer.

Britton.

An Approuer banished.

Bracton de coron, c.34.

19.H.6.47. 12.Ed.4.10 Fi.Cor.231 387. 2 A man imprisoned for felonie, may approue of treason, if he will, and in like sort, he that is imprisoned for treason may approue of felonie, if he wil: for when the Justices doe admit him to approue, they doe sweare him vpon a booke, to approue of all felonies and treasons that he doth knowe. And yet many doe affirme, that approuement must be onely of the thing, whereof the approuer is indicted, and of none other, and of that treason or felonie, which he himselfe with others did commit, and that approuement of all other offences is voide. As if one will appeale an other for robbing of him, viz. of the Approuer, it is voide: Or if one will appeale an other, for procuring the saide approuer to commit a felonie: Or that where he the saide Approuer had committed a felonie, the appellée knowing thereof did feloniously receiue him and comfort him, it is voide: because those offences hée could not commit, for he could not robbe himselfe, nor be accessorie to himselfe. Sed de hijs quære: Séeing the approuer is sworne to approue of all the felonies and treasons that he doth know.

Of what offences approuement may be.

Bracton de coron, c.33. 25.Ed.3.39

10.E.4.14. 40.Ass.p.39

Quære.

3 A man

Approouement in an Indictment, and not Appeale.

3 A man may approue in an indictment of felonie, but not in an appeale of felonie, for if he should approue in an appeale of felonie, he should thereby delay the Plaintife in the appeale to haue execution of him. And in like sort, if one that is indicted of felonie, doth become an approuer, and after an appeale is sued against him, upon the same indictment: in this case he shall surcease to procéede any further in his approouement. But upon an indictment of felonie, the prisoner which is arraigned may confesse the felonie, pray a Coroner, and so approue. And though some haue thought, that if a prisoner be not indicted, but doth stand at the barre, as one that is to be deliuered by Proclamation, if he will refuse the benefit thereof, confesse a felonie, and pray to become an approuer, that he shall be thereunto receiued: And some others haue béene of opinion, that if a man be in prison but for suspition of felony, he may confesse the felony before a Coroner, and become an approuer: But that cannot be by the Lawe, for a man cannot be attainted by his confession, if he be not indicted or appealed thereof before: and it is alwaies requisite, for him which shal become an approuer, that his confession be made upon such matter, upon which the Judge at all times at his pleasure, may giue iudgement to attaint him.

11.H. 7.5. Fi.Cor. 113 Fi.Cor. 442 Fi.Cor. 131

An Approuer must confesse the felonie.

Before whom one may approue.

4 One may become an approuer before those, who haue authoritie to assigne him a Coroner, as the Justices of the Kings Bench, the Justices in Eire, and the Justices of gaole deliuerie: But so can not Justices of Peace, and therefore a man can not become approuer before them. Neither can a man become an approuer in a Court Baron before the Steward and Sutors: Nor in the Countie court before the Shirife and Suitors: Nor before any other speciall Judge, unlesse his Commission doth extend thereunto.

2.H.4.19. 9.H.4.1.

How an Approuer shall vse himselfe.

5 He that will become an approuer, must when he is at the barre before the Judge, confesse the felonie, whereof he is arraigned, and pray that a Coroner may be assigned unto him to heare his approouement or appeale against others: for without confession of the offence, whereof he is arraigned, he cannot pray a Coroner. And this confession must be at the beginning, before hée hath pleaded any plea to the contrary therof: For if he wil pleade not guilty, he cannot after waiue that plea, and confesse the felonie, and pray a Coroner. And the reason is, because it cannot be intended, that hée will proue that, which he hath affirmed against others, when he hath shewed himselfe so false and unconstant in his answer before: for he is called an Approuer, viz. Probator, to the intent that he shall proue that which he alleadgeth against others, whereof there is small hope to be conceiued, when in the beginning he hath made a lie of himselfe: for if he will haue his approouement allowed for good, he must alwaies be found to speake trueth, without any lying. And when the Court doth perceiue that he hath made a lie, they presently take his approouement from him, and giue iudgement, that he shall be hanged. As, an approuer did appeale diuers, and the Shirife and Coroners did testifie, that there were none such in that countie, and without further inquirie, the approuer was adiudged to be hanged. And if upon the appeale of an approuer, processe be awarded against those which he doth appeale, and the Shirife returneth non sunt inuenti, iudgement shall be giuen, that the approuer shall be hanged. And in like sort it is, if an approuer doe appeale severall persons

No approouement after pleading.

An Approuer must tell truth

Fi.Cor. 441 2.H.7.3. 21 Ed.3.18 19 H.6.47. Fi.Cor.440 25.Ed.3.42 21.H.6.34 Fi.Cor.456

in

in seuerall counties, and processes be awarded against them, untill some of them be attainted, and some of them depend in processe not attainted, and the Justices be informed by credible persons of the same countie, wherein they were appealed, that there be no such men to their knowledge in rerum natura, the approuer shall be hanged. An approuer did appeale two men in London, and proces was awarded against them, and it was returned, that there were
Fi.Cor.460 no such men dwelling in the city of London, and the approuer agreeing to the same returne, saide that they were dwelling within the city of Lincolne, and he was not thereunto receiued, but was adiudged to be hanged: So that if there be any falshood or lying in the approuer, be it before his approuement or after, and that the court do perceiue it, they will take his appealing from him, and adiudge him to be hanged. And if they do otherwise, it is more of Approuement after pleading not guiltie.
12.Ed.4.10 fauour than of right: for of fauour the court may allow the prisoner to waiue his plea of Not guiltie, and to confesse the felonie, and to become an approuer. And if an approuer doe appeale one, who by his owne confession is out
21.H.6.35 of the Realme, he shall be hanged: for the appellee cannot be attainted at his sute; for though he should be outlawed, yet he may reuerse it at his returne for that cause.

6 When a prisoner upon his arraignement doth confesse the felonie, and praieth a Coroner, which is assigned unto him by the court, he must be sworn in the same court before his departing, to appeale of all felonies and treasons which he doth knowe: and the court shall appoint him a number of daies, wherein to make his appeale, in the which daies, and in euery of them hee ought to appeale: for if three dayes be appointed, and in two of them he doth appeale, and the third day he will affirme to the Coroner, that he can say no more, and the Coroner doth report the same to the court, iudgement shall be giuen, that he shall be hanged. An Approuers othe.
12.Ed.4.10.
26.Af.p.19.
Fit.Cor.439

7 An approuer shall haue wages of the King euery day that is assigned him by the court to approue in, viz. a penny a day. And some do affirme, that he shall haue no wages, untill he hath made his proofe by vanquishing some appellee in battell, or by conuicting him by verdict, and then he shall haue wages of the King for euery day. An Approuers wages.
Fi.Cor.439

8 When a Coroner is assigned to an approuer, the approuer must be let out of prison, to the intent that hee may approue or appeale of his owne free will being at liberty, without any dures: for if it be by dures, when he commeth againe before the Justices, hee may rehearse his appeale, and disauow it for that cause, which shalbe tried by the examination of the Coroner upon his othe. And if the Coroner do say, that the same appeale was not by dures, the appeale shall stand, and the approuer shall be hanged. And when the approuer hath made his appeale before the Coroner, he shall come againe before the Justices, and rehearse his appeale before them (for they will not reade his appeale unto him) and if hee doe faile in the rehearsall of his appeale, in anie word, otherwise than the Coroner hath recorded it, he shall be hanged: as if in his rehearsall he doe say, that there was a blacke horse stollen, where it it was recorded by the Coroner, a redde Horse: For the Approuer must declare the thing certainely, with all the circumstaunces thereof, without any varying or alteration: and he must know the person, whom he hath An Approuer set at liberty. An Approuers appeale must be certaine.
Fi.Cor.118
169.255.
26.Af.p.19
Bracton.

hath appealed, when hee is brought into question, for if he know him not, it is to be presumed, that they were neuer companions.

Processe against the appellees.

9 After an Approuer hath made his appeale before the Coroner, if the appellees be dwelling in the Countie, where the appeale is made, the Coroner hath authoritie to award processe against them vntill the Exigent, and to direct his processe to the Shirife to serue. But so he cannot doe, if the appellees be dwelling in another countie, for then he must not award processe against them, but referre it to the iustices, before whom he is to record the same appeale. And they may award processe as the Iustices of the Kings bench and Iustices in Eire may do, who may award processe by the common law, and Iustices of Gaole Deliuerie by the statute De Appellatis, made Anno 28. Ed. 1. which hath ordained; That whosoeuer shalbe appealed by any Approuers remaining in the Gaoles, which the Iustices of Gaole deliuerie shall deliuer, in what places soeuer of the Realme the persons appealed shall remaine, immediatly the Shirife of that countie, where such persons appealed be conuersant, or may be found, shall be commaunded by the Kings Writs vnder the testimonie of the same Iustices, that he shall apprehend those persons appealed, and conuey them to the Gaole, where the approuers, by whose appeale they be apprehended, be imprisoned. And the Shirife or Gaoler of that prison shall receiue them: and there they shall answer before the same Iustices. And if they put themselues vpon the country, the Iustices shall send by a iudiciall Writ to the Shirife of the Countie, where the felonie was committed, that hee shall returne an Enquest before them, at the place, where the approuers do remaine, at a certaine day.

29. Ed. 3. 42

St. 28. Ed. 1.

Pleas for the Appellee against the Approuer.

10 It is a good exception for the appellee in his owne defence to alleage against the approuer, that the approuer is a person attainted of treason, or felonie, and to shew how, viz. either by verdict, outlawrie, or abiuration, or in any other manner: for such a person is out of the Lawe, and so disabled to appeale or accuse others. And the same lawe is, if the approuer be a clerke conuict, for hee commeth now too late to confesse a felonie, when hee hath pleaded not guilty thereunto before, which was found false at his owne sute; and therefore it cannot be intended, that the thing hee saith now is true. And although hee had his clergie vpon confession of the felonie, yet hee shall not now become an approuer, for that he saide nothing at that time when hee ought to haue approued: and therefore the Lawe cannot intend, that hee hath any thing to say now that is true, seeing he would not speake it at that time, when hee might haue beene heard. But in the foresaid cases, if the approuer can shew any sufficient matter, which doth restore him to the lawe, as the Kings pardon, and such like, then the appellee shall answer to the approuer. S. Appeales. 92.

11. Ass. p. 27.
Fi. Cor. 387
443
21. Ed. 3. 17
17. Ed. 3. 13.

An Approuer conuict of felonie.

21. Ed. 3. 17

An Appellee cannot appeale others.

11 If he which is appealed by an approuer will confesse the appeale, and pray that he may become an approuer, and appeale others, hee shall not bee receiued thereunto, for seuerall causes: one is, for that he is appealed of felonie, and not indicted of felonie; and in an appeale, there lieth no approuement: another cause is, for that if his approuement should be of the same felonie,

lonie, he should thereby falsifie the appeale of the first approuer, in that he did not at the first discouer all his companions, being sworne thereunto. And a third cause is, for then by that meanes approuements would be infinite, and also the appellée is in a sort out of the lawe, for that the approuer hath deraigned an appeale against him.

Fi.Cor.113

12 It is a good exception for the appellée to obiect against the approuer, that the approuer is not in prison for any felonie or treason, but for debt, or trespasse, or some other offence: or to say, that the approuer is not in prison, but at large; for he cannot be an approuer, vnlesse he be first indicted of felonie, and doth confesse it before a Iudge, and then become an approuer.

21.Ed 3.18. Fi.Cor.231 — Approuer not in prison for felony, or at libertie.

13 It is a good plea (as some doe affirme) for him that is appealed, to say, that he is a lawfull man, and in the franke pledge, and in the Assise of our soueraigne Lord the King, and that hée hath a Lord, which will be his pledge. And if that be trauersed, and found for the appellée, he shall be discharged thereby. Sed quære.

Bracton. — The appellée an honest and credible man.

14 In an appeale by an approuer, the appellée may pleade, that the same approuer is a priest, not of perfect memorie, deafe, dumbe, a lazar, a naturall foole, a woman, a man aboue thréescore and tenne yéeres of age, or within age, or that he is mayhemed by some other, and not by the appellée, for that in these cases the approuer cannot deraigne or wage battell with him. S. Appeales. 93.

Fi.Cor.322 — General pleas in Barre of the appeale.

15 In diuers cases, if the appellant doe surcease to prosecute his appeale, the king may pursue it: for the appellant may by seuerall meanes leaue off to prosecute his appeale, as by Non-suite, Release, Retraxit, or a woman by taking a husband during the suite of appeale: for in all these Cases the appeale doth cease by the act of the partie; & therefore in which case soeuer that Cesser is after declaration in the appeale, the Defendant shall not goe at libertie, but shall be arraigned at the Kings suite vpon the same declaration: for that it doth appeare there is a felony committed, and the same is not yet tried. And the same Lawe is, if the appeale doe cease by the act of God, as if the appellant doe die: Or if it cease by the act of the Lawe, as if the appellant after his appeale made be hanged: Or if the appellant doe take the priuiledge of his Cleargie; for an appeale by an approuer is a great presumption against the Defendant, that he is guilty of the offence whereof he is appealed, and that is for the great punishment which the appellant is to suffer, if he at any time doe faile of his appeale, viz. death. And an appeale doth worke a greater presumption against the Defendant than an Indictment doth: for that it is vsed, if a man be appealed and indicted of one offence, and the Plaintife in the appeale after declaration is Non-suite; the Defendant shall be arraigned at the Kings sute vpon the declaration in the appeale, and not vpon the Indictment: But this presumption riseth where the appellant hath appeared to his suite, and declared: for vntill that time, it carieth not with it any presumption. Because any man may sue a Writte of

Where the King may pursue an appeale begunne. — 3.H.6.50. — 21.Ed.3.18 Fit.Cor.369 — 4.Ed.4.10 — 8.Ed.4.25.

appeale out of the Chauncerie in a strangers name, and finde pledges to prosecute it, and cause the Writ to be delivered to the Shirife of Record, that stranger not knowing thereof; in which Case it shall not be saide that strangers suite, untill he hath appeared in proper person thereunto, and declared: for untill that time, Non-suite in the appeale is not peremptorie to the stranger. Neither shall the Defendant be arraigned at the Kings suite, by this Non-suite any more than if hee had not beene Non-suite. But in that Case, if a stranger doe bring a new appeale against the Defendant, the Defendant shall aunswere him as hee should haue done if no such Non-suite had beene. But the Lawe is otherwise in an appeale commenced by Bill, for that suite of necessitie must be made by the party himselfe in his owne proper person, and his apparance must be recorded by the Shirife and Coroners, and the yeere, day, and place expressed, where, and when the felonie was committed, and who were principalles in the same felonie, and who were accessories. And so in an appeale by Writ, the Plaintifes Non-suite before declaration, doth giue the King no aduantage against the Defendant: but in an appeale commenced by Bill before the Shirife and Coroners, or in an appeale by an approuer it is otherwise, for in such an appeale, all the certaintie of the felonie is declared and comprised. In an appeale of murder against three, if one of them pleade Not guiltie, ready to defend himselfe, by his body, and so wageth battaile, upon which plea the Plaintife demurreth in lawe, which demurrer is adiudged against him; in this Case the same appellee shall be arraigned at the Kings suite: for that the felonie is not yet tried, nor he acquit thereof. And if one of the other appellees doe pleade, Not guiltie, and that the Plaintife doth demurre thereupon, and it is adiudged a good plea, and the same appellee is acquit against the appellant, yet he shall be arraigned at the Kings suite of the same murder. S. Appeales. 96.

7.H.7.5. Fi.Cor.384 — 22.Ass p.97 — 2 & 3.P.& M.Dy.121.

The Appellants release to the Appellee.

16 If the Defendant in an appeale do pleade a Release inrolled, and of record, made unto him by the appellant before the appeale commenced, he shall be presently delivered: But if it be made after the appeale commenced, the the Court will intend, that it is of purpose to defraud the King: and therefore in that case he shall be arraigned at the Kings sute, though he be acquit against the appellant by his release. Fit. Cor. 12

An Approuer confesseth his appeale to be false.

17 If an approuer, when an Enquest doth appeare upon the issue ioined betweene him and the appellee, and be ready to trie the same issue, will confesse his appeale to be false, yet notwithstanding the appellee shall be arraigned at the Kings suite. But if the approuer, when the appellee is in the field ready to deraigne battaile, will confesse his appeale to be false, the appellee shall goe quit, and not be arraigned at the Kings suite, and the approuer shall be hanged: for it is as much as if the appellee had vanquished the approuer in battaile. 21.H.6.34.

The appeale abating before declaration.

18 If an appeale commenced by Writ doe abate before declaration, so that the Court can not be informed of the yeere, day, and place, where, and when the felonie was committed: In that Case the Court doth use to examine the Coroner, if he be present, if there be any indictment depending of the same felony, or not: and if he say no, then to send to the Shirife of the Countie, where the felonie was supposed to be committed, to know if hee haue any indictment, or not, and in the meane time to let the Defendant to main-

mainprise: or otherwise the Court will set the Defendant at libertie. There was a time, when if a felon had bin taken with the manoure, and that the felon and the manoure had beene brought into the Court, the Iudges would haue arraigned the offendor vpon ẏ manoure without appeale or inditment: Sed obsoletum. A felon taken with the manoure.

19 In euery arraignement which is to be at the Kings sute vpon an Appeale begunne by the appellant, the declaration in the same appeale is intended to be once good, and true: for if it were neuer good, and abated for that cause, the appellee shall not be arraigned at the kings suite, notwithstanding the abatement be after declaration. And therefore if an appeale be abated by mis-naming of the Defendant, hee shall not be arraigned at the kings sute, though the abatement be by the Plaintifes owne confession. And yet in that case it might be said, that the appeale abated by couin, for that the said exception was not tried, but confessed by the Plaintife. And the same Lawe is, if the appeale shall be abated by mis-naming of the Plaintife, or of the Towne, or for lacke of a materiall word. And so it is, if in an appeale, the Defendant doe pleade, that the Plaintife is outlawed, or is attainted of treason, or felonie, or otherwise is disabled to maintaine an appeale: As, if a woman doe bring an appeale of the death of her husband, and the Defendant doth pleade, that shee and her said husband were neuer accoupled in lawfull marriage, or that shee hath married another husband: Or, that the appeale was not commenced within the yeere and day after the offence committed: Or, that the appellant hath an elder brother liuing to whome the appeale is giuen, and not to the Plaintife: And all those matters which shall be a Barre to the plaintife, to bring the appeale, shall also Barre the king to take any aduantage against the Appellee, vpon the same appeale: for in all these Cases it may appeare that the appeale was commenced without cause, and grounded vpon false matter. And yet it is otherwise, where the appeale was at the first grounded vpon sufficient and true matter. But in all the Cases aforesaid, though the king cannot take an aduantage of the appeale against the defendant, yet he shal compell him to answer to an inditment of the same felony, for that by these pleas the defendant is not discharged of the felonie, though he be discharged of the appeale. And further, if the appellee be discharged both against the party and also against the King, yet the Court may bind him to his good Abearing, if they shall thinke it meete.

No arraignement at the Kings suite vpon a false declaration. — 4.H.6.16 — Fi.Cor.121 — 17.Ass.p.26. — 11.Ass.p.27 — 18.Ed.3.35. — Fitz.Cor.3. 384.387. — 27.Ass.p.25 — S.Br.15. — If not an Appeale, yet an Inditment at the Kings suite. — Fi.Cor. 387 — Good abearing.

20 If an Excommunication be pleaded against the plaintife in appeale, notwithstanding the plea be thereby delayed, yet the Defendant shall not be arraigned at the kings sute, for the Plaintife may be absolued, and then proceede in his appeale. And therefore the appeale shal be continued vntill a certaine day, to the intent that the Plaintife may in the meane time procure his absolution: and during that time the Defendant shall be let to mainprise. But if the appellant be outlawed, though the Outlawrie be not for felonie, but for trespas, yet by that meanes the Defendant shalbe set at liberty, aswel against the king, as against the appellant. Notwithstanding in that case, there is no impossibilitie, but the Plaintife might purchase his charter of pardon, or reuerse the outlawrie for that it is erronious, and thereby be enabled to pursue his appeale.

13.Ed.4.8 — 3.Ed.3.10 — The plaintiffe in appeale excommunicate. — 17.Ass.p.25 — Fit. Vtlawrie 47. — The plaintiffe in appeale outlawed.

An Approuer pardoned, the Appellæ shall be discharged.

21 If one be appealed by an approuer, and the King doth pardon the approuer, he that is appealed by the approuer, shall be set at libertie, without being arraigned at the Kings suite: for by the pardon the felonie is extinct in him, and so he ceaseth to be an approuer, for the approuement shall continue no longer then the approuer is partaker of the felonie, whereof the approuement is made. 47.E.3.5. 47.E.3.16.

Vanquishing one approuer.

22 If thrée men doe become approuers seuerally against one man, of one and the same felony, and he ioyneth battell with them all, and doth vanquish that approuer which first ioyneth with him; by that meanes he shal be acquit against them all, and likewise against the King, and the other two approuers shall be hanged. But it is otherwise, if the approuement be of seuerall felonies: for in that case, though the appellæ doth ioyne battell with them all, and after vanquish that approuer which first ioyneth with him, he shall be remaunded to prison, vntill he hath ioyned battell with the other two: for that there must be seuerall trialls, where there be seuerall felonies, and seuerall issues. 7.Ed.3.11. 25.Ed.3.42

Examining an offendor condemned.

23 If a man would become an approuer, and cannot be suffered by the Lawe for some disablement, or for the impediments before mentioned, yet before he shal be put to execution, the Court will send the Shirife vnto him, to heare who they be that he can accuse, and thereupon cause the Shirife to indite them at his next Turne. 21.Ed.3.18

Sanctuarie, and Abiuration.

Sanctuarie in Greeke called *Asylum*, and by some in Latin termed *Templum misericordiæ* is a place priuileged by the King or chiefe gouernor of a country, for the safegard of the life of such a person as doth offend the king, his Lawes, crowne, and dignitie royall. Which priuileged places were deuised and instituted by the lawe of mercie vpon deuotion, and the great reuerence and honour that Princes & chiefe Rulers had to such places, wherein they graunted such priuiledges. As, first almighty God himselfe the chiefe Author of mercie gaue in charge to his seruant *Moses* (when the children of Israel were in their peregrination towards the land of Promise) that certaine Cities or places of refuge or Sanctuarie might be prouided for those to flie vnto, and to escape the hands of the reuengers of blood, who should by mischance and not willingly slay others: And after, the same people being setled in the same Land, he caused *Iosua* to execute the same commandement by assigning six cities to that purpose. And, long time after that, *Mulmutius Dunwallo* one of the renowned kings of the Brittons, who made many most worthy lawes for the well gouerning of his subiects (which were called *Mulmutius* Lawes) at the least 440. yeares before the natiuitie of our Sauior Christ ordained for Sanctuaries, places of priuiledge or defence of mans life, certaine Temples, and the foure great high waies which he before had caused to be made, or begunne, at his owne charges, viz, Fosse, Watling streete, Erming streete, and Ikeneld streete, and in some cases, and for some purposes euery plough: which Franchises or Liberties *Belinus* his sonne did after more fully effect and confirme. And some of the ancient Princes, Kings, or Gouernors in this Realme, graunted places of defence, or sanctuarie to such as should commit treason, & some others to such as should commit murder, robberie, burglarie, or other offences whatsoeuer, which in that point was further than the priuiledge which God gaue to his owne Sanctuarie, that was ordained onely for him which should kill another vnwillingly: for God commanded, that if any did slay his neighbor vpon malice prepenced, or by assault, he should be taken from his Altar, and put to death.

What Sanctuarie is.

Deut.19.

By whome Sanctuaries were instituted.

Iosua.20

Exodus 21

2 Abiuration is an othe that a man or woman doth take, when they haue committed felonie, and do flie to a Church, or churchyard for the safegarde of their liues, choosing rather to be perpetually banished out of the realme, than to stand to the Lawe, and to be tried of the felony: and this was one of saint

What Abiuration is.

Edwards Lawes that was King of this Realme before the Conquest, and instituted by him, which is also founded upon the Lawe of Mercy, that the Kings of this Realme did extend, for the great reverence that they did beare to the Temple of God, and to places dedicated to him, which was alwayes used sithence that time without alteration untill the one and twentie yeare of King Henry the eight. And this abiuration is an attainder in it selfe of felo- St.21.H.8.2.
nie that is confessed; which attainder by confession is the most strong that may be, for the vehement presumption that it hath of trueth: for it should be very absurd to say that he hath not committed such a felonie when the partie himselfe hath confessed it to the overthrow of himselfe and all his posteritie.

All Sanctuaries be extinguished.

3 By the Statute of Anno 32.H.8. it was enacted, That all Sanctua- St.32.H.8.12.
ries and places priviledged, which have beene used or taken for Sanctuarie (except parish churches and their churchyards, cathedrall churches, hospitalls, and churches collegiate, and all chappels dedicate, used as parish churches, and the Sanctuaries to everie of them belonging: and except such places and territories as hereafter be appointed to be places of tuition and priviledge, viz. Welles, Westminster, Northampton, Norwich, Yorke, Darbie, Launceston, and Westchester) shall be utterly extinguished, adnulled, and voide for ever. And by the Statute of Anno 22.H.8. it was ordained, St.22.H.8.14.
That if any person flie or resort to any parish church, Cemitorie, or other like halowed place for tuition of his life, by occasion of any murder, robbery, or other felony by the same person committed, and thereupon confesse any murder, felonie, or other offence before the Coroner, wherefore the same person by the Lawes of this Realme heretofore used, should abiure and passe out of the same, The same person thereupon shall abiure from all his libertie of this Realme, and from his liberall and free habitations, resorts and passages, to, and from the universall places of this Realme, which appertaine to the libertie of the Kings subiects undefamed, and shall forthwith be directed by the Coroner, taking and recording such abiuration, to any one Sanctuary within this Realme, which the same person will elect and chose, there to remaine as a Sanctuary person abiured during his life, and to be sworne before the Coroner so to doe, and to be marked with a hot yron upon the brawne of the thumbe of the right hand, according to the statute of Anno 21.H.8.2. And St.21.H.8.2
by the statute made Anno 1.Iac.25. it was enacted, That so much of all St.1.Iac.25
Statutes as concerneth abiured persons, and Sanctuaries, or ordering or governing of persons abiured, or in Sanctuaries made before the five and thirtieth yeere of the late Queene Elizabeths raigne, shall stand repealed, and be voide. And so all Sanctuaries being adnulled and extinguished by the foresaid statute of 32.H.8.12. saving churches, and churchyards, which were Sanctuaries by the common Law, and saving Welles, Westminster, Northampton, &c. erected and made by the said Statute of 32.H.8.12. & 33.H.8.15. which are also sithence extinguished and adnulled by the foresaide statute of 1.Iac.25. And therefore by no Lawes or Statutes that wee have in force, there be any Sanctuaries remaining: neither can any person take the benefit of Sanctuary in any place, or in any case, where there is no such thing in rerum natura (saving churches and churchyards) which never were Sanctuaries above fortie dayes at the uttermost, and that but in certaine Cases, and yet now out of use. But whether by the strict course of the common Lawes or any Statute in force, they be now to any intent in force, or not. Quære.

Abiuration by the cōmō Lawe out of the Realme.

Abiuration to a place within this Realme.

Quære. And for that so much of all stat. as concerneth abiured persons, or ordering, or gouerning of abiured persons, made before an̄ 35. El. be repealed and made void by the before rehearsed Statute of 1. Iac. 25. viz. the statute of 21. H.8.2. 22.H.8.14. 27.H.8.19. 32.H.8.3. 32.H.8.12. And by that means abiuration at the common law is restored to his former course, I will therefore write so much of abiuration, and abiured persons, as is warranted by the common lawes of this Realme onely, and not by any Statute, sauing by the statute of Articuli cleri, made an̄ 9. Ed.2.10. which is rather a confirmation or exposition of the common law, than a new law, and except so much as is contained or mentioned in the statute of 35. Eliz. 1. & 2. or in any other law made sithence that time, which I doe rather set downe that the Reader may knowe what the law hath bene, or is, then how it is vsed, and put in practise.

No abiuration for high treason.

4 Abiuration doth not lie for him which offendeth in high treason, because the Coroner cannot attaint him vpon his confession thereof, for that he is not his Iudge of that offence, neither can he be Iudge as Coroner, though hee haue a commission from the King to doe it. And if the offendor being in a Church would of purpose confesse a felonie, to the intent to escape Treason, yet if the Coroner be informed that hee is charged with treason, hee ought not to suffer him to abiure, and that for the Kings aduantage: for it is better for the King to attaint him of Treason, than of felonie, in respect of the Escheat, which in case of Treason doth wholly belong to the King, of whomsoeuer the offendors lands be holden. And the same law is in petit Treason; for the Coroner ought not to record his abiuration thereof, any more than hee may doe of high Treason: Neither the Coroner ought to let him passe by abiuration of another felonie, if he be informed that the offendor hath committed petit treason, and that for the grieuousnesse of the offence, though the King shall receiue no more benefit in petit treason, than in felonie. And the statutes which were made in the time of K. H.8. touching abiuration, be a speciall argument and proofe thereof; which doe onely make mention of abiuration for murder and felonie, but not for petit treason.

No abiuration for petit treason.

St.21.H.8.2 22.H.8.14. 27.H.8.19 32.H.8.12

Fi.Cor.420 9.Ed.4.28

No abiuration for the robber of a Church.

5 If a man doe robbe a Church and flie to another Church for the said offence, and there would abiure, he shall not be receiued thereunto, but shall violently be pulled forth of the Church, and thrust into prison. Quia frustra legis auxilium inuocat, qui in lege delinquit.

Fit. cor.313 9.E.4.28.

No abiuration for a man attainted.

6 If a man that is attainted of felonie, and in carrying to the gallowes to be put to death, doe escape from the Sherife, and flie to a Church, he cannot abiure, and though the Coroner would take his abiuration, and let him goe at libertie, the Sherife may take him againe, and put him to execution, notwithstanding the said abiuration, for it is void, and the Coroner in that case shalbe grieuously amerced for this escape, and so shall the towne where he was let at libertie; and the reason is, for that a man cannot haue two Iudgements for one offence. And so it is, and for the same reason, if a man that is attainted of felonie, and is carried to the gallowes, and hanged, breaketh the halter, falleth downe, and then riseth vp, and doth flie to a Church, he cannot abiure, but must be taken againe by the Sherife, & hanged vntill he be dead, according to his iudgement.

Fi.Cor.335

7 If

No abiuratiō for a man before abiured.

7 If a man doe abiure the Realme before a Coroner for felonie, and after doth returne into the Realme without the Kings pardon, and then flie to a Church, and would abiure againe, he shall not be allowed so to do, but shall be taken forth by violence, and put to execution, for that he was before attainted of felonie vpon his owne confession, and had his iudgement of abiuration, and cannot be twice attainted, or haue two iudgements. 9.Ed.4.28 8.H.4.3. Fi.Cor.410

Where an offendor may by violence bee drawne out of a Church.

8 If a man doe flie to a Church, claiming the priuiledge therof for the safeguard of his life, in some cases he may be drawne forth of the same by violence: as, if he come into the Church to claime the benefit thereof for an vnlawfull cause at the beginning, viz. for treason, robbing of a Church, beeing formerly abiured, or such like, in those cases he may be drawne forth of the Church by violence, by the people of the same towne: and in like sort, if he doe flie to a Church, and saith he doth take it for the safeguard of his life, and will not declare that he hath committed felonie, and that therefore he claimeth the priuiledge of the Church: in that case the officers of the towne may by strength take him out of the Church. But if he doe say that he doth take the Church for felonie, that is sufficient, without declaring what felonie, or the manner thereof: for he is not bound to shewe that but to the Coroner before whom hee doth make his abiuration, and then he must confesse and shew the yeare, day, and place, where, and when the felonie was committed, for that iudgement is to be giuen vpon his confession, which must be grounded vpon certaintie. 3.H.7.12. Bro.Cor. 180.

The offendors confessiō before the Coroner.

Tarrying in a Church aboue the time appointed.

9 If an offendors being in a Church were once lawfull, although he tarrie there aboue the time which the law hath appointed him, yet hee ought not for that cause be drawne out of the Church by violence, but meat and drinke shall be withholden from him, and euery person shall be forbidden to succour him: and he that doth relieue him shalbe punished at the Kings suit: which punishment some doe affirme shalbe, for a lay man death, and for a Clerke banishment; for he that taketh a Church for felonie, ought not to tarrie there aboue one night, if a Coroner will come vnto him, and be ready to take his abiuration, otherwise he may tarrie there fourtie daies. Fi.Cor.313 Britton. Bracton.

The manner of abiuration.

10 The manner of abiuration is, that he who taketh a Church, ought to declare that he doth take it for felonie which he hath committed: and when the Coroner commeth, he must confesse before him the felonie certainely, viz. the yeare, day, and place, where, and when hee committed the felonie, and pray to abiure the Realme, and to haue the tuition of the Church vntill he can prouide for his iourney: and this confession must be taken by the Coroner himselfe, and not by his deputie. And then he shal take an oath, which is his abiuration, in this manner: viz. Heare you this Master Coroner, That I A.B. am a theefe of two beasts (or a killer of a man) and a felon of the kings of England: and because I haue committed many offences and thefts in this Realme, I doe abiure the Kingdome of our Soueraigne Lord King James: And I must make haste towards the port of S. which thou hast giuen mee: And I must not goe out of the high waie; and if I doe, then I yeeld to bee taken as a theefe and felon of our Soueraigne Lord the Kings, & at ye port I will diligently seeke passage, and will not tarrie there but one flowing and ebbing Bracton. Britton.

The oath of abiuration.

if

if I may haue passage: And if I cannot haue passage in this time, I will go euery day vp to the knees into the sea, assaying to passe ouer. And if I cannot do it within fourtie daies together, I will returne to the Church as a thiefe and felon of our soueraigne Lord the King: So helpe me God, &c. And notwithstanding the words of the said oath, the offendor & not the Coroner ought to make the election of the port, whither he will goe, & where he will make his passage, and he must make his abiuration at the dore of the Church-yard.

Fi. Cor. 407 Britton. 11 He that doth abiure the Realme must haue vpon him but his coate, his shirt, and his breeches, and his head shalbe vncouered, & he must carrie a crosse in his hand, which (as Polidore saith) is a token that his life is saued by religion: and whatsoeuer he hath beside, is forfeited to the King, and neither the Coroner nor any of his seruants shall take any thing of the offendors for their fee. The attire of an abiured person.

St. 9. E. 2. 10 12 By the Statute of Lincolne made an. 9. E. 2. They they that abiure the Realme so long as they be in the high way shalbe in the Kings peace, and bee troubled of no man. And whilest they be in the Church, their keepers shall not tarie in the Church-yard, except necessitie, or perill of escape doe require it: and so long as they be in the Church, they shall not be compelled to depart, but may haue those things which be necessarie for their liuelihood, and may go forth to discharge nature. But if an abiured person be molested in the high way, and drawne out of the way, and imprisoned, yet that will not excuse him when he is againe at libertie, if he doe not within conuenient time after his libertie, returne to the way leading him to the port or place whereunto vpon his abiuration he made choice to goe. But if he doe goe out of the high way vpon ignorance, or to ease nature, that shall not hurt him, so that he doe returne to the high way in conuenient time, or doe his good will to returne. The vsing of persons abiured.

7. H. 7. 7. Fi. Cor. 14

13 After abiuration if the offendor doe any thing contrarie to his oath, viz. contrary to his abiuration, he shalbe put to execution, vnlesse he be a Clerke, and in that case shalbe saued from death by his Clergie: & because the Prelates and Clergie did complaine in Parliament, that though a Clerke ought not to be iudged by a temporall Judge, nor any thing may be done against him that concerneth life or member; neuerthelesse temporall Judges caused Clerks flying vnto the Church, and confessing their offences to abiure the Realme, and for that cause admitted their abiurations, although hereupon they cannot bee their Judges, and that so power was wrongfully giuen to Laie persons in the punishment of such Clerks. And if such should chance after to returne into the Realme, the said Prelates and Clergie desired such remedie to bee prouided therein, that the immunitie or priuiledge of the Church may be preserued vnbroken. Vpon which request by a Stat. made an. 9. E. 2. intituled Articuli cleri, it was enacted, That a Clerke flying to the Church for felonie, to obtaine the priuiledge of the Church, shall not be compelled to abiure the realme, but yeelding himselfe to the law of the realme, shall enioy the priuiledge of the Church, according to the laudible custome of the Realme heretofore vsed. Which said Statute being but a rehersall, restoring, and confirmation of the common law, is thought not to be repealed by the words of the foresaid stat. of 1. Iac. And so it appeareth by this stat. that if he which doth flie to a Church, will say that hee After abiuration broken, death.

St. 9. E. 2. 15

1. Iac. 25.

is

A Clerke need not abiure.

is a Clerke, he shall not be compelled to abiure, and if he doe abiure of his own good will, and thereby doth lose his lands, yet to saue him from execution hee shall haue his Clergie. S. St. 28. H. 8. 1. Clergie 5.

Where no felonie no abiuration for felonie.

14 A maried wife beeing desirous to bee deliuered from her husband, did flie to a Church, and acknowledged a felonie, where she neuer had committed any felonie, and desired to abiure: and her husband vnderstanding of it came to her, and then shee fled out of the Church and escaped, and towne or person were amerced for this escape: for there could no felon escape where no felonie was committed. Neither can there be any abiuration where no felonie is committed. And therefore an offendor cannot abiure for petit larcenie.

Fi. Cor. 415

Br. Cor. 182

The abiured pleadeth that he is not the same person.
The Kings pardon.

15 He that doth abiure, and is taken againe, and arraigned, may plead that he is not the same person which did abiure, and then that shalbe tried by the Coroner who tooke his abiuration: Or hee may plead the Kings pardon granted to him of the felonie and abiuration: for if the pardon make no mention of the abiuration, it is not good. S. Pardon 7.

Fi. Cor. 124

9. E. 4. 28.

A Recusant vsing conuenticles shall abiure the realm.

16 By the statute of an 35. El. it was ordained, that if any person or persons aboue the age of sixteene yeares, which shall offend against the said Acte (in persuading others to impugne the Queenes Ecclesiasticall lawes) shall not within three moneths after they shall be conuicted for their said offence, conforme themselues to the obedience of the Lawes and Statutes of this Realme, in comming to Church to heare diuine Seruice, and in making such publike confession and submission, as in the said Act is expressed, beeing thereunto required by the Bishop of the Dioces, or any Iustice of the Peace in the same countie, where the said person shall happen to be, or by the minister or Curat of the Parish: In euery such case, euery such offendor beeing thereunto warned or required by any such Iustice of Peace of the same Countie where such offendors shall happen to be, shall vpon his or their corporall Oath, before the Iustices of the Peace in the open Quarter Sessions of the same Countie where such offendors shall then bee, or at the Assises and Gaole Deliuerie of the same Countie, before the Iustices of the same Assises and Gaole Deliuerie, abiure the Realme of England, and all other the Queenes Dominions for euer (vnlesse her Maiestie shall licence the parties to returne:) and thereupon shall depart out of the Realme, at such Hauen or Port, and within such time as shall in that behalfe be assigned and appointed by the said Iustices, before whom such abiuration shalbe made, vnlesse the same offendor bee letted or staied by such lawfull and reasonable meanes or causes, as by the common lawes of this Realme are permitted and allowed in cases of abiuration for felonie. And in such cases of let or stay, then within such reasonable and conuenient time after, as the common law requireh in case of abiuration for felony, as is aforesaid. And the Iustices of peace before whom any such abiuration shall happen to be made, as is aforesaid, shall cause the same presently to be entered of Record before them, and shall certifie the same to the Iustices of Assises and Gaole deliuerie of the said Countie at the next Assises or Gaole deliuerie to be holden in the same countie. And if any such offendor

St. 35. El. 1

which

which by the tenour and intent of this act is to be abiured as is aforesaid, shall refuse to make such abiuration as is aforesaid, or after such abiuration made, shal not go to such hauen, and within such time as is before appointed, & from thence depart out of this Realme according to this present act, or after such his departure shall returne or come againe into any the Qu. Realmes or Dominions without her speciall licence in that behalfe first had and obtained: Then in euery such case the person so offending shalbe adiudged a felon, and suffer as in case of felonie, without benefit of Clergie. If any person or persons that shal at any time offend against this act, shall before he or they be so warned or required to make abiuration, according to the tenour of this act, repaire to some parish Church on some sonday, or other festiuall day, and then and there heare diuine seruice, and at Seruice time before the Sermon, or reading of ye gospel, make publike and open submission and declaration of his and their conformity to her Maiesties lawes and statutes, as in this act is hereafter declared & appointed: That then the same offendor shall thereupon be cleerely discharged of and from all the penalties and punishments inflicted or imposed by this act for any of the offences aforesaid. Prouided that no Popish Recusant or feme couert shalbe compelled to abiure by vertue of this act: Prouided also that euery person that shall abiure by force of this act, or refuse to abiure, being thereunto required, as is aforesaid, shal forfeit and lose to her Maiestie all his goods and cattels, and all his lands, tenements, and hereditaments, during his life only, and no longer. But his wife shal not lose her dower, neither shall his blood be corrupt. S. Felonie by stat. 9.

St 35. El. 2. 17 By a statute made an 35. El. 2. (intituled an act for the restraining of Popish Recusants to some certaine place of abode) it is ordained, That Recusants not conforming themselues to the obedience of the lawes of this realme, in comming to the Church to heare diuine seruice, which shall not vpon the request of two Justices of peace, or Coroner of the same countie, abiure ye realm, and depart for the same, and not returne without the Queenes licence, shalbe adiudged felons, and suffer and lose as in case of felonie, without benefit of Clergie. S. Fel. by St. 10. Popish Recusants shall abiure the Realme.

St. 3. E. 1. 10 18 By the stat. of West. 1. made an 3. E. 1. it is enacted, That he which committeth trespasse in parkes or ponds shall abiure, if hee cannot find suretie no more to doe the like offence. But that abiuration is not for felonie, neither shal he forfeit his lands or goods. Abiuration of a Trespasser.

Pleading

Pleading not guiltie.

HAuing made mention of one of the pleas which a prisoner brought to the barre to be arraigned of Treason or Felonie doth plead, viz. of the Confession of the offence, and shewed how many sorts of Confessions of felonie the law doth take notice of, & by what meanes she doth procéed against the parties confessing: I am now to treat of a second, or one other plea, that the prisoner vpon his arraignment doth plead in his own defence, which is the plea of Not guiltie. For when a prisoner by an appeale, or an Inditement, is charged with treason, or felonie, he may estrange himselfe from the offence, if he will, and ioyne the same issue, which the defendant oft times doth in an action of trespasse, & some other personall actions, viz. he may plead and take for his issue, Not guiltie. This plea

Pleading not guilty the most common plea.

of not guiltie is the most common and vsual plea, that he which is arraigned of treason or felonie, hath to plead vpon an inditement, or an appeale: and it is yͤ plea whereunto euery person that is arraigned shall be enforced, vnlesse it be in speciall cases, viz. where he hath matter of Iustification, or matter in Law to plead. And this plea of Not guiltie doth tend to the fact, that is to the felony, and therefore it receiueth great fauour in Law: for the Law doth allow this 7.Ed.4.15.
plea to him who is arraigned after he hath pleaded in abatement, or barre of 4.H.6.15
the appeale, or inditement, so that his barre doe not comprehend such matter 4.H.7.5. 10.H.4.4.
as doth confesse the felonie (as a Release of the appellant, or the Kings pardõ.) 9.H.4.2.
And that plea he shall haue also, though one of his pleas were matter in law: for though those pleas doe require diuers trials, yet in fauour of life hee shall 28.Ed.3.92.
haue both those pleas, as well as he shall haue when he doth plead matter tri- 22.E.4.39.
able by the Bishop, or by Record, viz. and moreouer not guiltie. Which pleas 27.Al.p.3 14.Ed.4.7

Pleading not guilty after other pleas.

he shall haue notwithstanding he doe not conclude, moreouer not guiltie, that is to say, he shall come time enough to plead not guiltie after the matter triable by the Bishop, or by Record, is found against him. And the manner of pleading in all those cases is to plead his plea, and to pray allowance thereof, and ouer to the felonie not guiltie.

Upon the plea of not guilty no coũcel allowed.

2 Upon this plea of onely not guiltie, the partie indited shall not haue coũcell learned in the law to plead for him, or to say any thing in his behalfe in the same

same plea (vnlesse it be in an appeale, which is the suit of the partie) for when ẏ offendor is put to answer to an inditement of treason or felonie, he must answer it in proper person, and not by atturney, or councel learned: For this plea of Not guiltie doth tend to the fact, ẏ which the party himselfe doth best know, and therefore hee can best make answer vnto it. And if his councell learned should plead his plea for him, and defend him, it may be that they would be so couert in their spéeches, and so shadow the matter with words, and so attenuate the proofs and euidence, that it would be hard, or long to haue the truth appeare. Also if the partie himselfe defend it, peraduenture his conscience will pricke him to vtter the truth, or his countenance, or gesture wil shew some to-
9.Ed.4.2. kens thereof, or by his simple spéeches somewhat may be drawne from him to bolt out the veritie of the cause, which would not be wonne of men learned in the law, who indeauour to speake prouidently, and artificially, which be the causes that the offendor shall answer in his owne person, and not by councell learned. And yet if the plea of the partie indited be such that it doth excéed his
1.H.7.15 learning and knowledge to answer, and plead vnto, then hee shall haue lear- Where councell shalbe allowed.
12.El. Dyer 296. ned councel assigned vnto him, though it be against the King. And one that is
7.H.4.36. in the Court at the time of the inditement or arraignment of a prisoner, may as Amicus Curiæ, informe the Court that there is a defect in the inditement, to the benefit of the prisoner. Informing the Court of a default.

Triall by Battell.

There is an auncient triall of the plea of Not guiltie by the common law, much used in former ages, which is triall by combate, viz. by Battell, which triall the defendant in an Appeale of felonie may choose, and combate with the Appellant, for the triall if he be guiltie or not of the felonie whereof the appellant hath commenced his appeale against him. And if the Appellee hath so good successe in that battell, that he doth therein vanquish the appellant, he shall barre him of his appeale for ever. And though this triall by battell is not so much in use as it was in the raignes of king Edward the 3. king Richard the 2. and king Henry the 4. yet is it at this day lawfull, and not so much disused, but it may be put in practise in an appeale, if the defendant will, and that there be no lawfull counter-plea thereof: Or else the defendant in an appeale may at his choyce plead not guiltie, and referre himselfe to be tried by the countrie. This triall in an appeale by battell shall be betweene the appellant and the appellee themselves, in their own persons, and not by Champions (as it is in a writ of right.) And this triall by battell is an auncient law of this realme, & it is also put in practise and allowed by the civill law; which it is thought the Romans learned and embraced, ever since that renowned combate that was fought in the time of Tullus Hostilius third king of the Romans, and of Metius Suffetius dictator of the Albans, betweene the three brethren Horatij Romans, and the three brethren Curiatij Albans, by the consent and in the presence of both the Captaines and Armies, for the perpetuall government of both the kingdomes: wherein M. Horatius vanquished, and slew in the field the three Curiatij, who presently before had killed his other two brethren, and by that meanes obtained to the Romans the perpetuall government of the citie and countrey of the Albans, and delivered his owne nation from continuall servitude.

Triall by battel, or by the countrey.

37.H.6.3

Tit.Liu.l.1

The forme of trial by battel.

2 The order and forme of triall by Battell is this: when the defendant in an appeale hath pleaded not guiltie, ready to defend the same by his body, hee must cast his gauntlet into the court, and if the Pl. wil reioyne to the Battel,

hee

Fit.Cor.385 hée must take vp the Gauntlet: But if the Plaintife will counterplead the Battell, then hée must let the Gauntlet lie: and then the Defendant may demurre in law thereupon, if he do let his gauntlet lie. If it be in an appeale of death, and that the appellant and the appellée doe ioyne in wager of Battell, the Appellant shall rehearse his appeale word by word, as he did at the first, and the appellée shall likewise make his defence, as he did at the first: and then the defendant shall wage the battel in this manner, viz. Thomas the ap-
17.E.3.2. pellée shall with his left hand take I. the appellant by the right hand, and lay
17.Ass.p.1
9.H.4.4 his owne right hand vpon a booke, and say thus: Heare you this, you man, which doe call your selfe John by your name of Baptisme, that I man, which doe call my selfe Thomas by name of Baptisme, such a day, and such an year, did not kill William your father by name, as you doe surmise, neither am I guiltie of this felonie, so helpe me God, and shall kisse the booke: and this I will defend against you by my bodie, as this Court will award. And after I. the Appellant shall with his left hand take T. the appellée by the right hand, and lay his owne right hand vpon the Booke, and say in this manner: Heare you this, you man, which by name of Baptisme doe call your selfe Thomas, that you furiously such a day, and in such a yeare, did kill William by name, my Father, so helpe me God, and shall kisse the Booke: and this I will iusti-fie against you by my bodie, as this Court will award. And the Court shall appoint them a day to make their combate, and the appellée shall put in pled-ges to the Court, to performe the battell, and to defend himselfe: and the plaintife shall put in pledges to deraigne the battell at the day assigned: And the Appellant shall goe at libertie, and the appellée shall bée kept in prison at ease, and haue sufficient meat and drinke. And the Marshall shall apparell the appellant and the appellée both alike at their owne costes, the night before the combate shall be fought, to the ende that they may bée in the field the next morning, ready to performe the combate, by the sunne rising. And the ap-pellées head shall be polled, but not the appellants: and the Marshall shall bring them attired into the field ready to performe the Battell. Which com-
19.H.6.35 bate shall be tried before the Iustices, who shall cause Proclamation to bée
Br. Battel 16 made when they be set, and the Appellant and the Appellée be within the lists,
Bracton de cor.ca.21 ready to atchieue the combate, That none, but the two combaters shall be so hardie to stirre, or make any noyse, whatsoeuer he shall sée, or heare, whereby the battell may be disturbed: And whosoeuer shall doe any thing contrarie to
Britton. the said Proclamation, shall bée imprisoned a yeare and a day. And they shall fight with weapons of small length, béeing bare headed, and hauing their hands and féet bare, with two staues of one length, horned at both endes. And either of thẽ shall haue a Scutchian foure cornerd, without any yron, for that
Bracton de one shall not hurt the other with the yron. And if the appellée can defend him-
coron.c.21. selfe vntill Starres may be séene in the firmament, then he shal goe quit from the appellant. And also when the appellant and the appellée be in the field ready to ioyne battell, or in the Battell, it is a sufficient vanquishment if the
21.H.6.34. appellant will confesse his appeale to be false: for by this acknowledgement,
Fi.Cor.98 he shalbe adiudged to be ouercome in the field, and barred of his appeale for e-uer. And on the other side, if the appellée doe confesse himselfe in the field to
Bracton de be vanquished, he shalbe presently hanged: As in an appeale the defendant
coron c.21. pleaded not guiltie, and made his choyce to trie it by Battel, and as they were
19.H.6.35. in the combate, ÿ appellant cast ÿ appellée to the ground, & did grieuously beat him, and the Iustices sent for the appellée, and when he was brought vnto

them, they demanded of him, if he would any more of the battell, or not: who answered, that he would not: and said further, that by the oath which hee had taken, hee was not guiltie of the felonie whereof he was appealed: to whom the Iustices said, That if he would any more of the battell, he should be laid in the same sort that he was when they sent for him: but he answered, that he would no more of the battell, and therefore hee was presently hanged.

The reason why the def. may be tried by battel in appeale.

3 The reason why in an appeale the Defendant shall bee admitted to trie his cause by Battell is, for that no euident or probable matter doth appeare against him to proue him guiltie of the felonie whereof hee is appealed, but onely the bare accusation of the Appellant, which is no witnesse of credit in his owne cause. And therefore seeing the appellant doth demaund iudgement of death against the Appellee by an appeale, and hath no other probable euidence to attaint him, but his owne accusation, it is more reason, that the appellant shall aduenture his life with the appellee for the triall thereof, if the defendant doe require it, than to put the triall thereof vpon the countrey (which for default of euidence may be ignorant of the truth thereof, and so giue a false verdit) and by that meanes to leaue it to God (to whom the truth of all things be knowne) to giue the verdit in this cause, by attributing the victorie or vanquishment to which partie it shall please him.

Counter-pleas to the battel.

4 If the appellant haue any vehement presumption, or sufficient testimony, to proue that his appeale is true, it will bee a good counter-plea, and sufficiently serue him to put the appellee from his triall by Battell: As, if the Defendant were indited of this Felonie before the appeale commenced, or 22.E.4.19.
was taken with the manoure, or was taken with a bloodie knife, or other wea- 20.E.4.6
pon, ouer the bodie of him that was slaine, or neere vnto him, whereby there 14.E.4.7.
was vehement suspition that he killed him, or that the defendant did lie a- 4.Ass.p.1
lone in the house with him that was killed, or that he and others did lie in the Bracton de
house with him that was slaine, and receiued no blowes or wounds in his de- corõ c.18.
fence, or that he made no Huy and Crie after the theeues or murderers to ap- Britton.
prehend them, or that he will not confesse which of those that were in the house with him, did kill the man that was slaine, or committed the felonie that was done, or that he receiued the man that was slaine into his house, which was seene to goe in aliue, and after was found dead there, and no meane proued how he came by his death.

Taken with the manoure.

5 If the Defendant be taken with the manoure (as in an appeale of death, with a bloodie knife, or other weapon) he shalbe barred from waging of battel. And so it shall be if he be taken with the manoure in an appeale of Robberie, 7.H.4.44
which manoure the plaintife must bring into the Court at the time when the Fit. cor.230
Appellee doth offer to ioyne in battell, or otherwise he must plead that the Ap- 4.Ed.3.9
pellee was taken with the manoure, which manoure hee would haue brought into the Court, but that he was not able to bring it: or else hee may say that the

the manoure is in the possession of another, and pray the Court to write for it. To which manoure when it commeth into the Court, the defendant shall haue no trauerse, or other exception, if the thing brought into the Court for the manoure, doe not varie from those goods, or things which be contained in the Appeale. And in appeale of robberie, if the Appellee be apprehended vpon fresh suit by Huy and Crie, and some of the money robbed be taken in his custodie, this is a sufficient taking with the manoure to put him from waging of Battell, though the money cannot be knowne from other money. And the reasons why in an appeale of robberie, the defendant being taken with the manoure, shall not wage battell against the appellant be, for that by the Appeale the plaintife doth endeauour to attaint the Appellee of felonie, and also to haue his goods againe. And it may be, that if it should be tried by Battell, the Appellee might vanquish the Appellant in combate (though the appellee be guiltie of the felonie) and by that meanes also retaine his goods stollen, without cause. And the manoure was accounted so pregnant an euidence in former ages, that the Justices would as readily arraigne a prisoner vpon the manoure taken in his possession, as vpon an inditment.

22.Ed.4.19 Fi.Cor.375

Taken with the manoure.

6 It is also a good counter-plea to the battell, for the Appellant to say, that the defendant when he was taken or arrested for that felonie whereof the appeale is sued, and therefore imprisoned, did breake the prison, and escaped, or did what he could to escape: for it is a very great presumption against him, that he is guiltie of the felonie whereof he is appealed, in that hee did breake the prison and flie, or would haue fled for the felonie: and that hee did not relie vpon, and trust to his innocencie, and be iustified and tried by the law. And the Appellee may reply to that counter-plea, and trauerse the arrest for felonie, or the breaking of the prison, if he will, or he may plead the Kings pardon for the breaking of the prison: which trauerse or pardon being tried, or allowed, he shalbe restored to his triall by battell.

Breaking of prison.

Fi.Cor.251 281 1.Asp.6.

1.As.p.3 Fi.Cor.154 157.

7 As there be impediments of the defendants part, why he may not wage battell against the appellant, so be there lets of the appellants part, that the appellee cannot wage battell against him: for as vehement presumptions of the defendants guiltinesse be causes to put him from waging of battell, so be vehement presumptions of the appellants infirmities, or weakenesse, sufficient barres to exclude the appellee from triall by battell with him. As, if the appellant be within the age of fouretéene yéeres, or aboue the age of thréescore and tenne yéeres, or within orders, or a woman, or be maihemed; whether he were maihemed by the appellee at the time that the saide appellee robbed him, or at any other time; or (as some doe affirme) whether he was maihemed by the appellee, or by any other. And some doe holde it for Lawe, that if the appellant be aboue the age of thréescore yeares, the appellee shall no more wage battell against him, than against an infant within age, or a woman. But if the appellee will wage battell being of that age, he may, for though he may discharge himselfe of battell, in respect of his saide age, if hée will, yet in that the Lawe hath giuen him his choice, whether he will be tried by battell, or by the Countrey, hée may refuse the benefit of his age, and wage battell.

Lets of trial by battell on the plaintifes part.

Fi.Cor.230 268. 22.E.4.20

Bracton.

Priuiledge of the Appellãts person.

8 In some cases the priuiledge of the person of the appellant shall put the appellee from the triall by battel with him: as the person of the King, when the defendant is arraigned at his suit in an appeale; for in an arraignment vpõ an Indictment at his suit, the partie indited shall not wage battell, for the vehement presumption that the Inditement is true, being found by the oathes of twelue lawfull men of the Countrey. And as the person of the King shall be exempt from battell, so shall all other, to whom the King shal please to grant such an exemption: As in former ages such a graunt hath beene made by some King of this Realme, to the Citizens of London, that battel shal not be waged against any of them in any appeale whatsoeuer, brought by any of them. And if a citizen of London will bring an appeale against another, and the defendant will offer to wage battell with him, though the Appellant would refuse the benefit of this priuiledge, and ioyne battell with him, yet the battell shall not be performed; for the Mayor and Comminaltie of London must sue a writ out of the Chauncerie, directed to the Judges, where that triall should bee made, rehearsing their libertie, and pray allowance thereof, to stay the trial by battell. And though in the foresaid case (and other cases, where counter-pleas to battell be pleaded) the plaintife doth count, that if the defendant will denie it, he is ready to proue it by his body, yet the defendant in his plea cannot take aduantage thereof, for those be but words of forme, and not of substance: and notwithstanding this conclusion, he may make his trial by the countrie, or otherwise as the law will.

The King.

Plo.com. 335.

Citizens of London.

Fi.Cor. 125 157.

Fi.Cor. 125

9 By the Statute of an 6. R.2. it was enacted, That if any Noble mans daughters, Ladies, or other women be rauished, and after the same rape committed, doe consent to the Rauishers, the husbands of such women (if they haue husbands) or if they haue no husbands liuing, then their fathers, or other their next kinsmen in blood, shall haue the suit to prosecute, and may pursue against the same offendors and rauishers in this behalfe, and to conuict them of felonie, though the same woman after the rape doe consent to the rauishers. And in this case the defendant shall not wage battell, but the truth of the matter shall be tried by the countrey. S. Felonies by Stat. 2.

St.6.R.2.6.

No wager of battell in appeale of Rape.

10 If one man doe appeale diuers men of one felonie, and they all ioyne in battell with the Appellant, he must fight with them all, one after another, if it doe not so chance that he is slaine by one of them, before he can performe the battell with the residue: which if it happen, all the residue of the defendants shall be discharged of the appeale. But if when the Appellant doth come into the field to fight with one of the Appellees, he will then confesse his appeale to be false towards him, yet that shall not discharge the residue of the appeale, but they shall proceed in their triall with the appellant. And likewise if one man be appealed by three men of seuerall felonies, and he doe plead not guiltie, ready to trie it by his bodie, in this case hee must fight with them all, one after another, and though he doe vanquish or kill one of them, this will not discharge him against the other. But if three men doe appeale one man but of one felonie, then if the Appellee doe vanquish one of them, he shalbe discharged against the other two. And in that case if the said three Appellants be Approuers, then the other two shalbe hanged.

One fighting with seueral men.

47.E.3.5. 19.H.6.35

Fi.Cor.98

Bracton de cor.ca.19

7.Ed.3.11

11 And all that is before written touching Triall by Battell, may be applied, as well to the appeale of an approuer, who confesseth himselfe to be a felon, as to an appeale commenced by a true man. An Appeale by approuer.

Fi. Droit. 57 12 If a man be appealed of felonie, and wageth battell with the appellant, and after he doth become blinde by infirmitie, and not by his owne procurement, he shall be discharged of the battel: (and so it is in a writ of Right:) for in this case the appellée hath pleaded such a plea as the Lawe doth allowe him: and his disabilitie to performe it commeth by the act of God. But if after the Defendant hath waged battell with the appellant, the same appellant shall become blinde, by what meanes soeuer, the appellée shall be arraigned at the Kings suite. S. Appeales. 96. The Appellée wageth battell, and then becommeth blinde.

Triall by Peeres.

Triall of the plea Not guiltie.

When the Defendant hath pleaded Not guiltie to an appeale, or an indictment, then the matter commeth to be tried betwéene the King and him, or the appellant and him, whether he be guiltie, or not. If it be in an appeale, it may be tried by Verdict, or by Battell, as the appellée will, sauing in certaine Cases: But vpon an Indictment there is no triall by battell, nor otherwise, sauing onely by verdict. In an Indictment of treason or felonie against one of the Peeres of the Realme, the triall is by his Péeres, which manner of triall in an appeale is not allowable.

The arraignment of a Péere of the Realme.

2 When a Péere of the Realme, and Lord of the parliament is to be arraigned vpon any treason, or felonie whereof he is indicted, and whereunto he hath pleaded Not guiltie, the King by his Letters patents shall assigne some great and sage Lord of the parliament to be high Steward of England for the day of his arraignement: who before the same day shall make a precept to his Serieant at Armes, that is appointed to serue him during the time of his Commission, to warne to appeare before him eightéene or twentie Lords of the parliament vpon the same day. And then at the day appointed, when the high Steward shall be set vnder the cloth of Estate, vpon the arraignement of the prisoner, and hath caused his Commission to be read, the same Serieant shall returne his precept, and thereupon the Lords shall be called, and when they haue appeared, and be set in their places, the Constable of the Tower shall be called to bring his prisoner into the Court, who then shall bring the prisoner to the Barre. And then the high Steward shall declare vnto the prisoner, the cause why the King hath assembled thither those Lords and him, and perswade him to answer without feare. And then hée shall cause the Clerke of the Crowne to reade his Indictment vnto him, and to aske him if hée be guiltie, or not; whereunto when hée hath aunswered Not guiltie, the Clerke of the Crowne shall aske him how he will be tried, and then he will say, by God & by his Péeres. And then the K. Serieants and

1.H.4.1. 13.H.8 13. 10.Ed.4.6.

Atturney

Atturney will giue Euidence against him, whereunto when the prisoner hath made answer, the Constable shall be commaunded to retire the prisoner from the Barre to some other place, while the Lords doe secretly conferre together in the Court: and then the Lords shall rise out of their places, and consult among themselues, and what they affirme, shall be done vpon their honours, without any othe to be ministred vnto them. And when they all, or the greatest part of them be agréed, they shall returne to their places, and sit downe. And then the high Steward shall aske of the yongest Lord by himselfe, if he that is arraigned be guilty, or not, of the offence whereof he is arraigned; and then of the yongest next him, and so of the residue, one by one, vntill he hath asked them all: and euery Lord shall answer by himselfe. And then the high Steward shall send for the prisoner againe, who shall be led to the Barre; to whom the high Steward shal reherse the verdict of the Péeres, and giue iudgement accordingly. But if an Earle the sonne and heire apparant of a Duke, or a Lord the sonne and heire apparant of a Marques, or Earle, be indicted of high treason, he shall be tried by Knights and Gentlemen, and not by Péeres: for he is not an Earle by Creation, but by Natiuitie. But if he be of dignity by creation, and a Lord of the Parliament, hee shall be tried by his Péeres.

38.H.8.Br. Treason 2

3 The foresaid manner of Triall séemeth to be appointed by the Statute of Magna Charta, which hath ordained, That no frée man shall be taken, or imprisoned or disseised of his fréehold, liberties, or frée customes, nor shall be outlawed, banished, or by any meanes brought to destruction: Neither wée will passe or sit in iudgement vpon him, but by the lawfull iudgement of his Péeres, or by the lawe of the Realme: We will not sell, deny, or deferre iustice or right to any. It appeareth by this statute of Magna Charta, that a Péere of the Realme shall be tried by his Péeres onely, in case where he is indicted at the Kings suite of treason, or felony, for the words of the statute be (we will not passe or sit in iudgement vpon him but by his Péeres:) But if an appeale of murder or other felony be sued by any common person against a Péere of the Realme, he shall be tried by common persons, and not by his Péeres. And because there was no mention made in the said statute of Magna Charta, how women, Ladies of great estate, because of their husbands Péeres of the Realme, married, or sole, viz. Duchesses, Countesses, or Baronesses, should be put to answer, nor before what Iudges they should be iudged vpon indictments of treasons or felonies by them committed: and for that the saide statute of Magna Charta doth onely make mention of a man: Therefore by a statute made Anno 20.H.6.9. it was enacted, That such Ladies of great estate, viz. Duchesses, Countesses, and Baronesses, which shall be indicted of any treason, or felony by them committed, whether they be married, or sole, shall be brought to their answer, and put to answer, and iudged before such Iudges and Péeres of the realme, as Péeres of the realme should be, if they were indicted or impeached of such treasons or felonies committed.

St.9.H.3. 29.

By whom Péeres appealed shal be tried.

10.Ed.4.6

St.20.H.6.9

By whom ladies shal be tried.

4 None of the foresaid statutes haue béene put in practise to extend to Bishops, though they enioy the name of Lords of the parliament, for they haue that name of Bishops in respect of their office, or function, and not in respect of

Bishops

of their nobilitie; neither haue they places in parliament in respect of their nobilitie, but in regard of their possessions, being ancient Baronies annexed to their dignities. If a Péere of the Realme be indicted of treason, or felonie, he may be thereupon arraigned in parliament, if it shall please the King: and then the Lords spirituall shall make one Procurator for them, for that by the Cannon lawe they cannot condemne any man to death. A Bishop was arraigned in the Kings Bench, (and not by any Lords of parliament) for that hée came to the parliament by summons, and departed without licence: and because this was an offence, as well to the King, as to the Péeres; and the King may commence a suite where he please for a trespas done to him, therefore this was accepted a lawfull indictment, though the complaint was made in an inferiour Court, for an offence done in an higher.

Arraignment in parliament. 10.E.4.6 3.E.3.19

Trial of treason committed in Ireland. 19.& 20.El. Dy. fo.360

5 If an Earle, or a Lord of Ireland doth commit treason in Ireland by open rebellion, he cannot be arraigned and put to his triall therefore in England: for he can neither be tried by his Péeres, nor by any Jurie of twelue men in England, because he is not a subiect of England, but of Ireland; and therefore his triall shall be in Ireland. And the custome there is to attaint a Péere by parliament, and not by his Péeres.

Misprision. The number of Péeres at the Triall.

6 This order of triall by the Péeres is likewise to be obserued, where one of the Péeres of this realme is indicted but of misprision of treason or felonie: in which triall the same forme shall be kept, as it shall be, where any Péere is indicted of treason or felonie, and arraigned thereupon. And the number of Péeres which shall be to trie a Péere indicted of treason, felonie, or misprision, shall be twelue at the least, and more if it shall please the King.

Triall by Péeres in all cases of treason and felony. St.33.H.8 23. St.35.H.8.2

7 In euery case where any offence or fact is of new made treason by any Statute, the Lords of the Parliament, and Péeres of the Realme offending therein, shall haue their triall by their Péeres, though the Statute doth not prouide for it by speciall words: as other inferiour persons offending in the like crimes, shal haue their triall by the verdict of twelue men, their péeres, viz. their equals; so that the words which be commonly put into new Statutes, that Péeres of the Realme offending therein, shalbe tried by their Péeres, bée not of necessity inserted. But because the course of the common law is in some sort altered by the statute of an 33.H.8.23. authorizing the King to graunt a commission vnto such persons, and into such shires as he will, for the triall of any murder committed in any other countie or place of the Realme whatsoeuer: And also by the Statute of 35.H.8.2. giuing the King like power to direct a commission into any countie of this Realme, and to any persons that he will, for the triall of treasons, and misprisions of treasons, committed out of the Realme: yet for that the triall in both those cases might be made by such persons, as the common law hath appointed, viz. of péeres by their péeres, it is so prouided and ordained by the special words of both those statutes.

Triall by the Countrie.

Triall by the Countrie, is a triall by twelue common persons of that vicenage or neighborhoode, where the treason or felony was committed: which kinde of triall seemeth also to be warranted and approued (though not at the first begunne) by the before rehearsed Statute of Magna Charta, which saith: Neither shall any passe or sit in iudgement vpon him, but by the lawfull iudgement of his Peeres, or by the Law of the realme. And thereupon it is accordingly vsed, that Knights, Esquiers, and Gentlemen of great estate being incited of treason or felony, be tried by their peeres, viz. by their equalls in degree, being also Knights, Esquiers, Gentlemen, or Merchants of good estate: and inferiour persons be likewise tried by their peeres or equalls, viz. by men of their owne degree, or (most commonly) by men of better or greater estate or degree.

Triall by the Country.

St. 9. H. 3. 29

1. M. Dy. 99

2 If he that is charged to be an offendour in petit treason, murder, or felonie, doe pleade to an Indictment found against him matter triable by an other Countie, than the Countie which did indict him, although by the common lawe he ought to haue beene tried in that forraine countie; yet now by the Statute of Anno 22. H. 8. he shall be tried by the countie which did indict him; the words of which Statute be these, viz. For more speedie trialles of murders and felonies, Be it enacted, &c. That all manner of forraine pleas, triable by the Countrie, hereafter to be pleaded by any person or persons arraigned vpon any Indictment for any petit treason, murder, or felonie, shalbe forthwith tried before the same Iustices, before whom such persons shall be arraigned, and by the same Iurors of the same countie, that shall trie the petit treason, murder, or felonie, whereof he shall so be arraigned, without any further respite or delay in whatsoeuer countie, or counties, place or places of this Realme, the matter of the same pleas be supposed or alleadged. This statute maketh no mētion of high treason, & therfore forrain pleas in high treason remaine to be tried in those forren counties, as they were at the cōmon lawe;

St. 22. H. 8. 14.

32. H. 8. 3

Triall of forraine pleas.

And

Appeale.

And so be they in an appeale: for this statute extendeth to Inditements onely. But if A. doe strike B. upon the Sea, and there giue him a mortall wound, whereof B. dieth in the Countie of L. in this case A. shall be discharged of the death of B. for they of the Countie of L. cannot inquire of the death without inquirie of the wound, and of the wound they cannot inquire, because it was giuen upon the Sea, and not in any Countie or place in this Realme. And they of the Admiralles Jurisdiction can not inquire as of a felonie of the wound, without inquiring of the death, and of the death they can not inquire, because it was within the body of a Countie, where by the statute of 13.R.2. & 15.R.2. they are forbidden to meddle.

Coke 2.93

A man stricken upon the Sea dieth upon the Land.

St. 13.R.2.5 St. 15.R.2.3.

The Processe against the Jurie.

3 The processe which shalbe awarded against the Jury to trie an issue in an appeale, is commonly a Venire facias, Habeas corpora, and Distringas, as it is used in other actions, sauing in the Kings Bench, for by the custome of that Court, the first processe against the Jurie, is an Habeas corpora, and after a Distresse, without suing a Venire facias. And some say, that in the K. Bench they use to haue no Habeas corpora at the first day, but a Venire facias, and then a Distresse, leauing out the Habeas corpora. The processe which is to be awarded against the Jury, is for the most part intended in an appeale: for in an Inditement though they may graunt processe against the Jury, yet it is not used by the Justices of Gaole deliuerie, because they doe take the pannell, which is returned by the Shirife, without making any precept unto him, for that they giue a generall commandement to the Shirife before their comming, to cause the Countrie to appeare before them. But so do not Justices of Oyer and Terminer.

27.H.6.10

Processe in an Appeale, not in an Inditement.

Fit. Enquest 55

Nisi prius for the defendant in appeale.

4 Although by the common Lawe a Nisi prius is grantable for the king, but not grantable against the king, where he is partie to the suite, or where the matter in question doth touch the kings right, or where he is party thereunto (but by aide praier,) unlesse his Atturney will assent thereunto: yet in an appeale of felonie, when the appellant and appellee be at issue, the Defendant may haue a Nisi prius to pursue the same issue, if there be any default in the Plaintife, that he doth not pursue it with effect, though the K. be in a sort party to that suite: for otherwise the appellee should continually remaine in prison to his utter undoing, and neuer haue remedy. Neither the Defendant in an appeale shall not haue a Venire facias with a prouiso, untill hee hath assigned some default in the Plaintife in the pursute of it. And yet the Plaintife may at his pleasure stay the Defendant in proceeding further with his processe, in praying a Tales upon the Defendants processe.

21.H.7.34 14.H.7.7 15.H.7.9 21.H.6.36

Remaunding of prisoners out of the K. Bench to be tried in the Countrie

5 Because diuers felons and murderers upon untrue surmises did oftentimes remoue as well their bodies, as their Inditements, by Writte, and otherwise, before the King in his Bench, and could not by the order of the Lawe be remaunded, and sent downe to the Justices of Gaole deliuerie, or of the peace, nor other Justices or Commissioners to proceede upon them, after the due course of the common lawe (for that a Record which is once remoued into an higher Court, can not by the common Lawe be sent backe to a more base and inferiour Court:) For the redresse whereof by a statute made An 6.H.8.

St.6.H.8.6 6.H.8.it was ordained, That the Justices of the K. Bench (for the time being) haue authoritie by their discretions, to remaund and send downe as well the bodies of all felons, and murderers, brought and remoued, or that shall be remoued or brought before the king in his Bench, as their indictments, into the counties whereas the same murders or felonies haue been committed or done, and to commaund all Justices of Gaole deliuery, Justices of Peace, and other Justices and Commissioners, and euery of them, to proceed and determine vpon all the foresaid bodies and indictments so remoued, after the course of the common law, in such maner as the same Justices of gaole deliuerie, Justices of peace, and other Commissioners, or any of them, might or should haue done, if the said prisoners or indictme͂ts had neuer bin brought into the said K. bench.

St.4.Iac.1. 6 By a stat. made Anno 4. Iac. it was enacted, That all offences of coniurations, witchcraft, & dealing with euill and wicked spirits, murder, manslaughter, felonious burning of houses and corne, burglary, robbing of houses by day, robberie, theft, the detestable vice of buggerie committed with mankind, or beast, and rape, heretofore done and committed since his Maiesties comming to the crown of England, or hereafter to be done or committed by any his Maiesties naturall borne subiects of this realme of England, or the dominions of the same, within the realme of Scotland, or the dominions thereof, and the accessories of, and to the same, shalbe from henceforth inquired of, heard, and determined before his Maiesties Just. of Assise, or his Commissioners of Oyer and Terminer, or Gaole deliuery, being naturall borne subiects within this realme of England, and none other, by good and lawfull men of the Counties of Cumberland, Northumberland, Westmerland, or any of the said counties, at the election of the said Just. of Assises, or Commissioners, in like maner and forme to all intents and purposes (the alterations hereafter in this Act expressed, only excepted) as if such offences had beene done and committed within the same Shire where they shalbe so inquired of, heard, and determined, as is aforesaid. At which trials, for the better discouerie of the truth, and for the better information of the consciences of the Jurie and Justices, there shall bee allowed vnto the party so arraigned, the benefit of such witnesses only to be examined vpon othe, that can be produced, for his better cleering and iustification, as hereafter in this Act are permitted and allowed.

Triall of felonies committed by English men in Scotland.

Witnesses allowed to him that is arraigned.

St.4.Iac.1. 7 Euery Justice of peace of the counties aforesaid, vnto whom complaint shalbe made, shall haue full power and authoritie by vertue of this Act, to bind ouer by recognisance in a conuenient summe taken to his Maiesties vse, as well the partie prosecuting, as any witnesses which he shall desire to produce (so as the said witnesses may haue their reasonable charges first tendred vnto them) to prosecute and giue in euidence before such his Maiesties Justices as aforesaid, as the case shall require.

The prosecutors and witnesses bound to giue euidence.

St.4.Iac.1. 8 Euery commander, procurer, counsellor, abettor, comforter, receiuer, or other accessorie of, or to any the offendors or offences aforesaid, so committed in Scotland, as aforesaid, offending within the realms of England or Scotland, shalbe produced, withall indicted, tried, iudged, and executed without delay, notwithstanding the principals, or any of them be not conuicted or attainted.

The accessory tryed, though the principall be not.

No clergie. No peremptorie chalenge aboue v. The words of the Inditement.

And that no such offendor either accessorie or principall shall be allowed the benefit of his clergy, nor admitted to his peremptory chalenge of aboue the number of fiue. And that euery inditment of any of the offences aforesaid, so committed as aforesaid, shalbe adiudged of as good force in law, notwithstanding the words (contra pacem, coronam, & dignitatem nostras) be omitted, as if the said words had been therein contained.

Euery Iuror must haue v. l. of freehold.

9 No Sherife, Undersherife, or other Minister, to whom it appertaineth, shall returne any Iuror to enquire of, or try any of the offences aforesaid, so committed as aforesaid, except euery such Iuror shall haue freehold in possession, to the value of v. l. by the yeare in the county where such inquirie and triall shall be, upon pain to forf. for euery Iuror that shalbe returned contrary to this Act, the summe of xl. l. to the K. and I. to be recouered by A. of debt, B. P. or I. in any of the K. courts at West. wherein no E. P. or W. &c. And the offendor shall or may challenge any Iuror that shall passe upon his life, for want of such freehold, as aforesaid. St.4. Iac.1.

The offendor shall forf. no lands.

10 No naturall subiect of his Maiestie, of the realme of England, or of the dominions of the same, shall for any the offences aforesaid, committed within the realme of Scotland, or for being accessory to the same, forfeit any lands, tenements, or hereditaments, either free, copie, or customary hold, neither shall the blood of such offendor be corrupted, nor the wife lose her dower, yet neuerthelesse the said offendors shall forf. to his Ma. his heires, and successors, their goods, chattels, and credits whatsoeuer. St.4. Iac.1.

A like Act made in Scotland.

11 And forasmuch as it is intended, that an Act like unto this shalbe ordained in the realme of Scotland, for the tryall and punishment of offendors, being his Ma. natural born subiects of the same realm, which shal commit any of the offences aforesaid within the realme of England, or the dominions therof, and shall after escape, or returne backe into Scotland: therefore be it enacted, That upon complaint made by any of his subiects of the realme of England, to any of the Iustices of Assise, Commissioners of Oyer and Terminer, or gaole deliuerie, or Iust. of the peace within the precincts of their seueral commissions respectiuely, being naturall borne subiects within the realme of England, concerning any such offences committed by any his subiects of the realme of Scotland, within the realme of England, in case where the offendor is returned into the realm of Scotland, as aforesaid, the said Iust. or commissioner, shal haue full power and authoritie, to bind ouer as well the said party complaining, or prosecuting, as any witnesses that he shall desire to produce (so as their reasonable charges be first tendred unto them) by recognisance in a conuenient sum to his Maiesties use, to prosecute and giue in euidence within the realme of Scotland: wherein if default shalbe made, and the same proued by certificat, or otherwise, before the Lord Treasorer, Chauncellor, and Barons of the Exchequer, or any of them in the Exchequer chamber, and a decree there made, that the same recognisance shall stand forfeited: then the court of Exchequer shall thereupon proceed for the leuying of the debt of the said recognisance, as if it were adiudged forfeited by the course of the common law. St.4. Iac.1.

Binding the complainant or witnesses to giue euidence in Scotland.

12 On

St.4.Iac.1. 12 On the other part, euery of his Maiesties subiects of the realme of Scotland, either party grieued, or witnesse, which shall prosecute in any the cases aforesaid, within the realme of England, and therby shall haue occasion to make his repaire hither, either voluntarie, or by the like bond (as is before expressed on the part of the realme of England) shall haue and enioy priuiledge and immunitie from all maner of arrests, concerning all offences, or other causes, as well capitall as others, committed, done, or occasioned, before he shall come into England as aforesaid (except treason or wilfull murder) so long as he or they shalbe necessarily going, comming, or abiding within the said realme of England, for the prosecution of the sayd offendors. Scottish men repairing into England to giue euidence, shalbe free frõ arresting.

St.4.Iac.1. 13 Prouided neuerthelesse, that euery such offence so committed as aforesaid, shalbe laid and alledged in the indictment or other declaration, to be done and committed in the realm of Scotland, according to the truth of the fact, and not in the counties where the trial is limited, to be had and made as aforesaid: any thing in this Act formerly contained to the contrarie notwithstanding. The offence shalbe laid where it is done.

St.4.Iac.1. 14 Prouided, that if any of his Maiesties subiects of the realme of Scotland, shall bee proceed with, and tryed in the Realme of Scotland, vpon the prosecution of any party grieued, and vpon euidence in open court, for any offence done or committed within the Realme of England, that no such person shalbe eftsons called into questiõ, or procéeded with for the same fact within the realme of England, but that it shalbe lawfull for euery such persons, to plead and alledge for himselfe, vpon his arraignment, that he was formerly lawfully acquited, conuicted or attainted of the same offence within the realme of Scotland, and that thereupon all further procéeding shal stay, vntill the Court haue sufficiently informed themselues by certificat from the realme of Scotland, or by any other good wayes, and meanes of the truth of the said allegations, which if they shall find true, the said person shalbe forthwith discharged of all further impeachment or procéeding. He that is once tried, shal not be eftsones called into question.

St.4.Iac.1. 15 No naturall borne subiect of the Realme of England, or the Dominions of the same, shall for any High Treason, Misprision, or concealement of High treason, Petit treason, or any other whatsoeuer offence or cause committed within Scotland, be sent out of England, where he is apprehended, to receiue his triall, vntill such time as both Realmes shall be made one in lawes and gouernment. None shalbe sent out of England to receiue his triall.

St.4.Iac.1. 16 At all such tryals the Iurors then and there sworne, or the greater part of them (who in respect of the great trust and charge which must now be layd vpon them, are by vertue of this Act, as before appeareth, to be persons of better conditions and qualitie, than the law required heretofore for Iurors in tryal of like offences) shall haue in their power and election according to their consciences and discretion vpon their othes, to receiue and admit onely such sufficient, good, and lawfull witnesses vpon their othes, either for, or against the partie arraigned, as shall not appeare to them, or the greater part of them, to be vnfit and vnworthy to bée witnesses in that case, either in regard of their The Iurors shall allow of, or reiect the witnesses.

hatred and malice, or their fauour and affection, either to the party prosecuting, or to the partie arraigned, or of their former euill life and conuersation.

Triall by Péeres. 17 Prouided, that if the offendor in any the cases aforesaid, shall be a Péere of the Realme, then his tryall therein shalbe by his Péeres, as is vsed in case of Felony or Treason, and not otherwise. St.4. Iac. 1.

1 Triall of him which woundeth a man in one county, whereof he dyeth in another. S.Principall &c.16.

2 Triall of a felonie committed in one countie, and accessorie thereunto in another. S.Principall &c 17.18.

3 Triall of Treason, Misprision of Treason, and Murders, where the King will. S.Indictments 10.

4 Indictments and trials of Treasons committed out of the Realme. S. Indictments 11.

Challenge.

Challenge.

1 When the prisoner standing at the barre hath pleaded not guiltie, and that the same issue is to bee tryed betweene the King and him, or the appellant and him, the law doth allow him to challenge, viz. calumniari, to take exception unto, or to desire to haue remoued, or put out of his Jurie certaine persons: And hee may therein haue more fauour than either of the parties to a suit shall haue in other tryals betweene partie and partie: For being arraigned of felonie, he may haue a peremptory challenge in fauour of life, which is to say, challenge without shewing cause. And though he can shew no cause to challenge him that he doth challenge, yet if his phantasie or affection doth not stand unto him, by this peremptorie challenge he may cause him to bee remoued and put from the Jurie. And by the common law this peremptorie challenge was permitted to the number of 35. persons, viz. to so many as would make up full three Juries (sauing one man) But sithence by a Statute made Anno 22. H. 8. it is enacted, That no person arraigned for any petit Treason, Murder, or Felonie, shall be from henceforth admitted to any peremptorie challenge aboue the number of twentie. And so by this statute, the number is abridged in three special cases, viz. in Petit treason, Murder, and Felonie: And so for High treason peremptorie challenge did remaine as it was at the common law, untill it was wholly taken away by the Statute of Anno 33. H. 8. which did ordaine, That peremptorie challenge should not thenceforth be admitted or allowed in cases of High treason, or Misprision of treason: And yet after that, challenge was againe reuiued in cases of High treason, by a statute made Anno 1. & 2. P. & M. whereby it was enacted, That all tryals hereafter to bee had, awarded, or made for any Treason, shall bee had and used onely, according to the due order and course of the common Lawes of this Realme, and not otherwise. And then if all tryals in Treasons shall bee according to the common Law, peremptorie challenge shall be allowed upon trial, according to the course of the common law, as well in Petit treason, as in High treason. A man being arraigned of High-treason, and pleading not guiltie, certaine of the Jurors were sworne and tried, the residue being drawne forth by challenge, and the Enquest remaining for default of Jurors, at another day the defendant did peremptorily

[Margin: Peremptorie Challenge.]

[Margin: St. 22. H. 8. 14.]

[Margin: Anno 32. H. 8. 3.]

[Margin: St. 33. H. 8. 23.]

[Margin: St. 1. & 2. P. & M. 10.]

[Margin: 32. H. 6. 20; 14. H. 7. 19]

challenge some of those that were first sworne, and the challenge was allowed in fauour of life. And in an Appeale of Robberie the defendant challenged a Iuror for a cause which was tryed against him, and then the Iurie remained for default of Iurors, and at another day hee challenged the same Iuror peremptorily, and he was allowed so to do. This peremptorie challenge is not to be taken, but where the life of the prisoner is in ieopardie by the tryall. And therefore if a man be outlawed of treason or felonie, and brought to the barre, and there doth plead misnaming, or some other plea in auoidance of the sayd outlawrie: in that case he shal not haue his peremptorie challenge, for that neither treason nor felonie is to be tryed by this issue, because they were at an end before by the outlawrie. If two, three, foure, or more persons, be indicted or appealed, and arraigned of one offence, and one enquest is charged to trye them al, if one of those persons arraigned do challenge peremptorily any of those Iurors, he shalbe drawne, and put out for them all, though one or some other doe desire that he may be sworne: for though they be all arraigned together, yet in the iudgement of law it is seuerall arraignments, for that their offences be seuerall, and not one, though they be indicted of one offence, and so euerie of the prisoners shall haue his challenge, so that he do not challenge peremptorily aboue the number of twentie persons. But if the Court will, it may diuide the panell, and also the Tales, and make them seuerall for euerie of the prisoners, and then euery prisoners challenge shal be by it selfe, and auaile himselfe onely that maketh it.

[Margin: 2.R.3.13. — Seuerance in challenge. — 9.Ed.4.27. Pl.Com. 100.]

[Margin: Challenge vpon cause.]

2 Besides the foresaid peremptorie challenge, which is grounded vpon opinion or phantasie, without cause, there is another kinde of challenge, which is called Challenge vpon cause, and is not allowable but vpon reasonable and good cause, ordained by the common lawes or statutes of this Realme: Whereof one challenge which was at the common law, and is also confirmed by statute, is a challenge of the indictors: for as Britton saith, when the defendant doth submit himselfe to be tryed by the countrey, and the Iurors doe appeare at the barre, they may be challenged, and the prisoner may say, This man ought not to bee of my Iurie, for he did indict me, and I doe presume of him, and of all my indictors, that they doe carrie the same affection towards me now, which they did when they indicted me: and this exception is to be alowed in case of death. And the same law is confirmed, and in a sort augmented by the statute de proditionibus, made Anno 25.Ed.3. by the which it was accorded, That no indictor shall bee put in Enquests vpon the deliuerance of the indictees, of Trespasse, or of Felonies, if hee be challenged for that cause by him that is indicted. And as it may appeare, this Statute is but a confirmation of the common law in this point, and so to be taken fauourably, and by that meanes it may be extended as well to Treasons as to Felonies. And also it may be construed, as well where the prisoner is indicted & arraigned vpon an Appeale, as where hee is indicted and arraigned vpon the inditment, though the same be not contained within the expresse words of the sayd statute.

[Margin: Britton. — 27.Ass.p.13. — Indictor. — St.25.E.3.3 — 8.H.4.3. — 7.E.4.4]

[Margin: Challenge for want of medietatē linguæ.]

3 There is another challenge vpon cause, which is to the Array, and that is, when an Alien is arraigned of Felonie, and pleadeth to an Issue, and the Enquest is returned all of English men, this is a cause of challenge,

by

St.28.E.3.13 by force of the Statute of Anno 28. Edw.3. which did ordaine, That in all manner of Enquests and proofes which be to be taken or made amongst aliens and Denizens, be they Marchants, or others, as well before the Mayor of the Staple, as before any other Iustices or Ministers, although the king be party, the one halfe of the Enquest or proofe shall be by Denizens, and the other halfe of Aliens, if so many Aliens be in the Towne or place where such Enquest or proofe is to be taken, that be not parties, nor with the parties in contracts, pleas, or other quarrels, whereof such enquests or proofes ought to bée taken. And if there be not so many aliens, then shall there be put in such enquests or proofes as many aliens as shall be found in the said Townes or places, which be not thereto parties, as afore is said, and the remnant of denizens, which be good men, and not suspitious to the one party, or to the other. At the

St.27.E.3.8 common Law, before this statute, and the statute of 27.Ed.3. this Triall per medietatem linguæ might haue béene obtained by the Kings graunt: as, if the

M.22.Ed.3. 14 King had graunted to a company of aliens, viz. of Almaines, Frenchmen, &c. that when any of them was impleaded, the one halfe of the Enquest should haue béene of their owne language: and after, to make that a generall Law, the statute of 27.Edw.3. was made. But séeing that statute did not remedie the mischiefe, where the King was party, the before rehearsed statute of 28. Edw.3. was prouided, which maketh mention generally of aliens: therefore it is not materiall of what Nation those aliens are, which shall be of the Enquest, so that they be aliens, though they be of another Nation then the party to the suit is. And because this Statute was ordained for the benefit of aliens, and of none but of aliens, and for that there were in this Realme of long time assembled some strangers together, with many English vagrant Rogues and Vagabonds, calling themselues Egyptians, which by their counterfeit spéeches, apparrell, and behauiour, could hardly be discerned one from the other: Therefore by a Statute made Anno 22. H. 8. it is Egyptians

St.22.H.8. 10. enacted, That if it happen any outlandish person, calling himselfe an Egyptian, or any such stranger, to commit within this Realme any Murther, Robbery, or Felony, and thereof to be indicted and arraigned, and to plead not guilty, or any other plea triable by the Countrey, then the Enquest that shall passe betwéene the King and such party, shall be altogether English-

St.1.& 2. P.&M.4. men. And by another Statute made Anno 1. & 2. Ph. & Ma. it was ordained, That if any of the said persons, called Egyptians, which shall bée transported or conueyed into this Realme of England, or Wales, doe continue within the same by the space of one moneth, that then hee or they so offending, shall by vertue of this act bée adiudged a Felon and Felons, and shall suffer death, losse of lands and goods, as in cases of Felony, and shall vpon the triall of him or any of them be tried by the County, and the inhabitants of the County or place where he or they shall be apprehended or taken, and not per medietatem linguæ, and shall lose the benefit of Clergy and Sanctuary. And whereas the words of the foresaid Statute of 28. Edw.3. be, That in all manner of Enquests and proofes which are to bee taken &c. those words are not to be construed of an Indictment, for that may be taken all of Denizens, though it doe concerne an Alien: But the Statute is to be intended of such Enquests, where the party is admitted to his challenge, and so he is not vpon an Indictment: for the party which is an alien may vpon

21.H.7.32. his arraignement haue the said challenge in the array, to shew that in the pannel there is not medietas linguæ, according to the statute, for he hath none other reme-

remedie being defendant. But if hee were plaintife it should bee otherwise: for then before the Venire facias awarded, hee must suggest, that he is an Alien, and pray Proces to summon the Jurie De medietate linguæ, according to the Statute: and further, hee must surmise in what parts beyond the seas hee was borne, to the intent that men of the same countrey may bee of his Enquest, if they may bee had: and if they will not signifie that before the Venire facias awarded, hee shall not suggest it after: neither shall he challenge the Array, or Polles for that cause, seeing it was his folly, that hee tooke not the benefit of the Statute in due time, and specially when hee knew himselfe to bee an Alien. And whereas the words of the foresayd Statute of 28. Edw. 3. bee (That are not parties, nor with the parties in contracts, pleas, or other quarrels, whereof such Enquests or proofes ought to bee taken) By these words it doth appeare, that the makers of this Statute would, that the parties should haue their Challenges to the Polles in those sayd cases. And therefore, though they haue not expressed but certaine cases, which induce hatred, or malice, yet by the mentioning of them, it seemeth, that they intended to allow all Challenges, which doe induce fauour, or otherwise. And the foresaid Statutes of 27. Edw. 3. & 28. Edw. 3. doe onely extend, where there is but one onely of the parties to the suit an alien: for if they be both aliens, the Enquest shall be all of Englishmen, and not de medietate linguæ, vnlesse the plea be depending before the Mayor of the Staple, and both the parties be Marchants of the Staple, or officers of the Staple, in which case then by the Statute of 27. Edw. 3. 8. the Enquest shall be all of aliens. If an alien be indicted of high Treason, he shall not haue his triall per medietatem linguę, but the triall shall be according to the due order & course of the common Lawes of this Realme. And if a Scot be indicted of Felony, he shall not haue his triall per medietatem linguæ, for that a Scot was neuer accounted an Alien, but rather a Subiect.

Lib. Int. M. 22. E. 3. 20. 21. H. 6. 4. P. 3. & 4. P. M. Dy. f. 144 St. 1. & 2. P. & M. 10. Dyer f. 304.

Treason. A Scot.

Challenge for want of sufficient freehold.

4 There is another Challenge vpon cause, viz. for want of sufficient Freehold, which is a Challenge of the Polles, and this Challenge was giuen by the Statute of 2. H. 5. which doth ordaine, That no person shall be admitted to passe in any Enquest vpon tryall of the death of a man: or in any Enquest betweene party and party in plea reall, or in plea personall, whereof the debt and dammages declared doe amount to fortie markes aboue all charges, if the same person hath not Lands and Tenements of the yearely value of fortie shillings aboue all charges, so that he be challenged for that cause by the party. And because many Marchants aliens, and other aliens, which neither had nor could purchase any Land in this Realme, were greatly discontented with the foresaid Statute of 2. H. 5. and were ready to depart this Realme, for that the same Statute did take away, or was expounded to diminish the chiefe force of the before mentioned Statute of 28. Edw. 3. 13. and by that meanes to abridge aliens of their Trials in most cases per medietatem linguæ. Therefore the more to encourage Marchants to continue here, and also others to come with their marchandizes into this Realme, by a Statute made Anno 8. H. 6. it was declared, That the same Statute made Anno 2. H. 5. should be no wayes preiudiciall to the foresaid first statute made 28. Edw. 3. nor was not meant that it should extend to any, but

St. 2. H. 5. 3. St. 8. H. 6. 29

but onely to Enquests to be taken betwéene Denizon and Denizon, and not to the other Enquests or proses mentioned in the sayd Statute of 28. Ed.3. viz. to Enquests to be taken betwéene Denizons and Aliens. And that the first statute of 28. Ed.3. should bée effectuall, stand in force, and be put in execution, according to the forme thereof, notwithstanding the later Statute of 2.H.5. and notwithstanding that Aliens haue not lands or tenements of the yearely value of fortie shillings, according to the purport of the sayd later statute of 2.H.5. And so by this statute, want of sufficient fréehold is the cause of Challenge to Aliens which bée impanelled with English men. But yet it séemeth to be a cause to challenge English men, who bée impanelled with Aliens, for the perclose of this Statute doth wholly relye vpon Aliens. This last rehearsed Statute of 8.H.6. willeth, That the intent of the other Statute of 2.H.5. should bée preferred before the words thereof, and so the Judges of the
9.H.6.27. law haue expounded it, for they haue allowed a Juror which had not fortie shillings of fréehold, to bée sworne in an Enquest, if others had so much land to his vse. And where the words of the statute be (If he hath not lands or tenements of the yearely value of fortie shillings) and doth not expresse in what Countie, yet they doe take it by intendment, that the lands must bée in the
9.H.7.1. Countie where the issue is to bée tryed. And for that the words be in the Pre-
M.12.H.7.4 sent tense (viz. if hée hath not) they doe expound it, that the Juror must haue
H.32.H.8. so much land in the same Countie at that time when he is sworne: for though
20. he had so much land when he was impanelled, yet if he hath aliened it, or that
P.21.H.6. the same was euicted from him by an auncient title before the time hee was
39. sworne, the challenge of insufficiencie shall bée allowed vnto the prisoner. And whereas the foresayd statute of 2.H.5. hath ordayned (That no person shall be admitted to passe in any Enquest vpon the tryal of the death of a man, if hée hath not lands of the yearely value of fortie shillings) this is not meant of the tryall of the death of a man which is slaine, but of the tryall of the death of a man which standeth at the barre vpon the question of his life or death. And then will this challenge serue for want of sufficient lands, vpon the triall of all maner of felonies and treasons. By the Statute of 33. H. 8. it is enacted,
St.33.H.8. That he which is arraigned of treason, murder, or manslaughter committed
22. within the Verge, shall haue no maner of challenge to any of the Jury, malice only excepted (and so shall haue no challenge for want of sufficient fréehold.)
St.3.H.7.14 And in like sort it is ordained by the Statute of Anno 3. H. 7. That hee which being the Kings seruant sworne, and whose name is in the checke Roll of the Kings houshold, vnder the degrée of a Lord, which is arraigned for conspiring with any other, to destroy any Lord of this Realme, or any other sworne to the Kings Councell: Or the Steward, Treasurer, or Controller of the Kings house, shall not haue any challenge but for mallice (and so shall haue no challenge for want of sufficient fréehold.) By a Statute made An-
St.33.H.8. no 33.H.8. it was enacted, That if a Commission of Oyer and Determi-
13. ner bée directed into any County, for the tryall of any person which doth confesse any Murther, to thrée of the Kings Councell, or is vehemently suspected thereof, no challenge for the Hundred or Shire shall bée allowed vnto him. But the challenge of any Juror for lacke of Fréehold, of the yearely value of forty shillings, shall bée allowed, as hath béene accustomed. And because Trials in Murthers and Felonies, in Cities, Boroughes, and Townes corporat within this Realme, hauing authoritie in the deli-

uerance

uerance of such offendors, were oftentimes deferred and delayed, by reason of challenge made by such offendors, of Iurors, for lacke of sufficiency of freehold, to the great hinderance of iustice: for the redresse thereof, by a statute made Anno 23. H. 8. it was enacted, That every person, being the kings naturall subiect borne, which either by the name of a citizen, or a freeman, or any other name, doth enioy the liberties of any City, Borough, or Towne corporat, where he dwelleth, being worth in moueable goods to the cleare value of forty pounds, shall bee admitted in tryall of Murthers and Felonies, in every Sessions and Gaoles of deliuery kept in and for the liberty of such Cities, Boroughes, or Townes corporat, albeit he hath no freehold. But this act extendeth not to any Knight or Esquire dwelling, abiding, or resorting to any such City, Borough, or Towne corporat: any thing in the same act to the contrary hereof notwithstanding. St. 23. H. 8. 13.

5 Upon the arraignement of a prisoner, the king by his prerogatiue might haue challenged every of the Iurors peremptorily by the common law, without shewing of any cause thereof, and by that challenge the same Iuror should haue béene presently drawne. But this was a great mischiefe and offence to the subiect, who by that meanes was infinitely delayed, and had often put out of the Iury the most discréet and indifferent men, which were returned for his tryall: For the remedy whereof, by a Statute intituled Ordinatio de inquisitionibus, made Anno 33. Edw. 1. it was established, That touching Inquisitions to bée made before any Iustices, wherein the king is any way a party, although it bée alleadged by those which doe prosecute for the king, that the Iurors of those Inquisitions, or any of them, bée not good for the king, those Inquisitions shall not therefore remaine to bée taken: But if they which doe pursue for the king, will challenge any of those Iurors, they shall shew a certaine cause of their challenge, and the truth of that challenge, whether it bée true, or not, shalbe inquired of, according to the Iustices discretion. But he that doth prosecute the sute for the king, néede not presently shew the cause upon his challenge (as a common person should do, if he were party against the king) for he may shew that cause when he hath perused the whole pannell. But if he that is arraigned, doe challenge any of the Polles, hee must shewe the cause upon his Challenge, which must be presently tried, for that it is in a plea of the crowne, wherein the king is a party.

Challenge for the king. — St. 33. E. 1. — 1. H. 5. 10. Fit. Chall. 105. 38. Ass. p. 22.

6 A man outlawed of Felonie shall haue his challenges upon an Issue taken, for the auoidance of the Felony: For though hée cannot challenge a worse man then himselfe, béeing outlawed for Felony, yet séeing it is in Issue to trie, whether hee bee an Outlaw, or not, and by this tryall, if it bée found for him, to defeat the same Outlawry, that opinion of him ought to bee holden in suspence, untill the said issue shall be tried against him.

An Outlaw of Felony. — Fi. Chall. 153. 165.

21.H.6.30. 24.H.4.19. 7 It is a good Challenge upon cause, to say, that one of the Jurors is an Alien, or a Villaine, or an Outlaw; for then hee is not Liber & legalis homo: For though an Alien borne hath dwelt in this Realme from his childhood, and be sworne in a Leet, or other Court, to the Kings obedience, yet he is not the Kings liege man: for the Steward of a Leet, nor any other, can make an Alien Legalis homo, but onely the King. A Juror, an alien, villaine, or outlaw.

Eui-

Euidence.

1 When a prisoner is indicted of Treason, or Felony, hath pleaded not guilty, is therupon arraigned, and finished his challenges, then euidence is to be giuen against him to proue him guilty, which euery person shall bée admitted to doe for the king. And because the euidence of those, that tooke the said offendor with the manner, did first accuse him, or brought him before the Iustices of Peace to be examined of the supposed offence, hath béene alwaies adiudged most pregnant and effectuall: Therefore by a statute made Anno 1. & 2. Ph. & Ma. it was ordayned, St. 1. & 2. P.&M. 13. That two Iustices of Peace at the least, whereof one of them to be of the Quorum, when any prisoner is brought before them for any manslaughter, or felony, before any bailement or mainprise, shall take the examination of the said prisoner, and information of them that bring him, of the fact, and circumstances thereof, and the same, or as much thereof, as shalbe materiall to proue the felony, shall put in writing, before they make the same bailement: which said examination, together with the said bailement, the said Iustices shall certifie at the next generall Gaole deliuerie to bée holden within their Commission: and that euery Coroner, vpon any inquisition before him found, whereby any person or persons shall bée indicted for murther, or manslaughter, or as accessorie or accessories to the same, before the murther or manslaughter committed, shall put in writing the effect of the euidence giuen to the Iury before him, béeing materiall. And as well the said Iustices, as the said Coroner, shall haue authority by this act to bind all such by Recognisance or Obligation, as doe declare any thing materiall to proue the said murther, or manslaughter, offences, or felonies, or to bée accessorie or accessories to the same, as is aforesaid, to appeare at the next generall Gaole deliuerie to bée holden within the County, City, or Towne corporat, where the tryall thereof shall bée, then and there to giue euidence against the party so indicted at the time of his triall, and shall certifie as well the same euidence, as such bond and bonds in writing as hée shall take, together with the Inquisition or Indictment before him taken and found, or before the time of his sayd tryall thereof to bée had or made. And likewise the said Iustices shall certifie all and euery such bond taken before them, in like manner, as is before said of baylements and examination. And in case any Iustice of peace,

Euidence against an offendor let to baile

or

or Quorum, or Coroner, shall offend in any thing contrary to the true intent and meaning of this act, then the Iustices of Gaole deliuery of the Shire, City, Towne, or Place, where such offences shal happen to be committed, vpon due proofe thereof by examination before them, shall for euery such offence set such fine on euery such Iustice of Peace, and Coroner, as the same Iustices of Gaole deliuery shall thinke méet, and shall estreat the same, as other Fines and Amerciaments assessed before Iustices of Gaole deliuery ought to bee. S. Mainprise 13.

2 Because the foresaid statute of 1. & 2. Ph. & Ma. 13. doth not extend to any such prisoners, as shall be brought before any Iustice of Peace, for Manslaughter or Felony, and by such Iustice shall be committed to ward, for the suspition of such Manslaughter or Felony, and not bayled: in which case the examination of such prisoner, and of such as shall bring him, is as necessary, or rather more, then where such prisoner shall be let to bayle: For the reformation whereof, by a statute made Anno 2. & 3. Ph. & Ma. it was enacted, That such Iustices or Iustice, before whom any person shall bée brought, for Manslaughter or Felony, or for suspition thereof, before he or they shall commit or send such prisoner to ward, shall take the examination of such prisoner, and information of those that bring him, of the fact and circumstances thereof, and the same, or as much thereof, as shall be materiall to proue the Felony, shall put in writing within two dayes after the said examination, and the same shall certifie in such manner and forme, and at such time, as they should and ought to doe, if such prisoner so committed or sent to ward, had béene bayled, or let to mainprise, vpon such paine as in the said former act is limitted and appointed, for not taking or not certifying such examinations, as in the said former act is expressed. And the said Iustices shall haue authority by this act to bind all such by Recognisance or Obligation, as doe declare any thing materiall, to proue the said Manslaughter, or Felony, against such prisoner as shall bee so committed to ward, to appeare at the next generall Gaole deliuery, to be holden within the County, City, or Towne corporat, where the triall of the said Manslaughter or Felony shall be, then and there to giue Euidence against the party. And the said Iustices shall certifie the sayd bands taken before them, in like manner, as they should and ought to certifie the bands mentioned in the said former act, vpon the paine, as in the said former act is mentioned, for not certifying such bands, as by the said former act is limitted and appointed to be certified.

St. 1. & 2. P. & M. 10.

Euidence against an offendor cōmitted to prison

3 And for that men should be the readier and more willing to giue Euidence against Robbers and other Felons, by a statute made Anno 21. H. 8. it was established, That if any Felon or Felons doe robbe or take away any money, goods, or cattels from any of the kings subiects, from their person, or otherwise, within this Realme, and thereof be indicted, and after be arraigned of the same Felony, and found guilty thereof, or otherwise attainted by reason of Euidence giuen by the party so robbed, or owner of the said money, goods, or cattels, or by any other by their procurement, then the party so robbed, or owner

St. 21. H. 8. 11

Restitution vpon attainder by euidēce.

ner, shalbe restored to his said money, goods, and cattels. Before which statute the party robbed or owner of the goods stolne could not haue had restitution, without suing of an Appeale against the Felon.

Euidence giuen by a stranger.

4 If the seruant be robbed, the master may giue euidence against the Felon, and haue restitution by this statute, if so be, that the goods robbed were the goods of the master: for the words of the statute be (The party so robbed, or owner.) Also if he that was robbed doth not giue Euidence himselfe, but procure another to giue the euidence, this is sufficient by the words of the statute, to obtaine restitution of his stolne goods.

There must be two accusors to giue euidence in Treason.

5 By a Braunch of a statute made Anñ 5. Ed. 6. it was ordained, That no person or persons shall be indicted, arraigned, conuicted, condemned, or attainted, for any Treasons that now be, or hereafter shalbe, vnlesse the same offendor or offendors be thereof accused by two lawfull accusors, which said accusors at the time of the arraignment of the party accused (if they be then liuing) shal be brought in person before the party so accused, and auow and maintain that which they haue to say against the said party, to proue him guilty of the Treasons or offences contained in the bill of inditement layed against the party arraigned, vnlesse the said party arraigned shall willingly without violence confesse the same. But after by the statute of An. 1. & 2. P. & M. it was ordained, That all tryals to be had, awarded, or made for any Treason, shall be had and vsed onely, according to the due order and course of the common lawes of this Realme, and not otherwise. Quære whether the said stat. of 1. & 2. P. & Ma. do take away the force of the foresaid stat. of 5. Ed. 6. which it is thought it doth not, but that the said statute of Anno 5. Ed. 6. doth remaine in force, seeing it was ordained onely for the accusation or euidence, and not for the time, place, or order of the triall.

St. 5. E. 6. 11. St. 1. & 2. P. & M. 10. T. 2. & 3. P. & M. Dyer 132.

Euidence in high Treason.

6 If there be an accusor of high Treason of his owne knowledge, or of his owne hearing, and he doth vtter it to another, that other may well be an accusor or witnesse. And likewise if the second man do vtter it to the third, and the third to the fourth man, euery of them may be an accusor or witnesse.

2. M. Dy. 98.

Euidence against abettors to offences

7 By the statute of Anno 5. Eliz. it is ordained, That no person or persons shalbe indicted for assisting, aiding, maintaining, comforting, or abetting of any person or persons, for any of the offences mentioned in the said statute, in extolling, setting forth, or defending of the vsurped power, and authority of the bishop of Rome, vnlesse he or they be thereof lawfully accused by such good and sufficient testimony or proofe, as by the Jury, by whom he shall be so indicted, shalbe thought good, lawfull, and sufficient, to proue him or them guilty of the said offences. S. Treasons 15.

St. 5. El. 1.

8 By

St.31.Eli.4. 8 By the Statute made Anno 31. Eliz. it is ordained, That such person and persons as shall bee impeached for any offence made Felony by that Statute (beeing intituled an act against imbesilling of armour, habiliments of warre, and victuals) shall by vertue of this act be receiued and admitted to make any lawfull proofe that he can, by lawfull witnesse, or otherwise, for his discharge and defence in that behalfe: any Law to the contrary notwithstanding. S. Felonies by Statute 33. Euidence on the def. part.

Verdict.

1 After the prisoner hath pleaded not guilty, hath been thereupon arraigned, and evidence given against him in open court, before the Judges and the Jury, the same Jury do depart from the barre to consider of their evidence & proofes, which being done, they return again to the court to give up their verdict, which as the issue of not guilty is generall, so may they deliver their verdict guilty, or not guilty, if they will, and that their evidence be cleare, and do induce them thereunto. But it is not alwaies requisit to give a generall verdict: for if the fact, whereupon the prisoner was arraigned, be such, that the Jury doe stand in doubt, whether it be felony, or not, they shall best discharge their consciences to give a speciall verdict, that is to say, a verdict at large, viz. a verdict, declaring at large the whole truth of the matter, which may be done as well in case of felony, as in an assise, or action of Trespas: as, they may deliver their verdict, that the prisoner which is arraigned for the killing of a man, did slay the same man in his owne defence: for he that is arraigned must plead not guilty (seeing that in his plea he cannot iustifie the killing of a man) and then the Jury in their verdict may declare the whole circumstance of the fact, and conclude, that he killed him in his own defence: for it is not a sufficient verdict for the Jury to say, that the prisoner killed the man in his owne defence, but they must shew the cause, manner, and circumstance of the fact, that the court may discerne & iudge, whether the fact which the prisoner hath committed, be felony, or not, whether the prisoner standeth in the Kings mercy, or not, and whether hee shall lose his goods, or not.

A verdict at large in felony

44.E.3.44 Fi.Cor.284 286.287. 47.Ass.p.31

2 As a Jury may give a speciall verdict, touching a man that killed another in his own defence, so may they give a speciall verdict, where he that is arraigned killed another by misfortune: Or where he which cōmitted the homicide, was not of perfect memory, or deafe & dumbe, or an infant without discretion: Or that the thing which was stoln was not worth above x.d. Or that he which is indicted & arraigned for committing of a murther, did kil the man by chance medley, or in his owne defence, and not of malice prepenced. And if two be indicted for cōmitting of a felony, & do plead thereunto not guilty, the Jury may find, that one of them committed the felony by the procuremēt of the other, but that he which was the procurer was not present at the cōmitting of the felony.

The verdict lesse penall thē the indictment

T.26.H.8.5 P.9.El.Dy.261. Pl.com.101 Br.Cor.221 Br.Appeale 122.

3 And as a Jury may giue a speciall verdict to attenuate an offence, and to make it lesse penall then is contained in the Indictment (as in the cases aforesaid) so may they by a speciall verdict aggrauate the offence, more then the Indictment did. As, a man was indicted and arraigned for the stealing of linnen Cloth to the value of two shillings, whereunto the prisoner pleaded not guilty, and the Jury found that he did rob the owner of the linnen cloth, to the value of x.s. and further, that he tooke it from the person of a man, whereupon hee was adiudged to be hanged.

The verdict more penall then the Indictment.

Fi. Cor. 115

4 When a man is indicted of the death of another man before the Coroner, vpon the sight of the body slaine, and after is acquite, the Jury which acquited him must find one that killed him, or els the meanes whereby he came to his death: and if they find that J. N. killed him, this shall serue for an indictment against J. N. for it is certaine, that there is such a person dead, seeing the Coroner did see him, and so recorded it, and therfore the maner of this persons death must not cease to be tried vntill it be found. But it is otherwise, where the prisoner is indicted before other Justices, because notwithstanding such an indictment, it may be there was no such person dead: for the body was not seene by the Justices, before whom that indictment passed, as in the other case it was by the Coroner: and therefore their record in that case, touching the death of a man, cannot be of so great force as the coroners is, vnles it be where the death of the man is notorious and generally knowne; then if he, which vpon an appeale or indictment of the death of that man is arraigned, & pleadeth not guilty, is by the Jury found not guilty, the Jury shalbe charged to inquire who killed him: as, a man was indicted and arraigned for the killing of another man, who thereunto pleaded not guilty, and the Jury found him not guilty: and because the man was knowne to be killed in the presence of many, the Justices charged the Jury to inquire and find who killed him, and the they found, that the same man which was killed, was in a Tauerne, and drunken, and fell vpon his owne knife by mischance, and so was the cause of his owne death.

Where a Jury shall find who killed the dead man.

24. H. 7. 2.
13. E. 4. 3.
22. As. p. 39
7. Eli. Dyer 238.
21. E. 3. 17
37. Ass. p. 13

Clergie.

What Clergy is. 1 Clergie is an auncient liberty of the holy Church, and it is when a prieſt, or one within holy orders, or any other in whō there is no impoſſibility to be a prieſt, is arraigned of Felony before a ſecular Judge, hee may pray to haue his Clergy, which was as much (before the ſtatute of 18. Eli.) as if he had prayed to be diſmiſſed of the temporall Judge, and to be deliuered to the Ordinary to purge him of that offence: and now ſithence that ſtatute, it is as much as if he ſhould pray (after the burning in the hand) to be enlarged, and deliuered out of priſon. And it appeareth by the ſtatute of Articuli Cleri, made Anno 9. Ed. 2. That a Clerke ought not to be iudged by a Temporall Judge, nor any thing may be done againſt him, that concerneth his life, or diſmembring of him: and though this priuiledge had his beginning from the Cannon Law, and not from the common Law of this Realme, yet it hath bin confirmed by diuers parliaments, and the temporall Judges haue ſo fauorably vſed it, that they haue graunted it to all that can read, although they be no prieſts, nor within holy orders (which is more then the Cannon Law requireth: for the Cannon Law expecteth no more then that it ſhalbe graunted to prieſts, and ſuch as be within holy orders.)

St. 18. Eli. 6. St. 9. E. 2. 15

Where no Clergy by the common Law. 2 None of them in whom there is any impediment to be Prieſt, can by the common Law haue the priuiledge of Clergy: as, he that is blind or maimed, or one ſuch as by no diſpenſation by the Lawes of the Church can be Prieſt, can haue the priuiledge of Clergy: Neither can any woman haue the priuiledge of Clergy. Fi. Cor. 461

Committer of Sacriledge. 3 He that hath committed Sacriledge, ſhall not haue the priuiledge of clergy by the common Law, if the Ordinary do refuſe him & the ſecular Judge do aſſent to his refuſall: and yet it is otherwiſe, if the Ordinary will clayme him for a Clerke, and receiue him. But if one that hath committed Sacriledge be arraigned of another felony then of that Sacriledge, for the which he doth pray his Clergy, and doth read well, and the Ordinary knowing that he hath committed Sacriledge, or ſome other grieuous crime, doth refuſe him, the ſaid offen-

Fi. Cor. 120. 283. 257. 26. Aſſ. p. 19. 27. Aſſ. p. 42

21.Ed.4.21 offendor shalbe hanged, though the Ordinary doth not shew to the Iudges the cause of his refusall. S.Br.24.

Fi.Cor.233. 26.Ass.p.19 9.E.4.28. 4. If one that is a priest, or within holy orders, hauing not the habit or tonsure of a clerke, do demaund his clergy, if the Ordinary do refuse him for it, he shalbe hanged: & so shall he be, if the court do refuse him for that cause, though the Ordinary do not refuse him. S.Br.5. Habite or tonsure of a clerke.

5 He that had his clergy once, should haue had it againe by the cōmon law, and so, oft times: but by the stat. of 4.H.7. it was enacted, That euery person (not being within orders) which once hath been admitted to the benefit of his clergy, being eftsoones arraigned of any such offence, shall not be admitted to the priuiledge of his clergy. And euery person so conuicted for murther, shalbe marked with an M. vpon the brawne of the left thumbe: and if it be for any other felony, he shalbe marked with a T. in the same place of the thumbe; and those markes to be made by the gaoler openly in the court before the Iudge, before the person be deliuered. And after by the stat. of 28.H.8. & 32.H.8. it was enacted, That such as be within holy orders shall be and stand vnder the same paines & dangers for their offences, and be vsed and ordered to all intents, as other persons not being within holy orders shalbe. Clergy allowed but once. St.4.H.7.13 St.28.H.8.1. St.32.H.8.3

6 He that killeth a man in his owne defence, or by misaduenture, by the common Law shall not haue his clergy: Neither shall he who committeth petite Larceny haue his clergy, and the reason is, for that in those cases he shall not haue iudgement of death. Br.Cor.183 Killing a man by mischance, or in his owne defence. Petit larcenie

7 He which had offended in high Treason by the common law, should not haue had his clergy, neither he which had offended in petit Treason, vntill by the stat. of Añ 25.E.3. pro Clero it was enacted, That all Clerkes, as well secular as religious, which shalbe from henceforth conuict before the secular Iustices for any manner Treasons and Felonies touching other persons thē the King himselfe, or his royall Maiesty, shall freely haue and enioy the priuiledge of holy Church, and shalbe without any impeachment or delay deliuered to the Ordinaries demaunding them. It appeareth by the statute of Anno 4.H.4. That the Clergie promised to the King in Parliament, that a Clerke conuict for Treason touching the King himselfe, or for being a common theefe notoriously detected, and deliuered to the Ordinary, shall not make his purgation. 19.H.6.47. Fit.Co.183 St.25.E.3.4 St.4.H.4.3 Offendors in Treasons.

8 He that had confessed a felony, could not haue had his Clergy by the common Law, vntill the stat. of Añ 9.E.2. viz. Articuli Cleri, was made: Because after his confession he could not purge him of that offence, and therefore it was in vaine to haue him deliuered to the Ordinary, to be tryed of that offence. But the spirituall men at that time intended, that the same confession of a Clerke before a Temporall Iudge was void, for that he could not be Iudge of St.9.E.2.15 Confession of felony.

of a Clerke: and therefore they obtained remedie by the said articles in two speciall cases, viz. Abiuration and Approuement: and by the equitie of the said statute, and in fauour of life, it is now permitted in all other cases of attainders.

Clergy taken away by seueral statutes. A Cutpurse.

9 By the statute of An. 8. Eliz. it is enacted, That no person or persons St. 8. El. 4.
which shalbe indicted or appelled for felonious taking of any money, goods, or cattels from the person of any other priuily, without his knowledge, in any place whatsoeuer, and thereupon found guilty by verdict of xij. men, or shall confesse the same vpon his or their arraignment, or will not answer directly to the same, according to the lawes of this Realme, or shall stand wilfully, or of malice, or obstinatly mute, or challenge peremptorily aboue the number of xx. or shalbe vpon such indictment or appeale outlawed, shall be admitted to haue the benefit of his or their clergy, but be excluded therof, and shall suffer death in such manner & forme, as they should if they were no clerks.

Forging of writings.

10 By the stat. of An. 5. El. it is established, That if any person or persons St. 5. El. 14.
being conuicted or condemned of any of the offences specified in that Statute (prouided against the forging of euidences & writings) by any of the waies or meanes in the same statute limitted, shall after any such his or their conuiction or condemnation eftsones commit or perpetrate any of the said offences, in the forme therin mentioned, that then euery such second offence or offences shalbe adiudged felony, & the parties thereof conuicted or attainted shall suffer death, losse, & forfeiture of their goods, cattels, lands & tenemēts, as in cases of felony, without hauing any aduantage or benefit of Clergy or Sanctuary. S. Forging &c. 8. and Felonies by Statute 27.

Buggery.

11 By the statutes of Añ 25. H. 8. & Añ 5. El. it is enacted, That if any do St. 25. H. 8. 6
commit Buggery with mankind or beast, the same offence shalbe adiudged felony, and that no person offending in the same shalbe admitted to his clergy. S. St. 5. El. 17.
Felonies by Stat. 11.

Egyptians.

12 By the statute of Añ 5. El. it is enacted, That euery person and persons St. 5. El. 20
of the age of xiiij. yeares, or aboue, calling himselfe an Egyptian, or being in company with them, or counterfeiting or disguising himselfe by his apparell, speech, or other behauior, like vnto the vagabonds, calling themselues Egyptians, and so doth continue at one or seuerall times by the space of a moneth, shalbe adiudged a felon, and shall lose the priuiledge and benefit of Sanctuary and Clergy. S. Felonies by Stat. 15.

Releeuing of a Jesuit or Priest.

14 By the stat. of Añ 27. El. it is enacted, That euery person which shall St. 27. Eli. 2.
wittingly & willingly receiue, relieue, comfort, aid, or maintaine any Jesuit, seminary priest, or other priest, deacō, or religious or ecclesiastical persō whatsoeuer, being borne within this realme, or any the dominions thereof, & heretofore (sithence the feast of S. Iohn the Baptist añ 1. Reg. El.) ordained, made, or

professed,

professed, or hereafter to be made, ordained, or professed by any authoritie or iurisdiction deriued from the Sea of Rome, being at liberty, or out of hold, knowing him to be a Iesuite, Seminarie Priest, or such other Priest, Deacon, or religious or ecclesiasticall person, as is aforesaid, shal for such offence be adiudged a felon without benefit of Clergy, and shal suffer death, lose and forfeit as in case of one attainted of felony. S.Felonies by Stat. 22.

St.18.El.6. 15 By the Statute of Anno 18. Eliz. it is ordained, That if any person or persons shall fortune to commit or doe any manner of felonious Rape, Rauishment, or Burglary, or shall vnlawfully and carnally know and abuse any woman child vnder the age of tenne yeares, and shal be thereof found guilty by verdict, be outlawed, or confesse the same vpon his arraignment, he shall suffer paines of death, and forfeit as in cases of felony, without any allowance or priuiledge of Clergy. Rape. Burglary.

St.3.H.7.2 16 By the statute of An 3.H.7. it is enacted, That if any person or persons shall take any maid, widow, or wife, which hath any lands or goods, or is heire apparant to her auncestor against her wil vnlawfully, such taking, procuring, and abetting to the same, and also receiuing wittingly the same woman so taken against her will, & knowing the same, shalbe felony: and such misdoers, takers and procurators to the same shalbe reputed & taken as principall Felons. But this act doth not extend to any person taking a woman, onely clayming her as his ward or bondwoman. And by the stat. of 39. El. it is ordained, That euery such person & persons as shalbe conuicted or attainted of or for any offēce made felony by the foresaid act of añ 3.H.7. or which shalbe indicted & arraigned of or for any such offence, & stand mute, or make no direct answere, or challenge peremptorily aboue the number of xx. shal in euery such case lose his and their benefit of Clergy. Prouided alwaies, that this act shal not extend to take away the benefit of Clergy, but onely from such person and persons as hereafter shall be principals, or procurers, or accessaries before such offence cōmitted. S.Felonies by Stat.5.

Taking a woman against her will. St.39.El.9. Ward. Bondwoman.

St.1.Iac.12 17. By the statute of An.1.Iac. it is enacted, That if any person or persons shal vse, practise, or exercise any inuocation or coniuration of any euil & wicked spirit, or shall consult, couenant with, entertaine, imploy, feede, or reward any euill & wicked spirit, to or for any intent or purpose, or take vp any dead man, woman, or child, out of his, her, or their graue, or any other place where the dead body resteth, or the skin, bone, or any other part of any dead person, to be imploied or vsed in any maner of Witchcraft, Sorcerie, Charme, or Inchantment, or shall vse, practise, or exercise any Witchcraft, Inchantment, Charme, or Sorcerie, whereby any person shall be killed, destroyed, wasted, consumed, pined, or lamed in his or her body, or any part thereof: then euery such offendor or offendors, their aidors, abettors, and councellors, being of any the said offences duly and lawfully conuicted and attainted, shall suffer pains of death as a felon, or felons, and shall lose the priuiledge and benefit of Clergy & Sanctuary: and if any person or persons shall take vpon him or thē by Witchcraft, Inchantmēt, Charme, or Sorcery, to tell or declare in what place any treasure Coniuration. witchcraft.

of

Telling where things lost may be found. Prouoking to loue. Destroying of men or cattell.

of gold or siluer should or might be found or had in the earth, or other secret places, or where goods lost or stolne should be found or become, or to the intent to prouoke any person to unlawfull loue, or whereby any goods or cattels of any person shalbe destroyed, wasted, or impaired, or to hurt or destroy any person in his or her body, although the same be not effected and done: and being once conuicted of the same offences, as is aforesaid, do eftsones perpetrate and commit the like offence, then euery such offendor being of any the said offences the second time lawfully and duly conuicted and attainted, shall suffer pains of death as a felon, and shall lose the benefit and priuiledge of clergy and sanctuarie. S. Felonies by Stat. 29.

Stabbing or thrusting.

18 By the statute of Anno 1. Iac. it is enacted, That if any person or persons shall stabbe or thrust any person or persons that hath not then any weapon drawne, or that hath not then first stricken the party which shall so stabbe or thrust, so as the person or persons so stabbed or thrust, shall therof die within the space of sixe moneths then next following, although it cannot be proued that the same was done of mallice forethought: yet the party so offending, and being thereof conuict by verdict of twelue men, confession, or otherwise, according to the Lawes of this Realme, shalbe excluded from the benefit of his or their Clergy, and shall suffer death as in case of wilfull murther. S. Homicide 24. *St. 1. Iac. 8 S. Murther 24.*

A Recusant not abiuring, or returning.

19 If any such offendor, which by the tenor and effect of the act made Ann. 35. Eliz. (intituled an act to retaine the Queenes Subiects in due obedience) is to be abiured the Realme, shall refuse to make such abiuration, as by that statute is appointed: Or after such abiuration shall not goe to such Hauen, and within such time as is appointed, and from thence depart the Realme, according to the said statute: Or after his departure shall returne againe into any of the kings Realmes or Dominions, without his speciall licence in that behalfe first had and obtained: then in euery such case the person so offending shalbe adiudged a felon, and suffer as in case of felony, without benefit of clergy. S. Felonies by Stat. 9. *St. 35. El. 1.*

Abiuration of a Popish Recusant.

20 If any such offendor, which by the tenor and intent of the act made Ann. 35. Eliz. (intituled an act for the restraining of Popish Recusants to some place of abode) is to be abiured the Realme, shall refuse to make such abiuration: Or after such abiuration made shall not goe to such hauen, and within such time as is appointed, and from thence depart out of this Realme according to the said act: Or after such departure shall returne and come againe into any of the kings Dominions, without his speciall licence in that behalfe first obtained and had: then in euery such case the person so offending shall be adiudged a felon, and lose as in case of felony, without benefit of Clergy. S. Felonies by Stat. 11. *St. 35. El. 2.*

A Souldier departing fro his captaine.

21 By the statute of Ann. 18. H. 6. it is enacted, That if any souldier, man of Armes, or Archer, which hath taken parcell of his wages of his Captaine, and *St. 18. H. 6. 15.*

and is entred of record the kings souldier (except notorious sicknes or impediment by Gods visitation doth let, which he shall imediately certifie his captaine, and repaie his money) or els being in the enemies countrie in garrison, or els where, in the kings seruice, where he is appointed to serue, doth depart without licence of the kings lieutenant, deputie, high admirall, viceadmirall, captaine, or in their absence of their deputies, he shalbe taken, iudged, and executed as a felon. And by the Stat. of Anno 2. & 3. Ed. 6. he shal not haue aduantage of his Clergie or sanctuarie, S. Felon. by Stat. 21. St. 2. & 3. Ed. 6. 2.

St. 39. El. 17 22 By the Stat. of An. 39. El. it is ordained, That if any idle and wandring Souldier or Mariner doe not settle himselfe to labour, seruice, or other lawfull course of life, without wandring; or otherwise repaire to the places where he was born, or to his dwelling place, and there remain, betaking himselfe to some lawfull trade or course of life: Or comming from his Captaine, shall not haue a testimonial of a Iustice of peace, &c. or shal counterfeit or forge such testimoniall, or haue with him any such testimoniall forged, knowing the same to be forged, being retained into seruice, or shall depart within the yeare without the licence of him that retained him into seruice, Then he shalbe iudged as a felon without the benefit of clergie. S. Fel. by Stat. 3. Wandering souldiers and mariners.

St. 43. Eli. 13 23 By the Stat. of An. 43. El. it is established, That whosoeuer shal without lawfull authoritie take any of the kings subiects, against his or their wills, and carry him or them out of the counties of Cumberland, Northumberland, Westmerland, or the Bishoprick of Durham, or to any other place within any of the said counties, or detayne, force, or imprison him or them as prisoners, or against his or their wills to raunsome them, or to make a pray or spoile of his or their person or goods vpon deadly feude, or otherwise, shalbe taken to be felons, and suffer death without benefit of Clergy, Sanctuary, or Abiuration, &c. S. Felonies by stat. 36. Taking away any person against his will in Cumberland &c.

St. 1. E. 6. 12. 24 By the stat. of Anno 1. Ed. 6. it is ordained, That no person or persons that heretofore hath bin, or that at any time hereafter shalbe in due form of the law attainted or cōuicted of murther of malice prepēced, or of poisoning of malice prepenced, or of breaking of any house by day or by night, any person being then in the same house, where the said breaking hath bin, or shal be committed, heretofore hath bin, or hereafter shalbe therby put in feare or dread, or of, or for robbing of any persō or persons in the high way, or neere to the high way, or for felonious stealing of Horses, Geldings, or Mares, or of felonious taking of any goods out of any parish church, or chappel, or being indicted or appealed of any of the same offences, & thereupon found guilty by verdict of xij. men, or shall confesse the same vpō his or their arraigment, or will not answere directly according to the laws of this realme, or shal stand wilfully or of malice mute, shal not be admitted to haue or enioy ẏ priuiledge or benefit of his Clergy or Sanctuary, but shalbe put from the same. And that in all other cases of Felony (other then such as are before mentioned) all and singular person and persons Murther. Poysoning. Burglary. Robbery in the high way. Stealing of horses Sacriledge. Clergy allowed in all other felonies.

which

which shalbe arraigned, or found guilty upon his or their arraignment, or shal confesse the same, or stand mute in forme aforesaid, or will not answer directly in forme aforesaid, shall haue & enioy the priuiledge and benefit of his or their Clergy and Sanctuary, in like maner and forme as he or they should or might haue done before the 24. of Aprill, Anno 1. H.8.

25 Because it was doubtfull by the words mentioned in the foresaid act of 1. Ed. 6. 12. whether that any person being in due forme of Law found guilty, or otherwise attainted or conuicted for felonious stealing of one Horse, Gelding, or Mare, ought to be admitted to haue and enioy the priuiledge and benefit of his Clergy or Sanctuary: Therefore by a stat. made Anno 2. & 3. Ed. 6. it is declared and enacted, That all and singular person and persons feloniously taking or stealing any Horse, Gelding, or Mare, shall not be admitted to haue or enioy the priuiledge or benefit of his or their Clergy or Sanctuary, but shalbe put from the same, in like manner and forme, as though he or they had bin indicted or appealed for felonious stealing of two Horses, two Geldings, or two Mares of any others, and thereupon found guilty by verdict of twelue men, or confessed the same upon their arraignment, or stand wilfully or of malice mute. But he that is accessary to the stealing of Horses or Mares, shal haue the benefit of his Clergy, for that the foresaid statutes shalbe taken strictly, which maketh mention expressely but of the principall.

Stealing one Horse. — St. 2. & 3. Ed. 6. 33.

Accessaries to stealing of Horses. — P. 1. M. Dy. 99.

26 By a statute made Anno 5. & 6. Ed. 6. it was rehearsed and ordained, That where in the parliament holden at Westminster 15. die Ianuarij An. 25. H.8. it is recited, That at the parliament holden at West. an. 23. H.8. amongst other things it was ordained, That no person or persons, which after that time should happen to be found guilty after the lawes of this land of any manner of petit Treason, or for any wilfull murther of malice prepenced, or for robbing of any Churches, Chappels, or other holy places, or for robbing of any person or persons in their dwelling houses, or dwelling places, the owner or dweller in the same house, his wife, childrē, or seruants then being within, and put in feare and dread by the same: Or for robbing of any person or persons in or neere about the high way: or for wilfull burning of any dwelling houses, or barnes, wherein any graine or corne should happen to be: nor any person or persons being found guilty of any abetment, or procurement, helping, maintaining, or concealing of or to any such petite Treason, Murthers, or Felonies, should not from thenceforth be admitted to the benefit of his or their Clergy, but should be utterly excluded thereof, and suffer death, in such manner and forme, as they should haue done for any the causes or offences abouesaid, if they were not Clerkes. Which act extended but only where such offendor was conuicted in such County or place, where such offence was cōmitted and done, and not where he or they did such offence in one County, and were taken with the manoure in another County. Wherefore it was considered, That for as much as diuers and many Felons and Robbers, that commit and do diuers & many great heinous robberies & burglaries in one shire, & conuey the spoile and robbery into any other shire, and there be takē, indicted, and arraigned

St. 5. & 6. Ed. 6. 10.
St. 25. H. 8.
St. 23. H. 8. 1

arraigned of felonie, for the felonious stealing of the same goods, in the same other Shire than where the same Robberies or Burglaries were done and committed, and not of the same Robberie nor Burglarie, for that it was not done nor committed in the same Shire where they bee so indicted and arraigned, and that by reason thereof such felons, robbers, and burglarers, had and enioyed the priuiledge and aduantage of their Clergie: For redresse whereof it was enacted in the same Parliament holden in the sayd fiue and twentieth yeare of the said late King, That if any person or persons, after that time, after such robberie or burglarie by him or them done in one Countie, should be indicted of Felonie, for stealing of any goods or cattels in any other Countie within this Realme, and thereupon arraigned, and found guiltie, or stand mute of malice, or challenge peremptorily aboue the number of twentie persons, or would not vpon his or their arraignment directly answer to the same felonie, that then the same person and persons so arraigned, and found guiltie, or standing mute of malice, or challenging peremptorily aboue the number of twentie persons, or that would not directly answer to the law, should lose and bee put from the benefit of his or their Clergie, in like manner and forme as they should haue beene, if they had beene indicted, arraigned, and found guiltie in the same Countie where such robberie or burglarie, as is aforesayd was done or committed, if it should appeare to the Iustices before whom any such felons or robbers should be arraigned by euidence giuen before them, or by examination, that the same felons or burglarers should haue beene put from their Clergie, in case they had beene indicted, arraigned, and found guiltie in the same countie where the same robberies or burglaries were committed or done, as in the same statute made in the said fiue and twentieth yere among other things more plainely appeareth. And where in the Parliament

St.1.E.6.12 holden at Westminster, the fourth day of Nouember, in the first yeare of the raigne of our Soueraigne Lord the King that now is, it is ordayned and enacted amongst other things, That no person or persons that before that time had beene, or at any time hereafter should bee in due forme of law attainted or conuicted of murder of malice prepensed, or of poysoning of malice prepensed, or of breaking of any house by day, or by night, any person beeing then in the same house when the same breaking had bin, or after that time should bee committed, beeing put in feare or dread, or of or for robbing of any person or persons in the high way, or neere the high way, or for felonious stealing of Horses, Geldings, or Mares, or of felonious taking of any goods out of any Parish Church, or other Church or Chappell, or beeing indicted or appealed of any of the same offences, and thereupon found guiltie by verdict of twelue men, or should confesse the same vpon his or their arraignement, or would not answer directly according to the lawes of this Realme, or should stand wilfully or of malice mute, should not bee admitted to haue or enioy the priuiledge or benefit of his or their Clergie or Sanctuarie, but should bee put from the same. And that in all other cases of Felonie (other than such as be before mentioned) all and singular person and persons, which after the first day of March then next following, should bee arraigned or found guiltie vpon his or their arraignement, or should confesse the same, or stand mute in forme aforesayd, or would not answer directly in forme abouesayd, should haue and enioy the priuiledge and benefit of his or their Clergie, and the libertie and priuiledge of Sanctuarie, in like manner and forme, as hee or they might or should haue done before the foure and twentieth day of Aprill, in the first yeare of the raigne of the sayd late King Henrie the eight, as in the sayd Act made in the sayd first yeare, among other things more plainely appeareth. By reason of which article and clause, contained in the sayd Act made in the sayd first yeare, the sayd Statute made in the sayd fiue and twentieth yeare of the sayd late King, which did put such felons and burglarers from their Clergie, that doe such offence in one Countie, and after are taken with the goods stollen in another Countie, and there indicted, arraigned, and found guiltie, was made void: By reason whereof diuers and many persons that sithence the sayd first yeare, haue committed such Robberies and Burglaries in one Countie, and after haue beene taken with the manner in another Countie, and there indicted, arraigned, and found guiltie, haue had and enioyed their Clergie, which they could not haue had, in case the sayd Act made in the sayd fiue and twentieth yeare had stood in force, to the great boldening and comfort of such offendors: Be it enacted, That the sayd Act made in the sayd fiue and twentieth yeare, touching the putting of such offendors from their Clergie, and euerie article, clause, and sentence contained in the same, touching Clergie, shall from henceforth touching such offences to be committed and done, stand, remaine, and be in full strength and vertue, in such manner and forme, as it did before the making of the sayd Act made in the said first yeare of the raigne of our said Soueraigne Lord that now is, any clause, article, or sentence comprised in the said Act made in the said first yeare, to the contrarie thereof notwithstanding. This Statute of 5.& 6.Ed.6. doth not reuiue the whole before rehearsed Statute of 25.H.8. (being before repealed by the last braunch of the before specified Statute of 1.Ed.6.12.) but reuiueth onely so much thereof, as concerneth the stealing of goods in one Countie, and after carying them into another Countie, as it appeareth by the words of the same Statute. And neither the sayd Statute of 25.H.8. nor this Statute of 5. & 6.Ed.6. doe extend to Appeales, but onely to Indictments: so that in an Appeale brought in the Countie whither the goods robbed or spoyled were carryed, if the defendant be conuict thereof, the defendant may haue his Clergie at this day.

Stealing of goods in one County, and carrying them into another.

St.5.& 6.E.6.10.

27 By a Statute made Anno 5.& 6.E.6. it was rehearsed and established, That whereas at the Parliament holden at Westminster by prorogation anno 23.H.8. it was then and there among other things ordained, That no person or persons, which after that time should happen to be found guiltie after the lawes of this Realme, for any manner petit Treason, or for any wilfull murder of malice prepensed, or for robbing of any Churches, Chappels, or other holy places, or for robbing any person or persons in their dwelling houses, or dwelling places, the owner or dweller in the same house, his wife, his children, or seruants then being within, and put in feare or dread by the same, or for robbing of any person or persons in or neere about the highwayes, or for wilfull burning of any dwelling houses, or barnes, wherein any graine or corne shall happen to be: nor any person or persons being found guiltie of any abetment, procurement, maintaining, or concealing of any, or to any such Petit treasons, murders, or felonies, should from thenceforth be admitted to the benefit of his or their Clergie, but vtterly to be excluded therof, & suffer death in such maner and forme as they should haue done, for any the causes or offences abouesaid, if they were not Clerkes (such as be within the holy orders (that is

St.5.& 6.E.6.9.

St.23.H.8.1

to

St.32.H.8.3 to say) of the orders of Subdeacon, or aboue, all only excepted, as by the same act among other things more plainely appeareth) the which act was made to endure untill the last day of the next parliament, and after that at the Session of the parliament holden at Westminster by prorogation in the 32. yeare of the raigne of the said late king, the same act with other acts was made to continue for euer. Sithence the making of which statute it hath been doubted, that if such robberies and felonies haue bin committed and done in dwelling houses and dwelling places, the owner or dweller in the same house, his wife, his children, or seruants, being then put in feare or dread by the same, shal not lose the benefit of their clergy, if the offendors be therein found guilty by the laws of this Realme, unlesse the same robbery or felony be committed & done in the very chamber, house, or place, where the owner or dweller in the same house, his wife, children, or seruants shall happen to be, or lie at the time of such robbery and felony cōmitted & done, and put in feare and dread, although the owner or dweller in such house & houses, his wife, his children or seruants at the time of such robbery & felony committed and done, were or lay in other places within the precinct of the same dwelling houses, nigh unto the house or place where such robbery & felony shall happen to be done: Or if it happen that the owner or dweller within the same house where such robbery & felony shal happen to be done, his wife, children, or seruants to be asleepe at the time of such robbery & felony committed & done, although the same robbery were done in the chamber or place where the owner or dweller in the same house, his wife, children, or seruants, then lay, the offendors being found guilty thereof, according to the lawes of the land, should not lose the benefit and aduantage of his clergy. And where also it hath bin in question, and doubted, that if such robberies & felonies happen to be committed and done in any booth or boothes, tent, or tents, in any faire or market, the owner of the same, his wife, children, or seruants happen to be within the same at the time of the committing of such felonies, and put in feare and dread, the offendors therein being found guilty, after the lawes of this realme, should not lose the benefit of their Clergy. For the true declaration & explanation of the same doubts or questions before recited, be it enacted, That if it happen any person or persons to be found guilty according to the laws of this realme, for robbing of any person or persons in any part or parcell of their dwelling houses or dwelling places, the owner or dweller in the same house, or his wife, his children, or seruants, being then within the same house or place, where it shal happen the same robbery and felony to be committed & done, or in any other place within the precinct of the same house, or dwelling place, that such offēdors in no wise shalbe admitted to their clergy whether the owner or dweller in the same house, his wife, or children, thē and there being, shalbe waking or sleeping. And that no person nor persons which shall happen to be found guilty after the lawes of this realme, of, & for robbing any person or persons in any booth or tent in any faire, or market, the owner, his wife, his children or seruants, or seruant, then being within the same booth or tent, shall not from henceforth be admitted to the benefit of his or their clergy, but utterly be excluded thereof, and suffer death in such manner & forme as is before mentioned in the said act, made in the said 32. yeare of the raigne of the same late king for robberies and felonies committed and done in dwelling houses and dwelling places, the owner or dweller in the same, his wife, children or seruants then being within the same, and put in feare and dread, without hauing any respect or consideration, whether the owner or dweller in such boothes and tents, his wife, children, or seruants being in the same boothes or tents

Margin notes: St.5.& 6.E.6.9. — Robbing of houses. — Robbing of booths or tents

tents, at the time of such robberies and felonies committed, shalbe sleeping or waking.

This statute mentioneth onely where one is found guiltie after the lawes of this Realme: and therefore it is to be considered, if the offendor doe confesse the felonie, or stand mute, or challenge peremptorily aboue twentie persons, or will not answer directly to the felony, whether he shall haue his clergy or not, because he is out of the words of this statute. Also this statute doth not take away the benefit of Clergie from the offendor, but where the owner, his wife, children, or seruants were within the house at the time of the offence committed: for if none of them but a stranger did lye within the house by the licence of the owner, at the time of the offence committed, then is the offendor out of the danger of this Statute. And so he that is attainted by outlawrie, or by battell, is out of the cases of all the foresaid statutes which doe take away Clergy.

Attainder by outlawrie, or by battell.

One was indicted, for that he did feloniously take xl.s. in mony nūbred, from the person of J.S. and he had his Clergy in this case, for that it was not robberie, because it was not found by the indictment, that the person of J.S. was put in feare by assault and violence. 5.El.Dyer.224.

28 Because diuers lewd persons, understanding that the penaltie of robbing of houses in the day time (no person being in the house at the time of the robberie) is not so penall, as to doe a robberie in any house, any person béeing therein at the time of the robberie, which hath and doth imbolden seueral lewd persons to watch their opportunitie and time to commit and doe many haynous robberies, in breaking and entring diuers honest persons houses, and specially of the poorer sort of people, who by reason of their pouertie are not able to kéepe any seruant, or otherwise to leaue any body to look to their house when they go abroad to heare diuine seruice, or to follow their worke to get their liuing: For the preuention whereof, by a statute made Anno 39. Elizab. it was enacted, That if any person or persons shall bée found guilty, and conuicted by verdict, confession, or otherwise, according to the lawes of this Realme, for the felonious taking away in the day time, of any money, goods, or cattell, being of the value of fiue shillings or vpward, in any dwelling house, or houses, or any part thereof, or any outhouse, or outhouses, belonging and vsed to and with any dwelling house or houses, although no person shall bée in the sayd house or outhouses, at the time of such felonie committed: then such person and persons shall not be admitted to the benefit of his or their clergy, but shall bée vtterly excluded thereof. S.39.El.15.

Robbing a house in the day time.

Commandement or counsell of felonies.

29 By the statute made Anno 4. & 5. P. & M. it was enacted, That al and euery person and persons that shall malitiously commaund, hyre, or counsell any person or persons to commit or doe any Petit Treason, wilfull murder, or to do any robbery in any dwelling house or houses, or to do or commit any robberie in or néere any highway in the Realme of England, or in any other the Quéenes Dominions: or to commit or doe any robberie in any place within the Marches of England, against Scotland: or wilfully to burne any dwelling house, or any part therof: or any barne then hauing corne or graine in the same: then euery such offendor and offendors, and euery of them, being outlawed of the same, or being thereof arraigned and found guiltie by the order of the law, or being otherwise lawfully attainted or conuicted of the same offence, or being St.4 & 5. P.&M.4.

arraigned

arraigned thereof, do stand mute of malice or froward mind, or doe challenge peremptorily aboue the number of xx. persons, or will not answer directly to such offence, shall not haue the benefit of his or their clergy. Euery Lord and Peere of the realme hauing place and voyce in Parliament, vpon euery inditement for any of the offences aforesaid, shall bee tryed by his Peeres. A man was indicted of the robberie of another in his mansion house, he being in his house, and put in feare: And another was indicted, for that he did feloniously before the sayd robberie procure and counsell the principall to commit the sayd robberie: in which inditment of the accessorie, this word (malitiously) was omitted: for the default of which word, this accessorie had his clergie, for this word (malitiously) shall haue relation to all the aforesaid offences of Petit treason, murder, robberie, and burning of houses.

P.2.Eliz. Dyer 183.

Malitiously omitted in the inditment.

30 By the before specified Statute of Anno 1.Ed.6. among other things it is enacted, That in all and euerie case and cases, where any of the kings subiects shall and may vpon his praier, haue the priuiledge of Clergie, as a Clerke conuict that may make purgation: in all those cases, and euerie of them, and also in all and euerie case and cases of felonie, wherein the priuiledge or benefit of Clergie is restrained, excepted, or taken away by this Statute (wilfull murder and poysoning of malice prepenced only excepted) the Lord and Lords of the Parliament, and Peere and Peers of the Realme hauing place and voice in Parliament, shall by vertue of this Act, of common grace, vpon his or their requests and prayer, alledging that he is a Lord or Peere of this Realme, claiming the benefit of this Act, though he cannot read, without burning in the hand, losse of inheritance, or corruption of his bloud, be adiudged, deemed, taken, and vsed, for the first time onely, to all constructions, intents, and purposes, as a Clerke conuict, which may make purgation, without any further or other benefit of Clergie, to any such Lord or Peer from thenceforth, at any time after, for any cause to be allowed, adiudged, or admitted: Any law, custome, statute, or other thing to the contrarie notwithstanding. By this Statute a Lord of the Parliament shall haue the priuiledge of his Clergie, where a common person shall not, viz. for the breaking of a house by day or night, or for robbing of any in the highway, and in all other cases excepted in the sayd statute of Anno 1.Ed.6. sauing in wilfull murder and poysoning. But in all other cases wherein Clergie is taken away by any statute made sithence the sayd statute of Anno 1.Ed.6. he is in the same degree that a common and inferiour person is. But the Court will not giue him the benefit of this statute, if he doth not require it. If a Lord of the Parliament doth confesse his offence vpon his arraignment, or doth abiure, or is outlawed for felony, it seemeth that in these cases he may haue the benefit of this statute, viz. his Clergie: for that by the Statute of 18.Elizab.6. hee nor any other need to make his purgation, but shall bee forthwith deliuered out of prison by the Iustices: sed quære.

St.1.E.6.12. S.Br.24.

Where a Lord of the Parliament shal haue the benefit of his Clergie.

31 In all the foresaid cases of wilfull murder, breaking of houses, robbing in or neere the highway, buggerie, stabbing, and such like, where a man is put out of his Clergie by statute, it is necessarie, that in the inditment mention should be made of the offence, in such manner as the same offence is expressed in the statute, or otherwise the offendor shall haue his Clergie: for if the inditment be onely murdrauit, without adding ex malitia præcogitata, the partie

P.9.Eliz. Dyer 261.

The inditment must bee according to the statute.

meant to be indicted of wilfull murder, shall haue his Clergie; and so of all the residue: for his attainder or conuiction is vpon the matter contained in the appeale or indictment: and if in the appeale or indictment no matter is contained which doth put him out of his Clergie, then it cannot be sayd that hée is attaint or conuict of any matter contained in the Statute, which should cause him to lose the benefit thereof. And the Iudge is to haue speciall regard and consideration, when those words be put into the indictment, that they which do giue euidence do proue the same words well and substantially, as well as the principall fact: and if they doe not, the Iudge is to admonish the Iurie thereof, viz. that there is no proofe of those words by the euidence, and that therefore they are not bound to find them, if they doe not know them of their owne knowledge. Or otherwise for default of good examination, the life and lands of any man may be lost by the malice of another which will put false words in an indictment, that cannot be proued by euidence.

The words of the indictment to be proued.

when Clergy shalbe demanded.

32 By the auntient law of the Realme, if a Clerke of any order or dignitie had béene taken for the death of a man, or other felonie or offence, and imprisoned, and the Ordinarie had demaunded him, the temporall Iudge ought to haue deliuered him presently to the Ordinarie, his Officiall, or to some other by his warrant, without inquiring of him, viz before his indictment: Not to the intent that the Ordinarie should set him at libertie, but kéepe him in prison vntill the offendor were purged of his cryme: For it was then holden for law, that the King could not kéepe him in prison, whom hée could not iudge, neither could hée disgrade any of his Clergie, because hée could not admit any to his Clergie. But because the Statute of Westminst. 1. doth ordaine, That they which bée indicted of Felonie in the Kings Court, by the solemne othe of lawfull witnesses, shall bée deliuered to the Ordinarie vpon his request, according to the priuiledge of holy Church, but yet in no manner without due purgation: Therefore they that came after this Statute, chaunged the sayd auntient law, for they would not deliuer the prisoner vnto the Ordinarie, vntill hée was indicted, and also arraigned, and that it was enquired by an Enquest of Office, whether hée were guiltie or not. In which case, if he were found not guiltie, they would discharge him: and if he were found guiltie, his goods should bée forfeited, his lands taken into the Kings hands, and his bodie deliuered to the Ordinarie. And the cause of chaunging this law was, that the Ordinarie might take greater charge of the prisoner, being now indicted, than before, and to benefit the King by the forfeiture of the prisoners goods, and to bréed a greater feare in Clerkes after, that they should not offend. Which alteration was obserued for law, vntill the raigne of King Henry the first, at which time the Iudges would not admit a prisoner to demaund his Clergie vpon his arraignment, but put himselfe first to answer to the Felonie, and if hée were found guiltie of the Felonie, at his owne suit, then to heare him demaund his Clergie, and not before: which is a more reasonable law than the former: for before hee should haue forfeited his goods vpon an Enquest of Office, whereunto hée could haue no challenge: and now he shalbe tryed at his owne suit, and shall haue his challenge to the Enquest: and then if he be found guiltie, hée shall forfeit his goods: and for the sauing of his life and his lands, hée is to pray his Clergie. Which hath bin vsed euer sithence, and is obserued for law at this time, vnlesse the prisoner himselfe will refuse the benefit thereof, and pray to haue his booke, without hearing the

Bracton.

St.W.3.E.1

Fitz.Cor. 233.386. 417. M.40.E.3. 42.

3.H.7.1. & 12.

the verdict: As if a prisoner after an Enquest is charged upon him, and before their returne againe, will say that he is a Clerke, and desire his booke at his perill: in this case the Court hath allowed him his Clergie, and yet after hath receiued a verdict, as well in fauour of life, as in fauour of the King, for if he be found not guiltie, the prisoner shall be discharged, and if he bee found guiltie, the King shall haue his goods as forfeit: And the request of his booke in that case, is more for the prisoners disaduantage than the Kings, for it may bee a meane that the Jurie understanding thereof, will the rather find him guiltie of the felonie, than otherwise they would haue done. Clergy demanded before verdict.

26.Ass.p.19 33 If a prisoner doe say, that hee is no Clerke, yet after if before iudgement hee doe pray his Clergie (where Clergie is allowable by the law) and then doth read as a Clerke, hee shall haue his Clergie, notwithstanding his former words. But it hath beene a question, whether the Judges ought to allow any man his Clergie without praying of it, though the offendor be Fi.Cor.254 indicted by the name of Priest, Clerke, &c. or that by some other meanes the Judges themselues doe know that hee is a Clerke, or that without praying of his Clergie they shall giue iudgement of death against him. And in this case some doe affirme, that if the prisoner doth not pray his Clergie, hee shall not haue it, though the Judge doth upon his owne priuat knowledge understand that hee is a Clerke: for the Judge must in those cases proceed according to his iudiciall knowledge, and as by record things bee found, proued, and tryed before him, and not according to his owne naturall knowledge. And they bee the rather so induced to thinke by the words of the aforesayd St.1.E.6.12 statute of 1.Edw.6. which ordayned, That a Peere of the Realme shall (upon request) haue the benefit of his Clergie, and so inferre, that without request he shall not haue it, nor any other without request, which is to haue it upon request. Denying to be a Clerke, and yet is. Whether clergie is allowable without request.

34 The temporall Court shall be Judge to allow or disallow of Clergy, and 15.H.7.9. not the Ordinary: for it was entred into the roll of the court, legit vt Clericus, ideo tradatur Ordinario, by which words it doth appear, that the court doth giue allowance therof: for the felony being the act which is cōmitted is temporal, and the Judge which did commit him to the Ordinary is temporal, & so is the authority wherby he did commit him. And the Ordinary should haue bin puni- St.18.El.6. shed if before the stat. of 18. Eli. he had letten to baile or at liberty any prisoner cōmitted to him, or if he had imprisoned him too straitly, or too easily, or would not haue suffered him to haue made his purgation: and in that case the king might haue sent his Writ unto the Ordinarie, commaunding him to suffer his prisoner to make his purgation, or might haue pardoned him, or Fitz.Cor. 44.17 set him at liberty, without making his purgation: and if one read as a Clerke, and yet the Ordinarie will refuse him, notwithstanding hee shall haue the benefite of his Clergie: and on the other side, if the Ordinarie will say that hee doth read as a Clerke, whereas in truth hee doth not read as a Clerke, the Court must giue iudgement that hee shall bee hanged, and cause execution to bee done of him. And further to proue, that the Temporall Court is Judge of the reading, the Court doth appoint the verse or place to the prisoner to read, and not the Ordinarie: Who shall allow of clergy.

And

And also doth set a fine vpon the Ordinary, for saying that the prisoner doth read as a Clerk, where he doth not, which the court could not do, if the reading were referred to the Ordinarie. 34.H.6.49. 21.Ed.4.21. 9.E.4.28.

A felon doth read vnder the gallowes.

35 If a felon doth not read as a Clerke before the Judge at the time of his arraignment, whereupon he is adiudged to be hanged, yet in fauor of life, if hee do demand it at another time vnder the gallows if any of the Judges do passe that way, and doth read as a Clerke, he shall haue the benefit of his Clergie, although there be no Ordinary there to demaund him: But this is in case where the felon is arraigned and iudged before the Just. of the K. Bench; or else in case where he is arraigned and iudged before the Just. of gaole deliuerie, and it is entred by the Court, non legit vt Clericus, and then for some cause he is repried vntill the next Session, and then againe he is demanded if he can read, and then he can and doth read: in this case he shall haue his Clergy in fauor of life. And though he was taught to read in the gaole, this shall saue his life, but the gaoler shalbe punished for it. 34.H.6.49. 3.& 4.El. Dy. fo.205.

36 The Court vpon the suit of the prisoner may allow him the priuiledge of his Clergie in the absence of the Ordinarie, or without the aduice of the Ordinarie, or without demanding of the Ordinary, vtrũ legit vt Clericus an non: and so the court need not expect the presence of the Ordinary, if he faile of his attendance: for the court doth vse the Ordinary but as a minister in this cause, to confirme their iudgement in allowance of Clergie, and to heare his opinion, if the prisoner be worthy of Clergy or not: Because the maner and order is, for the Ordinary to deliuer a booke to the Just. who open it, and assigne the verse that the prisoner shall read: and the Ordinary receiuing the booke of the Justices, doth come to the prisoner, and command him to read that verse, which being done, the court doth demand of the Ordinary, vtrũ legit vt Clericus an non? and the Ordinarie doth answer, legit, or non legit: and then the court doth allow that which the Ordinarie saith, if it be true, or otherwise not. And moreouer the Ordinarie was in former times vsed by the Justices to another purpose, viz. to know if the prisoner were within orders or not, which the temporall court could not take knowledge of, for if he were within orders, he should haue had the priuiledge of the church, whether he did read or not, by shewing the letters of his orders, or by the Ordinaries certificat, vntill the stat. of anno 28. H.8. was made, by the which it was ordained, That such as be within holy orders, shalbe and stand vnder the paines and damages for their offences, and be vsed and ordered to all intents, as other persons not being within holy orders shall be. And further, it may be that the offendor hath bin a committer of sacriledge, an heretike, or an Apostata, or some other grieuous offendor, so that the court hearing the Ordinary willing to refuse him, would also refuse him. 9.E.4.28 St.28.H.8.1

To what vse the Ordinarie is imployed.

Clerks within Orders shalbe vsed as others be.

What is reading as a Clerke.

37 There is a difference of reading, for it may be that the prisoner may read two or three words of the verse that is assigned vnto him by the court, but not the whole verse, which is a kind of reading, but not such a reading as a Clerke ought to make: for if hee will read as a Clerke, hee must read the whole verse. But although at the first hee beginneth with spelling, and after doth read as a Clerke, yet in fauour of life he shalbe allowed for a Clerke, 9.Ed.4.28.

and

4.Eliz. Dyer 215. and the forme of entry upon request of Clergie, is, Et tradito ei libro, legit vt clericus.

38 Though the Court may giue allowance of Clergie in the Ordinaries absence, yet that shall not excuse the Ordinary of his attendance in proper person, or by his deputie, upon paine of a fine to be assessed upon him by the Court: which deputy ought to haue and bring with him sufficient letters of the Ordinarie, under his seale, testifying the authoritie which the Ordinary hath giuen him: And though his warrant be but to challenge Clerkes arraigned (and not Clerks conuicted) yet the warrant is good ynough, and shalbe allowed. And if two seuerall persons do claime to be Ordinaries, the Court ought not to allow either of them, but must write to the Metropolitan to make certificat who of right ought to be Ordinarie.

The Ordinaries attendāce. 25.E.3.40. Contention who is Ordinarie.

Fi.Cor.432 Britton. 39 He that is indicted by the name of a Clerke, or appeareth to the Judge to be a Priest, shall not upon his arraignment stand at the bar in fetters. And so was the law in antient time for euery prisoner, as Britton reporteth.

A Priest shall haue no fetters.

40 Bigamie in times past was a counterplea to clergy, viz. to alledge, that he who demandeth the priuiledge of his clergy, was maried to such a woman, at such a place, within such a dioces, and that the said woman dyed, and that he maried another woman in such a place in the same or another dioces, and so hée is Bigamus: Or if he hath béene but once maried, to say, that she which hée maried was a widow, and before had bin the wife of such a man: which allegation should haue bin tried by the bishop of the dioces where the mariage was alledged to be solemnized: And it being certified by the bishop, that he was Bigamus, the prisoner should haue béene put from his clergie: Which was by a Constitution made at the Counsell of Lions, as it appeareth by the stat. of Bigamie, made anno 4. Ed. 1. for before that Counsell of Lions, euery man that had bin twice maried, or had maried a widow, should haue had the priuiledge of clergie. But that law was sithence altered by the stat. of anno 1. Ed. 6. wherby it is enacted, That if any person or persons by this stat. or by any other stat. or lawes of this realme, ought to haue or to be admitted to the benefit of his or clergie, that the same person or persons shalbe from henceforth admitted and allowed to haue his or their clergy, although they or any of them haue bin diuers and sundrie times maried to any single woman or single women, or to any widow or widowes, or to two wiues, or mo: Any law, statute, or usage, to the contrarie notwithstanding. And though, some haue affirmed, that the foresaid stat. of 1. Ed. 6. was abrogated by a braunch of a stat. made 1. & 2. P. & M. 8. which did repeale all stat. prouisions, and articles made against the sea of Rome, since the xx. yere of K. H. 8. and the Pope by his decretals brought in the same exception of Bigamy, which was obserued and obeyed as a common law, untill the said stat. of 1. E. 6. But that foresaid stat. of 1. & 2. P. & M. 8. was also after repealed by the stat. of an. 1. El. 1. for the which and some other causes, it is agréed and holden for law, that the before rehearsed stat. of 1. Ed. 6. doth stand and remaine in force, and Bigamus shall haue his Clergie.

St.4.Ed.1.5. St.1.E.6.12 S.Br.24. St.1.Ed.6. 3.Eliz.Dyer fol.201.

Bigamus shal haue his Clergie.

41 It is a good counterplea to him who demaundeth his Clergy, to say, that he had another time the benefit of his Clergie, when he was arraigned of another

Another time conuict.

another felony, and shew the certainty therof, when and where he was arraigned, and had his Clergie, to demaund iudgement if hée shall haue his Clergie againe: Which counterplea was ordayned by the statute of Anno 4. H. 7. for by the common law, if a man had once enioyed the benefit of his Clergie for felonie, and after committed felonie againe, yet he should haue had the priuiledge of his Clergie againe, and so often as hée had committed felony, vntil the said statute did restraine him by these words: viz. Where vpon trust of the priuiledge of the church, diuers persons haue bin the more bold to commit murder, rape, robberie, theft, and all other mischiuous déeds, because they haue béen continually admitted to the benefit of their clergie, as oft as they did offend in any of the premisses: In auoidance of such presumptuous boldnesse, it is ordained, That euerie person (not being within orders) which once hath bin admitted to the benefit of his Clergie eftsoones arraigned of any such offences, be not admitted to haue the benefit or priuiledge of his clergy: and ẏ euery such person so conuicted for murder, to be marked with an M. vpon the brawne of the left thumb, & if it be for felony, the same person to be marked with a T. in the same place of the thumb: & these markes to be made by the gaoler openly in the court before the Iudge, before such person be deliuered to the Ordinarie. Prouided alwayes, if any person at the second time of asking his clergie, because hee is within orders, hath not there ready his letters of his orders, or a certificat of his Ordinarie witnessing the same, that then the Iustices before whom hee is so arraigned, shall giue him a day by their discretion, to bring in his said letters or certificat. And if he faile, and bring not in at such a day his said letters, nor certificat, then the same person to lose the benefit of his clergie, as he shall doe that is without orders. By which stat. it doth appeare, that he that is within orders is excepted, and that he may haue his clergie the second time, vpon the shewing of his letters of orders, or his Ordinaries certificat of the same, this statute notwithstanding. But after by the statute made Anno 28. H. 8. & 32. H. 8. it was enacted, That all such persons as be, or shall be within holy orders, which by the lawes of this Realme ought or may haue their clergie for any felonies, and shalbe admitted to the same, shalbe burned in the hand, in like maner and forme as lay Clerkes béene accustomed in such cases, and shall suffer and incurre after, all such paines, damages, and forfeitures, and bee ordered and vsed for their offences of felony, to all intents and purposes, as lay persons admitted to their clergie, be, or ought to be ordered and vsed by the lawes and statutes of this Realme: Any lawes, statutes, prouisions, customes, &c. notwithstanding. The force and effect of part of which said statutes of 28. H. 8. & 32. H. 8. is in some sort attenuated by a braunch of the stat. of Anno 1. Ed. 6. (as some do conceiue it) which doth ordaine, That in all other cases (sauing such as be mentioned in the sayd Act) all and singular person & persons, which shall be arraigned, or found guiltie vpon his or their arraignement, or should confesse the same, or stand mute, or would not answer directly, should haue and enioy the priuiledge and benefit of his and their clergie, the libertie and priuiledge of Sanctuarie, in like manner and forme, as he or they might or should haue done before the foure and twentieth day of Aprill, Anno 1. H. 8. at which time a man within orders should haue had the priuiledge of his clergie seuerall times: And by this Statute he shall not be burned in the hand as a lay man shall. But yet in all those cases wherein a man is put out of his Clergie, by the Statute of Anno 1. Ed. 6. and also in all other cases wherein Clergie is taken away by any Statute made sithence Anno primo Edw. 6. a man within orders is as well put out of his Clergie, as a lay man, eue-

Margin notes: St. 4. H. 7. 13. — How the conuict shalbe marked. — St. 28. H. 8. 1 & 32. H. 8. 3. — How offendors that be within orders shalbe vsed. — St. 1. E. 6. 12. S. Br. 24.

euery of those Statutes being generall and without exception.

42 Because diuers persons haue béene in times past indicted, arraigned, and some of them Clerkes conuict, and some of them Clerkes attainted, and some of them outlawed for Murder, Burglarie, Robberie, and other Felonies, before Justices of Peace, Justices of Gaole deliuerie, and Justices of Oyer and Terminer, within diuers, Cities, Counties, Franchises and Liberties within this Realme: The records of which attainders, outlawries, and conuictions, many times by the negligence of the Clerke of the Crowne, Clerke of the Peace, Clerke of Assise, and such other as haue had the order, rule, kéeping, and gouernance of the same Records, haue béene imbeciled, and not readie to be obiected against such persons as haue béen newly arraigned before the King in his Bench, or before other the Kings Justices, for the like and such other offences by them committed or done: And for that it hath not béene knowne certainely, whither to resort for the same Records, because they were not certified into any place certaine, by reason whereof sometimes such persons and like offendors, which haue béene newly arraigned, as is aforesayd, haue had the benefit of his or their Clergie, where they ought not, ne should haue had the same, if the said Records had béene then present in the same place where such person or persons were so newly arraigned, or else certified into some other place certaine, where the same Records might haue bin séen, sent for, or written for, to haue béene obiected against such person or persons so newly arraigned, whereby as well the King, as also all other persons, haue many times lost their Escheats, and other aduantages and forfeitures, that they should haue had by meane of the sayd attainders, to the great losses of the King and other persons: and also the sayd offendors haue had their Clergie, where they ought not to haue had, to the great boldnesse and encouragement of like offendors: For the reformation whereof by a Statute made Anno 34. & 35. H. 8. it was enacted, That the Clerke of the Crowne, Clerke of the Peace, and Clerkes of Assise for the time being, where any such attainder, outlawrie, or conuiction shall so bée had, shall not onely certifie a Transcript briefly and in few words, containing the tenor and effect of euerie such indictment, outlawrie, or conuiction, and Clerke attainted, before them so to be had, made, or pronounced, that is to say, the name, sirname, and addition of euerie such person and persons, as shall be so indicted, and thereupon outlawed, conuicted, or Clerke attainted: and the certaintie of the sayd felonie, or other offence, whereupon he or they shalbe so outlawed, conuicted, or Clerke attainted, and the day and place of his outlawrie, conuiction, and attainder, and the day and place where and when the said felony or other offence whereupon the said person or persons shalbe so indicted, outlawed, or Clerke attainted, shall be made and done, before the K. in his bench at West. in the county of Midd. there to remaine of record for euer, among other the K. records there, within xl. daies next after any such attainder, conuiction, or outlawrie shall be had, made, or procured (if the terme be thẽ) & if not, within xx. dayes next after the beginning of the terme next following the said xl. daies, but also shall deliuer a transcript of euerie such indictment, whereupon the said person & persons shal fortune hereafter so to be conuicted, or Clerkes attainted, to the Ordinary, to whom the body of the said person or persons shall be committed, at the time that the sayd person or persons shall bee committed, the sayd Ordinarie paying to euerie such Clerke as shall write the sayd Transcript, for euerie copie of such indictment, twelue

St. 34. & 35. H. 8. 14.

Certificat into the K. bench of outlawries, attainders, & conuictions.

twelue pence for his paines, vpon paine that euery Clerke of the Crowne, Clerke of the peace, and Clerke of Assise for the time being, before whom such Indictment, Attainder, Outlary, or Conuiction shalbe so had, made, pronounced, or remaine, for the non-certifying of euery such record, and deliuering of the copy of such Indictment to the said Ordinaries, according to this statute, to lose and forfeit forty shillings, the one moity thereof to be to the king, and the other moity to him that will sue for the same, by action of Debt, Bill, Information, or otherwise, in any of the kings Courts of Record, wherein no Wager of Law, Essoine, or Protection shalbe allowed: and the clerke of the Crowne in the kings Bench shall receiue the said certificats and transcripts at such time as they shall be tendered and profered vnto them by the said clerkes of the Crowne, clerkes of the peace, and clerkes of assise, or by their deputy or deputies, without taking any thing for the same, vpon paine of forfeiture of forty shillings for euery such certificat by him refused. Prouided alwaies, that if there be any more persons contained and named in any such Indictment other then such person so attainted, conuicted, or outlawed, that then such clerke of the crowne, clerke of assise, or clerke of peace, with whom the record of such attainder, outlary, or conuiction shall remaine, shall within the time before in this act limitted certifie the transcript of such indictment, outlarie, or conuiction onely concerning such person or persons so indicted and attainted, outlawed, or conuicted into the kings Bench at Westminster, as is aforesaid: which transcript so certified shall be had and taken as good, effectuall, and auaileable in the Law, to all intents and purposes, against such person and persons, against whom it shall be so obiected, alledged, or pleaded, as if the very record thereof, whereupon he or they were so indicted, were there present. And be it enacted &c. That the said clerke of the crowne in the kings Bench, for the time being, shall at all such times as the Iustices of Gaole Deliuerie or Iustices of Peace in euery County within this Realme of England doe write vnto him for the names of such persons, which be so attainted by Outlarie, or clerkes attainted or conuicted, and certified into the said Bench, shall incontinently without delay certifie the said names and surnames of the said persons, with the causes why and wherefore they were conuict or attainted, vnto the Iustices of Gaole deliuery, or Iustices of Peace, vpon paine and penalty to forfeit for euery name of such persons which shall be so written for, and not certified by the said Clerk of the Crowne in the kings Bench to the said Iustices, fortie shillings. Prouided, that this Act, nor any thing therein contained, shall not extend to the Clerkes of the Crowne, Clerkes of the Peace, Clerkes of Gaole deliuerie, neither to any of the Prenotaries within the Counties of Wales and Chester, or within the Counties Palantine of Lancaster and Duresme, or any of them, to make any transcript of any such attainder, conuiction, or outlawrie of any person or persons conuicted, attainted, or outlawed, before the Kings Iustices of his Counties of Wales nor Chester, or Countie of Lancaster, Duresme, or any of them, but that the same Records shall and may remaine and be in the custodie and keeping of the sayd Clerkes and Prenotaries, in such maner and wise as they are at this day: this Act or any thing therein contained to the contrarie notwithstanding.

43 Though the deliuering of him to the Ordinarie who hath the benefit of his Clergie, and making of purgation, bee taken away the Statute of

18. Eliz.

18.Eliz.6. yet because both deliuering to the Ordinarie, and making of purgation were vsed by the space of many generations in this realme, and seuerall lawes, statutes, and some prouinciall councells were made and ordained, touching the ordering, direction, and gouernance of those which as Clerks conuict or attaint were committed to the Ordinary, and were to make purgation, or not: I will therefore briefly set downe the effect of some of those laws, as antiquitie did retaine them. He which had the priuiledge of his Clergie, and was deliuered to the Ordinarie that did demaund him, was not set at libertie, to goe wandring vp and downe the Countrie, but was safely and straitly kept in the Bishoppes prison, hauing for foode vppon the Sonday bread, ale, and pease, and vpon all the other daies, courser bread, and small drinke once in the day onely (or in the Kings prison, if the Bishop would haue it so) vntill hee had purged himselfe of the crime wherewith hee was charged, or otherwise had failed of his purgation and could not make it. And if the Bishop would not admitte him to make his purgation, then the King would direct his Writte to the Bishoppe, commaunding him to suffer the same prisoner to make his purgation: or the King at his pleasure might pardon the prisoner, or cause him to be set at libertie without making any purgation. And when a Clerke was to make his purgation, the King was to be made priuie thereunto, who did direct his Writ to the Shirife of the countie where the offendor was prisoner, commaunding him to make proclamation through his Countie, that if any man could shew cause why such an offendor, viz. A.B. prisoner in the Kings or Bishoppes prison should not make his purgation, that then he should appeare such a day, and in such a place, and shew the same cause. And in London the Preacher at Paules Crosse did likewise notifie, that A.B. prisoner in such a prison was to make his purgation in such a Diocesse, at such a place, vpon such a day: at which day assigned, whether any crime or not, to giue euidence against him, they vsed to bring forth the prisoner, and to arraigne him of the principall fact, and if hee pleaded or saide that hee was not guiltie thereunto, then an Enquest of Clerkes was charged. And if by the saide Enquest of Clerkes he was found not guilty of the same offence, then he was set at libertie: and if hee were found guiltie, he was disgraded.

In what sort a clerke deliuered to the Ordinarie was vsed.

15.H.7.19.

The manner of making purgation.

There be two sorts of Clerkes, whereof the one is a Clerke conuict, and the other is a Clerke attainted. A Clerke conuict is hee who praieth his Clergie before Judgement be giuen against him of death, and hath his Clergie allowed vnto him: such a Clerke before the Statute of 18.Elizab. might haue made his purgation, sauing in certaine especiall cases. As a common thiefe could not make his purgation, notwithstanding that hee were but a Clerke conuict: for it is better for the common wealth to haue such an incorrigible person continually to remaine in prison than to goe at libertie to doe more hurt. And likewise, a Monke that was a Clerke conuict, should haue beene deliuered to his Abbot, to haue remained in the Abbey continually, without making his purgation. And also in an appeale, if the Defendant had beene conuict by verdict, and had enioyed his Clergie as a Clerke conuict, he should not haue made his purgation: for if hee had made his purgation, then the Plaintife in the appeale should haue recouered his goodes without cause, for that by the purgation it doth appeare that hee was not guiltie of the felonie.

A Clerke conuict.

Fi.Cor.247

Fi.Cor.417

Fi.Cor.10, 147.

A Clerke attainted is he who praieth his Clergie after Judgement of felonie giuen of him: Such a Clerke could not haue made his purgation, for that

Clerke attainted.

when he was condemned of felony by iudgement, hée could not contrarie to that Iudgement be purged thereof; that iudgement remaining in force: and therefore there was none other remedy for him, but to purchase the Kings pardon, or else hée must haue remained in prison during his life. And whether this Iudgement of death did follow either vpon Confession before the
Clergie after Confession. Coroner, vpon abiuration, or before the Iustices vpon his arraignement, or vpon triall by verdict of twelue men, if this iudgement were once giuen, hée should not after make his purgation. And though, after his confession of the felony, and before Iudgement giuen against him thereupon, he doth pray his Clergie, he shall haue it, and might haue made his purgation: for that the confession being before a secular Iudge, who is not his Iudge, is voide.
Approuer. And for that cause the statute of Articuli Cleri cap. 16. doth ground, That an approuer shall haue the benefit of his Clergie: and yet he hath confessed his offence before a secular Iudge. And it is not to be interpreted that the benefit of this Statute is to be extended onely to saue the approuers life, and not to set him at libertie by making his purgation, for then hée should haue but part of the benefit of Clergie, and not the whole which is contrary to the saide Statute of Articuli Cleri: If an approuer had waiued his appeale, & holden him to his Clergie; he should haue made his purgation, because the Temporall court doth dismisse him, as a man in whom it hath no iurisdiction: which waiuer of the appeale did not waiue the confession that hée had made before. And though an approuer in some Cases should not haue made his purgation, yet that was in such cases onely, where he did not pray his Clergie vntill Iudgement was giuen against him of felonie. If one that shall abiure the Realme for felony, had come againe into the Realme without the Kings licence, whereupon he was taken and brought to the Barre, and that it was demaunded of him, whie hée should not be put to death, and he had demaunded his Clergie, and that was allowed: yet he should not haue béene deliuered to the Ordinarie, but sent to prison againe, vntill hée had obtained the Kings pardon. For Clergie would haue serued him for the felonie, but not to excuse the contempt which he made by comming againe into the Realme without the Kings licence: But it had béene otherwise if he had prayed his Clergie at the time when he fled to the Church. By the entrie into the Roule of the Court which made mention of the prisoners deliuerie to the Ordinarie, it appeareth, that the making, or not making of
In whom rested the making of purgation. purgation did rest much in the Temporall Court, and not in the Ordinarie: for if he were not to make his purgation, then the entrie was, Quod talis commissus est Ordinaria absq; purgatione facienda: and if hée were to make his purgation, then the wordes, Absque purgatione facienda were omitted: and in all cases where the Temporall court had determined that purgation did not lie (as in the case of Clerke attaint, or such like) if the Ordinarie had admitted the prisoner to haue made purgation, and thereby set him at
Escape for suffering purgation. libertie, he should haue bin charged with an escape: for the authority whereby he was committed to prison, was temporall, and he receiued him from the temporall court, or otherwise the Ordinary could not haue retained him in prison. And therefore the temporall court had somewhat to doe with setting him at libertie out of prison. If one had béene conuicted of diuerse felonies, and had béene admitted to his Clergie, in that case hée ought to haue made purgation for them all. But the force of the foresaide Lawes, touching committing of clerkes to the Ordinary, and making of purgation is altered by the

St.9.E.2.16 — Fi.Cor.128 — 27.H.6.7 — 13.E.4.3 — Fi.Cor.56 247 — Fi.Cor.155 — Fi.Cor.232

before

St.18.El.6 before mentioned statute of Anno 18. Eliz. whereby it was enacted, That euerie person and persons which shall be admitted and allowed to haue the benefit or priuiledge of his or their Clergie, shall not thereupon be deliuered to the Ordinarie, as hath béene accustomed, but after such Clergie allowed and St.4.H.7.13 burning in the hand, according to the statute in that behalfe prouided, shall forthwith be enlarged & deliuered out of prison by the Justices before whom such Clergie shall be graunted, that cause notwithstanding. Prouided neuerthelesse, that the Justices before whom any such allowance of Clergie shal be had, shall and may for the further correction of such persons to whom Clergie shall be allowed, detaine and kéepe them in prison, for such conuenient time, as the same Justices in their discretions shall thinke conuenient, so as the same doe not excéede one yéeres imprisonment: Any lawe or vsage heretofore had to the contrary in any wise notwithstanding.

Clergie allowed without deliuery to the Ordinarie.

The Kings
Pardon.

THe Kings Pardon is a barre to an Indictment of treason or felonie: which graunting of Pardon is one of the most ancient and honourable prerogatiues that is annexed to the Imperiall Crowne of this Realme, being an authoritie in a sort to reuiue a dead man, and to continue him in life, whom the Lawe adiudged to die. And it is only granted vpon a good hope that the king hath of the amendment of the life of that subiect, who hath offended his lawes, and whose crime his owne conscience doth assure him that he may pardon, notwithstanding his othe taken at his coronation, (which othe is, that he will to the vttermost of his power, cause equall and right iustice to be done in all iudgements, and discretion in mercy and truth:)

The Kings oath at his coronation

for as Bracton saith: The King at his coronation, by an oathe taken in the name of Jesus Christ the sonne of God, ought to promise his subiects thrée things: The first, that he will commaund, and doe his whole indeuour during his raigne, that true peace may be performed to the Church of God, and all his people: The second, that he will by all meanes restraine euery kind of rapine and oppression: The third, that in all Judgements he will commaund iustice and mercie to be obserued, that by his mercifull dealing with others, the God of mercie may take commiseration vpon him, and that by his iustice all his people may enioy peace.

Bracton

2 Because authoritie to remitt and pardon Treasons, Murders, Manslaughters and other felonies, with diuers others of the most ancient prerogatiues, and authorities of Justice, appertaining to the imperiall Crowne of this Realme, were seuered and taken from the saide Crowne, by sundrie gifts of the Kings of this Realme, to the great diminution and detriment of the royall estate of the same, and to the hindrance and delay of iustice: For reformation whereof, by a statute made Anno 27.H.8. it was enacted, That no person or persons, of what estate or degrée soeuer they be, shall haue anie power or authoritie to pardon or remit any treasons, murders, manslaughters or felonies whatsoeuer they be: nor any accessories to any treasons, murders, manslaughters, or felonies: or any outlawries for any such offences aforesaid, committed, done, or diuulged, by, or against any person or persons in any parts of this Realme, or Wales, or the Marches of the same. But that the King his heires and successors kings of this Realme, shall haue the whole and

St.27.H.8. 25.

None but the king shal pardon treasons, felonies, &c.

and sole power and authoritie thereof united and knit to the imperiall crowne of this realme, as of good right and equitie it appertaineth: any graunts, vsages, Acts of parliament, or any other thing to the contrary notwithstanding.

3 But because the Kings of this Realme haue not had that circumspection in graunting of pardons, which Bracton doth thinke fit, and haue béene many times deceiued in their grants by false suggestions: and for that offendors in times past were greatly encouraged, and lesse feared to offend, in respect that pardons of manslaughters, robberies, felonies, and other trespasses against the Peace, were so easily graunted: For the redresse whereof, by St.2.Ed.3.2 a statute made Anno 2.Ed.3. it was ordained, That no such charters should be graunted, but where the King may doe it by his oathe, that is to say, in case where a man doth kill an other in his owne defence, or by misfortune: which saide Statute was after rehearsed and confirmed by an other Statute St.4.E.3.13 made Anno 4.Ed.3. And also by another Statute made Anno 14.Ed.3. the St.14.Ed 3.10. effect of the same was rehearsed and confirmed, and it was moreouer ordained, That if any charter of pardon were from thenceforth graunted contrarie to the purport of the said Statutes, that then the same should be accompted as voide. In which cases onely the K. may grant pardon of felonie, &c.

4 And though there be wordes large enough in the foresaide Statutes to make frustrate all those charters of pardon, which be graunted against the forme of the same Statutes: yet by putting into the Charters of pardon these wordes, viz. Non obstante aliquo statuto, actu, ordinatione in contrarium edito, the force of those Statutes be cleane taken away, and not onely of those, but also of all other in which this clause of Non obstante is inserted: for it is a dispensation of the Statute, and commonly put in euerie Letters patents. But because the Kings of this Realme, were oft times deceiued in granting of charters of pardon, by the false and vntrue suggestion of others: St.27.E.3.2 Therefore, to auoide those abuses, by a Statute made Anno 27.Ed.3. it was accorded, That in euery charter of pardon of felonie, which shall be graunted at the suggestion of any person; the suggestion, and the name of him that maketh it, shall be comprised in the same charter. And if after the suggestion be found vntrue, the Charter shall be disallowed, and accounted nothing worth: And the Justices before whom such Charters shall be alleaged, shall enquire of the same suggestions, and if they finde them vntrue, they shall disallow the Charters, and procéede further as the Lawe requireth. Non obstante in a pardon. The suggestion comprised in the pardon.

5 Because the Commons did complaine in Parliament of the outrages, mischiefes, and dammages which did come to the Realme, by treasons, murders, & rauishments of women commonly done & committed, and the rather, for that charters of pardon were too easily granted thereof: and did desire the King, that such charters of pardon might no more be granted in those Cases. Whereunto the K. did answer, that he would yéeld to their petition, sauing ye prerogatiue, and regal authority, which his progenitors before that time had: And to the intent that the King would be certainely informed before, of what St.13.R.2.1 offences he did graunt pardon; Therefore by a Statute made Anno 13.R.2. Stat. 2. the King did graunt with the assent of the Parliament, That no

The offences that be specified in the pardon.

Charter of pardon shall be allowed before any Iustice for murder, for the death of a man slaine by awaite, assault, or malice prepensed, treason, or rape of a woman, vnlesse the same murder, death of a man slaine by awaite, assault, or malice prepensed, treason, or rape of a woman be specified in the same Charter. And if a Charter of the death of a man be alleadged before any Iustice, in which Charter it is not specified, that hee of whose death any such is arraigned, was murdered or slaine by awaite, assault, or malice prepensed, the same Iustices shall enquire by a good Enquest of the visne where the dead was slaine, if hee were murdered, or slaine by awaite, assault, or malice prepensed. And if they shall find, that he was murdered or slaine by await, assault, or malice prepensed, the charter shalbe disalowed, and further therein shalbe done as the Law requireth: which saide stat. was after confirmed by the statute of Anno 16. R. 2. And therefore, whereas, if a man before this Statute, had counterfeited the Kings great or priuy Seale, and the King had pardoned him all felonies, homicides, robberies, and other trespasses; by the common Lawe his pardon should haue beene allowed, and he discharged, which sithence would not be allowed, vnlesse the treason were specified in the charter of pardon. St. 16. R. 2. 6 2. Ed. 3. 24

6 For that many common and notorious Theeues indited of seuerall felonies, murders, and rapes in diuers countries, and vpon the same, as well before the Kings Iustices, as before the King himselfe, being arraigned of the same felonies, for the sauing of their liues, did in times past become approuers, to the intent, that in the meane time by Brocage, and great gifts bestowed vpon certaine persons, they might purchase and obtaine their charters of pardon: and then after their deliuerance became more notorious Theeues, than they were before: for the redresse whereof, and to the intent to punish him with discredit and forfeture who pursueth such a charter, there was a statute made Anno 5. H. 4. which doth ordaine, That if any man or woman doe desire or pursue, or cause to be requested or pursued for any charter of pardon, for any felon arraigned of felonie, murder, or rape, which for the safegard of his life doth become an approuer: then the name of him or her which pursueth such charter, shalbe put in the same charter, making mention that the same charter is graunted at his request and instance. And if he to whom the charter is granted, after his deliueraunce becommeth a felon, the same person who pursued for his charter, shall forfeit a hundred pounds, to be leuied to the Kings vse.

Sute for an Approuers pardon. St. 5. H. 4. 2

Pardon of the felonie, but not of the attainder

7 If a man be attainted of felonie, and the King doth pardon him all felonies, this is not sufficiēt, neither wil it auaile him, because in the charter there is no pardon of the attainder. As one abiured the Realme for the death of a man, and returned againe without the Kings licence, and beeing brought to the barre, he pleaded the kings pardon, and because it made no mention of his abiuration, which was his attainder, it was disalowed. If the King do by Act of parliament grant a generall pardon of all felonies, except burglarie, and an offendor is attainted of burglary, he shal haue no benefit of this pardon: for ẏ offence of burglarie doth remaine notwithstanding the attainder thereof.

9. Ed. 4. 28. 11. H. 4. 15 46. Fi. Cor. 124 S. Abiuration 15 Co. l. 6. 13

Pardon of the attainder, but not of the felonie.

8 If a man commit felonie, and is attainted thereof, if the King do pardon him the attainder, and the execution, this will not auaile him, because the felonie doth yet remaine vnpardoned.

8. H. 4. 22. Co. li. 6. 13

22.Ed.4.7 28 & 29 H. 8.Dyer f.34 — 9 If the king doe pardon two, thrée, or moe men, all felonies by them, or any of them committed, this will not auaile them, because felonie is alwaies seuerall: & though the sequell of the Charter be seuerall, yet it shall not make that which in the beginning of the Charter was ioynt, to bee seuerall: But it is otherwise if the beginning of the Charter had béene seuerall, & the sequell ioynt. — A ioynt pardō to two or thrée

3.H.7.15 — 10 If the King graunt to a man, that he shalbe quit of the escape of prisoners out of his prison, béeing there for felonie, or Treason: yet this will not discharge him of voluntarie escape, but onely of negligent escape: for voluntarie escape is felonie, and the King cannot licence a man to commit felonie, but he ought to restraine him of the doing thereof. — Grant to be quit of escapes of felons.

11.H.4.41. — 11 Euery prisoner shall take aduantage of a generall pardon graunted by Act of Parliament, without pleading of it. And the court shall giue him the aduantage thereof, though he doth waiue and refuse the benefit of the same Act: but ye is to be intended, where the act is general, without any exception: For if there be any persons excepted in ye same pardon grãted by Act of Parliament, then he ought to plead, that he is not any of those which is excepted, and that he was not adherent to T. and so must plead to euery point and thing excepted in the said Act of Parliament, to the intent to proue himselfe enabled to enioy the benefit of the said pardon: (vnlesse in the said Act of Parliament there be mention made, that euery person may take aduantage of it, without pleading of it:) And if he that doth plead that pardon be of the same name that any of those is, which is excepted in the pardon, hee then must in pleading declare the same, and shew that he is another man, and not he which is excepted in the pardon: or otherwise he shall come too late to plead it after. And if he plead it before the Justices in the countrey, where the Kings atturney is not present, the Justices shall cause proclamation to be made, that if any will speake for the King, let him come forth, &c. — A generall pardon by Parliament.

8.E.4.7 Pl.com,401

12 The partie whom it doth concerne ought not onely to plead the Kings pardon granted vnto him by his Charter, without Parliament, but hee must also shew it vnder Seale, for that the custodie thereof belongeth onely to him, and to none other: And therefore though he will say that he was at another time arraigned of the same felonie, at the Kings suit, in such a countie, where he pleaded the said Charter, and that was allowed, which allowance is of Record: yet that is no good plea without shewing the Charter. But the court of fauour will respite the partie that pleadeth it, to bring in the Charter at ye day assigned. — The Kings pardon must be shewed vnder seale

H.11.H.4. 41.

13 When a man doth plead the Kings pardon of any homicide, robberie, felonie, or other trespasse, he ought also to bring with him a writ of allowance, testifying that he hath found suretie, according to the Statute of an 10. Ed.3. which hath established, That if the King doe grant to any person any Charter of pardon of any homicide, robberie, or felonie, then he to whom the same is granted shall come within thrée moneths next after the making of the same, before the Sherife and Coroners of the Countie where the felonie was done, and shall find sixe good and sufficient mainpernors, for whom the said sherife — A writ of allowance of the Kings pardon

St.10.E.3.3

and

He that hath a pardon shal find sureties for his good abearing

and Coroners will answer, that he from thenceforth shall beare himselfe well and lawfully. And the maineprises shalbe sealed, and returned into the chancerie, within thrée moneths after the end of the said thrée moneths. And if hée which hath such Charter will ayd himselfe thereby, and hath not found such mainprises, or after such mainprise found, doth beare himselfe otherwise against the peace, than he ought, his charter shalbe accounted void, & of no force.

The good behauiour broken after a pardon.

14 A prisoner that was indited & outlawed of felonie, pleadeth the Kings pardon of the same felonie and outlawrie, but shewed no writ of allowance, testifying that he had found suretie in the Chauncerie according to the foresaid Statute of 10. Ed. 3. neither did he make mention in his plea, that he had foūd suretie according to that Statute: nor yet did he vouch the Record thereof in the Chauncerie: therefore the Justices had no cause to allow of his Charter of pardon. And the same offendor after his pardon graunted was indited before the Justices of peace of the countie where he dwelt, that he did beat and woūd A. B. against the Kings peace, and thereof was conuict before the same Justices of peace, by his owne confession, which Record of his conuiction was sent into the Kings Bench by the said Justices of peace: and for that he had borne himselfe otherwise than he ought toward the peace, his charter of pardon was adnulled, he had iudgement of death, and was hanged. 3. H. 7. 7.

A pardon must agrée with the inditement

Where a charter may vary from the inditment

15 A Charter of pardon ought to agrée with the Indictment, in the name, surname, and addition of the partie, to whom the same Charter is graunted, to the intent, that he may be knowne to be the same person which is indited: or otherwise it is not allowable, sauing in some speciall cases: As, in appeale of 11. H. 4. 39.
death, where the plaintife was non-suit after declaration, and the defendant was arraigned at the Kings suit vpon the declaration, whereunto he pleaded the Kings pardon, which did not agrée with the appeale, in the name of him ỷ was slaine, nor in the day, but agréed with the inditement in the death of the selfe same man, to the which inditement this pardon had before time bin pleaded and allowed. And for that it may well be intended of the same death, séeing one man cannot haue two deaths, it was allowed, notwithstanding the variance. Two men were outlawed in appeale of murder, and they purchased 28. & 29. H.
their pardon, and had a Scire facias against the Plaintife in the appeale, 8. Dy. 34.
and also a Scire facias against the Lords mediate or immediate, and the pardon did not agrée with the inditement in the additions, but the parties toke an auerment, that they were the same parties which were indited: and an exception was taken to the pardon, for the words of the pardon were, Pardonauimus &c. W. B. & L. B. omnes & omnimodas vtlagarias versus præfatos W. B. & L. B. seu versus eorum alterum promulgatas: which words in the premisses of the pardon be ioynt, where they should haue been Pardonauimus &c. W. B. & L. B. & eorum alteri, because that euery felonie is seuerall, and for these seuerall felonies they should haue had seuerall pardons: And yet the pardon was allowed. If a man be indited of felonie by the name of A. B. yeoman, and after the King doth pardon him by the name of A. B. gentleman, esquire, 20. H. 7.
knight, or &c. all manner of felonies; he may plead this pardon, and auerre that Kel. fol. 58.
A. B. yeoman, and A. B. gentleman, or &c. be one person, and this pardon will discharge him: for it may be he was a yeoman at the time of the inditement, and after made gentleman by the King, or by some office.

16 When

4.E.4.10 16 When after non-suit in appeale the Kings pardon is allowed, it is vsed to enter the pardon and alowance vpon the bill of appeale: and therefore if there be any inditement of the same felonie against the defendant, it shalbée good for him to cause these words to be entred and indorced vpō the inditmēt, viz. Cesset processus faciendus super indictamentum, eo quod defendens acquietatus recessit ab Appello. The pardon and alowance entred vpon the appeale.

4.Ed.4.10 17 All this matter of pardons is (in effect) to be referred to inditments, because the Kings pardon is no plea to the parties appeale, for the felon shalbée put to death notwithstanding that: But it is a good plea against the King, when the appeale is determined. And if it be determined by act in law, and not by the act of the partie, the pardon shall not be allowed without warning of the partie: as in appeal, the plaintife doth pursue it vntill he hath outlawed the defendant, in this case by the Outlawry the appeale is determined: and yet if the king doe pardon the defendant, the pardon shall not bée allowed, vntill hée hath sued a Scire facias against the party, at whose suit he was outlawed: And if at the day of the Scire facias returned, the partie doe appeare, the Appellant may pray execution of him, notwithstanding the pardon: but if the Appellant be returned warned, and doth make default, ẏ Charter shalbe allowed without further suit. In an appeale of murder the defendant pleaded not guiltie vpon his arraignment, and by the enquest was found guiltie of manslaughter, and then prayed, and had his Clergie: Whereupon by force of the Statute of an̄ 4.H.7.13. he being a conuict person, ought to bée marked by the Gaoler openly in the Court: which marking or burning in the hand the king did and may pardon, though it be in an appeale; for burning in ẏ hand is no part of the iudgement, but onely a meane to notifie to the Judge, vpon an offendors second conuiction, that he once before had his Clergie vpon a former conuiction. And for that it was ordained by the Statute of an̄ 18. El. 6. That after Clergie allowed, and burning in the hand, the prisoner shall be forthwith enlarged, and deliuered out of prison: which act doth extend as well to the case of the Appeale, as to the case of an Inditment: Therefore the King hauing pardoned the burning in the hand, the partie was also discharged of his imprisonment. A pardon no plea to an appeale. Co.l.50. & 100 3.El. Dyer 201 261 St.4.H.7.13 The Kings pardon of burning in the hand. St.18.El.6

2.R.3.8 18 A Scire facias vpon a Charter of pardon may be graunted against an appellant, though the appellée, which doth pray it, sheweth not any release of the appellants made vnto him, or any such other matter in discharge of ẏ appeale; for he shall come time enough to shew that, when the appellant doth appeare vpon the Scire facias. And the appellée may haue a Scire facias against the appellant, though in the Charter there be not this clause, viz. ita quod stet rectus in curia. Upon a pardon, a Scire facias against an appellant.

Fi.Char.17 19 An appeale was brought against a principall and accessorie, the principall was pursued to an Outlawrie; whereupon an Exigent was awarded against the Accessorie, returnable at a certaine day, at which day the Plaintife was Non-suit in his Appeale, and then the Principall came with a Charter of Pardon, and prayed allowance thereof, for that the plaintife was Non-suite, which would not bée graunted by the Court, for that the Non-suite doth not aide an appellee that is outlawed.

non-suit

non-suit did not ayde him, seeing the appeale was determined before against him by the Outlawrie.

The Kings protection.

20 A man beeing arraigned of felonie pleaded not guiltie, and beeing demanded how he would be tried, he shewed forth the Kings protection, and said that the same was a sufficient discharge for him, and would make none other answere: whereupon the Justices agreed, that he should be put to his penance, viz. to his paine fort, & dure. And yet at another time, one béeing found guiltie of felonie, shewed the Kings Charter, which did not containe any pardon, but onely that the King had retained him to goe with him into Gascoigne, & that was allowed, and the Justices did surcease to procéed any further against him.

8. Ed. 4. 29

Fi. Cor. 239

Pardon of a felonie before it was committed.

21 A. was indicted for that he did the 13. day of February, an 13. Regin Eliz. strike B. whereof the said B. died ẏ 18. day of June then next following. A. upon his arraignmēt pleaded the generall pardon by Parliament, by which all felonies, offences, misdemeanours &c. in the act not excepted, which might bée pardoned, before, and untill the 14. day of February were pardoned, released, and discharged against the Quéene: and auerred, that neither hee, nor the said offence were excepted in the said pardon, and praied to be discharged. And he was discharged by the said pardon, for that the wound giuen by the prisoner was the cause of the felonie, the giuing of which wound was an offence & misdemeanour against the Crowne, the which was pardoned by the Act of Parliament, and by that meanes all acts ensuing upon the same offence were pardoned.

Plo. com. 401.

Standing

Standing mute, or answering indirectly.

As sometime he that is arraigned of felonie is so farre both from making confession of the felonie whereof he is indited, and also of pleading not guiltie thereunto, that hee will make no answer at all, but stand mute of malice, and euill will: or otherwise plead such matter which is no answer to the felonie whereof hee is arraigned, or such a peruerse plea, which is no direct answer to the offence whereof he is indited: Or if he doe answer to the offence, yet he will so conclude his plea, that the same plea can haue no triall: In all which cases he shall be put to his penance for contemning the law, and refusing of the ordinarie triall deuised by the law, that is to say, he shall be put to paine grieuous, and durable, otherwise tearmed, to paine fort & dure, and as it is commonly tearmed, he shalbe pressed to death. Which paine is called grieuous, for that it is so heauie and weightie that hee is not able to endure it: and it is called durable, because the offendor shall neuer haue ease or reliefe of it, but shall die in it.

Stand mute, or not answering directly.

Fi.Cor.233 283,359 4.Ed.4.11 Kel.fol.70.

2 The paine grieuous and durable was not at the common law, but ordained by the Statute of Westminst.1. made an 3. Ed.1. whereby it was enacted, That notorious felons openly knowne of euill name, who will not put themselues vpon enquests of felonies which men doe prosecute before the Justices at the Kings suit, shalbe put in hard and strong prison, as they which refuse to be tried by the law of the Realme: But this is not to be intended of prisoners which be taken for light suspition. By which Statute it doth appeare, that none shalbe adiudged to this paine, if there be not euident or very probable matter to conuince him of the offence whereof he is arraigned, or otherwise that he is a notable theefe, or openly knowen to be of an euil name: which the Judge ought strictly to examine before hee proceed to iudgement against him.

Felons refusing lawfull triall.

St.3.E.1.12

3 The

Pennance onely upon an inditment, and not upon an appeale.

3 The iudgement of pennance is only to be giuen when a prisoner is arraigned at the Kings suit, and not where he is arraigned at the parties suit: for the words of the Statute be (and will not put themselues upon enquests of felonies which men do prosecute before the Justices at the Kings suit;) and therefore in an appeale prosecuted at the suit of the party, the iudgemēt of pennance, viz. of paine grieuous & durable, shall not be giuen, but another iudgement, that is to say, that the offendor shalbe hanged. And an offendor shal haue this iudgement of pennance at the K. suit, although that suit be begun before his due time, viz. within the yeare after the offence committed, where the king ought to haue taried untill the yeres end for the interest of the party, who was to pursue his appeale within the yeare. 21.Ed.3.18 40.Ass.p.40

Pennance for piracie.

4 If a man be indicted and arraigned before Commissioners to heare and determine, for Piracie and Robbery committed upon the sea, and he wil stand mute, and not answere directly, he shall haue iudgement of pennance, viz. of painefort, & dure: and that is by force of the statute of Anno 28.H.8. which hath ordained, That all Treasons, Felonies, Robberies, Murthers, and confederacies committed upon the Sea, or in any other Hauen, River, Creeke, or place, where the admirall hath, or pretendeth to haue iurisdiction, shalbe inquired, heard, tried, determined, and iudged in such shires & places in the realme, as shal be limitted in the kings Commission or Commissions, to be directed for the same, in like forme, as if any such offences had béene committed upon the land. And such Commissions shalbe had under the great Seale directed to the Admirall, or his Lieutenant and Deputy, and to thrée or foure such other, as shalbe appointed by the Lord Chancelor, as often as néed shal require, to heare and determine such offences after the common course of the laws of this land, used for Treasons, Felonies, Robberies, Murthers, and Confederacies of the same, committed upon the land within this Realme. And if any person happen to be indicted for any such offence done upon the Seas, or in any other place aboue limitted, then such order, proces, iudgement, and execution shall be used and made to and against euery such person so indicted, as against Traytors, Felons, and Murderers, for Treason, Felony, Robbery, Murther, or other such offences done upon the land: and such as shalbe conuict of any such offēce by verdict, confession, or proces, shall suffer such paines of death, losse of lands, goods, and cattels, as if they had bin attainted and conuicted of any of the said offences done upon the land. 7.El. Dyer 242. St.28.H.8. 15.

No pennance for high Treason.

5 The foresaid statute of West.1. maketh mention only of felons and felonies: and therefore in high Treason, whether it be by inditment, or by any other meanes whatsoeuer, the offendor shal not haue the said iudgement of pennance, viz. of paine grieuous and durable, but shall haue another iudgement, that is to say, as of a Traitor conuict. 15.E.4.33 M.3.& 4.El. Dy.205 300

No pennance for a man before attainted.

6 If a man that is attainted of Felony be brought to the barre, and asked what cause he can shew, why he should not be put to death, and he will stand mute, 8.H.4.2 26.Ass.p.19

mute: in this case he shalbe hanged, and not put to his penance, for hee cannot put himselfe vpon an Enquest of felonie, because he was attainted thereof before, and so he is out of the case of the stat.

7 If a man vpon his arraignement doth confesse the felony, and before iudgement at another day he will stand mute by fraud, and so it is found: in this case he shalbe hanged, and not put to his penance, for his iudgement shall be giuen vpon his confession. And so it is, if he do demur in law vpon any point which is adiudged against him, he shalbe hanged: for in both those cases he is out of the puruiew of the foresaid stat. of West. 1. And in like sort he shalbe hanged and not put to his penance, if he be indicted and arraigned for a murder, or manslaughter committed within the Kings Palace, or where hee doth abide, according to the stat. of Anno 33. H.8. if he do stand mute, or will answer indirectly.

14.E.4.7. St.33.H.8. 12.

Standing mute after confession.

Demurring in law.

8 In all cases where a man vpon his arraignement doth stand mute, before he shalbe hanged, put to his penance, or otherwise suffer death, it shalbe inquired, if he do stand mute by fraud, or by the act of God: for if it bee by the act of God, the Court ex officio ought to inquire, if he be the same person, and of all other pleas that he might haue pleaded, if hee had not beene mute, to haue staid execution. And this inquirie is but of office, and shall be made by the Marshals seruants, and others. But if it be in case where an issue is ioyned by the consent of the parties, and after when the Enquest doth come, the prisoner doth stand mute, there the Court shall charge the Enquest which appeareth therewith, without putting any of the Marshals seruants vnto them, and so change that which was a Jurie by the consent of the parties, to an Enquest of office. And their charge shall be to enquire of the time when he did speake, and if he be mute of malice, or in delay of his execution, or by the act of God. But this charge or inquirie, ought not to be made or giuen, where the prisoner did speak to the Court when he was at the bar, and after the same day, because he would not ioyne issue, or challenge peremptorily aboue the number appointed to him by the law, be adiudged to his penance: for then it doth appear to the court that he doth it of malice. And the same law is, if a prisoner after his confession, or attainder, hath continually remained in prison, and is brought before the same Justices before whom hee did confesse his felonie, or was attainted, to answer why execution should not be done of him, and he will stand mute: in this case there needeth no inquirie to be made, if he be the same person or not, for that doth appeare to the Justices by his continuall remaining in prison. But it is otherwise if he goe at libertie after his attainder, by abiuration, outlawrie, and such like.

43.Ass.p.30 M.8.H.4.1. 10.E.4.19

Inquirie of him that standeth mute.

9 The iudgement in the sayd penance, viz. in the said paine heauie, and grieuous, is, That the prisoner shall be sent to the prison from whence hee came, and put into a meane house, stopped from light, & there shalbe laid vpon the bare ground, without any litter, straw, or other couering, and without any gar-

4.E.4.11. 14.Ed.4.7. 8.H.4.2.

The Iudgement in penance.

garment about him, sauing something to couer his priuie members, and that he shall lie vpon his backe, and his head shalbe couered, and his féet bare, and that one of his armes shall be drawne with a cord to one side of the house, and the other arme to the other side, and that his legges shall be vsed in the same manner, and that vpon his bodie shalbe laid so much yron and stone as he can beare, and more, and that the first day after he shall haue thrée morcels of barlie bread, without any drinke, and the second day he shall drinke so much as he can thrée times of the water which is next the prison doore, sauing running water, without any bread: and this shalbe his diet vntil he die. And he against whom this iudgement of penance shalbe giuen, shall forfeit to the king his goods, but he shall forfeit no land.

The forfeiture.

Fitz. Escheat. 10.

Iudgement

Iudgement and Execution in Treasons, Felonies, &c.

Hauing written of Treasons & Felonies, & shewed who be principals, and who be accessories therein, how the offendors therein are to be pursued by Appeales, or inditements, what pleas they may plead, & how they are to be tried, that the truth of each persons innocency, or guiltinesse may appeare: I am now to treat of ẏ iudgement & execution which by the lawes & statutes of this Realme must follow therupon. As first, if he that is arraigned of treason or felonie, be acquit thereof, there is none other iudgement, but that the Court doth discharge him, paying his fees. Iudgement where the prisoner is acquit.

2 The iudgement of a man attainted of high Treason is, that he shall bée led backe againe to the place from whence he came, and from thence be drawn vpon a hurdle to the place of execution, and there be hanged by the necke, and then be cut downe aliue, and his intrals and priuie members be cut from his bodie, and be burned in his sight, and his head to be cut off, and his body to bée diuided into foure parts, and then to be disposed at the Kings pleasure: Sauing that the iudgement of a man which is attainted for clipping the Kings money, contrarie to the Statute of an 25. Ed. 3. 2. shalbe onely, that he shalbée drawne and hanged; though it was high treason by ẏ common law, & so is expounded & confirmed by that Statute. But if any man shalbe attainted of treson, for cōmitting any of the offences made high treason by either of ẏ Stat. of an 1. M. 6. 1. & 2. P. & M. 11. 5. El. 11. 18. El. 1. 5. El. 1. 13. El. 2. 23. El. 1. 27. El. 2. 3. Iac. 4. he shalbe adiudged a traitour, and shall haue iudgement, and suffer, as in cases of high treason, viz. he shalbe drawne, hanged, and quartered, as is before mentioned. And though there be no mention made thereof in the iudgement, yet he that is attainted of treason or felonie by verdict, confession, outlawrie, or abiuration, shall also forfeit his lands and goods, his wife shall lose her dower, and his blood shalbe corrupted, sauing in certaine cases. Iudgement in high treason of a man. 6. El. Dyer 230. S. Treasons

3 The iudgement of a woman, which shalbe attainted of high Treason, or

The iudgement of a woman traitour. or petite treason, is, That she shall be ledde backe againe to the place from whence shee came, and from thence be drawne vpon a hurdle, to the place of execution, and there be burned to death. But if one man doe murder another, and the wife of him that was murdered be accessorie to her husbandes death, the murderer and the wife both shall be hanged, and she shall not be burned, because she was but accessory. 1.R.3.4 8.El.Dy. 254.

Iudgement of a man in petit treason. 4 The iudgement of a man attainted of petit treason, is, That hee shall be ledde backe againe to the place from whence hee came, and from thence drawne vpon an hurdle to the place of execution, and there to be hanged by the necke, vntill he be dead.

Iudgement in felonie. 5 The iudgement of a man attainted of murder, burglarie, robberie, or other felonie, is, That he shall be ledde backe againe to the place from whence he came, and from thence carried to the place of execution, and there be hanged by the necke vntill he be dead. And the like iudgement is giuen against a woman, being attainted of anie of the same offences.

Misprision. 6 The iudgement in misprision of treason, is, That the offendor shall forfeit to the King his goodes and his lands during his life, and shall be perpetually imprisoned during his life.

Attainder of treason by the common lawe 7 In the foresaide iudgement giuen in high treason by the order of the common Lawe, there can be no errour assigned, but it is as strong as if it had beene done by Act of Parliament: For the Statute made Anno 33.H. 8. hath ordained, That if any person or persons shall be attainted of high treason by the course of the common Lawes or Statutes of this Realme, that in euery such case, such attainder by the common Lawe, shall be of as good strength, value, force, and effect, as if it had beene done by authoritie of Parliament. St.33.H.8. 20.

Iudgement of pennance. 8 The iudgement of him who being indited of felonie, will stand mute of malice, or not answer directly, or will refuse lawfull triall, being called Pennaunce, or paine fort & dure, is, That the prisoner shall be sent to the place from whence he came, &c. S. Standing mute, &c. 9. P.4.E.4. 11.

Iudgements in felony by Iustices of Nisi prius. 9 As touching those who shall giue iudgement against the offendors aforesaide, it is ordained by the Statute of Anno 14.H.6. That the Iustices before whome Inquisitions, Enquests, and Iuries shall be taken by the Kings Writte called Nisi prius, according to the forme of the Statute thereof made, haue power of all the cases of felonie, and of treason, to giue their iudgements, as well where a man is acquitte of felonie, or of treason, as where he is thereof attainted, at the day and place, where the saide Inquisitions, Enquests, and Iuries shall be taken, and then from thenceforth to St.14.H.6.1

award

awarde Execution to be made by force of the saide Iudgements.

10 Because it oft times falleth out, that an offendor is found guiltie of treason or felonie before some Iustices of Gaole Deliuerie, for the which Iudgement of death should or might ensue, and yet that person is repried to prison, without iudgement at that time giuen against him; and then before the next Gaole deliuerie the same Iustices of Gaole deliuerie doe die, or be remoued, and others be assigned Iustices of Gaole deliuerie in their places by the Kings Commission, which (as many did conceiue it) could not giue iudgement of that prisoner, so repried by the former Iustices, by warrant of the foresaide Statute of 14. H.6.1. or for some other cause: For the remedy whereof by a Statute made Anno 1. Edw 6. it is enacted, That in all Cases where any person shall be found guiltie of any Treason, Murder, Manslaughter, Rape, or other felonie whatsoeuer, for the which iudgement of death should or may ensue, and shall be repried to prison without iudgement at that time giuen against him: Those persons that at any time shall by the Kings Letters patents be assigned Iustices to deliuer the Gaole, where anie such person found guiltie shall remaine, shall haue full power to giue Iudgement of death against such person so found guiltie, and repried, as the same Iustices before whome such person was found guiltie might haue done, if their Commission of Gaole Deliuerie had remained in full force.

St. 1. E. 6. 7.

Iudgement by new Iustices.

11 The Iudgement in petit Larceny is, that the offendor shall be ledde backe againe to the Gaole, Stockes, or place from whence hee came, and there to remaine a weeke, a moneth, or, &c. and then in such a Citie, Borough, Market towne, Village where the fact was done, or other place assigned by the Iustices, to be tied to a carte, stripped from the girdle vpward, and whipped vntill his bodie doe bleede, once, twice, or thrice, &c. according to the Iustices discretion.

Iudgement in petit larcenie.

12 If a woman be indicted and arraigned of felonie, it is no plea for her to say, that shee is with childe, but she must pleade to the felonie, Not guiltie; and if she be found guiltie, then shee may alleadge, that shee is with childe: and then the Marshall or Sherife shall be commanded to returne an enquest of twelue women before the Iustices, who being then sworne to examine and trie the trueth, shall take that woman into a chamber, and search and trie whether she be quicke with childe, or not: and if she be found to be quicke with childe, then execution of her shall be staied vntill she shall be deliuered: But if shee be not quicke with child, she shalbe hanged presently, for it will not auaile her to be yong with childe: And yet whether shee be with child, or not, Iudgement shall not be delayed, but shalbe presently giuen against her, that she shalbe hanged: but only the execution of that iudgement shal be stayed. If after she is repried and deliuered of her childe, and before the next Gaole deliuerie she be with child againe, though she be quicke with childe, execution shall not be staied, but she shalbe put to execution presently. And yet in that case the truth of the matter being inquired of, and found, the shirife, marshall, or gaoler

Stay of a womans execution being with childe.

22. As. p. 71
25. Ed. 3. 42.
12. As. p. 11
23. As. p. 2.
Fitz. Cor. 240. 253.

which had the custodie of her, shalbe fined, for keeping her so slackly, that shee had the company of a man.

A man hanged falleth downe before he be dead.

13 If a man attainted of felonie, be adiudged to be hanged, and the sherife doth carrie him to the place of execution, and doth hang him, and he breaketh the Rope, and falleth downe before he be dead: In this case the sherife must take him, and hang him againe, for his iudgement is, that he shalbe carried to the place of execution, and there be hanged untill he be dead: And so untill he be dead, the iudgement is not fully executed. Fi, Cor, 335

Forfeiture.

Forfeiture.

A Fter an offendor is attainted of treason, or felonie, and hath had iudgement of death, hee shall presently thereby forfeit his goods, and also his lands (sauing in certaine cases hereafter expressed) though it be not mentioned in the iudgement. And notwithstanding there is a difference betweene treason and felonie, concerning the forfeiture of lands; yet touching the forfeiture of goodes, they be all one, for they shall be forfeited to the King, as it appeareth by the Statute intituled Prerogatiua Regis, which hath ordained, That the King shall haue all the goodes of felons which be condemned, and which be fugitiue, wheresoeuer they be found: and if they haue any freeholde, it shall be forthwith seised into the Kings hands, and the King shall haue the profites thereof, by the space of a yeere, and a day, and the land shall be wasted and destroyed in the houses, woodes, and gardeins, and in all things belonging to the same, (except men of certaine priuiledged places.) And after the King hath had the yeare, day, and waste, the land shall be restored to the chiefe Lord of the same Fee, vnlesse that before hee redeeme the same yeere, day, and waste of the King, by payment of a fine. But there is a custome in the countie of Gloucester, that after a yeare and day, the lands and tenements of felons in that Shire, shall reuert, and be restored to the next heire to whom they ought to haue descended, if the felonie had not beene committed. And in Kent in Gauelkinde (the Father to the Bough, the Sonne to the Plough,) there all the heires males shall diuide their inheritaunce, and likewise women: but women shall not make partition with men: And a woman after the death of her husband, shall be endowed of the moitie: And if a woman doe committe fornication in her widdowhoode, or take any husband, she shall lose her Dower.

A felon shal forfeit lands and goods

St. 17. Ed. 2 16

22. Ass. p. 96 Fit. forfeiture 35.

2 A man being indicted before the Coroner of the death of an other man, and if it be further found by the same indictment, that hee did flie for the said felonie,

Forfeiture of goods.

felonie, although after he be acquitte of the same felonie, and notwithstanding that the Enquest which did acquitte him, doe say that he did not flie for the felonie, yet his goodes shall be forfeited to the King: For the King shal take holde of that Record which is most for his benefit, and that is the Coroners Record. And in like sort, if one that is indicted of felonie, is acquitte thereof by verdict, if the Jury which did acquitte him will say, that he did flie for the felonie, he shall forfeit his goodes, which he had at the time of the verdict giuen: which being an auncient lawe of this Realme, is grounded vpon this reason, that notwithstanding his acquitall of the felonie, yet he is to be suspected of the felonie, for the vehement presumption which is risen of him, as well in respect of his flying away, as by the inditment. And though the Enquest which did finde, that he fled for the felonie, be as touching that part of their verdict, but an Enquest of office, yet it is not trauersable, because it is onely touching goodes, for the which goodes no trauerse against the King is allowed by the Lawe, for the Lawe doth accompt goodes inter minima, & de minimis non curat lex. And though goods be in comparison of mans life, or his lands, in the eie of the Law ecalled and accompted Minima, yet they be not of so small value, or so little to be regarded, but the Judge, or the Coroner ought with all due circumspection foresee, that the Jurie be not vpon ignoraunce or small euidence seduced to finde an vntrueth, to the vtter vndoing of the partie indicted or accused. And in like sort, if a man be indicted and arraigned of felonie, and it is found by the Enquest, or the Coroners Roll, that hee fledde for the felonie; he shall forfeit his goodes, though hee hath the Kings pardon of the felonie: for the charter of pardon doth containe the presumption of him, that he is guiltie of the felonie.

Flying for felonie.

7.Eli.352 Dy.238. Co.l.5.109

Fitz.forf. 32. Fi.Cor.290 344.

Fi.Cor.308 338.

3 If a man be indited before the Coroner as accessorie to the death of an other man, and it be found, that he fled for the felonie: in this Case hee shall forfeit his goodes, if hee were accessorie before the felonie committed. But if it be found before the Coroner, that hee was accessorie to the felonie after the offence committed, and that he fled for the felonie, hee shall not forfeit his goodes: for the Coroner hath no authoritie to meddle with any that was accessorie after the homicide committed, but onely with such, by whose meanes the dead man was slaine, or who were the causes of his death, which the accessorie after the offence committed could not be. And therefore when hee indicted one for receiuing of a murderer, and that he fled, this inditement of the receipt of the murderer was voide, and consequently the finding of the flying. But if one man be indicted of felonie as principall, and another as accessorie after the offence committed before Justices; and the principall is attainted by verdict, and the accessorie is acquitte, and it is found, that hee did flie for the felonie, he shall forfeit his goodes: for that Justices assigned haue authority to enquire, as well of accessories after the felonie committed, as of accessories before the felonie.

An accessorie fled for the felonie.

4.H.7.18

The diffrence of the Coroners and the Justices authoritie.

4 If one be indicted but of petit larceny, and vpon his arraignement be thereof acquit, and it is found, that hee did flee for the felonie, he shall forfeit his

The forfeiture for petit larcenie.

Fi.Cor.406

his goods. And likewise if he be attainted of petit larceny, he shall forfeit his goods, but not his lands.

5 This flying away, whereupon the forfeiture of goods doth ensue, may be as well, where the offendor doth flie before arrest, as where he doth flie after arrest: as if a man that is vehemently suspected to haue committed a murder, or other felonie, is attempted to be arrested by the Shirife, Coroner or anie others, and hée doth flie away, and is pursued, and because hée will not yéelde himselfe to the Kings peace, and be taken, is slaine in the pursuite, by those that would haue arrested him, or by some others, that did come to assist them, and that be presented of record before the Justices, hauing authoritie to enquire thereof: In this Case his goodes shall be forfeit to the King: although being slaine, hée could neither be acquit, nor attainted of the felonie, whereof hée was suspected. And yet if this man had béene taken aliue, and that it had béene found, that he had fled for the felonie: if hée had not also béene indited of the felonie, hée should haue forfeited nothing: for without an inditment it could not be proued, that a felonie was committed, and he could not flie for a felonie, if none such were done. S. Bra.30.

Forfeiture vpon flying before arrest.

Fi.Cor.289 290.312.

Forfeiture without attainder.

42.Ass.p.5.

6 If Processe be awarded vpon an appeale or inditment of felonie against any person, who doth absent himselfe, and not appeare, vntill the Exigent shall be awarded against him; this long absence, which is a flieing in Lawe, shall cause him to forfeit his goodes, although after he be acquit of the felonie. And the reason is, for that it doth appeare of Record, that hée did flie, or withdraw himselfe, when he absented himselfe vntill the Exigent was awarded against him. But if he hath any reasonable excuse of his absence, as that he was in prison at the time of the Exigent awarded, or beyond the Sea, or such like reasonable excuse, then he shall not forfeit his goodes: and yet if the Defendant in an appeale, were out of prison, at the time of the awarding of the Exigent against him, and after when the Outlawrie was pronounced against him, he was in prison, by his imprisonment he may reuerse the Outlawrie, but he can not reuerse the awarding of the Exigent, which was lawfully awarded against him, whereupon the forfeiture of his goods did accrue to the King. And the like Lawe is, if the King had pardoned the felonie, before the Exigent awarded, and the offendor had found suretie in the Chauncerie according to the Statute of Anno 10. Edw.3.3. yet if the Exigent were after awarded against the offendor, the offendors goodes should not be forfeited: for it doth appeare of Record, for what cause the goodes were saued, viz. because the felonie was pardoned, and therefore the awarding of the Exigent against him, vpon an inditment of felonie, is reuersable, whereupon he should forfeit his goods.

22.Ass.p.81 41.Ass.p.13 Co.l.5.110

Forfeiture vpon the Exigent awarded

Fitz. forf. 19.31.

43.E.3.18.

7 If an appeale be pursued against two, viz. against one of them as principall, and against the other as accessorie, and the Exigent is awarded against the accessorie, before the principall is outlawed, the accessorie shall not forfeit his goodes, though hée did flie for the felony: for the Statute of Westminster

43.Ed.3.17 St.3.E.1.14

No forfeiture by the accessorie untill the principall be attainted.

minster 1. hath ordained, That no person shall be outlawed upon appeale of commaundement, force, aide, or receipt, untill the principall shall be attainted. And yet the appellor shall not let to attach his appeale at the next Countie, as well against the accessorie, as against the principall. But the Exigent against the accessorie shall staie, untill the principall be attainted by Outlawrie, or otherwise. But this is intended of an appeale commenced by Bill, and not by Writ; for in an appeale by Writ, it doth not appeare who is principall, and who is accessorie, untill the appellant hath declared against them. St.3.E.1.14 43.Ed.3.17.

Forfeiture notwithstanding appearance and pleading.

8 If an Exigent be well awarded against the defendant, and then hee doth appeare, and the appellant doth count against him, notwithstanding there be a default in the Writte or Count, whereuppon the Writte doth abate, yet the defendants goodes shall be forfeit: for by the awarding of the Exigent, the goodes shall be forfeit, and no Count which the plaintife can make after, shall cause the defendant to haue his goods againe. And when the defendant hath appeared and pleaded, the processe is determined, which processe is the Kings title, and thereunto the defendant hath made no aunswer. 43.Ed.3.17.

The forfeture of a Clarke conuict.

Homicide by misaduenture.

Killing in his owne defence.

Felo de se.

Standing mute.

9 A Clarke conuict shall forfeit his goodes, viz. (he that is indicted or appealed of felonie, and thereunto pleadeth Not guiltie, and uppon his arraignement doth desire to be tried by his Countrie, which findeth him guiltie of the felonie, and then hee praieth his Clergie before iudgement of death is giuen against him, is called a Clarke conuict.) He that committeth homicide by misaduenture, shall forfeit his goodes: And so shall hee which doth kill a man in his owne defence, forfeit his goods: And likewise he that killeth himselfe, and is felo de se, shall forfeit his goodes: And he that being indited of felonie will stand mute, not answer directly, or challenge peremptorily aboue twentie persons, shall forfeit his goodes. 4.H.7.2.

Forfeiting of a right or action.

Forfeiture of a trespasse.

Forfeiture of a debt.

10 In some cases an offendor shall forfeit a right, or a thing whereof hee hath no possession but onely an action, or title thereunto; As if goodes be wrongfully taken, or holden from the possession of the owner, and after the owner is attainted of treason or felonie, those goodes shall be forfeited to the King: and the Court of the Kings Exchequer may award processe against the possessor of them, to bring them into the same Court. And so the King shall haue the benefite of an action of trespasse, which the partie attainted might haue had against the other for those goodes wrongfully taken, or holden away. But if he that was attainted, were beaten or mayhemed by another, the King shall not haue an action of trespasse of battery, appeale of mayheme, or other remedy against that partie, which did the foresaid iniurie to the person attainted, for that the money to be recouered by the action of trespasse is reduced to no certaintie. And if money be owing to a man by obligation, or simple contract, and after he to whome the money is payable, is attainted of treason or felonie, that obligation and duetie shall be forfeited to the King. And if one man or more be bound by obligation to two men, 6.H.7.9. 39.Ass.p.63 30.Ed.3.4 Fi.Cor.343.

or

or more, for the paiment of a summe of money, or any other dutie, and one of the Obligees is outlawed, or attainted of treason or felonie, the King shall haue the whole Obligation, and the money or dutie arising or payable thereby; and the King, or he to whom the King will giue the same debt, shall haue an action in his owne name to recouer it: which action shall bee maintainable, though there be variance betweene the action and the specialtie. And in like sort, if a man be Receiuer to another of his money, and hee to whom he is receiuer be attainted of Treason or Felonie, after office found thereof, the King may haue a Scire facias against the Receiuer to receiue this money, and by that meanes the King shall haue the benefit of the action of account, which the partie attainted might haue had. And in some cases an offendor in treason or felonie shall forfeit an interest in lands, whereof he himselfe neuer had, or could haue possession, but an authoritie to dispose: As if hee that hath the reuersion of lands in fee simple, whereof another hath the possession for the terme of yeares, doth graunt and assure this land to others, to the use of himselfe for terme of his life, and after his deccase, to the use of the Executors and Assignes of the grauntor, for the terme of twentie yeares next after the death of the grauntor, the remainder ouer in taile, and after the grantor is attainted of treason by Act of Parliament, and all his lands, tenements, goods, and cattels which he had to his owne proper use, were forfeited to the King, and uested in his actuall possession without office, and the grauntor died intestate without assignement of this lease: In this case, the King shall haue this terme of twentie yeares as forfeit to him, for it was an interest in the grauntor, and did, and might well remaine in him in expectancie, notwithstanding his estate for the terme of his life; and if the grauntors executors should haue had this lease, they must not haue enioyed it to their owne use, but as assets in their hands. And though the King shall haue such goods, debts, money due upon accounts, and interest in lands, as were due to the partie attainted of treason, or felonie, yet he shall not pay such debts as the said person attainted did owe.

Margin notes: 19.H.6.47. 28.H.8. Dy.30. 50.Ass.p.5 28.Ed.3.92 — Ioynt debt forfeited. — An account forfeited. — Forfeiting of an interest. — 14.El.Dy. 309 — The King shall not pay the attainted persons debts — Fi.Cor.317 334.

11 As in the cases aforesaid, and some others, a person attainted may forfeit goods, debts, and rights, whereof he hath no possession, but onely an action, or title: so in some other cases, hee may forfeit goods, whereof he hath no propertie, but onely a possession: As if a man deliuer money out of a bagge, or corne out of a sacke, to another to keepe, and to restore againe when the owner will require it, if the partie to whom the money or corne was deliuered be attainted of Treason or felonie, the money or corne shalbe forfeited to the King, and the partie who deliuered the same, hath no remedie to recouer it, for the first owner who deliuered it cannot proue that it was his money when it was out of a bagge, or that it was his corne when it was out of a sacke, for that one sort of money cannot be knowne from another, nor one sort of corne from another. But if the money were deliuered in a bagge, or the corne in a sacke, then the owner that deliuered it may come unto the Iustices before whom the offendor is attainted, and shewe the deliuerie of it, and signifie that it was to be restored upon his request: whereof the Iustices shal enquire by an Enquest of office, and if his suggestion be found to bee true, hee shall haue his money or corne againe: But if the money or other thing deliuered

Margin notes: Forfeiting of goods wherein the offendor hath no propertie. — Fi.Cor.317 323 delivered by the owner be converted to another commoditie, then the law is otherwise: as if a man deliver money to another to buy wooll, or some such other commoditie, and to worke it, lay it up, or to keepe it in his house, and the partie to whom the money is delivered, doth buy wooll, or &c. and bringeth it to his owne house, and then is attainted of Treason or Felonie, the King shall have the wooll, or &c. as forfeit, and the partie who delivered the mony is without remedie to recover his money, or the wooll, or &c. for though hee might have had an action of Account against the partie to whom hee delivered his money, if he had lived, and remained unattainted, yet hee shall have no action or remedie against the King.

Fitz. Cor. 334.

Forf. for default of pursuit.

A felon hath no property in goods stolne.

12 If a man doe steale goods at divers times from severall men, and he is attainted at the suit of one of them, for the goods stolne from him, but is not attainted at the suit of the others: by this attainder the felon shall forfeit to the King not onely his owne goods, but also the goods stolne from those other, at whose suit hee was not attainted, though hee had no propertie, but onely a possession in those goods: for a felon hath no propertie in goods stolne, but it doth alwayes remaine in the right owner, which propertie in this case, for default of pursuing the felon, is forfeited to the King.

44. E. 3. 44.

Forf. of other mens goods & his owne.

13 In like sort, if a man doe steale goods from another, and before his attainder, hee doth kill himselfe, hee shall forfeit to the King not onely his owne goods, but also the goods which hee did steale from that other, though hee had no propertie, but a possession in the stolne goods: for the owner of these goods having not prosecuted and given evidence against the offendor, to attaint him of Felonie, either by Appeale or Indictment, can neither have restitution of these goods by the common law, nor by force of the Statute of 21. H. 8. 11.

Fi. Cor. 318

Forf. where a woman killeth her husband.

14 In the time of King Edward the second, it was holden for law, That if a wife did kill her husband, and after did flie, all the goods within the house, and without, the corne in the barnes, and yard, and that which was growing on the ground, should be confiscat and forfeit to the King: And their reason was, for that when the husband is killed, and no will was made by him of his goods, they ought to remaine to his wife, and then shee being in case, that by the committing of this treason shee cannot have them, they bee forfeit to the King, and confiscat. But that law seemeth to bee altered by the Statute of Anno 31. Ed. 3. which hath ordained, That where a man dyeth intestat, the Ordinarie shall depute the next and most lawfull friends of him which dyed intestat, to administer his goods. And moreover, by the Statute of 21. H. 8. it is further enacted, That if any person die intestat, or the Executors named in any such Testament, refuse to prove the sayd Testament, then the Ordinarie, or other person or persons having authoritie to take probate of Testaments, shall graunt the administration of the goods of the Testator, or person deceased, to the widow of the same person, or to the next of his kinne, or

Anno 8. E. 2. Fi. Cor. 423

St. 31. E. 3. 11.

St. 21. H. 8. 5

to both, as by the discretion of the same Ordinarie, shall bee thought good, taking suertie of him, or them, to whom shall be made such Commission, for the true administration of the goods, cattels, and debts, which he or they shall be so authorised to administer. By which two Statutes it doth appeare, that the law doth not cast the interest of the husbands goods dying intestat upon the wife, nor giue her such a title thereunto, as shee may either possesse, alien, or forfeit them, untill she be authorised by the Ordinarie. And in the meane time betweene the husbands death, and that the administration of the goods of the intestat be graunted to some person or persons, the interest of the goods is in the Ordinarie, as appeareth by the Statute of Westmunst. 2. 13. Edward. 1. 19.

P. 10. Ed. 4. 1 — 15 If hee that is made Executor, or which hath taken letters of Administration of the goods of one which dyed intestat, be attainted of Treason or felonie, he shall not forfeit the goods of the Testator, or intestat, because those goods bee the Testator or intestats goods in his custodie, and he hath not them to his owne use, but a right of disposing of them, towards the performance of the Testators will, or to pay the intestats debts: And whereas the law doth allow a woman couert to make a will, and to ordaine her husband her Executor thereof, or to make any other person her Executor (by her husbands consent) of her Parophanalia, or Jewels of value, and of such debts as were due to her as Executrix to another, and of such Obligations, Recognisances, and other specialties as were before mariage made, or acknowledged unto her, and of such goods as were taken wrongfully from her, before the mariage betweene her husband and her, for the recouerie whereof the husband may haue his actions as Executor to his wife, but not as husband to his wife, neither would they euer haue beene recouered, if she had not made an Executor; and when they bee recouered, the Executor shall stand chargeable to others for debts due and payable by his wife, so farre as the same goods recouered will extend: In this case, if the husband, or that other which is made Executor to the woman couert, shall bee attainted of Treason or Felonie, the goods of the wife, or the money recouered, shall not bee forfeited to the king, because the Executor hath them, but towards the performance of the womans will, and to satisfie those debts and legacies which shee did stand charged to pay.

Executor shall not forfeit his Testators goods.

39. H. 6. 27. 12. H. 7. 22. 18. E. 4. 11. 4. H. 6. 31. M. 33. H. 6. 31.

16 If any person that is joyntenant, or tenant in common with another, of goods, bee attainted of Treason, or Felonie, the whole goods shall bee forfeited to the King. And if a lease for the terme of yeares be made to the husband and wife of certaine landes, and the husband bee attainted of Treason, or Felonie, the whole terme shall bee forfeited to the King. And likewise it is of felo de se, if a lease bee made to him and his wife for the terme of yeares, hee shall forfeit to the King the whole terme.

Jointenants forfeiture.

Fitz. Trauerse 33. 50. Ass. p. 5. Pl. Com. 258.

Confiscation of goods. 17 The law in some cases doth giue another title to the King of goods that late were another persons, and doth not terme it a forfeiture, but a confiscation of goods, and that is, when the goods were not claimed, or title pretended vnto them by any other: As if a man be indicted for the felonious stealing of another mans goods, where in truth those goods were his owne, and the goods be brought into the Court as a manouce against him; and it is asked of him, whose those goods be, and he doth disclaime to haue any propertie in them: by this disclaimer he shall lose the goods, though they were his owne: and though he be acquit of the felonie, the goods by this disclaimer shall bee confiscat to the King: but if he had not disclaimed in them, the goods should haue béene restored vnto him. Fitz.Cor. 355.368. Fitz.Cor. 391.

Confiscation by disclaimer in his owne goods.

Confiscation by disclaiming in the goods of others. 18 If goods be found in the possession of a felon, which he doth disauow, and after he is attainted for the stealing of other goods, but not of those: In this case the goods which he did disauow shalbe confiscat to the King: But if hée had béene attainted for the stealing of those goods, they should haue bin termed goods forfeit, and not goods confiscat. Fi.Cor.368. Fitz.Forf. 24.

Confiscation of goods left out of an appeale. 19 If one doe bring an Appeale of Robberie against a felon, and leaueth out of his Appeal some part of the goods robbed: in this case the King shal haue those goods which be left out of the Appeale, for the plaintife cannot enlarge his Appeale, nor recouer those goods left out. And therefore séeing the felon can make no executor, nor any can be administrator to him, and so no other person is intituled to haue those goods, the King shall haue them as confiscat, according to the old text, Quod non capit Christus, capit fiscus: And the appellant shalbe thus punished, by the losse of his goods, for his negligence, attenuating, concealing of the robbers offence. Fitz.Cor. 100. Co.li.5.110

Confiscation by a false appeale. 20 If a man bring an Appeale of Robberie against another, which tooke the Appellants goods lawfully, and not feloniously (viz. found them in the high way) & it is so found by verdict: in this case, though the appellée hath no cause to detaine them against the appellant, for that they were his owne goods, yet the plaintife shall lose them for his false appeale, and they shall bee confiscat to the King; and also the appellant shall bée committed to prison, for charging the defendant with robberie, whom he did know came lawfully by the goods, and so for malitious séeking of a mans bloud without cause; and the defendant shal be discharged. Fitz.Cor. 367. Co.li.5.110

A waife. 21 There is another kind of forfeiture of felons goods to the King, which is called a waif, and that is, when a felon vpon huy and cry, or other pursuit after him, or for feare to bee taken, or otherwise to ease himselfe of carriage, doth without Huy and crye wayue, cast away, or goe from the goods that hée did steale, and hath in his possession, or some part thereof, and doth flye away, whereupon the Kings Officers, or some other in the Kings right, doth seise those goods: In this case the goods so seised be called a waife, and the King shall retaine them to his proper vse, if the owner of them doth not make fresh Co.li.5.109

Seising of a waife.

fresh suit after the felon, to attaint him for those goods. And if the owner doe make fresh suit after the felon, hée shall haue his goods againe, notwithstanding the waiuing and seising of them. And this forfeiture of goods by waise, is a penaltie which the law imposeth vpon the owner of those goods, for default of fresh suit against the felon, and for omitting his duetie in pursuing and apprehending of the felon, being a pernitious and corrupt member of the Com-
St.21.H.8. 11. monwealth. And by the Statute of 21.H.8. the Iustices before whom any felon or felons shalbe found guiltie, or otherwise attainted by reason of euidence giuen by the partie robbed, or owner of any money, goods, or cattels robbed, or by any other by his procurement, haue power to award from time to time, writs of Restitution, for the said money, goods, or cattels, as though any such Felon or Felons were attainted at the suit of the party in Appeale.
Co.li.5.109 But if a felon doe steale goods, and carrie them into a Mannor, and there leaue them, or leaue them in his owne house, or in the house of any other, or in the custodie of any other, or hide them in the ground, or in any secret place, and after doth flie, these goods shall not be adiudged in law to be waiued, nor shall bée forfeited: for if the felon hath not the goods with him when he doth flie, or doth waiue them for feare to be taken, they shall not be accounted waiued or forfeited, but the owner may take them againe without fresh suit, for that there is no default in him.

22 If a felon do steale goods, and after doth waiue them, the owner of them may reseise the same goods, and carrie them away twentie yeres after the waiuing of them, if in the meane time no Officer of the Kings, nor of any Lord of a libertie, hath seised them before the owner: But if any Officer of the Kings, or of any Lord of a Franchise hath seised them before, then the owner must sue an Appeale against the felon, and so he may haue his goods againe, if hée hath made fresh suit: or else the owner must procure the felon to be indicted, arraigned, and found guiltie, or otherwise to be attainted by euidence giuen by himselfe, or by some other by his procurement, and by that meanes obtaine a writ of Restitution to be awarded by the Iustices before whom the sayd felon shall be arraigned, according to the foresaid statute of 21.H.8.11. And the like law is, if a felon do steale goods, and doth not waiue them, nor any Huy and crie is made vpon him, but one in the Kings right doth take the goods from the felon, vpon suspition that he hath stolne them, yet the owner vpon fresh suit shall haue restitution of them againe, for it may be, that the owner had not intelligence of the stealing of his goods a long time after they were stolne, and then could not make fresh suit, nor leuie huy and crie.

The owner seiseth goods waiued.

21.Ed.4.16.

23 There can be no waife but of goods stolne (sauing in certaine cases) for if one do take goods as a trespassor, and doth goe from them, no man can seise
P.12.E.4.5 them as a waife: And therefore in an action of Trespas of goods taken away, if the defendant do iustifie for a waife, it is a good issue for the plaintife to ioine, that the goods were not stolne. And if a man do fly for a felonie, and leaue his house & goods, yet those goods shall not be a waife, for that they were not stolne. And in some speciall case there may be a waife, though there be no stealing, as
29.E.3.29. vpon a huy and cry leuied, a man that hath committed no felony doth leaue his owne goods, and doth flie to a church, those goods may be seised to the Kings vse for a waife.

No waife but of stoln goods.

waif of goods not stolne.

No waife of goods stolne from an Alien

24 If the goods of an Alien which hath the Kings safe conduct both for bodie and goods, be stolne from him, and by the felon bee after wayued, and refused, yet those goods cannot bee claimed or seised by the Officers of the King, or of any Lord of a Franchise, for a waife: for when the King hath graunted to the Alien safecondnct both in bodie and goods, and this is a couenant betweene the King and him; then if a felon doe steale his goods, and after waiue them, it is no reason that the Alien should lose them, and be put to sue against the felon, but he must sue to the King vpon his couenant: And therefore the K. cannot haue those goods as waife, and by the same reason hee cannot graunt them to another, neither can any haue them by prescription. 13.Ed.4.10

Forf. of lands
Tenant for yeares.
T. for life.
T. in tayle.
T. in the right of his wife, or church.

25 As he that is attainted of Treason or Felonie, shal lose his goods, debts and rights, so also shall he forfeit his leases for terme of yeares of lands, the lands which he holdeth by extent of Statutes, Recognisances, or Judgemẽts, his leases for the terme of his owne or another persons life of lands. And because tenant in taile is in diuers respects but tenant for the terme of his owne life, of his lands intailed, therefore if he commit Petit Treason, or Felonie, he shall forfeit his said intailed lands, but for terme of his owne life. And he that hath land in anothers right, shal forfeit for high Treason, petit Treason, Murder, or other felony, no longer or greater estate than he hath in the same lands: as a man seised in the right of his wife of lãds, or in the right of his church, shal forfeit no further estate in the same lands, but during his owne estate therein: as it doth appeare not onely by the rules of the common lawes, but the same is also confirmed by the Statute of 5. Ed. 6. 11. hereafter rehearsed. Fitz. Forf. 13.

The forf. of lands in tayle.

26 By the common law Tenant in tayle beeing attainted of high Treason, should haue forfeited the lands whereof hee was so seised of an estate in tayle, but onely for the terme of his owne life, and the same, after his death, should haue discended to his heirs: But now by the Statute made Anno 26. H. 8. and Anno 5. Ed. 6. it is ordained, That euerie offendor and offendors, being hereafter lawfully conuict of any manner of high Treason, by presentment, confession, verdict, or Proces of Outlawrie, according to the due course and custome of the lawes of this Realme, shall lose and forfeit to the King, his heires and successors, all such lands, tenements, and hereditaments, which any such offendor or offendors shal haue of any estate of inheritance, in his own right, in vse, or possession, by any right, title, or meanes within this realme of England, or elsewhere within any the Kings dominions, at the time of any such Treasons committed, or at any time after: As if the King giue land to the husband and wife, and the heires males of their two bodies lawfully begotten, the remainder thereof to the heires males of the body of the husband lawfully begotten, reseruing the reuersion to himselfe: and the husband and wife haue issue a sonne, and the husband committeth high Treason, is attainted thereof, and executed; and this attainder is confirmed by Act of Parliament, and all the offendors lands bee giuen to the King: Sauing to all Straungers their right, other than to the Donor in Tayle, and his heirs: In this case, after the death of the wife, the King shall haue the land: for that by reason of the fathers attainder of Treason the estate Taile was forfeyted and extinguished by force of the sayd Statutes of Anno 26. H. 8. and Anno 5. Edw. 6. and the blond corrupt, and the heire disabled, for

St. 26. H. 8. 16.
St. 5. E. 6. 11
16. El. Dyer 332.

An estate taile forfeited and extinguished.

for that in his lineall conueyance of his discent to the land, hee must deriue
Br.Dene 61 himselfe heire as well to his father as to his mother. And in like sort if a man
Co.li.1.103 seised of lands in fee simple, maketh a feoffement thereof to certaine persons to the vse of his wife for the terme of her life, the remainder thereof to the vse of the heires of his owne bodie lawfully begotten; & after the feoffor hath issue a sonne, and is attainted of high Treason, and executed: In this case his sonne shall not inherit this land as heire to his father, whose bloud was corrupt by his attainder, but the land shall be forfeited to the King by the foresayd Statute of 26.H.8. And as tenant in taile by committing of high Treason shall by force of the foresayd Statutes of 26.H.8. & 5.Ed.6. forfeit those lands whereof he hath the possession, reuersion, or remainder in tayle: so shall hee likewise forfeit to the King by committing of high Treason, those lands whereunto hee
Pl.Com. 547. hath but a right in taile. As if the King giue lands to a man, and to the heires males of his bodie lawfully begotten, reseruing the reuersion to himselfe, and the tenant in tayle hath issue a sonne, and dyeth, and the sonne doth enter and make a feoffement in fee to a stranger of the same land, and then hath issue a sonne, and committeth high Treason, and is attainted thereof, this land shall bee forfeited to the King: for by this feoffement made by tenant in tayle to a straunger, there passed none other estate from the same tenant in tayle, but onely an estate for the terme of his owne life, and so the tayle, and the right of the tayle remained in the tenant in tayle, and by his attainder the estate in tayle is extinguished in the Kings reuersion in fee simple. And the King shall bee sayd rather to haue this land reuerted vnto him, as if all the issue of tenant in tayle were dead, than by forfeiture: for the wordes of the Statute of 26.H.8. be, All persons attainted of Treason, shall loose and forfeit to the King, his heires and successors, all lands and tenements which such offendor shall haue of any estate of inheritance at the time of the Treason committed, or at any time after: Sauing to all others and their heires (other than the offendors in Treason, their heires and successors) all their rights and possessions, &c. which they had at the day of the Treason committed, or after. And by these generall wordes, That they shall loose and forfeit all lands and tenements, which they haue of any estate of inheritance, and by excluding the heire in the Sauing, lands tayled shall bee forfeited: and the lands in this case cannot be aptly termed to be forfeited to the King and his heires, where hee had the fee simple before, but are rather to be sayd reuerted to the King, the tenant in tayle dying without any issue, which, by his attainder of Treason, and the corruption of
Co.li.7.33. his blood, could inherit this land. And if the King by his letters Patents vnder the great Seale doe create an Earle, and giue him the title and honour of an Earledome to him and the heires males of his body begotten, and the grantee hath issue two sonnes by seuerall women, and then dyeth, and his eldest sonne doth enioy the same Earledome, and after committeth Treason, by leuying of warre in the Realme against the King, and is attainted thereof, and then dyeth without issue of his bodie begotten: by this attainder the same shal be forf. to the K. and not discend to the brother of the half blood, nor to his heirs: for this Earldom and name of dignity may be intailed according to the stat. of
St.13.E.1.1 W.2. De donis conditionalib', for that it concerneth land, & must be supported and maintained with land to vphold the countenãce & charge of ỹ owner thereof: And therfore this Earldome being by the K. giuen to the Earle & the heires males of his body begotten, is an inheritance which may discend from one heire male to an other, and then by the speciall wordes of the before rehearsed Statute of 26.H.8. and 5.Ed.6. it shall be forfeited to the King by the said heires attain-

Forf. of a right in tayle.

Forf. of name or title of dignitie intailed.

attainder of high treason: for it was in the same heire an hereditament, and whereof he had an estate of inheritance. And moreouer, when the King at the first did giue to this Earle, and the heires males of his body begotten, the foresaide great title of honour, though there was no condition expressed in the same grant, yet there was a secret condition implied therein, viz. that the said grauntée, and the heires males of his body should be assistant and seruiceable to the King his heires and successors by his Councell in the time of peace, and by his force and prowesse in the time of warre: Therefore when the heire male of this Earle the first grauntée did take Councell to breake the peace of the King, and leuied warres and imployed his force and power against him, he first brake the same secret condition, which was annexed to his ancestors graunt of the Earledome: And so there is reason and cause whie his said title of honour depending vpon the same condition should therewith cease and determine, and that the same should returne againe to the Crowne from whence it was deriued.

The forfeture of lands in fee simple.

27 Besides the forfeitures aforesaide, euery person that is attainted of high treason, petit treason, or felonie, shall also forfeit his lands in fée simple, which he hath in his owne right, in vse, or possession: sauing that the attainder of treason by force of the Statute of Anno 5. El. 1. (ordained against the maintaining of the authoritie of the Bishops and Sea of Rome) shall not extend to make any corruption of bloud, the disheritance of any heire, forfeiture of any dower, nor to preiudice the right or title of any person, other than the offendor or offendors, during his or their naturall liues onely. And sauing that the attainder of treason, by force of the Statute of Anno 5. Eliz. 11. (prouided against the clipping, washing, filing, or rounding of money) maketh no corruption of bloud in the heire, or forfeiture of dower in the wife. And sauing that the attainder of treason by force of the Statute established Anno 18. El. 1. (against impairing, diminishing, falsifying, skaling, or lightning of money) maketh no corruption of bloud, nor the wife to lose her dower: for he that is attainted of that treason shall suffer death, and forfeit all his goods, and chattels to the King, and all his lands during his life onely. And likewise sauing that the attainder of felonie by force of the Statute made Anno 1. Iac. 12. (against coniuration, witchcraft, enchantment, charme, and sorcerie) maketh no corruption of bloud, nor the forfeiture of the heires or successors inheritance of any land, nor of the wiues title of dower. And further sauing that the attainder of felonie by force of the Statute prouided Anno 1. M. 12. against vnlawfull assemblies, maketh no corruption of bloud. And moreouer, sauing that the attainder of felonie by force of the Statute ordained Anno 5. El. 14. against the forging of Euidences, and writings, maketh no corruption of bloud, nor forfeiture of land or dower. And furthermore sauing that the attainder of felonie by force of the Statute of Anno 31. Eliz. 4. (prouided against the imbeseling of the Quéenes ordnance, armour, or artillery) maketh the offendor to forfeit no lands, tenements, or hereditaments, any longer than during his life, no corruption of bloud, nor the wife to forfeit her dower. And the same lawe is, if an Englishman doe commit any felonie in Scotland. And if a man haue an annuitie to him and his heires, and he doe commit high treason, and is attainted thereof, he shall forfeit to the King the same annuitie by force of the before recited Statute of Anno 26. H. 8. 13. for that the same annuitie is an inheritance.

30. H. 6. 5. St. 5. El. 1. St. 5. El. 11 St. 18. El. 1 St. 1. Iac. 12 St. 1. M. 12 St. 5. El. 14. St. 31. El. 4 St. 4. Iac. 1. S. Triall by the country 10.

The forfeture of an annuity.

Co. li. 7. 34 S. Br. 56.

28 He that is attainted of high treason, petit treason, or felonie, shall also forfeit such lands, whereof he hath neither possession, reuersion, or remainder, but onely a title, or right, or cause of action. As if a man be disseised of lands, and then the disseisee committeth high treason, after an office found thereof, the king may seise those lands as forfeited and escheated unto him, in respect of the same persons attainder of treason. And if the disseisee be attainted of petit treason, or felonie, the Lord of the Fee, of whom the same lands be holden, may enter into the same lands, as escheated unto him, in respect of the attainder of his lawfull tenant. But the Lord cannot haue a writ of escheat, or other action to recouer the same land, because his tenant died not, or was not seized thereof, but his onely remedie is to enter. And if a man make a lease for the terme of life of his land, and after committeth felony, and then the tenant for the terme of life dieth, the Lord may enter, but cannot haue a writ of escheat. Forfeiting of a title to land. Co.l.3.10 6.H.7.9

29 As he that is attainted of treason, or felony, shal forfeit his lands, so shal the Lord to whom those lands be forfeited, haue the euidẽce of the same lands, as escheated or forfeited unto him, to maintaine his title in the same lands escheated, and to proue how his late tenant came by and held the same lands. Forfeiting of euidence. 49.H.6.14

30 Though it is ordained by the statute of Magna Charta, That iustice shall not be sold, deferred, or denied to no man: neither shall any man be condemned but by lawfull triall: and that it be further established by the statute of Anno 5. Edw. 3. That no man shalbe attached nor forejudged of life, lands, or goods, against the forme of the great Charter, and the Law of the Realme: So that the Law of the Realme doth allow to euery man that is an offendor, his answere and lawfull triall, be his crime supposed to be neuer so great, and the proofe thereof neuer so manifest. But if a man that is arrested of Treason or Felony, or being vehemently suspected to haue committed Treason or Felony, is attempted to be arrested, be so wilfull, stubborne, or rebellious, that he will not yeeld to be iustified and tried by the Law, but will either kill himselfe, or giue cause to other men to slay him, for resisting and not submitting his obedience to the Law, then he shal forfeit his goods, so that this offence be found and presented by twelue men before the Coroner, or some Iustices after his death: for in this case the default is in the offendor, and not in the Law, that he came not to lawfull triall of his offence; for the law requireth no more, but that the supposed offendor shalbe safely kept sub custodia legis, by imprisonment or maineprise, untill it be tried whether he be an offendor or not. But though the person thus slaine, shall for his disobedience forfeit his goods, being not attainted either of treason or felonie, yet in the like case, he shall not forfeit his lands if hee bee slaine in arresting or after arrest, or otherwise die before he be attainted, as it appeareth by the Stat. of an̄ 34. Ed. 3. 12. which hath established, That for forfeitures of dead persons not attainted, nor adiudged in their liues, their heires or land-tenants shall not be impeached, or challenged, nor of any other forfeiture, except the forfeitures in old time adiudged, after the death of the persons by presentment in Eyre, or in the Kings bench, or of felons of themselues, or others. And yet some doe affirme, if a man doe leuie warre, or open rebellion against the King, or is assistant to his enemies, St.9.H.3.29 St.5.E.3.9 Forfeiture without attainder. Fi.Cor.289 290.312. S.Br.5. St.34.E.3.12.

mies in the field, and then is slaine in battell, he shall forfeit his lands & goods: And others doe adde thereunto, that the same his Treason and manner of death, must also after his death be found by a Jurie super visum corporis, before the chiefe Justice of England, being the soueraigne Coroner of the realm, and he must returne it into the Kings Bench, and make a Record therof, and then that person shall forfeit his lands and goods. And upon those words of the sayd Statute of 34. Ed. 3. viz. (Except the forfeitures in old time adiudged after the death of the persons by presentment in Eire, or in the Kings Bench, or &c.) some doe inferre, that if a presentment in Eire, or in the Kings Bench, be made of such an open rebellion, and battell thereupon foughten, and of those that manifestly shewing themselues to bee open enemies or rebels to the King, were slaine therein, that by the words of the same Statute, they shall forfeit their lands. But if a man bee arrested for counterfeiting the K. great or priuie Seale, for forging of his money, or for a priuy conspiracie of the death of the King, or &c. and is slaine in resisting the said arrest, or for a rescous attempted before or after the sayd arrest, hee shall forfeit his goods, but not his lands. And if he bee arrested for any of the sayd offences, and committed to prison for the same, and after doth dye in prison before he bee attainted of any of the sayd offences, he shall neither forfeit lands nor goods, though he be taken with the manoure, viz. found hand hauing, and backe bearing: for though it is a mischiefe that a man committing high Treason, shall forfeit neither life, lands, or goods, yet the law doth rather beare with that mischiefe, than to suffer such an inconuenience, that a man onely accused, or but only a supposed offendor, should bee attainted, and forfeit his lands and goods, where being preuented by death, viz. by the hand of God, hee cannot come to answer, and defend himselfe, and by that meanes cannot bee condemned by such lawfull tryall which is meant and specified in the before rehearsed Statute of Magna charta: But for the auoiding of questiō and doubt in the case aforesaid, they which haue beene knowne parties to such open and manifest rebellions, haue been of late yeares attainted by Act of Parliament, and their lands and goods giuen as forfeit to the King: As it appeareth by the stat. of Anno 29. H. 6. 13. El. 29. El. 35. El. 3. Iac.

Co.li.4.57 Pl.Com. 262.263.

St.29.H.6.1 St.13.El.16 St.29.El.1 St.35.El.5. St.3.Iac.2.

The forf. of the yeare, day, and wast.

31 There is another forfeiture besides the losse of life, lands, annuities, and goods, wherewith the law hath deuised to punish those that doe commit petit Treason, or Felonie, and be attainted thereof, which is called in Latine the forfeiture of Diem, annum, & vastum the forfeiture of the yeare, day, and wast, which is executed upon the houses and lands of the offendor, that be holden of any other, sauing of the king: That is, the felons houses and lands shall bee seised into the Kings hands, where they shall remaine by the space of a yeare, and day, and then the houses shall be throwne downe to the ground, the trees shall be pulled up by the roots, the medowes shalbe ploughed up, and all things which the felon did build or plant, shalbe cast downe, digged up, and supplanted: Which punishment was ordained in despight of offendors, and to shew to others, how much the law doth detest murderers, committers of burglarie, robberie, and other felonies, and as much as may be to terrifie and discourage others to attempt or practise the like.

Fi.Cor. 310 290.327.

Fitz.Cor. 358.

32 It appeareth by Bracton, that by the common law the King should haue had but onely the wast of a Felons lands, viz. the benefit to pull downe his houses, root vp his trees, plough vp his medowes, and such other commodities, as he could haue raised by spoyling and wasting of the felons houses, trees, and lands, and that then the land so wasted should haue beene presently deliuered to the Lord of the fee of whom the same lands were holden, which wast and spoyle was then made without redemption. And after by a composition made betweene the King and the Lords, it was agreed, That the King should haue the benefit of the felons lands a yeare and a day, to redeeme the spoyle and wast which hee might make of the sayd felons lands. And the K. graunt by the great Charter made Anno 9. H. 3. tendeth to the same effect, viz. Wee will not hold the lands of those that bee conuict of felonie, but a yere and a day, and then they shall bee deliuered to the Lords of the fees. And so it seemeth, that King Henrie the third, and King Edward the first, did hold themselues satisfied with the yeare and day of the felons lands, without taking the wast thereof. But after Anno 17. Ed. 2. the Kings Prerogatiues royall beeing expressed, or enacted by Parliament, amongst others it is ordayned, That the King shall haue all the goods of felons which be condemned, and which be fugitiue, wheresoeuer they bee found: And if they haue any freehold, it shall bee forthwith seised into the Kings hands, and the King shall haue the profits thereof by the space of a yeare and a day, and the land shall bee wasted and destroyed in the houses, woods, and gardens, and in all things belonging to the same (except men of certaine places priuiledged) And after the King hath had the yeare, day, and wast, the land shall bee restored to the chiefe Lord of the same fee, vnlesse that before he redeeme the same yeare, day, and wast, of the King, by the paiment of a fine. But there is a custome in the Countie of Glocester, that after a yeare and a day the lands and tenements of Felons in that Shire, shall reuert and be restored to the next heire to whom they ought to haue discended, if the felonie had not beene committed. And in Kent in Gauelkind, the father to the bough, the sonne to the plough, there all the heires males shall diuide their inheritance, and likewise women: but women shall not make partition with men.

[Margin: By what means the K. came by the yere, day, and wast. — St. 9. H. 4. 3 22. — St. 17. E. 2. 16]

33 By force of which stat. of Prerogatiua Regis, euer sithence that time the King hath had all the three things aforesaid, viz. the yeare, the day, and the wast of the lands of him which was attainted of felonie, as one of the prerogatiues annexed to the Crowne, in all cases where the felon had such an estate in his land, that he might forfeit the same after his death, and that hee himselfe might lawfully haue made wast in the same, without being impeached therefore. And therefore if the felon be but tenant for the terme of life, or for the terme of yeares of lands, the king shall not haue the yeare, day, and wast of them, after the felons death, for then he might wast another mans inheritance. But if a man that is seised of lands in the right of his wife, do commit felonie, and is attainted thereof, the king shall haue the profits of the land during the husbands life, if the wife doe liue so long. And some doe affirme, that the king shall haue the yeare, day, and wast of the said wiues lands, after the felons death, because the felon during his life might haue committed wast therein, and for that the felon had such an estate in his wiues lands, that by the common law he might in his life haue made alienation of them, and driuen his wife

[Margin: The yere, day, and wast of lands, of what title, shalbe forfeited. — Bracton de Corona, cap. 13. — Fitz. Cor. 327.]

wife to her Cui in vita, to haue recouered them. But that seemeth to be helped (if any such law were before) by the Statute of An. 32. H. 8. whereby it is or- Sta. 32. H. 8. 28
dained, That no fine, feoffement, or other act, made, suffered, or done by the husband onely, of any lands, tenements, or other hereditaments, being the inheritance or freehold of his wife, during the couerture betweene them, shall in any wise be, or make any discontinuance thereof, or be preiudiciall or hurtfull to the said wife, or her heires, or to such as shall haue title, interest, or right to the same, by the death of such wife: But the same wife, or her heires, and such other to whom such right shall appertaine after her decease, shall and may then lawfully enter into such lands, &c. according to their rights and titles therein, notwithstanding such fine, feoffement, or other act (fines leuied by the husband and wife, whereunto the said wife is partie and priuie, only except.) By which Statute the wife after the death of her husband, may enter into her owne land, notwithstanding any attainder, forfeiture, or other act done by her husband.

No yere, day, and wast of lands holden by ioynt purchase.

34 A man seised of land in fee simple, holden of a common person, did infeoffe thereof the husband and wife, and their heires, the husband committed felonie, and was attainted thereof, the King seised the land into his hands, for his yere, day, and wast, and after the Kings said terme expired, the Lord of the 4. E. 3. 47.
fee of whom the same land was holden, did sue in the Chauncerie to haue the same land restored to him, to whom, by warrant, the Escheator did deliuer the same land, vpon whose possession the wife of the felon attainted did enter, and the said Lord of the fee reentred vpon her, whereupon the sayd woman brought an Assise against the sayd Lord, and recouered the land: Because the fee simple of the same land being in the wife, by reason of the ioynt purchase with her husband, the K. ought not to haue had the yeare and day after the felons death, nor the Lord of the fee the land after by Escheat.

Tenant in tayle.

35 If tenant in tayle generall or speciall, or tenant in franke mariage of land, do commit petit Treason, or Felonie, and is attainted thereof, and executed, the King after his death shall neither haue the yeare, day, or wast in the felons land; nor the Lord of the fee shall haue the land by Escheat, but after the felons death the same land shall discend, reuert, or remaine secundum formam doni, to the next heire in tayle of the felon, or to him in the reuersion or remainder thereof: for in this case the felon was in effect but tenant for the terme of his owne life, and thereby could not forfeit a greater estate in his land, than that which he had. And in like sort, if he that hath land by fresh disseisin, or is tenant in fee farme of land, vpon condition to pay the vttermost yearely value thereof, or hath land in Mortgage, to be redeemed by the Mortgager, vpon condition of payment of money, or other condition, doth commit petit treason, or felonie, and is attainted thereof, the King shall not haue the yeare, day, and wast, for that would tend to the preiudice of others, not partie to the offence, who haue, or may haue a better right and title to the same lands than the felon attainted.

A disseisor. Tenant in fee farme. A mortgagee.

Fi.Cor.310 36 If a man that is owner of land in antient demesne, which hee may sell without consent of the Lord, doe commit petit Treason or Felonie, and is attainted thereof, the King shall haue the yeare, day, and wast, notwithstanding that he hath used to surrender the land into the Lords hands by a rod in the Court, upon euerie alienation thereof. But if he be owner of the land in auntient demesne of a base tenure, it is otherwise. Tenant in antient demesne.

Fitz.Cor. 290. 37 A man that tooke a Church for felonie escaped, and the towne pursued, and killed him, because he would not yeeld himselfe; and this matter was presented before the Justices in Eyre, and they adiudged, that his goods, and the profits of his lands, should be forfeited to the King, from the time of his flying untill the presentment; and also that the King should haue the yeare, day, and wast. But this land shall not come to the Lord of the fee by Escheat, because hee was not attainted of felonie. S.Br.30. The yere, day & wast without attainder.

Fi.Cor.332 38 The King shall not haue the yeare, day, and wast of the lands of a clerk conuict, neither shall the Lord of the fee haue the forfeiture thereof, for that the offendor is not attainted, but onely conuict of felonie. And if the land of the felon attainted, be but of the yearely value of three or foure shillings, or of so small value, that it will cost more to obtaine it by suit out of the Kings hands than it is worth, then the King shall not haue the yeare, day, and wast thereof. Fi.Cor.327 The yere, day and wast of a Clerke conuict. Land of small value.

St.17.E.2.16 39 The words of the foresayd Stat. of Prærogatiua Regis be (If they haue any freehold, it shall bee presently seised into the Kings hands) This word presently, ought to bee intended immediatly after the Office found, and not before: And therefore if an Office of that land bee not found untill it bee many yeares after the felons attainder, yet from the time of the Office found, untill a yeare and a day after, the King shall haue the Felons lands. And also the King shall haue the profit of the Felons lands, from the time of his attainder, untill the Office bee found thereof, though it bee twentie years betweene the attainder and the Office: for the heire of the felon cannot haue it in respect of the corruption of bloud: And the Lord must not haue it by Escheat, untill the King bee intituled unto it by Office, and untill one yeare and a day after, and untill the King hath wasted it, unlesse the Lord doth agree with the King in the meane time, for the sayd yeare, day, and wast. And moreouer, the Lord cannot at any time enter into the same land as escheated unto him, untill hee hath sued a writ to haue it deliuered unto him out of the Kings hands: for after a writ is awarded to find the land of him that is attainted of Felonie, another Writ shall bee directed, to enquire if the King hath had the yeare, day, and wast: and that beeing found, the Lord shall haue the land out of the Kings hands, and not before: because though the attainder of the Felon was found, and that the King ought to haue had the yeare, day, and wast, yet it may bee that the King neuer had the profit

When the K. shall haue the felons yeare, day, and wast.

49.E.3.11. Fitz.N.B. fol.144. Fitz.Trauerse 48. 4.E.3.47. Regist.fol.165.

profit thereof, but was interrupted by some person, or by some casuall meanes.

The yere, day, and wast, not grantable frõ the Crowne.

40 This commoditie to the King, and forfeiture of the felon, of the yeare, day, and wast, is such a benefit to the King, and so firmely and highly annexed to the Crowne, that it cannot be seuered from it, or granted to any other: neither can any person claime it by colour of any franchise or libertie. But after the King is intituled vnto it by Office, hée may graunt or commit the land to another during the yeare and day, and also giue him authoritie to take the benefit of the wast. Fit.Cor.310

What goods of felons the king shal haue

41 The words of the foresaid Stat. of Prærog. Regis be (The K. shal haue all the goods of felons which be condemned, and which bee fugitiue) which is as much to say, as he shall haue all their goods, mouable and vnmouable: for the King shal haue the corne growing vpon the land of the felon attainted, and the issues and profits of the land, which he hath in his owne right, or in the right of his wife, during the time of his life, or vntill he doth purchase his pardon. But touching the profit of fugitiues lands, there is a difference betwéene a flying presented before the Coroner, and a flying found by verdict vpon an acquitall: for vpon a flying presented before the Coroner, he shall forfeit the profits of his lands, vntill his death, or vntill he be acquit, or vntill he hath purchased the K. pardon: but vpon a flying found by verdict, vpon acquitall, he shall forf. no issues of his lands, for by his acquitall the land is discharged, and consequently the issues thereof.

Forfeiture vpon flying. Fi.Cor.296 344.

From what time forf. of land shal haue relation.

42 The law hath restrained offendors in Treason and Felonie to certaine times, to make alienation of their lands and goods, and hath prefixed limits whereunto the forfeiture of their said lands and goods shall haue relation; and yet with this difference, That as sone as any Treason or Felonie is committed, the offendor therein is restrained to make any alienation of his lands, for then it is not his land, but by the committing of the Treason or Felonie, hee hath forfeited all the estate which he had therein. And therefore, if betwéen the time of the committing of the Treason or Felonie, and of the offendors attainder thereof, the offendor doth make any alienation or assurance of his land, after the time that the offendor shall be attainted of the same Treason or Felonie, the said assurance shall bée void, whether the same attainder bée by verdict, confession, or outlawrie: for the forfeiture of the land shall haue relation from the time of the offence committed.

Pl.Com. 263. 30.H.6:5. Bracton. Fitz.Forf. 30. Bracton l.2. 13.

From what time the forf. of goods shall haue relation.

43 The forfeiture of goods and chattels shall not looke backe so farre as forfeyture of landes, nor shall haue relation from the time of the Treason or Felonie committed, but from the time of the Attaynder of the Treason, or Felonie: And therefore if one doe commit Treason, or

Fi.Forf.30 Felony, and in the meane time betwéene the Treason or Felony committed, and the offendors attainder thereof, the offendor doth giue away his goods, this is a good gift, for as yet they be not forfeit, but be his owne to maintaine himselfe and his family, vntill he be attainted of Treason, or Felony, and by the Law adiudged not worthy to possesse or enioy goods, nor to haue sustenance. And therefore, if vpon a fugam fecit presented before the Coroner, one doe forfeit his goods, he shall not forfeit those goods that hée had at the time of the Felony committed, but he shall onely forfeit those goods which he had at that day, when the fugam fecit was presented against him. And in like sort, if one that is indicted of Felony be acquit thereof by verdict, and in their
Fi.Cor.296 verdict the Jury doe find, that the prisoner did flye for the Felony, in this case the same prisoner shall forfeit those goods which hee had the day of the verdict giuen, and not any goods which he had before. And so it is, if one be conuict by
7.H.4.41. verdict, the goods shall be forfeited which the offendor had the day of the verdict giuen, and not those which he had before. And he that is outlawed of Treason or Felony, shall forfeit those goods which he hath at the time of the Exigent awarded, and not those which he had before, and hath aliened. But if a man doe commit a Treason or Felony, and is arrested thereof, and as he is in carrying to a Justice of Peace to be examined, or to the Gaole by the Constables, or others, doe breake away, or in making of rescous or resistance is slaine by those which do so carry him, because he will not yéeld, and be iustified by the
Fi.Cor.290 law: in this case those goods shalbe forfeited, which he had at the time of the felony committed. And so it is, if one commit a Felony, and when the Shirife, Coroner, Constable, or others do attempt to apprehend him, he is slain because he doth resist, and will not yéeld to be arrested, the goods shalbe forfeited which he hath at the time of the felony committed.

St.3.E.1. 44 It appeareth by the statute of 3. Ed. 1. intituled Officium Coronatoris, That if any person be found guilty before the Coroner of the death of another, presently the Coroner shall goe to his house, and inquire what cattell hée hath, and what corne he hath in his graunge, and what on the ground, and if he be a Fréeman, what land he hath, and how much it is worth by the yeare: and when they haue so inquired of all things, they shall cause the land, the corne, and cattell to bée priced, as if they should be forthwith sold, and immediatly they shall be deliuered to the whole Towne, to answere for the same before the Justices. And in like sort, when it is found before the Coroner, that
22.Ass.p.96 one did flye for a Felony, the Shirife shall presently seize his lands into the Kings hands by word, without Enquest, and also shall seize all his goods into the Kings hands, and shall appraise them by an Enquest (as well of Villaines as of Fréemen) and the prices shalbée inrolled in the Coroners Roll, and deliuered to the Towne, to answere to the King for the same: for by that which is found before the Coroner, the goods bée forfeited, without
43.E.3.24 further inquiry. And so may another Officer of the Kings seize the goods of a Felon before attainder, and if the Felon doth find surety, the Officer must leaue them in his custody. But whether hée doth find surety, or not, the Officer ought not to carry them away, but must leaue them in the custodie of the Felons neighbours: For if one bée indicted of Felony, his
7.H.4.31 goods shall not be remoued forth of his house vntill he be attainted, but shalbe kept by his neighbours all the time of his imprisonment, and the Felon shalbe

Who shal seise and kéepe Felons goods, and when.

maintained with them. And according thereunto there is a writ in the Register, viz. Quod tenementa & bona taliter capta, videantur & imbreuiantur, & saluo custodiantur per balliuum ipsius capti, qui securitatem Regi inueniet ei respondendi, si &c. saluis inde ipsi capto & familiæ suæ necessarijs quamdiu fuerit in prisona. By which writ it doth appeare, and also by the assertions of Bracton and Britton, that one which is indicted or imprisoned for Felony, shall not bee put out of the possession of his goods, untill he be conuict of Felony, but he must haue reasonable maintenance of his goods for him and his family, untill he bee conuict, and then that which doth remaine shalbe the kings. And yet the felon must not disorderly sell or wast his goods: and so this difference is to be obserued in seising of a Felons goods, viz. where the goods be forfeited before the felony tried, and where they be not forfeited untill the felony tried: For if they be forfeited before the felony tried, they shalbe presently seised upon the forfeiture of them, though there be no conuiction of felony (as in the foresaid cases, where one is found guilty before the Coroner of the death of another, or where it is found before the Coroner, that one did flie for a felony:) But if they be not forfeited untill the felony tried, then they shall not be seised, untill the Felon be conuicted. Registrum.

The goods of a prisoner shal not be seised untill he be attainted.

45 And because that diuers persons were often arrested and imprisoned for suspition of Felony, sometime of malice, and sometime of light suspition, and were kept in prison without baile or mainprise; and for that sometime shirifes, escheators, baylifes of Liberties, and others, did seise and take away the goods of some persons arrested or imprisoned for Felony, before the same person was conuict or attainted of the same Felony, contrary to the common law: Therefore partly to confirme the common law, and partly to giue to the party grieued a more ample recompence for his wrong receiued then the cõmon law before did, viz. to giue him the double value of his goods so takẽ or seised, where the common law gaue him the single value, and partly to giue him a spædy remedy to recouer the same, there was a stat. made Anñ 1. R. 3. by the which it is ordained, That no Shirife, Undershirife, Escheator, Baylife of Franchise, or other person, shall take or seise the goods of any person arrested or imprisoned, before the same person or persons so arrested or imprisoned be conuict or attainted of such felony, according to the law of England: or otherwise that the same goods be in some manner lawfully forfeited, upon paine to lose the double value of the goods so taken, to him or them which be endamaged therby, by action of Debt in this behalfe to be pursued, by like proces, iudgement, & execution, as is commonly used in other actions of Debt pursued at the common law, wherin no wager of law, essoine, or protection shall be allowed: This stat. of 1. R. 3. extẽdeth only to those that be arrested or imprisoned: for notwithstanding this statute, the shirife may seise the goods of them which be at liberty and indicted of felony, at the second Capias, by force of the stat. of 25. E. 3. as it appeareth Appeales 59. St. 1. R. 3. 3 St. 25. E. 3. 14

Who shal haue the custody of felons goods forfeited.

46 The custody of the goods of those which be conuict of Felony, or which be Fugitiues, after they be forfeited, doth belong to the Towne where the same goods be, or where the Felon doth dwell: and therefore upon a fugam fecit presented before the Coroner, the goods ought to be seised by the Shirife, 22. Ass. p. 56.

rife, and prayſed by an Enqueſt, and the appraiſement muſt bée inrolled in the Coroners Roll, and the goods ſhalbe deliuered to the towne, to anſwere to the king for them: and though the goods be not deliuered to the towne, yet if
Fi.Cor.366 the goods were in the Felons poſſeſſion at the time of his conuiction, or flying, the towne ſhall anſwere for them. And ſome do affirme, that the ſhirife and the Dozeners may ſeize Felons goods into the kings hands, and the ſhirife ſhall deliuer thoſe goods to the towne, to anſwere to the king at the comming of the Iuſtices in Eyre: But if neither the Shirife nor the Dozeners doe ſeize the ſame goods, yet the towne ſhall anſwere to the king for them at the comming of the Iuſtices in Eyre: For as ſoone as a fugam fecit is found before the Co-
Fi.Forf.32 roner, the towne ſhalbe preſently charged with the goods of him that did flye away. And though it be preſented before the Iuſtices, that a Felon was deliuered to the ſhirife with the manoure, and with all his goods, yet the towne ſhalbe charged with the ſaid Felons goods, though the ſame was found, and preſented with intent to eaſe or diſcharge the ſame town. And in like ſort, not-
Fi.Cor.300 withſtanding it doth appeare by the Coroners Roll, that the goods of a Felon were deliuered to one man of the town, yet the king ſhall leuy thoſe goods of the whole towne. But when the ſhirife doth come to leuy thoſe goods of the town, by the ſhirifes conſent they may be leuied of him only who had them in cuſto-
Fit.Co.181 dy. One that was indicted of Felony, appeared at the Exigent, and pleaded, and was acquit, and his goods being forfeited, becauſe he did not come in before the Exigent awarded, were praiſed by the Enqueſt, which acquitted him at forty ſhillings: and the ſame Enqueſt found what towne was charged with them, which ſaid preſentment of the Enqueſt was inrolled, and it was adiudged, that the ſame towne may ſeize the ſame Felons goods in what place ſoeuer they can find them. And becauſe the towne where the Felons goods be, ſhall anſwere for them, therefore they which doe take into their poſſeſſion any of the ſame Felons goods, and other goods which do belong vnto the king as Deodands, and ſuch like, are to be amerced by the Iuſtices in Eyre, if the ſame goods be not deliuered vnto them by the towne, which hath the charge of them, for that the ſame towne hath the cuſtody of them. But by a Statute
St.31.E.3.3 made Anno 31. Ed. 3. the towne ſhalbe eaſed of this charge, if they can ſhew what other perſon hath detained thoſe goods, and that they could neuer haue poſſeſſion of them: the words of which ſtatute be: If any man or towne be charged in the Exchequer by the Eſtreats of the Iuſtices, of the goods of Fugitiues and Felons, and he will alledge in diſcharge of himſelfe, another that is chargeable, he ſhalbe heard, and right ſhalbe done. And therfore if it be found by office before the Eſcheator, that the goods of a man attainted of Felony be in the cuſtody of ſuch a perſon: in this caſe a Scire facias ſhalbe awarded vpon the ſame office againſt the ſaid perſon, to ſhew if he hath any thing to ſay why he ſhould not anſwer thoſe goods. But if it be found by the Enqueſt, which did attaint the Felon before Iuſtices of Gaole deliuery, Iuſtices of Oier and Determiner, or Iuſtices of Peace, that any perſon doth detaine the goods of a Felon attainted, the ſaid Iuſtices cannot award proces thereupon againſt the party, that doth detaine the ſame goods, but they muſt ſend their Eſtreats into the Exchequer, and the officers of the exchequer will award proces againſt the ſame party to leuy the ſame goods. And yet if he that is preſented to detaine the ſame goods, do find himſelfe grieued therewith, he cannot haue a Trauerſe in the Exchequer to that which is found by the Iury, becauſe the court of Exchequer hath not the record before thē, neither can he trauerſe the ſame before the Iuſtices of Gaole deliuerie, Iuſtices of Oyer and Determiner, or Iuſtices of

peace, for that they cannot award a Supersedeas to the Barons of the Exchequer to surcease their Proces. But his onely remedie in this case is, to procure a Certiorari to remoue the Record into the Kings Bench, and there to tender his trauerse, and auerrement, and to haue a Supersedeas from thence to the Barons of the Exchequer, to surcease their Proces. And the same law is, if the like thing be found by an Enquest in the Kings Bench, after they haue deliuered their Records thereof into the Exchequer. And a man which was indicted for the taking of goods of one that was attainted of Treason, was put to the answer thereof: So that sithence the sayd statute of 31. Edw. 3. others haue beene charged with felons goods, as well as townes. But the Sherife was alwayes charged with the profits of felons & fugitiues lands, according to the extent thereof, and not any towne: And so he was charged with goods cōfiscat: as, where vpō an indictment of felonie, the manoure is brought into the Court, and the partie indicted doth disclaime therein, by this disclaimer the King shall haue the manoure, and the Sherife shall be charged therewith. And the same manoure shall be praysed by the Enquest that doth trye the felonie: and if it be found by the same Jurie, that it was impaired by the Constable, or any other who had the same in keeping, the Sherife shalbe commaunded to leuie so much in value, as it was impaired by the said Constable, or other. And in some cases the Sherife shall be charged with a felons goods, and not the towne where the felon did dwel, or where his goods remained: but that must be by agreement betweene the said Sherife and the towne.

The Sherife charged with felons lands.

Fi.Cor. 390

Fitz.Cor. 355.368.

Fitz.Cor. 250.308.

47 In High treason the King shall haue the forfeiture of the offendors lands, of whom soeuer they be holden, and that by the common law: for the offence committed is not to any subiect, but to the Soueraigne gouernour himselfe, his Crowne, and Realme, which is an offence of so high a nature, that it cannot be recompenced with all that the offendor hath, and then it should bee lesse counteruailed, if any other should bee partaker with the King therin. And the meane Lords shall receiue no losse thereby, for they had nothing in the land but a Seigniorie out of it: And if they hold ouer of the King by the like seruices, then haue they lost nothing, for that they be discharged of their charge and seruices, which they did hold by, which was as much as they receiued of the tenant perauaile: And if they held of the King by lesse rent than their tenant perauaile held of them, they shall haue the surplusage of that which was holden of them, of the king, by the way of petition. And if the king doe not keepe the land so escheated vnto him in his hands, but will assure it to another, hee must reuiue the tenure in the Mesne Lord, to hold of them of whom it was holden before the attainder. It appeareth by the statute of Prærogatiua Regis cap. 12. That the Kings and whole Court of Parliaments meaning was at that time when it was published and established by Parliament, which were the Prerogatiues royall, annexed to the Crowne of England by the common law, That of such lands as did escheat to the King, the seruice of the Lord of the fee should be reserued: for the words of the Statute bee these, viz. The King shall haue escheat of the lands of Normans, to whose fee soeuer they belong: Sauing the seruice appertayning to the chiefe Lordes of the same Fee. And King Henrie the third gaue the Escheates of Normans landes to bee holden of the chiefe Lordes of the Fee, by Seruices and Customs due and accustomed thereunto. Some of which Normans dwelling in Normandie at that time had lands in England, and were subiects to the King

To whom the forf. of lands for high treason shal accrue

Fitz. Assise 124.

Fitz. Petition 19.

St. 17. Ed. 2. 12.

King of England, and did forsake their obedience to the King of England, and became subiects to the K. of Fraunce, the King of Englands enemie, and therby did forfeit those lands which they had in England, by the common law, and they did escheat to the king.

48 In Petit Treason, and Felony the king shal not haue the escheat of the offendors land, vnlesse it be holden immediatly of him: but the king shal haue the profits of the said offendors land by the space of a yeare and a day, and the land shall be wasted and destroyed in the houses, woods, and gardeins, and in all things belonging to the same, and then it shall bee deliuered to the chiefe Lord of the fee, of whom the same land is immediatly holden. And yet in some cases the King shall haue the forfeiture of the land of him which doth commit Petit Treason, or Felonie, though the land be holden of others, and not of him, as it appeareth by the Statute of Prærogatiua Regis, which hath ordained, That the king shall haue the escheates of lands of Archbishops and Bishops, freeholders, when such tenants be attainted of Felony committed in time of vacation, whilest their temporalties were in the Kings hands, to bestow in what sort it shall please him: Sauing to such Prelats the seruice that to them is due and accustomed. And therefore sauing in the cases aforesaid, the mesne Lords of whom the lands be immediatly holden, shall haue their escheats of their freeholders lands, that haue committed Petit Treason or Felonie, which land after the King hath hath had the yere, day, and wast thereof, they must haue deliuered vnto them out of the kings hands; by suing out of a writ. S.Br.39.

Who shal haue the forf. in petit treason and felony.

St:17.E.2, 14.

49 If any stranger, or other (sauing the King) doth intrude into that land whereof the felon attainted was seised at the time of the felony committed, the immediat Lord of the fee of whom the same land is holden, may enter vpon him, and put him out, or else he may haue his writ of Escheat against him: In the which writ he must rehearse the iudgement giuen against the person attainted, viz. if he were attainted by outlawrie, to alledge, Eo quod prædictus A. feloniam fecit pro qua vtlagatus fuit, and if he were attainted by abiuration, to say, Pro qua regnum nostrum abiurauit, and if he were attainted by confession or verdit, to say, Pro qua suspensus fuit: and if hee doe alledge one of those iudgements, in the stead of another, his writ shall abate. And yet he need not rehearse the manner of the felonie in his writ, nor in his count, but generally that he committed felonie. And though there be error in the iudgement, yet the Lord shall haue a writ of Escheat, and the tenant shall not falsifie the iudgement by the errour.

The Lords remedy for lands escheated vnto him.

Fitz.Escheat 14. Fitz. Escheat 8. Fitz.Escheat 6.

46.E.3.4. 50 If land escheat to the auncestor, because his tenant was attainted of felonie, and the auncestor dyeth before he doth bring his writ of Escheat, or doth enter; In this case the heire may haue a writ of Escheat, and suppose that the partie attainted did hold of his auncestor.

The heirs remedie for land escheated to his auncestor.

Fitz.Escheat 17. 51 If a lease of land be made for the terme of life, reseruing to the lessor a rent, and the lessor payeth his seruices to the chiefe Lord, and then the lessor is where the Lord shall haue his writ of Escheat, and where he may enter.

attainted of felonie, and after the tenant for terme of life dyeth: In this case the Lord paramount may haue a writ of escheat of the land: for the rent which was reserued vpon the lease, doth come in stead of the land, and so in the construction of law he died seised of the land. But if no rent had béen reserued, the Lord might haue entred into the land as escheated vnto him, but could not haue recouered it by a writ of Escheat, no more than if his tenant being disseised, had bin attainted of felony, in which case his only remedy is to enter. 6.H.7.9.

The forme of a writ of Escheat.

52 This is the forme of the writ of Escheat. Rex vicecomiti B. salutem: Præcipe A. quod iuste & sine dilatione reddat B. decem acras terræ cum pertinentijs in N. quas C. de eò tenuit, & quæ ad ipsum B. reuerti debent tanquam Escaeta sua, eò quod prędict' C. feloniam fecit pro qua suspensus fuit, vt dicitur: Vel pro qua vtlagatus fuit, vt dicitur: vel pro qua regnum abiurauit, vt dicitur. Et nisi &c. And though the indictment was executed in other maner than is rehearsed in the writ, yet the writ shall not abate, as if he were Decapitatus & non suspensus, for the execution of the iudgement is not material, so that he had such a iudgement, for the action is true, though the writ be not true. Register. fo.165.

The K. remedie for land escheated to him.

53 In all cases of felony, if the king ought to haue the escheat, he must haue an office found for him before he can enter: for vntill the office found, the king hath but a possession in law, and not in déed, notwithstanding the death of him which is attainted. But by the stat. of an. 33. H. 8. the king shal haue the lands, goods, cattels, and all other things of the offendors attainted of high Treason, without any office: the words of which stat. be these, viz. If any person or persons shalbe attainted of high Treason, by the course of the common lawes, or statutes of this realme, in euery such case euery such attainder by the common law, shalbe of as good strength, value, force, and effect, as if it had bin done by authoritie of Parliament. And the K. his heires and successors, shall haue as much aduantage by such attainder, as well of vses, rights, entries, conditions, possessions, reuersions, remainders, and all other things, as if it had béen done and declared by authoritie of Parliament, and shalbe déemed and adiudged in actuall and real possession of the lands, tenements, hereditaments, vses, goods, chattels, and all other things of the offendors so attainted, which his Highnes ought lawfully to haue, and which they so being attainted ought or might lawfully lose and forf. as if the attainder had bin done by authoritie of Parliament without any office or inquisition to be found of the same: Any law, statute &c. notwithstanding. By force of which stat. the King shall be in actuall and reall possession of those lands which do escheat vnto him by any attainder of high Treason, without any office or inquisition thereof found: though for those lands which do escheat vnto him by any attainder of felonie, there must be an office found for him, before he can enter, according to the antient course of the common law. St.33.H.8. 20.

An office of those lands which do escheat for felonie.

Forf. of title of Dower.

54 By the common law any man attainted of Treason or felonie, should haue forfeited that title which his wife had by their espousals to be endowed of his lands, to the intent, that if the care of his owne life could not stay him from the committing of felony, or treason, yet the loue which he did beare to his wife and children, should restrain him thereof, whom he was assured by that wicked

act

act to vndoe, and vtterly to deprine them of all likelihood wherewith to maintaine them. And some do affirme, that this law was at the first deuised, to punish the wife, and to auoid her dower, for that it was intended, that the wife gaue consent vnto, or at the least did know of the Treason, or Felonie, which her husband committed, and either by intreatie, persuasion, or some other meanes, might haue withdrawne him from it. But the common law in that St.1.E.6.12 case is altered by the stat. of Anno 1. Ed.6. whereby it is enacted, That albeit any person or persons, of what estate, condition, or degree he or they be, shal fortune to be attainted, conuicted, or outlawed of any Treason, petit Treason, Misprision of treason, Murder, or Felony whatsoeuer, yet that notwithstanding, euerie woman that is, or shall fortune to be wife of the person so attainted, conuicted, or outlawed, shalbe endowable, and enabled to demaund, haue, and enioy her dower, in like maner and forme as though her husband had not beene attainted, conuicted, or outlawed: Any statute, law, custom, &c. notwithstanding. But after, some part of the foresaid stat. of Anno 1. E.6. was altered St.5.& 6. E.6.11. by a braunch of a stat. made Anno 5. & 6. Ed.6. whereby it was prouided and enacted, That the wife, or wiues, whose husband, or husbands hereafter shalbe attainted of any Treasons whatsoeuer they be, shall in no wise be receiued to aske, challenge, demand, or haue dower of any the lands, tenements, or hereditaments of any the person or persons to be attainted of treason, as is aforesaid, during the said attainder in his force. And yet sithence the foresaid stat. of 5. & 6. Ed.6. it was specially prouided and ordained by the stat. made Anno 5. El.1. & Anno 5. El.11. & An.18. El.1. That the husbands attainder of treason, by force of any of the foresaid stat. should cause no forf. of dower in the wife S.Br.27.

Br. Appeale 117. Fitz. Iudg. 225 Plo. Com. 261. 55 If in an Appeale the Appellee do wage battell, and the Appellant doth slay him in the field, the Appellee shall forf. all his goods & chattels, but his land shall not escheat: for inheritance is so greatly fauoured, that it shall not be forf. without attainder by iudgement. But if the Appellant do vanquish the Appellee, then his land shalbe forf. for when he is vanquished and not killed, iudgement shalbe giuen, that he shalbe hanged, and by that meanes he shall forf. his land. What the Appellee that wageth battell, shall forf.

6.H.8. Dyer 2. 56 If a man seised of land in fee, doth grant a rent charge out of the same to another for the terme of the life of the grantee, pro bono cōsilio suo impendendo, with clause of distres within the same land, if the grantee of this rent charge be attainted of treason, and committed to prison, yet hee shall not forf. this rent charge to the K. for it is incident to the cause for the which it was giuen, viz. to the counsell to be giuen by the grantee to the grantor, which was a trust that the grantor reposed in the grantee to giue him counsell, which trust the grantee cannot assigne or forf. to another. And though the grantee of this rent charge be attainted of treason, and imprisoned, yet the grantor may come or send to him for his counsel, and he may giue it him, and so there wil be no fault in him. But if a man do purchase a rent charge for the time of his life, out of another mans lands, in consideration of a summe of money paid by the grantee to the grantor, and after the grantee is attainted of treason or felony, the same rent charge shalbe forf. to the K. and paid to him during the life of the grauntee. S. Br. 27. A rent charge pro consilio not forfeited.

57 Out

The forfeitures of an Outlaw.

57 Out of all which foresaid forfeitures, the words of Bracton may be verified, who writeth, That a man outlawed (or otherwise attainted of Treason or Felony) shall forfeit his coũtrey and kingdome, and shall become a banished man, who in English is called an Outlaw. And in former times he hath béene tearmed a Friendlesse man, and so he hath séemed to forfeit his friends: for if any man after his Outlary doth willingly féed him, receiue him, kéepe company with him, or hide him, he shal be punished in the same sort that the Outlaw shall. Also he shall forfeit all things which be peaceable, séeing that from the time he is an Outlaw, he carieth a Wolues head, so that all men may kill him without punishment, and specially if he defend himselfe, or flie away, in such sort that he may be hardly apprehended. But if he doe not flie, or defend himselfe, then he that killeth a man so taken, shal answere for him, as for any other man, for that life and death be in the kings hands, vnlesse there be a custome to the contrary, as in the Counties of Hereford and Glocester. And he shal forfeit the benefit of Law: for he which being outlawed will be so bold, as to returne without the kings licence, shall die without law, or further examination in iudgement. And he cannot appeale others, for he hath lost the benefit of law, and carieth with him his iudgement vpon his head, & he can haue no defence, so long as the Outlary standeth in force. It is vpright iustice, that he shal perish without law and iudgement, who refuseth to liue according to the law. And he shall forfeit his right and possession of all things that he hath gotten, or may get. And all bonds, obligations, homages, fealties, oathes, and other contracts made with him, be dissolued, which can neuer be reuiued but vpon a new contract, though he be restored. And he shal forfeit all his tenements and hereditaments from him and his heires, and euery action that was due to him before his Outlary, though he be after restored by the kings pardon. And Outlary of felony, and euery other iudgement of felony, doth dissolue all the gifts & sales of land that he made sithence the time of the felony committed. The outlawes goods shalbe the kings, for he cannot be outlawed in any other place, but in the kings Court, as in the County Court, or in the Hustings of London.

Bracton, de coroñ, c. 13

Cor-

Corruption of Blood.

1 BY attainder of Treason, or Felony, commeth corruption of Blood: that is to say, that the offendors children cannot be heires to him that is attainted, nor to any other auncestor. And if the offendor were a Nobleman, or a Gentleman before, by this attainder he is become ignoble, and not onely he himselfe, but also all his children, hauing respect to the Nobilitie, which they had by their birth. And this corruption of Blood is so grieuous, that it cannot bee salued otherwise then by authoritie of Parliament. But if the King will pardon the offendor, it will cleanse the corruption of blood of those children, which be borne after the pardon: and they which be borne after the pardon, may inherite the land which their auncestor purchased at the time of the pardon, or after; but so cannot they which were borne before the pardon. And also he that is attainted of Treason or Felony, shall not bee heire to his father, but his disabilitie shall hinder others to be heire, so that during his life, the land shall rather escheat to the lord of the fee, then discend to another.

Corruption of blood salued by Parliament only

27.Ed.3.77. Fi.Petit.20 But if he that is attainted doe die without issue of his body, during the life of his auncestor, then his younger brother, sister, or cousin shall inherite: for

Fi.Discent 6. if the eldest sonne be hanged, or doth abiure the Realme for Felony, during

26.As.p.2. the fathers life, it is no impediment, but that the youngest sonne may inherite.

29.As.p.11 And if he which is attainted of Treason or Felony in the life time of

13.H.4.8. his auncestor, doe purchase the Kings pardon before the death of his aun-

Fit. Discent 17. cestor, yet he shall not be heire to his said auncestor, but the land shall rather escheat to the lord of the fee. But if the eldest sonne be a Clerke conuict in the life of his father, and after his father dieth, in this case he shall inherite his fathers land, because he was not attainted of Felony, for by the common Law hee should haue inherited after hee had made his purgation. And now by

Fi.Cor.382 St.18.Eli.6. the Statute of Anno 18. Eliz. hee shall bee forthwith enlarged after burning in the hand, and deliuered out of prison, and not committed to the Ordinary to make his purgation, and so he is in case, as if he had made his purgation.

2 If

where corruption of blood shall preiudice tenant by the courtesie.

2 If a man that hath land in the right of his wife, haue issue, and doth commit Felony, for the which he is attainted, and the king doth pardon him: in this case, if his wife doe die before him, he shall not be tenant by the courtesie, for the corruption of blood of that issue. But it is otherwise, if he hath issue after the pardon, for then he shall be tenant by the courtesie, although the issue which he had before the pardon be not inheritable. 13.H.7.17.

The eldest sonne attainted of felony during his fathers life.

3 If a man seised of lands hath issue two sonnes, and the eldest is attainted of Felony in the life of his father, and is executed for the felony, or otherwise dieth during the life of his father, and after the father dieth seised of the land, the land shal discend to the youngest sonne, as heire to his father, if the eldest sonne hath no issue then liuing. But if the eldest sonne, that was attainted, hath any issue in life, which should haue inherited but for the attainder, the land shall escheat to the lord, and not discend to the younger brother, for that the blood of the eldest brother is corrupted. 32.H.8. Dyer 48.

where an attainder, but no corruption of blood.

4 S.Forfeiture 27, That the attainder of Treason or Felony in certaine cases, shal not extend to make any corruption of blood, the disinheritance of any heire, forfeiture of any dower, nor to preiudice the right or title of any person, other then of the offendor or offendors, during his or their naturall liues only.

Re-

Restitution of stolne goods.

1 Hauing written of Robberies, and other Felonies, and declared how Felons are to be prosecuted by Arrest, Appeale, Indictment, Arraignment, Tryall, and Iudgement, and what they shall forfeit, I meane now to shew, how true men, whose goods were robbed, stoln, or feloniously taken from them by such Felons, shall be restored to their goods againe. As it is necessary for the Commonwealth, that Felons should be punished, least the impunity of some should incourage them, and also allure others to commit the like offences: so is it fit, that they chiefely, whose goods were taken from them; and therby haue tasted the smart, and receiued the losse by the Felons, and are more likely to know who they be, and where they be, then others are, should doe their uttermost endeauor to procure those Felons to be apprehended, brought to their answers, and to haue them punished according to their demerits: that is to say, he that was robbed or whose goods were stolne from him, ought presently after the felony committed to pursue the Felon so hastily, that (if it be possible) he may take him with the manoure, and thereupon bring his appeale against him, and conuince him of the Felony. And the said speedy and diligent pursute of his, is called Fresh suit, which thing being found by a Iury, the king ought to make restitution to the appellant of his goods contayned in the appeale, which his officer or any other to his use did seize. But if it be not found by a Iury, that the owner did make Fresh suit, the said owner shall lose his goods, and the king shall haue them, although the Felon be conuict at the same parties suit. For as the Law doth so abhorre Felonies and Felons, that it punisheth a Felon with the losse of his life, his lands, goods, and all that he hath: so doth it in such sort condemne the concealing, wincking at, or slacke pursute of a felon, that it punisheth a true man with the forfeiture of his goods stolne from him, for omitting his duty in making fresh sute after, prosecuting, and pursuing to death of a knowne Felon. If the manoure wherwith the Felon is taken be portable, or otherwise may be conueniently done, it ought to be brought into the Court before the Iustices: and if it be in a chest, boxe, cloakebag, or male, the appellant must declare the goods particularly which be in it,

What is fresh suit.

Fi.Cor.379.

Fi.Cor.392.

before

before it be opened, or that he can haue it restored vnto him againe. And if the Fresh suit be made by the seruant of him that is robbed, and not by the party himselfe, yet it is sufficient to procure him restitution of his goods. And if the Felon which committed a Robbery or other Felony be not taken by the space of a yeare after the Felony committed, yet if the party that was robbed, or whose goods were stolne, do his endeuour to apprehend the Felon, and make diligent and speciall inquiry for him, and after he is taken, though not at the suit of the party robbed, or &c. yet that shal be adiudged a sufficient Fresh suit, and vpon his appeale brought, and the offendor conuicted, he shal haue restitution of his goods robbed or stolne. 7.H.4.43.

Fresh suit by the seruant.

2 Though in former times it was not adiudged sufficient for the appellant to conuict the offendor of Felony, but he must haue attainted him thereof, before he could haue had restitution of his goods: and if the Felon were in that case, that he could not be attainted at the owners suit, he should not haue had restitution of his goods, but they should haue bin forfeited to the king, were the suit neuer so fresh. As, if the felon being pursued by the party robbed with huy and cry, did flie to a Church, and made his abiuration: or that the Felon was in prison, and died before the owners appeale commenced. But now the law is otherwise construed: for it is thought to be a great extremity, that the party which was robbed should lose his goods, when he hath done all that hee could, & that there was no default in him. And therefore it is now agreed, that if after the appeale commenced the Felon do die in prison, or do breake the prison, and flie to a Church, and there abiure, the Fresh suit shalbe inquired of, and if it be found, the party robbed shall haue restitution of his goods. And in like sort, if the offendor will stand mute of malice, or challenge peremptorily aboue the number that the law doth appoint him, or will demaund his clergy: in all these cases the Fresh suit shalbe enquired of, and if it be found, the appellant shall be restored to his goods, and yet in these cases the Felon is not attainted. But because the appellant hath done his indeuor, and all that is in him, to attaint the Felon, it is reason that he shall haue restitution of his goods.

what conuiction shalbe sufficient to giue the owner restitution of his goods.

Fi.Cor.319 H.8.E.3.10. Fi.Cor.379 380. 26.Ass.p.32 Fit. Forfeit. 15. 8.H.4.1. 10.H.4.5

3 Restitution shalbe graunted and made to the owner of his goods stolne, as soone as the Felon shalbe attainted or conuicted by his appeale, & the Fresh suit shalbe found, though the appellant doth not pray, or sue execution of the body of the appellee: for the appellant hath prosecuted the suit so farre, that hee hath brought the felon to the kings mercy; so that the appellant, nor any other for him, can stay or release the execution, but only the king: and therefore it is reason, that he now should haue restitution of his goods. And some do affirme, that when the appellant hath so farre prosecuted the appellee, that he is outlawed, that the appellant shall haue restitution of his goods, without inquirie of the Fresh suit, because he hath pursued the suit against the offendor, so farre as he can. If an appeale be sued against the principall and accessorie, and the principall is attainted, and the Fresh suit is found, the appellant shall haue restitution of his goods, without suing against the accessory. And though he doe continue his suit against the accessory, yet that shall not hinder his restitution, for that he hath procured the attainder of the principall Felon: and whe-

when the owner shall haue restitution.

21.Ed.4.73. Fit.Co. 392 21.Ed.4.16. 21.E.4.16. 10.H.4.5.

whether the accessorie bee attaint, or acquit, yet the appellant shall haue restitution of his goods. And in like sort, if an appeale be sued against two as principals, and one of them is attainted, and the other is acquited, and the Fresh suit is found, the appellant shall haue restitution of his goods, for that it doth appeare, that the appellant was robbed of his goods, and had cause to sue: for though the appeale be found false in part, touching him that is acquit, yet that shall not preiudice the appellant, seeing that falsehood commeth not of his owne declaration, but by the verdict of the Jury. If one man do robbe diuers men, whereupon they doe bring their seuerall appeales, and the Felon is attainted at the suit of one of them, and that it is moreouer found that he hath made Fresh suit: in this case the residue shall not haue restitution, untill the Felon be found guilty at their seuerall suites, and the Fresh suit also seuerally found.

4.E.4.11.

4 Before Restitution can be awarded of Felons goods, an enquirie is to bee made of the Fresh suit before the Justices, and not before the Shirife, (though it be but an Enquest of Office) and it is to bee done by the Jury, that doth find the defendant in the appeale guilty of the Felony, unlesse it bee in case, where the defendant doth confesse the appeale of the plaintife, and then it shall be inquired by the Uisne, where the Felony was committed by the people of that County where the appeale is brought, except it bee brought in London: for London hath such a priuiledge, that they shall not bee drawne to appeare upon Juries out of the Citie: and the Kings Justices cannot goe into the Citie, and take the same by Nisi prius, because it is but an Enquest of Office: and therefore in that case they doe inquire of it by people of the County where the Felon was taken, and from thence shall the Uisne come. But first the Court is to inquire of the Defendant in the appeale, if hee doe clayme any propertie in the goods, or not, and if hee clayme nothing therein, then it must enquire, if the goods were the plaintifes at the time of the Robbery committed, and moreouer inquire of the Fresh suit.

Before whom and by whom inquirie of fresh suit is to be made.

1.H.4.5. 2.R.3.12. Fit. Forfeit. 15.

5 By the common Law there was no helpe for the party robbed by indictment of the Felon to recouer his goods againe, or to haue restitution of them: for although the enquest which tried the Felon upon his arraignment, would after they had found him guilty of the Felony, haue said, that the party robbed had made Fresh suit, yet that would not haue auailed to haue procured him restitution of his goods. And therefore to redresse that enormitie, there was a statute made Anno 21.H.8. by which it was enacted, That if any Felon or Felons hereafter doe robbe or take away any money, goods, or cattels from any the Kings Subiects, from their person, or otherwise within this Realme, and thereof the said Felon or Felons be indicted, and after arraigned of the same Felony, and found guilty thereof, or otherwise attainted by reason of euidence giuen by the party so robbed, or owner of the said mony, goods, and cattels, and that as well the Just. of Gaole deliuery, as other Justices, before whom any such Felon or Felons shalbe found guilty, or otherwise attainted, by

Restitution upon attainder by indictment.

Fi.Cor.460. St.21.H.8.11.

by reaſon of euidence giuen by the party ſo robbed, or owner, or by any other by their procurement haue power by this act to award from time to time Writs of Reſtitution for the ſaid money, goods, or cattels, in like manner, as though any ſuch Felon or Felons were attainted at the ſuit of the party in appeale. And ſo by force of this Statute the party robbed ſhall haue reſtitution of his ſtolne goods, vpon euidence giuen by him, or by any other by his procurement againſt the Felon, though he neuer made any freſh ſuit. S. Euidence 3.4. Appeales 55.

Dama-

Dammages in Appeale.

1 IUstice and reason doe require, that when a mans life, his fame, and credit, his lands, his goods, the disheritance of his posterity, the corruption of his blood, and all that he hath in this world to forfeit, hath bin put in hazard, and brought into question and triall, without iust desert, or other ground, but only vpon the malicious accusation of some one or moe persõs, and that he is found a true and lawfull man, & duly acquit by the country of the offence, whereof he was appealed, that he should haue recompence for it against his false accusor: and if his accusor be not sufficient, then against him or them that did procure or abet him to pursue the appeale. And therefore the common law did giue dammages to the defendant in
48.Ed.3.22 an appeale, and assigned him a meane to recouer them, when he was acquit of the felony. But because the dammages which were to be recouered against the procurors, or abettors, were to be recouered by writ originall, viz. by a writ of Conspiracy, and not otherwise, which was not so speedy a remedy, as the great malice and wickednesse of the offence required, the stat. of West.2. was made
St.13.E.1.12 for the quicker redresse thereof An 13. Ed.1. the words whereof be these, viz. For as much as many through malice, intending to grieue others, do procure false appeales of homicide, and other felonies, to be sued by appellants, hauing nothing wherewith to satisfie the king for their false appeale, nor to answer to the party damages. It is ordained, that when any which is appealed of felony imposed vpon him, doth acquite himselfe in the K. Court in due manner, either at the appellants suit, or the kings, the Iustices before whom the said appeale shalbe heard and determined, shal punish the appellant by one yeres imprisonment: and neuerthelesse, such appellant shall yeeld to the appellée damages by the Iust. discretion, hauing respect to the imprisonment or arrest that the party hath sustained by reason of such appeale, and to the slander which he hath receiued by the imprisonment, or otherwise, & also he shal pay a grieuous fine to the K. And if the appellants be not able to recompẽce the damages, inquiry shalbe made by whose abetmẽt the appeale was maliciously cõmenced, if the appellée desire it. And if it be found by the same Enquest, that any man is abettor through malice, he shalbe distrained by a iudiciall writ to appeare before the I.

The punishment of the appellant and abettors, whẽ the appellée is acquit.

 at

at the appellées suit: and if he be lawfully conuict of such abetment by malice, he shall be imprisoned, and restore dammages, as is aforesaid of the appellant. In an appeale of the death of a man there shall no Essoine lie for the appellant for any cause, in whatsoeuer court the appeale shalbe determined.

No Essoine for the Appellant in appeale of death.

The appeale must be commenced vpon malice.

2 And whereas the words of the foresaid stat. of West. 2. be, (For as much as many through malice) it doth thereby appeare, that if the defendant in an appeale be to recouer dammages, it ought to be in respect, that the appeale was grounded rather vpon malice then vpon good matter. And therefore if the defendant were indicted of that Felony wherof the appeale was sued, before the suit of the appeale, although the def. be after acquit thereof, yet he shall not recouer dammages, because it shalbe intended, that the indictment induced him to bring the appeale, and not malice. But the law is méere contrary, if he were not indicted vntill after the appeale commenced: Or if there be any such variance betwéene the appeale and the indictment, that the acquitall of him vpon the one, is not the acquitall of him vpon the other, as if he be indicted as principall, and appealed as accessory, vel e conuerso. And yet it is otherwise, if the variance be not in a matter of substance: for such a variance shal not so preiudice, but that the acquitall vpon the one shalbe also an acquitall vpon the other. By the letter of the said statute of Westm. 2. this word (Malice) doth only referre it selfe to Abettors and Procurors, but yet it is commonly taken to extend as well to the appellant, as to them.

St. 13. E. 1. 12. 40 Ed. 3. 42. 22. Ass. p. 39. 32. H. 6. 2. 14. H. 7. 2.

The Statute extendeth to all felonies.

3 The said stat. of West. 2. saith, when any is appealed of felony, this word felony is not only intended of such offences, which were felonies at the time of making the said statute, but also of all other offences which haue béen made felony by stat. sithence the said statute. And therfore in an appeale of rape (which was made felony by the same stat. of West. 2.) the plaintife was nonsute when the Enquest was to be taken, and the def. was arraigned at the kings suit, and found not guilty, and the Jury was charged to inquire of the abettors.

St. 13. E. 1. 12. Fi. Cor. 275. 381.

The defendant acquited by battell.

4 The words of the said statute of West. 2. be (When any doth acquit himselfe in due manner) which may be intended as wel that the defendant shal recouer dammages, where he doth acquite himselfe by battell, as where he doth acquite himselfe by the country. But that acquital by battell is to be construed in this manner, where the appellant when he is in the field will acknowledge his appeale to be false; for that is a kind of vanquishment: for it must not bée intended, where the appellant is slain in the field, séeing when the person of the appellant is dead, the dammages be also gone for euer, without any recouery to be had of them.

St. 13. E. 1. 12. Fit. Cor. 98.

5 It is to be noted, that there is an acquitall in law, as well as an acquitall in déed: for if two be appealed, one as principall, and the other as accessory, and the

the principall is acquite, by this acquitall the accessory shall recouer his dama- Where the
ges against the appellant, if the Enquest which tried the principall, were also accessory in
2.&3.P.& charged vpon the accessory, though they gaue no verdict of the accessory: for in appeale shall
M.Dy.120. this case the accessory shall haue a writ of Conspiracy by the common Law, be- recouer dama-
33.H.6.2. cause by a meane he put his life in ieopardy. But it is otherwise, if the princi- ges.
pall be acquit, and the accessory did not appeare, but depended in proces: for in
41.As.p.24 that case he ought expressely to be acquit by verdict, or otherwise, he shal not re-
couer dammages by force of this statute, neither shal he haue a writ of Conspi-
racy by the common law.

St.13.E.1.12 6 These words of the foresaid stat. of West. 2. be of great moment (viz. whē Where the def.
any which is appealed of Felony doth acquite himselfe in due maner) for if the is said to ac-
def. doth barre the plaintife of his appeale, he cannot recouer damages thereby quite himselfe
against the plaintife, except the barre be such as doth acquite the def. of the Fe- in due maner,
lony. And therefore if the def. doth plead, that the appellant is a bastard, or hath and where not
an elder brother, or was neuer accoupled in lawfull mariage, or such like pleas
in barre, and by these pleas doth barre the plaintife, yet he shall not recouer da-
mages against him, for the def. may be indicted againe of the same Felony, and
27.Ass.p.25 attainted, notwithstanding by either of these pleas he is discharged of the ap-
Fi.Cor.77. peale, as well against the king, as against the appellant: for those pleas which
do not try the def. innocency in the Felony, do neuer giue him dammages any
more then if he had pleaded in abatement of the writ of Appeale such a plea as
had abated it. For notwithstanding such a plea doth discharge him of the ap-
peale as well against the K. as against the party, yet it doth not discharge him
Fit.Cor.12. of the felony. And the like law is, if in an appeale the def. do barre the appellant
by a demurrer in law, yet he shal not recouer damages against him, for the def.
innocency in the felony doth not by that meanes come to triall. And so it is, if
22.Ass.p.77. in an appeale of the death of a man the def. do plead to issue, & is foūd by verdict
to kill the man in his owne defence, or by misaduenture, in these cases he shall
recouer no dammages against the appellant, for this is no acquitall of the Fe-
lony, because the def. is inforced to purchase his pardon to purge him of the Fe-
lony: and besides it doth appeare, that this appeale was not commenced vpon
Fi.Cor.386. malice. In like sort, if the def. in an appeale vpon his arraignmēt will demand
his Clergy, & the Court wil take an Enquest of office, to inquire whether he be
guilty, or not, and the enquest doth find him not guilty, yet by this acquitall he
shall not recouer damages, for in that he demaunded his clergy before triall, he
did rather in a sort confesse the Felony by implication, then otherwise. But if
he had refused his clergy, and put himselfe vpon the enquest, who had acquited
him, then he had bin acquite in due manner, according to the foresaid statute, &
should haue recouered his damages. And so it is, if the def. in an appeal hath the
release of the appellant, or the K. pardon, & will waiue them, & plead not guilty,
& put himselfe vpon the countrey, and is acquit, he shall recouer damages, & yet
he hath done a thing of record (viz. by purchasing the K. pardon) wherin by im-
plication he doth confesse the Felony. But if it were a pardon by act of Parlia-
11.H.4.40 ment, he could not waiue it. If the def. be acquit erroniously without due pro-
ces, he shal not recouer his damages against the plaintife, for that the words of
the foresaid statute of West. 2. be: Se acquietauerit in curia Regis modo debito.
9.H.5.2 As, where the def. doth appeare by the Exigent, vpon whom the Shirife hath
returned Cepi corpus defendentis, where he should haue returned Exigi feci,

and the defendant doth appeare vpon the Euidence, and without taking aduantage thereof, pleadeth not guilty to the appeale, and it is so found for him: yet some do affirme, that he shall not recouer his dammages, because he is acquit erroniously without due proces. But others vpon greater reason do hold, that the Error in the proces is not materiall, so long as there is no Error in the writ of appeale, declaration, or pleading: for the def. is arraigned vpon the originall Writ, and not vpon the meane proces. Fi.Cor.444.

Acquite at the K. suit is only vpō an appeal

7 The foresaid statute of West. 2. hath ordained, (That when any which is appealed of felony, doth acquite himselfe, either at the appellants suit, or at the Kings suit:) This suit of the K. is alwaies intended vpon an appeale, when the def. is arraigned vpon an appeale, after that the appellant hath declared in his appeale, and is Nonsute: for if the def. were acquite at the kings suit, vpō an indictment of the same Felony, yet he shall recouer no dammages. And the manner how he shall recouer dammages, being acquite at the kings suit, doth somewhat vary from recouering of dammages at the parties suit: for when it is at the kings suit, he shall not recouer his dammages, though he be acquite, vntill he hath sued a Scire facias against the appellant, to bring him into the Court againe, being out of the Court before by his Nonsute. But if he be acquit at the appellants suit, he shall haue his iudgement to recouer dammages, without suing of any further Proces. And if a woman that is appellant be Nonsute, and after doth take a husband, the Scire facias shall bee awarded against the wife onely. St.13.E.1.12 Fit.Damag. 77.

B.

what Justices may inflict the penalty vpon the appellant.

8 And though the foresaid statute of West. 2. hath prouided, That the Justices before whom the said appeale shalbe heard and determined, shall punish the appellant by a yeares imprisonment: that punishment cannot be inflicted by the Just. of Nisi prius: and yet by the statute of Anno 14. H. 6. the Justices of Nisi prius haue power to giue iudgement in Treason and Felony tried before them, and that as well where the defendant is acquite, as where he is attainted. But yet they be not such Justices, as this statute doth meane: For that all the plea of Appeale was not heard before them, but a parcell, viz. the triall onely. St.13.E.1.12 St.14.H.6.1 2.& 3.P.& M.Dy.120. 14.E.4.14. 22.E.4.18.

The dammages for seueral persons assessed seuerally

9 And whereas the said statute of West. 2. would haue the Justices in assessing of dammages for the defendant in an appeale, to haue respect to his imprisonment, arrest, & slander: Therefore in an appeale brought against diuers, if they be all acquite, the dammages shalbe taxed seuerally, that is to say, euery of the defendants shall haue his dammages taxed by himselfe: for it may bee, that one hath cause to recouer more then the other: as, if one were appealed as principall, and the other as accessory; or that the one were a gentleman, or a man of greater estate, and the other of a meaner degree. But yet this Recouery of dammages must be intended in one, who is by the law enabled to recouer dammages: for if an appeale be brought against a woman couert onely, without her husband (as it must be vnles the husband committed felony with his St.13.E.1.12 8.H.5.6. Fi.Dam.77. Fi.Cor.276.

his wife) the wife shall not recouer dammages, though she be acquite. And yet if the appeale be brought against the husband and wife together, & they be both acquite, then the dammages shalbe seuerally taxed, that is to say, the husband shall recouer for his owne imprisonment, and the husband and wife shall recouer iointly for the imprisonment of the wife.
Fitz. Iudg. 108.

St. 13. E. 1. 12
9. H. 5. 1
41. Ass. p. 8.
10 Though the foresaid statute of West. 2. doth ordaine, That the appellant shall be grieuously fined to the king, yet that is to be intended, where the appellant shall yeeld dammages to the defendant: for if the case be such, as that the appellant shall not render dammages to the def. then he shall not pay a fine to the K. but shalbe amerced only: as, where an appeale doth abate by misnaming, the appellant shalbe only amerced. And yet if the appellant be Nonsute after declaration, he shal pay a fine to the king, and the Court will award proces against him for the same fine: and though the defendant be after acquite at the kings suit, by which meanes he shal recouer dammages against the appellant, yet the appellant shall not pay a new fine to the king, for that he hath paied it before. And if the defendant be found guilty, when he is tryed at the kings suit, the appellant hath no remedy to recouer the fine, which he hath paied before: for by the common Law, the plaintife in an appeale should haue paied a fine for his Nonsute, which is the cause that a fine shalbe paied by the appellant presently vpon his Nonsute.
Where the appellant shall pay a fine to the king.

St. 13. E. 1. 12
8. H. 5. 6.
8. Ed. 4. 3.
11 And for that the words of the said statute of West. 2. be, If the appellants be not able to recompence the dammages, inquiry shalbe made, by whose abetment the appeale was commenced: by those words it is to be gathered, that if dammages be not to be recouered against the appellant, there shall neuer any inquiry be made of the abettors, as in ẏ cases aforesaid. And where the words of the statute be, If the appellant be not able to recompence the dammages, it is intended all the dammages: for if the appellant be sufficient to render part of the dammages, but not the whole, inquiry shalbe made of the abettors, and they shall pay the residue.
In what case inquiry shal be of the abettors

St. 13. E. 1. 12
12 The foresaid statute doth ordaine, That inquiry shalbe made of the abettors, if the appellée do desire it: so that the Court of Office ought not to inquire thereof, but at the appellées request. And if an appeale be brought against two, and one of them is acquit by verdict, if the Court do inquire of the abettors at the request of the same defendant, and the Enquest doth find, that there be no abettors, and after the other defendant is arraigned, and also acquite, and if he do request also, that inquiry may be made of the abettors, the verdict of the former Enquest, wherunto he was not priuy, neither against which he shall haue any remedy, being but an Enquest of Office, shall not bind him; but according to the words of the said statute, inquiry shall be made againe at his request of the abettors: for though it be commonly inquired of the abettors, by the same Jury which doth trie the def. yet their inquiry therein is but an Enquest of office: for if they do find abettors, the abettors when they doe appeare, may tra-

uerse

uerse all that the Enquest hath found: As if they haue found that the appellant was not sufficient, or that such a man, or such a one were abettors: because they that be supposed abettors, may say by protestation, not confessing the felonie, for their plea, that the appellant is sufficient, or that they were no abettors: for the words of the said statute be (And if they be lawfully conuict of such abetment by malice) which doth proue that they shal haue their answer to that which was found by the Enquest. And also it is a good answer for him that is charged to be an abettor, to shew sufficient matter to proue, that the defendant ought not to recouer his damages against the appellant, or that the defendant was not lawfully acquit, but erroniously. But if the abettors would take exception to the inquisition found, for that the enquest did not find at what day, yeare, and place the abetment was made, that is no good exception: for in that they haue found the abetment, they haue performed the words of the statute (which be, That inquirie shall be made by whose abetment) and that they haue found: And touching the yeare, day, and place, the defendant in the Appeale must adde to the inquisition, and so supply that which wanteth.

What pleas the abettors may plead. 8.Ed.4.3. Fi.Cor.386 Fi.Cor.45 M.22.E.4.

13 Because the said statute hath ordained, that after by an Enquest an abettor is found, he shalbe distrained by a iudiciall writ at the appellees suit, to appeare before the Iustices: Therefore it is to be gathered by words of the said statute, that the proces against abettors is distresse infinit: for this proces of distresse is alwayes pursued by him that is acquit, who for his speedie remedie may prosecute it, although the apppellant be not in the Court: as where the Appellant was nonsuit in the Appeale, and the defendant was arraigned at the Kings suit, and acquit, and his damages taxed, and the abettors found: in this case the defendant shall haue proces against the abettors presently, although the iudgement of damages shalbe suspended, vntill a Scire facias shall be awarded and returned against the appellant. And the defendant who is acquit in an Appeale, may be nonsuit in the proces which hee doth pursue against the abettors, and begin againe if he will, for that nonsuit is not peremptorie to him.

Proces against the abettors. St.13.E.1.12 Fi.Dam.77. Nonsute in the proces against the abettors. Fit.Co.386

14 There is an original writ to be pursued by the Appellee, who is acquit by verdict, against the abettors, for their abetment, wherein he may count against abettors, of greater damages than were assessed by the Iustices in the Appeal: for of those damages taxed in the Appeale, there will lie no Attaint, because the inquirie touching them is but of office. And the defendant in the Appeale cannot compell the Iustices to increase those damages, and therefore it is reason that he should releeue himselfe by this action.

A writ against the abettors by the appellee. Fitz.Act.sur stat.28.

15 The same remedie which is giuen by the foresaid stat. of West.2. to the def. in an appeale of Felony, if he be acquite, is giuen by the stat. made An. 1. R. 2. to him who is falsely indicted for pursuing in a spirituall Court a matter pertaining to the temporall iurisdiction, after that he is acquite thereof: The words of which stat. be these: The Prelates & Clergy of the realme do greatly complaine, for that people of holy Church suing in the spirituall court for their tithes, & other things, which ought of right, and of auncient time were wont to appertaine to the same spirituall court, & that the Iudges of spirituall courts, & other

Procurors of indictments for suits in spirituall Courts. St.1.R.2.13

other persons dealing therein according to the Law, be maliciously and vnduly for that cause indicted, imprisoned, and by the secular power horribly oppressed, and also enforced by violence, by oathes, by grieuous obligations, and by many other meanes vnduly compelled to desist, and vtterly to leaue off from the things aforesaid, contrary to the liberties of the holy Church. Wherefore it is enacted, That all such Obligations made, or to be made by duresse, or violence, shalbe of no value. And touching those which do procure by malice such indictments, & themselues to be indictors, after that the same indictees be thereof acquite, such procurors and indictors shall haue and incurre the same paine which is contained in the statute of West. 2. touching those which do procure false appeales to be made. And the Iustices of Assise, or other Iustices, before whom such persons indicted shalbe acquite, shall haue authority to inquire of such indictors and procurors, and to punish them duly, euery person according to his desert.

A Writ

A Writ of Conspiracie.

Where a Writ of Conspiracy doth lie.

1 A Writ of Conspiracy doth lie, where two or three persons, or more, of malice, and by co[...]in, doe conspire and deuise to indict another person falsely, and after he which is so indicted is acquited, in this case he shall haue a writ of Conspiracy against those, who did so conspire to indict him. But this writ doth lye against two persons at the least, which doe so conspire: for if one person, of malice and his own false imagination, doth labour and cause one to be falsely indicted, the party which was so indicted shall not haue a writ of Conspiracy, but an action vpon the case against him, who caused him to be falsely indicted. 28. Ass. p. 12. 11. H. 4. 2.

2 At the common law a writ of Conspiracy did lie as well vpon an acquitall in an appeale, as it doth at this day on an acquitall vpon an inditment. But there hath growne a question thereof sithence the stat. of West. 2. was made, for that in the writ of Conspiracy, in the Register, it is noted for a rule, and also it is affirmed by some others, That a writ of Conspiracy doth not lye vpon an appeale, for that the said stat. of West. 2. gaue to the def. dammages against the appellant and the abettors, and so in a sort prouided for him another remedy. But to say generally, that the def. shall not haue a writ of Conspiracy vpō an acquital in an appeale, for that he may haue damages against the appellant and the abettors, is no sufficient reason: for the said stat. doth not giue to the def. inquiry against the abettors, but vpon his owne request, and therefore if he will omit to desire it, he shal haue the remedy ordained by the common law: which law is not changed by the foresaid stat. of West. 2. that is in the affirmatiue, & doth not restraine the benefit giuen by the common law. And it may be, that the damages assessed by the enquest of office, will not be so beneficiall vnto him, as the damages which wil be giuen by a Jury, that is taken at the parties suit, whereunto he shall haue his challenges, and an attaint, if they giue a false verdict. Also in a Writ of Conspiracy proces is to be awarded by Capias and Exigent, which proces is not to be graunted vpon an inquiry, according to the stat. of West. 2. So that if the abettors be not distrainable, the def. in an appeal shalbe without any remedy. And further, the damages which the abettors are

St. 13. E. 1. 12. Registrum

Fit. Na. Bre. 114.

are to pay by force of the said statute of West.2. be the dammages that the defendant hath recouered against the appellant, which dammages the abettors are to pay for the defendant, or for his insufficiencie, or nonabilitie, and not for themselues. And so it may be said, that they may satisfie for themselues in a writ of Conspiracie to be brought against them, or otherwise their offence shalbe vnpunished. And therefore notwithstanding the said statute of West. 2. a Writ of Conspiracie doth lye at this day, as well where the defendant is acquited vpon an appeale, as where he is acquited vpon an Indictment. And accordingly there is a Writ of Conspiracie in the Register deuised for that purpose, amongst other Writs of Conspiracie. But in an appeale founded vpon an indictment, if the defendant be acquite vpon the appeale, he shall not haue a Writ of Conspiracie, because it cannot be intended to be founded vpon malice, when it is founded vpon an Indictment. And likewise, if an Appeale be founded vpon an Indictment, although the appellant be Nonsute after declaration, and the defendant be arraigned, and acquite at the Kings suit, yet the defendant shall not haue a Writ of Conspiracy, causa qua supra.

Conspiracy maintenable vpon acquittall in an appeale or indictment.

33.H.6.2. 40.Ed.3.42 22.Al. p.39 14.H.7.2.

3 He against whom a Writ of Conspiracie is to be brought, must be charged, that he conspired with others to indict the plaintife falsely and maliciously, without any good or lawfull cause, or els the Writ will not lye: and therefore if by the conspiracie of two or moe one is indicted of Murther, and vpon his arraignement it is found, that he did kill the man in his owne defence, or by misaduenture, or by any other meanes which by the Law is iustifiable, he shall not haue a Writ of Conspiracie: for the Indictment was framed vpon good cause, viz. the death of a man, and neither vpon falsehood, or malice: and in like sort, if he that is indicted or appealed of Felony, doth purchase his Charter of Pardon thereof, and pleadeth it, he shall not haue a Writ of Conspiracie, for by that pardon sued he doth in a sort confesse the committing of the felonie, and so cleere the falshood or malice of any which did deuise to indite him. And yet notwithstanding the obtaining of his pardon, he may waiue it, and plead not guiltie, and then if he be acquit of the felonie, he may haue his writ of conspiracie. But if the pardon be by act of Parliament, he cannot waiue it: for the Iustices ought to allow him his pardon without pleading of it, if it be a generall pardon.

The indictment must be false, which giueth the writ of Conspiracy

22.Asp.77 Fi.Cõsp.21. 24. 11.H.4.40. 7.E.6. Dyer 85. 28.H.8. Dyer 28.

4 If two be indited or appealed of felonie, the one as principall, and the other as accessorie, and the principall hath his charter of pardon, or doth die before he be attainted, the accessorie shall not haue a writ of conspiracie against the parties that sued the appeale, or deuised to indite the principal and him, for that it is not yet discussed, but standeth indifferent whether the conspiracie were false or true.

33.H.6.2

A conspiracie doubtfull.

5 If after a conspiracie for an inditement agreed vpon, to be preferred by two or more, the same conspirators be sworne vpon an Enquest to enquire of felonies, and they with the residue of the Enquest that be sworne with them, do indict him of felony, against whom they did before conspire, in this case he shall

21.E.3.17 7.H.4.31. 27.Ass.p.12 30.Ass.p.21 33.Ass.p.77

The conspirators doe become inditors

shall not haue a Writ of Conspiracy against them, because it cannot be inten-
ded false and malicious, when they did it by vertue of their oathes, and also did
it with others besides themselues. And the same Law is, if after the conspi-
rators be sworne vpon the Enquest of inquirie, and haue spoken and confer-
red with their companions, the Iustices shall remoue them from the En-
quest, yet in that they were once sworne, and the conspiracie thereby dischar-
ged, this remouing them from the Enquest which commeth after, shall not 20.H.6.5.&
make them to bee againe in danger, and charge of the Writ of Conspiracie. 35.

A Iustice of peace.

And so it is of a Iustice of Peace; he shall not be charged by a Writ of Con- 27.Ass.p.12
spiracy, for any thing which he doth in open Sessions as a Iustice of Peace, 11.E.4.18
for he is a Iudge of record, and sworne to execute his office duly, and may in- 21.E.4.67.
forme for the kings benefit, and to punish offendors as well as he can. But the 47.Ed.3.17.
Law is meere contrary, if one who is no Iustice of record doth it, for he shal be
charged by a Writ of Conspiracy, if he do it with others. And in like sort, if 35.H.6.14.

A giuer of Euidence.

one doth come into the Court, and discouereth a felony, and is sworn, and doth 27.Ass.p.12
giue euidence to the Enquest, he shall not thereupon be charged in conspiracie, 20.H.6.5.
if he doth not before conspire with others falsely and maliciously. In a writ of 9.H.4.11.
Conspiracy the def. pleaded, that when the Iurors had taken their oathes vp- 21.H.7.
on the inditment, he was sworn to informe them: But because an act done by Kel.81.
him only without others, cannot be said to be any conspiracy, and so was no 35.H.6.14.
answer to that wherewith the plaintife charged him, for that cause he wayued 27.Ass.p.12
his plea, and pleaded not guilty: for he that is to be charged with a conspiracy,
must be charged, in respect that he did it with others, and falsely, and malici-
ously.

Who be conspirators.

6 And for that it might be knowne to all men, whom the Law did construe
to be conspirators, and were worthy to be punished as conspirators: Therefore
there was a stat. made An 33.Ed.1. which defineth them in this manner, viz. St.33 E.1.
Conspirators be they, which bind themselues by oath, couenant, or other alli-
ance, that euery one shall helpe and maintaine others purpose, falsely and ma-
liciously to indict, or to moue and maintaine suites: and also that cause infants
to appeale others of felony, whereby they are imprisoned, and much grieued:
and such as retaine men in the country with liueries, or fees, to maintaine their
leud enterprises, and to subuert the truth, as wel the takers as the giuers. And
Stewards and Bailifes of great Lords, who by their seigniory, office, or pow-
er, doe vndertake to maintaine or vphold other quarrels or suites then such
which concerne their Lords, or themselues.

A conspiracie must be by more then one.

7 The foresaid statute doth define conspirators to be those, which bind St.33.E.1.
themselues by oath &c. By which words it doth appeare, that a conspiracy can-
not be committed by one person alone, but by two at the least: and therefore
this Writ of Conspiracy will not be maintained against one alone, though it
were begun against diuers: for as soone as it shal appear, that all but one be dis- 28.Ass.p.12
charged therof, by their discharge, that one shal also be discharged. But this dis- 22.Ass.p.77
charge ought to be such a one, as may be a discharge to all intents, as acquitall 11.H.4.16.
of all by verdict sauing one, is an acquitall of that one also. And so it is, if al but
one be discharged by matter in Law, as if they plead, that they were inditors,
or such like matter in Law, which will discharge them: for in those cases they
be

be acquit of the conſpiracie to all intents. But if in a writ of Conſpiracie ſued
14.H.6.25. againſt two, one of them is attainted, and the other doth barre the plaintife by a demurrer in law, yet that ſhall not diſcharge the other which is attainted, if the barre doth not containe matter to proue that he did not conſpire, or could not conſpire. And ſo it is, if in a writ of Conſpiracy brought againſt two, the one doth appeare & plead, and his plea is found againſt him: in this caſe iudge-
24.E.3.34. ment may be giuen againſt him, though the other be not attainted: and yet in
27.E.3.80. that caſe ſome doe affirme, that in a writ of Conſpiracy againſt two, one of thē ſhall not anſwere, vntill his companion doth appeare, for the inconueniency which may enſue, viz. that the one may be foūd guilty, and the other after may be acquit of the ſame conſpiracy. But if he that did firſt appear, wil plead without his companion (though the law doth not inforce him thereunto) and that the verdict do paſſe againſt him, and he found guilty of the conſpiracy, iudgement ſhalbe giuen againſt him, as is aforeſaid, though after his companion be acquited of the ſame conſpiracy: Nam volenti non fit iniuria. Where one only charged in Conſpiracy

8 As a writ of Conſpiracy will not lie againſt one perſon only, no more wil it be maintained againſt two, who do repreſent but one perſon, as the husband No writ of Conſpiracy againſt the husband and wife
40.Ed.3.19. and wife: for a writ of Conſpiracy is not to be brought againſt them, ſeeing the
38.E.3.3. husband and wife by common intendment ought to haue but one will, which will of the wiues is (or ſhould be) ſubiect to the will of the husband: So that when they conferre and ſpeake together, all ſhall be intended the ſpeech and act of the husband, and nothing of the wife. But it is otherwiſe, if ſhe do any act alone without her husband, as if ſhe doe commit Treaſon or Felony &c. But
Fi.N.B. 116.L. a writ of Conſpiracy will lye againſt the husband, his wife, and a third perſon.

9 The common forme of the writ of Conſpiracy in the Regiſter is this, The forme of the writ of Conſpiracie.
Regiſter. fo.134. viz. Rex vicecomiti N. Salutem &c. Si A. fecerit &c. tunc pone &c. B. & C. quod ſint coram nobis &c. oſtenſuri quare conſpiratione inter eos apud M. pręhabita, præfatum A. de quodam equo furtiue apud R. capto & abducto indictari, & ipſum ea occaſione capi, & in priſona noſtra N. quouſque in curia noſtra coram dilectis & fidelibus noſtris I. & S. iuſticiarijs noſtris ad Gaolam noſtram N. deliberandam aſſignatis, ſecundum legem & conſuetudinem regni noſtri acquietatus fuiſſet detineri falſo & malitioſe procurauerunt ad graue damnum ipſius A. & contra formam ordinationis in huiuſmodi caſu prouiſæ. Et habeas ibi nomina plegiorum & hoc breue. Teſte &c. Which foreſaid writ is founded vpon a verdict: but if it be a writ of Conſpiracy founded vpon the plaintifes Nonſute in an appeale, then the words of the writ be theſe, viz. Quouſque idem A. per conſiderationem curiæ noſtræ inde quietus receſſit:
35.H.6.46 Though in the Writ of Conſpiracie it is not alledged, that the place where the Conſpiracie was deuiſed, was within the Countie, and within the iuriſdiction of thoſe Iuſtices before whom the plaintife was acquit, yet the writ is good, notwithſtanding the omiſſion of that allegation: for it ſhalbe intended to be made within the ſame county, vntil the contrarie ſhalbe ſhewed. But it
3.H.6.72. muſt needs be expreſſed in the writ, before which Iuſt. the acquitall of the pl. was, but not the manner of the acquitall, nor how hee was acquited. And

neither in this writ, nor in other writs of Conſpiracie mentioned in the Regiſter, all the indictment néed not to be rehearſed, but briefly the ſubſtance thereof, and it is ſufficiently in forme, if the writ of Conſpiracie doe agrée with the indictment, which it ought to do. 19.H.6.34. 47.Ed.3.16.

A writ of conſpiracy for the acceſſorie.

10 In the Regiſter there is a writ of Conſpiracie for the Acceſſorie in felonie, when hée is acquit by verdict, and another writ for him vpon the acquital of the Principall (if his life were put in ieopardie by the ſame Enqueſt that acquited the principall) but yet theſe two writs doe differ in forme, for the firſt is Quouſq; coram præfatis Iuſticiarijs noſtris inde ſecundum legem & conſuetudinem noſtram acquietatus fuit: And the other is, Quouſq; principal' ſecundum legem &c. acquietatus fuiſſet, & idem acceſſorius quietus receſſit. And it is ſufficient, if in the writ brought by the acceſſorie hee make mention of his owne impriſonment, and not of the principals. 33.H.6.1. And this forme of quietus receſſit, is vſed alſo when a writ of Conſpiracie is brought vpon an acquitall in an Appeale at the Kings ſuit, after the parties nonſuit. In a writ of Conſpiracie the plaintife may ſuppoſe that the conſpiracie was made in two Townes, because in one day the Conſpirators may meete in ſeuerall Townes. 22.H.6.49.

Conſpiracy in two townes.

Barres in conſpiracie.

11 In a writ of Conſpiracie it is a good plea for the defendants to plead in barre of the Action, a concord betwéene the plaintife and them: And ſo it is to plead any matter which will proue the acquitall of the plaintife erronious, for then was not the plaintife lawfully acquit according to the Statute of Weſtminſt.2. 21.H.6.28

Iudgement in conſpiracie

12 When any is conuict in a writ of Conſpiracie at the ſuit of the partie, the iudgement is none other, but that the plaintife ſhall recouer his damages, and that the defendants ſhall bée taken. 43.E.3.33. But if one be indicted and conuicted of conſpiracie, at the Kings ſuit, the iudgement is more grieuous, for then the iudgement is, That they ſhall loſe their frée law, to the intent, that they ſhall not after that time be put in Iuries or Aſſiſes, nor otherwiſe produced as witneſſes to teſtifie truth: and if they haue to do in the Kings Court, they ſhall make their Attourney to ſue for them, and that they ſhall not approach within twelue miles of the Kings Court, and that their lands, goods, and cattels ſhall bée ſeiſed into the Kings hand, and their houſes waſted, and their wiues and children thruſt out of doores, and their trées pulled vp by the rotes, and their bodies taken and impriſoned. 27.Aſp.59 46.Aſp.11. 24.E.3.34. And this is tearmed a villainous iudgement, becauſe it bringeth villanie and ſhame to him that receiueth it.

13 And becauſe that wicked offence of conſpiracie ſhould bee inquired of, and puniſhed, as well by indictment, as by writ, there was a Statute made Anno 28.Ed.1. called Articuli ſuper chartas, whereby it was ordayned, That in right of Conſpirators, falſe informers, and imbracers of Enqueſts, Aſſiſes, and Iuries, the King hath prouided remedie by a Writ out of the Chauncery. St.28.E.1. And from henceforth the King will, that his Iuſtices of the one

Bench

Bench & the other, and the Iuſt. aſſigned to take Aſſiſes, when they come into the countrey to do their office, ſhall make enquiry thereof at any mans plaint without writ, and ſhall without delay do right to the plaintiffes. And the Iuſtices may be commaunded by a writ directed unto them out of the Chancery, to execute the ſame ſtatute, although the ſtatute of it ſelfe is a ſufficient warrant and authoritie for them ſo to doe: which remedie mentioned in the foreſaid ſtatute, was intended to be ordained by another ſtatute, called the ſtatute of Conſpiratoꝛs, made Anno 20. Edw. 1. at Berwike upon Tweed, which doth prouide a writ of Conſpiracie againſt conſpiratoꝛs, maintainers of falſe quarels, and champertoꝛs, and expreſſeth the forme of that writ.

Regiſter. fo. 118. — Inquirie of Conſpiracies by Iuſtices. — St. 20. E. 1.

14 But becauſe the foreſayd Statute of Articuli ſuper chartas did prouide onely a remedie at the plaint of the partie, and did not giue the Iuſtices in the ſayd Statute mentioned power to enquire of, heare, and determine conſpiracies, at the ſuit of the King, neither did it giue authoritie to the ſaid Iuſtices, to adiourne the ſuit, if for ſhortneſſe of time it could not be determined in the countrey: Therefore by a ſtatute made Anno 4. Edw. 3. the ſame enormities were redreſſed by theſe words, viz. Where, in times paſt diuers people of the Realme, as well great as other, haue made alliances, confederacies, and conſpiracies, to maintaine parties, pleas, and quarels, whereby diuers haue béene wrongfully diſherited, and ſome ranſomed and deſtroyed, and ſome for feare béeing maymed, and beaten, durſt not ſue for their right, nor complaine, nor the Iurors of Enqueſts giue their verdicts, to the great hurt of the people, and ſlaunder of the Law, and common right: Therefore it is agréed, that the Iuſtices of the one Bench, and of the other, and the Iuſtices aſſigned to take Aſſiſes, whenſoeuer they come to hold their Seſſions, to take Enqueſts upon Niſi prius, ſhall enquire, heare, and determine as well at the Kings ſuit, as at the ſuit of the partie, of ſuch maintainers, bearers, and conſpiratoꝛs, and alſo of champertoꝛs, and of all other things contained in the ſayd Article, as well as Iuſtices in Eire ſhould doe, if they were in the ſame Countie. And that which cannot be determined before the Iuſtices of the one Bench or of the other, upon the Niſi prius, for ſhortneſſe of time, ſhall be adiourned into the places whereof they be Iuſtices, and there ſhall be determined according to right and reaſon.

St. 28. Ed. 1 — St. 4. E. 3. 11. — Inquirie of conſpiratoꝛs at K. or parties ſuit.

15 Notwithſtanding the foreſaid Statutes, there were ſuch deuiſes and practiſes to execute malice and reuenge, and deſire to put others in perill of their liues, lands, and goods, that ſome would frame indictments or appeales againſt others of the K. good and obedient ſubiects, of Treaſon, Felony, or treſpas, in ſeuerall forrein counties, liberties, and franchiſes, where the ſaid perſons did neuer dwel nor conuerſe, and there they were purſued to the Exigent, and ſometime outlawed, before that they could know of it: For the remedie whereof there was a ſtat. made Anno 8. H. 6. wherein amongſt other things it was enacted, That if any perſon ſhall be indicted or appealed of felony, treaſon, or treſpas, in a forein county, he ſhal in an action upon the caſe, recouer treble damages againſt euery procurer of ſuch indictment, or appeale, after hee is duly acquited by verdict. And the like proces ſhalbe in the ſame, as in an action of Treſpas vi & armis. S. Appeales 61.

St. 8. H. 6. 10 — Procurers of an indictment or appeale in a forein county

A Writ of Conſpiracie.

An offence ſuppoſed to be in a place where there is none ſuch.

16 Becauſe diuers people vpon malice, enuie, and deſire of reuenge, did oft-time cauſe the K. liege people to be appealed or indicted in diuers counties, of Treaſons or Felonies, ſuppoſing by the ſaid appeals or inditments, that the ſaid Treaſons or Felonies were committed in one certaine place, whereas there is no ſuch place within the ſaid county where the ſaid inditmēt is found, nor any ſuch place in the county, as is declared by the ſaid Appeale: Therefore by the ſtat. made anno 7. H. 5. anno 9. H. 5. & anno 18. H. 6. it was ordained, That the ſaid Appeals and inditments, and the proces thereupon ſhalbe void, and adiudged of no force. And that the ſaid Appellées and Indictées may haue their writs of Conſpiracie againſt their indictors, procurors, and conſpirators, and recouer their damages. And that the indictors, procurors, and conſpirators ſhalbe puniſhed by impriſonment, fine and ranſome, for the K. aduantage, by the Iuſtices diſcretion.

St. 9. H. 5. 1.
St. 18. H. 6. 12.

The

The Coroner and his Authoritie and dutie in Felonies &c.

1 A Coroner is an antient officer of trust in this realm, ordained to be a principall preseruer and keeper of the peace, to make record of the pleas of the Crown, and of his owne view, and of abiurations, and of outlawries, and of Appeales and accusations of felons made before him, and of nonsuits of plaintifes in Appeales, and of all things done in the Countie which belongeth to the Office of the Coroner. And also an Appeale shalbe entred of Robberie or Larcenie in the presence of the Coroner in the Court of any free man which hath a franchise of Infang theefe. Which Coroner shall be chosen into the same Office vpon the death, or other auoidance of another, by force of the Kings writ directed to the Sherife of that Countie where that Office is void, by death or otherwise. And the same election shall be in the full County Court by warrant of the Kings writ: The tenor of which writ is as followeth.

The Coroners Office.

Election of the Coroner.

2 James by the grace of God &c. To the Sherife of the Countie of Buckingham Salutation &c. Because L. one of our Coroners of the Countie is deceased, as we are informed, we do commaund thee, if it bee so, that thou doest cause another Coroner to be chosen in thy full Countie, by the assent of the same Countie, in the place of the same L. according to the forme of the statute therefore made and prouided: Who taking his othe according to the custom, shall from thenceforth do and performe all things which doe appertaine to the Office of a Coroner in the Countie aforesayd. And cause such a one to bee chosen which best can, and will attend that Office. When a Coroner is chosen he shall continue in his Office vntill the King hath otherwise determined his pleasure, or that the King doth dye, or that there be another King: for he is not changeable euerie yeare, as the Sherife and Escheator is. And then the Sherife shall giue him an othe, That he shall lawfully and without demaunding

The writ de Coronatore eligendo.

How long a Coroner shal continue in his Office.

4.E.4.44

of any reward, make his enquests and inrolments, and do all things which do belong to the office of the Coroner.

3 And because many meane men, and of small discretion, were divers times chosen into the sayd Office of Coroners, and for that it is expedient that discreet, lawfull, and sage men should meddle in the same Office; therefore by the Statute of Westminst. prim, made Anno 3. Edw. primi, it was ordained, That all Coroners of Shires shall bee chosen in the full Counties, by the Commons of the same Counties, of the most meet and worthie people, which may bee found in the same Counties, to execute the sayd Offices, and of the most sage and wise Knights, which doe best know, can, and will attend unto the same Office, and which will lawfully attache and present the Pleas of the Crowne. And the same Statute was after rehearsed and confirmed by the Statute of Anno 28. Edw. 3. by which it was ordained, That Coroners of Counties shall bee chosen in the full Counties, by the Commons of the same Counties, of the most fit and lawfull persons of the same Counties: Allwayes saving to the King and other Lords, which ought to make such Coroners their Franchises. But by the Statute of Anno 14. Edw. 3. no Coroner shall bee chosen, if hee have not sufficient land in fee in the same Countie, whereof hee may answer all manner of people. And because this Statute is in the negative, therefore the not satisfying of it, is a sufficient cause to remoove a Coroner from his Office. And hee is sayd to have sufficient land, if hee hath land in the Countie whereupon hee may live according to his degree, to execute that Office. And whereas the foresayd Statute of 28. Edw. 3. hath ordayned, That a Coroner shall bee chosen by the Commons of the sayd Counties, that is intended by the freeholders of the same Counties, and by none other.

Margin: Who shalbe Coroners, & by whom they shalbe chosen. — A Coroner must have sufficient land. — St. 3. E. 1. 10 — St. 28. E. 3. 6 — St. 14. E. 3. 8 — Fi. N. B. 164.

4 The foresayd Statute of Westminst. prim, committeth the Office of Coroners to Knights and none others: and therefore in former ages it was a cause amongst others, to discharge a Coroner of his Office, that hee was no Knight: But because those words were put into the Statute onely to the intent that the Coroner should have sufficient within the same Countie: for which cause, if that be performed, the intent of the Statute is observed.

Margin: Whether Coroners ought to be knights. — St. 3. E. 1. 10

5 And also the same statute doth ordaine, That such shall bee chosen Coroners, which do know, can, and will attend unto the said Office: And therefore if any be chosen, which do not know, cannot, or will not attend unto the same office, they shalbe remoued and discharged of that office by the K. writ, wherein the cause of his discharge shall be rehearsed: either because he is imployed in other affaires of the K. or that he is sicke of some grieuous and long infirmitie, or that he is lame, or that he is not meet for that office (viz. by force of some clause contained in the said statute of West. 1.) or that hee hath not sufficient lands within the same Countie, or that he hath the palsey, or that hee is dwelling in the uttermost part of the Shire, or that he is chosen Sherife, or verderer of a forrest. But if any of those causes surmised be false, whereby the Coroner

Margin: Causes to remoue a Coroner. — Co. J. 5. 57. — Fitz. N. B. 165. N.

roner is discharged of his Office by false suggestion, then he may sue for a commission to be awarded out of the Chauncerie, to enquire of the same suggestion. And if it be found false, and returned so into the Chauncerie, then there shall be a Supersedeas awarded out of the Chauncerie, to the Sherife, that hee shall not remoue the sayd Coroner. And if he be remoued, that hee shall suffer him to enioy the sayd Office as he did before. But it is sometimes vsed, and most commendable for him that is chosen Coroner, if he perceiue in himselfe any of the foresayd impediments, to purchase a writ out of the Chancerie, to discharge him of the said Office. Register. fo.177.

6 And because the sayd Coroner should doe iustice and right to all persons, without extortion or exaction, the foresayd statute of West.1. doth further ordaine, That Sherifes shall haue counter-rolls with the Coroners, as well of Appeales as of Enquests, of Attachments, and other things which do belong to his Office. And no Coroner shall demaund or take any thing for the execution of his Office, vpon paine of a grieuous forfeiture to the King. Which said Statute was also confirmed by a statute made at Excester, anno 14. Edw. 1. And by the statute made Anno 1.H.8. it was enacted, That vpon request made to a Coroner to come and enquire vpon the view of any person slaine, drowned, or otherwise dead by misaduenture, the sayd Coroner shall diligently doe his Office, vpon the view of the bodie of euerie such person or persons, without any thing taking therefore, vpon paine to euerie Coroner that will not endeuour himselfe to doe his Office as is aforesaid, or that hee taketh any thing of any person, for doing of his Office vpon euery person dead by misaduenture, for euerie time fortie shillings. And the Iustices of Assises, and Iustices of Peace, within the countrey where such default of Coroners be, haue authoritie to enquire thereof, and to determine the same, as well by examination as by presentment. But by a statute made Anno 3.H.7. it was prouided, That a Coroner shall haue for his fee vpon euerie Inquisition taken vpon the view of a bodie murdered, or otherwise slaine, iij.s.iiij.d. of the goods and cattels of the murderer, if he haue any, and if he haue no goods, the Coroner shall haue his fee of such amerciaments as any towneship shall be amerced for escape of any such murderer. And though by the common law the Coroner hath a fee, a penie of euerie Uiffnage, as appendant to his Office, at the comming of the Iustices in Eire, yet that fee is not repugnant to the foresayd statute of Westminst.1. for hee taketh not that to execute his Office, but as a fee of right incident to his office, though he do nothing in the execution of the said Office.

Where a Coroner may take a fee, and where not.

St.3.E.1.10 St.14.E.1. St.1.H.8.7. St.3.H.7.1. Fitz.Cor. 321.372.

7 It appeareth both by the stat. intituled Officium Coronatoris, and by Bracton, that if any Coroners be aduertised by the K. Bailifes, or other honest men of the countrey, to come to those that be slaine, sodainly dead, or wounded, or to house breakers, or to any place where treasure is found, they shall immediatly come and forthwith commaund foure, fiue, or sixe of the next townes, that they appeare before them in such a place: and when they come, the Coroners vpon their othe, shall inquire, if they did know of that man that was killed, where he was first slaine, whether in the field, or in the house, bed, Tauerne, or in any companie, and who were there. Likewise they shal inquire who were culpable, either of the act or force, and who were present, either men

St.3.Ed.1. Bracton de Corona, cap.5.

Of what things Coroners shall inquire.

Murder.

Inquirie of the offendors.

men or women, and of what age they be, so they can speak, and haue discretion: And they which be found guiltie by inquisition in the foresaid maner, shalbe taken, deliuered to the Sherif, and committed to the gaole: and as many of them as be not found guiltie, shalbe attached, vntill the comming of the Iustices, and their names inrolled. And if any man be sodainly slain, and found in the fields or woods, it is to be considered whether he were slaine there or not: if hee were brought thither, their steps that brought him (if it may be) shall bee followed, and so shall the tracke of horse and cart. And also it shall be inquired, if he that was slaine were knowne or vnknowne, and where he lodged the night before: And if any be found guiltie of the death of such, immediatly the Coroners shal come to his house, and inquire what cattell he hath, and what corne in his graunge, and what on the ground; and if he be a free man, what free land hee hath, and what it is worth by the yeare, beside the Lord of the fees seruice: but the land shall remaine in the kings hands, vntill the Lord of the fee hath made a fine for it. And when they haue enquired of all things, then they shal cause them to be priced, as if they should straight way be sold, and the bodie of him that is dead shall be buried. Moreouer, the Coroners shall enquire of them which be drowned, sodainly slaine, or strangled by the signe of a coard tyed strait about their neckes, or about any of their members, or vpon any other hurt found vpon their bodies, or some other manifest token, and shall attache the finders, and al other in their company. A Coroner ought to inquire of treasure that is found, who were the finders, and who are suspected thereof, which may be gathered by some mans delicat liuing, and frequenting of Tauernes, which (vpon suspition) shall be attached by foure, or sixe, or two pledges. If any be appealed of Rape, he shall be attached by foure or sixe pledges, if the appeale be fresh, and the signe of the truth apparant, or an open outcrie leuyed: But if it be without any manifest token or outcry, two pledges shall suffice. Upon Appeale of Maihem, if the wounds be mortall, they which bee appealed shall bee forthwith apprehended, and kept vntill it be knowne whether he that is hurt shall recouer or not: if he dye they shall be retained, if he liue they shall be attached by foure or sixe pledges, according to the bignesse of the wound: If it be for a Maihem, then there shall be no lesse than foure pledges: if a small wound be, then two will serue. The length, breadth, and deepenesse of all wounds ought to be viewed, and with what weapons, and in what part of the bodie the partie was hurt, and also how many wounds there be: how many be culpable, and who gaue the wound: all which things shall bee inrolled in the Coroners roll. Horses, boats, carts, commonly called Deodands, wherby any person shall perish, shall be valued and deliuered to the whole township, which shalbe answerable therefore. Whosoeuer layeth hands vpon the wreck of the sea, shalbe attached by sufficient pledges. The price of the wrecke shalbe valued, and deliuered to the towne to answer, &c.

A man found slaine.

Sodainly slaine.

Treasure troue.

Rape.

Maihem or wound.

The length, breadth, and deepnesse of wounds.

Deodands.

Wrecke of the Sea.

The Coroner shall execute his Office in his owne person.

8 It doth first appeare by the words of this stat. that the Coroner ought to do his office in his owne proper person, and not by Deputie, viz. They shall presently come to those that bee slaine, or sodainely dead. And so also it is declared by the Statute of Excester, and proued by the foresayde definition of the Office or Authoritie of a Coroner, viz. That a Coroner shall make a Record of his owne view: which is, that hee shall see the dead bodie when hee doth make the inquirie, or otherwise the inquirie is not good: For if hee will inquire of any dead person without the sight of

St.3.Ed.1.

St.14.E.1.

Fi. Cor.107

of him, this is without authoritie, and so void. And therefore if the bodie bee buried before his comming, hee must record it in his Rolles, to the intent that the towne where he was buried may be amerced for it, by the Justices in Eire vpon the sight of the Coroners Rols. And yet notwithstanding the Coroner must digge the bodie out of the ground, and make his enquirie vpon the sight of the bodie, as he should haue done if it had not been buried. If one be indicted before the Coroner vpon the sight of the body, and then the body is by the Coroners commandement buried, and after, for that the indictment is not sufficient, the Coroner doth take the body out of the earth, and indict the offendor againe: this is lawfully done, being vpon the sight of the bodie, though the bodie had beene buried fourteene dayes before. If a dead bodie that is slaine, or sodainely dead, be suffered to lye vpon the ground vnburied to putrifie, or to yeeld an euill sauour, without sending for the Coroner, the towne where the same bodie did so lye vnburied, shall bee amerced. And likewise if a prisoner do dye in prison, and the keeper of the prison doth not send for a Coroner, he shall be amerced. And though a Coroner shall make a record of his owne view, and enter the same into his roll, yet by the statute of Magna Charta no Coroner, Sherife, Constable, Escheator, or other Bailife of the K. shall hold pleas of the Crowne.

Margin: The Coroner shall see the dead body. — Fitz. Cor. 329. Britton 4. 21. E. 4. 70. 2. R. 3. 2. — A body buried taken vp againe. — Fi. Cor. 339 — Fi. Cor. 421 Britton. — St. 9. H. 3. 17 — Pleas of the Crowne.

9 The said statute of West. 1. ordaineth, That if any Coroners be aduertised by the Kings Bailifes, or other honest men of the countrey, they shall presently come and make inquisition: whereby it appeareth, that if the Coroner shall be slacke and negligent in comming to doe his office, after the Bailifes or men of the countrey haue sent for him, he shall be punished. And if he omit to doe his office, as to make inquirie of, or to enter into his roll the death of a man, or any other thing which by the law he is to doe, or make a record of, hee shall bee committed to prison. And by the statute of Anno 3. H. 7. If any Coroner be remisse in viewing of a dead bodie murdered, or slaine, and do not enquire of them that haue done the murder, or death, of their abettors, and consenters, who were present thereat, and their names: or so found, doe not inroll, certifie, and deliuer his inquisition to the Justices of the next gaole deliuerie in the Shire where the inquisition is taken, that the same Just. may proceed against such murderers, if they be in the gaole, or else certifie the inquisition into the K. Bench, the said Coroner shall forfeit to the King for euery offence v. l.

Margin: St. 3. Ed. 1. — The Coroner must presently do his office. — Fitz. Cor. 291. — St. 3. H. 7. 1. — Coroners shall inquire and certifie at the gaole deliuerey

10 The foresaid statute of West. 1. as touching inquisition, doth only extend to a dead person: whereby it seemeth that a Coroner cannot inquire of any other felony, but of the death of a man: Sauing that in Northumberland the Coroner doth inquire of all felonies: But that authoritie they maintaine by prescription. A presentment was made before the Coroner, that a felon being apprehended for stealing, was led to a church by certaine persons: and this was adiudged a void presentment, because he cannot inquire thereof by vertue of his office: but if he had receiued the kings writ, or commission to haue made inquirie thereof, hee might haue done it. And yet some do affirme, that he may inquire of the rape of a woman, and of breaking of prison (being other felonies different from the death of a man) and of Sturgeon, and Whales taken. If a man be slaine in the armes or braunches of the sea, where one may see

Margin: St. 3. Ed. 1. 35. H. 6. 27 — The Coroner shall inquire onely of the death of a man. — 27. Ass. p. 55 — Slaine in an arme of the sea.

see the ground on both sides, the Coroner shall inquire thereof, and not the Ad-
mirall, because the countrey may take knowledge thereof: which prooueth, Fi.Cor. 399
Admirall. that by the common law the Admirall had no iurisdiction but vpon the mayne
Sea, before the Statute of 13.R.2. & 2.H.4. were made. And though the St.13.R.2.5
Coroner cannot enquire of any other felonies, but of the death of a man, yet 2.H.4.11.
by the Statute of West.1. made Anno 3.Ed.1. it was ordained, That if the St.3.Ed.1.9
Sherife, Coroner, or any other Bailife within Franchise or without, for re-
A Coroner concealing a felon, or not arresting him. ward, intreatie, or any affinitie, doe conceale, consent, or procure to conceale
the felonies done in their liberties: or otherwise will not attach or arrest such
felons, whereas they may, or will not do their offices for the fauour that they
beare to such offendors, and be thereof attainted, they shall be one yeare im-
prisoned, and make a grieuous fine: And if they haue not whereof to make
fine, they shall be three yeares imprisoned. So that a Coroner may attach or
arrest any maner of felon whatsoeuer, though he cannot inquire of him.

The force of a Coroners record. 11 It is contained in the before specified Statute of Westminst. 1. That
all things ought to bee inrolled in the Rolles of the Coroner: Which prooueth
that the same inrolment is the Coroners Record, and that the sayd Record is
of great force: for if the thing inrolled be within the compasse of the Coroners
authoritie, it shall be of greater credit than the Record of any other: For if a Bro.Cor.
thing be found before the Iustices in Eyre, contrary to that which was entred 352.
The first Coroner. into the roll of the Coroner, it shall be void. And the Record of the first Coro- Fitz.Cor.
ner, viz. the Record of him which first sitteth vpon the view of the bodie, shall 107.
be preferred before the Record of the second Coroner, who doth after sit and
Approuer. inquire of him. If a man become an Approuer before the Coroner, and doth Fitz.Cor.
Dures. appeale others, he shall not be receiued to say after, That he did it by dures of 118.
imprisonment, but shall bee estopped thereof by the Coroners Record. And in
Abiuring before the Coroner. like sort, if one hath abiured the Realme before the Coroner, and after doth re- 12.Ass.p.29.
turne, and is arraigned, and doth plead, that he is not the same person: if in Fi.Cor.124
this case the Coroner doth record him to be the same person, he shal be condem-
Confession of breaking of prison. ned. And the same law is, if a man be arraigned of breaking of prison, he shall 25.E.3.42.
be estopped, to plead not guiltie thereunto, if the Coroner doth record, that he Fitz.Cor.
did at another time confesse it before him. And if an Approuer to prolong his 243.435.
Approuer. life, doe appeale others, where there be none such, and that bee testified by
the Coroner, the Approuer shall be hanged, without further enquirie of the 25.Ed.3.24.
approuement.

Who ought to appeare vpon the Coroners inquisition. 12 By the Statute of Marlbridge made Anno 52.H.3. it was ordayned, St.52.H.3.
That vpon an inquisition to be taken by a Coroner of the death of a man, 24.
euerie one of the age of twelue yeares ought to appeare, except they haue a rea-
sonable excuse of their absence.

The Coroner may take appeals. 13 And though the foresayd Statute of Officium Coronatoris doe make
mention but of certaine Appeales, as an Appeale of Rape, Mayhem, &c. yet the
Coroner with the Sherife hath authoritie to take Appeales of Robberie and
other Felonies, and also to take the Appeale of an Approuer, in this sort and
manner following, viz. he may take an Appeale of Robberie, or other felonie
committed in the same countie where he is Coroner, and not elsewhere. But

he

he may take the Appeale of an Approuer, of an offence committed in any countie of England; and the reason of this difference is, because by the approuement the Approuer is attainted of Felonie, but so is not the offendor in the other case, and therefore if in the former case he should receiue such an Appeale of Robberie, or other Felonie, it could not be tryed by a Jury of the countie where he is Coroner, for that the felonie was committed in a forrein countie. And yet in the foresaid case of approuement in another countie, the Coroner cannot award Proces thereupon, but he must enter it into his roll, and send it to the Justices of Gaole deliuerie, who shall award Proces vnto the Sherife of that forreine countie, to apprehend him which is so appealed. And as the Coroner may take the Appeale of an Approuer in another countie, so vpon the same reason he may take the abiuration of one which hath confessed a felonie committed by him in another countie.

Fitz.Cor. 437. Fitz.Cor. 461.

14 If the Coroner shall find any person drowned in a daungerous pond or pit, he must commaund the towne where the same pond or pit is, to stop it vp, and enter the same his commandement into his Roll: And if after it bee found before the Justices in Eire, that the same pond, or &c. is not stopped vp, the whole towne where it is shalbe amerced.

Fitz.Cor. 416.

Stopping vp a place of danger.

15 Though there be diuers Coroners in a Countie, yet it is not requisit to haue more than one to enquire vpon the sight of a dead bodie. And in like sort one is sufficient to giue iudgement vpon an Outlawrie, and in Redisseisin it is sufficient to haue two Coroners. But where Proces is to bee awarded to the Coroners, in default of the Sherife, there all the Coroners within the Countie ought to serue, or otherwise it is not good: for they execute that office as ministers, and not as Judges, as they doe in other cases. And by the statute of Anno 23. H.6. euery of the Coroners shall bee present in his proper person at the assessing of the wages of the Knights of the same Shire for the Parliament, with the Sherife, Vndersherife, Baylifes, and others that will be present to assesse the wages of the sayd Knights, after the deliuerance of the Kings writ De solutione feodi Militum Parliamenti, and proclamation thereof made, vpon paine of forfeiture of euery of them making default, xl.s. to the King.

14.H.4.35. 39.H.6.41. St.23.H.6. 11.

Where the presence of all the Coroners is requisit, and where but of some one of them.

16 By the Statute made Anno 1. & 2. P. & M. it is ordained, That euery Coroner vpon any inquisition before him found, whereby any person shall bee indicted for murder or manslaughter, or as accessory to the same before the murder or manslaughter committed, shall put in writing the effect of the euidence giuen to the Jurie before him, being materiall. And he hath authoritie to bind all such by Recognisance, or Obligation, as doe declare any thing materiall to proue the sayd murder or manslaughter, or to be accessorie to the same, to appeare at the next generall gaole deliuerie to be holden within the countie, citie, or towne corporat, where the tryall thereof shall be, then and there to giue euidence against the partie so indicted, at the time of his tryall, and shall certifie as well the same euidence, as such bond in writing which he shall take, together with the Inquisition or Indictment before him taken and found, at, or before his sayd tryall to be made. And if any Coroner shall offend in any thing to the contrarie

St.1.& 2. P.&M.13.

The Coroner must record the euidence, and bind the parties to giue it.

contrarie, then the Iustices of gaole deliuerie for the Shire, Citie, Towne, or place where such offence shalbe committed, vpon due proofe thereof by examination before them, shall for euerie such offence, set such fine on such Coroner, as they shall thinke meet.

Inquirie of a man slaine within the K. house & verge.

17 Forasmuch as heretofore many felonies that haue béene committed within the Verge, haue béene vnpunished, because the Coroners of the county haue not béene authorized to inquire of felonies done within the Verge, but onely the Coroner of the Kings house, which neuer continueth in one place, by reason whereof there can be no triall made in due manner, nor the felons put in Exigent, nor outlawed, nor nothing presented in the Eire, which hath beene great damage to the King, and to the hindrance of his peace: For the redresse whereof by a Statute made Anno 28. Ed. 1. intituled Articuli super chartas, it St. 28. E. 1. 3 was ordained, That if the death of a man (where the Coroners Office is to make view and Enquest) doth chaunce in any countie where the Kings house is, and within the Verge, the Coroner of the same countie shalbe commanded with the Coroner of the Kings house, to execute his office, and to inroll it. And that thing which cannot be determined before the Steward, shall bee committed to the common law, so that Exigents, Outlawries, and Presentments, shal be thereupon made to the Iustices in their circuits, by the Coroner of the countie, as well as of other felonies done out of the Verge: Neuerthelesse they shal not omit by reason hereof, to make attachmēts freshly vpon the felonies done. Which foresaid statute, for so much thereof as doth touch or concerne the K. house onely, is in part altered by the statute of Anno 33. H. 8. whereby it is or- St. 33. H. 8. 12. dayned, That all Inquisitions vpon the view of persons slaine within any of the Kings Palaces or houses, or any other house, at such time as he shall bee abiding in his royall person, viz. (within Edifices, Courts, places, gardens, orchards, or houses within the Porters ward of any of the house or houses aboue rehearsed, or within any gardens, priuie walkes, orchards, tylt-yards, wood-yards, tenice playes, cocke fights, bowling allyes, neere adioyning to any of the houses aboue rehearsed, and being part of the same, or within two hundred foot of the standard, of any outward gate or gates of any of the houses aboue rehearsed, commonly vsed for passage out or from any of the house or houses aboue specified) shalbe taken by the Coroner of the houshold of the King or his heires, without adioyning of any other Coroner of any Shire, by the othes of twelue or more of the Yeomen officers of the Kings &c. houshold, returned by the two Clerkes Comptrollers, the Clerkes of the Checke, Clerks Marshall, or one of them for the time being, of the foresayd houshold, to whom the sayd Coroner shall direct his Precept (which Coroner &c. shall be assigned by the L. Steward for the time being.) And the said Coroner shall from time to time for euer without delay, certifie vnder his Seale, and the Seals of such persons as shalbe so sworne before him, all such Inquisitions, Indictments, and Offices, vpon the view of all dead bodies which shall bee slaine within any of the K. Palaces or houses, or other house aforesaid, before the sayd L. Steward, and in his absence before the Treasurer, Comptroller, and Steward of the Marshalsey, or before two of them, whereof the said Steward of the Marshalsey to be one. And such Inquisitions and Offices so certified, shal be taken as good to all intents, as any Inquisition taken vpon the view of the bodie of any person being dead, by any Coroner of any countie of this Realme, hath béene, or shalbe adiudged.

Inquirie if a man be slaine within the K. house & verge.

18 Where-

Se. 28.E.1.3 18 Whereas the foresaid stat. of 28. E. 1. hath ordained, That if the death of a man doth chance in any county where the K. house is, and within the Verge, the Coroner of the same countie shalbe commanded with the Coroner of the K. house to execute his office, and to inroll it. But if a murder or manslaughter be found within the countie of M. within the Verge, by an Inquisition taken before one which is then both one of the Coroners of the county of M. and also Coroner of the K. house, and then & there one is indicted of the same murder or manslaughter, this is a good indictment: for the intent and meaning of the said stat. of 28. Ed. 1. is performed, though not by two persons, yet by one man having two offices, and also the mischiefe recited in the said Act, is avoyded: for though the Court doth remove, yet the Coroner of the county may proceed. One man Coroner of the K. house, and of the county.

Co. li. 4. 46.

Who ſhall be Iudge of Treaſon and Felonie.

1 HAuing written at large of Treaſons and Felonies, and ſhewed what ſorts, and how many of either of them there be, and which of thoſe were deliuered vs by the common law, and which ordained by ſtatute: And declared who be principals, and who be acceſſories in the ſaid crimes: how the offendors therein, vpon a pricke and guilt of conſcience, doe ofttimes breake priſon and indeuor to eſcape, and how by Huy and cry, and other means they be apprehended, and brought to be tryed by the iuſtice of the law: how they be accuſed by Appeals or Indictments, in what ſort they ſhalbe reſtained and kept ſub cuſtodia legis, in priſon, or by mainpriſe, or bail, vntil they haue anſwered their ſaid offences: And alſo hauing expreſſed what pleas the partie accuſed hath to plead for himſelfe, or other helps to defend himſelfe, by whom and what means thoſe pleas ſhalbe examined, and what fauours bee afforded him in the tryall therof: and what iudgement, execution, & forfeitures the law doth inflict vpon thoſe that in contempt of her do commit the ſaid capitall and moſt grieuous offence: And further, hauing dilated how a true man being vpon malice, and falſly charged with felony by an Appeale, or Indictment, ſhall, in ſome ſatiſfaction of his diſcredit and loſſes, recouer damages againſt the appellant, his abettors, or the conſpirators: And hauing laid open the authority & duty of the Coroner, who is a moſt antient officer of truſt in this Realm, & a ſpeciall preſeruer of the peace of the King and the kingdome, I am now laſtly to write who ſhall bee Iudge in the foreſaid Treaſons and Felonies, and ſhal inflict puniſhment vpon euerie tranſgreſſor of the ſaid lawes according to his deſert. Wherein is to be conſidered, that the dead letter of the common or ſtatute law, cannot be that Iudge, to inquire of felons, examine them, commit them to priſon, indict them, arraigne them, allow them their lawfulll triall, examine their cauſes, and yeeld them iuſtice according to their ſeueral demerits by acquital, or condemnation: but it muſt be Lex loquẽs, viz. That Iudge muſt be a man of learning and vprightneſſe, which by his mouth will ſpeake and attribute to euery perſon, that which the wiſdome and integritie of his heart doth conceiue to be iuſt, lawfull, and due vnto them. And though that Iudge ought ſo to be countenanced and

pro-

protected by the regall authoritie, that he shall not néed to feare the face of any man for doing of iustice, and shall be enabled to crush and suppresse all offences within his iurisdiction; yet the king himselfe cannot be that Iudge, nor sit in iudgement in causes of treason or felonie, because he is one of the parties to the iudgement: for al treasons & felonies be done, & be supposed to be done contrary to the peace, crowne, & dignitie of the K. And further, the escheates and other fort. of lands, leases, goods, and cattels, which do come by the attainder of any person of treason or felonie, do for the most part by the law accrue to the king: And so if the King might be Iudge, hee should bee Iudge in his owne cause, which Ius gentium doth not permit. But the King by his Commission may commit that authoritie to others, who may iudge betwéene him and the supposed offendor. And the King ought to make choyce of such a man to be Iudge as is wise, and doth feare God, who hath truth in his mouth, and no couetousnesse in his heart, who will neither decline from the troden path of iustice, to the right hand nor to the left, for the hope of prosperity, or feare of aduersitie, nor will draw the Kings sword to reuenge his owne wrongs; who will denie iustice to none, neither himselfe will expect or take reward of any; who will fréely licence all persons to prosecute their right, giue full eare to the widowes complaint, further the cause of the orphan and fatherlesse, and suffer none that hée can helpe to receiue wrong; who will not feare the countenance of the mightie, nor disdaine the basenesse of the poore, whom neither hatred, fauor, or priuat affection will moue, but without respect of persons will yéeld to each wight, that which his cause requireth; who will remember, and neuer forget, that God hath endowed him with knowledge and vnderstanding, that he hath made a couenant with him, to shew him what true iustice and iudgement is, that all his actions bée continually in Gods sight, and that euerie moment from heauen the King of Kings doth behold them: And finally, who duely respecting both the commissions which he hath receiued from God and his prince, will so indifferently temper iustice with mercie towards the poore prisoner standing trembling before him at the barre, as he will hope for mercie when himselfe shall make his last and great account before the God of iustice and mercie.

The K. cannot be Iudge in Treason or Felonie.

What sort of men ought to be Iudges.

Ecclesiast. 17

2 Whereas diuers antient Prerogatiues and Authorities of iustice, appertaining to the Crown of this Realm, were seuered and taken from the same by sundrie gifts of the Kings Progenitors, Kings of this Realme, to the great diminution of the royall estate of the same, and to the hindrance and delay of iustice: for the reformation whereof, by a Statute made Anno 27. H. 8. it was enacted, That no person or persons, of what estate, condition, or degrée soeuer they bée, shall haue any power or authoritie to make any Iustices of Eyre, Iustices of Assise, Iustices of Peace, or Iustices of Gaole deliuerie, but that all such Officers and Ministers, shall bée made by Letters Patents, vnder the Kings great Seale, in the name, and by authoritie of the King and his heires, Kings of this Realme, in all Shires, Counties, Counties Palantine, and other places of this Realme, Wales, and the Marches of the same, or in any other his Dominions, at their pleasure and wills, in such maner and forme, as Iustices in Eyre, &c. bée commonly made in euerie Shire of this Realme: Any graunts, vsages, Acts of Parliament, or other thing notwithstanding.

St. 27. H. 8. 25.

None shall make Iustices but the King.

Who shall be Iudge of Treason and Felonie.

The Iudge vpon the arraignment of a Peere of the Realme.

3 When a Peere of the Realme, and Lord of the Parliament, is to be arraigned vpon any Treason or Felonie, whereof he is indited, and whereunto he hath pleaded not guiltie, the King by his letters patents shall assigne some noble and sage Lord of the Parliament, to bee high Steward of England for the day of his arraignement, who before the same day shall make a Precept to his Serieant at Armes, that is appointed to serue him during the time of his Commission, to warne to appeare before him xviij. or xx. Lords of the Parliament, vpon the same day. &c. S. Triall 2.

1.H.4.12. 13.H.8.23. 10.Ed.4.6.

4 Where Treasons, Misprisions of Treasons, Murders, Manslaughters, and other malicious strikings, by reason whereof blood hath been shed, against the K. peace, were often committed within the limits of the Kings palace, or house, or other houses where his Maiestie was abiding in his royall person: which offences when they be done, be best knowne by his Highnesse Officers of his houshold, and by his seruants of his Checke roll: And if his Maiesty shall happen to remoue from such his palace, or house, or other house where such offences were done, before the tryall and determination thereof, then such offences might not lawfully be tryed, heard, and determined by and before the sayd Officers, but bee remitted to bee tryed and determined by the order of the Common law, by reason whereof the punishment of the sayd offendors, in such cases, hath beene long time delayed, and sometime their offences forgotten, and not remembred, and so they escaped vnpunished: For the redresse whereof, by a Statute made Anno 33.H.8. it was enacted, That all Treasons, Misprisions of Treasons, Murders, Manslaughters, Bloudsheds, and other malitious strikings, by reason whereof bloud shall be shed, against the Kings peace, which shall bee done within any the Palaces or houses of the King or his heires, or within any other house or houses, at such time as his Maiestie shall bee then abiding in his royall person, shall bee inquired of, tryed, heard, and determined within any of the Kings houses, or other house where his Maiestie shall bee abiding, before the Lord Steward of the Kings houshold, and in his absence, before the Treasorer, and Comptroller of the K. houshold, and Steward of the Marshalsey for the time beeing, or two of them, whereof the Steward of the Marshalsey to bee one, by vertue of their offices, without any Commission, or other authoritie to them giuen. And whether the King shall bee remooued from the house where such offences shall bee done, or not, before they be inquired of, heard, and determined, yet such offences shall be inquired of, tryed, heard, and determined before the Kings Officers of his houshold before named, or two of them, by the Inquisition and verdict of his houshold seruants in his Checke roll, at such Palace or house where his Maiestie shall bee at any time abiding, in manner and forme as is hereafter expressed. The two Clerkes Comptrollers, Clerkes of the Checke, and Clerkes Marshals for the time being, of the K. houshold, or one of them, vpon a Precept to them, or any of them made by the Lord Steward, or in his absence, by the said Treasorer and Comptroller of the Kings houshold, and the said Steward of the Marshalsey, or by two of them, whereof the sayd Steward of the Marshalsey to be one, shall haue power to summon, warne, and returne the names of twentie foure persons, being yeomen officers of the Kings said

St.33.H.8. 12.

Iudge of treasons and felonies committed in the K. house.

sayd houshold in the sayd Checke roll, to inquire of such Treasons, Misprisions of Treasons, Murders, Manslaughters, and other malitious strikings, by reason whereof bloud shall bee shed, against the Kings peace, before the sayd Lord Steward, and in his absence before the sayd Treasorer, Comptroller, and Steward of the Marshalsey, or before two of them at the least, whereof the Steward to bee one. And it shall bee lawfull to the sayde Lord Steward, and in his absence, to the sayd Treasorer, Comptroller, and Steward of the Marshalsey aforesayd, or two of them, whereof the sayd Steward to bee one, before whom such Returnes shall bee so made as is aforesayd, to cause such number of the sayd foure and twentie persons so returned, aboue the number of twelue persons, as to him or them shall seeme expedient, to inquire of such Treasons, Misprisions of Treasons, Murders, Manslaughters, or other malitious strikings, by reason whereof bloud shal bee shed, against the Kings peace, within the sayd Palaces, or other the sayd houses, at any time committed. And if any person or persons bee indicted by the sayd Jurie so sworne before them as is aforesaid, or by Inquisition before the Coroner of the sayd houshold, and certified before the sayd Lord Steward, or in his absence before the sayd Treasorer, Comptroller, and Steward of the Marshalsey, or two of them, whereof the sayd Steward of the Marshalsey to bee one, Then immediatly the said Lord Steward, or &c. Treasorer, Comptroller, and Steward of the Marshalsey, or two of them, whereof &c. before whom the sayd Presentment, Inquisition, or Indictment shall bee so found, or certified by the sayd Coroner, shall arraigne before them euerie such person so indicted, according to the course of the common law, and forthwith after issue ioyned betweene the King and the prisoner so arraigned, the same day and place, or any other, shall make another Precept to the sayd Clerks Comptrollers, Clerkes of the Checke, and Clerkes Marshals of the said houshold, or to one of them, to summon and returne one Jurie of foure and twenty persons, to appeare before the sayd Lord Steward, or &c. Treasorer, Comptroller, and Steward of the Marshalsey, or two of them, whereof the sayd Steward of the Marshalsey to be one, at such day, time, and place, and vpon such paine as shal be then limited of the Serieants and Gentlemen Officers of the Kings chamber, and of the sayd houshold, which shall take wages by the K. Checke roll. And the sayd Steward, or &c. Treasorer, Comptroller, and Steward of the sayd Marshalsey, or two of them, whereof the sayd Steward to be one, before whom such Jurie shall bee so returned, shall cause twelue of the same Jurie to bee sworne, truely to try between the King and such person, as shall bee so indicted and arraigned of such Treasons, Misprisions of treasons, Murders, Manslaughters, and other malitious strikings, by reason whereof bloud shall bee shed, against the Kings peace, or any of them. And if any such person or persons so arraigned be found guiltie of any Treason, Misprision of Treason, Murders, or Manslaughters, then hee shall haue iudgement of life and member, and suffer such paines of death, and shall forfeit all their mannors, lands, tenements, goods, and cattels, in like manner as if the same person and persons had beene found guiltie of any of the sayd offences by the order of the common law, without the benefit of Clergie, or Sanctuarie. Prouided alwayes, that the tryall of Peeres for any offence before mentioned shalbe as it hath beene vsed in times past.

St.3.H.7.14 5 By the stat. made Anno 3.H.7. it was ordayned, That the Steward, Trea-

Iudges of conspiracie in the K. house. Treasorer, and Comptroller of the Kings house for the time beeing, or one of them, shall haue authoritie to inquire by twelue sad-men, and discréet persons, of the Checke rol of the Kings houshould, if any seruant admitted to be his seruant sworne, and his name put in the Checke roll of his houshold, whatsoeuer he be (seruing in any office or rome reputed and taken vnder the estate of a Lord) make any confederacies, cōpassings, conspiracies, or imaginations, with any person or persons, to destroy or murder the K. or any Lord of this realm, or any other person sworne to the kings Counsel, Steward, Treasorer, or Comptroller of the Kings house: And if it be found before the said Steward for the time being, by the said xij. sad men, that any such of the K. seruants, as is abouesaid, hath confederat, compassed, conspired, or imagined, as is abouesaid, hee so found by the inquirie, shall bée put thereupon to answer. And the Steward, Treasorer, and Comptroller, or two of them, haue power to determine the same matter according to the law: and if he put him in tryall, then it shall bée tryed by other twelue sad men of the said houshold. And if such misdoers shall be found guiltie by confession, or otherwise, the said offence shall be iudged felonie. S. Felonie by Stat. 1.

Iudges within the Verge. 6 The Iustices of the Kings Bench, the Iustises of Oyer and Terminer, Iustices of Gaole deliuerie, and Iustices of Peace, haue power to inquire, heare, and determine all murders and felonies within the Verge, for that their authoritie and iurisdiction is generall through the whole countie, and so it hath béene allwayes vsed. Co. li. 4. 47.

Iudges of the K. Bench. 7 The Iustices of the Kings Bench, without hauing Commission, may heare and determine all maner of Treasons and Felonies. And by the Stat. of Anno 35. H. 8. & Anno 5. Ed. 6. it is enacted, That all manner of offences being alreadie made or declared, or hereafter to be made or declared, by any lawes and statutes of this Realme, to be Treasons, Misprisions of Treasons, or concealments of Treasons, & done, perpetrated, or committed, or hereafter to bee done, perpetrated, or committed by any person or persons, out of this Realme of England, shall bée inquired of, heard, and determined before the Kings Iustices of his Bench, for Pleas to be holden before himselfe, by good and lawfull men of the same Shire where the sayd Bench shall sit, and be kept, or else before such Commissioners, and in such Shire of this Realme, as shall bée assigned by the Kings Commission, and by good and lawful men of the same Shire, in like manner and forme to all intents and purposes, as if such Treasons, Misprisions of Treasons, and concealements of Treasons, had béene done and committed within the same Shire where they shalbe so inquired of, heard, and determined. Prouided allwayes, that if any Peeres of this Realme shal be indicted of any such Treasons, or other offences, then they shall haue their triall by their Péeres, as heretofore hath béene accustomed.

St. 35. H. 8. 2. St. 5. E. 6. 11.

Iudges of Treasons committed beyond the Seas.

Dy. fol. 287 & 298.

8 By the Stat. intituled De finibus, made Anno 27. Ed. 1. and also by the Stat. of Anno 4. E. 3. it is ordayned, That good and discréet persons (other than of the St. 27. E. 1. 2. St. 4. E. 3. 2.

Iudges of gaole deliuery

of the Benches, if they may be found sufficient) shalbe assigned in all the shires of England, to take Assises, Iuries, & Certifications, and to deliuer the gaoles. And the Iustices assigned to deliuer the gaoles, shall haue power to deliuer the same gaoles of those that shalbe indicted before the gardeins of the peace. And the said gardeins shall send their inditements before the Iustices. And they shall haue authoritie to inquire of Sherifes, Gaolers, and others, in whose ward such indicted persons shal be, if they make deliuerance, or let to mainprise any so indicted, which be not mainpernable, and to punish the said Sherifes, Gaolers, and others offending against this Act. And by the stat. of An. 3. H. 7. it is enacted, That the wife or heire of any person murdered, or slaine, as case shall require, may commence their Appeale in proper person, at any time within the yere after the felony done, before the Sherife & Coroners where the said felonie and murder was done, or before the King in his Bench, or Iustices of Gaole deliuerie.

St. 3. H. 7. 1 — *Iudges in appeale of murder or manslaughter*

9 To the intent to inable the Iust. of Nisi prius to giue iudgement of such persons as be either attainted or acquit of treason or felonie, by a stat. made an. 14. H. 6. it was established, That the Iust. before whom Enquests, Inquisitions, and Iuries shalbe taken by the K. writ of Nisi prius, according to the form of the stat. thereof made, shall haue power of all the cases of felony, and of treason, to giue iudgement. Though this stat. of 14. H. 6. doth giue authoritie to Iustices of Nisi prius to giue iudgement as wel vpon acquital, as vpon attainder of treason, or felonie, notwithstanding if in an Appeale the defendant bee acquit before them, they cannot award damages against the plaintife, nor inquire of abettors: for their power by this stat. extendeth but to treason and felonie onely, whereof they may giue iudgement, and of nothing else: for the awarding of damages, and inquiring of abettors, doth yet remaine as it was at the common law.

Iustices of Nisi prius Iudges in felonie & treason — *St. 14. H. 6. 1* — *10. Ed. 4. 14* — *Awarding of damages, and inquiring of abettors.*

10 By the stat. of Anno 33. H. 8. it is ordained, That if any person or persons, being examined before the K. Counsell, or thrée of them, vpon any maner of murders, do confesse any such offences, or that the said Counsell, or thrée of them, vpon such examination, shall thinke any person so examined, to bée vehemently suspected of any murder, then in euery such case, by the kings commandement, the K. Commission of Oyer and Terminer, vnder the great Seale, shalbe made to such persons, and to such Shires, or places, as shalbe appointed by his Highnesse, for the spéedie tryall, conuiction, or deliuerance of such offendors: which Commissioners shall haue authoritie to inquire, heare, and determine all such murders within the Shire, and places limited by their Commission, by such good and lawfull persons as shall bee returned before them by the Sherife, his minister, or other hauing power to returne writs & proces for that purpose, in whatsoeuer other Shire or place within the K. dominions, or without, such offences were cōmitted. But Péers of the realme being indicted of the said offence, shall be tried by their Péeres. This stat. was also made for the triall of treasons, and misprision of treasons, by speciall commission. But by the stat. of an. 1. & 2. P. & M. it was enacted, That all trials to bee made for any treasons, shalbe only vsed according to the course of the common law.

St. 33. H. 8. 23. — *Iudges of murders by speciall commission.* — *St. 1. & 2. P. & M. 10.*

11 Where

Who ſhall be Iudge of Treaſon and Feloníe.

11 Where Traitoꝛs, Pirats, Theeues, Robbers, Murderers, and confederatoꝛs vpon the Sea, many times eſcaped vnpuniſhed, becauſe the tryall of their offences hath heretofoꝛe beene oꝛdered, iudged, and determined befoꝛe the Admirall, oꝛ his Lieutenant, oꝛ Commiſſarie, after the courſe of the Ciuile lawes, the nature whereof is, that befoꝛe any iudgement of death can be giuen againſt the offendoꝛs, either they muſt plainly confeſſe their offences (which they will neuer doe without toꝛture oꝛ paines) oꝛ elſe their offences muſt be ſo plainely and directly pꝛoued by witneſſes indifferent, ſuch as ſaw their offences committed, which cannot bee gotten but by chaunce at few times, becauſe ſuch offendoꝛs commit their offences vpon the Sea, and many times murder and kill ſuch perſons being the ſhip oꝛ boat where they commit their offences, which ſhould bee witneſſe againſt them in that behalfe: and alſo ſuch as ſhould beare witneſſe, bee commonly Mariners, and ſhipmen, which, becauſe of their often voyages and paſſages vpon the Sea, depart without long tarrying and pꝛotracting of time, to the great coſts and charges as well of the King, as ſuch as would purſue ſuch offendoꝛs: Foꝛ refoꝛmation whereof, by a Statute made Anno 28. H. 8. it was enacted, That all Treaſons, Felonies, Robberies, Murders, and Confederacies, committed in, oꝛ vpon the Sea, oꝛ in any other Hauen, Riuer, Creeke, oꝛ place where the Admirall oꝛ Admirals haue, oꝛ pꝛetend to haue power, authoꝛitie, oꝛ iuriſdiction, ſhall bee inquired, tryed, heard, determined, and iudged in ſuch Shires and places in the Realme, as ſhall bee limited by the Kings Commiſſion oꝛ Commiſſions, to be directed foꝛ the ſame, in like foꝛme and condition, as if any ſuch offence oꝛ offences had beene committed oꝛ done in and vpon the land: And ſuch Commiſſions ſhall bee had vnder the great Seale, directed to the Admirall oꝛ Admirals, oꝛ to his oꝛ their Lieutenant, Deputie and Deputies, and to thꝛee oꝛ foure other ſuch ſubſtantiall perſons as ſhall bee named oꝛ appointed by the Loꝛd Chauncelloꝛ foꝛ the time being, from time to time, and as oft as neede ſhall require, to heare and determine ſuch offences, after the courſe of the common lawes of this land, vſed foꝛ Treaſons, Felonies, Robberies, Murders, and Confederacies of the ſame, done and committed vpon the land within the Realme. And ſuch perſons to whome ſuch Commiſſion oꝛ Commiſſions ſhall bee directed, oꝛ foure of them at the leaſt, ſhall haue authoꝛitie to inquire of ſuch offences, and euerie of them, by the othes of twelue good and lawfull inhabitants of the Shire limited in their Commiſſion, in ſuch manner and foꝛme, as if ſuch offences had beene committed vpon the land within the ſame Shire. And euerie Indictment found and pꝛeſented befoꝛe ſuch Commiſſioners, of any Treaſons, Felonies, Robberies, Murders, Manſlaughters, oꝛ ſuch other offences committed oꝛ done in oꝛ vpon the Seas, oꝛ in, oꝛ vpon any Riuer, Hauen, oꝛ Creeke, ſhall be good and effectual in the law. And if any perſon oꝛ perſons happen to be indicted foꝛ any ſuch offence done vpon the Seas, oꝛ in any other place aboue limited, then ſuch oꝛder, Pꝛoces, Judgement, and execution ſhal be vſed, had, done, and made, to, and againſt euerie ſuch perſon and perſons ſo being indicted, as againſt traitoꝛs, felons, and murderers, foꝛ treaſon, felonie, robberie, murder, oꝛ other ſuch offences done vpon the land, as by the law of this Realm is accuſtomed. And the trial of ſuch offence oꝛ offences, if it be denied by the offendoꝛ oꝛ offendoꝛs, ſhalbe had by xy. lawfull men inhabited in the Shire limited in ſuch commiſſion, which ſhall be directed as is afoꝛeſaid, and no challenge to be had foꝛ the Hundꝛed. And ſuch as ſhalbe conuict of any ſuch offence oꝛ offences, by verdict, confeſſion, oꝛ pꝛoces by authoꝛitie of any ſuch commiſſion, ſhall haue and ſuffer ſuch pains of death, loſſes

St. 28. H. 8. 15.

Judges in piracie where the Admirall hath iuriſdiction.

No challenge foꝛ the hűdꝛed

losses of lands, goods, and cattels, as if they had béen conuicted of any treasons, felonies, robberies, or other the said offences done vpon the land, without benefit of Clergie, or Sanctuarie. Prouided alwayes, that this Act shall not extend, or be preiudiciall to any person or persons, for taking of any victuals, gables, ropes, anchors, or sayles, which any such person or persons compelled by necessitie, taketh of, or in any ship which may conueniently spare the same, so the same person or persons pay out of hand for the same victuall, gables, ropes, anchors, or sayles, mony, or mony worth, to the value of the thing so taken, or doe deliuer for the same a sufficient bill obligatorie, to bée payd in forme following, viz. if the taking of the same things bée on this side the straits of Marrok, then to bée payd within foure monethes: and if beyond the said Straits, then to be paid within twelue monethes next ensuing the making of the sayd bill. And that the makers of the sayd bils well and truely pay the same debt, at the day to be limited within the said bills. Prouided alwayes, that whensoeuer any such Commission for the punishment of the offences aforesayd, or of any of them, shalbe directed or sent to any place within the iurisdiction of the fiue Ports, that then euery such Commission shall bee directed vnto the Lord Warden of the sayd Ports for the time being, or to his deputie, and vnto thrée or foure such other persons as the Lord Chauncellor for the time béeing shall appoint. And that when any Commission shall be directed vnto the fiue Ports, for the inquisition and tryall of any of the offences expressed in this Act, that euerie such inquisition and tryall to be had by vertue of such Commission, shall be made and had by the inhabitants in the said fiue ports, or the members thereof: Any thing in this Act to the contrarie notwithstanding. So much of this stat. as concerneth the triall of treasons, is altered by the stat. of Anno 1. & 2. P. & M. 10. and the same made triable onely by the course of the common law. Taking things vpon necessitie. Commissions directed into the fiue ports.

St. 18. E. 3. 2 12 The Iustices of peace of euery county by vertue of the K. commission to them directed, and by force of the stat. of Anno 18. Ed. 3. be Iudges in felonie, and haue authoritie to heare and determine felonies: the words of which stat. be these, viz. Two or thrée of the most worthy men of counties, shalbe assigned kéepers of the peace by the K. commission: and at what time néed shall bée, the same, with other wise and learned in the law, shall be appointed by the K. commission, to heare and determine felonies, and trespasses done against the peace in the same county, and to execute punishment reasonably, according to law, reason, and the maner of the fact. And the words of the kings commission which doth authorize Iustices of peace to be Iudges of Felonie, and to heare and determin felonies, amongst others, be these, viz. Iacobus Dei gratia Angliæ, Scotiæ, Franciæ, & Hibernię Rex, fidei defensor &c. Prædilectis A. B. C. D. E. H. &c. Salutem. Sciatis quod assignauimus vos, & quoslibet duos, vel plures vestrum (Quorum aliquem vestrum A. B. C. D. vnum esse volumus) Iustitiarios nostros, ad pacem nostram in comitatu nostro Buckingham conseruandam, & ad inquirendum per sacramentum proborum & legalium hominum de comitatu prædicto (per quos rei veritas melius sciri poterit) de omnibus & omnimodis felonijs, transgressionibus &c. ac de omnibus & singulis alijs malefactis & offensis de quibus Iustitiarij nostri pacis legitime inquirere possunt aut debent per quoscunque aut qualitercunque in Comitatu prædicto factis siue perpetratis, Vel quæ in posterum ibidem fieri, vel attemptari contigerit, &c. Et ad omnia & singula Felonias &c. indictamenta prædicta, ceteraq; omnia Iust. of peace Iudges in felonie. The words of the commission of the peace.

&c sin-

& singula præmissa secundum leges & statuta Regni nostri Angliæ (prout in huiusmodi casu fieri consueuit & debuit) audiendum & terminandum. And though it doth plainely appeare by the words of the foresayd Commission, that the King doth giue authoritie to Justices of Peace, to inquire of, heare, and determine all manner of Felonies, viz. as well of such as bee made Felonies by Statute, as of such offences as were Felonies by the Common law: yet because there hath beene a scruple and question moued by some, that the foresaid Statute of Anno 18. Edw. 3. did meane, and was to bee expounded to giue authoritie to Justices of Peace, to inquire of, heare, and determine those felonies onely which were at the time of the making of that Statute, felonies, viz. That were felonies by the Common law, and not to giue them authoritie to inquire of, heare, and determine those offences as felonies, which were made felonies by seuerall Statutes ordained sithence that time, and that the Kings Commission authorised by that Statute, did giue them no further authoritie than that Statute meant: Therefore not to adde to the law, but to satisfie euerie reader, and to make that thing more plaine and perspicuous to all men, which to some did seeme doubtfull, the makers of the stat. of anno 8. El. 3. touching the transporting of sheepe, and of the stat. of anno 25. H. 8. 6. ordained against buggery, and of the stat. of anno 18. H. 6. 19. established to punish Souldiers that depart from their Captains without licence, and of the stat. of an. 39. El. 4. & an. 1. Iac. 7. touching dangerous and incorrigible rogues, and of the stat. prouided an. 39. El. 17. against wandering souldiers and mariners, and of the stat. of an. 22. H. 8. 11. established against the cutting downe of powdike, and of the stat. of an. 43. El. 13. enacted against the carrying away of any persons against their wils out of Cumberland, Northumberland, Westmerland, or the Bishopricke of Durham, did by speciall words ordaine, that the J. of the peace of the counties wherein any of the foresaid seuerall offences were committed, should haue authoritie at their generall Quarter Sessions, to inquire of, heare, and determine the said offences. And the like authoritie was giuen by the said seuerall stat. to the Just. of Assise, and Just. of Gaole deliuerie, to inquire of, heare, and determine the said offences in the counties where the same were committed within their seuerall commissions. And by the stat. of an. 1. E. 4. it was ordained, That the J. of peace of euery county, shal haue authoritie and power to arraigne and deliuer all person and persons indicted or presented before the Sherifes, Undersherifes, their Clerks, Bailifs, or Ministers, or any of them, in their Turnes or Lawdayes. And as of other felonies, so J. of peace may inquire of murder, because wilfull murder is felony. But Just. of peace cannot inquire of treason, for neither the before mentioned stat. of 18. E. 3. nor the words of their commission, do authorise them so to do.

[Margin: St. 1. E. 4. 2. — 3. H. 7. 5. — 5. E. 6. Di. 69 — 9. H. 4. 1. — Murder. — Treason.]

13 There be some that haue libertie of Soc and Sac, Tol and Them, Infangtheefe and Outfangtheefe: these in their own courts may giue iudgement of him who is found within their liberty possessed of any manifest theft, as if he be hand hauing, and back bearing, and that Sathaber (viz. he whose the goods be) do pursue him: for unlesse he be in possession of the goods (though another doth pursue him as a theefe) yet that Court, Hundred, or Wapentake, cannot hold plea of such a theft, nor make inquirie by the Countrey, whether such a man which was not possessed of the goods, bee culpable, or not. Neither shall any wage battell without possession. It is called Infangtheefe, where a Theefe is taken possessed of goods stolne within any such

[Margin: The Lord of a Mannor Judge in felonie. — Bracton de Corona, cap. 35. 2. R. 3. 10. — Kel. fol. 150 — Infangtheefe.]

Man-

Mannor or Libertie, who is commorant and dwelling within the same libertie, and one of the said Lords owne people. Outfangthæfe, is a thæfe that is a stranger, comming from some other place into the Mannor of the Lord who hath such a libertie, and is there taken with the manoure. And yet he that hath such a libertie, cannot fetch one of his owne people who hath committed larcenie out of his libertie, and bring him into his libertie, and iudge him there according to his libertie; for euery person must receiue the punishment of the law where he hath offended the law: But he may giue iudgement as well against his own people, as against strangers committing larcenie, that be taken within his libertie. And in this libertie of Infangthæfe and Outfangthæfe, and in waife and stray, and wreck of the sea, a man may prescribe, but so he cannot do in goods of felons and fugitiues, for they do belong to the Crowne, and cannot passe without the Kings graunt.

Outfangthæf.

46.Ed.3.15
14.H.4.15

Fitz.Prescription 65

14 The custome of some countrey is such, that if one hath committed burglarie, or other felonie, and he be pursued by huy and cry from towne to town, and so taken flying, he must be beheaded in the presence of the inhabitants of foure townes, and so by the vsage of that countrey he is accounted a felon: And this must be recorded in the Coroners roll, and after the Coroner must present it before the Iustices, and they will adiudge him a felon. And so he must be first put to death, and after iudged a felon.

A felon first executed, and then iudged.

FINIS.

The generall Titles of this Booke.

Yy 18 Ap-

A briefe

A briefe effect of euery Braunch or Chapter in this Treatise.

Menace, Aſsault, Batterie, Impriſonment, Maihemìng. *Fol.* 1.

Peace, or good abearing.

84 The Sherife, Constable, and seuerall other officers be conseruators of the Peace.

85 Euery able person, when need requireth, must be a conseruator of the Peace.

86 Menaces, Assaults, Batteries, &c. in some cases are punishable in the Starre-chamber.

Riots, Routs, vnlawfull and Rebellious Assemblies. Fol. 24.

Force, and Forcible Entries. *Fol.*34.

9 A warrant to the Shirife to make restitution.

10 Restitution awarded out of the Kings bench.

11 No restitution, but where force is found by inquisition.

12 Where no restitution against three yeares possession.

Where restitution notwithstanding three yeares possession.

13 A *Supersedeas* to stay restitution.

14 Where force found, and yet no restitution.

15 A *Mittimus* to send to the Gaole such as doe hold land by force.

16 A Iustice may enquire of Forcible Entries, without complaint.

17 In an action of forcible entry the writ must be *Vi & armis*.

18 Who may bring an action of Forcible entry.

19 He that hath title, entereth by force.

20 Hee that hath possession, sueth a Writ of Forcible Entry.

21 Forcible entry of a Rent or Common.

22 Forcible entry to the vse of another.

Forcible detaining by words onely.

23 Iointenants or Tenants in common expelling each other by force.

24 Who may bring a Writ of Entry vpon the Statute of *5. Richard. 2.*

25 Turning a water-course by force.

26 The plea of not guiltie in Forcible entry

The finding of the speciall matter doth charge or discharge the defendant of force.

Presentment of Forcible entry.

27 One action for entring and detaining with force.

28 A writ vpon the Statute of North-hampton.

29 What shalbe said to be force.

Force by number of seruants.

Force by number of weapons.

30 Who may make a Forcible entry.

31 What force is lawfull to the persons of men.

32 Where the house of a man may be broken by force, & where not.

33 A particular person may defend himselfe and his by force.

34 The Writ of *Vi laica remouenda*.

35 Where force shalbe remoued for the K. Incumbent, where not.

Forgerie. *Fol.* 43.

1 Forgerie, Periurie, and Maintenance doe tend to the breach of the Peace.

2 The enormitie of Forgerie.

A repeale of former Statutes of Forgerie.

3 Forging of deeds, whereby anothers landes shall bee troubled.

4 For-

Periurie, Subornation. *Fol.* 48.

12 Per-

Maintenance, Champertie, Embracerie, and buying of Titles. Fol. 56.

Main-

Deceit, Couin, Collusion, Fraud 67.

1 The multitude and enormities of deceits and frauds.

2 The reward for paines, and punishment for deceits of officers towards the Law.

A Iudge.

A Clerke.

A Serieant.

A Pleader.

A Philozer.

An Exigenter.

No office of Iustice shall be sold or bought.

No man shalbe Iustice of Assise in his owne County.

3 Who shalbe Atturneyes.

Sollicitors.

The penalty for following a suit in anothers name.

What acts done by Atturneyes in seuerall cases shall bee adiudged deceit.

4 The Law reiecteth deceitfull and fraudulent acts.

A fine leuied of land to defraud the right owner thereof, shall bee void.

5 A fine leuied of auncient demesne land, to defraud the Lord of his Seigniorie, is voidable.

6 How a recouery of land by deceit shalbe auoided.

7 A *Scire facias* vpon a recouery by deceit auoided.

A recouery of debt by deceit auoided.

A iudgement to auoid the meaning of a Statute.

The executors shall haue remedy for a deceitfull recouery against the Testator.

8 Deceit vpon a recouery in a *Quare impedit*.

Deceit vpon a recouery in wast.

9 Deceit vpon a recouery in a *Pracipe in capite*.

10 Where a good Title shal be impaired by a couenous recouery thereof.

11 A Warranty deuised by deceit.

12 Deceit by getting of a Protection.

13 Deceit by purchasing of a writ to charge another.

14 Deceit by purchasing of a writ in anothers name.

Deceit for procuring one to sue another.

15 Deceit by acknowledging of a statute in anothers name.

Deceit by doing of a iudiciall act in anothers name.

16 Deceit by forging of a resignation of a Benefice.

17 Deceit by conueying of land to one man, which before was bargained to another.

18 Deceit by not performing of his Warranty.

19 Deceit by confession of an action, wherein hee hath no interest.

20 Deceit by the aliening of the goods of his wife, from whom hee meaneth to be diuorced.

21 Sale of goods in open Market by deceit and couin.

22 A fraudulent assurance to defeat the discontinuee in tayle of his plea of Assets per Discent.

Extortion, Exaction. Fol. 82.

4 Extortion in a Serieant, Crier, or Marshall of a Iudge.

5 Extortion in a Coroner.

6 Extortion in a Sherife, vnder-Sherife, or Baylife, for making of arrests &c.

7 Extortion in a Sherife, for sparing to returne a Iuror.

8 Extortion in a Sherife, for the seruing of an Execution.

9 Extortion in the Chirographer of the common place.

10 Extortion in the kings auditors, or their Clerkes.

11 Extortion in the Kings Receiuers.

Extortion in them who do pay fees or pensions.

12 Extortion in officers of the Exchequer.

13 Extortion in a Clerke of the Signet or priuy Seale.

14 Extortion by officers of the faculties.

15 Extortion by Gouernours vpon such as be made prentices or freemen.

16 Extortion by the officers of the Court of Wards.

17 Extortion in taking of Obligations for the payment of first fruits.

18 Extortion by Escheators.

19 Exaction by the Admirall &c. vpon them who trauaile for Fish.

20 Extortion by the marshall of the kings house.

Extortion by a seruitor of bills in the marshals Court.

21 Exaction by Muster-masters to spare the taking of souldiers.

Exaction by captaines of their souldiers.

22 Extortion by taking of Scauage of Marchants.

23 Extortion by the Clerke of the Statutes or &c.

24 A preuention of extortion by atturneyes, in taking of excessiue fees.

An atturney delaying of a suit, or demaunding more then is due.

25 A preuention of Extortion in stewards of Courts.

26 Extortion in gaugers, searchers, and packers of fish.

Extortion in Ordinaries and their Officers for probat of Testaments, Administrations, &c.

28 Extortion in an Ordinarie for the seale of a Citation.

29 Extortion in Parsons, Vicars, &c. for Mortuaries.

30 Exaction for presenting or collating to a benefice.

31 Exaction for admitting to a benefice.

32 Exaction for resigning, or exchanging of a benefice.

33 Exaction for making of ministers, or giuing licence to preach.

34 Exaction for a voice in electing of a fellow or scholler into a Colledge, or &c.

35 Exaction by taking money to resigne a place in a Colledge, &c.

36 Exaction by gathering money, which should discharge the fifteene of a Towne.

37 Extortion by taking of an amerciament in a Court Baron.

Oppreßion. *Fol.* 91.

Treasons. Fol. 109.

8 The

A briefe effect of euery Braunch

*Homicide. Fol.*120.

1 Homicide by Iustice.
By necessitie.
By chaunce or misfortune.
By will.
2 Homicide by Iustice.
The order of law not obserued in the execution of iustice.
3 None may kill a man that is outlawed, or attainted in *Præmunire.*
4 Killing of a felon that wil not be arrested.
Euerie person may arrest a felon.
Killing of such as be vnlawfully assembled.
5 Killing of him that is in carying to the gaole.
6 Killing of a prisoner attempting to escape.
7 Killing him that attempteth robberie or burglarie.
8 Killing of an offendor in a Parke &c.
9 Vnitie of possession in a chase or mannor.
10 One killing of another in combat.
11 Homicide vpon necessity in defence of his house from burning.
Homicide in defending himself from robberie.
12 No forfeiture for Homicide vpon necessitie.
13 Killing of another in his owne defence, in his owne house.
14 Necessitie ineuitable requisit in homicide in his own defence
The definition of Homicide in his owne defence.
15 Where in Homicide in his owne defence his goods shall bee forfeited, and where not.
16 Killing a man in his own defence, found by verdict.
17 The prisoner indicted for killing in his owne defence, must plead, not guiltie.
18 How he shall be discharged that killeth a man in his owne defence.
19 What is Homicide by misaduenture.
20 The like order in misaduenture, as in his owne defence.
21 What is Homicide by murder.
What is Homicide by manslaughter.
22 The name of murder.
Murder more grieuous than felonie.
23 Wilfull poysoning is murder.
24 Stabbing to death is murder.
25 Murder by killing of a Constable comming to part a fray.
Murder by killing of a Sherife or his Officers in seruing of Proces.
Murder by killing of a watchman.
26 Murder and Manslaughter committed in the death of one man.

or Chapter in this Teratiſe.

Felonie

A briefe effect of euery Braunch

Felonie by the Common Law. Fol. 129.

32 No

Felonie by Statute. Fol. 133.

27 In what case forging of euidence is felonie.

28 In what case a banished rogue shalbe a felon.

29 Felony by practising of coniuration, witchcraft, inuocation, &c.

30 Felonie in hunting in the night, or with visors, and denying of it.

31 Felony by vnlawfull assemblies aboue twelue persons, &c.

32 Felonie in wandring souldidiers or mariners, that will not settle to worke.

33 Felonie in imbeciling of the Kings Armour, Ordnance, Shot, &c.

34 Felonie in cutting downe Powdike.

35 Felonie in not taking the othe for the King, or not entring into bond.

36 Felonie in forcible carrying any person out of Cumberland, &c.

37 Felonie in breaking of prison.

Principall and Accessorie. *Fol.* 141.

1 There is no Accessorie in high Treason.

2 Accessory before the offence committed.

3 Procurement of felony.

4 Comming purposely to doe Manslaughter.

5 A will to assist a felon.

6 In company, but not assenting to a felonie.

7 Holding a man vntill hee be slaine.

8 One thing commanded, and another effected.

9 Counselling to rob one, and another is robbed.

Commaunding to beat one, and another is killed.

Commaunding to burne one house, and another is burned.

Counsell to doe one act, and another is done.

The felonie commanded, committed in another manner.

10 The felonie commaunded, countermaunded.

11 Counselling to poison one and another is poysoned.

12 A commanding or ayding to rape or robberie.

13 Accessories after the offence. What act of the Accessorie maketh him a felon.

14 Receit of a felon attainted in the same countie.

15 Receit of a felon attainted in another countie.

16 Indictment and triall of an Accessorie in one countie, to an offence done in another.

17 Receiuing of stolne goods.

18 Receiuing of a felon.

19 Accessory to an Accessorie.

20 Rescue of a felon.

21 A wife not accessory to her husband.

22 A wife may bee a principall felon.

Accesso-

Breaking of Priſon, and Reſcous. *Fol.* 148.

4 Neg-

Eſcape. *Fol.*149.

28 Con-

Pursute by Huy and Cry. *Fol.* 152.

A briefe effect of euery Braunch

Appeales of Felonie. *Fol.156.*

35 The

Indictments. Fol. 169.

Mainprise and Baile. Fol. 180.

Con-

or Chapter in this Treatise.

*Confession of the offence. Fol.*184.

*Approuer. Fol.*185.

6 Brea-

Triall by Peeres. Fol. 196.

Triall by the Countrey. Fol. 198.

Challenge. *Fol.*201.

Euidence. *Fol.* 204.

Verdict. *Fol.*206.

Clergy. *Fol.* 207.

4 The

The Kings Pardon. Fol. 218.

Standing mute, or answering indirectly. Fol. 222.

Iudge-

Iudgement and Execution. *Fol.*224.

Forfeiture. *Fol.*226.

Corruption of Blood. Fol.239.

Reſtitution of ſtolne goods. Fol. 240.

Damages in Appeale. Fol.242.

9 The dammages for seuerall persons assessed seuerally.

10 Where the appellant shall pay a fine to the king.

11 In what *cases* inquiry shall be made for the abettors.

12 What pleas the abettors may plead.

13 Proces against the abettors.

Nonsute in the proces against the abettors.

14 A writ against the abettors by the appellee.

15 Procurers of indictments for suits in spirituall courts.

A Writ of Conspiracie. Fol.245.

1 In what case a Writ of Conspiracie doth lye.

2 Conspiracie maintenable vpon an acquitall in an indictment or appeale.

3 The indictment must be false which giueth the Writ of Conspiracie.

4 Conspiracie doubtfull whether true or false.

5 The conspirators do become indictors.

A Iustice of Peace.

A giuer of Euidence.

6 Who be conspirators.

7 A Conspiracie must bee by more then one.

Where only one shalbe charged in Conspiracie.

8 No Writ of Conspiracie against the Husband and the Wife.

9 The forme of the Writ of Conspiracie.

10 The writ of Conspiracy for the accessarie.

11 Barres in a writ of Conspiracie.

12 Iudgement in Conspiracie.

A villanous iudgement.

13 Inquiry of Conspiracie by Iustices.

14 Inquiry of Conspirators at the kings or parties suit.

15 Procurers of an indictment or an appeale in a forraine county.

16 An offence supposed to bee done in a place where there is none such.

The Coroner and his authoritie and dutie in Felonies &c. Fol.249.

1 The office and duty of a Coroner.

2 The Writ *de Coronatore Eligendo.*

3 Who shall be Coroners, and by whom they shalbe chosen.

4 Whether Coroners ought to be knights.

5 Causes to remoue a Coroner.

6 Where

Who shall be Judge in Treason and Felony. Fol.253.

mitted out of the Realme.

8 Iustices of Gaole deliuerie Iudges in Felony.

9 Iudges of *Nisi prius* Iudges in Felony &c.

10 Speciall commissioners Iudges at the arraignement of a Murderer.

11 Iudges of piracie or offences done vpon the sea.

12 Iustices of Peace Iudges in Felony.

13 The Lord of a Mannour Iudge in Felony.

Infangtheefe.

Outfangtheefe.

14 A Felon first executed, and then iudged.

FINIS.